The African Slave in
Colonial Peru
1524-1650

The African Slave in Colonial Peru
1524-1650

FREDERICK P. BOWSER

STANFORD UNIVERSITY PRESS
Stanford, California
1974

Stanford University Press
Stanford, California
© 1974 by the Board of Trustees of the
Leland Stanford Junior University
Printed in the United States of America
ISBN 0-8047-0840-1
LC 73-80619

To France Vinton Scholes and Engel Sluiter

Preface

The past thirty-odd years have witnessed a steady growth of scholarly interest in the role of the African in the Americas. The majority of these studies deal with the black man in the United States, Brazil, and the Caribbean islands during the eighteenth and nineteenth centuries, and with good reason. During this period African slavery both reached its apogee and met its end in those areas, leaving behind a legacy of racial bitterness and strife that, however subtle the form, continues to the present day.

By comparison, the institution of slavery on the Spanish American mainland has received considerably less attention, and this is an unfortunate historiographical development. Along with Brazil, the colonies of Peru, Mexico, and New Granada (which in the period under study coincided roughly with the modern republic of Colombia) were the most important centers of African slavery in the Western Hemisphere during the sixteenth and seventeenth centuries. A study of the function and evolution of slavery in those areas can teach us much about the institution. If we turn to the broader issue of race relations, the importance of these colonies is greater still. During more than three hundred years of Spanish American slavery, only in Peru, Mexico, and parts of New Granada were relations between European and African influenced to a significant degree by a third racial element, the Indian. Economic, social, and sexual contact among these three groups produced gradations of racial animosity and acceptance that had profound effects on the societies in question and that were without parallel in the hemisphere.

It was with all of these considerations in mind that I decided in 1963 to begin an intensive investigation of the role of the African in colonial Peru. Of the three colonies, Peru was the most attractive subject for study, for several reasons. For one thing, only in Peru, and much to the distaste of the Spanish Crown, did forced Indian labor on a massive scale coexist with African slavery. For another, the important question of the colored population's acceptance and assimilation was most easily studied there, since slavery in Peru was above all an urban institution. As a denizen of the cities, the Afro-Peruvian thus had unique opportunities for advancement. Finally, a far greater quantity of historical documentation was available for Peru than for Mexico or New Granada.

When I began research a decade ago, only the useful monographs of Emilio Harth-terré and Alberto Márquez Abanto, who concerned themselves with the skilled Afro-Peruvian and with Afro-Indian relations, were available to serve as a base. Since that time, I have been able to profit from the splendid researches of James Lockhart concerning the Afro-Peruvian during the early colonial period. Basically, however, the foundations of this book rest on extensive archival research conducted in Peru, Spain, and Portugal, as detailed in the Bibliography, pp. 419-22. In this regard I was fortunate in having a wealth of material to draw on. Coastal Peru was so dependent on black labor, and slavery became such a part of the fabric of life, that virtually every agency of civil and ecclesiastical government generated documents having to do with the Afro-Peruvian, from official correspondence, fiscal records, lawsuits, and censuses, to marriage licenses, bills of sale, contracts, bail bonds, wills, and letters of manumission. On the basis of this mound of documentation, it was possible to study in some detail the pattern of slavery in Peru, including the slave trade, both in the Atlantic and in the Pacific; the contribution of the Africans to the Peruvian economy; the devices that were developed to control slaves of such radically different language and culture; the simultaneous efforts that were made, consciously and otherwise, to assimilate the Afro-Peruvians and to encourage them to identify with the society and values of the Spaniards; the phenomenon of racial mixture; the processes of liberation; and, finally, the emerging role of the free colored population. In short, to the greatest extent possible this book attempts to trace the complex interaction between Spaniard, African, and Indian within the socioeconomic structure of colonial Peru.

However, this vast and rich fund of documentation has one serious flaw: the African slave, and even the free person of color, was rarely viewed as a person, as a thinking being with feelings and needs unrelated to the body. This was an age with a profound indifference to the lower classes so long as those unfortunates performed their work and routinely commended their souls to God. Spaniards duly noted the need for numbers of blacks and browns in Peru, and occasionally their vices and unruliness were deplored—but usually in the mass, not as individuals. Therefore, and despite the close personal ties that prevailed between many Spanish masters and their African servants, it is extraordinarily difficult to make the black man come alive, to know anything of his world view, of his spiritual life and perceptions, or of his most deeply felt aspirations and frustrations. An occasional glimpse of life is to be had from a few sources—for the slave, from legal actions seeking manumission or marriage, for the free person of color from a somewhat broader range of notarial records—and I have used documentation of this sort to the fullest in an effort to make those of African descent something more than cardboard figures.

For several reasons (aside from the sheer mass of the documentation), I found the year 1650 an appropriate terminal date for this study. First, the Treaty of Westphalia (1648) signaled the end of Iberian claims to monopoly of the colonial world, including the Atlantic slave trade; thereafter, the flow of slaves to Peru became a much more complex and international affair requiring separate monographic treatment. Second, within Peru, the slave who had been merely a luxury a hundred years earlier had become a necessity by 1650; by that date the institution of slavery had acquired a firm grip on the coastal economy, a situation that was to endure into the nineteenth century. Finally, by the middle of the seventeenth century the status of the black man, both slave and free, and the attitudes that would make for the near-disappearance of those of African descent were fixed in law and popular opinion. A study of Peruvian slavery after 1650 would no doubt yield many interesting variations in detail but few changes in the basic pattern.

A final word concerning the scope of this book. The Peru of this volume corresponds roughly with the boundaries of the modern republic, though official consideration of the use of African labor in silver mining makes a few references to Upper Peru (Bolivia) necessary.

This study has received very generous financial support from various sources, and I am grateful to them all. In chronological order, they are the Foreign Area Fellowship Program; the University of California (Berkeley) and its Bancroft Library; the Center for Research in International Studies at Stanford University; the Mabelle McLeod Lewis Memorial Fund; and the National Endowment for the Humanities.

The staffs of the various archives and libraries in Spain, Peru, and Portugal were uniformly courteous and helpful. My special thanks go to Diego Bermúdez Camacho and Macario Valpuesta Cortés of the Archivo General de Indias (Seville) and to Felipe Márquez Abanto of the Archivo Nacional del Perú (Lima). I must also single out for praise Mrs. Vivian C. Fisher of the Bancroft Library for her unfailing cheerfulness in processing microfilm shipments that were often very tangled indeed.

The path of research is greatly smoothed with the comfort of friends, and several deserve my warmest gratitude. Among them are David Brading, from whom I have received the joys of companionship and learned many of the intangibles of scholarship over the years; and Margaret Crahan, Rolando Mellafe, Arturo Flores Vera, and Paul Ganster, who have provided valuable assistance at various stages of research. I acknowledge a debt more personal than academic when I thank Señora Nora Bryson de Andrade for the benefit of her wisdom and knowledge of things limeña. This book would never have been completed without the assistance of my wife, Barbara, an unfailing source of patience, cheerfulness, and support during the long period of research, writing, and revision. Finally, my appreciation goes to my teachers. I want to thank Professor John H. Rowe for much of what I have learned about colonial Peru, and to express my gratitude to James F. King for wise advice and help at critical moments. I have dedicated this book to the two professors who have most influenced my interests. Its flaws are mine, its virtues those they endeavored to instill.

F.P.B.

Stanford, California
March 1973

Contents

1. The Beginnings of African Slavery in Peru   1

2. The Atlantic Slave Trade to Spanish America   26

3. The Peruvian Slave Trade   52

4. The African and the Peruvian Economy: A General Survey   88

5. African Versus Indian Labor: A Royal Dilemma   110

6. The Black Artisan   125

7. The Control of the African: Crime and Sedition   147

8. The Control of the African: Cimarrones and the Santa Hermandad   187

9. Physical and Spiritual Concerns   222

10. The Free Person of Color: Manumission   272

11. The Free Person of Color: Acceptance and Advancement   302

12. Conclusion   324

Appendixes
A. The Colored Population of Lima   337
B. Lima Slave Prices, 1560-1650   342
C. African Ethnic Names   346
D. Glossary   347

Notes   353
Bibliography   419
Index   429

Author's Note

Few problems are more confusing to the student of colonial Peruvian history than that of currency. Until the 1570's commercial transactions in Peru were usually expressed in gold pesos (called *pesos de oro* or *pesos ensayados*), considered to be of a fineness of about 22 or 22.5 carats and of a presumed value of 450 *maravedís*. In practice, however, much more silver than gold was in circulation. Official coinage was not struck in Peru on a systematic basis until 1572, when the royal mint was moved from Lima to Potosí to be closer to the mining centers. Before then, the silver that made Peru famous around the world changed hands in bar form or in crude lumps, and the value of both varied widely. To reflect these realities, transactions were often expressed in pesos of "current silver" (*peso corriente*), worth about 300 *maravedís* each. The *peso ensayado* itself was subject to an official change of value in 1592, when Philip II ordered that the gold peso used in payments to the treasury be valued at 425 *maravedís* (or 12.5 *reales*), the reduction to cover the cost of coining the silver bullion at the mint. This unit of value also crept into commercial transactions.

To make matters still more confusing, for several decades in the last part of the sixteenth century and the beginning of the seventeenth, an imaginary unit called the *peso de a nueve* (worth nine *reales*, or 306 *maravedís*) also appears in government records and notarial documentation. Finally, in the seventeenth century still another monetary unit slowly gained currency, the famous *peso de a ocho* (piece of eight) of eight *reales*, or 272 *maravedís*, each.

One source I have consulted (Pike) suggests that the *peso ensayado* of the 1570's was worth about U.S. $.75 (1972). It would be more to the point, however, to know the peso's buying power. In this connection I will merely refer the reader to the text, where there are various useful hints, e.g., that the estimated cost of feeding a black slave in the urban area of Lima in the 1560's was one *real* a day; that in the 1630's one could buy a man's woolen outfit of the cheapest quality for about 4.5 pesos.

In this book, I have attempted to strike a balance between the need for simplicity and the confusion of historical reality. In Chapter 1, reference is to the gold peso of 450 *maravedís*. Elsewhere, I have usually converted all pesos into units of eight *reales*, a convention that is of particular importance in Appendix B, and all exceptions to this rule of conversion have been noted in the text. For more information on Spanish currency, see Haring, *Spanish Empire*, pp. 306-10; Lockhart, *Spanish Peru*, p. 82; Phelan, *Kingdom of Quito*, p. 341; Pike, *Aristocrats and Traders*, p. xiii; and Lohmann Villena, "Apuntaciones," pp. 80-81.

A few words also need to be said about the racial terminology employed in this book. I have opted not to use the term Negro for persons of African descent since many are now offended by the word, though I have retained it in direct quotations. Black has been used as a substitute, but I also use that word in a strict sense to refer to "pure" Africans. A Spaniard of the colonial period would have done the same, i.e., all persons of color were called *negros*, though more precise racial classifications were employed as the occasion demanded. Most people today still use "black" in the same dual sense, and it has been so used in this book—with a minimum of confusion to the careful reader, I hope. I wish, however, to alert my readers to the fact that the distinction between such terms as black and mulatto assumes particular importance in Chapters 9-11.

The African Slave in
Colonial Peru
1524-1650

The borders between Peru and the neighboring countries are modern ones. The northern and southern borders, for instance, do not demarcate the Lima Audiencia district, which was only vaguely limited. As for the eastern border, the Andes more or less marked the extent of Spanish colonization in the period under study.

CHAPTER ONE

The Beginnings of African Slavery in Peru

On hearing of the Spanish discovery of the Western Hemisphere many Europeans of the late fifteenth century must have sensed that the consequences for both the discoverers and the discovered would be profound. Spain would enrich herself with the treasures from these vast and mysterious new possessions, but she would give of her culture in return. The inhabitants of the New World would become Spaniards and Christians, whether through suasion or force, and a new Spain would take shape in America. But surely there were few observers in 1500 who foresaw that the Spanish colonization of the New World would ultimately involve millions of enslaved people from still another continent, Africa.[1] Yet it was only twenty-five years after the epochal first voyage of Columbus that the commitment to African slavery was made, and the greatest forced human migration in history began.

A curious set of circumstances gave slavery on the Iberian Peninsula a new lease on life on the very eve of the discovery of America. Established in Spain since Roman times, the institution of slavery was greatly strengthened during the Middle Ages by a stream of captives taken during the more or less continuous warfare between the Moors and the Spaniards. In addition, between the thirteenth and fifteenth centuries Italian merchants carried on a thriving trade in slaves on the Black Sea, and Tartars, Circassians, Armenians, Georgians, and Bulgarians by the thousands were offered for sale in the slave marts of Italy and Spain. There were also Africans to be bought or captured from the Arab traders. Supplied from all these sources, parts of Spain had become thickly populated with slaves, when the Black Sea marts were abruptly sealed off by the Turkish capture of Constantinople in 1453.[2]

But even as the slave trade was dying in the Mediterranean basin it was coming to new life elsewhere. In these same decades Portuguese ships were nosing south along the Atlantic coast of Africa, to establish direct contact with African societies and break the monopoly of commerce in blacks formerly enjoyed by the Arabs. Early dealings in slaves were modest, overshadowed by those in gold and ivory, but by the 1460's Portuguese traders were supplying both their own countrymen and the Spanish with considerable numbers of Africans, and Lisbon became a thriving slave mart. Spanish merchants soon followed the Portuguese lead,[3] and by the end of the fifteenth century Turkish expansionism and Iberian commercial enterprise had served to transform the status of the African from that of one slave among many to the single remaining source of cheap, alien servile labor.

But just as the ultimate importance of this development cannot be overemphasized, its initial scope should not be exaggerated. The slave trade between Africa and the Iberian Peninsula began as, and remained, a modest affair.[4] Indeed, Spanish interest in Africa was so slight that, after an interval of warfare with Portugal in the late 1470's, Spain ceded the exploitation of the mainland to the Portuguese in return for the Canary Islands. Columbus's discoveries further blinded Spain to the ultimate importance of Africa. Ferdinand and Isabella hastened to secure papal confirmation of authority in America and induced Pope Alexander VI to issue the bull *Inter caetera*, which drew an imaginary boundary line from north to south 100 leagues west of the Azores and the Cape Verde Islands staking out everything beyond as a Spanish sphere of exploration. A subsequent bull, *Dudum siquidem*, extended the grant to include "all islands and mainlands whatever, found or to be found . . . in sailing or traveling towards the west and south, whether they be in regions occidental or meridional and oriental and of India." The Portuguese were disturbed by the reference to India, a territory soon to be reached by sailing around Africa, and ostensibly to protect their African interests, refused to accept the validity of the papal grants unless the line was drawn 270 leagues farther west. The Spanish monarchs, who perhaps still shared Columbus's delusion that he had reached Asia, agreed to the change, and the Treaty of Tordesillas in 1494 formalized the concession.[5]

It was the Portuguese who benefited most from Tordesillas. Portugal received the true route to India, the assurance that Spain would remain a minor colonial power in Africa, and the not inconsequential American territory of Brazil. In return, Spain got the rest of the New World, an entity only dimly perceived (if at all) at the time, and at the moment the bargain seemed a bad one. In 1499, when Vasco da Gama returned to Lisbon in triumph from India, the Spanish were scratching around in the small and quickly exhausted gold deposits on the Caribbean islands. In the process a native population of several millions rapidly declined, victims of the harsh Spanish labor system and European diseases against which they had no immunity. As the natives died off the Crown began (reluctantly at first) to authorize the importation of more and more blacks to take their place, but subject to certain stipulations. To protect the remaining natives from possible contact with African idolatry, only Christian blacks, i.e., slaves who had been born in Spain or Portugal or who had resided there long enough to be baptized, were allowed to go to America, and even then their owners first had to obtain a royal license for each, a permit that increasingly involved payment of a fee and customs duties.[6] By 1517, however, the government recognized that African labor had to be imported on a larger scale to ensure the economic survival of the islands, and in the next year the first substantial shipment of slaves directly from Africa to America was authorized, 4,000 blacks over an eight-year period.[7]

Still, it is doubtful if the implications of this move, which underlined the Spanish concessions made in Africa, were realized at the time. Beginning in 1519, with the discovery and conquest of Mexico, Spanish eyes were turned elsewhere. In Mexico the Spaniards found the elements necessary for a great colonial empire: highly civilized natives who were accustomed to subordination and who lived in a region that showed evidence of mineral wealth. And Cortés had scarcely conquered Mexico when Francisco Pizarro promised to duplicate the achievement in Peru.

Pizarro was one of many conquistadores who gravitated to the Isthmus of Panama and achieved a measure of wealth, yet were urged on by the news of the spectacular success of their compatriots in Mexico. Hearing persistent tales of wealthy native kingdoms to the south of Panama, Pizarro formed a company for the purpose of Pacific exploration. African slaves were relatively numerous in Panama by this date, at least in part because of the decline of the native population, and blacks figured in all the expeditions undertaken by the company between 1524 and 1528.[8] An African slave helped to save the life of Pizarro's most prominent associate, Diego de Almagro, for example, and later, in 1528, when Pizarro discovered the city of Túmbez, a black sent along to observe the place was seized by the incredulous natives and vigorously scrubbed in an effort to remove what was presumed to be the dye on his skin.[9]

The explorers' observations at Túmbez convinced them that the conquest of the territory they had discovered was beyond their resources and beyond any backing they might expect from the skeptical citizens and officials of Panama. Pizarro accordingly went to Spain and there succeeded in enlisting official support, formalized in 1529 in a document called the Capitulations of Toledo. Among other things, it licensed him to import, duty free, fifty African slaves (at least a third of whom were to be women) into the land he had pledged to conquer, plus two slaves for his personal use. Other men who embarked for the new colony in various official capacities were granted similar permits for the payment of a modest fee.

This trickle of black slaves from the Iberian Peninsula to the new territory continued during the early years of colonization. Between 1529 and 1537 the Crown granted licenses to some thirty individuals to import at least 363 African slaves. Pizarro and his kinsmen led the list by far with 258 permits, and most of the rest went to prominent government officials and colonists for household servants. The importation of twenty Africans was also authorized for the building of roads, bridges, and other public works.[10] This same period also saw the introduction of blacks for commercial purposes. At least two such permits were issued. The first went in 1535 to two slave traders, who were granted an unspecified number of licenses for trade with Peru; and the second, in the following year, permitted a partnership that had obtained a monopoly of all the wool and yarn available for export from Peru to bring 100 black slaves into the region to aid the enterprise.[11]

The main flow of blacks to the area in this early period came, not from Spain or Africa, but from other parts of Spanish America.[12] The fame of Peruvian riches quickly spread to the other Spanish settlements and caused a veritable gold rush to the region. Quite naturally, Spaniards who came in search of fortune carried their African slaves with them. In 1534, for example, when Pedro de Alvarado and his followers set sail from Guatemala to lay claim to a portion of the new territory, some 200 blacks accompanied the party. The attempt failed, but the majority of the slaves were sold and remained in Peru.[13] In 1535 one observer informed the Crown that 600 Spaniards and 400 African slaves had embarked from Panama for Peru in the previous six months. Indeed, the dimensions of the exodus to Peru grew so great that the Caribbean islands, where the gold deposits were nearing exhaustion, faced virtual depopulation. Despite the efforts of the government to prevent migration, Spaniards desperate to reach Peru were not above stealing a boat with which to spirit themselves and their blacks away from the islands and toward the new El Dorado. As late as 1538 one conquistador came to Peru from Santo Domingo, allegedly with the permission of the governor of the island, with "many horses, arms, slaves, and much mining equipment and other things necessary for war and for mine labor, which together were worth more than 16,000 pesos in gold."[14]

The chroniclers of the conquest of Peru preferred to concentrate on the exploits of Spaniards, and therefore we have little information on the participation of blacks. Two notable cases are those of an African assistant to the master of artillery on the 1531 expedition of conquest, a man so highly respected as to bear the title of Captain until the bitter partisanship of the civil wars caused his death at the hands of the Pizarro faction;[15] and of Juan Valiente, one of some 150 blacks who accompanied Diego de Almagro on his expedition to Chile in 1535. Valiente, a runaway slave from Mexico, survived the rigors of Almagro's Chilean venture and later attached himself to the expedition of Pedro de Valdivia, who was more fortunate in his attempt at colonization. Valiente went to Chile with Valdivia as a free soldier with his own arms and horse, and for his services in the new colony was awarded both a grant of land and the privilege of Indian labor.[16]

On the whole, however, there seems not to have been much room for a real African role in the early development of Peru. In the first place, the Spanish could rely on a substantial number of Indian slaves, particularly natives captured during the conquests of Central America and Mexico. Indeed, during the early years of the Peruvian conquest Indian slaves from these two regions were more numerous than their black counterparts.[17] In addition, the natives of Peru were also held in bondage, in fact if not in name. As James Lockhart observes, the Spanish conquerors appropriated, "as servants and mistresses, Indians who thenceforth traveled about the country in their personal retinue. Torn

Fig. 1. A black slave of a Spanish *corregidor de indios* flogging an Indian

out of the indigenous social context, many such Indians lost their geographical context as well. A large proportion of them settled down with their masters in parts of Peru remote from their birthplaces, so that even they shared a certain degree of foreignness with the Negroes and foreign Indians."[18] Further, as early as 1534 Pizarro began to reward his followers with *encomiendas*, broad powers to commandeer the tribute and labor of a specified number of natives in a certain district, a lucrative enough reward to attract virtually all of the prominent conquistadores.[19]

Withal, a slight demand for black slaves continued, perhaps in large part because the Spanish did not entirely trust the newly conquered Indian. The 1535-36 revolt of the Inca Manco confirmed that the natives bore no great love for their conquerors, and the Spanish reaction was to place greater reliance on blacks, who helped suppress the rebellion.[20] Indeed, the Spanish were now forced to reconsider the whole question of the black man.[21] What made the African such a loyal servant was his utter foreignness. Unlike (say) a Nicaraguan Indian, he could not desert his master and melt into the native population. More important, he had no desire to do so. Of necessity, the African identified with everything Spanish more rapidly than did the Indian—to the point, in fact, where many blacks, in imitation of their white masters, terrorized native villages and even accumulated staffs of cowed Indian servants. This led, at least during the early period of Peruvian colonization, to a strong mutual hostility between Indian and African that benefited both the Spaniard and his black slave.[22] Prized by the master for his fidelity, the black man rapidly came to occupy an intermediate position between Spaniard and Indian rather than the place beneath the Indian to which the law had consigned him. Missionary priests who lived in near-isolation among the Indians often had a black slave to serve as both servant and companion, and many of the Spaniards attempted to achieve a measure of security by leavening the ranks of their native servants with African slaves. Indeed, the identification of some blacks with everything Spanish appears to have been almost total, as in the case of Margarita, slave of Diego de Almagro. Margarita waited on Almagro faithfully while in Panama, accompanied him during the conquest of Peru, and remained with him during the imprisonment that ended in his execution. A grateful Almagro freed her on his death. In liberty, Margarita took her former master's name, founded a chaplaincy in the Mercederian convent at Cuzco to perpetuate his memory, and during the civil war period loaned money to the Spanish Crown to defeat its enemies.[23]

In addition to the prospect of loyal service, the ownership of black slaves brought prestige. Black slaves, says Lockhart, "were one essential part of the general pattern of Spanish ambitions. No encomendero felt happy until he owned a large house, land, livestock, and—most to the point here—Negro servants. Most Spaniards could not hope to achieve this goal in its entirety, but they aimed at least for two essentials, a house (which could be rented) and Negroes. One of the most important yardsticks for a Spaniard's contribution to any of the various war efforts was the number of Negro servants he brought to the battle with him." That this was indeed a yardstick of prestige is evident in the petition of the conquistador Juan de Pancorvo seeking confirmation of an encomienda grant, in which he went to great pains to mention the numerous black slaves he had in his entourage.[24]

Many Peruvian blacks must have been puzzled by the behavior of their seemingly invincible masters in the years after 1536. Victory over the Incas brought only disunity. The partnership between Pizarro and Almagro, so effective in hard times, collapsed under the strain of dividing the spoils of success, and the colony was plunged into civil war. Pizarro's adherents defeated and executed Almagro only to witness the assassination of their own leader and to be forced, in the early 1540's, to rally around the royal standard in the successful fight against Diego de Almagro the Younger. These events had scarcely passed when in 1542-43 the Crown promulgated the New Laws, a body of legislation that sharply limited conquistador control over the Indian population, and then sent the tactless Viceroy Blasco Núñez Vela (1544-46) to enforce them. Armed with lands, Indian tribute, and retainers, the conquistadores preferred combat to submission, with Gonzalo Pizarro at their head. The New Laws eventually prevailed, albeit in drastically modified form, but peace did not come to the colony for well over a decade.[25]

In all this strife, blacks played a part on both sides of the shifting lines of combat. Though in most cases African slaves "went as pages, and stayed in the tents at battletime,"[26] blacks were prominent enough at the major battles of the Peruvian civil wars to be mentioned by contemporaries and chroniclers of the period. At the decisive battle of Chupas, for example, the defeated army of the younger Almagro is reported to have included some 1,000 blacks;[27] and in the 1546 battle of Añaquito against Núñez Vela, Gonzalo Pizarro's victorious army was assisted by as many as 600 black auxiliaries.[28] A year later, his fortunes in decline, Pizarro nevertheless won the battle of Guarina, fought in the Peruvian highlands, and after the victory African slaves were used to scour the battlefield for enemy soldiers to execute.[29] When Pizarro was finally defeated in 1548, blacks were once again present in large numbers on both sides. Even more significant was the role played by skilled Africans in the supply of the royal army. Black artisans were employed to manufacture harquebuses, swords, and lances, and an African woman was commissioned to supply the force with rosaries. Clearly, the black craftsman was already a part of the colonial economy.[30]

The victory of the royal forces precipitated a sweeping redistribution of the black slaves within the colony. To maintain himself in power, Pizarro had rewarded his followers with the blacks, livestock, and liquid assets known to belong to his enemies, and the victorious Crown now followed the same strategy. Slaves who belonged to Pizarro's adherents were either confiscated and auctioned for the Crown's financial benefit or, perhaps more often, passed silently into the hands of the victors.[31] Further, in 1550 seven of the most prominent supporters of the Crown were granted approximately 1,700 duty-free slave licenses as compensation for their expenses.[32] What became of the permits is unknown. Many times recipients of this form of royal largess sold their licenses to slave merchants, who then shipped the Africans to various destinations, but at this date Peru must have seemed a likely market, and these permits may well have served to swell the black population.

The last rebellion to torment Peru during this period was that led by Francisco Hernández Girón between 1553 and 1554. Once again, the issue was the Crown's authority over the Indian population, but this time many conquistadores, with the example of Gonzalo Pizarro fresh in their minds, did not dare to challenge the royal will. Desperate to increase his following, Hernández did what no Spanish commander before him had ever had the nerve to try: he offered freedom to all slaves who would join him and armed his black followers for participation in battle. It appears that an original nucleus of 150 blacks was formed from captured slaves and those belonging to Hernández's adherents. With vague promises of freedom and the immediate inducement of military trappings, this number was doubled by black recruits from the

Arequipa, Guamanga (Ayacucho), and Nazca areas. This contingent, trained and commanded by a black general named Juan, a slave carpenter, and "disciplined and divided into companies, with banners and drums, armed with pikes and harquebuses," served as a squadron in the army Hernández gathered. The blacks gave good account of themselves in battle.[33] The Crown on its side employed Africans in the military preparations to put down the rebellion, and many of its supporters brought their blacks to assist them in what proved to be a victory.[34]

Despite the tumult of the years of conquest and civil war, commercial life began in the new colony, including, in a modest way, the trafficking in African slaves. Predictably, the lure of the spoils of conquest prompted the creation of many companies for trade in merchandise, horses, and slaves between Peru, the mother country (via Panama), and other Spanish American areas, and commerce within the new colony was also lively.[35] In the beginning, everybody with anything to sell participated. The governor of Panama was quick to appreciate the commercial opportunities afforded by the conquest and dispatched an associate with a quantity of clothing, horses, and blacks to sell in exchange for silver.[36] Even Viceroy Núñez Vela was prompted to join in, arranging for agents in Portugal to transport sixty blacks to the colony for sale. His brother likewise traded in "dry goods, horses, and blacks" before the pair of them lost their lives in the Gonzalo Pizarro rebellion.[37] Increasingly, however, the bulk of Peruvian commerce passed into the hands of full-time merchants, and the civil strife that raged within the colony had little impact on the activities of these men. As Lockhart notes, most merchants "enjoyed the status of near-neutrals in the wars since everyone needed them and they were not candidates for the encomiendas over which the wars were fought."[38]

The majority of these merchants, some of them Corsican and Portuguese, probably dealt in slaves, but only in a small way: ordinarily even the largest traders handled lots of from ten to twenty blacks, and these on an irregular basis, and most simply brought a slave or two along with other general merchandise. Slaves changed hands in equally small lots. The two largest sales of blacks recorded between 1532 and 1560 (in Lima in 1543) involved only twelve individuals each.[39] Most transactions involved only one slave, who often was sold in conjunction with a horse, various articles of clothing, or other items. In 1535, for example, Diego de Almagro purchased in one lot an African slave, a quantity of clothing, shoes, and weapons, forty-eight horseshoes, 1,400 horseshoe nails, some soap, two currycombs, and a hoof parer—all for 800 pesos. Similar transactions could be multiplied at will.[40]

Despite the relatively small demand for blacks in the early decades of Spanish Peru, slave prices slowly increased. In 1534, when most Spaniards confidently assumed that the services of the natives were theirs for the asking, and when prices paid for blacks were momentarily depressed by the discovery that Peruvian Indians were killing many more blacks than imported Indian slaves, the top price for an African was little more than 150 gold pesos. By the late 1530's, with Spanish confidence shaken by the Inca revolt, the general run of blacks were selling for from 100 to 250 pesos each, against 50 to 150 pesos for their Indian counterparts, and skilled slaves of both races might fetch as much again. Slave prices remained stable in the 1540's until the worst of the civil conflict was over, when the upper figure rose to 300 pesos. Prices paid for blacks increased more rapidly during the 1550's, and by 1557 ranged from 250 to 500 gold pesos.[41]

Commerce in blacks, always supplemented by the trickle of slaves who accompanied their masters to the colony, produced an estimated Afro-Peruvian population of some 3,000 by the mid-1550's, with approximately half this number concentrated in the capital of Lima*—not a large figure, but then the number of Spaniards could not have been much greater. Most of those concerned with colonial development at the time did not except a significant increase in the black population. However important as a symbol of opulence, the African was expensive and available only in limited numbers, and was therefore considered to be of little significance to the future of Peru.

Still, the Spanish had no intention of developing the colony by their own muscle. Even the most humble of the Spanish immigrants viewed themselves as members of a conquering race and shunned manual labor. Many of the first to come were little more than adventurers bent on living off whatever could be exacted from the native population by force, and even when conditions stabilized the Spaniard was a man who "always idle . . . , very delicate, and fit for little manual labor."[42] Unwilling to work with his own hands, the Spaniard intended to have the Indian work for him. In Peru the Spanish had conquered an aboriginal population that was large and accustomed over centuries to the requisi-

* See Appendix A for the Lima situation in the period studied.

tion of tribute and labor by a central authority, and it was the Indian who was expected to work the mountain mines and the agricultural enterprises of both coast and highlands.

In the beginning, then, all concerned with the colonization of Peru looked to the Indian for labor. But the attitudes and interests of the home government and the colonists soon began to diverge. Most of the conquerors and settlers of Peru favored the unrestrained exploitation of the natives, though few would have put the matter so bluntly, but the Spanish Crown was unwilling to sanction this policy. Though fully aware that Peru could not prosper without cheap labor, the monarchy could not ignore an increasingly vocal group of men, of whom Bartolomé de las Casas was the most conspicuous, who were outraged by the excesses of the conquest and who questioned whether Spain had any title to America at all, much less to the services of its aboriginal inhabitants.[43] Ultimately, the Crown was forced to concede to the Indian the status of free vassal within its dominions. There is little reason to doubt the sincerity of this concession, but certainly more than humanitarian considerations figured in the policy of the government. For one thing, the Crown was determined to prevent the rise of a conquistador aristocracy capable of challenging its authority in the American colonies, and to this end royal control over Indian labor was essential.

The New Laws of 1542-43 had been designed to attain the moral and political goals of the Crown, and though civil war forced the abrogation of this legislation in Peru, the policies of the home government did not change.[44] These policies were designed to channel Indian manpower into the development of the colony, but with a minimum of harshness toward the native and with a maximum of government control. These goals were firmly, if cautiously, pursued by a victorious Crown. In particular, the enslavement of the Indian was regarded as intolerable except in extreme cases of rebellion, and by 1550 Indian slavery had all but disappeared from the colony.[45] Moreover, in the succeeding years the Crown broke the hold of the Spanish encomenderos over their native charges.[46] Encomenderos were forbidden to demand tribute in the form of unpaid labor, and the amounts of other forms of tribute were fixed; and the government rejected appeals to assign encomienda grants in perpetuity. The installation of *corregidores de indios*, royal officials who exercised judicial and political authority in Indian areas similar to that of a governor, further reduced the encomenderos' power over the natives. By the end of the 1570's it was clear to all that the Crown, and not the conquistadores and their descendants, held mastery over the native population.

In these same years the Crown began having second thoughts about the employment of the African, particularly in the mining industry. Mine labor was among the most arduous of occupations in the colonial economy, and there was ample precedent for the use of blacks in the industry. During the early decades of Spanish Peru Africans were prominent in the mining of gold, a metal found largely in placer deposits in the hot, low-lying parts of the colony. Indian labor was used where available, but the native population was sparse in many such regions, the mortality rate was appalling, and mine operators were often forced to import blacks to take up the slack, particularly since the climate was presumed to agree with the African. Such was the case, for example, during the 1542 gold rush to the Carabaya area in the jurisdiction of Cuzco. The black mining gangs were ordinarily small, numbering from ten to fifteen men, with perhaps a slave woman to cook for them, though larger work forces were occasionally required. In Lockhart's view, black gold miners had a far worse lot than the rest of their fellow Africans, "tramping in gangs from one steaming river site to the next, out of contact with either the Indian or the Hispanic world, except for their Spanish overseer."[47]

But it was silver, not gold, that gave Peru its reputation for wealth, and for years the government considered sparing the natives by using blacks in the silver mines, located in the bleak Peruvian highlands. The Crown was in a position to call the tune, since by law subsoil rights were royal property, and the question was therefore not merely one of labor but whether the mines were to be worked directly or left to public exploitation in return for substantial royalties.

Apparently Viceroy Núñez Vela initiated the discussion in 1544, arguing that if the Crown followed the customary practice of permitting the public development of such claims, private entrepreneurs would be willing to invest money in slaves to extract the silver, and there would be no need to use Indian labor for the task.[48] At that date, the colonists were eager enough to work the mines, but they were reluctant to purchase expensive Africans when cheap Indian labor was available in the vicinity. Would-be developers argued that the cost of operations in the difficult highland terrain was very great, particularly with respect to supply and transport, and that no profit would remain if they were forced to purchase Africans who soon sickened and died in the cold climate.[49] It may well be that blacks did have a difficult time adjusting to the frigid *sierra* (as expressed in the still-current Peruvian saying *el gallinazo no canta en puna**), but mine labor exacted a heavy toll among the native population as well. The blunt fact was that the Spanish mine operators were concerned with mortality rates in the labor force only in relation to profits. The nearby Indian, who represented no capital investment, was preferred to the distant African, and the colonial mining interests were determined to make their views prevail.

With the chaos of the Gonzalo Pizarro rebellion, the questions of the ownership and labor force of the mines were left hanging for a time. However, once Pizarro had been defeated by Pedro de la Gasca, who continued to govern Peru in the name of the Crown, royal supervision over the highland mines at Porco and Potosí, then worked by Indians, was quickly established. Gasca soon became convinced that the government should decide one way or the other who was to exploit these properties, and pressed for the Crown itself to mine the silver with the aid of African slaves.[50] He argued that Porco could be profitably worked with African slaves: the climate was temperate, and the native population of the area could feed and clothe the blacks. Indeed, if African women were imported to perform these tasks, the black miners would be self-sufficient. Gasca admitted that the climate of Potosí was more severe, but he observed that Gonzalo Pizarro had used black mine labor in that location, and the governor had no doubt that the Crown could profitably employ Africans there to supplement the Indians who were already skilled in the work. As at Porco, the nearby natives could be relied on to supply the black miners with food and clothing. Gasca also argued that the cost of transporting the slaves to Peru could be met by importing more than were needed for the mines and selling the surplus.

Gasca's proposals for the Porco mine were endorsed and made more specific in 1551 by Juan de Cáceres, a royal treasury official. He advised the government to import into Peru the necessary equipment and 200 blacks, preferably between the ages of twenty-five and thirty. Half of the slaves should be female to ensure that the males would be well fed

---

* In literal English, the turkey buzzard doesn't sing in the highlands. The gallinazo, a black-colored vulture with a bare, reddish head, is common along the Peruvian coast, but is not seen in the cold tablelands of the Andes.

and reasonably contented, and therefore less liable to run away. The females could divide their time between domestic chores and helping the men in the mines. Cáceres, too, proposed that the nearby Indians supply the bulk of the slaves' food and clothing.[51]

The Council of the Indies, responsible for the governance and prosperity of the American colonies, was interested in these proposals, and questioned Gasca on his return to Spain about the wisdom of encouraging the export of slaves to Peru, "where they say there is a shortage of them," for work in the mines and other enterprises. The tone of the Council's inquiry, which stressed the financial advantages to be gained by the Crown through the sale of slave licenses, leaves little doubt that an affirmative reply was desired.[52] At approximately the same time, however, another official report was filed from Peru insisting that the climate of the highlands was too cold to employ African slaves at mine labor, and that those who did not die would attempt to run away to escape the rigors of the altitude.[53]

Confronted with this conflicting testimony, the Crown was unable to reach a decision on the question of mine labor, and in 1554 a new investigation of the matter was begun by the Council of the Indies. Opinions were solicited from many prominent colonists or ex-colonists resident in Spain. Further, the Council did not concern itself merely with the question as it related to the claims at Porco and Potosí, but extended its inquiry to the problem of mine labor throughout Peru. The government wished to know if Africans could perform mine labor at a profit, whether the natives of the area could feed and clothe them, and how many slaves and Indians would be involved. It was interested, too, in finding out whether the Indian might not in fact be used to better purpose than the black, asking witnesses if there were natives who would be willing to work in the mines (perhaps for a share of the ore extracted), and if it would be useful to allow Indians held in encomienda by the Crown to pay their tribute in this fashion. In addition, the Council wanted the witnesses' opinion on whether the Crown should work the silver mines on its own account or lease them to others for a percentage of the bullion extracted.[54] Clearly, the Council wished to tap the mineral wealth of Peru but to do so without compromising the liberty of the native population. African labor was regarded as the possible solution to the problem.

However, except for Pedro de la Gasca, who continued to advocate the importation of blacks, all of the witnesses declared that the mines should be worked by salaried Indian labor. Some of the most interesting testimony came from Hernando Pizarro, who had experimented with blacks on his mining claim. Pizarro recalled that he had ordered 120 slaves to be shipped from Seville, but owing to mistreatment en route and the carelessness of his agents scarcely thirty of them had arrived in Peru. As a result of this unhappy experience, Pizarro urged the Crown to purchase blacks from slave traders in Peru if the mines were placed under royal administration; the higher initial cost would be more than offset by the elimination of the risks involved in transporting slaves from either Spain or Africa in the care of unconcerned agents. But even then Pizarro did not think the employment of blacks in the mines would be profitable: most Africans could not withstand the frigid climate, and still others rapidly sickened and died from the smoke of the furnaces required to found the silver.

The other witnesses shared Pizarro's pessimism, and one of them, Jerónimo de Soria, presented to the Council an absorbing document that calculated the cost of working a mine with African labor. According to Soria, at least thirty male slaves would be required to work a claim, and if these men were to be well fed and content, thereby preventing runaways and general mischief-making, an additional thirty female blacks were necessary. Figuring that each couple would cost 647 pesos a year to maintain, against a potential maximum earning power of 750, Soria suggested that at best one would get a return of 103 pesos a year per couple. Since each couple delivered in the highlands would cost 600 pesos if unskilled or 800 if skilled, this meant that a life expectancy of six to eight years would have to be assumed for each slave before the purchase price was even recovered and any real profit cleared. On the other hand, Soria pointed out, if the mines were thrown open for private exploitation, with the customary 20 per cent of production going to the Crown, the government would receive 150 pesos of the estimated 750 produced by a couple (slave or otherwise) in a year and assume no risk at all. Soria's cost estimates were somewhat inflated,[55] but the weight of his testimony in combination with Pizarro's was sufficient to persuade the Crown to let private individuals take on the task of exploiting the highland mines. In addition, plans for the large-scale employment of Africans in the mines were shelved, and the government consented to the use of Indian mine labor.

During the second half of the 1550's this decision seemed a wise one. The silver mines of highland Peru were relatively small, the ore rich, and the local labor supply sufficient. But the employment of the African in mining was not quite forgotten in government circles. The metal in this case was gold, and the chief proponent of black labor was the viceroy Marqués de Cañete (1555-61). Cañete became interested in the matter in 1556 with the discovery of rich gold deposits in the sparsely populated Chachapoyas area. Convinced by a group of prominent churchmen that it would be inhumane to force Indians from other areas to undertake such hard labor in an alien climate, particularly one suitable for the employment of Africans, Cañete urged the Crown to send 3,000 blacks, a third of them female, and the necessary mining equipment to the colony for sale to private individuals. In this way the cost of the enterprise would be quickly recovered, and no hardship would be imposed on the Indians. Moreover, the government would gain additional revenue when the mines were opened up and the royalties on the ore began to be paid.[56]

The Crown refused to be drawn into a venture that required large capital expenditures for African slaves, but in the meantime—and without royal authorization—Cañete had gone ahead with another plan. Gold had been discovered in the tropical province of Carabaya, and Cañete proposed to settle the idle free coloreds of Peru in this favorable climate to work the ore deposits. To this end, in 1557 he appointed a Spaniard to govern the projected settlement and gave him 2,000 pesos with which to bring free blacks and mulattoes from anywhere in the colony to settle there. The scope of Cañete's experiment is not known, but at least sixteen free persons of color were taken to the site from the Lima area.[57] As it happened, the mines of Carabaya did not live up to official expectations. Worse from the Spanish point of view, the free coloreds who settled there soon became "the owners of agricultural land, cultivated by Indian labor." Fifteen years later, the town they had founded, San Juan del Oro, was still in existence and had thirty to forty heads of household, most of them mulatto.[58] Thus ended the only official attempt to work the mineral wealth of Peru with persons of African descent, though, as we shall see, various plans and projects toward that end continued to be formulated.

In the 1560's and 1570's, however, the government pondered larger problems. In the early years of colonization the employment of Indian labor to develop the colony had been seen by Spanish officialdom as purely a moral issue, but in the second half of the sixteenth century a practical, and urgent, dimension was added to the problem. In the first place, the Crown had confidently stripped the encomendero class of the right to coerce Indian labor only to discover that without coercion the native population, caught up in subsistence agriculture at the village level, displayed little interest in participation in the larger economy. To be sure, the operation of the encomienda as a labor institution had exposed the Indian to the opportunities available in Spanish towns, with the result that many natives stayed on to work after their labor obligations to the encomenderos had been fulfilled, and many others were prompted to come to the towns to seek extra income in times of economic distress. Moreover, native nobles, who with the consent of the encomendero had been accustomed to renting out work gangs of their subjects to other Spaniards as a way to raise the tribute money, did not lose sight of this opportunity after the encomenderos were forbidden to demand personal service as tribute. In addition to all these, the Spanish could rely on the *yanaconas*, a servant class of Indians who had long since lost all ties to clan or village and who did not come under the authority of the encomienda.[59]

Even so, once the labor function was divorced from the encomienda, the number of Indians who offered themselves for hire was too few and subject to too many fluctuations to satisfy Spanish demand. In any case, by the second half of the sixteenth century the Peruvian Indian population had been drastically reduced. There were many reasons for this decline. A bloody civil war among the Incas had just ended when the Spaniards arrived, and the conquest and civil war periods exposed the natives to twenty-odd years of famine, overwork, property loss, cultural shock, and general mistreatment. Even more devastating were the unfamiliar European diseases—smallpox, measles, typhoid—which spread among the native population with catastrophic effect.

Relatively little research has been done on demographic trends during the colonial period, but the most reliable estimates to date indicate that between 1525 and 1571 the aboriginal population fell from as many as 6,000,000 persons to some 1,500,000, and that the total continued to shrink, though less rapidly, until well into the eighteenth century. The loss was most severe along the Peruvian coast, where perhaps as much as 90 per cent of the population, or approximately 1,000,000 people, died by the end of the 1540's. The chronicler Pedro de Cieza de León, who traveled over much of Peru during this period, was horrified by the destruction of native life along the coast. The case of the Chincha Valley south of Lima was but one of many he cited: "And the inhabitants of this valley were so numerous that many Spaniards say that when it was conquered by the Marquis [Pizarro] and themselves, there were ... more than twenty-five thousand men, and I doubt that there are now five thousand, so many have been the inroads and hardships they have suffered."[60] With the exception of a few provinces, the highlands were not as hard hit, perhaps because communications (and therefore the spread of disease) were difficult, but even so a third of the population probably vanished.[61]

As the labor market became tighter and tighter the *mita* (or *repartimiento*) system became increasingly important as a means of coercing the natives to work. The mita was an outgrowth of the Inca past. To provide labor for public works and other state purposes, the Inca rulers instructed their provincial governors to rotate such service among the families under their jurisdiction. No man who performed this service (*mit'ayoq*) was required to serve again until all the rest had had a turn (*mit'a*). In the beginning the Spanish conquerors relied on the system unconsciously. When the governor or encomendero of a certain district needed an unusually large number of laborers for a specific project, the native leader was instructed to furnish the men, and he understandably fell back on Inca practice and raised his quota by the traditional method. In later decades colonial authorities systematized the practice, allotting to each Indian province a certain quota of men to be furnished on a rotating basis for service in designated Spanish areas and enterprises. Indeed, the Spanish Crown made a superficial improvement on Inca practice by insisting that native labor under the mita system be paid. However, the legal wage for mita service was never as high as that commanded by the Indian in the free labor market, and the mitayo was still obligated for the payment of his regular tribute assessment. In these circumstances the Indians had little enthusiasm for the system, and severe official pressure was frequently necessary to raise the required quota of native labor.

Even if the natives had willingly performed such labor service, the mita system was doomed to falter for the simple reason that so many Spaniards tended to settle along the Peruvian coast. For some of the large landowners of the coast, whose plantations supplied wheat, cotton, sugar, grapes, and other crops to the urban centers of Peru, the mita appeared to be a convenient source of native labor for construction, farm work, and general service. But since this was the very area where Indian population losses were most severe, the quotas could be filled only by compelling mitayos to travel great distances.* They were paid nothing for the trip and a mere *real* as a daily wage on arrival, scarcely enough for the day's food.

In fact, the operation of the mita system along the coast was not only hampered by a declining Indian population; it gave impetus to the trend. Mita service inevitably increased the chances of exposure to European disease and forced natives of the highlands to come to a radically different climate to put in long hours to back-breaking labor without proper rest or nourishment. The Spanish, like the Incas before them, gradually became aware that such a sharp climatic change followed by heavy labor often meant serious illness or death. Indeed, in 1563 the Crown forbade the practice of sending Indians accustomed to one climate to labor in another,[62] but this legislation remained a dead letter for many years.

Yet the government was not interested in improving the situation if it meant the expenditure of royal funds. In 1567, for example, Governor Lope García de Castro (1564-69) proposed that the Crown purchase some fifty blacks at a cost of 14,000-15,000 pesos to help build bridges at sites where the climate would damage the health of highland Indians, but the government turned a deaf ear to the suggestion.[63] Seven years later, in 1574, the Crown was informed that death usually claimed more than half of the mitayos who came down from the highlands to work in Lima, Trujillo, and other coastal towns. The government was urged to put a stop to the practice and to insist that only African slaves be employed for such service, but the would-be reformer apparently was not favored with a royal reply.[64]

The Crown would probably have been more concerned with the operation of the coastal mita if there had been more complaints from this sector of the economy. But the faltering of the forced-labor system in

* As early as the 1560's, for example, mitayos were required to come to Lima from as far away as Jauja, a ten-day journey by foot, to assemble daily in the plaza of the capital and hire themselves out to residents who wanted houses built or fields cultivated. The native ruler of Jauja finally refused to order his subjects to come to the capital and was jailed for his pains.

mid-century seems not to have created any real crisis for Spaniards along the coast, since many had relied on African slaves, yanaconas, and free Indian labor to provide the core of their work force for years. This was true even of encomenderos, who might have been expected to give strenuous support to the concept of forced Indian labor. In the early 1550's, for example, the encomendero Jerónimo de Villegas operated his eight farms in the Arequipa district with black and yanacona labor, and in 1556 one Doña Beatriz de Santillán, who enjoyed tribute revenues of 7,000 pesos, also possessed "slaves and other estates" valued at 25,000. The strongest evidence of a realistic turning away from exclusive reliance on the Indian comes from a 1562 report to the Crown prepared by Viceroy Conde de Nieva (1561-64) and the commissioners appointed to investigate the question of granting encomiendas in perpetuity. The report, which favored the idea, observed that the encomenderos held many slaves who cultivated their lands.[65] Another indication of the role of the African in supplementing the available number of natives comes from a decree of 1567 enjoining colonial officials to take steps to prevent the reported abuses inflicted by the black slaves of encomenderos on the Indians.[66] In short, though they petitioned for cheap mita labor, coastal Spaniards and even some highland encomenderos proved highly flexible when the situation demanded. African slaves, mitayos, yanaconas, and free Indians were used as occasion and opportunity warranted, and little effort was made to cling to a mita system that was manifestly inadequate. However much these Spaniards valued symbolic dominance over the Indian, common sense dictated that alternative sources of manpower be considered, and this realization would shortly pave the way for a greatly increased commerce in African slaves.

The situation was different in the mining areas of the Peruvian highlands, where the quality of the ore extracted began to decline in the 1560's. To keep production figures up, mining operations became more extensive and more difficult, and the developers began to petition the Crown to do something to increase the supply of cheap labor.[67] A decade earlier, when the government had yielded to the arguments of those who contended that the native population was the only sensible source of mine labor, it had been easy enough to tolerate the employment of the Indian on a small scale. But now the Crown was asked to organize a labor system that involved thousands of natives from several provinces to satisfy the needs of the mines, and despite the unfavorable testimony collected during the 1550's, the African and even the Spaniard were considered as alternatives.

Viceroy Nieva bluntly informed the Crown in 1563, however, that the choice was between the virtual economic extinction of the colony ("If there are no mines there is no Peru") and the large-scale employment of Indian mine laborers. To the suggestion that Spaniards be employed for the task, Nieva replied that there were not enough of them, and even if there were, his countrymen would "rather die than put hoes in their hands." As for Africans, the viceroy shared the prevailing view that they were not fit for work in the sierra climate, and argued that in any case it would be dangerous to import that many slaves: the Africans already outnumbered the Europeans (or so Nieva claimed), and the number of black criminals increased daily. Nieva flatly stated that forced Indian labor in the mines, with adequate compensation and good treatment, was the only solution.[68]

Nieva's advice was reluctantly accepted for the moment, but with the advent of the great Francisco de Toledo (1569-80) as viceroy, another determined effort was made to solve the labor question. The strategy agreed on by Toledo and the Crown was to lighten the labor burden of the Indian as much as possible and still avoid the massive importation of African slaves by pressing all free blacks, mulattoes, and various other racial mixtures who were not gainfully employed into the labor force. The concept was hardly an original one. Viceroy Cañete, among others, had made similar attempts to force those who were neither respectable Spaniards nor slaves nor Indians into the mainstream of colonial economic activity—partly for their labor and partly so the authorities could keep better tabs on this potentially troublesome segment of the colonial population.* But Toledo's effort was unique in its scope, and its failure heralded the beginning of African slavery as an important labor institution in Peru.

Toledo began the project in February 1570 with a letter to the Crown proposing that the free blacks and mulattoes of the colony, many of whom were supposedly resident in the Indian towns and oppressing the inhabitants, be forced into the service of Spaniards in the principal

---

* Forcible employment of free coloreds as a control device is discussed at length in Chapter 7.

cities. If this did not fully relieve the pressure on the available supply of mitayos, he suggested that the regulation could be extended to *mestizos* (offspring of Spanish men and Indian women). Four months later, he modified his plan, proposing that free blacks and others of African descent be compelled to work for wages in the mines, and mestizos in the cities.[69] The following year, during an inspection tour of the viceroyalty, Toledo met with the Cuzco city council to discuss methods of forcing these groups into the labor market. The result was legislation ordering free blacks and mulattoes to hire themselves out to, and take residence with, Spanish masters.[70]

Within three years the home government, which had been considering similar legislation for the American empire as a whole, came to the support of Toledo. In 1574 the Crown ordered censuses of the free blacks and mulattoes in every American colony along with estimates of the amount of tribute they ought to pay the government.[71] The intent was first to increase royal revenues through the tribute assessment, but the idea was also to force free blacks and mulattoes into the work force to earn the wages with which to pay the assessment. The law was slow to take hold, however. In 1576 the Crown attorney in Lima could report merely that the mixed blood population of Peru was numerous but undisciplined, and that much effort would be required if they were to contribute to the economy.[72] The Crown reaffirmed its stand in a 1577 decree that commanded free blacks and mulattoes to hire themselves out to Spanish masters so that their whereabouts might be known and the tax easily collected.[73] But this measure, too, remained a dead letter, in large part because Viceroy Toledo had lost his earlier conviction that the labor problems of Peru could be solved without resort to a further extension of the mita.

Toledo seems to have given little attention to the labor problems of the coast, except to lament that the importation of more African slaves would probably be necessary.[74] Rather, he concentrated his formidable administrative skills on the mining highlands, and there he found that nothing short of instituting the mita on a massive scale would turn the trick. By the end of his tenure, Toledo had organized the mining mita in the form that endured with slight modifications for over a century, with the bulk of the manpower assigned to the mercury mine of Huancavelica and to the silver-producing areas of Potosí, though some smaller gold and silver mines were also favored. The mita for Potosí, for example, drew laborers from the whole highland area between Cuzco and Tarija, which possessed a population of perhaps 450,000 Indians. Of this number, Toledo provided that one-seventh of the adult males (14,248 men in 1578) were to go to Potosí each year to serve for a twelve-month period. Similar quotas were established in the other mining districts. This system imposed a nearly intolerable burden on the Indians of the affected provinces, and many of them were led to flee to avoid service, abandoning their lands and villages to become so-called *forasteros*. Their departure inevitably increased the burden on those who remained, however much it may have eased the labor situation in those areas to which they fled.[75]

In fairness to Toledo, the full horrors of the mining mita did not become manifest until after his departure; and the viceroy consistently defended the justice of his measures and was at pains to mention the lack of alternatives. Ambitious schemes to find substitutes for Indian labor vanished from his later correspondence, replaced by assertions that there were neither enough Spaniards nor enough blacks and mulattoes to ease the load on the highland Indians. In any event, Toledo claimed, there were already too many blacks in Peru for the authorities and the white citizenry to feel secure, though he conceded that still more slaves would be needed to serve an expanding coastal economy.[76] In the circumstances Toledo urged that the royal conscience soothe itself with the thought that the mining mitayos were paid for their labor and, according to the letter of the law, well treated. In its turn, the home government accepted Toledo's decisions, since there seemed to be no other way to satisfy the labor demands of the Peruvian mines and continue the flow of needed revenue to the Crown.

In a larger sense, and leaving moral judgments aside, the policies of Toledo and their acceptance by the Crown were prompted by Peruvian realities that were to endure for several centuries. Short of outright enslavement and the most ruthless exploitation, a dwindling native population could not be made to sustain the different, if complementary, economies of coast and sierra. Since the bulk of the remaining Indians were concentrated in the highlands, it was logical that Toledo and his successors should earmark them for work in that area and leave the coast to rely on the African. Toward the end of Toledo's tenure, Spaniards who lived along the coast began to sense the drift of official policy, and the result was a sharp increase in the demand for blacks. Beginning in the 1580's a link was forged between Peru and Africa that would have been unthinkable twenty years before. An almost incidental camp-follower during the conquest and civil wars, the very symbol of ostentation for *nouveaux riches* conquistadores, the black slave now became one of the keys to the economic development of Peru.

CHAPTER TWO

The Atlantic Slave Trade to
Spanish America

Peru was not the only American colony to look to Africa for the man-power to supplement a dwindling native population. Mexico, New Granada, and other areas of the Spanish American mainland experi-enced similar labor shortages in the late sixteenth century, and the result was a substantial increase in the volume of the Atlantic slave trade.[1] The Spanish and their Portuguese cousins regarded this devel-opment with moral complacency, largely because of the subtle process by which the African was transformed in the sixteenth-century Euro-pean mind into the "Negro," a man who was not merely the only available slave but was in fact born to bondage.

In this respect, the Amerindian and the African fared very differently. Many Europeans pictured the Indian as uncorrupted and childlike in his innocence, certainly as a creature from a New World where the Gospel had never been heard. Churchmen and the more compassionate conquistadores labored to shield this noble savage from exploitation. But no Las Casas ever came to the aid of the African. The black man's historical connections with Christianity were at once too close and too distant to arouse the sympathy that the Amerindian evoked. There was, for example, the myth of the *bon nègre*, "dating back to the manger of Bethlehem and [based] on Europe's respect and predilection for the legendary Christian kingdom of Ethiopia."[2] By the beginning of the fifteenth century at least, and perhaps earlier, Caspar, the youngest of the Three Magi, was depicted as an African in European art and litera-ture. In the vague area of popular belief that separated Christian dogma from superstition, however, these favorable connections with Europe were counterbalanced by the legend of Ham's curse, which held the blackness of the Africans to be a punishment visited on them by God.[3]

Moreover, the African, already stamped in the Iberian mind as a pagan of "the Old World, the world of antiquity and of the Bible, which at least had been exposed for many centuries to the word of God," was also associated with the infidel Moors, through whose agency the Spanish and Portuguese had first obtained African slaves. As more and more unchristian Africans were discovered, the vision of Christian Ethiopia soon gave way before the myth of Ham's curse and the reality of the Islamic presence in Africa, with the result that few questions about the morality of African bondage were raised in the Iberian world for centuries.[4]

Some have plausibly argued that the Spanish never shared the northern European's virulent prejudice toward the African, ascribing their relative liberality to the cosmopolitanism of the Mediterranean area; to the indirect influence of Islam, which, before Catholicism, had reconciled proselytism with the slave trade; and to the skins of the Spanish themselves, darkened by contact with the Moors, a development that helped weaken the moral connotations of color so vivid in the minds of northern Europeans.[5] Indeed, it seems reasonable to assert that the Catholic Spanish extended their hierarchical view of the world to include relations between the races. If the Spanish were the best of all physical types, then the African was "near" (*próximo*), as a royal decree phrased it. In the corporate society the Spanish created in the New World, a place was easily found for the African that promised him equality in the next world while preserving Iberian superiority in the present.[6] At any rate, whatever the degree of his racial prejudice, the Spaniard was quite prepared to enslave the African, soothing his conscience with the thought that the temporary debasement of the black man's status was more than compensated for by the salvation of his soul.

If no agonizing doubts concerning the morality of African slavery plagued Spanish officialdom, the Crown was nevertheless determined to regulate both the quality and the quantity of the slave trade. Free trade in slaves between Africa and America was unthinkable in official circles for two reasons. For one thing, many Spaniards, particularly ecclesiastics, feared that the black man would hamper the Christianization of the Indian, either as an idolatrous pagan or, worse, as an Islamic infidel.* It was for this reason that in the beginning only blacks born in the power of Christians, or who had at least resided on the Peninsula long enough to be baptized, were permitted in America. When the need for direct shipments of slaves from Africa was recognized, the Crown had to content itself with an attempt to exclude slaves suspected of Islamic leanings, such as the notorious *esclavos Gelofes* (Wolofs) of the Guinea area, many of whom not only were infidels but were prone to insubordination as well. These measures were not rigorously enforced, but the government remained sensitive to the charge that the slave trade was flooding America with blacks who were heathens and enemies of the Faith.[7]

The Crown also regulated the slave trade for its own financial advantage, finding there were substantial gains to be made in charging a fee for the royal permits to take blacks to America. To be sure, many such permits were granted free of charge to reward faithful servants or even to pay debts, with the expectation that the licenses would then be sold to slavers.[8] Perhaps the most spectacular example of this practice was Charles V's grant of 4,000 licenses in 1518 to a Flemish favorite, who quickly sold the permits to a firm of Genoese merchants for 25,000 ducats. As American demand for blacks increased, licenses obtained in this fashion became the objects of speculation, to be sold at high bid to slave traders for use in the Atlantic trade.[9] In addition, small numbers of permits continued to be issued free of charge to government officials and ecclesiastics posted to Spanish America for blacks in their service.[10] However, as the financial difficulties of the Spanish Crown increased, caused by a seemingly endless succession of wars in Europe, more and more slave licenses were sold in large blocks directly to the slave traders —and at higher and higher prices. The charge per license, a modest two ducats at the outset in 1513, rose steadily from the 1530's on, and by 1560 reached thirty ducats.[11] The government realized that slave traders would merely pass this increased cost along in the American market, but after an attempt to establish ceilings on the price of Africans failed in the 1550's,[12] no further action was taken to stop the upward spiral.

Despite American complaints that blacks were high priced and in

---

* The Spanish Crown's dread that there might be converts to Islam among the blacks sent to America may account for the curious fact that the African, unlike the Indian, was not granted the status of neophyte in the Faith.

short supply, for many decades the Spanish Crown was reluctant to remedy the situation. More than concern for its own revenues from the slave trade was involved. By the middle of the sixteenth century, if not before, the consequences of the Treaty of Tordesillas had become clear to the Spanish government. The demand for blacks in America was growing, but Spain was cut off from the sources of supply in Africa and had to depend on Portugal for slaves. Since the Spanish needed slaves for America, and the Portuguese silver for Asian commerce, it seems that both nationalities might have profited from the situation. But Spain, determined to monopolize the commerce of her American possessions, did not see it in this light. To the Spanish Crown the slave trade with the Portuguese was a necessary evil that drained off American silver into foreign hands, a commerce to be carefully regulated and even restricted.

Ironically, and unfortunately for the Spanish economic aims, the steady rise in the price of slave licenses during the sixteenth century made the Portuguese more and more prominent in the Spanish American slave trade in a direct sense. Until the middle of the century or so, Spanish merchants (and often Italian and German slavers), supplied with slaves from Portuguese Africa, were active in the trade, but in the 1560's and 1570's Portuguese commercial houses and syndicates played an ever-greater role. The development was an altogether logical one. More than any other group, Portuguese merchants were familiar with the barter arrangements and sources of supply in Africa, and they already controlled the slave trade to Brazil. In addition, Portuguese firms had the financial resources necessary to absorb the higher license fees, sell slaves on credit to Spanish colonists always pressed for cash, and still make a profit.[13] The Spanish Crown had no choice but to see the Portuguese grab the lion's share of the Spanish American slave trade, but the necessity was resented.

In 1580, however, the situation changed drastically. In that year, Philip II of Spain fell heir to the Portuguese throne, and during the sixty-year dynastic union of the two Iberian empires that followed, the plans and decisions of high government officials were formulated more and more as if for a single imperial system. Legally, out-and-out administrative integration was impossible. Under the Spanish Hapsburgs, Portugal remained an autonomous kingdom, with her overseas territories administered by Portuguese officials; and accordingly the coast of Africa remained under the political and commercial domination of the Portuguese. But imperial policy was now framed in Madrid, and precisely at the moment when American demand for blacks increased sharply the Spanish Crown found itself in a position to manipulate African supply. For all practical purposes, dynastic union nullified the Treaty of Tordesillas, or so Spanish officialdom reasoned. If the American empire was in need of Africans, Spain was now in a position to provide them on her own terms.

Those terms were soon made clear. The Portuguese Crown claimed a monopoly of African commerce, but in fact had for long contented itself with the imposition of customs duties on the articles exported, including slaves, and even these revenues were not collected directly. Rather, the West African coast was divided into a number of areas or "contracts," with the collection of royal duties farmed out to private individuals for a specified number of years in return for a lump sum. These contractors in turn concluded agreements (*avenças*) with slave traders wishing to export Africans from their regions, and collected the duties involved, whether the slave was bound for Lisbon, Brazil, or Spanish America. After dynastic union, the Spanish government began to sign supplementary agreements with the Portuguese contractors earmarking a certain number of slaves from the various African areas for Spanish America. In such cases, the Spanish Crown dispensed with the license fee and instead collected a percentage of the slave's sale price in America: one-third for a slave from São Jorge da Mina, São Tomé, or Angola, and one-fourth for one from Cape Verde-Guinea.

To illustrate, in 1589 a company formed by four individuals made the successful bid for the Cape Verde-Guinea contract. Under this agreement, the company paid a lump sum annually to the Portuguese Crown and in return was authorized to collect the customary government revenues, including the duties on 3,000 slaves, who were to be exported at the rate of 500 a year over the contract's six-year term. A subsequent agreement with the Spanish Crown in 1590 allowed all these blacks to be exported to Spanish America in return for 25 per cent of the sale price. Most of the avenças needed to implement the agreement were concluded with slave merchants in Seville in the following year, and by 1593 the requisite number of slaves had been contracted for. In this instance, which was probably fairly typical, the contractors sold the bulk of the licenses but kept some to use for their own profit. We may note that the majority of the slaves were earmarked for the Caribbean port of Cartagena, which in these years became the chief slave depot for the surrounding area and Peru. The contract for Angola, let at approximately the same time, was also supplemented by an agreement that permitted the exportation of slaves to Spanish America.[14]

These arrangements between Spanish Crown and Portuguese contractor were merely a temporary stopgap, however, while discussion of the reorganization of the Spanish American slave trade within government circles—slowed by the morale-shattering defeat of the Invincible Armada in 1588—continued to seek a better solution, prompted in part by vociferous complaints from the colonies about the scarcity and high price of blacks.[15] That solution was implemented between 1593 and 1595, when the idea of further agreements with the contractors for Portuguese Africa was shelved, and the sale of slave licenses for Spanish America was placed under monopoly contract (*asiento*). Six such agreements were concluded during the period of dynastic union.[16]

The asiento was a long-term contract between the Spanish Crown and an individual or company for what was in fact only a semi-monopoly of the sale of licenses for the exportation of slaves to Spanish America.* The number of licenses to be sold each year, at prices that ranged as high as forty ducats each,[17] was invariably pegged at several thousand. Most of these were sold in small lots. The asentista was obligated to pay the Crown an annual lump sum that was slightly less than the total value of the licenses, and derived his profit from the difference between these two figures plus whatever he could make on the few licenses he was allowed to use himself. The asentista was thus essentially a middleman between the government and the slave merchant, an agent responsible for finding buyers for the licenses, smoothing out any differences between the slave merchants and government officials, collecting (with the aid of factors) the contract's revenues, and helping enforce the regulations that governed the trade.

To administer the slave trade by means of a monopoly contract was

---

* No asentista ever exercised true monopoly control over the slave trade. In the first place, a certain number of licenses were usually reserved for the Crown's use, and, as financial needs grew increasingly desperate, these were often sold as a block. See, for example, the documents on the contract concluded with Antonio Fernandes d'Elvas in 1615, in AGI, Indiferente General 2795 and 2829. See also Scelle, *La traité négrière*, 1: 443-44. In the second place, it was specified in all asientos that the Crown might make supplementary arrangements with the African contractors for slave exportation to Spanish America as in the past, though the government never saw fit to exercise this privilege.

not a new idea: the asiento had been experimented with and abandoned early in the sixteenth century. In the 1590's, however, circumstances argued for a new period of trial. First, despite the Crown's newfound power to manipulate the Portuguese supply of blacks, the pattern of the Spanish American slave trade remained haphazard. Individual slave traders still chose their own destinations and clustered around the silver-rich ports of Cartagena and Veracruz to the detriment of other areas also in need of blacks. Monopoly contract was seen as the best way to rectify this situation. Accordingly, all the asientos concluded in this period meticulously reserved for the Crown the right to determine the destination of slaves shipped to Spanish America. In practice, the government rarely exercised this right, but Spanish bureaucrats were no doubt comforted by the thought that the asiento could respond quickly to colonial complaints of labor shortages.[18]

Financial considerations also favored the revival of the asiento. To meet imperial expenditures, the government had sold interest-bearing bonds on a mammoth scale ever since the time of Charles V, and to facilitate their sale, had secured the payment of the interest (and eventually the principal) on these bonds, known as *juros*, against specific government revenues. By the 1590's government income from slave licenses had come to be heavily mortgaged to pay the interest on the juros assigned to it.[19] In these circumstances the Crown was anxious that revenue from the slave trade be not only as large as possible, but also predictable. One monopoly contract obligating an individual or group of impeccable financial credentials for the annual payment of a lump sum seemed a more reasonable means of attaining this goal than several price-sharing agreements with African contractors.

It should be stressed that the asentista could do no more than sell a slave trader an export license valid for Spanish America; the slaves represented by this license had to come from Portuguese Africa, and no legal guarantee could be issued in Spain that these blacks would be available. In practice, however, the overwhelming majority of the slave merchants who dealt with the asentista were Portuguese colleagues of the African contractors and had no need to fear that the contractors would deny them access to slaves on the African coast. Further, all of the asentistas during this period were also Portuguese, and many themselves held contracts for certain regions of the African coast. For example, João Rodrigues Coutinho, with whom an asiento was concluded in

1601, was both the governor of Angola and the contractor for that territory, and Antonio Fernandes d'Elvas, asentista from 1615 to 1622, held the contracts for both Angola and Guinea. The Spanish Crown, ruling the Portuguese empire with the assistance of a viceroy and a Council of Portugal, assured that this would be the case, and such men were pivotal figures in the slave trade, simultaneously Spanish asentistas and African contractors, with extensive connections and interests on the Iberian Peninsula, in Spanish America, and in Brazil.

The asiento proved to be an imperfect instrument for the regulation of the Spanish American slave trade. In the first place, the early asentistas, princes of the slave trade though they were, overestimated the profits to be made from their contracts and obligated themselves to pay the Crown amounts they could not meet without going bankrupt or resorting to illegal operations in Spanish America. Of the six asientos signed under the dynastic union, the first four, which spanned the years 1595-1622, satisfied neither contractor nor Crown: the first was terminated by the government on suspicion of fraud, the financial collapse of the second was prevented only by the death of the contractor, and the third and fourth ended in bankruptcy. In financial terms, the last two asientos, concluded in 1623 and 1631, appear to have been moderately successful, but even so the Crown and the Spanish mercantile community had little cause to be pleased. The fact was that the asentistas found themselves powerless to control the activities of their clients, the Portuguese slave merchants, and these men, sensing Spanish commercial weakness, used their authorized operations in Spanish America as a blind to flood the area with contraband slaves and merchandise.

To some degree, the actions of the Spanish Crown itself were responsible for this situation. Unquestionably, the Crown was sincere in its desire to supply the American colonies with African labor, and with the sources of African supply assured by dynastic union, it was possible to set a figure on how many slaves were needed each year in the Spanish American economy and to make the asentista responsible for fulfilling that quota. However, the government consistently underestimated American demand for blacks, and perhaps deliberately so, for even under dynastic union Spain appears to have been determined to hold to a minimum the amount of American silver that passed into Portuguese hands as a result of the slave trade. But if this was the idea, the policy backfired. Portuguese merchants, quick to sense that American demand for blacks exceeded the quotas of the asiento, used bribery and a variety of other tricks to sell many more slaves than they were licensed to import.

Spain might have been less disturbed by a Portuguese-dominated slave trade to the American colonies, whatever the extent of contraband, if the larger issue of her commercial monopoly had been satisfactorily resolved. From the early days of colonization Spain had sought to exclude foreign commercial participation in America and had granted monopoly control of colonial commerce to the merchant guild of Seville. But her attempts to monopolize this trade were doomed by the collapse of Spanish industry and by the rigidity and expense of the convoy system on which the trade depended. As goods carried legally to America became more and more expensive Portuguese merchants, eager for profit, began supplementing their legitimate cargoes with quantities of illegal slaves and merchandise. The extent of this contraband is subject to debate, but there was enough of it at least to enrage the Seville merchants, who claimed that Portuguese smuggling, masked as legitimate trade in blacks under the asiento, drained off large quantities of bullion that would otherwise have flowed through legal channels to support the convoy system and the fabric of Spanish empire.[20]

By the turn of the seventeenth century, the Seville monopolists were sufficiently incensed to begin a propaganda campaign against the Portuguese slave trade to Spanish America, and they waged it relentlessly until the dissolution of dynastic union in 1640. With powerful allies in the Spanish bureaucracy, most notably the officials of the Casa de la Contratación in Seville, which regulated commerce with the colonies, Spanish merchants attacked the Portuguese on more than simple economic grounds. Portuguese slave traders were not merely smugglers who robbed Spain of silver; they were also Jewish heretics who practiced their faith in secret behind a public facade of Catholic orthodoxy and who inundated the American colonies with blacks indoctrinated in their own false beliefs. These beliefs, embellished with African superstitions, were in turn spreading among the Indians. The Seville merchants questioned whether African labor was worth all the smuggling and undermining of the Church's work among the Indians, but they stopped short of appealing for the abolition of the slave trade.[21]

The high tide of Seville's opposition to Portuguese participation in the slave trade occurred between 1608 and 1615. In 1608 the merchants secured a royal decree barring foreigners from trade in Spanish America unless they had resided there for twenty years, ten of them either in marriage to a native or in possession of a home or other real property.[22] Portuguese slave merchants were quick to respond to this threat and warned that both Spain and Portugal would lose the revenues from this trade if the decree were not rescinded. Whether moved by this petition or by other considerations, the Spanish government did not apply this legislation to Portuguese slave traders.

But the determined Seville merchants continued the attack, using their considerable influence to block the conclusion of a new asiento in 1610 and forcing the government to reconsider the Portuguese role once more. Spokesmen for the guild were particularly critical of the clause in previous asientos that allowed slave traders to depart for Africa and Spanish America from Seville, Lisbon, or the Canary Islands. The partisans of the Seville monopolists contended that officials at the other two locations took their inspection duties much less seriously than those of Seville did, permitting slave merchants to sail with great amounts of contraband. At a minimum, the guild argued for a mandatory inspection of all slaving vessels at Seville, but it wanted much more. As the discussion of the proposed asiento continued, the guild and its partisans urged that the Portuguese be required to sell their blacks in Seville to Spaniards, who would then transport the slaves to America on the annual convoys; and further, that if a new asiento was decided on, the asentista should be a Spaniard. Though these restrictions would diminish the revenue from the slave trade, the Seville circle argued, much more would be gained by eliminating Portuguese contraband to the obvious benefit of Spanish shipping. In short, the Seville monopolists pressed for the elimination of the Portuguese from American commerce.

The Portuguese quickly countered the new attack, denying the old charges of smuggling and heresy, while dismissing the Sevillian proposals as economic madness that could only increase contraband activity. The Portuguese further claimed that the arrangement would violate the autonomy of Portugal and her colonies, and that the loss of revenue would cripple the African possessions, which were administered with income from the slave trade. Thus weakened, Portuguese Africa would be lost to foreign enemies.

In 1611 the Spanish Crown brushed the Portuguese arguments aside and granted the Seville guild everything it had asked for. All slaving vessels were to be inspected at Seville before sailing for Spanish America, and all Africans were to be brought to the port for transportation to the colonies by Spanish vessels in the annual convoys. Only if there were no Spanish buyers for the slaves would Portuguese merchantmen be allowed to take blacks to Spanish America for sale, but even then they must sail with the convoys. Under these conditions the Crown found no takers for a new asiento, and between 1611 and 1614 legal commerce in slaves reached the vanishing point. Meanwhile, contraband in blacks flourished at the expense of the Spanish purse. Compromise with the Portuguese was necessary to conclude a new asiento in 1615. The Crown abandoned the idea of having slaves carried to Spanish America on the annual convoys but continued to insist on the inspection of all slaving vessels at Seville before they set sail for the colonies. To reduce the risk of contraband still further, blacks now had to be imported exclusively through two ports, Cartagena and Veracruz. After inspection at these locations, the merchant could take his slaves for sale wherever he chose. These rules were modified in 1623 to permit slave ships to sail from Lisbon again, and thereafter the majority chose to do so.[23]

The Seville merchant guild mounted no more major challenges against Portuguese dominance of the slave trade during the last decades of dynastic union, but distrust and bitterness continued between the nationals of the two countries, feelings that were intensified by Iberian reverses at the hands of the Dutch in the colonial world. With regard to the slave trade in particular, Spain discovered that even dynastic union could not restore what had been bargained away at Tordesillas. Anxious for revenue and determined to keep as much American silver as possible in Spanish hands, the Crown consistently pegged the volume of the legal slave trade at a figure too low to satisfy colonial demand. Contraband was the inevitable result. But rather than face up to its causes, the Spanish Crown, urged on by the Seville monopolists, responded with futile legislation and blamed the slave trade for the growing commercial weakness of Spain, in which it actually played little part. Since the labor needs of Spanish America could not be denied, the slave trade was tolerated as a necessary evil until the Portuguese revolted in 1640, but so burdened by regulations as to ensure the very contraband the Spanish government wished to prevent.

On the positive side, dynastic union gave Spain a measure of control over the slave trade to her American colonies that she had not known before and would never enjoy again. Friction between Portuguese and Spanish commercial interests may well have prevented the slave trade from fully satisfying American demand for blacks (at least legally), but it is also true that the commerce in human flesh between Africa and America increased significantly after the middle of the sixteenth century, and particularly after dynastic union in 1580. Scholars have put the figure for the period between 1551 and 1640 at anywhere from 169,900 blacks to 350,000. Given the widespread smuggling and the paucity of surviving documentation concerning even the legal trade, the true number will never be known; however, it is safe to say that several hundred thousand slaves were imported into Spanish America during this period, the great majority handled by Portuguese merchants.[24]

During most of the sixteenth century the bulk of the Africans bound for Spanish America came from the West African coast and specifically from the section between the Senegal and Niger rivers known as the Ríos de Guinea. Africans from this area were long preferred by the Spanish for their industry, cheerfulness, and adaptability,[25] and, bowing to colonial preference, the Spanish Crown consistently encouraged the shipment of Guinea blacks to its American possessions: the agreements concluded with the African contractors in the 1580's provided that only a fourth of the sale price of Guinea slaves go to the Crown as against a third for blacks from other areas; the asientos concluded after 1595 stipulated that the largest possible number of slaves be from Guinea; and in 1635 an attempt was made to route all the slaves from this region to Spanish America.[26]

Beginning in the late sixteenth century, however, the English, French, and Dutch began to challenge Portugal's claim to monopoly in Guinea, and she was powerless to remedy the situation. Portugal did not have the naval strength necessary to patrol the Guinea coast; Spanish maritime power was tied down elsewhere; and, in any event, such an operation would have cost far more than duties from the slave trade. The effect of foreign competition was to increase the quantity of barter goods required per slave and to prompt many Portuguese slave merchants to move farther south in search of cheaper prices.[27]

An alternative source of "black ivory" were the peoples of the Bights of Benin and Biafra and those of the Congo-Angola areas, a trade engaged in by many of the Portuguese settlers on the island of São Tomé.* The economy of the island, a booming sugar colony until eclipsed by the growth of the Brazilian plantations in the late sixteenth century, absorbed many of the slaves from the mainland, and many others were sold to Atlantic slave merchants. Throughout the period under study, São Tomé continued to serve as a stopover for slavers, a place where the human cargo could be rested and refreshed, but the island's importance as an intermediary between the Atlantic merchants and the peoples of West Central Africa did not endure much beyond the middle decades of the sixteenth century.

In the 1570's the Portuguese government made the decision to colonize actively in Angola, and in 1575, with the founding of São Paulo de Luanda, that region began its rise to prominence in the African slave trade.[28] The Bantu peoples of these regions were of a relatively rudimentary civilization compared with the Guinea slaves, and some Spaniards were inclined to dismiss them as useless and prone to illness, though docile. The Bantu, however, knew how to work metal, to weave and make pottery, and to domesticate animals, including cattle. More important still, they seemed to be available in inexhaustible numbers. As one enthusiastic official wrote the Crown in 1591, the thickly populated hinterland of Luanda would furnish a copious supply of slaves "until the end of the world."[29]

Beginning in the late 1580's Angola began to supply an increasingly high percentage of the Africans bound for Spanish America, though it is difficult to determine how great the shift away from Guinea was and to strike a balance between the respective contributions of the two areas. In terms of the official destinations of slavers leaving the Peninsula, Guinea experienced a precipitate decline in the seventeenth century. In the period 1606-10 roughly 53 per cent of the slave ships named Guinea as their destination, but the figure never rose higher than 33 per cent thereafter and fell to a minuscule fraction in the decade before Portu-

---

* The areas of Congo and Angola, like all of those of the West African coast at this date, were only vaguely defined. I accept here C. R. Boxer's definition of the Congo as the region bounded on the west by the sea and on the north, south, and east by the Zaire (or Congo), Dande, and Kwango rivers; and of Angola as the area between the Dande and Longa rivers with a hinterland extending several hundred miles into the interior. *Salvador de Sá*, p. 224. See also Curtin, *Atlantic Slave Trade*, pp. 104-5; and the map in Boxer, *Portuguese Seaborne Empire*, p. 95.

guese independence. In contrast, the number of ships bound for Angola never fell below 71 per cent in any five-year period after 1615, and the proportion reached 93 per cent in 1636-40.[30]

These official declarations should not be taken too seriously, however, since the availability and price of slaves at destination often caused a change of plans on arrival. Walter Rodney is one of several scholars who have attempted more realistic estimates. He contends that until 1640, in the best years at least, some 3,000 slaves were exported annually from Guinea, the majority destined for Spanish America. Boxer thinks that about 15,000 blacks were exported from Angola during an averagely good year in the early seventeenth century, with perhaps a total of 5,000 going to Cartagena and Veracruz for distribution and another 1,500 to Buenos Aires.[31] More precise figures are available for Angola for a twenty-month period in 1624-26, when 75 ships called at Luanda and transported 17,708 slave "pieces";* of these, 30 vessels with 9,070 blacks were bound for Spanish America.[32] Philip Curtin's estimates are considerably more conservative; at the highest rate, in the years 1616-20, he puts the average number of slaves exported from Angola to Spanish America at 2,892.[33] Finally, scattered data from Peruvian notarial records, as presented in Tables 1 and 2, indicate that Guinea supplied some 55 to 56 per cent of the slaves exported to Peru between 1560 and 1650, other West African areas 11-12 per cent, and Angola the rest. Indeed, as the sample of *bozales* (slaves exported directly from Africa to Peru) shows, before the revolt of Portugal disrupted the slave trade the flow of blacks from Angola equaled or ex-

---

* A slave "piece" equaled a prime slave, the Spanish *pieza de Indias*. King, "Evolution of the Free Slave Trade Principle," p. 36, identifies a piece as a man or woman between the ages of eighteen and thirty and at least seven Spanish *palmos* tall. Molinari, *Trata de negros*, p. 47, defines the term as encompassing Africans fifteen to thirty years of age who were robust and had no physical defects or missing teeth. Various fractions of the piece corresponded to those who by age, health, or physique fell short of the standard. Boxer, *Salvador de Sá*, p. 231, using 1678 information, identifies a prime slave as one aged fifteen to twenty-five. Slaves eight to fifteen years old and from twenty-five to thirty-five were counted as two-thirds of a piece, and those under eight and up to forty-five as half. Suckling infants were not counted, and all slaves over forty-five or diseased were valued by arbiters. During the period under study, however, and perhaps later as well, the term piece had two meanings: it was used precisely on the African coast and in Spanish American ports to determine the payment of duties, but it was also widely and loosely employed to refer to any adult slave, regardless of age or physical condition, as the slave traders' records I cite in Chapter 3 show. For a good description of the *palmeo* operation by which the number of pieces was determined, see Chandler, "Health and Slavery."

TABLE I

Area	1560–62	1564–66	1568–73	1575–77	1578–79	1580–82	1585	1589–91	1595
Senegambia and Guinea-Bissau									
Bran	37	24	22	22	11	19	32	51	81
Biafara	26	25	34	24	18	22	30	59	41
Berbesi	11	8	5	6	1	1	4	3	1
Jolofo	8	14	8	11	9	7	9	5	9
Mandinga	8	16	6	8	7	4	13	11	16
Nalu	5	2	2	1	—	4	—	4	4
Bañol	3	4	4	3	4	3	6	12	34
Casanga	2	5	4	3	3	2	6	3	3
Fula	2	—	—	1	—	1	—	—	—
Bioho	1	7	2	5	3	2	5	9	5
Guinea (unspecified)	—	—	—	1	—	—	—	—	2
Folupo*	—	—	—	—	—	—	—	—	—
Soso	—	—	—	—	—	—	—	—	—
Balanta*	—	—	—	—	—	—	—	1	1
SUBTOTAL	103	105	87	85	56	65	105	158	197
Other West Africa									
Terranova	15	13	20	10	8	3	10	—	3
Zape	11	15	26	15	10	14	17	10	8
Cocoli	1	—	2	3	3	2	—	1	2
Bleblo	—	1	—	—	—	—	—	—	—
Arara/Arda[a]	—	1	—	—	1	—	—	—	—
Caravali	—	—	—	—	—	1	—	—	—
Mina	—	—	—	2	—	—	—	—	—
Lucumi*	—	—	—	—	—	—	—	—	—
SUBTOTAL	27	30	48	30	22	20	27	11	13
Central and Southern Africa									
Congo	9	10	11	16	7	10	15	12	13
Mozambique	4	4	7	1	—	3	2	7	5
Anchico	2	—	—	—	—	—	—	—	2
Benguela (shipping point)	—	—	—	—	—	—	—	—	—
Angola	—	—	—	4	2	1	8	26	132
Alonga	—	—	—	—	—	—	1	—	—
Malamba/Malemba*	—	—	—	—	—	—	—	—	—
Mosanga	—	1	1	3	2	—	—	—	—
SUBTOTAL	15	15	19	24	11	14	26	45	152
TOTAL	145	150	154	124	89	99	158	214	362

SOURCE: These data are taken from the notarial records listed in the Bibliography, pp. 420–21. For full details on my sampling techniques, see Appendix B.

NOTE: Sixteenth– and seventeenth–century nomenclature is used here. For the modern equivalent or geographical location, or both, see Appendix C. Curtin, *Atlantic Slave Trade*, is followed except in the case of the asterisked names, on which see (in order) Sandoval, *De instauranda*, pp. 60, 91–92, 78, and 96.

[a] The orthography of the notarial records of the period is so contradictory that a separation of these groups is nearly impossible.

Ethnic Origins of Afro-Peruvians, 1560-1650

1600	1605	1610	1615	1620	1625	1630	1635	1640	1645	1650	Total
61	65	39	39	80	71	58	71	38	20	8	849
29	49	39	28	45	35	31	29	19	3	8	594
1	2	2	—	—	—	—	—	—	—	—	45
2	9	10	6	4	7	1	2	4	1	2	128
9	16	17	12	34	29	23	30	15	4	6	284
4	4	2	6	23	17	5	4	11	3	2	103
20	31	20	13	42	54	17	21	19	5	1	316
2	1	1	3	5	2	1	2	1	—	—	49
—	—	1	1	—	—	—	1	1	—	—	8
5	4	11	11	19	15	36	17	14	5	4	180
5	11	—	—	—	—	1	1	—	—	1	22
—	21	13	18	29	19	49	60	13	8	7	237
—	1	—	—	7	1	4	2	—	3	—	18
2	5	2	5	12	10	9	10	12	4	2	75
140	219	157	142	300	260	235	250	147	56	41	2908
6	—	2	7	16	4	4	3	8	4	7	143
7	4	5	5	15	12	7	19	6	7	1	214
2	—	1	1	4	1	9	22	9	2	2	67
—	—	—	—	—	—	—	—	—	—	—	1
2	1	2	9	61	12	2	2	1	—	1	95
—	1	—	—	27	33	11	5	5	2	3	88
1	—	—	—	3	3	1	—	—	—	—	10
—	1	—	2	2	2	2	3	1	2	2	17
78	7	10	24	128	67	36	54	30	17	16	635
12	14	21	15	18	10	13	15	22	13	11	267
4	3	1	—	1	3	1	1	2	—	—	49
3	4	1	2	2	1	—	2	—	—	1	20
—	—	—	2	—	—	—	—	—	—	—	2
90	62	59	44	95	165	144	243	152	73	55	1355
—	—	—	—	—	—	—	—	—	—	—	1
—	—	—	—	—	—	—	—	11	6	12	29
—	—	—	3	—	1	—	—	1	—	—	12
109	83	82	66	116	180	158	261	188	92	78	1735
267	309	249	232	544	507	429	565	365	165	136	5278

TABLE 2

Area	1560–62	1564–66	1568–73	1575–77	1578–79	1580–82	1585	1589–91	1595
Senegambia and Guinea-Bissau									
Bran	5	7	7	1	—	2	15	27	49
Biafara	1	7	8	1	2	4	7	15	12
Berbesi	2	—	—	—	—	—	—	1	1
Jolofo	—	—	—	—	—	—	1	4	4
Mandinga	—	4	—	—	—	1	1	4	8
Nalu	1	—	1	1	—	—	—	1	2
Bañol	1	—	1	—	1	1	3	7	22
Casanga	1	—	1	2	—	2	1	1	—
Fula	—	—	—	—	—	1	—	—	—
Bioho	—	1	—	—	1	—	—	4	4
Guinea (unspecified)	—	—	—	—	—	—	—	—	—
Folupo	—	—	—	—	—	—	—	—	2
Soso	—	—	—	—	—	—	—	—	—
Balanta	—	—	—	—	—	—	—	—	—
SUBTOTAL	11	19	18	5	4	11	28	64	104
Other West Africa									
Terranova	—	—	1	—	—	—	—	—	—
Zape	2	3	6	—	—	1	1	—	3
Cocoli	—	—	—	—	—	—	—	1	—
Arara/Arda	—	1	—	—	—	—	—	—	—
Caravali	—	—	—	—	—	—	—	—	—
Mina	—	—	—	—	—	—	—	—	—
Lucumi	—	—	—	—	—	—	—	—	—
SUBTOTAL	2	4	7	0	0	1	1	1	3
Central and Southern Africa									
Congo	—	1	—	1	—	—	1	2	4
Mozambique	—	—	—	—	—	—	—	2	—
Anchico	—	—	—	—	—	—	—	—	2
Angola	—	—	—	—	—	—	—	8	104
Malamba/Malemba	—	—	—	—	—	—	—	—	—
SUBTOTAL	0	1	0	1	0	0	1	12	110
TOTAL	13	24	25	6	4	12	30	77	217

SOURCE: Table 1 and notarial records listed in Bibliography, pp. 420–21.
NOTE: Sixteenth– and seventeenth–century nomenclature is used. For modern equivalents, see Appendix C.

Ethnic Origins of Peruvian Bozales, 1560-1650

1600	1605	1610	1615	1620	1625	1630	1635	1640	1645	1650	Total
24	37	8	10	45	44	38	57	18	—	—	394
8	32	15	4	25	14	14	13	7	—	—	189
—	2	1	—	—	—	—	—	—	—	—	7
—	5	1	—	2	5	1	2	1	—	—	26
2	7	11	3	20	23	13	22	6	—	—	125
1	4	—	3	20	13	2	3	—	—	—	52
7	20	6	5	26	42	8	13	5	—	—	168
—	—	—	—	3	2	1	1	1	—	—	16
—	—	—	—	—	—	—	—	—	—	—	1
1	—	5	5	16	11	31	15	6	—	—	100
—	11	—	1	—	—	—	1	—	—	—	13
4	18	6	9	17	9	34	45	6	—	—	150
—	1	—	—	7	—	4	1	—	—	—	13
2	3	—	1	3	6	5	4	3	—	—	27
49	140	53	41	184	169	151	177	53	0	0	1281
1	—	—	3	6	—	—	—	—	—	—	11
2	2	—	1	12	7	6	15	3	—	—	64
1	—	—	—	3	2	7	18	4	—	—	36
1	—	—	4	57	8	—	—	—	—	—	71
—	—	—	—	25	28	4	—	—	—	1	58
—	—	—	—	—	3	—	—	—	—	—	3
—	—	—	1	2	1	1	—	—	—	—	5
5	2	0	9	105	49	18	33	7	0	1	248
1	6	2	4	4	3	1	2	1	—	—	33
—	—	—	—	—	—	—	—	—	—	—	2
1	2	—	—	1	—	—	2	—	—	—	8
66	14	12	23	53	120	88	177	51	2	1	719
—	—	—	—	—	—	—	1	3	—	—	4
68	22	14	27	58	123	89	182	55	2	1	766
122	164	67	77	347	341	258	392	115	2	2	2295

ceeded that from Guinea in only four years: 1595, 1600, 1635, and 1640. On the basis of this mixed evidence, the most one can conclude is that despite the spectacular rise to prominence of Angola in the slave trade, Guinea remained a major supplier of blacks to Spanish America.[34]

Let us now briefly consider the process by which the clients of the Spanish asentistas and the African contractors obtained their slaves. The Portuguese possessed ample papal authority to take Africans captive forcibly, but this tactic was characteristic of only their very earliest contacts and, save for the hostilities in Angola, was soon discarded in favor of barter.[35] Slavery was a common practice on the West African coast when the Portuguese arrived, a punishment imposed on prisoners of war and persons convicted of such crimes as adultery, murder, and theft. In addition, in times of severe famine many Africans sold themselves into slavery to ensure survival. But these traditional sources of slaves soon proved insufficient to satisfy European demand, and the lure of barter goods led the tribal chiefs to abuse their authority by extending the imposition of bondage to less serious and even fabricated offenses. European demand for slaves also encouraged intertribal warfare with inevitably destructive results. In the words of Boxer, the Africans "were often obtained from the inter-tribal wars in the interior, [and] the growth of the slave trade presumably worsened the existing state of violence and insecurity—or at any rate did nothing to help lessen it. The African chiefs and headmen were those who benefitted most from trading with the Portuguese, and . . . most of them were always willing partners in the slave trade." Indeed, some groups, such as the Bioho in Guinea, seem to have done a thriving business with the Portuguese on the basis of dawn raids on the villages of their neighbors.[36] Occasionally, even the Portuguese slave merchants seem to have had uneasy consciences over the fact that the known demand for blacks encouraged warfare and raids among the tribes.[37]

Barter arrangements varied somewhat from area to area and were largely independent of the control of both the contractor and the Portuguese government, though the government did make ineffective attempts at regulation.[38] Along the Guinea coast the principal barter items were textiles (some of the fancier varieties came from India), wine, garlic, beads, and iron. By the second decade of the seventeenth century iron seems to have replaced textiles as the most popular barter commodity.[39] At the same time, mounting competition, both among the

Portuguese and between them and foreign traders, increased the amount of barter goods required to procure a slave. According to one complaint, where eighty pieces of cloth had been sufficient to purchase a slave in 1615, 250-300 pieces were required in 1620. This claim is probably exaggerated. For example, in 1611, when the Portuguese were lobbying against the proposal to ship blacks bound for America via Seville, they claimed that a Guinea slave cost between 140 and 156 pesos in barter goods.[40] As we shall see in Chapter 3, the prices paid for slaves in Peru during this period indicate that there was no such increase of the magnitude implied in the 1620 complaint, a jump that would have made Guinea slaves unsalable in the American market. Mounting barter costs in Guinea certainly favored the development of new sources of supply in Angola, where the Portuguese were more in command of the situation, but it is clear from the data in Tables 1 and 2 that Guinea slaves continued to be competitive in Spanish America.

In the Guinea area, both the barter goods flowing inland and the slaves herded toward the awaiting ships passed through the hands of a group of tough adventurers known as *tangomaos* (or *lançados*) who lived in or near the various ports.[41] The tangomaos were long the targets of both the Portuguese Crown and the contractors, since they evaded the payment of duties whenever they could and dealt with Iberian and northern European alike, but most attempts to break their hold during our period failed. The tangomaos were a fact of life with which the slaver had to deal. As Boxer notes, "Many of them settled in the Negro villages, where they and their Mulatto descendants functioned as principals or intermediaries in the barter-trade between Africans and Europeans." Moreover, "Some of them were able to marry into the ruling families, while others made advantageous agreements with local chiefs, either on their own account, or on behalf of the European principals for whom they might be working. Their influence was for long a source of envy and astonishment to other European traders who frequented Upper Guinea." These middlemen either went into the interior themselves to barter for slaves or sent their black or mulatto agents, known as *mochileros*, to do the task for them. In this fashion, a constant stream of slaves reached the coastal ports, but, even though the Portuguese Crown imposed the death penalty for tax evasion, duty was paid on only a fraction of this total.[42]

In Angola the Portuguese obtained some slaves by way of war or tribute, but here too they relied in good part on barter. Boxer provides this description of the procedure:

Under normally peaceful conditions, slaving agents called *pombeiros* or *pumbeiros* (from a native word meaning "hawker") roamed the interior regions, purchasing slaves from the local chieftains and taking them to Luanda. . . . The pombeiros were mulattoes, or often pure Negroes, who would be sent out by their Portuguese masters at Luanda with anything up to a total of a hundred and fifty Negro slaves as carriers to transport the palm-cloth, cowries, wine, and other merchandise for which slaves were purchased in the interior. These pombeiros would stay away from one to two years before either sending or bringing back to the coast chain-gangs of five or six hundred slaves. Although usually very loyal to their European masters, it was not unknown for them to default on their employers and to make off with the slaves and the merchandise. Some of the most trusty pombeiros did not return to Luanda for years on end, but stayed up-country and received periodically merchandise from the coast in exchange for slaves. The original form of currency had been a kind of cowrie shell known as *njimbu* or *zimbo*, which was found on the island of Luanda, and imported extensively from Brazil. The *zimbo* was gradually supplanted by the use of *panos* or palm-leaf cloth, and by rock salt, brandy, gunpowder, and other European commodities of relatively small intrinsic value.[43]

The pumbeiros used much of this merchandise at large fairs or slave marts in the interior of Angola, events that lured African slave merchants called *genses* from as far away as 600 miles or so.

Captives taken in the Portuguese colonists' continuing hostilities with the interior tribes were another fruitful source of slaves. This enterprise was entrusted largely to black mercenaries after 1614. In the words of a contemporary observer, "Ordinarily those resident in the colony have *negros de guerra* who fight for our side, and all that they take in the interior is for their masters, and therefore these slaves cost them nothing."[44] According to the same source, even those blacks who had to be purchased were cheap enough, costing at most some twenty Spanish pesos' worth of goods each. These captives were then sold for more than twice their cost to Atlantic slave traders. The colonists stretched their margins of profit still further by inflating the price on the stocks of fresh food the slave ships had to lay in before departing for the Americas. A cow, for example, might cost the slave merchant nearly as much as a black. In turn, the merchants carried in all manner of manufactures and foodstuffs, which they sold for allegedly exorbitant prices in return for slaves. Both parties thus sold dear and bought dear, and probably neither gained any decisive advantage over the other.

Little is known about the disposition and treatment of the slaves taken along the Guinea coast prior to embarkation, but in Angola they were kept at Luanda in large buildings, or barracoons, pending shipment.[45] Captives often arrived in bad condition, having marched in many cases from a point hundreds of miles in the interior with little food, but once in Luanda, good business practice dictated that they be fattened up. Therefore, the blacks were fed well, and their skins greased with palm-oil for a healthy appearance. Sick captives were quarantined, and if no ships were available the others were set to agricultural work.[46]

Usually the day before embarkation the slaves were assembled in a nearby church, or perhaps in the main square of the port, to be baptized. As far as the civil and ecclesiastical authorities were concerned, it was essential that this sacrament be performed, since the missionary aspect of the slave trade was usually cited as the most compelling reason for its existence. Even so, the spectacle was tragicomic. Ordinarily, the slaves had not received any religious instruction, or indeed even been told of the existence of the Christian God. As a prelude to the perfunctory ceremony to follow, the priest walked among the rows of captives, assigning a Christian name to each and handing him a paper with his name written on it lest he forget it. This done, the priest made a second swing through the black ranks, sprinkling a little salt on the tongue of each slave, and then a third swing to apply holy water, "and hurriedly," on each. The ceremony over, the priest addressed the following words to the assemblage through an interpreter: "Look, you people are now children of God; you are going to the lands of the Spaniards where you will learn the things of the Holy Faith. Think no more of the lands you are leaving, and don't eat dogs, rats, or horses. Now go with a good will." Obviously, the captives had no idea of the meaning of the ceremony, and their interpretation was likely to be of the gloomiest sort. Even the best informed were mystified and unmoved.[47]

The foregoing is an account of the situation in Angola; an even more cynical lack of concern seems to have prevailed in Guinea. Though there were occasional attempts at reform in the first decades of the seventeenth century, pushed usually by the Jesuits, very little was achieved. Missionary workers were few and of poor quality, surrounded by a largely unscrupulous lay population, and their ranks were drastically thinned by tropical diseases. Those who survived "were more active in the slave-trade than in saying mass or doing any priestly office." In short, everything conspired to form insuperable obstacles to continuous and expanding missionary movement. In Africa, unlike America, the vineyard of the Lord was never worked with any particular diligence during the sixteenth and seventeenth centuries.[48]

Embarkation was a pitiful spectacle. It was not merely that the African was leaving his native land never to return, as he must have sensed. In addition, the odd ceremony of baptism increased the confusion and gave rise to lurid rumors that spread through the cargo: they were being carried away to be eaten; the Spaniards intended to make oil or lard from their fat. In the circumstances, as the slave traders soon learned, many captives preferred to jump overboard and drown rather than face this anticipated fate. Consequently, the slaves were chained six together, often with iron rings around the neck as well, and then bound two by two with foot shackles. As a further precaution, they were kept below decks, with the hatches battened down, even in port. Conditions in the hold soon grew so fetid and unsanity that "a Spaniard could not stick his face through the hatchway without becoming nauseated," and this on a voyage to Cartagena that might take over two months.[49] These conditions were frequently aggravated by overcrowding. The slave ships of the period were usually small ones of under 200 tons on which 600 Africans or more were sometimes loaded. These *tumbeiros*, or "coffins," as the ships were called by many, were usually lightly manned, perhaps with a European crew of only ten or a dozen men plus an occasional black interpreter. The captives were therefore allowed to take exercise and fresh air on deck only in small groups and at infrequent intervals to minimize the risk of mutiny and suicide. Since the crew was so small, many cargoes seem to have been fed only once a day, and a poor meal at that: a bowl of cornmeal or millet mush and some water.[50]

The combination of poor care and overcrowding helped to spread disease among the slaves, to the point where the Spanish asentistas assumed their merchant clients would load from 10 to 20 per cent more slaves than they had licenses for, and pay extra for any excess cargo lucky enough to survive the Atlantic crossing.[51] If all this were not enough, there was the added danger of shipwreck. Little is known on the subject as it relates specifically to slaving vessels. Certainly the contemporary report that "every day brings us news of great disasters and shipwrecks" is an exaggeration. Yet just as certainly accidents did occur, and the results were apt to be grim, as in the case of a slave ship from Angola that hit a sand bank and sank within sight of Cartagena, losing all but thirty of the reported 900 blacks on board.[52] For the merchant there was the protection of insurance if he escaped alive, but this was small consolation to the shackled slaves below deck when disaster struck.[53]

Still, if some slave traders were willing to risk overloading their ships to ensure an ample return, and others were simply callous, a larger and more careful group tried to profit from experience. Even so harsh a critic of the system as the Jesuit Alonso de Sandoval, who worked among the slaves arriving at Cartagena in the early seventeenth century, conceded that prevailing conditions on the Atlantic crossing, though still bad, had at least shown some improvement during his time.[54] In this period, for example, some of the slave traders operating between Angola and Cartagena began to put in at Pernambuco (before that city's capture by the Dutch in 1630), Maranhão, or Jamaica to replenish their supplies and to give their cargoes some respite from the fetid holds of the ships.[55] Indeed, thanks to steps like this, the Portuguese slave traders acquired a reputation for efficiency among their foreign competitors. After the Dutch seizure of Luanda in 1641, for example, the first director there filed an official report to the effect that the Portuguese could ship 500 slaves in a small ship with a lower mortality rate than the Dutch could expect in transporting 300 on a large ship. The secret, he claimed, was better care and feeding. The Portuguese washed down the deck every other day "with bad vinegar"; they cooked "warm hot-pot for their slaves twice daily, once with African beans, the next time with maize, and all well-cooked with a good big spoonful of palm-oil mixed therein, together with a little salt, and sometimes a large hunk of dried fish in each dish." A portion of mush was also served daily, and "a little nigger-wine [was kept] especially on hand for the sick." Further, every slave was furnished with several pieces of old cloth to use as clothing.[56]

It must also be recognized that even the most humane trader was powerless to stop the spread of disease once it took hold below deck. The Portuguese merchant Manuel Bautista Pérez, for example, who later came to dominate the Peruvian slave trade, was noted for the care he took with his cargoes. Active in the Atlantic slave trade since 1612, Pérez was certainly no greenhorn when he made his 1618 voyage from

Guinea to Cartagena with a cargo of 508 slaves. Yet of this number, ninety were lost in the crossing (forty from scurvy alone) for a mortality rate of some 17 per cent, a figure that Pérez called a "punishment from God."[57]

However well or ill they treated their cargoes, for the great majority of slave traders who supplied the Peruvian market, the sight of Cartagena or some other Caribbean port signaled the end of the journey. A few of the asientos concluded during this period permitted the merchants to venture inland and offer the slaves for sale, instead of disposing of them at a lower price in the port cities.[58] Most Atlantic traders, however, were content to sell their cargoes in Cartagena (perhaps to a relative or business associate), pay whatever duties could not be evaded, and return to the Peninsula, usually to begin the process anew.[59] Any other method of operation, leaving to one side the cumbersome details of transshipment across the Isthmus and down the Pacific coast, would have meant an intolerably long interval before the trader realized a return on his investment. By and large, then, the intercolonial trade in blacks was handled not by the Atlantic slave traders, but by the middlemen of Cartagena, Puerto Belo, and Lima, whose activities will be discussed in the next chapter.

To sum up, the Atlantic slave trade was a sordid but complex business in which Portuguese merchants based in Lisbon and Seville played an all-important part. Their capital, their initiative, their knowledge, their search for profits, made the slave trade function. The Spanish government also had a central role in commerce in blacks. The flow of Africans to the American colonies was dependent on royal consent and subject to government regulation, and the Crown viewed the slave trade with mixed emotions. The black slave was seen as a vital source of labor for the development of Spanish America, and the duties placed on importation provided modest revenues for a financially hard-pressed Crown. However, the concessions made at Tordesillas and the economics of the trade required that traffic in Africans be entrusted to Portuguese merchants. These men wanted payment in silver, a necessity Spain resented in an age when bullion was deemed to be the standard of national wealth. As it happened, growing American demand for blacks in the late sixteenth century coincided with the dynastic union of the two Iberian empires, and for the moment Spain's dilemma seemed solved. With the African coast now under the de facto control of the Spanish Crown, American demand for blacks could be calculated and met, government revenues could be assured by monopoly contract, and the resulting flow of silver would remain within the empire. But the Crown consistently underestimated both American need for slaves and Portuguese desire for silver. The result was widespread contraband in blacks and, after the Spanish convoy system began to falter in the seventeenth century, in merchandise as well. Government attempts to placate the outraged merchant guild of Seville took the form of futile legislation that did little to limit contraband and at the same time added to the growing friction between the Spanish and the Portuguese during the last decades of dynastic union. These tensions within the imperial structure might well have been endured if it had not been for the reverses both nations suffered during this period at the hands of the Dutch throughout the colonial world, reverses that doomed the Iberian attempts at monopoly stated in the Treaty of Tordesillas and precipitated the successful Portuguese bid for independence in 1640. Yet with all the internal friction and outside aggression, the Iberians during this period pressed thousands of Africans, as a result of a "justice which God alone understands,"[60] into the development of the Spanish empire in America, and Peru was one of the chief beneficiaries.

CHAPTER THREE

The Peruvian Slave Trade

For Africans bound for Spanish America the sight of the Caribbean coast often meant merely that the midpoint of the voyage had been reached; many of them were destined to live out their days thousands of miles away in Peru, and, as in the case of bolts of cloth and other merchandise brought to the New World for sale, the selection of which of them would make the trip to Lima was subject to the vagaries of the marketplace. The Atlantic slave trader quickly disposed of his cargo, usually in two or three large lots, which might then be further fragmented into slave groups of even two or three Africans. "Thus," as the Jesuit Alonso de Sandoval remarked of Cartagena, "it is doubtful which will be those who will remain here . . . because many times after having been purchased for service here, they are resold for shipment out of town."[1]

In this frantic process of sale and resale, the African's condition was often momentarily even worse than it had been during the Atlantic voyage. Exhausted by the journey, naked, often dying of thirst but too timid to ask for water, and thoroughly frightened, the slaves were usually lodged in the patio of their purchaser's home or in a nearby corral. By day, there were the slave sales, the *feria de los negros*, and the unfortunate blacks were subjected to the attentions of a multitude of people, "some carried there by their greed, others by curiosity," and in the case of the Jesuits, "by compassion."[2] By night, divided by sexes, they were herded into "damp, thick-walled structures, undoubtedly constructed of adobe, in which crude tiers of sleeping platforms had been erected of rough planks. The only entrance, a small door, was bolted. A small, high window provided the only ventilation, and sanitary facilities, if any, consisted simply of tubs. Hopelessly incurable slaves spent their remaining hours in these fetid cabins," and all this in the sweltering heat of Cartagena.[3]

Slave merchants made an effort to feed their blacks well, since an emaciated slave was certain to bring a poor price, but Sandoval remarks that the very abundance, after the miseries of the voyage, seemed to sicken the African. Whatever the truth of this assertion, most cargoes succumbed to widespread illness on arrival. Slaves purchased by relatively poor men seemed to survive this crisis better than those bought by the rich, for the poorer owners had more to lose and tended to their slaves personally, whereas the richer men tended to be preoccupied by many enterprises and usually entrusted their slaves to majordomos whose carelessness turned more than one cargo "into a hospital of sick men, from which the cemetery is peopled with the dead." In addition to wounds, bruises, abscesses, and physical defects of every description (including maimed and missing limbs), scurvy, dysentery, and yaws were common among slaves cargoes. Less frequently, but with more serious consequences, cargoes were riddled with typhus, measles, smallpox, yellow fever, or malaria.[4] Since next to nothing was known about the treatment of these diseases, there was little to do but let them run their course, and many of the slave traders and their customers soon grew callous and indifferent to the problem. Sandoval recalled entering one patio to find two dead slaves, "stark naked, lying on the bare ground as if they were beasts, face up, their mouths open and full of flies."[5] Dead blacks were often thrown naked into the street until someone could take them away for burial or were left to lie where they died, covered with flies, while buyers milled around ignoring them as they would a dead dog. Traders with some sensitivity for the conventions of society wrapped the corpses in shrouds of old matting and threw them into a convenient corner for later burial.

In all this confusion and wretchedness, the Jesuits worked very hard to secure good treatment for the African, and the early efforts of the Society among the slave cargoes at Cartagena, led by such men as Sandoval and Saint Peter Claver ("the slave of the black slaves"), constitute one of the Church's finest hours in the New World. Mindful of the slaves' physical and psychological needs, the Jesuits brought them clothing, water, a sweet or some trinket, and, above all, kind words. But spiritual concerns were uppermost in their minds, and acutely aware of the defective baptisms that had been performed in Africa, many priests made truly heroic efforts to bring the dying into the Church before they expired, to secure medical attention for the ill, and, finally, to baptize the healthy in proper fashion. As a symbol of baptism, the slaves were given a tin medallion on a cord to hang around their necks, and the absence of such a symbol served to alert the Jesuits of Lima that an African had yet to be catechized. As was only natural, the blacks returned this humanity with gratitude and loyalty, and many a slave who lost his medallion immediately asked for another.[6]

The location of Cartagena made it a natural distribution point for African slaves into New Granada, the West Indies, and even New Spain, but it was in Peru that the great slaving port found its most important market. As one anonymous observer said bluntly of the city in the early seventeenth century, "here come many ships loaded with blacks brought by merchants from Guinea, and to here come merchants from Peru to buy them."[7] The statement oversimplifies the tangle of mercantile relationships that prevailed in the intercolonial slave trade, but it accurately reflects the importance of the ties between Cartagena and Lima.

As we saw in Chapter 1, for much of the sixteenth century the Peruvian slave trade was a small-scale, loosely organized enterprise. Merchants and ships' captains plying the route between Panama and Callao leavened their cargoes of merchandise with a slave or two, and often individual Limeños instructed these traders to buy slaves for them on the Isthmus where prices were cheaper. To some extent, this pattern continued to prevail in the seventeenth century. This is evident, for example, in the voyage of Alonso de Miranda, master of the *Nuestra Señora de la Alegría*, who arrived in Panama on June 1, 1609, after a voyage of five and a half months from Callao; lingered on there until close to the end of the year on-loading cargo, including 127 slaves he had been charged to purchase for various individuals in Paita, Santa, and Callao; and finally put back in again at Callao on October 25, 1610, after nearly two years' absence. Unquestionably, Miranda's trip took longer than most (he experienced two unaccountable delays on his return that forced him back to Paita twice), but it demonstrates that the slow, fragmented commerce in slaves so typical of the sixteenth century was not unknown in the seventeenth.[8] Some Spanish shipowners also dabbled on occasion in the trade themselves. For example, Gaspar Martín, captain of the *San Pablo* on the Panama-Callao run, who appears ordinarily to have hauled mainly merchandise, joined with his Portuguese partner in 1623 in purchasing a lot of 124 slaves in Panama for resale in the Lima area.[9]

Beginning in the last decades of the sixteenth century, however, and in response to the increased Peruvian demand for blacks (as reflected in the sharp upswing in prices*), men who may more properly be called slavers came to dominate the Panama-Callao commerce in Africans. There was stiff competition among the merchants of Spanish America in a market with a limited quantity of slaves, but the Lima traders possessed one formidable advantage: Peruvian silver. The demand for blacks was no doubt as great in Hispaniola and Venezuela as it was in Peru, but agricultural products were no match for the lure of bullion. The merchants of Lima were therefore able to skim off the cream of the Cartagena supply, and the Peruvian capital became to the Pacific coast what Cartagena was to the Caribbean: a distribution point for African slaves destined for Ecuador, Chile, and the rest of Peru.[10]

As the slave trade grew in importance, so did the predominance of Portuguese merchants. That the Spanish tended to grow somewhat hysterical on this score, denouncing the Portuguese as a pack of secret Judaizers whose illegal machinations drained Spanish bullion off to Lisbon, should not be allowed to obscure the fact that the Portuguese did indeed dominate both Atlantic and intercolonial commerce in Africans. The result was "a veritable Portuguese colonization" centered around Cartagena.[11]

The officials of the Casa de la Contratación, aware of the influx, and sympathetic as usual to the interests of the Seville monopolists, more than once urged the Crown to remedy the situation. In 1610, for example, they lamented the large numbers of rich and powerful Portuguese resident in Cartagena and elsewhere, men who through bribery turned royal officials in America into willing accomplices in their illegal activities. Unless the situation were remedied, the Casa feared, these merchants would greatly damage the legal trade of the convoy system, thereby reducing royal customs duties and placing the maritime lifeline between Spain and America in grave jeopardy. The blame for their growing numbers was placed squarely on the asientos concluded with the Portuguese, which allowed twenty or more slave ships to be dis-

---

* For detailed data on Peruvian slave prices, which I shall be discussing here and there throughout this chapter, see Appendix B, pp. 342-45, especially the graphs.

patched from Africa "full of Portuguese who pose as sailors and who bring slaves to sell, and all of them remain in the Indies, trading." Indeed, it was claimed that control of commerce in the Tierra Firme (Isthmus) area had already slipped almost entirely into the hands of the Portuguese. Ships now came directly from Portugal in flagrant violation of the law, but the local government officials made no move to oppose such activities.[12]

The partisans of the Seville monopolists may have exaggerated the extent of Portuguese contraband operations, but not by much. As one observer bitterly noted in 1600, every slave trader who obtained licenses for 100 Africans casually loaded five times that number and ran into no difficulties with the authorities in Cartagena; he merely distributed between twelve and twenty slaves among the parties concerned, and was then given free rein to sell the rest of his cargo. The slave trader Manuel Bautista Pérez, whose activities will be studied in detail later in this chapter, matter-of-factly listed in his account book for 1618 that he had bribed the governor, treasury officials, and various minor functionaries of Cartagena with slaves and cash totaling 6,170 pesos to get them to let him land twice as many slaves as his registry called for. Even the convoy system was riddled with fraud—to the point where the newly appointed corregidor of Ica, Gregorio Rico, felt obliged to write the Crown from Puerto Belo about the scandalous numbers of illegally imported slaves who had made the voyage with him.[13]

As we have seen, the Spanish Crown was never able to resolve the problem of contraband. The slave trade was impossible without the participation of Portuguese merchants, men who could not resist profiting from the American demand for slaves. The Crown responded to the shrill protests of the Seville monopolists about the Portuguese with legislation and investigation, but neither was effective. In 1595 the Spanish passed a law permitting slave merchants to exceed the authorized number of slaves provided they showed the accurate number on their manifests and paid the appropriate duties.[14] But obviously the Portuguese merchants would not pay duty when evasion was so easy. And government attempts to investigate the situation were thoroughly blocked. The new viceroy, the Príncipe de Esquilache (1615-21), for example, was told to investigate the persistent incidents and rumors of fraud in the slave trade at Cartagena while in route to Peru to assume office. As Esquilache admitted in his report to the Crown, his stay in

Cartagena was too short to get to the bottom of the matter, but even so every avenue of inquiry he had attempted to pursue had been filled with obstructions. The guards assigned to prevent the unloading of slave ships before inspection, and who "alone knew the truth" concerning the frauds, had fled and could not be found for questioning. Even the Jesuits would not reveal what they knew, and catechizing among the recently arrived slaves as they did, they doubtless knew a great deal. Esquilache observed that certain parties maintained estates outside the city for the sole purpose of receiving slaves who had been fraudulently disembarked on the coast before the ships entered the harbor, but he could provide no further specifics. The viceroy closed his report with the recommendation that a detailed investigation of the matter be made by officials of integrity, armed with sufficient authority to detain those involved regardless of their rank and influence.[15] The Crown chose not to act on this suggestion, however, and the illegal slave traffic continued to keep pace as best it could with the American demand throughout the period under study.

The Crown did, however, have an instrument at its disposal that could bring the Portuguese merchants to heel, and one that could strike with great selectivity. This was the Holy Office, which had tribunals in both Cartagena and Lima. Many of the Portuguese seem in fact to have been Jews, and even those who were not sometimes had to prove it in a judicial process that took years to complete. In the meantime, their assets passed into the hands of the Inquisition for administration. In short, the arrest of one merchant by the Holy Office struck fear into the hearts of many others, and perhaps no other agency of the Spanish Crown, whatever the intent of the inquisitors in any particular case, was so effective in thinning the ranks of Portuguese traders in Spanish America.[16]

To take a case for Cartagena, we may mention that of Luis Gomes Barreto, a man of sixty-five years and a respected member of the community at the time of his arrest in 1636. Barreto had been born in Viseu, but his parents moved to São Tomé a few years later. After a commercial apprenticeship in Lisbon with his elder brothers, Barreto took the modest capital they gave him and followed his parents to the island. He spent a year there, and then made two trips to Brazil with slaves. These voyages were apparently quite profitable, for Barreto was able to go next to Angola and buy a load of blacks on his own account.

These he sold in Cartagena and Santa Marta, and then took ship for Spain. Within two months, he sailed again from Seville for Angola and returned to Cartagena with more slaves. Barreto repeated this process, but then the pleasures of married life caused him to abandon further voyages to Africa. This did not, however, mean an end to his activities in the slave trade. Barreto now made four separate voyages to Lima with blacks for sale. At the conclusion of the last one, in 1607, he had become wealthy enough to purchase the office of Depositary General in Cartagena. Using the port city as a base, he continued to ship Africans to Lima until the time of his arrest. Barreto was able to talk his way out of the charges against him, but continued rumors of his Judaizing caused a second arrest in 1650. Two years later, at the age of eighty-two, he was condemned to a short period of exile from the city, a mild penalty though sufficiently hard on an old man.[17]

By far the most spectacular of the Holy Office's investigations of the Portuguese merchants centered in Lima. Initiated in 1635, the inquiry lasted four years and eventually involved eighty persons, twelve of whom were burnt at the stake or otherwise dispatched in an auto da fé on January 23, 1639.[18] One of the most prominent merchants arrested was Manuel Bautista Pérez, who was identified by the Holy Office as the spiritual leader (*capitán grande*) of the Lima Jews. Charged also as Jews were Sebastián Duarte, Pérez's business associate and brother-in-law, and several other dealers in slaves. Pérez and Duarte never confessed to this ancestry, but were (as the expression went) relaxed to the secular arm anyway. Both were apparently executed in the prison of the Holy Office and then burnt in effigy. In accordance with the standard practice of the Inquisition, their assets were seized by the Holy Office, and more important for our purposes, so were their voluminous records, which provide detailed information on the Pacific coast slave trade during this period, as well as some hint of the lives of the men involved.[19]

Pérez, who may well have been the wealthiest merchant in Peru at the time of his arrest and who certainly dominated the colony's slave trade, was a native of Ança in the Portuguese bishopric of Coimbra.[20] He was active in the slave trade at least as early as 1612, though at first only as an agent for a considerable number of investors. As we have seen, his 1618 voyage from Guinea to Cartagena, made in partnership with a merchant who remained in Portugal, had a disastrous mortality rate, and Pérez decided on arrival that the only way to salvage the venture was to take a cargo of slaves for sale to Lima. The 227 blacks he sold there brought such a handsome profit that he was moved to make the Peruvian capital his permanent base of operations.[21] For several years thereafter, Pérez annually made the voyage from Lima to Cartagena and back to buy and sell slaves, but he finally realized that durable partnerships were the secret of success in the intercolonial slave trade. That is, it was much simpler and more profitable for him to remain in Lima the year round, selling slaves sent to him by agents on the Isthmus and in Cartagena. To this end, Pérez formed partnerships with several Portuguese resident in the Caribbean area, including Luis Gomez Barreto. His most reliable supplier, however, was his brother-in-law, Sebastián Duarte. Duarte, too, was a native of Portugal who had come to Spanish America, and thence to Lima, with a cargo of Africans, making the trip in 1622. There is no evidence that Pérez sent for him, but there may well have been previous ties in Portugal between the families of the two men. In any event Duarte was soon married to one of Pérez's sisters, and the older man set his brother-in-law up in a dry goods store in Lima. More important, Pérez was soon relying on his brother-in-law and various Duarte relatives to procure slaves for him in the Caribbean area, blacks he then sold with great success in Lima and elsewhere in Peru.[22]

At the time of his arrest Pérez had accumulated a fortune of close to half a million pesos and had begun diverting his assets from trade to more gentlemanly pursuits, including silver mines in Huarochirí and plantations around Lima. In the words of Henry Charles Lea: "His confiscated house has since been known as the *casa de Pilatos*, and his ostentatious mode of life may be judged by the fact that when his carriage was sold by the tribunal it fetched thirty-four hundred pesos." Pérez may well have been Jewish, but he never owned to it, and died impenitent after an unsuccessful suicide attempt in the jails of the Holy Office. His public life was one of almost garish devotion to Catholicism. His business records abound with thanks to the Lord (though not specifically to Jesus); priests educated his children; and perhaps in return for substantial donations, "he was greatly esteemed by the clergy who dedicated to him their literary effusions in terms of the warmest adulation."[23] Duarte, we may assume, led a life of similar comfort.

Shrewd traders like Pérez and Duarte did not deviate radically from the pattern of the Peruvian slave trade as it had operated since the conquest period. On Pérez's initial voyage to Lima in 1618 he carried not only blacks but also over 12,000 pounds of yellow wax, and he continued this practice of diversifying his wares in later years. In the Caribbean area he and Duarte purchased emeralds, pearls, wax, saffron, fine woods, and large quantities of imported fabrics from Europe, the Orient (*tafetán de China* via the Manila Galleon), and Mexico (*tafetán de México, seda de Mixteca*) to sell to the affluent in Lima.[24] This trade was designed to minimize risk, to buy cheap on the Isthmus and sell dear in Peru, and more often than not the strategy worked. In 1633-34, for example, Pérez and Duarte, in partnership with a third party, purchased some 10,600 pesos' worth of pearls in Cartagena and resold them in Lima for over 16,000 pesos. Not all of Pérez's ventures were successful, to be sure. In 1623, for instance, he lamented that he found few takers for some fabrics he had purchased in the Caribbean because a ship loaded with similar merchandise had arrived from Mexico four days before he himself reached the city.[25]

All the same, it cannot be emphasized too strongly that Pérez and his associates, unlike their predecessors, were first and foremost slave traders. Their greatest profits came from commerce in human flesh, and this was the main reason for their frequent trips to the Caribbean. Pérez and Duarte preferred to buy their blacks from Atlantic merchants they knew and trusted,[26] but once in Cartagena they usually accumulated their cargoes according to the dictates of the market. Blacks were haggled for in both large and small lots over a considerable period of time, and often a lot was rejected one week only to be purchased the next, when a price had been agreed on or when it became obvious that these were the only Africans available to round out the cargo. For example, it took Duarte from December 15, 1632, to January 5, 1633, to purchase a total of 193 slaves from twenty-one individuals in Cartagena. Two of the sellers were sailors, one a druggist, and two others held the degrees of doctor and licenciate, respectively. Duarte's largest purchase involved thirty-nine slaves, which he bought from one seller in two transactions. Another larger lot consisted of thirty-four slaves, purchased from one seller in three transactions.[27] Pérez and Duarte also bought slaves for friends and associates in Peru, and sold small parcels of blacks belonging to people on the Isthmus and in Cartagena in Lima for a share of the profits.

Such dealings required substantial sums of money. When Duarte left Lima for Cartagena on May 26, 1633, for example, he carried with him silver in the amount of 214,343 pesos. Of this sum, 147,405 pesos was earmarked for debts incurred on previous voyages, leaving a working capital of 66,938 pesos for a slave cargo and expenses. But Duarte was expected to use credit as well as cash in his transactions. For example, over half the cost of the 193 slaves he purchased in 1632-33 was covered by promissory notes payable in either a year or two years.[28]

A further example may serve to underline the complexity of credit transactions as they involved the slave trade. A nephew of Duarte's, who was stationed in Cartagena in 1629-33 to secure a steady supply of blacks for the associates to sell in Peru, purchased a lot of 122 slaves for 44,510 pesos. He paid 9,000 of this amount in cash, pledged 16,000 more in his uncle's name, and signed a personal note for the balance. He then turned around and sold sixty-nine of the slaves in Panama, in the name of the company, for some 28,000 pesos, taking 75 per cent of this amount in short-term notes (of three, six, and twelve months). The interest on such notes could range as high as 17 per cent.[29]

During the period when the enterprises of Pérez and Duarte flourished, slave prices in Cartagena remained relatively stable, though there was some fluctuation through time and the price of Angolan slaves slowly increased. In 1620 Pérez reported that slaves from Guinea could be purchased for about 270 to 315 pesos, and the best slaves from Angola for 200. Though the price of Guinea slaves increased for a time—in 1629 Duarte paid as much as 380 pesos for a large number of them—by 1632 the supply was plentiful enough to bring the range back down to 295-342 pesos. In the same year Duarte had to pay between 280 and 326 pesos each for Angolan slaves, but by the following year his top price had dropped to 305 pesos.[30]

This relative stability of what we may term the wholesale price of blacks in Cartagena was reflected in the retail market of Lima, but the Spanish Crown had no reason for self-congratulation. The comparatively minor fluctuations in slave prices during the last decades of the asiento period had little to do with the Crown's monopoly arrangements, but were the result instead of massive smuggling. A few examples from the Duarte-Pérez ledger books will serve to indicate the scope of these operations. For every slave imported into Cartagena from Africa, a merchant was supposed to have a *fe de entrada*, an official document certifying that the proper duty had been paid, and that the black was part of a shipment authorized under the asiento. Yet, only sixty-six of the 177 slaves Duarte purchased in Cartagena between August 1 and August 14, 1633, were so certified. Similarly, of 222 blacks he had purchased the year before, 148 had been illegally imported.[31]

Slavers operating between the Caribbean and Peru, however, were subject to inspection by royal treasury officials at three different points —Cartagena, Puerto Belo, and Panama—and had a final examination of their documents at Callao. It was important, therefore, that their papers be in order, that an effort be made to demonstrate that all slaves had been legally imported. One common method employed to this end was to purchase a fe issued for a slave of similar origin and physical description. In 1634, for example, the Pérez operation purchased twenty-nine fes from a shipowner for seventeen pesos each;[32] plainly, fraudulent certifications cost less than the legal license fees, or the traders would have simply declared the slaves and paid the duty. Forgery was almost certainly also widely employed, and, if all else failed, Spanish officials along the way were bribed into silence. We have already seen how casually Pérez used this last technique, and bureaucrats no doubt came to expect a gratuity as a matter of course. Duarte reported on one occasion tipping the treasury officials at Panama twenty pesos for "the good and prompt dispatch of the ship," and for Puerto Belo he cryptically recorded an expense of thirty pesos "for the good services of the guards" (*por la buena negociación al guardia*).[33]

It should be emphasized that the life of even the most experienced merchant was one of constant stress. To be sure, the price of slaves in Cartagena fluctuated very little over the long haul, but this was not necessarily true of every cargo, and bargaining in the port city was a strenuous business. A merchant had to decide whether to buy the slaves he was offered, even if they seemed over-priced and inferior in quality, or to await another slaver, which might be late in arriving and whose human merchandise might in any case be no better than what was currently on the market. Slaves were smuggled into Cartagena and sold with an apparent ease that masks the number of contacts and the discretion required of the merchants who bought them. Meanwhile, as these delicate negotiations went on, the slave merchant had to preserve his cargo against the heat and stench of Cartagena, while taking care that his expenses did not erase his anticipated profits. Large sums had to be spent for food and medical care for the blacks, and cash trickled away in many minor ways. In Cartagena alone, a merchant had to pay house rent and various fees to notaries and port officials for the preparation of the ship's registry; and thereafter he paid freight charges for the blacks to be hauled to Puerto Belo, a voyage of nine or ten days.

Prominent traders like Pérez and Duarte ordinarily spent a considerable amount of time in Puerto Belo.[34] Occasionally a slave or two would be purchased there or accepted on consignment. But this was not the reason they went to the city. For one thing, Puerto Belo was the site of fairs held on the arrival of the mercantile convoys from Spain, and the merchants frequented these events to add to their stocks of merchandise. More important, the city was a mandatory checkpoint in the slave trade. In the sixteenth century runaway blacks became so troublesome on the Isthmus that the Crown banned further importation into the area. The ban was never entirely effective, but slave merchants bound for the Pacific coast were required to register their cargoes with the royal officials at Puerto Belo and to swear that none of the blacks would be sold in Tierra Firme. The officials at Panama on the Pacific side of the Isthmus were charged with examining this registry to be sure the promise had been complied with.[35]

While the merchants haggled over the price of cloth in Puerto Belo their blacks were rested and fattened up, meaning additional expenses for housing and maintenance. Then came the crossing of the Isthmus, a short but hard journey through the lush vegetation of the tropical rain forest, ordinarily accomplished in two days. Healthy slaves made the trip on foot, but the sick and mothers with infants, plus any merchandise purchased at Puerto Belo, had to be transported by mule or by barge down the Chagres River. Additional expenses were incurred for the mules and a muleteer-guide, for ferry service across the Chagres and Piquirí rivers, and for an overnight stay at one of various rude inns along the way. Particular care had to be exercised on the Isthmus crossing because desperate blacks usually chose this part of the journey to attempt an escape, perhaps to join one of the runaway groups that plagued the area during much of the sixteenth and seventeenth centuries. Despite their vigilance, Pérez and Duarte lost several slaves in this way during the course of their various journeys. Perhaps in part to prevent such escapes, the associates selected one black to be the "captain" of the slave gang during the trip. This man was probably also responsible for the general welfare of the slaves and may have acted as interpreter.

Pérez and Duarte ordinarily spent at least a month in Panama before departing for Callao. Arrangements had to be made for shipping, and additional slaves were invariably accepted on consignment and sometimes purchased. More important, perhaps, there was still more merchandise to buy, contraband goods from the Orient and Mexico that came from Acapulco. Here, in addition to expenses for maintenance, the slave merchants had to purchase quantities of food and medicine for the Pacific voyage, and some gave their blacks a fresh (and doubtless much-needed) change of clothing at this point. Miscellaneous costs included the preparation of a new ship's registry for inspection at Callao, the carting of the slaves to the docks at Perico, tips to the soldiers who supervised this operation, and the payment of various brokerage and messenger fees.[36] Ordinarily, the saying of some Masses for a safe voyage was arranged, and then the last leg of the journey began.

Most slave ships bound for Callao customarily made at least one stop along the way, particularly at the port of Paita or at the ports of Guanchaco, Santa, and Saña in the Trujillo area. Fresh supplies of meat and produce were taken on at these stops, and slaves were sold for use in the nearby plantations. In favorable weather it was possible to put in at a port or two and still reach Callao within thirty days or less. Occasionally, all or some of the slaves were unloaded at Paita or Trujillo, refreshed, and marched overland or taken by mule to Lima, with the merchant or an agent selling part of them along the way. From time to time Pérez and Duarte employed this strategy, and so did other slave merchants. In 1625, for example, Cristóbal Serrato and Gerónimo Rodríguez, residents of Panama, formed a partnership to sell thirty-nine slaves in Peru. The blacks were unloaded in the Trujillo area, where eighteen were sold. One died, and the others were sold in Lima (nine) and Cuzco (eleven). By year's end, the partners were in Lima to divide the profits and make their way back to the Isthmus.[37]

The mortality rate was heavy on the journey to Peru. It was the rare colonial slave merchant who did not have part of his cargo sicken in Cartagena or on the Isthmus, there to be left for recuperation or death, and widespread sickness sometimes even disrupted the voyage from Panama to Callao. In 1618, for example, a cargo of blacks who belonged to prominent Lima slave dealers was so riddled with illness that the ship had to put in at Paita, where the majority of the slaves took some six weeks to recuperate. (In this case, the major ailment was described as cancerous sores so severe as to require a number of amputations. The foot of one of the slaves was described as being so cancerous that "not a drop of blood" fell when it was cut off.)[38]

The high mortality rate during this second stage of the blacks' long journey cannot be blamed entirely on the colonial slave merchants. These men realized that adequate food and medical care were necessary to protect their investments, and, according to the standards of the time, did what they could. The blacks owned by Pérez and Duarte, for example, were fed a varied diet of beef, pork, corn, plantains, barley, bread, salt fish, and eggs, prepared with lard and vinegar as the ingredients required. Sick slaves were given an even more lavish variety, depending on their condition, which might include fowl, molasses, oranges, sugar, red wine, quinces, garbanzos, squashes, and cassava bread. Pérez and Duarte (and, we may assume, most of their fellows) were always careful to keep on hand a large stock of salves, powders, and oils for the care of their cargoes, and barbers and surgeons were called in as the occasion required for emetics, bleedings, and more serious operations. The fact is, however, many of their medical remedies were worthless—sugar to gargle away a severe sore throat, honey and mustard for lockjaw—and much faith was placed in the efficacy of the bezoar stone.[39] Despite an abundant diet, this primitive medical care could not stem the tide of sickness and death among blacks who had been herded for months from one cramped and filthy ship's hold or compound to another.

Moreover, some colonial slave traders, too, succumbed to the temptation to overcrowd, and often with disastrous results. The Jesuit Sandoval mentions one slave ship bound for Puerto Belo on which, "the blacks being many and the space tight," nearly the whole cargo sickened and died, along with the Jesuit priest on board who worked frantically to catechize and baptize the blacks before death.[40] Additional evidence of widespread overcrowding comes from 1632, when the *Nuestra Señora del Rosario* sank outside of Callao with a heavy loss of life and property: twenty-three Spaniards and 120 Africans; 1,500 chests of dry goods and 150 cakes of crude wax. Another forty-seven Spaniards and four Africans managed to escape in a skiff. The Conde de Chinchón (viceroy, 1629-39) considered the matter grave enough to merit a letter to the Crown, in which he blamed the accident on the carelessness of the

pilot but observed also that practically all ships left Panama for Callao
so badly overloaded and so badly ballasted that it was a wonder there
were not more such tragedies.[41]

In general, it appears that a slave trader who operated between Cartagena and Lima could count himself lucky if he did not lose more than
10 per cent of his blacks. Let us take three of Pérez's and Duarte's cargoes. In one, consisting of 264 blacks hauled from Cartagena to Lima
in 1628-29, twenty-eight died in shipment and another eleven in Lima
before sale for a mortality rate of 15 per cent; in the second, a year later,
thirty-two in a total of 234 died, a rate of 14 per cent; and in the third,
in 1633-34, the rate fell to 13 per cent, with a loss of forty-nine blacks
out of 377.[42] There were, of course, extreme cases, such as a low 4.5 per
cent loss of life in a Pérez-Duarte shipment in 1630-31 and an appalling
21 per cent in a Pérez cargo in 1620-21. The full horror faced by slave
trader and black slave alike, however, tends to be somehow lost in these
percentages. A more graphic way of presenting the last figure is to say
that in just 136 days in 1620-21, Pérez lost sixty slaves, or approximately
one black every other day, some from measles, some from smallpox,
but most with the cause of death unspecified and presumably unknown
—and this merely between Cartagena and embarkation in Panama.[43]

Apart from being a problem for the slave traders, diseased blacks
were also a public-health problem, a matter that was of increasing concern to the officials of Lima. At a city council meeting in 1620 it was
suspected that three ships from Perico, which were loaded with over
1,800 blacks and were expected momentarily at Callao, might be carrying contagious diseases, since the weather had been unusually hot (and,
presumably, since the ships were so overloaded). Accordingly, the proposal was made that the slaves be kept aboard until inspected by a competent doctor under the supervision of one of the municipal justices, "as
has always been done on other occasions." After discussion, the council
decided to ask the viceroy for permission to make the inspection in
accordance with past practice, as certified by many similar decrees in
the possession of the city clerk.[44] The fears of the municipality must
have struck a responsive chord within the viceregal government. At a
city council meeting four years later, there was mention of an ordinance
issued by the recently arrived viceroy, the Marqués de Guadalcázar
(1622-29), barring the entry of slave cargoes into Lima without government permission.[45]

The 1624 council meeting produced still another innovation. The city authorities observed that slave traders usually brought their blacks into the heart of town and lodged them in crowded quarters, which caused whatever diseases they might have to spread in the city. To get around the problem the council proposed that a large compound for newly arrived slaves be built on the other side of the Rímac River in the San Lázaro district, near the slaughterhouse, which was far enough away from the town for the wind to carry the "corrupted air" in the opposite direction and yet quite near the plaza. Not only would the public health be served, but there would be other advantages. The slave traders would be spared the expense of renting quarters in the center of town, which could not be had for less than 500 pesos, and more housing would be freed for the city's residents; water and meat for the slaves would be accessible, and medical assistance more easily administered; once the location became known, buyers would come to the compound as a matter of course; and, finally, the city would realize some revenue from the rent of the quarters, which could be applied to public works. The council unanimously agreed to ask the viceroy's permission for the project, and for a supplementary decree requiring that all newly arrived slaves be sold at the compound when construction was completed.

The viceroy gave the council even more than it had asked for: on November 21, 1624, Guadalcázar imposed a head tax of one peso on all incoming slaves for the construction of four separate quarters in the San Lázaro district.[46] But little more seems to have been done until the administration of the next viceroy, Chinchón. On March 14, 1630, Chinchón ordered that each incoming slave cargo be detained at least a league away from Lima, separated by sexes, until a team of three physicians could certify that its members were free of smallpox and measles, "which they always carry with them." For a time at least this regulation was enforced.[47] In 1633 Chinchón reported to the Crown that four houses had been built in San Lázaro, with separate quarters for male and female slaves above the age of ten, and that the city was enjoying the rents therefrom. Even the slave merchants were reported to be pleased.[48] The Crown confirmed the action in the following year. These four compounds apparently formed the core of the black district of Lima called Malambo.[49]

On arrival in Lima the slave trader was confronted with an array of duties and taxes to pay. The city levied a two-peso head tax on all incoming blacks to finance a patrol for the apprehension of runaway slaves.[50] An ad valorem tax (*alcabala*) was estimated and collected on each slave at the customs house, and after 1627 an additional sales tax in an equal amount (called the tax of the "Union of Arms") was imposed for support of the Spanish war effort.[51] Finally, every slave imported into Lima was subject to a value-added tax (*almojarifazgo*) of 5 per cent of the difference between the prevailing prices in Lima and Panama.

As good businessmen, slave traders resented the imposition of any tax on their operations, but the almojarifazgo was more fiercely opposed than most. In the beginning the Crown conceded that no customs duty was owed on a slave at the first American point of importation (e.g., Cartagena); the license fee relieved the slave trader of paying any other import duties. The question that provoked disagreement between Crown and merchant was whether the slave, in common with European articles reshipped from one colonial port to another, should be taxed on any increase in value accruing thereby. Ever needful of revenue, the Spanish Crown slowly answered the question in the affirmative. The government failed in its first attempt to impose a value-added tax on slaves transported from the Isthmus to Peru in 1542-44;[52] but in 1562 it made a new attempt to set a 5 per cent duty on any increase in the value of goods, including slaves, shipped from Panama to Callao. For more than a decade, slave merchants fought the legality of the tax, claiming that all customs duties on blacks were embodied in the license fee, but in 1572 Viceroy Toledo succeeded in imposing the royal will.[53]

In the end, the almojarifazgo on blacks was collected on a purely arbitrary basis. The treasury officials of Panama and Lima found themselves much too busy to maintain a constant exchange of information on the fluctuating price of slaves in both cities, and so the Lima officials merely assumed that the poorest black, by reason of age or physical condition, increased fifty pesos in value between Panama and Peru; the minimum duty on blacks therefore became two and a half pesos per head. Slaves of better quality were appraised on a scale that was usually in multiples of this minimum, up to a maximum of twenty pesos, an amount that was rarely exceeded.[54] Occasionally, if an excessive duty had been charged, the treasury officials reversed themselves and granted a small refund.[55]

After a merchant had cleared his slaves through customs and the medical inspection, and housed them in a convenient location, the sales began. The demand for slaves in Peru was fairly constant over the years, but short-term fluctuations could be quite disconcerting to the slave merchants. For example, Pérez had found both demand and prices high on his initial Peruvian venture in 1618-19; in a letter to an associate he had gloatingly anticipated that the entire cargo would be sold for an average of 600 pesos per slave. On his very next voyage, however, conditions had changed drastically. Mortality among his cargo had been high; Lima was glutted with slaves; agricultural prices were depressed, and few planters wished to pay cash; and all this had caused some of his competitors to unload their cargoes at very low prices on credit (*a precios que es vergüenza decirlo*).[56]

Over the long haul, these market fluctuations probably served to concentrate the bulk of the Peruvian slave trade in fewer and fewer hands. A merchant of Pérez's stature could absorb an occasional reverse. He had the financial resources to sell on credit and still buy more slaves in Cartagena. Moreover, his widespread network of familial and business relationships enabled him to station agents in the Caribbean ports and in the wine-growing areas of the Peruvian south coast, while he himself remained free to work the Lima market. People no doubt preferred to buy slaves from an established merchant like Pérez; he had a reputation to protect, and, unlike a fly-by-night trader, could be contacted by a dissatisfied customer. By 1632 Pérez was so well known in the colony that he was filling the requests of customers almost 400 miles away.[57]

Pérez's ability to remain full-time in Lima was a very important asset. In the seventeenth century slaves were not immediately snapped up in Lima by hordes of eager buyers, but had to be sold slowly over many months. Pérez, for example, received two lots of slaves, totaling 344 blacks, on February 4 and March 13, 1634. By May 20 he had sold only 201 of them, and as late as August he had still to find buyers for seventy-two.[58] But Pérez could afford to take his time. Duarte or another associate could hurry back to Cartagena for more slaves while Pérez remained in Lima seeking the highest possible price for the cargo.

As credit sales became more common Pérez complained of the development, but it slowly worked to his advantage. Prior to the 1620's slave traders seem to have frowned on credit sales. In 1595, for example, a Spanish landowner explained to an associate that he had been unable to purchase badly needed slaves because he was short of funds, and all blacks were being sold for cash.[59] Pérez himself stated in letters to his partners that long-term sales on credit were uncommon prior to the depressed conditions of 1623, when his desperate competitors threatened to "destroy" the trade by accepting promissory notes payable in eighteen months' to two years' time for their blacks.[60] However much Pérez deplored this innovation, he had no choice but to go along, though he tried always to secure at least partial payment in cash. Nevertheless, by the 1630's he was selling many slave lots entirely on credit, with payment to be made in two or even three years' time, usually in equal annual installments. Since Pérez and other slave traders preferred to send their silver to the Isthmus in the safety of the royal galleons, these annual payments were ordinarily due thirty days before the fleet sailed. To give an example of the extent to which credit arrangements came to prevail in the Lima slave market, in 1634 Pérez sold 299 slaves for a total price of 179,355 pesos; of this sum, only 50,482 pesos was received in cash.[61] Pérez had sufficient capital to operate under the new arrangements, but many of his smaller competitors were probably forced to reduce their operations still more, if not to suspend them altogether.

For those with the requisite capital, business connections, and experience, however, there were substantial profits to be made in the Pacific coast slave trade. Even in one of their worst years, 1630, Pérez and Duarte got a healthy 10 per cent return on their investment in 189 slaves; on an outlay of 100,035 pesos, including 73,680 pesos for the slaves, they realized a net profit of 10,785 pesos. And the next year was even more rewarding. In 1631 they netted 18,915 pesos on 140 slaves they purchased at Cartagena for 49,889 pesos, making something over 30 per cent profit on a total investment of 62,861 pesos.[62]

Clearly, the partners had driven a harder bargain in the Cartagena market in 1631, perhaps because slaves were more plentiful than the year before, and they had kept expenses down. Both were keys to success in a Lima market that fluctuated, though not severely, in the fifteen years or so that Pérez and Duarte were active in the trade. To an extent, the Pacific coast trader was at the mercy of forces he could not control; the availability and price of slaves in Cartagena were subject to the dictates of the government, the prevailing barter conditions in Africa, and the mortality rate on the Atlantic crossing. Thus, Pérez and Duarte had had to pay an average of 411 pesos per black in 1630 as against an average price of only 356 pesos in 1631. Expenses on the run from Cartagena to Callao could be carefully budgeted to some degree, but here too there were factors beyond the slaver's control. A sickly cargo required more time for rest and recuperation, thus raising costs for maintenance and medical care. Shipping might be difficult to obtain, or other commercial dealings might force the slave trader to spend more time on the Isthmus, and every day that passed between purchase and sale increased costs. Accordingly, whereas the 1630 cargo cost 139 pesos per slave put down in Lima, a year later the cost per slave fell to 88 pesos for a shorter and less difficult voyage.

Finally, Pérez dealt in quantity, and this was a key factor in his success. It was not uncommon for him to receive 300 or 400 slaves a year, and at profits of up to 135 pesos per slave, he was thus able to accumulate a formidable amount of capital with which to support his credit operations. The beauty of his permanent residence in Lima was that when his agents sent him slaves in this quantity in one lot, he could afford the considerable time it took to sell a cargo of such size. It took him, for example, close on to three years to dispose of a lot of 402 slaves Duarte sent him in early 1632. By June 1 of the following year he had sold the bulk of them, 372, but it took him at least another year to sell another eighteen. As of August 1, 1635, he still had twelve on hand and expected to have difficulty unloading them because of their ill health and deformities.[63]

The dealings of Pérez, Duarte, and other slave merchants inevitably aroused resentment. Debtors are rarely favorably disposed toward their creditors, and were even less so in this case since the one group was predominantly Portuguese and the other mainly Spanish. At a meeting of the Lima city council in 1620 it was charged that three powerful, but unnamed, slave dealers had conspired to keep slave prices at a high level and were refusing to sell a slave for less than 700 or 800 pesos. These figures are too high, but it is true that slave prices in Lima reached a level in 1620 that had not been seen since the 1580's, and many buyers may have been priced out of the market. Apparently, one of the councilmen had ransacked the municipal archives and had found the decree of the 1550's by which the Crown had vainly attempted to fix the sale price of slaves in the American colonies. It is not clear whether or not the council knew that this legislation had been revoked, but in any event appeals were made first to the viceroy and then to the Crown to restore the price ceiling.[64] The councilmen failed in their attempts, but as it happened, supply caught up with demand, causing slave prices to fall in Lima during the 1620's and the early 1630's. Nevertheless, resentment against the Portuguese continued, and many Limeños probably welcomed the arrests made by the Holy Office in 1635.

It is difficult to say with any exactness how many blacks were imported into Peru in the period under study, since no body of documentation has been discovered from which a reliable, continuous estimate of the volume of the Peruvian slave trade could be extracted.[65] Consequently, one can only fall back on the statements of contemporary observers and supplement these with estimates based on what scattered hard data there are. We may begin by examining various estimates of the number of slaves who passed through Cartagena in the early decades of the seventeenth century. By that time Cartagena had become the focus of the slave trade to South America, and Peru was the prime market. One author, relying on the annual reports sent by the Jesuits to their superiors in Spain, states that in the years 1607-10 Cartagena received between twelve and fourteen slave ships per year, a total that suggests the annual importation of some 4,950 blacks.[66] In 1615 the Crown gave credence to a report that between 2,000 and 4,000 blacks entered the port annually for sale. Another observer, writing around the same date, estimated that between ten and twelve ships arrived every year from Angola, with nearly as many from Guinea, but this estimate implies a huge volume of slaves. The usually reliable Sandoval, a decade or so later, set the number of ships arriving per year at between twelve and fourteen, carrying a minimum of 3,600 Africans.[67] These general estimates may be supplemented by two pieces of recorded evidence on the volume of the slave trade to Cartagena. The first, based on treasury accounts for the years 1585-90, shows a total of 6,884 slaves, or about 1,147 a year, but this is for a period when the colonists complained bitterly about the shortage of blacks and therefore may be atypical. The second figure is for the interval between the annual convoys of 1619 and 1620, during which 2,411 Africans were imported into the city; of this total, at least 666 were unlicensed and had to be declared on arrival.[68] Given the above evidence, and allowing for contraband and for temporary periods of scarcity and saturation, it seems reasonable to assume that Cartagena received as many as 1,500 slaves in the best years between 1580 and 1600, and a minimum of 2,000 blacks annually between 1600 and 1640.

The overwhelming majority of blacks who entered Peru came more or less directly from Africa via Tierra Firme. These were the bozales, Africans who had yet to acquire the rudiments of Spanish language and culture. However, as in the formative years of the colony, a trickle of Africans came to Peru from the Iberian Peninsula and from other regions of Spanish America. In a sample of 6,890 slaves sold in the Lima market in the period 1560-1650, 448 (6.5 per cent) came from these areas as follows:[69]

Area	No. of slaves	Area	No. of slaves
Spain (esp. Seville)	97	Puerto Rico	10
Tierra Firme	75	Guatemala	7
Hispaniola	60	Nicaragua	5
New Granada (esp.		Cuba	5
Cartagena)	50	Bolivia (upper Peru)	4
Portugal	45	Venezuela	2
Mexico	41	Honduras, Jamaica, Para-	
Chile	25	guay, Tucumán (Argen-	
Ecuador	17	tina), and Brazil	1

Some of these Africans came to Peru as servants along with their masters and were subsequently sold, but others came in small lots of a dozen slaves or less and were intended for immediate sale. As we have seen, Pérez and Duarte, along with other merchants, dealt on a consignment basis with Spaniards living elsewhere in Spanish America who hoped to dispose of a few unwanted blacks in a profitable Peruvian market.[70] Indeed, the Crown indulged in the same practice. Between 1603 and 1606, for example, the government sent some unwanted blacks held in Mexico for auction in Peru, and similar arrangements were frequently made for the disposal of runaway blacks captured on the Isthmus, troublesome foes who conspired with English corsairs.[71]

So far as contraband activities in the Peruvian slave trade are concerned, the available evidence indicates that for most of the period the smuggling of blacks on the Panama-Callao run was insignificant. There were serious abuses, to be sure, as witness the Lima city council's complaint in 1573 that the municipal head tax on blacks was being systematically evaded by ship captains who landed their slave cargoes on the beach before entering Callao,[72] but the worst of the abuses undoubtedly occurred before the government had a direct interest in the flow of Africans to Peru. This charge came at the very beginning of royal attempts to profit from the Pacific slave trade through the almojarifazgo, and, with the successful imposition of this duty, Crown officials seem to have exercised greater vigilance over commerce in blacks. The next reference to contraband in surviving documentation is for 1604, and only five cases are recorded between that date and 1618. These involved a mere seventy-seven slaves and total penalties of some 2,200 pesos. The 1618 case involved a healthy fine of 1,000 pesos for the illegal importation of four slaves,[73] but in several instances the culprits were simply required to pay the owed freight charges and customs duties.

The last and most spectacular case of smuggling before 1650 occurred in 1629, when officers and members of the crew of the royal fleet in the Pacific were charged with conspiring to carry some eighty slaves valued at 40,000 pesos illegally from Panama to Callao. None of the blacks, allegedly bozales, were ever found, and, despite royal efforts to press the investigation, no culprits were ever singled out for punishment. From the evidence uncovered, most of these blacks had belonged to the ships' crews and were carried to Lima, at least ostensibly, for household service. In the opinion of the investigating official, this practice "could not be avoided, nor is it the custom to charge freight for or to declare" slaves who were brought to Peru in this fashion.[74]

In short, blacks were certainly brought into Peru illegally over the years, but their numbers rarely gave cause for official alarm and cannot be considered a major factor in any estimate of the volume of the Pacific coast slave trade. It will be noted, in this connection, that prominent slave traders like Pérez never figured in these incidents for the simple reason that they confined their contraband activities to the Caribbean area where there was the most to gain. For these men, interested primarily in obtaining a sufficient number of slaves from the Atlantic traders, legally or illegally, an attempt to avoid the relatively minor duties imposed on arrival at Lima was not worth the risk.

With these considerations in mind, we turn now to the specific question of the probable number of blacks who entered Peru in the period under study. There are no dependable year-by-year figures for the period down to 1623, but it is clear that the African population of the colony grew steadily during the sixteenth and seventeenth centuries, at least until the temporary suspension of the slave trade in 1640. As early as 1565 the Spanish authorities were worried about the security problem posed by the growing black population, and some thirty years later the Lima city council, alarmed by the large number of African inhabi-

tants, proposed to the Crown that an additional tax be imposed to restrict their "daily" importation.[75] The city had indeed had a sizable
influx of blacks. Its African population, perhaps no more than some
4,000 in 1586, rose to 6,690 in 1593, 11,130 in 1614, and 13,137 in 1619,
and probably numbered some 20,000 in 1640. And it was not so much
the number of blacks, but their rising proportion that was alarming to
the city leaders. After 1593 Lima was a city whose population was half
African, and it remained so until 1640. Demographic data for the rest
of the colony are fragmentary, but a figure of some 30,000 Africans for
the whole of Peru by 1640 seems reasonable (see Appendix A).

Further, this rate of growth was maintained despite the well-estab-
lished fact that the Africans' rate of reproduction in Peru, as elsewhere
in Latin America, was not high enough even to maintain demographic
stability, let alone provide an increase in numbers. The average lifespan
of a slave in Spanish America has yet to be determined; the most that
can be said for Peru is that if many blacks lived to a ripe old age, then
there is also evidence that the mortality rate among Afro-Peruvians was
far higher than among Spaniards. The best demonstration of this disparity in death rates that has come to light is a racial breakdown of
burials listed for the four parishes of Lima (Cathedral, Santa Ana, San
Sebastián, and San Marcelo) for the years 1608-10, which show 1,666
for blacks, 805 for Spaniards, 388 for Indians, 138 for mulattoes, 36
for mestizos, and 12 unknown (listed as condemned to death by hanging).[76] At roughly the same time the two races were very nearly in balance in the city: the 1614 census lists 11,867 Spaniards and 11,130 blacks
and mulattoes. There is additional evidence that the death rate among
the black population was particularly severe. In 1640 the Lima city
council protested the imposition of the Union of Arms tax with the
claim that 1,200 black agricultural workers on the surrounding estates
died each year. Again in a 1646 petition to the Crown to resume the
African slave trade, the council claimed that some 2,000 blacks worth
a million pesos died every year within the city's environs (i.e., a death
rate of 10 per cent per annum if we assume an African population of
20,000); and that replacement being impossible, agriculture was falling
into ruin for lack of hands. In 1650 the Conde de Salvatierra (1648-55)
noted in a viceregal report that more than half the slave population
had died since 1642.[77] Though these claims were no doubt exaggerated,
since pleas to the Crown were usually couched in the direst of terms,

it is apparent that the growth of the African population of Peru during this period was due not to natural increase but to importation.

As we have seen, that importation began in a limited way. Until the 1580's no more than 500 blacks passed through Lima in an average year, and often there were considerably fewer. Municipal revenues from the head tax during the sixteenth century have not been preserved, but a rough idea of city expenses for the years 1555-88 can be determined from the records of a suit filed by a group of merchants to abolish the tax.[78] These show an expenditure of 15,841 pesos in head-tax revenues for the period on salaries, supplies, bounty payments, commissions, and unpaid loans, and it is unlikely that any large surplus was left in the fund in 1588. On the basis of the four-peso-per-head rate then in force, the figures work out to a total of 3,960 slaves, or 128 per year. To be sure, as we shall see in Chapter 8, the city did not take proper precautions in collecting this revenue, and some of the funds found their way into the pockets of the collection agents. In addition, this total reflects neither those Africans who were sold by slave merchants along the Peruvian coast on the way to Lima nor those who were secretly unloaded just outside Callao. But even if we assume these taxes reflect only a third of the volume of the Peruvian slave trade, the total number of blacks imported in an average year would still have been only some 400.

Additional evidence that the slave trade to Peru was on a small scale during most of the sixteenth century comes from the almojarifazgo records. Generally, these accounts are too all-encompassing to be useful, but those for 1575, which are quite detailed because of royal pressure to ensure compliance, document the importation of only 226 African slaves.[79] Since the application of this duty to blacks was resented, and importation may therefore have been light while the slave traders tested the government's will, a reasonable assumption would put the annual average of blacks imported into Peru between 1555 and 1588 at 250-300.

To state the matter this way, however, obscures the fact that many more African slaves entered Peru between (say) 1578 and 1588 than during the earlier period. With the failure of Viceroy Toledo to reconcile a shrinking pool of Indian labor with the demands of a growing colonial economy, the prices commanded by Africans in the Peruvian market rose spectacularly, and so did their numbers, as the colony committed itself to black slavery to sustain economic growth. Beginning in the 1590's, this trend is easier to evaluate. For example, according to census data, the African population of Lima grew at an average rate of

211 per year between 1594 and 1611. If we assume that two-thirds of the blacks imported into the city remained there, with the rest going to other parts of the colony or to Ecuador, Chile, or upper Peru, and that the number of deaths among Afro-Peruvians exceeded the number of births by 3 per cent per annum, a figure that seems conservative enough, then the average annual volume of the slave trade during this period would have been in the neighborhood of 600-800 blacks. Between 1615 and 1619 the rate of increase in the Afro-Peruvian population of Lima almost doubled, to some 400 blacks per year. Employing the same crude method of calculation would put the volume of the slave trade during this period at around 1,100-1,200 Africans per year. Between 1620 and 1640 the growth rate seems to have slowed somewhat, if the estimate of a total Peruvian black population of around 30,000 in 1640 is accepted. This would suggest an importation rate of 1,000-1,400 slaves in an average year.

These purely arbitrary calculations square well enough with Crown figures on the volume of the Peruvian slave trade. On the basis of head tax paid in Lima, 1,501 slaves were imported through the city in 1623, 916 in 1624, 759 in 1625, 768 in 1626, and 806 in 1627.[80] And in a later period royal treasury officials recorded these figures on the Lima trade:*

Year	No.	Year	No.	Year	No.
1636	950	1640	229	1644	8
1637	889	1641	132	1645	17
1638	1,149	1642	537	1646	7
1639	670	1643	15	1647	8

We should not be deceived, however, by the precision of these figures. In the first place, another 10 per cent or thereabouts should be added to these totals to account for slaves who were smuggled into Callao. In the second place, as Pérez lamented, depressed economic conditions and an overabundance of bozales in the Lima market meant relatively hard times for slave traders in 1623, and the figures for the following years may reflect a resulting caution on their part; conse-

---

* AGIC 1720-21, 1722b, 1726-27, 1728a, 1729-30, 1732. The drastic drop in the 1640's is the result of the revolt of Portugal and the temporary disruption of the slave trade. The few blacks imported after 1643 were mostly sailors, some from as far away as Nicaragua. Their shipmaster-owners doubtless had made the trip to Lima for other reasons, but once there could not resist the prices offered for their crews. Indeed, in 1648 the Chilean authorities prevailed on the Crown to forbid the exportation of slaves from Chile to Peru. The intent of this decree must have been to prevent Chilean slaveowners from stripping the colony of blacks in response to the higher prices in Peru. Konetzke, *Colección*, 2.1: 438-39.

quently, these figures may be atypical for both the period before 1623 and the period between (say) 1630 and 1635.[81] In addition, the arrest of Pérez and other slave merchants in 1635 must have disrupted the flow of blacks to Lima to some extent, and this disruption may be reflected in the official figures for 1636-39. It is necessary also to take into account those slaves who were imported via Paita, Trujillo, Arequipa, and other towns along the Peruvian coast, a number that seems to have fluctuated wildly from year to year.[82] There is no logical way to strike a balance between these various factors for any given year, but it seems safe to assume that an upward revision of the head-tax totals of 20 per cent would prevent any possible underestimation of the volume of the Peruvian slave trade. That is, in an average year during the first four decades of the seventeenth century, Peru received some 1,000-1,500 slaves, and on rare occasion received as many as 2,000.[83]

Most of these blacks were rude bozales, for whom Spanish ways were a mystery. Pacific coast traders like Pérez dealt almost exclusively in such slaves. But another type of slave was also available in the Lima market in large numbers: the ladino, a black who to a greater or lesser extent was Spanish except for skin color and lingering ties with his African tribal group and its culture. However poorly grasped or inwardly despised, the language, religion, and culture of the Spaniard were known to the ladino, and he moved with some ease in the Spanish world. Most ladinos were sold not by professional slave merchants, but by Peruvian slaveholders, and these sales could be made for assorted reasons. The most common were a need for money, the temptation of a high price, a desire to upgrade a work force, a change of residence to another colony, and a lapse of some sort on the part of the slave.

Some ladinos were African-born but Hispanicized through years of residence in Spanish America; others, called *criollos*, had been born in the power of Spaniards and Portuguese. Considering the low rate of natural increase among slaves, criollos were a relatively numerous group. Of the 6,890 slaves in the sample I referred to earlier, 763 (11 per cent) were born in the colony,[84] and another 167 (2 per cent) came from the Atlantic islands off the African coast, the bulk of them from the Cape Verde Islands and São Tomé.[85] Adding to these totals the 448 slaves who came to Peru from the Peninsula or from other parts of Spanish America (see p. 73), most of whom were born in those areas, we find criollos representing some 20 per cent of the blacks offered for sale in the Lima market (1,378 out of 6,890). The African-born blacks in the sample broke down this way: 2,381 (34.5 per cent) were bozales, and 3,031 (45.5 per cent) were blacks who had spent some time in Spanish America (most no doubt in Peru) and were at the time of sale in process of becoming ladinos. In short, Peru relied on Africa for nearly 80 per cent of her black slaves, but of those offered for sale at any given moment in the Lima market, only about one-third were bozales.[86]

An examination of Lima slave transactions reveals that by and large Spanish purchasers preferred slaves fresh from Africa to all but the best of the ladinos (see Tables B.1-B.3, pp. 344-45). Father Sandoval mentioned this preference in his classic work and explained that the Spanish liked the bozales because they were frightened and docile whereas ladinos (and particularly criollos) were considered too knowing of Iberian ways to be easily disciplined. In other words, many Spaniards chose to train a bozal rather than face disciplining a ladino or a criollo, and not a few even regarded the Christian faith as subversive of obedience, the first step in transforming their docile blacks into potential troublemakers (see Chapter 9).

The Peruvian chronicler Felipe Guamán Poma de Ayala, writing at the beginning of the seventeenth century, however, did not find so decided a preference for the bozales. He himself thought the blacks fresh from Guinea far and away the best slaves—humble, and once they understood Christianity, good and faithful. "In spite of this," he wrote, "the Spanish say that black bozales are worthless, but they do not understand what they say; because instead of running them down they should teach them with love, bring them up well, and indoctrinate them; in this fashion one of these bozales will be worth two black criollos. Saints will come from the bozales." For the American-born slaves, Poma had little but contempt:

They are rebellious, liars, thieves, pickpockets, highwaymen, gamblers, drunks . . . ; many times they kill their own masters out of sheer wickedness; they are liars and nincompoops, they mouth the words and have the rosary in their hands, but they are hypocrites; they think only of stealing, they neither listen nor pay attention to sermons and preachings; whippings and beatings matter not to them; the more punishment they receive the more wicked they become, and there is no method or form to correct them. . . . While drunk or gambling they kill each other, and they teach their knaveries and their bad habits to the bozales.[87]

The evidence suggests that more and more Spanish buyers during this period came to share Poma's opinion of the two groups and to lump the more Hispanicized of the African-born along with the criollos. However, Spanish preference for bozales was not so pronounced in the purchase of female slaves. Aside from the obvious factor of sexual attraction, this may be due to the fact that female slaves were largely employed in household tasks that made a degree of acculturation desirable.

The preferred bozal, for the Peruvians as for the Spanish in general, was the "Guinea" slave. This preference, however, was not confined to the Guinea slave narrowly defined, but was broadly extended to all blacks from West Africa. To illustrate, according to notary records for 1620 (when all African regions were well represented in the Lima market), of the 142 bozales aged sixteen to twenty-five sold who can be identified by ethnic origin, seventy-four were African from Senegambia/Guinea-Bissau (the true Guinea slave). They brought an average price of 642 pesos, and forty-seven blacks from other West African regions went for only slightly less, 630 pesos on average. Twenty-one slaves from the Congo and Angola, however, fetched only about 577 pesos each. This same pattern prevailed throughout the period.

Whatever a potential buyer's preferences with regard to origin and culture, if he sought a prime slave in the Lima market, i.e., a black whether male or female between the ages of sixteen and thirty-five, he could anticipate spending in the neighborhood of 500 pesos. He might have to pay over 600 in a year when slaves were scarce, perhaps as little as 425 if the market was glutted, but prices more often than not equaled or exceeded 500 pesos, especially for blacks between the ages of sixteen and twenty-five. Slaves below fifteen and over thirty-five were usually considerably cheaper. Age, origin, and culture, however, were not the only criteria. Strength, health, and docility were also highly prized qualities. Many buyers had specific needs. Supposing a housekeeper was desired, the ability to cook and sew would be a more important consideration than age or attractiveness, though contemporaries reported that many slaveholders preferred their female blacks to be attractive. Race mixture, so widespread in colonial Spanish America, seems to confirm the assertion. Perhaps a potential buyer was in the market for a watchman. In this case, an aged black man of sixty years or more might be adequate. In short, many factors might induce a buyer to favor one slave over another, and these varied from transaction to transaction.

The majority of transactions in the Lima market involved at most a handful of slaves, and more often than not only one. But there was an occasional large purchase, like that of the lime dealer Alonso Sánchez, who bought twenty-one bozales in a single transaction in 1621 for 12,000 pesos, payable in two equal installments over a three-year period. The various religious orders also customarily purchased large blocks of slaves from time to time, presumably for use on their rural properties. Usually, as in the Sánchez case, large transactions were made at least in part on credit.[88] A surprisingly high 39.5 per cent of the slaves in my sample were women (2,726 of 6,884), of whom 11.8 per cent were sold with at least one small child. Even among the bozales, 34.5 per cent (824) were women, a proportion that may in part have been the result of a 1524 royal decree requiring all black cargoes destined for America to be at least one-third female in the hope of discouraging illicit sexual unions and allaying general discontent among the male slaves.[89] However, the ratio of men to women among bozales was probably also determined by the realities of slave procurement in Africa and by American demand for black female slaves. These percentages argue that females changed hands with less frequency than males, since (as Appendix A indicates) the sexes were very nearly in balance in seventeenth-century Lima.

Slave buyers were very concerned to detect what the Spanish called *tachas*, the physical or moral defects of the blacks they were offered. Only 847 of the 6,890 slaves in my sample were declared defective in any way by their owners, and the tachas were in some cases unimportant. The biggest single impairment among the 388 slaves with physical infirmities, for instance, was missing teeth, affecting sixty-one blacks (about 16 per cent of the total). Other major groups of physical defects were: maimed or missing digits (forty-seven persons) and limbs, including hands and feet (thirty-eight); body ulcers or sores (thirty-one); and body wounds or scars, or both (eighteen). Forty-eight persons were simply listed as sick. The vast majority of the 459 slaves listed as morally defective were claimed runaways (408), and many of these were branded also as thieves or drunkards. Fifteen slaves were supposedly argumentative, and two were charged with being possessed by the devil.[90]

These figures suggest a remarkably healthy and well-adjusted slave population. The great majority of the blacks sold in the Lima slave market were in good health, at least if outward appearance was any guide, and many of the others did not have serious physical impairment. Miss-

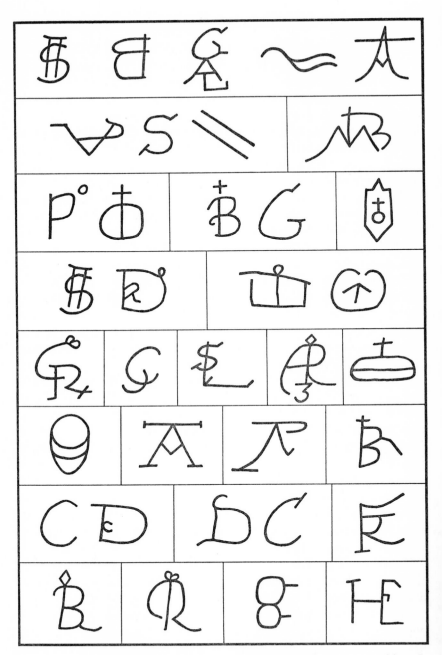

Fig. 2. Slave brands recorded in Lima notarial documents. A sequence of brands (as in the top row) indicates the black changed hands one or more times

ing teeth, for example, did not affect the slave's working ability. Moreover, many sellers claimed that their slaves were sick to avoid future lawsuits in the event of illness. The same holds true for moral defects. As the volume of the slave trade mounted in the late sixteenth century, many sellers branded their slaves as drunkards, thieves, and runaways or simply as runaways, but these epithets were designed as much to forestall future claims for refunds as to be descriptive of the slaves being sold.

It is nevertheless true that the purchaser had to be alert in slave transactions. A mortally ill slave might be palmed off as healthy, and a notorious runaway or thief sold to an unsuspecting buyer from out of town. Commercial law attempted to prevent such unscrupulous dealings expressly obliging the seller to state the defects of his slaves, to the best of his knowledge, in the bill of sale (*carta de venta*). A conscientious notary prepared such documents with meticulous care. Properly done, the document bore the name and place of residence of both buyer and seller (and frequently their position or occupation); the Christian name, origin, sex, age, defects, and price of the slave, together with the credit arrangements; the date of the transaction and the names of the witnesses; and the signatures of the buyer, the seller, and the notary. The legal language in the bill of sale for a black was the same as for any other object; in commercial law the African had no more dignity than a horse. And when, in theory, all the slave's defects had been recounted, down to the brands on his arms, chest, and face (see Fig. 2) and the buyer signed the document, he thereby acknowledged that he was aware of the slave's shortcomings and accepted them.*

These legal safeguards depended on the honesty of the seller and the shrewdness of the buyer, and were not always effective. In 1572, for example, an anonymous and bitter petition addressed to the Lima city council charged that unruly slaves and unscrupulous masters were between them successfully defrauding the gullible public. According to the complaint, the master of a black who was a thief or runaway was more severely punished than the guilty slave, since the real offender at most

---

* At some point in the 17th century the Crown began branding each slave on the right breast with "a capital R surmounted by a crown...fashioned from a single piece of heavy silver wire" (Chandler, "Health and Slavery") to certify legal importation. I do not know if this practice started before 1650; the royal brand is not mentioned in the Lima notary records, perhaps because of its universality. But brands were widely used by slave traders, and as Fig. 2 indicates, their private marks were scrupulously recorded.

got a whipping whereas the owner had to pay a heavy fine for the black's transgression or fees for his apprehension, or both. After a few such incidents, the master sold the culprit to an unsuspecting buyer, and the result was a lawsuit when the buyer discovered the truth. The petitioner proposed a savagely simple remedy: a runaway (*huidor*) should be branded with the letter H on the cheek, and a thief (*ladrón*) with the letter L. In this way, sales under false pretenses could be easily avoided. The city council adopted the measure after some discussion, but the Audiencia quashed the idea a month later.[91]

As the number of slaves exchanged mounted in the decades after 1580, so did buyer suspicion, but the realities of commerce in blacks forced the slow adoption of a double standard with regard to the responsibilities of the seller. Professional slave traders like Pérez, who dealt almost exclusively in bozales, were not expected to make a moral judgment concerning every black they sold; such a procedure would have been meaningless and ludicrous. Slave merchants were expected to do little more than certify that the black was healthy, though the law demanded that they also disclose any vices they had observed. Accordingly, in contracts signed by professional slave dealers, the phrase was usually inserted that the black was sold "according to the common custom and usage by which *negros bozales* are sold in this kingdom." Occasionally, an exceptionally cautious trader would add that the black was sold as a *costal de huesos* [or a *costal lleno de huesos*] *con alma en boca*; that is, as if he were in perfect physical condition even though he might actually be close to drawing his last breath (lit., have his soul in his mouth), with his bones soon ready to be put in a bag for burial.[92] However, to allay the fears of buyers, many slave merchants permitted them to inspect minutely the naked bodies of the bozales, often with the aid of a physician; and Pérez, together with many of his competitors, allowed customers to take slaves home on a trial basis, which might last for weeks or months, before the deal was concluded.[93]

A different set of expectations prevailed for individuals who were not professional slave merchants and who sold blacks of some residence in the colony. Under these circumstances, even if the slave had been held for only a short time (and blacks changed hands frequently during this period), the seller was under considerable and growing pressure to make a moral as well as a physical judgment of the black in question. Some slaveholders continued to sell their blacks without comment, thereby offering an implicit assurance that their charges were free of defects—a practice that was particularly common before the 1580's, when the number of slaves who changed hands in any given year was low. But more and more sellers, especially in the seventeenth century, began explicitly guaranteeing that the slaves they sold were perfectly sound in all respects. Other slaveholders chose to enumerate the real or alleged faults of their blacks in the bills of sale (e.g., an African might be sold with the almost ritualistic assertion that he was a drunkard, thief, and runaway, or with, say, the more truthful assertion that his physical health was impaired by a hernia). Still other masters offered and sold slaves, and made explicit in the bills of sale that no assurances at all were offered concerning their physical and moral qualities, but this course often aroused buyer suspicion.

No legal formula protected the dishonest seller from the outraged buyer, but at least the lack of guarantee to some extent sheltered the seller from the charge of misrepresentation, and slaves sold on this basis often brought handsome sums, paid by men who perhaps trusted their own judgment more than the honesty of those with whom they dealt. All the same (as Table B.4, p. 345, indicates) a seller who could in good conscience certify, whether implicitly or explicitly, that his slave was without defects usually got a better price than one who listed the faults of his black or refused to guarantee soundness.

Given the annual exchange of thousands of slaves in Peru, there were inevitably a certain number of dissatisfied buyers and a still smaller number of lawsuits to recover the purchase price. Spanish law here attempted to strike a balance between the interests of buyer and seller and at the same time discourage undue litigation. A disgruntled buyer could sue for cancellation of the transaction only if he could prove intentional misrepresentation. And over and above his purchase price (or the cancellation of his debt), he could claim only court costs plus reasonable compensation for any expenses incurred in connection with the slave's defect—for medical care and supplies, say, in the case of a sick slave, or for fees to lawmen and jailers in the case of a delinquent one. Ordinarily, legal action to void a sale had to be initiated within six months of the purchase, though more liberal judges sometimes ruled that this six-month limit was to be measured from the date the buyer first noticed the slave's defect.

In any case, the law was designed and largely interpreted to encourage honesty on the part of both seller and buyer. As we have seen, no legal formula could shield the seller from a dissatisfied customer, even if the slave had been sold with no assurances whatever, provided the buyer could prove willful deceit on the seller's part. However, Spanish courts, clogged with litigation throughout the colonial period, discouraged suits over trivial defects, and in general heard only those where there was evidence that the medical or more defects of a slave made him or her nearly useless, or even a burden, to the buyer. Spanish jurists were aided in their efforts by the policies of prominent professional dealers like Pérez, who were solicitous of their good names. Such dealers not only tried to avoid dissatisfaction by selling blacks on a trial basis but also preferred to settle out of court and thus avoid costly litigation.[94] Some buyers contented themselves with the small reductions in the purchase price the sellers offered, others battled through the courts to achieve the same result.[95] Still another consideration made buyers think twice before initiating legal action. Satisfaction was frequently slow in coming, since both parties had the right to present witnesses to support their cases. Litigants often found that prospective witnesses had left the colony or were traveling within it, and tracking them down and taking their depositions was a slow and costly business. This difficulty, together with legal fees, threatened to outweigh any financial settlement reached in the courts, and many discontented buyers doubtless dropped their plans for suits and vowed to profit by bitter experience.[96]

A few examples will illustrate the varieties of redhibition. In 1634 Doña Catalina Pardo y Cárdenas sued Licenciado Álvaro Núñez de Cabañas for a refund of the 590 pesos she had paid for Ana Angola and her infant child. Doña Catalina claimed that Núñez had sold her the slave as healthy, but it had later turned out that Ana's feet were so afflicted with buboes she was unable to walk. Núñez replied that Ana had always been healthy in his possession and claimed that her ailment had been acquired "because in summer, in the full rigor of the sun, she went about every day, all day, selling fruit," for her mistress's profit. Doña Catalina denied that she had ever mistreated Ana, and, in testimony most damaging to Núñez, the slave herself affirmed that her ailment was an old one. Doña Catalina won her case in the diocesan court of Lima. Núñez appealed to the bishop of Ayacucho, as was customary, but in 1636 refunded the purchase price and took Ana back.

To take a suit involving moral defects, we may cite one initiated by

Doctor Don Juan de Urbina, a lawyer himself, against Bachiller Pedro López, a priest, over Isabel Jolofa, aged twenty-two and sold with full assurances for 360 pesos in 1634. Three years later, Urbina charged that Isabel was in fact a runaway and a thief at the time of sale, that López knew of these defects, and that the slave had subsequently stolen property from him worth 500 pesos. Urbina went on to claim that these defects, combined with the fact that Isabel was "married, very small, and of little utility [*de poco trabajo*]," made her actual value perhaps 200 pesos. He sued for a refund of his money plus the value of the goods stolen from him, though he indicated that cancellation of the bill of sale or a reduction of Isabel's price to 200 pesos would also be satisfactory. López replied that he had intended to sell Isabel with a full declaration of her defects, but since the bill of sale had already been prepared, he had contented himself with a verbal statement that was later put in writing. He contended further that Isabel was a good cook who was worth at least 600 pesos, that he had purchased her for 425, and that he had sacrificed her at the 360 price. As late as 1638 the case was unresolved and was no doubt settled out of court.[97]

More rarely, a seller sued for nullification of a transaction. In 1628, for example, María de Garay, recently widowed, complained that she had been tricked into selling her mulatto slave for 450 pesos when in fact he was worth twice that much. The buyer, Gaspar de la Cueva, replied that the price was a fair one, and that María was not the naïve, poverty-stricken widow she claimed to be. Cueva won the case.[98] In other instances, women who were tricked into selling valuable slaves in their husbands' absences successfully sued for restitution of their blacks plus the estimated wages they would have earned in the interval.[99]

Against this background of charges and countercharges of fraud and deceit among (mostly) individuals, the skill, diligence, and acumen of merchants like Pérez might excite an admiration were it not for the fact that they dealt largely in human flesh. Yet it must always be remembered that these men were products of their time; they saw eye to eye with their clients in both Africa and America, and they served a need whose morality was openly questioned by few. The activities of such men were the inevitable consequences of the fact that the Spanish empire in America could not rest on the labor of the Indian alone, but also needed the African. On that point we turn now to examine how the black African's labor was used in Peru.

CHAPTER FOUR

The African and the Peruvian Economy: A General Survey

The increased flow of blacks to Peru in the decades after 1580 benefited most segments of the Peruvian economic system, and perhaps none more so than agriculture. Blacks first became important in the truck gardens (*chácaras*) that sprang up around the Spanish towns soon after the conquest. These small plots were irrigated, at least along the arid coast, and were planted in a wide variety of grains, fruits, and vegetables. A few animals were often grazed on them as well. Each chácara required only a small number of slaves to perform routine agricultural tasks on a year-round basis, often with little or no direct Spanish supervision; and Indians were employed on a seasonal basis to help with the harvesting. The blacks sometimes lived in the nearby town, going out daily to work in the fields, and sometimes right on the chácara. After the middle of the sixteenth century, more and more of these agricultural units appear to have relied almost exclusively on slave labor even at harvest time, perhaps in response to the dwindling number of natives, though occasionally free persons of color were also employed, apparently in the smaller and more isolated chácaras. From a very early date, as Lockhart indicates, Africans were also employed on the estates farther from the urban areas, devoted in the main to livestock. On very large ranches, there were teams of black herdsmen, but more typical was the isolated slave who cared for a relatively few pigs, cows, or goats. According to Lockhart, "Herdsmen were more closely attached to the stock than to the land; whereas field Negroes were sold along with the land they worked, herdsmen were sold together with the herds." In time, free coloreds were employed in this activity also.[1]

Though chácaras were important to Peruvian agriculture throughout the period under study, during the last decades of the sixteenth century and in response to growing markets, large areas of Peru came to be dominated by estates of considerable size, worked mainly by blacks. Often such enterprises were dependent neither on a single crop nor on a single market. In contrast to Brazil and certain West Indian sugar islands, African slavery and large-scale agriculture in Peru were not synonymous with monoculture, though some areas did tend to specialize in a single crop (e.g., the south coast in vineyards), and most sugar plantations seem to have produced little else. For example, the farm of Lorenzo Pérez Noguera in the Lima area, worked by sixteen blacks in 1637-39, sold quantities of olives and olive oil, fodder, wood, plantains, oranges, barley, and wheat worth nearly 2,800 pesos. A cleric in the Moquegua Valley, between Arequipa and Arica, used his lands and nineteen slaves in the production of wine and sugar, and the hacienda of Acaray in the Guara Valley, with twenty-three slaves, though devoted primarily to sugarcane, also grew wheat.[2] Other slaveholders cultivated two or more holdings, each with its own specialization; one combined sugar plantations in one area with a diversified truck garden in another, a second the cultivation of vineyards with the pasturing of goats, and a third ranching in the province of Guaylas with farming in the valley of Lurigancho.[3] There were also slaveholders who concentrated on the production of a single crop in widely scattered holdings.[4]

Some slaveholders drew only part of their incomes from agriculture. For example, the assets Francisco Velásquez Talavera listed in his will in 1571 included not only slaves, livestock, and four chácaras, but also extensive hunks of urban real estate in Lima, a textile mill in the valley of Santa Lucía de Chanchan, and sizable investments in mortgages.[5] Among men of similar substance were Andrés Dávila, a resident of Arequipa, who owned two vineyards, a chácara, and a store, in addition to a townhouse and twenty-six slaves (and this, in 1640, after a good portion of his wealth had gone to provide for many children); Bartolomé Verdugo, who in his will in 1633 listed holdings in land and slaves in Cañete, houses in Lima and Callao, and two ships at anchor at Callao; and Bartolomé de Heredía, whose possessions in 1598, when he sought to have his estate entailed, consisted of a farm outside Lima, which had over 555 acres planted in wheat, two orchards, a house and chapel, livestock, and thirteen blacks, plus rental property in Lima worth some 20,000 pesos, a residence there (staffed by ten black servants), and assorted personal possessions valued at around 5,000 pesos.[6]

Other Peruvian agriculturalists were of much more modest means. Some preferred to own a black work force and rent the lands on which their slaves were used.[7] Others rented not only the lands they cultivated but the slaves as well. In 1632, for example, Juan Bautista Moreno rented a chácara in the valley of Lati, together with thirteen blacks, for one year. His landlord was obligated to maintain the work force at that level, with replacements if necessary, or to reduce the rent of 1,350 pesos by four reales per day for each absent black. In a similar agreement of 1600, the owner of a vineyard in Ica leased his property for three years together with six slaves, undertaking either to replace blacks who sickened or fled for over a month's time or to pay the tenant five reales per man per day. The landlord also made himself responsible for the costs of his slaves' clothing and religious instruction during the term of the lease.[8]

In short, Peruvian agriculturalists were as diverse as the crops they cultivated, and probably had little conception of themselves as a "class" or interest group. The labor force they relied on was equally mixed. Where possible, Indians were employed, whether mitayos, yanaconas, or forasteros, both on a year-round basis and as extra hands at harvest time,[9] but increasingly Africans had to be purchased to sustain Peruvian agriculture. For example, between 1635 and 1638 the Jesuit College of San Pablo in Lima spent 35,533 pesos for African slaves to work its agricultural holdings, and smaller operators made proportionately heavy capital expenditures.[10] Several of the factors responsible for this development have been mentioned: the reluctance of the Indian to leave the traditional village economy and work for wages; the decline of the native population and the consequent abuses of the mita system; and the Spanish Crown's growing distaste for that system and determination to curtail it.

Agriculture was one of the first segments of the Peruvian economy to feel the impact of the Crown's labor policy. The first pinch came when the government prohibited the employment of Indians in sugar mills and vineyards. The Conde del Villar (1585-90) and his successor, the Marqués de Cañete (1590-96), vigorously enforced this policy in Peru, and the inevitable result was to spur the demand for Africans.[11] In an abortive attempt to abolish the mita in 1601 (a move that is discussed in Chapter 5), the Crown extended the prohibition to olive groves, but sought to mollify Peruvian agriculturalists by stating that the intention was not to deprive them of Indian labor. The government wanted the natives to be given the opportunity to hire themselves out to employers of their own choosing, but conceded that Indians could be forced to work if absolutely necessary to sustain Peruvian agriculture. Even so, forced agricultural service was to be performed within a reasonable distance from Indian villages in order to spare the natives the hardships of long journeys and to ensure their medical and religious care by the resident priest.[12]

Royal efforts to eliminate the agricultural mita were less than a complete success, as demonstrated by a 1626 letter to the Crown from a priest in Trujillo lamenting the frightful death rate among the mitayos in that area.[13] Nevertheless, government policy was not entirely without effect. In the Lima area, for example, by 1623 only 500 mitayos were working the wheat fields, cattle ranches, sugar plantations, and orchards that contributed so greatly to the capital's wealth. Thirteen years later, Viceroy Chinchón reported that mita labor was used only to irrigate the wheat fields around the city.[14]

By 1640 Lima agriculture was so heavily dependent on African labor that the suspension of the slave trade provoked public protest and considerable economic distress. Indeed, the city council in 1646, with the support of the viceroy, the Marqués de Mancera (1639-48), petitioned the Crown to lift the ban and predicted the economic ruin of the colony if it did not. The council claimed that thousands of blacks engaged in agricultural occupations and valued at some 8,000,000 pesos had died since 1640. Since no replacements could be obtained, some landholders had been forced to suspend their operations or to reduce them drastically, and the result had been steadily increasing food prices. As for the Peruvian-born blacks, the council argued that there were not enough criollos to fill even the need for household servants, much less take up the slack in agriculture, and that in any event most of them were too arrogant and lazy to make good farm workers. The Crown was urged to find a temporary way to supply the area with blacks, perhaps by requisition from Cartagena, until the slave trade was resumed.[15]

Few areas of Peru were as dependent as Lima on African labor, but the black slave nevertheless played an important agricultural role in many other parts of the colony, particularly on the plantations in the coastal river valleys. We may begin our survey in northern Peru with

the city of Trujillo and the surrounding valleys, an area that produced
large quantities of sugar, wheat flour, and conserves for export to the
settlements of the Isthmus. In addition, cotton was grown for the manufacture of flour sacks and also of candle wicks, which were shipped
throughout the colony for use in churches and silver mines. "Many
Indians and blacks" were employed in Trujillo agriculture, and others
were occupied in household service. In 1604 the city alone had 1,073
blacks (121 of them free), against 1,021 Spaniards and 1,094 Indians;
the number of Africans in the surrounding district must have been much
greater.[16] Moving south along the coast, the district around the *villa* of
Santa, near the river of the same name, was one of livestock ranches,
fields of sugarcane and wheat (this last crop marketed in Lima), and
fruit orchards. In the early seventeenth century there were reportedly
some seventy Spanish families in the town, most of whom possessed
African slaves for their farms.[17]

The Africans employed in agriculture in the coastal valleys south of
Lima probably constituted the most numerous group of blacks outside
the capital. Cañete and Lunaguan were the first of these valleys, worked
by "many Indians and blacks," and producing fruit, wine, wheat, corn,
and potatoes for sale in the Lima market. Farther south were the famous
wine-producing valleys, beginning with Pisco and Condor, and here
the concentration of blacks was very heavy. Served by the port of La
Magdalena, this area was described by a seventeenth-century writer as
"one of the richest to be found in all the Kingdom." With the aid of
irrigation, the Condor Valley alone produced 100,000 jugs (*botijas*) of
wine a year. Sugarcane was also grown in quantity in both Pisco and
Condor. Some 10,000 Africans were reportedly employed by the estates
of the two valleys. The same observer noted that "on every farm they
have a Negro village for the exploitation of the vineyards," and that
"every Negro costs at least 500 pesos, and [from 50 to 150 pesos more]
if he is of good tribe and well built."[18]

An estate owned by Captain Pedro de Vera Montoya and his wife is
typical of the scale of operations in these two valleys. In 1622 they possessed a vineyard of over 205 acres producing 6,500 jugs of wine annually and with an ultimate production capacity of 10,000 jugs; eighty
black slaves of different nations and ages, three or four of them female;
a sugar mill to process loaf sugar and molasses, and land in cane yield-
ing 3,300 jugs of molasses; approximately 500 goats and sheep; a mill

to grind wheat and corn into flour; an orchard of "many fruit trees"; a plant for the manufacture of wine jugs, and two Africans skilled in the task; thirty-six mules; the plantation headquarters, "La Garpultaya," and attached wine cellars; a blacksmith's forge and all other necessary equipment, including an African smith; 400 olive trees producing 200 jugs of olives and twenty jugs of olive oil; 20,000 willow trees planted to supply the farm with wood; and wheat fields producing over 1,100 bushels a year. The total annual value of the estate's agricultural products in that year was estimated at 20,000 pesos.[19]

The vineyards of the Ica Valley to the south, together with those of the smaller surrounding valleys, were said to be producing about 400,000-500,000 jugs of wine a year and quantities of raisins in the early 1600's. In addition, wheat, corn, and many kinds of fruit were cultivated. One observer estimated that between 8,000 and 10,000 slaves were required to farm this area. Some of the wine was sent via Morro Quemado and Pisco to Lima and Arica, and large quantities were transported by land to Castrovirreina, Huancavelica, Ayacucho, and other highland towns.[20]

During the late 1540's and early 1550's the neighboring valley of Nazca was a sugar-producing area, dominated by a large mill producing 30,000 pesos' worth of the product annually and employing several hundred slaves. The mill was owned by Pedro Gutiérrez de Contreras, a comrade of Pizarro's who became one of the richest of the conquistadores, but it was destroyed during the Hernández Girón rebellion. Thereafter, only the name of the valley, "El Ingenio de la Nazca" (The Sugar Refinery of Nazca), testified to this early economic role.[21] The grape supplanted sugar as the principal crop, and wine production in the early seventeenth century reached 70,000 jugs of very high quality per year. Some of the wine was exported through the port of Caballos to Lima, but most was sent by llama to Ayacucho, Cuzco, and other highland settlements. As in Pisco and Ica, numerous blacks were employed in the vineyards.[22]

Still farther south along the coast were the valleys of Camaná and Vitor. Though these were important agricultural areas, with much acreage given over to vineyards, the scale of operations appears to have been much smaller than in the wine-growing valleys to the north, and the number of slaves per establishment fewer. The largest holding mentioned in documents was a vineyard in the Camaná Valley that was worked by over thirty slaves in 1607 and produced some 4,000 jugs of wine a year.[23] The soil around the towns of Arica and Tacna, the southernmost points of coastal Peru, contained too much sulfur and alum for the profitable growing of olives and grapes. However, fertilized with guano, it yielded abundant crops of wheat, corn, and other cereals, which were produced with the aid of "many" Africans and Indians.[24]

The native population was large enough to provide most of the labor in the agricultural operations of the highlands, but in certain areas of the sierra Africans composed a significant segment of the population. In Cajamarca in the north, for example, with an agricultural economy similar to Trujillo's, there were 141 black slaves and eight free mulattoes in a total population of 662 in 1632.[25] In Huánuco, which one observer claimed had the best climate in all Peru, "many" blacks cared for the orchards and prepared the exquisite conserves therefrom, or harvested the sugar, wheat, and corn in the outlying fields.[26] Ayacucho (then Guamanga) and the surrounding valleys of Yucay, Viñaca, Huamanguilla, and La Quinua produced grapes and other fruit, as well as wheat, corn, and other cereals. Much of the land was also devoted to livestock. In the early seventeenth century the city had some 400 Spaniards and mestizos, "plus a large service contingent of native Indians, yanaconas, Negroes, and mulattoes."[27] Blacks also worked in the nearby valley of Abancay. In 1647 one of the wealthy sugar producers there, Doña Leonor Costilla Gallinato, had holdings and slaves whose combined worth was 100,000 pesos.[28] Doña Leonor also owned estates in the vicinity of Cuzco valued at an equal amount, worked by blacks and devoted to the cultivation of wheat, corn, and other cereals.

Though Cuzco was predominantly an Indian town, other agriculturalists based in that city likewise relied on "large numbers of Negro slaves and mulattoes" for their cattle ranches, mule herds, sugar mills, vineyards, and fields of wheat, corn, and other cereals and crops.[29] In the nearby tropical province of Vilcabamba, blacks were used in the cultivation of sugar.[30]

A few generalizations can be made about the slaves gangs who worked Peruvian plantations.[31] First, the size of the slave population resident on most estates during this period was relatively modest and rarely exceeded forty slaves of all ages. A survey of forty-one agricultural enterprises, for example, shows this distribution:

Number of slaves	Number of estates	Number of slaves	Number of estates
0-5	3	21-25	4
6-10	8	26-30	4
11-15	6	31-35	4
16-20	7	36-40	2

Only three plantations had more than forty slaves, and only one of these more than 100. These data would be more meaningful if correlated with the size of the landholdings involved and with the proportion of African to Indian labor, but such information is so rarely available that further generalization is impossible.

Second, it is clear that the male slave was dominant in the Peruvian countryside, in sharp contrast to urban areas such as Lima, where the proportion of males to females tended to be more or less equal (see Appendix A). In a sample of 1,939 rural slaves over 82 per cent (1,603) were males.[32] This sexual imbalance was in large part responsible for the inability of the black population of Peru to sustain itself without new infusions of slaves from Africa. Clearly, mortality rates among both infant and adult slaves must also be considered, since, as we have seen, there is some evidence that the mortality rate was considerably higher among Peruvian blacks than among whites. The available data do not permit the historian to strike a balance between these factors, but everything seems to have acted as a spur to the slave trade. For example, a sample of 365 rural blacks reveals the following age distribution:

Age	Males	Females
under 8	11	7
8-15	13	3
16-25	34	9
26-35	105	13
36-45	66	15
over 45	75	14

It will be noted that 46 per cent of the slaves were age thirty-six or older. More important, the "over 45" category represents 24 per cent of the sample, and of these blacks nearly half (48 of 89) were sixty years of age or older. Yet, the number of slaves in the vital 8 to 15 age group, who might have been looked to as replacements for their aging fellows in the work force, make up only 4 per cent of the total. If this sample represents conditions in rural Peru, and given widespread complaints about the high death rate among adult Peruvian blacks, it is small wonder that the agriculturalists of the colony were alarmed by the suspension of the slave trade in 1640.

Blacks were also extensively employed in the transportation system that linked the various parts of the colony together and tied Peru to the outside world. Ox- or mule-drawn carts were used to haul merchandise, silver, and other commodities back and forth between the principal coastal cities and the ports that served them, and mule trains were used on the routes that connected the coast with the highlands. In both cases, blacks cared for and loaded the animals and carts. The largest of the mule trains numbered as many as eighty animals. In the sixteenth century the going was so rough that it was considered necessary to have one muleteer to supervise three mules; by the seventeenth the ratio had become one for every ten animals. The work was hard, in no small measure because the bridges across most Peruvian rivers were mere suspension spans of vegetable fiber. Each time a stream was crossed, the mules had to be unloaded, the merchandise carried across on the backs of Africans and Indians, and the animals reloaded on the other side.[33] Many merchants and plantation owners had their own mule trains and black muleteers; and such pack trains were often sold as a unit: animals, blacks, and equipment.[34] Others, the Crown among them, preferred to rely on professional mule drivers, arranging for such transportation as the need arose. In 1625, for example, royal officials paid seventeen black haulers ten reales each to transport 200 jugs of olive oil from a farm near Lima to Callao to provision the royal fleet.[35] However, such ad hoc arrangements were awkward during emergencies— for example, when the Dutch fleet appeared in the Pacific in 1624 and threatened Pisco, Lima officials were forced to appropriate sixty-six privately owned mules and several African muleteers in order to send a relief expedition[36]—and as royal efforts to defend Peru grew in scope, long-term contracts to supply blacks, mules, and equipment to meet the government's transportation needs were let with private individuals.[37]

The African also played an important role in trade and navigation along the Pacific coast, since both private shipping and the royal fleet relied heavily on black seamen. Most of the Spaniards, Africans, and Indians of Callao, which was far and away the busiest Peruvian port, ranking in importance with Panama in the Pacific, were said to be sailors.[38] Private shipping consisted of light vessels ranging from very small boats, used to transport produce short distances along the coast and "manned only by a Spaniard assisted by a Negro and a couple of Indians," to ships of some 300 tons with crews of twenty men or less.[39] The great run was the trip from Callao to Panama and back, plied (for example) in 1608-10 by the *Nuestra Señora de la Alegría*. The ship made the first leg of the journey staffed by the co-owner, a shipsmaster, a notary, four Spanish sailors, and four black sailors, plus a female slave who probably did the cooking. On the return voyage to Callao, the number of black sailors rose to six and the number of whites to seven.[40] Blacks were also extensively employed on the merchant ships running between Callao and various Chilean and Ecuadorian ports and those that sailed (legally or otherwise) to Acapulco and Central America.[41] Few blacks in private shipping rose above the lowly station of sailor, though there is one case of a mulatto captain who commanded a ship called the *San Nicolás*.[42] The Callao waterfront also had a fair number of black stevedores, part of a "large service contingent of Negroes and mulattoes, slave and free, and Indians, who come in and help both in the harbor activities and the service of its residents, and in the transportation of the merchandise and products."[43]

Until the last decades of the sixteenth century the royal navy was represented in the Pacific by a mere galleon or two, and from time to time black slaves owned by the Crown were to be found among the crews.[44] However, beginning in the 1580's the Crown strengthened the royal fleet substantially against the threat of intrusion by the English or the Dutch. By the seventeenth century the fleet usually consisted of three or four galleons, two or three galleys, and numerous small craft. Rather than pay large sums for slaves to man these vessels, the Crown preferred to hire sailors, and many of these seamen were blacks.

Between 1584 and 1641 the Crown employed at least 926 black sailors at a cost of over 100,370 pesos.[45] Twenty-three were free men of color; the rest were owned by 510 masters. All blacks aboard the royal ships were classified as cabin boys (*grumetes*), and ordinary pay for their services was half that of a Spanish seaman. In addition, the Crown provided board. This wage, which came to sixteen and a half pesos of nine reales per month (reduced after 1632 to fifteen pesos of eight reales), was a good return for the owner of a robust black with no particular skill, and life at sea and military discipline in port held runaways to a minimum. The one possible drawback was that the Crown did not pay the master the bulk of the wages earned by his blacks until the end of their period of service, a matter of months or years. In the 1620's, for example, three blacks who belonged to a Lima cleric worked at varying intervals for a total of 103 months on the royal vessels, but at the time the last slave left the fleet he had still to collect over two-thirds of their wages. Despite the slowness of payment, many masters hired out from two to four of their slaves to the royal fleet, and it was not uncommon for a slaveholder to have six to eight blacks so employed (a few had even more), though they did not all necessarily serve at the same time. The masters of the 903 black sailors referred to above included lawyers, notaries public, royal treasury officials, and members of both the secular clergy and the Augustinian, Franciscan, and Jesuit orders. Seventy-five of the 903 were owned by women, many of them widows, who considered this a safe and profitable way to employ their blacks, and many others belonged to Spaniards who served the royal military establishment in various capacities, ranging from the commander of the garrison at Callao to common soldiers and sailors.

One of the most difficult problems connected with the royal navy was recruiting oarsmen for the galleys, a job that was perhaps the most arduous in the navy and yet was the most poorly paid: ten pesos per month. Most slaveholders were not tempted by such low wages, forcing the Crown to fill the ranks with criminals, a measure that further reduced the attractiveness of the task for free men.[46] In the 1580's the Crown was still attempting to use hired labor to man the oars of the galley and galliot stationed at Callao, and a high percentage of those it employed were free blacks and mulattoes, some perhaps unskilled and anxious for any sort of work, others pressed into service by the authorities.[47] But later in the decade, when the Villar administration had two galleys built, it quickly became clear that they could not be fully manned, even though as many criminals as possible were condemned to galley service. The Peruvian authorities therefore urged the Crown to purchase from 150 to 300 Africans for the task. The government displayed its usual reluctance to invest large sums in blacks, and the proposal was accepted only after several years' consideration.[48]

The plan was blocked, however, by the accession of the Marqués de Cañete as viceroy in 1590. Cañete was against the use of galleys altogether, charging that the strong currents of the Pacific and the rough coastline with its few harbors made such vessels useless for the Callao-Panama run, the purpose for which they were intended. The viceroy was equally pessimistic with regard to oarsmen. There was not enough convict labor to man even one of the vessels. The importation of royal slaves would be not only expensive, but essentially useless: the majority would soon die, Cañete stated, since the African's constitution was not equal to the task. And hiring black oarsmen in Peru would require substantial expenditures for no particular nautical advantage. In view of all these difficulties, the viceroy used the galleys in the harbor of Callao only during the critical months from December to February, when enemy ships could enter the Pacific through the Strait of Magellan, largely to preserve the fiction that the port possessed such vessels. In an emergency Cañete proposed to protect shipping at Callao by drafting blacks from all over the city to man the galleys, plus a sufficient number of soldiers to fire their cannon. During the rest of the year, the vessels became floating prisons to house forty to fifty black, mulatto, and Indian convicts, who were used in the royal shipyards and in the construction of a new complex of government warehouses at Callao. The convicts could be held here with only eight soldiers guarding them, an expense their labor more than compensated for.[49]

The policies Cañete adopted apparently remained in force about twenty years, for an observer writing around 1615 mentioned a galley at Callao that served "only as a jail for malefactors and for blacks" who had been condemned to labor on the various royal construction projects at the port.[50] However, the galleys came back into official favor in the 1620's and 1630's, when three of them were in continuous operation. Since no salaries were disbursed to oarsmen during this period, though black grumetes were consistently employed, the benches must have been manned by criminals, many of whom were no doubt blacks.[51] This supposition is confirmed by the debate in official circles at this same time over the feasibility of condemning criminals to serve in the Huancavelica mercury mine rather than on the galleys (see Chapter 7). In 1628 Viceroy Guadalcázar argued that the needs of the Callao galleys for manpower were too great to consider the measure.[52]

The next viceroy, Chinchón, was equally concerned to maintain the galleys in operation, and indeed considered them so necessary that he had two new ones built. But his successor, the Marqués de Mancera, returned to the position of Cañete, repeating all the objections he had voiced fifty years before. Mancera was particularly shocked by the lack of experienced oarsmen. In a letter to the Crown he stated that Chinchón had proposed in time of emergency to man the galleys with blacks who had been condemned to serve in various hat and clothing factories, and to supplement these by drafting other persons of color to complete the crews. In Mancera's view, even conceding that there would be time to put the plan into effect and that the Crown had the right to take such steps, the black draftees would be inexperienced and therefore worse than useless. Further, granted that such an expedient could be employed in emergencies, the viceroy saw no way in ordinary times to obtain the 500 blacks necessary to operate the galleys on the Panama-Callao run. To purchase this many slaves would be extremely expensive, and since the African's lifespan was short, constant replacements would be required. Mancera therefore proposed to dry-dock the galleys and use them only in the event of enemy attack, when such vessels could transport royal revenues to Panama and free the rest of the navy for defense duties.[53] There is no record of further action in the period under study.

Although African labor was important to Peruvian agriculture and transport, blacks were perhaps most conspicuous as retainers and household servants in the urban areas along the coast and in many parts of the highlands. This was particularly true of the capital of Lima, where blacks were employed on a lavish scale. High civil and ecclesiastical dignitaries were accompanied in the street by as many as four armed black lackeys; and in an environment where, as one chronicler observed, there was no one who did not take himself for a gentleman, others strove to imitate this example. (As we shall see in Chapter 7, the resulting number of armed blacks posed formidable problems for law-enforcement agencies.) Black retainers were also something to be displayed on public occasions. For example, in a night procession of the religious brotherhood of merchants during Holy Week of 1637, all the slaves of those captains of commerce marched behind their masters with lighted torches in their hands. The aristocratic ladies of Lima made an equally brave show, using liveried black servants to carry the sedan chairs that bore them to church and to social calls, and as coachmen on their richly appointed carriages.[54]

Some Indians were still available for household service along the coast,[55] but the requirements of stylish living and the desire for prestige prompted the expenditure of impressive sums for Africans who served as cooks, laundresses, maids, wet nurses, handymen, and gardeners in Spanish homes. For example, Doña Francisca de Peñalosa, who worked fourteen slaves on her chácara in the Carabayllo Valley near Lima and an undetermined number on a south-coast vineyard, also maintained a household staff of twelve blacks in her residence in Lima; and Don Nicolás de Rivera y Dávalos, who employed seventy-one slaves on his farms near Lima, had a staff of sixteen blacks to serve him in the capital.[56] More than one government official, contemplating the probable reaction of the slave population in the event of foreign attack, deplored the excessive number of African household servants, which saw as many as thirty blacks in attendance for one household, maintained as much for ostentation as for service.[57] Others were more sanguine, among them Viceroy Chinchón, who assured the Crown that the large numbers of black household servants would be an asset instead of a liability in the event of foreign aggression. During the Dutch threat of 1624, he pointed out, several blacks had deliberately sacrificed their own lives to save those of their masters.[58]

The Peruvians of moderate means were quick to follow the example of the rich and the important. For example, Antonio Messia, who held a minor position in the bureaucracy as the receptor general of judicial fines levied by the Audiencia, left little more on his death in 1635 than his office (something that could be sold in this period[59]), a coach and mules, and a little furniture, but he had six slaves as well. And in 1615 Rodrigo Benítez, a sergeant in the rural constabulary, listed his total possessions as 900 pesos (a third of it owed in back salary), a modest home, eight horses and mules, and five blacks.[60] Those who lived in near-poverty also stretched their resources to include the ownership of blacks. Indeed, according to one seventeenth-century observer, there was "no one, no matter how poor," along the coast who did not have a black slave to serve him.[61] This statement is exaggerated, but not by much, since servants were considered de rigueur for anyone with pretensions to respectability. A man like Juan Hidalgo de Balderas, with few assets beyond a little cash and worked silver, some clothing, and a horse, possessed two male slaves. The even less fortunate Isabel Jiménez, a widow, could list in her will no more than a female servant and a pitiful amount of furniture and personal effects, and the estate of Doña Marta de Oviedo, who died in 1625, was smaller still, consisting

NEGROS
COMOLLEBAEVITÃTA

paciencia y amor de Jesucristo los puenos
negros y negras y el villaco de su amo no
tiene caridad y amor de progimo

Fig. 3. A Spanish master punishing his slaves

of five blacks and little else.[62] Even the Indians of Peru, both nobles and commoners, came to possess substantial numbers of African slaves.[63] In short, the cathedral chapter of Lima did not overstate by much the situation in the coastal communities when they said of black labor that "there is no other in this Kingdom."[64]

Yet I do not want to leave the impression that the urban residents of Peru owned slaves simply to establish their own social status. Black labor may have been profligately employed in many instances, but by the standards of the age it was indispensable to the operation of many households. Moreover, despite the presumably high morality rate among blacks, slaves were regarded as valuable investments. For example, there were few women of quality, at least in Lima, whose dowries did not include slaves, and ordinarily blacks constituted a substantial part of the value of the property they brought their husbands.[65] Shrewd and hardworking individuals used their savings to buy slaves, as in the case of the Indian Inés de Escobar, who recalled in her 1615 will that twenty-five years earlier she and her Spanish husband, a tailor, had possessed only a lot, a mule, a saddle, and the tools of her husband's trade; the labor of these decades had gone into three houses, four blacks, and various personal effects.[66] Blacks accumulated in this fashion were often used as collateral for loans,[67] or became objects of speculation, to be traded from hand to hand, often within months, in response to fluctuations in value.[68]

Even more important, in terms of direct financial benefit, many urban slaveholders hired out their slaves and lived on the resulting income. The famous Peruvian chronicler Poma de Ayala lamented the "wickedness" of this practice, declaring that the worst offenders were women, "who, with little fear of God or of the authorities, mistreat [the blacks] and demand of them daily wages of eight and twelve and four reales as tribute, and give them nothing to eat or to wear. . . . There is no justice for the poor creatures, and many flee as a result."[69] Poma's lurid statement serves to underscore the economic importance of the hiring-out system to one segment of Spanish society in particular, the gentle-woman of little means. In 1610, for example, the widow María de Cabrera possessed only odds and ends "of little value" and a female slave, and supported herself solely on the slave's monthly wage of twelve pesos. María Osorio, likewise a widow, was more comfortably fixed, but she too relied heavily on the wages of two blacks, a male serving on a ship in the Pacific, and a female hired out in Callao.[70] Some Spanish men found it convenient to purchase blacks to support their mistresses and illegitimate children.[71] In short, for those who lived in the urban areas of Peru, and particularly for the weak and the near-helpless, ownership of blacks was not entirely an extravagance. The earnings of slaves often meant the difference between a degree of comfort and ruin.[72]

The authorities, anxious to prevent the theft and prostitution that resulted when greedy and inconsiderate masters forced their slaves to seek employment without supervision (see Chapters 7 and 8), attempted to control the situation by requiring formal contracts between employer, slave, and master. These *cartas de alquiler* were particularly important in the case of unskilled blacks, who were the most likely to be driven to desperate measures to bring in earnings. To the periodic distress of the authorities, masters and slaves did not always respect this requirement, but many slaveholders were so dependent on the hiring-out system that enforcement was often ticklish. In 1636, for example, after several black women had been arrested for wandering about looking for work in violation of the law, the Lima city council was moved to ask the viceroy to suspend the ordinance as prejudicial to the "many poor people" who depended on slave earnings. Evidently the viceroy took no action.[73]

In any event, when the requirement of a formal employment contract was respected, a study of these documents reveals that (the royal navy apart) unskilled blacks were rarely hired out for more than a year,[74] and the majority were employed as domestics and menials with duties so varied as to be unspecified in the contracts. In addition, there was considerable demand for nursemaids and wet nurses. Wages were predictably low, with the grumetes of the navy by far the highest paid. Domestics in their teens received some five to six pesos a month and adults anywhere from eight to twelve pesos, the variation perhaps based on their reputation or appearance. Nursemaids and wet nurses, ordinarily hired for less than a year, were the most highly paid domestics, and in the seventeenth century commanded as much as thirteen to fifteen pesos a month. Occasionally, however, even females in this line of work were hired out for as little as eight and a half pesos a month.[75]

The African slave was no less important to the semiprivate and public sectors of society, and specifically to the monasteries, convents, and hospitals. There was both an ostentatious and a serious side to the role of slaves in such service. On the first count, the most obvious example was Lima's richest convent, La Encarnación, which housed some 400 women in the early seventeenth century. A considerable number of these women had taken holy orders and devoted their lives to religious contemplation and charitable activities, but others were the daughters of the rich, placed in the convent for an education until marriage could be arranged. Most were served by female blacks. According to one observer, the minimum fee to enter the convent was 6,000 pesos, and double that or more for those who desired a separate apartment with a female slave and some spending money.[76]

Such extravagances aside, blacks played a vital role in many hospitals and charitable institutions. For example, in 1607 the hospital of Santa Ana, which cared for the Indian population of Lima, possessed twenty-seven African slaves who served as practical nurses, bookkeepers, cooks, laundresses, and the like, and in general performed every required service except the practice of medicine itself.[77] The founders of such institutions were usually careful to include slaves among their endowments. For example, the first Viceroy Cañete, who was active in the founding of the hospital of San Andrés for Spaniards and an orphanage for mestizos, ensured that both would have a sufficient number of Africans to perform the necessary tasks. And when, in 1593, Cristóbal Sánchez de Bilbao and his wife donated the bulk of their worldly possessions to establish the convalescent hospital of San Diego in Lima, two blacks were included in the grant.[78] In addition, many individuals donated slaves to these institutions, some contributing on a grand scale, like the teamster Juan Maço de Dueñas, who donated eighteen blacks to San Andrés Hospital along with real estate, cash, carts, and livestock. More often the contribution was more modest, as in the case of Pedro de Rojas, who gave a single slave to the Indian hospital of Santa Ana.[79]

Africans also served many government agencies. Black drummers and fifers paced the march of the royal forces. Black janitors and stevedores worked at the royal customhouse, armory, and storage facilities at Callao. Blacks swept the chambers of the Audiencia and the streets of Lima, and periodically tidied up the municipal jail. In Lima law-enforcement officers made their rounds accompanied by several armed slaves, and blacks also acted as gatekeepers at the city jail. From the 1540's special police officers known as *cuadrilleros* were used by the city of Lima to apprehend runaway slaves; both free persons of color and Africans owned by the municipality or by private individuals served in this capacity. Occasionally, blacks in the employ of the Crown were the property of the agency involved, but in most instances they were hired from private citizens or were owned by government officeholders. Black drummers and fifers, for example, were usually owned by the captains of the military companies they played for, and at a salary of twenty pesos a month, they represented a handsome source of supplemental income to these officers. Similarly, the weighmaster of the royal customhouse at Callao used one of his own slaves as a janitor there, for which service the Crown paid fifteen pesos.[80]

Many persons of color, both slave and free, were involved in the provision and preparation of foodstuffs for consumption in Peruvian towns. For example, there were blacks active in the fishing population that operated, according to Lockhart, "along the coast, near Arequipa, Lima, and Piura, and perhaps in other places as well."[81] The Peruvian fishing industry during this period was a small-scale operation, a matter largely of companies under constantly changing ownership that possessed two or three small boats, each manned by one Spanish fisherman and a few black slaves. Blacks soon became skilled at the task, and one, the free mulatto Pedro de Meneses, came to own his boat and slave assistants.[82]

The city of Lima and its port of Callao were particularly dependent on black labor for provisions. Blacks worked in the Lima slaughterhouse and meat market, some of them owned by the city, others by the various individuals who contracted to operate the establishment; and royal officials used blacks to butcher, cure, and salt the meat used aboard the navy ships.[83] Slaves and free blacks of both sexes were extensively employed in the preparation and sale of the bread, pastries, candied fruit, and preserves so dear to the Spanish palate, and also prepared more substantial fare—hardtack—for consumption by the sailors employed by the Crown.[84]

Though the viceroy or the Audiencia occasionally intervened in the control of mercantile operations in Lima, the municipal council had broad authority in this area, and that authority extended to overseeing the food supply. The council members established market prices and were responsible for ensuring that the capital received adequate provisions. The city authorities did not object to the use of blacks in the preparation and marketing of foodstuffs and other commodities so long as these activities were subject to control. But they were increasingly suspicious of the more or less independent operations of a growing number of blacks, who obtained and sold merchandise wherever they could. In the first place, it was feared that these operations were blinds for theft and prostitution. Further, it was charged that blacks used coercion to buy articles from the Indians for resale at higher prices.[85] From time to time black vendors of foodstuffs were also accused of engaging in a variety of sharp and unhygienic business practices. In 1551, for example, the city attorney complained that the African and Spanish women who prepared and sold baked goods also commonly treated buboes, preparing the sarsaparilla that was thought to cure the sickness, and sometimes even medicating the afflicted areas. The council ordered the vendors to confine themselves to one activity or the other and to practice neither until they had publicly declared their choice of profession.[86]

The issue of black vendors came to a head in the 1570's, and under circumstances that were most embarrassing to the Lima authorities. In 1571 the criminal branch of the Audiencia complained to the Crown that members of the city council were using their authority to control the supply of much of the food sold in the city and alleged that the councilmen's slaves ranged far into the countryside to purchase meat and produce for resale in the city markets at artificially high prices, with the resulting profits going to their masters.[87] These allegations were probably true, and in the following year the municipal council adopted two measures in an attempt to demonstrate its zeal for the public welfare. First, persons of color were forbidden to buy or sell foodstuffs anywhere within five leagues of the city under penalty of 100 lashes and a ten-peso fine. Second, no master could allow his slaves to sell any merchandise in the streets without a municipal license under penalty of a fifty-peso fine. Black vendors, and females in particular, were ordered to present themselves before the city council to obtain such licenses. These measures were not enough to satisfy the Audiencia, and in 1574 it forbade all African mercantile activity, a decision that reduced the sale of municipal retail licenses by one-sixth.[88] This move went too far, since the black merchants filled a genuine and growing need, and they soon resumed their trade.

There was little official effort to restrict colored mercantile operations in the subsequent decades. In 1622, for example, an appeal to the viceroy from the Lima city attorney to prohibit blacks from selling articles from door to door got no response.[89] Indeed, in the seventeenth century black vendors were a very visible part of the life of the capital, numerous enough even to constitute a public nuisance. In 1613, for example, the city authorities were told the street behind the viceregal palace leading to the church of San Francisco was so clogged with black and mulatto fishmongers and their customers, and so full of bad odors, that the area was effectively closed to all traffic. To remedy this situation, fishmongers were ordered to transfer their operations to a small square in front of the municipal slaughterhouse.[90] Black female vendors of foodstuffs were particularly prominent. According to Father Buenaventura de Salinas y Córdova, much of the fruit that was produced in such lavish variety in the surrounding chácaras and orchards was sold in Lima's main square by women—"mulattoes, blacks, Indians, and mestizos [sitting beneath] awnings to protect themselves from the sun. The Indian women place everything they sell on the ground on blankets and mats, and the mulatto and black women their goods on wooden tables." Each woman by mutual agreement had her customary place, and everything was arranged with much precision. So colorful was the fruit market, said Salinas, that visiting it was a favorite form of diversion for Lima's upper classes. Black women also roamed the streets selling doughnuts, milk, whipped cream, cheeses, and, in summer, the beverages chicha and mead.[91] Among males, by 1650 the free black water vendors of Lima were numerous enough to organize themselves into a guild.[92]

Many blacks and mulattoes also operated or owned *pulperías*, something of a small combined grocery store, delicatessen, and tavern. As will be discussed later, during much of the sixteenth century the authorities in a largely futile attempt to discourage theft, frowned on the sale of wine to blacks, and likewise tried to block persons of color from working in or owning establishments that sold alcoholic beverages. Evidently, the blacks who worked in pulperías were suspected of accepting stolen goods from their fellows in exchange for alcohol, and fencing the goods at a handsome profit. Whether these suspicions were justified or not, in 1568 the Lima city council limited to twenty-five the number of persons permited to sell wine by the drink and forbade blacks of both sexes to engage in this activity. While in Cuzco in 1572, Viceroy Toledo heard complaints concerning taverns operated by free colored women, establishments that specialized in the sale of chicha and that were allegedly contributing to widespread drunkenness among both the Indians and the blacks. Toledo ordered the taverns closed and prohibited the manufacture and sale of chicha.[93]

Despite these efforts, the colored pulperos continued their operations and even flourished. In 1595, for example, the city of Lima again forbade the issuance of tavern licenses to blacks and mulattoes, and any permits possessed by these groups were ordered revoked. However, the mulata tavernkeeper Magdalena de Santiago successfully appealed the decision before the council and was allowed to retain her business. The issue was revived in 1618, when a member of the council charged that many pulperos in Lima obtained the required license and then turned the management of their establishments over to blacks and mulattoes. Further, many colored persons had secured licenses of their own in one way or another. It was alleged that various unspecified evils came from this practice, probably a reference to traffic in stolen goods. The council pledged strict enforcement of existing ordinances on the subject, but very little change was observed.[94] In succeeding decades free persons of color, and women in particular, became if anything even more prominent in the operation of pulperías, though they were usually required to post bond. Others, women again prominent among their number, operated small shops identified in the records simply as *tiendas*. In 1645, for example, María de Morales, a free mulatto and widow of a notary public, rented space for one of these tiendas for a year at seven pesos per month.[95]

In a letter to the Crown in 1636, Viceroy Chinchón, who shared the racial prejudices of his day, but combined with these humanity and a willingness to express himself frankly in official correspondence, summarized the African's contribution to the Peruvian economy. In coastal Peru, he declared, there was "no service but theirs" in the homes, bakeries, building trades, and mechanical arts, on the Crown's ships and those of private individuals, and "in the countryside for the farms of wheat, corn, barley, and fruit, and grass for the livestock, for sugarcane and its refinement, and for the vineyards. . . . All this black labor is necessary for the maintenance of human life, since neither the Spaniards who come from Castile nor those born here, when they incline to this sort of work, which is very improbable under present circumstances, are sufficient for the tenth part, or even less, of what is required."[96] However expensive, irksome, feared, or disturbing to the morally sensitive, the African slave and his descendants were above all a necessity.

CHAPTER FIVE

African Versus Indian Labor:
A Royal Dilemma

African slavery and forced Indian labor transformed Peru into the richest of the Spanish American colonies in the sixteenth and seventeenth centuries, but the Crown viewed both sources of manpower with displeasure and distaste. The morality of African slavery went largely unquestioned. It was the slave trade itself that was objectionable, a necessary evil that drained off valuable silver into Portuguese hands. In addition, many government officials considered the black man a potential enemy to be carefully watched. The Spanish Crown, therefore, was hardly happy about the entrenchment of African labor along the Peruvian coast. But the alternative, the mita, a system almost universally deplored for the cruelty and destructiveness of its operation, was even more distasteful. Few Spanish officials in Peru defended the mita except on grounds of economic necessity, and no Spanish monarch from Charles V to Philip IV ever reconciled himself to the institution. Many official attempts were made to abolish, restrict, or ease the mita, with black labor often proposed as an alternative, but almost all of them failed. Royal concern for the Indian may have been greater than fear of the African, but in the end financial considerations outweighed both. The government was not prepared to sacrifice its own revenues to improve the lot of the Indian, and found the private sector of the economy to be equally reluctant. Nevertheless, a brief review of these efforts provides an interesting study of the conflict between moral dictates and imperial aggrandizement, a characteristic of Spanish activity in America.

No aspect of the forced Indian labor system caused greater official distress than the mining mita. As we have seen, the Crown finally sanctioned the massive employment of natives in the mines at Viceroy Toledo's urging. Nevertheless, the government was reluctant to abandon the idea of substantial African participation in the Peruvian mining industry, and the possibility of black labor in the mines continued to be studied. Finally, in the late sixteenth century, the Crown entered into two agreements to implement this goal.

The first took the form of a ten-year contract concluded in 1580 with Ventura Espino, a Peruvian mine operator, who undertook to work all the mines in the Audiencia districts of Lima, Charcas, and Quito, of whatever metal and including not only those currently held by the Crown but also any he discovered during the period of the contract.[1] Espino agreed to furnish the necessary equipment, to provide skilled workmen as required, to bear the cost of any litigation that might arise from the implementation of the contract, and to give the Crown 40 per cent of the metal extracted, or double the usual share paid by other leaseholders, free of all operating costs. The Crown in its turn gave Espino the right to import 1,000 black slaves (a third of whom had to be female) from Africa or from "the provinces of Brazil." The first batch of 400 were to be imported in the first year of the agreement, the others in batches of 100 over the next six years. All were to be used exclusively for mining operations and could not be sold en route or in Peru, and for each Espino was to pay the standard license fee of 30 ducats within two years of importation.

Both parties realized that even 1,000 slaves might be insufficient for a project of this magnitude. Accordingly, Espino agreed to bring from Spain any skilled laborers and craftsmen he needed, and the Crown agreed to supplement the black labor force with mita Indians as necessary. A decree was issued ordering the viceroy to supply the contractor with the required native labor, but with the curious stipulation that the Indians were not to be forced to work against their will. In short, the contract with Espino seems to have been both a serious attempt by the Crown to demonstrate the feasibility of using African labor in mining operations and a subtle warning to other developers to place less reliance on the mita or risk the reversion of their claims to the government.

Espino ran into difficulties almost at once. First, his resources proved to be much more limited than his ambitions. August 1582 found him still in Spain, unable to arrange the necessary sureties to guarantee the project. The Crown finally permitted him to sail to Peru without posting these bonds, and the permit for the 400 slaves who were to have been imported in 1581 was extended.[2] Espino finally arrived in Lima in 1583, accompanied by sixty men, only to be confronted with more problems.[3] Viceroy Martín Enríquez (1581-83), who apparently had favored the project, had died, and the Audiencia, governing in the interim, was adamantly opposed to it, as were the royal treasury officials. Espino's opponents argued that the existing system of individual leases was more profitable than the proposed unified administration under Espino.[4] In addition, it was alleged that Espino had failed to bring the necessary slaves and equipment, and the Audiencia used this charge as a pretext to delay implementation of the new agreement while appeals for cancellation were sent to Spain. Espino's prospects grew even dimmer with the arrival of a new viceroy, the Conde del Villar, for he too was hostile to the project. During this long period of waiting Espino saw his plans for a mining empire founded on black labor slowly crumble, and his financial position declined to the point where he was forced to cede virtually all interest in the contract and complete powers of administration to three principal creditors. He died shortly thereafter. The new leaseholders petitioned the Crown for an extension of the agreement and for orders that would force the colonial bureaucracy to comply with its terms, but their pleas were denied in 1589.

The government body that turned a deaf ear to the entreaties of Espino's assignees was a committee composed of members of the councils of the Indies and the Treasury,[5] and their decision was probably influenced by the financial arguments of Peruvian officials. However, the failure of the Espino contract did not dampen official interest in the African as an alternative to mita labor, though it may have made Spanish bureaucrats more skeptical of ambitious proposals to that end. In any event, two years earlier, in 1587, the committee had conducted a searching review of possible ways to improve the Indian's situation and had concluded that further consideration should be given to the use of blacks in Peruvian mines, particularly in the gold mines of the tropical areas.[6] Whether by coincidence or by design, the committee had scarcely made its recommendation when precisely such a project was presented for their consideration.

Late in 1587 or early in 1588 a citizen of Potosí named Pedro Cornejo de Estrella called the attention of the Council of the Indies to the number of potentially rich mines in Peru that could not be worked because of ventilation and drainage problems.[7] Estrella claimed that a mechanism of his invention (which was never explained) could alleviate these problems and put the mines back into production. Estrella offered to demonstrate the mechanism's utility in the gold deposits of Carabaya province, whose tropical climate exacted its toll on the highland natives brought down to work the mines. In return, Estrella asked for a permit to import 150 African slaves free of royal duties to assist the operation and for the exclusive use of his invention for a period of twelve years. The proposal was forwarded to the joint Indies-Treasury committee for evaluation, and its members were impressed by Estrella's arguments. However, with customary caution the committee recommended in February 1588 that only fifty slave licenses be granted free of charge, and that Estrella be allowed to purchase another fifty for the standard fee, payable within four years. The Crown approved the recommendation, but even more cautiously stipulated that Estrella's mysterious invention must show results within two years or he would have to pay the license fee on all 100 slaves.

Estrella's venture fared no better than Espino's. He too had difficulty establishing the credit of his guarantors, and in desperation he offered to buy all 100 slave licenses if the Crown would approve the bonds and grant him permission to take three assistants to Peru—a carpenter, a blacksmith, and a brassworker. Finally, in August 1591 the Crown extended the limits of his contract for another two years and permitted him to sail with the fleet of 1592. As luck would have it, his ship sank, probably almost before the voyage was under way, and the government was forced to prolong the agreement for still another year. Estrella eventually made his way back to America only to die in debt shortly thereafter, his project uninitiated.[8]

It will be noticed that the Espino and Estrella contracts involved minimal risk to the Crown and did not call for the expenditure of a single royal peso. This was standard government policy. However much the plight of the Indian was deplored, the government consistently refused to promote the alternative of African slavery with its own funds, though several imaginative projects were forwarded to Spain. One suggestion, advanced in 1574, proposed a massive colonization effort in the underdeveloped parts of the colony, with a royal trade and retail monopoly importing African slaves for sale to the settlers to work the fields and mineral deposits, particularly in tropical areas where the Indian population was sparse.[9] A similar proposal came in 1591 from the Dominican friar Tomás Durán y Ribera, who pointed to the heavy mortality rate among the Indian mitayos and proposed that the situation be remedied by placing the slave trade under royal monopoly. According to Durán, this measure would ensure the massive importation of Africans, thereby reducing the labor obligations of the Indians, and at the same time produce a substantial amount of revenue for the royal coffers.[10] A crushing lack of interest greeted both proposals in Spain. The Crown would not become a slave dealer.

The Crown was not averse, however, to the most imaginative proposal of all—that the Indian communities themselves invest in Africans. This curious project involved the Apurímac, a deep river that bisects the route between Lima and Cuzco.[11] In the late sixteenth century the Apurímac was spanned by an Incaic-type suspension bridge of vegetable fiber. The swaying of such a bridge must have made crossing disagreeable even to the Incas, and the use of horses and mules by the Spanish made the span even more unsuitable and increased the frequency of repairs. The Indian provinces of the Cuzco area had maintained the bridge since Inca times as a part of their labor tax, and some 250 men were obliged to serve without pay each year to renew the cables. Maintenance was difficult and dangerous at best, and with the use of highland Indian labor in the tropical climate the mortality rate was further increased. When the second Marqués de Cañete came to Peru in 1590, he was under royal instructions to improve the colony's communication system. He soon considered one obvious improvement—the construction of a permanent stone span across the Apurímac—which would greatly facilitate transport between Lima and Cuzco and eliminate the need for intensive maintenance, with consequent hardship and loss of life to the natives.

Originally, a force of Indians was proposed to construct the bridge, but the Protector General of the Indians, Don Antonio de Torres Fresnada, heard of the project and objected.[12] Torres argued that at least 500 Indians would be required for the project, and that few of them would have any experience in European construction techniques. Moreover, the hard work in an unfamiliar climate would decimate the Indian population of the area. Torres countered with the proposal that African slaves be purchased for the job; the money could come from the funds of the Indian communities that were now charged with maintaining the span,[13] and the other inhabitants of the region could be assessed for the necessary provisions during construction. When the project was complete, the blacks would belong to the Indian villages on a pro rata basis.

Cañete accepted this proposal, and in 1595 ordered that 100 Africans, a third of whom were to be women, be purchased for the project. Sixty-eight blacks were acquired immediately, at a cost of 330 *pesos ensaya-dos* each, from a slave lot that had just arrived in the capital. Half of the sale price was paid in cash, and the balance was to be paid within six months. Another 3,000 pesos was assigned to feed, clothe, and transport the slaves to the construction site. Since the money from the Indian communities was not actually in the government's possession, the above sums were borrowed from the revenues of the vacant episcopal see of Cuzco and from other funds. At the same time, the viceroy directed a member of the Audiencia, Alonso Maldonado de Torres, who was in Cuzco on other business, to take a total of 40,000 pesos from the community funds of the fourteen Indian districts involved to pay the loan and to cover the cost of the thirty-two slaves yet to be purchased. Maldonado moved swiftly with the assessments, and by the end of the year a large part of the money seems to have been pledged. In the meantime, Cañete informed the Crown of his action and secured royal approval.[14]

At this point, however, the project soured. Cañete was at the end of his term as viceroy, and his successor, Don Luis de Velasco (1596-1604), considered a stone bridge too ambitious and ordered that a wooden one be built instead. But Velasco did favor the use of black slave labor, paid for by the Indian communities, and the number of Africans purchased to complete the span swelled to over 130 during his tenure. On this score, both Cañete and Velasco overreached themselves. The Indian communities either could not or would not come up with the money pledged to pay for the slaves, and, when the wooden bridge was completed, the authorities had no choice but to send the blacks to the capital for sale at auction. Even that went awry, for the sale was marked by fraud, and as late as 1610 the Crown was attempting to clear up the matter and recover the proceeds.[15] Thus, the actions of two viceroys momentarily saddled the government with the ownership of over 100 slaves, a situation that never occurred again during the period under study.

Although the Crown remained firm in its determination to avoid using its own resources to promote African slavery in Peru, it continued trying to restrict the enforced employment of Indians and to encourage the use of black labor. As we have seen, in the late sixteenth century Indian labor was barred from sugar mills, vineyards, and textile factories, a measure the Peruvian viceroys attempted to enforce with some vigor. Further, in the 1590's the Crown returned to an issue first widely discussed in Toledo's day: the employment, on a forced basis if necessary, of the free colored population. Proposals both specific and general flowed from Spain on this subject. In 1593, for example, the Crown asked Viceroy Cañete if the delivery of mail in Peru might not be entrusted to free blacks and mulattoes (along with idle Spaniards and mestizos), thereby freeing the 500 to 600 Indian couriers (*chasquis*) who currently performed this service. The Crown cited reports that the chasquis were infrequently paid, and that this service was a heavy burden on the Indian population.[16] Cañete responded that though the mail system was indeed a hardship on the Indians, to rely on the groups the Crown suggested would expose the native villages along the roads to even greater abuses than those already suffered. Cañete promised to study the matter and to effect the appropriate remedies. The Crown agreed to await the viceroy's proposals, and the question seems to have been dropped for the moment.[17]

In general terms, too, the Crown pressed for the employment of idle free persons of color. The royal view continued to be that the addition of free coloreds to the labor force, together with vagabond Spaniards and mestizos, not only would reduce the burden of the mita but also would cut the rate of turbulence and crime in Peru. For example, in 1595 Viceroy Velasco was ordered to round up the idle elements of the colony and force them to learn a trade.[18] In 1596, the Council of the Indies recommended that free blacks, mulattoes, and *zambaigos* (Afro-Indians)[19] be obliged to work, but warned that they should not be employed side by side with the natives lest the Indians be exposed to abuse.[20] These decrees and recommendations had very little impact in Peru for the simple reason that the free colored population was too small to have any significant effect on the labor situation, but they presaged the most ambitious government reform since the promulgation of the New Laws: in 1601 a royal decree was issued abolishing the mita.

The Crown had always been uneasy about the morality of coerced native labor, and continuing complaints against the mita system from both ecclesiastics and government officials were given added weight by the slow but relentless decline of the Indian population. By the turn of the seventeenth century the Crown had become convinced that the process could be reversed only by altering the means by which Peru recruited its manpower; hence the decree of 1601.[21] The new legislation had been framed after exhaustive examination of past promulgations and after prolonged deliberation by the Council of the Indies, during which the opinions of most prominent officials or ex-officials with American experience had been solicited. The results were long on moral fervor but somewhat short on practical solutions.

The decree began with a bitter denunciation of the abuses common under the mita system, and condemned the cynical advice and deceit of certain unnamed colonial officials, which had served to blind the royal vision. The need for Indian labor was conceded, but it would be permitted only under conditions that would ensure good treatment and instruction in the Faith and only to the extent that all idle Spaniards, mestizos, and free persons of color were unable to meet the demand for manpower. Brief mention was made of the encomienda system, and encomenderos were again forbidden to commute tribute for personal service. Nor were Spaniards to detain Indians in their service, whether for debt or any other reason, or treat them as personal property.

The Crown specifically ordered several reforms. In agriculture, as we have seen, Indians were not to be used in certain enterprises and were to be forced to work only if absolutely necessary, and then at a reasonable distance from their villages. The mining mita posed a thornier problem. The Crown, for a start, was determined not to do anything that would decrease the production of precious metals. Within that limitation, it proposed as a first step that the viceroy make every effort to persuade the mine operators to use as many Africans as possible in their work crews. For the rest, Indian workers were to be offered inducements to accept employment in the mines on a permanent basis. To this end a census was to be made of the Indians living in the immediate vicinity of each mining settlement to determine if they could supply the necessary labor for the mines. Where more hands were needed, other Indians were to be attracted to settle in the area with promises of land. All idle Spaniards, blacks, and mixed racial groups in the vicinity were also to be pressed into service. In addition, since the mitayos had suffered great loss of life in the frequent drainage projects necessary to keep the mines in operation, blacks were henceforth to be employed for this task. Finally, to allow time for the new regulations to be adopted, the operation of the mita was to continue for another year to prevent a drop in silver production.

Clearly, the intent of this legislation was to place all Indian labor on a voluntary basis, a goal long cherished by the Spanish kings. After some six decades of colonial rule, it was hoped that the Peruvian Indian would at last break away from the life of the village and cheerfully work for an employer of his own choosing at a wage agreed upon between them. Forced labor for wages under the mita, with all the attendant abuses, would no longer be necessary, and the Indian population would increase as a result. In the interval, African slaves and the free coloreds of the colony could supply whatever additional manpower was required.

But the Crown also foresaw that the Indians might be just as unwilling to participate now as they had been in the past. Thus, in the case of agriculture, local magistrates retained their power to compel Indians to work if the occasion demanded. Similarly, the sweeping reforms intended for the mines were not all they appeared to be on the surface. Secret instructions to Viceroy Velasco, issued on the same date as the legislation, acknowledged that it might take longer than a year to reorganize the labor supply for the mines. In that event, the viceroy was to call a council of the highest ecclesiastical and secular dignitaries to determine whether or not the mita should continue to function in the interim.[22] In short, the Crown's desire for reform was tempered by the realization that the disruption of the colonial economy and the consequent decrease of its own revenues were too high a price to pay.

During the next eight years the Crown tried to breathe as much life into the legislation as financial considerations would allow. The new viceroy, the Conde de Monterrey (1604-6), was given the same royal instructions that Velasco had received: idle Spaniards, blacks, and mixed breeds were to be compelled to engage in useful occupations; those who knew a trade were to practice it, and those who did not were to learn one or serve a Spanish employer in some recognized capacity; in Lima and other cities where there were few Indians and many blacks, Indians were to be excused where possible from janitorial service in the churches and monasteries, repair work on roads and bridges, and odd jobs during feast days; and when Indians had to be used, they were to be fully reimbursed.[23] Monterrey was troubled by the growing number of mulattoes, zambaigos, and mestizos who were useless to the economy through lack of skills, but he died in office without proposing a solution. The Crown instructed Monterrey's successor, the Marqués de Montesclaros (1607-15), to take all necessary steps to integrate these groups into the economy,[24] but little appears to have been accomplished in this regard.

Indeed, very little was being done to implement any of the legislation of 1601. To be sure, the number of blacks continued to increase in the agricultural and urban areas of the coast, but this was perhaps more in response to a sheer shortage of labor than to any official pressure to restrict the mita. Still less was done to abolish the mining mita, though its horrors had been documented many times. In 1603 Viceroy Velasco had turned to the members of the Lima Audiencia, to members of the various religious orders, and to everyone else he could think of for advice on how best to deal with the issue of forced Indian labor in the mines, and their response was unanimous: the king's orders could not be implemented without ruining the colony. Most people to whom Velasco talked defended the justice of the mining mita and trotted out the much-used argument that it would be impractical to employ blacks because the climate would kill them. And one man who advised Velasco, Pedro Muñiz, dean of the Lima cathedral, had no qualms about Indian mine labor, but he did object to the idea expressed in the royal decree that blacks might substitute for Indians in the most dangerous task, observing that blacks "are our neighbors like the rest."[25]

Quite naturally, the beneficiaries of forced mining labor had no desire to substitute expensive blacks of uncertain longevity for miserably paid Indians, and colonial authorities were understandably reluctant to challenge the mining interests without the full backing of the Crown. This backing, despite the brave words of 1601, the government refused to give. In 1604, for example, Viceroy Velasco reported that Peruvian mines could be worked with blacks only if the Crown were to permit the massive importation of Africans under royal auspices for sale on liberal credit terms to the mine operators. Even so, a limited number of mitayos would have to be employed, but in such a way, it was hoped, as to spare the villages involved from the rigors of the old regime. The Crown did not pursue the matter beyond directing Montesclaros in 1608 to explore the idea and offer an opinion.[26] A year later, reluctant as ever to invest its own funds in the slave trade, the government inquired about the possibility of settling free blacks, mulattoes, and zambaigos in Spanish-type towns in the highlands, where these groups would be obliged to pay tribute and work in the mines.[27]

Colonial authorities no doubt sensed that the Crown was interested in palliatives rather than basic reform, a fact that was confirmed by a decree of May 26, 1609.[28] Formally admitting the failure of the policy of relying on voluntary Indian labor in conjunction with African slavery, the government restored the mita system in both mining and agriculture along the lines laid down by Toledo. The Crown expressed the hope that the Indian, in the fullness of time, would voluntarily participate in the economy. In the meantime the viceroy should try to induce the colonists to import as many African slaves as would be consistent with both the prosperity and the public safety of the colony; and to take suitable steps to press the unemployed, of whatever category, into the work force. On the second point, in a separate decree of the same date the Crown ordered the viceroy to see about using as many Spaniards as possible in menial tasks in the hope of encouraging the darker members of Peruvian society to follow their example.[29] Another decree, also of that date, directed the viceroy to consider anew the feasibility of importing Africans to work the mines.[30]

Montesclaros was slow to comment at length on the Crown's many proposals of 1609, and when he did so nearly two years later it was in a style so vague and guarded as to be almost incoherent. The viceroy opposed the idea of founding settlements for idle Spaniards and blacks in order to bring them into the labor force, arguing that it was difficult enough now to control these groups when they were concentrated primarily in the cities; if they were to be scattered in isolated mining towns as the Crown had suggested, the task would be well-nigh impossible. Local law enforcement agencies were too weak to protect the Indian villages from the inevitable rascality of these sluggards. Though the decline of the Indian population was deplorable, Montesclaros said, the manpower problem would be better solved by applying an enlightened mita policy than by launching any dubious new projects. The viceroy believed that Africans were unsuited for extensive use in the mines because the climate damaged their health and because they would bully the Indians whenever possible, but he thought the Crown might import Africans for sale to the plantations that supplied the mining centers with food. If the project was to succeed, the buyers must be warned to take proper care of the slaves and cautioned that mitayos would not be assigned to replace dead blacks. In addition, direct viceregal supervision of the distribution of such slaves would be the only way to ensure that they were in fact sold at modest prices to replace Indian labor. Even so, the measure might not halt the decline of the Indian population. Montesclaros refused to predict the number of Africans that might ultimately be required but stated that one or two trial shipments on the royal account would probably indicate the demand with little or no financial strain on the Crown's part. Finally, the viceroy acknowledged that from the paltry production of many mines it was clear the mitayos were often being used for other tasks, but he argued that interference without royal support would spell disaster for any official because of the inevitable protests that would be lodged.

Within a week of this letter Montesclaros sent another, addressing himself again to the proposal that free blacks, mulattoes, and other castes be settled in towns and obliged to work in the mines and pay tribute. This time he used a new argument against the measure: it would give the blacks and castes too clear an idea of their numerical superiority. Meanwhile, he reported, every effort was being made to establish tribute payments among blacks and mulattoes in order to force them to seek employment.[31] Upon receipt of these two communications the Crown abandoned any attempt at reform for over a decade.

The local authorities, however, did not entirely abandon the idea of substituting slave labor for Indian labor. This was done in at least one major project—the construction of a new bridge across the Apurímac River.[32] The wooden span built at the orders of Viceroy Velasco in the early seventeenth century was soon washed away, and evidently not even a suspension bridge was put in its place, since in the 1610's passengers and merchandise had to be ferried across the river. To remedy this situation, Viceroy Esquilache concluded a contract in 1618 with Bernabé Florines, an architect, and Francisco de la Fuente, the municipal clerk of Cuzco, to build a stone bridge across the Apurímac within three years. The project, to be financed by an excise tax on all merchandise, bullion, and currency entering Cuzco from both Lima and Potosí, was to involve as little Indian labor as possible. A mita force of twenty-four Indians was assigned to the project, but they were expressly barred from doing anything but light work (e.g., sawing wood, mixing lime) in the highlands and were on no account to be brought down to the construction site. For the heavy labor the partners agreed to purchase thirty-two blacks (including eight females). Two Spanish masters were to be engaged to teach the art of stonecutting to the slaves and to any Indians who might be hired if additional labor was needed.

From the beginning the project was marked by delays and reverses. Fuente withdrew from the partnership quite early in the game, and Florines seems to have had great difficulty getting a new backer. He finally found a new partner in 1620, Captain Pedro Guevara de Armenta. Guevara agreed to launch the project with 10,000 pesos for the purchase of slaves and to share with Florines any profit deriving from their sale when the job was complete and after all debts had been satisfied. Armed with these resources, Florines began work on the span and hired a free black, who presumably knew something about stonecutting, to supervise the slaves. But the difficulties continued. Florines appears to have built a temporary bridge of some sort across the Apurímac, only to have it washed out almost immediately. He continued the work on the permanent span until at least 1624, but the project was never finished, and the fate of the slaves involved is unknown.

In the 1620's and 1630's royal consideration of African versus Indian labor was more fitful than before, perhaps in large part because of the increasingly desperate and expensive conflict with the Dutch. Nevertheless, opposition to forced Indian labor was not quite dead. In 1622, for example, the Crown questioned the Lima Audiencia and the Tribunal of Accounts about the feasibility of importing blacks on the royal account for sale to the mine operators. Both responded, as many authorities had earlier, that in the case of the silver mines past experience had demonstrated the climate to be injurious to the health of African slaves; and that though the gold mines could indeed be worked by blacks, those who were trying to exploit these deposits were so poor they would have to purchase the slaves on credit. Many would be unable to pay and would seek greener pastures elsewhere, taking the slaves with them, and to locate these debtors and initiate lawsuits would cost more than the outstanding debts. The consensus was that slave-trading was best left in private hands, an opinion that the Crown accepted.[33] Five years later the Crown made a similar proposal with regard to the gold deposits of the Loja district (today part of Ecuador). Viceroy Chinchón, after consulting the Audiencia, the Tribunal of Accounts, and the treasury officials, advised against the idea for the same reasons given in 1622, and once again the Crown accepted the advice.[34] This was roughly the period when the government began talking about condemning criminals (of whatever color) to the Huancavelica mercury mines instead of to galley service, but the idea was never pursued. In sum, outside of the gold mines in such tropical provinces as Vilcabamba, the African's role in Peruvian mining consisted of the rare slave here and there who served in a supervisory capacity.[35] Despite all the efforts and good intentions of the Crown, the extraction of the silver ore on which it so heavily depended remained the unhappy task of the Indian.

Government interest in other aspects of the labor situation in Peru did not revive until the 1640's. In the early years of that decade, Viceroy Mancera ordered that the estimated 350 Indian mail couriers of the colony, men whom he described as overworked and underpaid, be replaced by free persons of color, mestizos, and Spaniards. In effect, this decision followed the suggestion made earlier to Viceroy Velasco, a policy that Mancera stated had been allowed to lapse.[36] In 1644, perhaps emboldened by the viceroy's action, Don Francisco de Valenzuela, the Protector of the Indians, suggested to the Crown that the percentage of natives obligated for agricultural mita service at any one time be reduced from one-seventh to one-tenth. On the surface, the proposal could hardly have come at a more inauspicious time. Portugal was lost, the slave trade in disruption, Spanish military power in both Europe and America at low ebb, and the Crown's dependence on Peruvian silver greater than ever—scarcely the moment to tamper with the labor system of Spain's richest American colony. Nonetheless, the home government not only agreed to consider the proposal, but in fact broadened its scope. A 1648 decree to Viceroy Salvatierra hearkened back to the Crown's surrender in 1609 to the mita system, and inquired if perhaps the number of blacks was now sufficient and the Indian's willingness to participate in the economy great enough to abolish or reduce forced native labor, at least on the plantations.[37] It was Salvatierra's unpleasant duty to inform the Crown of the realities of Peruvian life. Lima, the viceroy stated, could ill afford to spare even those few Indians who had been allotted for irrigation duties, since the black population had declined by half in the years following the suspension of the slave trade. Other agricultural areas along the coast were suffering similar labor shortages, and even some parts of the highlands were feeling the strain.

No remedy was in sight until the slave trade resumed. Salvatierra deplored the continuing population losses among the Indians but stated that to tamper with the mita system in present circumstances would cause food prices to rise to ruinous levels.[38] These arguments were good enough for the Crown. In 1651 the viceroy was informed that representations from all over Spanish America had prompted consideration of the best means of reviving the slave trade, and that for now the attempt to reform the mita system was being abandoned.[39]

Measured by its own goals, the Crown's policies with regard to both forced Indian labor and African slavery fell far short of success. The Spanish government viewed the two as alternative and even temporary sources of manpower. The mita was to be tolerated until the Indian came to accept the idea of voluntary labor; meanwhile, the African slave, and even the free person of color, could be used to spare the native from performing the most brutal tasks of the colonial economy. In time, it was reasoned, the Indian would work of his own accord, the mita could be abolished, the native population would thereby increase, and perhaps even African slavery would dwindle to insignificance. Instead the economic and demographic realities of Peru transformed the mita and black slavery into complementary and enduring institutions. In the highlands, and wherever the Indian population remained relatively dense, the natives supplied the bulk of the labor, usually under conditions of coercion. In these areas, the reform proposals and legislation of decades failed to reduce native labor obligations significantly. The failure was largely the Crown's own doing: it lacked the will and the resources to make African slavery an alternative to the mita, perhaps because it foresaw the economic disruption that such a move would cause. Royal distaste for the forced labor system was genuine, but attempts at reform were in the realm of wishful thinking. Only along the Peruvian coast did African labor come to predominate, and even this development was as much a result of Indian population decline as a reflection of the royal will. The slow dichotomization of Peru into African coast and Indian sierra was due by and large to the failure of royal labor policies, not to their success.

❧

CHAPTER SIX

The Black Artisan

African slavery in the Americas is firmly associated with plantation labor and household service, but nothing could be more misleading than to think of the slave as merely a great strong black with a hoe in his hand or a deferential servant in the master's home. It is not that these images are untrue, but that they obscure the African as artisan. To be sure, the majority of Afro-Peruvians performed tasks that demanded little training for proficiency, and that, by the same token, did little to advance the black man in the social and economic structure of the colony. Nevertheless, some Africans were able to achieve a measure of success in the arts and crafts, for the Spanish and Indian craftsmen of Peru were unable to keep up with colonial demand, and it was the skilled African who took up the slack. Many African-born slaves already knew how to weave fabrics and to work metals and woods; all that was lacking was training in European techniques and conventions.[1] Spanish artisan-slaveowners were quick to take advantage of this fact, and other slaveholders were not far behind. The demand for skilled labor was so great that Peruvian-born slaves were also trained as craftsmen under the apprenticeship system, and everyone profited. Masters pocketed the handsome wages earned by black artisans, and allowed their charges a degree of independence largely unknown by unskilled slaves. Occasionally, slave artisans were even allowed to apply a portion of their wages toward the purchase of freedom, and free blacks soon came to appreciate that the arts and crafts held great opportunities for them and their children. In short, the skilled trades constituted a major avenue of advancement for the free colored population of the colony.

The black artisan was most prominent in the cities and towns of Peru, but his importance in the rural areas should not be minimized. In the early decades of colonial rule, Spanish artisans—most commonly smiths —routinely trained gangs of slave blacks capable of working without direction for sale to the wealthy in remote areas of the colony, and this practice doubtless continued in later years.[2] By the late sixteenth century most Peruvian vineyards and sugar plantations possessed blacks skilled in the operations essential to the function of these agricultural enterprises. For example, the black slave population of the sugar hacienda of San José de Quipico in the corregimiento of Chircay in 1636 included a sugarmaster and six assistants, three purgers, two carpenters, two potters, one blacksmith, and one charcoal-maker.[3] Some of the southern vineyards obtained their earthenware jugs from large factories located in the village of Córdoba, between Ica and Pisco, whose skilled black workers were valued at 4,000 pesos each.[4] And many other vineyards kept slaves of their own to make the jugs or wineskins they needed.[5] Slaves adept at masonry and adobe-making were a common feature of the Peruvian plantation, as were charcoal-makers. In 1640, for example, Doña Catalina de Espinosa sold eight black charcoalmakers on her *carbonería* in the Casma Valley, along with their implements, for 300 pesos each.[6]

The skilled black played an even more vital role in the urban areas. For example, black carpenters, shipwrights, joiners, and caulkers made up a good part of the work force in the government shipyards at Callao and Guayaquil after the decision was taken in the late 1580's to keep the royal navy on what was essentially a war footing. Between 1587 and 1641 expenditures for black artisans employed at the royal shipyards totaled nearly 93,000 pesos.[7] During this period 377 blacks worked at the shipyards, of whom twenty-seven were free, twenty-four were owned by the Crown (at a cost of over 14,000 pesos), and the remainder were owned by 141 individuals. Seventy-four of the private owners were Spanish carpenters and shipwrights who worked side by side at the shipyards with their black assistants. Probably they and most other Spanish craftsmen trained their slaves on the job, for that way the black could earn wages from the beginning of apprenticeship, and the master soon recovered his investment and acquired a valuable helper. Many of the other privately owned slaves had special skills and were simply hired out by their masters. Their owners, as in the case of the black sailors, included a number of military men and a high percentage of women, many of them widows of craftsmen. The clergy were also represented. The Jesuits hired out a caulker, and the Augustinian monastery at Callao four black sawers. Occasionally, a slaveholder hired out blacks to serve on the royal vessels and employed others to help build the ships. For example, Captain Antonio Cabral Pimentel, who owned eleven slave sailors, also hired out Andrés Biafara as a shipwright and Gaspar Bran as a caulker at the royal shipyards. Of the free black craftsmen, many were apprentices or ex-apprentices of Spanish craftsmen, and some may have been former slaves who had been allowed to divert a portion of their wages toward the purchase of freedom.

The wages paid at the shipyards were good in comparison with those earned by skilled workers in other trades. Caulkers and shipwrights were the most favored, presumably because their tasks required considerable skill. In these specializations a slave apprentice ordinarily received between four and six reales daily, and a black journeyman might earn as much as four pesos a day for his master, or about 100 pesos a month. Next in the wage scale came the sawers, who were usually paid two and a half pesos a day, though some might earn as little as eight reales. Joiners made still less: the highest recorded salary was two pesos a day, but ordinarily remuneration varied between eight and fourteen reales. All the above figures are for the period before 1630. After that date the Crown began trying to economize, and salaries paid to both white and black craftsmen at the royal shipyards were steadily reduced in the next ten years. Finally, in 1640 Viceroy Mancera established maximum wages of three pesos per day for Spanish craftsmen of whatever specialty and two pesos for blacks, an action approved by the Crown.[8]

Skilled blacks were vital to all phases of the Peruvian construction industry, including the procurement and processing of the necessary materials. According to Lockhart, a substantial amount of slave labor was used in the "quarries and kilns for the production of tile, brick, lime, and cut stone" that were to be found in the vicinity of most Peruvian towns.[9] Indeed, black labor was used extensively in building the very cities of Peru, or at least those with a sizable African population. For example, four of the six bricklayers engaged to build the royal mint at Lima in 1569 were black. The highest-paid of these was a slave; he earned ten reales a day, against three and a half pesos for the one

Spaniard hired and eight reales, or one peso, for the other non-black, an Indian. The other three black bricklayers seem to have been free; two of them earned a peso a day, the third only four reales. There was, in addition, a free black lathe operator on the job, hired to make certain hoisting equipment.[10] Over the years black artisans, both free and slave, were employed to build, repair, and remodel the *casas reales* at Callao (the complex of government buildings consisting of the custom-house, the arsenal, and the royal warehouses).[11]

With the increasing Dutch penetration of the Pacific during the first half of the seventeenth century, the Crown began building major land fortifications in Peru, and here too the African played his part.[12] The push for this project began in 1623 with word of the approach of a large Dutch fleet. When these reports were confirmed in the following year, Viceroy Guadalcázar immediately ordered every seaport, and particularly Callao and Pisco, to make all possible preparations, including fortifications, to meet the threat. To construct the defensive works around the port of Pisco, more than 500 blacks, some of them bricklayers and adobe-makers, were requisitioned from the neighboring wine-producing valleys.[13] The port of Callao was surrounded by numerous trenches and minor adobe fortifications, and was further guarded by a fort named San Ignacio, which was erected within three months. The total number of laborers involved in this construction is unknown, but twenty-five bricklayers alone were used, and of these eighteen were blacks (four of them free). No distinction was made between black and white bricklayers with regard to wages; depending on ability, both earned between twenty reales and eight reales a day.[14] One person who took part in the work later claimed to have supervised fifty blacks, both bricklayers and common laborers, and another stated that he had contributed the labor of six African slaves during the emergency.[15]

The Dutch threat passed, but the Spanish remained apprehensive about the future, and in 1625 Guadalcázar ordered the construction of a more elaborate fortification at another point along the Callao harbor.[16] This structure, designed as a permanent garrison for 400 soldiers (and for as many as 2,000 in an emergency), cost the Crown a total of 44,000 pesos. A good part of this sum went for the wages of African labor in one phase or another of the operation. Most of the adobes used, for example—some 234,000 of the 290,000-plus needed—were supplied by African adoberos. Ten black bricklayers worked at the construction site. They had each agreed at the outset to lay 550 bricks a day for a wage similar to that paid in 1624, but later they were given two reales per day in overtime to speed the work, and began laying 1,000 bricks a day. Over 125 African common laborers were also employed on the project; many of them were simply paid in wine at a considerable savings to the Crown. In 1631 African bricklayers were hired to modify the structure, which came to be known as San Felipe de Guadalcázar in honor of the viceroy.[17]

The last and most impressive addition to the royal fortifications at Callao, a wall built mainly of stone and enclosing most of the town, was begun in 1641. Nearly 450 skilled and unskilled laborers were occupied in the undertaking, a large but unspecified number of whom were reported to be blacks. Viceroy Mancera, the prime mover of the project, informed the Crown that the wall would probably be completed in eighteen months, provided the men were kept working six days a week.[18]

The city of Lima also employed Africans in various building projects over the years. For example, blacks owned or hired by the municipality assisted in the construction, and occasional repair and remodeling, of the buildings that housed the city council, the municipal jail, the slaughterhouse, and the city meat and fish markets. Many of these projects were planned and supervised by Francisco de Gamarra, a free black mason who was prominent in the construction industry of the capital in the late sixteenth and early seventeenth centuries. Gamarra in turn occasionally subcontracted part of the work to one or other of his colored colleagues.[19] One of the most massive projects undertaken by the city was the construction of a water system. For this project, which involved a central fountain, a storage tank, and numerous water mains, the city bought a privately owned tile factory in 1565 and used twelve to thirteen of its own slaves over the next nine years to manufacture and place the water pipes.[20]

Bridges were essential to Lima, situated as it is on both sides of the Rímac River, and blacks worked on both of the important spans completed during the period under study. For the first of these, a brick bridge constructed between 1557 and 1560, royal funds were used to help defray the cost of the equipment and the black workmen.[21] In 1606 this structure collapsed as a result of an earthquake, and two years later a new stone bridge was begun. The city bought eighteen skilled slaves

for the task (who were sold to the Crown to work in the royal shipyards on completion of the project in 1610), and several free mulatto
and black masons were also hired for the job.²² In the ensuing years
large numbers of blacks and Indians were employed to construct and
maintain cutwaters to protect the bridge against the high waters of the
winter months.²³ How many of the blacks working at the repair and
strengthening of the bridge were skilled laborers is unknown.

Many black artisans also took part in the construction of the churches,
monasteries, educational institutions, and hospitals of the colony. In
the beginning, the bulk of these men were brought over from Spain.
In 1543, for example, the Crown sent from Spain—at its own expense
and duty-free—three slaves skilled in carpentry, bricklaying, and black-
smithing to help in the construction of the various Dominican monasteries. Again in 1549 the government authorized the duty-free importation of two slaves, a carpenter and a bricklayer, both purchased in
Spain, to help build the Lima cathedral; a similar concession involving
three blacks with the same skills (and their wives) was granted to the
Indian hospital of Santa Ana in 1579.²⁴ As time passed, however, most
of the skilled labor needed was found in Peru. One could buy craftsmen
at the Lima market at will. Or one could simply buy unskilled blacks
and train them on the job, as the contractors charged with building the
Cuzco cathedral did with the nineteen bozales they purchased in Lima.²⁵

Skilled black labor was also donated to religious and educational
institutions on either a temporary or a permanent basis. In 1574, for
example, when the University of San Marcos purchased the former Augustinian convent of Lima for its operations three professors donated
the labor of their slaves and building materials to make the necessary
alterations, and in 1618 one person pledged the labor of 200 blacks for
the construction of a proposed convent in Saña.²⁶ As we have seen,
those connected with the founding of an institution often took care to
see that it was permanently staffed with slaves. This was true of the
Lima convent of Santa Clara, founded in 1589 by Francisco de Saldaña.
Saldaña donated not only several buildings to house the organization
but also nine slaves. As business administrator for the convent, Saldaña
continued to solicit donations for the institution, and by 1606 Santa
Clara possessed a tidy annual income from mortgages, additional real
estate in the city, agricultural property, and twenty-nine African slaves,
many of them artisans, who were assisting in the remodeling of the
institution's quarters.²⁷

In general, however, such institutions did not maintain a pool of craftsmen to handle the occasional major job but merely retained a handful of slaves to take care of routine maintenance and repair. When a large project was contemplated, the institution turned to its patrons for donated labor and to the marketplace, where it could hire whatever skilled workers it needed. In 1584, for example, construction of the permanent quarters of the Inquisition in Lima was begun exclusively with hired labor, including fifteen black craftsmen—eleven sawers, three plasterers, and one lathe operator.[28] The practice of hiring skilled labor was a boon to the operations of free colored artisans. We have already noted that one black mason, Francisco de Gamarra, was extremely active in the construction industry in the 1570's and after. Though plainly the most prominent free man of color so employed, he was not the only one. Among the others were the free mulatto Juan de Mora, a journeyman architect, who in 1595 undertook to build a portal for a chapel in the church of La Merced, and the free mulatto joiner and furniture maker Fernando Joseph, who in 1639 was hired to assist in the construction of the choir stalls in the Lima cathedral.[29]

Black artisans, slave and free alike, also played a prominent role in the construction of residences and other buildings for private patrons. In 1600, for example, Agustín de Acosta, a bricklayer and the slave of Jorge de Acosta, undertook to finish the house of Diego de Herrera, a saddlemaker, for 120 pesos.[30] Cases of free men of color in this line of work date from as early as 1553, when Andrés Moreno, a mulatto, contracted with Don Bartolomé de Quiñones to make doors for his residence; and the aforementioned Francisco de Gamarra filled at least five private contracts between 1578 and 1598.[31]

In private construction the patron ordinarily provided the materials, but arrangements concerning additional help and room and board were quite varied. In one contract, in which the free mulatto bricklayer Rafael Manrique undertook to build some houses, the employer was to supply the adobes and to pay Manrique twenty-two pesos for each 1,000 adobes laid; Manrique in turn was to pay the wages of any assistants he might need. Others secured more generous terms. The free mulatto carpenter Gregorio López hired himself out in 1605 for ten reales a day plus board for four months; and in 1648 Diego de Lagama, a mulatto who specialized in the building and remodeling of residences, did even better. A sugar planter hired him to build a house, agreeing to give him 1,200 pesos, room and board, and the services of three slaves.[32]

Another important occupation among Africans was metalworking, in which art the Jesuit Sandoval found Guinea blacks to be particularly adept.[33] Ironworking was essential to the Spanish conquest, and black slaves participated in the field from the start, first simply by keeping the forges supplied with charcoal (a major problem since wood was scarce near most Spanish towns), then serving as apprentices, and finally becoming skilled smiths in their own right.[34] Once the heartland of Peru had been won, African ironworkers continued to play a role in the new expeditions of exploration and conquest that departed for the peripheral areas. This was true, for example, in the case of the ill-fated Ursua-Aguirre Amazonian venture of 1559. Likewise, we find a black ironworker, acquired at a cost of 1,435 pesos along with forge and tools, accompanying Álvaro de Mendaña's expedition to the South Seas in 1567.[35] Earlier, during the Peruvian civil wars, and perhaps thereafter, black swordsmiths and gunsmiths were employed in the royal armory.[36] Indeed, by the 1550's the Spanish smiths of Lima were so disturbed over African competition that they urged the authorities to bar black ironworkers from operating their own shops. To justify this discrimination, the Spanish alleged that their black competitors made picklocks and engaged in other unspecified illegal practices. Evidently the authorities found these charges convincing, since they ruled that black ironworkers had to practice their trade under Spanish supervision.[37] In theory blacks were now condemned to perpetual journeyman status, but the ruling was forgotten or simply ignored after a period of years, for in 1625 Francisco Bañol, a free black, referred to himself as a "master blacksmith" in a legal document and operated his own shop without official interference.[38]

Far fewer blacks became silversmiths, goldbeaters, or gilders. Lockhart explains this phenomenon for silversmithing during the early colonial period by noting that such men "were more assayers and general experts on metals and mining than producers, and what productive work they did was often of high technical difficulty."[39] Further, these were all prestigious skilled trades that the Spanish wanted for themselves. Despite the very considerable demand for worked silver and gilded objects, therefore, references to blacks who practiced these trades are infrequent, and the individuals were usually slaves of Spanish craftsmen. In 1635, for example, the Lima city council allowed a Spanish silversmith to employ a slave gilder in his operations, over the strenuous opposition of the gilders' organization, after five fellow craftsmen testified that the black was so skilled, particularly at the gilding of brass, that no Spaniard in the colony could rival him.[40] A year earlier, another Spaniard secured municipal approval to set up shop with the help of six black goldbeaters, one of whom was described as one of the most skilled in the city.[41] References to black silversmiths can also be found in the documentation, but rarely as independent craftsmen.[42] In the 1630's, for example, there were at least 200 silversmiths working in some fifty shops in Lima, but Salinas y Córdova, who reported these figures, made no mention at all of skilled blacks.[43]

As we have seen, the city of Lima employed slaves in the manufacture of tile pipe for the municipal water system, and African participation in this craft remained significant. One observer, writing in the first decade of the seventeenth century, mentioned a tile and brick manufacturer who had 400 slaves serving in his operations; and in 1641 Juan del Corral, one of the most important makers of decorative tiles in Lima, had a thirteen-year-old black apprentice.[44] In at least one instance slaves were also involved in the making of glass. These were the slaves of the master glassmaker Pedro de la Barrera, who tried to set up operations in Ica in the late 1620's. Barrera, a native of Seville, appears to have set out from that port with a contingent of skilled blacks he had purchased with borrowed money. Most of these slaves soon died, however, forcing Barrera to rent others (at eight pesos monthly). By 1629 the luckless Barrera had managed to purchase ten blacks to assist him, but at this point he was so deeply in debt that he lost his entire estate to creditors. The fate of the blacks, one of whom was described as a journeyman glassmaker, is not known.[45]

Perhaps in part because of previous experience as herdsmen in Africa, many blacks engaged in tanning and leatherwork. As early as 1574 there is a record of a free black setting up shop as a saddlemaker in Lima; and in the same year, Garci Hernández de Medinilla, a man of modest means and seemingly not connected with the business himself, listed two black leatherworkers among the six slaves in his will.[46] An unusual example of black participation in this trade involves the manufacture of sheepskin bags in which mercury was transported from the Huancavelica mine to the Upper Peruvian mining centers. In the seventeenth century the Crown let the transportation contract to private individuals, and among the expenses was the manufacture of the bags, which were purchased in lots of one dozen. Blacks were usually employed to make these bags at a wage of seven or eight reales per day. The bags must have been quite small and the process of the simplest, since incredibly large quantities were produced by few hands in a short period of time. In one instance, for example, a supervisor and four blacks turned out 24,000 in three days. The Crown was a steady customer, however, purchasing over 162,000 bags between 1612 and 1615 alone.[47]

Blacks also played an important part in the manufacture of wearing apparel and related items, though in this field (as in so many others) fear of competition on the part of Spanish artisans led to guild regulations barring persons of color from achieving the rank of master and thus, at least in theory, from owning a shop. In Lima, for example, this prohibition was adopted by the tailors and hosiers guild, the lacemakers and borderers guild, and the dyers guild. Little is known about the policies of guilds in other Peruvian cities, but in 1591 the tailors guild of Cuzco likewise excluded the black man.[48] The intention of these regulations was to use the skilled person of color where necessary, but to freeze him at journeyman status so as to leave the Spanish craftsman in control of the market. This policy was not uniformly successful, and in time colored artisans came to dominate many branches of the apparel trade. At least as early as 1590, for example, the city of Lima permitted blacks to work as cobblers, subject to examination and municipal approval, and by the late 1620's there were more than forty black and mulatto shoemakers working in their own shops in competition with twenty-four Spaniards and six mestizos. The situation was much the same among the tailors at this time, when Lima had over 100 black, mulatto, Indian, and mestizo "examined masters," as well as numbers of journeymen from these groups, as against only fifty Spaniards practicing the trade.[49]

African labor was also extensively employed in the manufacture of hats, but under quite different circumstances. Here, though there were some small entrepreneurs in the field, employing perhaps six or seven slaves,[50] the trend was to large operations and the specialization of labor. For example, the hat factory acquired in 1625 by Juan Bernardo Jaramillo employed thirty-one slaves: four framers, five beaters, nine carders, and thirteen fullers. The factory cost Jaramillo 14,764 pesos, 12,600 of which represented the value of the skilled blacks. In 1623

Antonio de Rivera Zambrano, who manufactured both hats and textiles in his mill in the San Lázaro district of Lima, and who marketed his products in Potosí, Cartagena, and Quito among other places, listed sixty-eight skilled slaves in his will: seventeen carders, eleven beaters, ten framers, and thirty fullers. According to Salinas y Córdova, Lima had eighteen hat factories in 1630, each employing from forty to a hundred blacks and "some Indians."[51] Clearly, there was little room for the independent colored artisan in the manufacture of hats.

In the Peruvian textile industry, the composition of the labor force was different still. Despite the Crown's prohibition of the use of native labor, Indians continued to manufacture most of the cloth produced in the colony, though many scattered references in surviving documentation indicate that black labor was important in some of the textile mills on the outskirts of Lima.[52] Since labor conditions in these establishments were notoriously bad, most of the blacks employed were almost certainly either slaves or convicts, not free persons of color.

With regard to the general distribution of blacks by craft, Lockhart, who has closely studied this question for the early colonial period, finds that they "were especially well represented in basic trades like carpentry and tailoring. A disproportionate number of Negro artisans were blacksmiths and swordsmiths, practitioners of those most basic trades of all, which made the whole Spanish conquest and occupation possible. All the trades involving mass production, like tanning or confectionery, needed and employed Negroes." In high-prestige trades like silversmithing and stonemasonry, however, the number of blacks fell off sharply.[53] This picture did not change much during the 1560-1650 period.

In the bills of sale I examined in the Peruvian notarial records, 121 slave artisans were involved. Their specializations were as follows:

Trade	No. of slaves	Trade	No. of slaves	Trade	No. of slaves
Tailor	16	Blacksmith	10	Carpenter	6
Sawer	12	Cobbler	9	Candlemaker	4
Bricklayer	12	Charcoal-maker	8	Hosier	3
Hatmaker	12	Leatherworker	8	Wheelwright	3

The group also included two potters, two carders, and two boilermakers. Each of the other slaves practiced a different trade, but none of their specializations fell outside the general categories I have been discussing (e.g., metalworking, wearing apparel, and construction).

Black artisans became increasingly numerous and increasingly important with every passing decade in the period before 1650, and no group was more responsible for this development than the Spanish craftsmen themselves. As Lockhart indicates, from the very beginning of the colonial period Spanish artisans purchased African and Indian slaves to increase their productivity, and many strained to do so even though they were not well established themselves. Some purchased high-priced blacks who already had the needed skills, but most saved themselves the expense by buying unskilled slaves and training them. Artisans quickly became one of the largest slaveholding groups in Peru, and blacks were vital to the operation of their shops in the early decades of Spanish Peru when craftsmen were still relatively few and the demand for their products high. Many Spanish artisans also made handsome profits in these early years by training units of slaves in a particular skill, most notably smithing, for sale to others, especially those in the more isolated areas of the new conquest. In 1554, for example, a Spanish smith sold a forge, two Spanish-born black ironworkers, and two African-born helpers to a lawyer bound for Chile for 2,000 pesos, a price sufficient to buy "a mansion or a ship." The Spanish craftsman's role of foreman and trainer became an increasingly important part of his operations as more and more Spaniards, seeing the profit to be made from the earnings of trained blacks, purchased either skilled slaves, to be hired out, or inexperienced lads to be farmed out as apprentices.[54]

Slaveholders with the most varied economic interests thought it to their advantage to own skilled blacks. To cite a few examples: Pedro de Saavedra y Aguilera, a hereditary councilman of the city of Huánuco, with investments there in urban real estate, agricultural properties, and livestock, owned Bartolomé de la Cruz, a black cobbler; Francisco Hernández Irola, who speculated in real estate, cloth, wax, and ecclesiastical tithes, owned Antón Mina, a journeyman bricklayer; and the cleric Alonso de Estrada, who produced wine in the Moquegua Valley, owned a mulatto tailor named Juan.[55] Less affluent slaveholders, and women in particular, were often quite dependent on the earnings of their skilled blacks. For example, in 1645 Doña Francisca de Chávez could list in her will little more than her Lima home (mortgaged for 1,000 pesos), some furniture, four female blacks and their children, and Lázaro Criollo, a cobbler.[56]

A relatively substantial investment was required to purchase a slave artisan in the marketplace. According to Emilio Harth-terré, a moderately skilled and healthy slave would have cost at minimum about 565 pesos in the sixteenth century, and slightly more, about 600 pesos, in the 1650's.[57] The data I gathered from Peruvian notarial records are in very rough and superficial agreement with this assertion; the average purchase price of the 121 skilled blacks in my sample, for instance, was 624 pesos. At the same time it is important to note that such averages obscure as much as they reveal. First, the prices paid for skilled blacks during this period fluctuated along the same general lines as those paid for unskilled males (see Appendix B), albeit at a higher level. My sample of skilled slaves, taken at five-year intervals, is too small to graph, particularly since prices paid for blacks varied sharply from skill to skill, but the purchase price of three black tailors, all in the 26-35 age bracket, will serve to illustrate these fluctuations: Juan Bañol went for 390 pesos in 1610, when the market was steady and perhaps stagnant; Sebastián Angola for 700 in 1620, when high prices again prevailed; and Antonio Enríquez for 550 in 1640, when the market was depressed.[58]

Still, the general balance between supply and demand did not alone determine price fluctuations. The age, health, and personality of the slave, his technical competence, the labor situation in his particular craft, and, ultimately, the prestige attached to his trade were also factors. Advancing age, particularly in combination with physical defects, sharply reduced the value of skilled slaves. In 1577, for example, when blacks who were of prime age and condition but unskilled were bringing an average price of 390 pesos, a black tailor named Juan de Valenzuela was sold for a mere 300-odd pesos, primarily because he was forty-five years old and had a hernia. Older slaves, however skilled, were commonly sold for less than 200 pesos.[59] During this period, most black artisans were sold fully guaranteed against moral defects; any who were not were usually sold at a reduced price.[60] The question of technical competence, though rarely discussed in bills of sale, probably played a considerable part in determining a slave's price. In 1650, for example, and admittedly in a period of rising prices, the bricklayer Juan Angola was sold for the handsome sum of 700 pesos despite his fifty years and his owner's refusal to certify his good health or character.[61] Moreover, it is possible to discern a rough hierarchy of desirable skills among slave artisans. With some consistency black carpenters, potters, and metalworkers were purchased for prices ranging between

1,000 and 2,000 pesos, and other craftsmen for substantially lower amounts, though bricklayers, smiths, and leatherworkers occasionally commanded such sums.[62] Finally, some buyers and sellers of skilled blacks unquestionably drove harder bargains than others, and the occasional master, hard-pressed for cash, may have been forced to sell his slave at an artificially low price. In short, though generalizations are difficult, one can safely say that slave artisans of assured good health and character could not be had during this period for much less than 500 pesos, and that quite often prices were considerably higher.

Even at these prices, the purchase of a skilled black was a profitable investment, and this despite the fact that only the exceptional colored artisan could equal the earning power of his Spanish counterpart. According to the calculations of Harth-terré and Márquez Abanto, which agree with my own findings, a common black laborer earned approximately four reales, a journeyman as much as twelve reales, and an excellent "master" (in fact if not in name) twenty reales for a day's work (usually twelve hours). That is, skilled blacks in the last two categories earned in the neighborhood of 37.5 and 62.5 pesos a month, respectively, if we use the royal formula of five holidays in every thirty-day interval. Clearly, there was much individual variation. Highly skilled blacks, such as those employed by the royal shipyards, earned considerably higher wages than these during much of the period, and a colored artisan of mediocre talents would probably have been paid less than the going rate in any given craft. In general, however, this scale of wages appears to be roughly accurate and was relatively steady until 1650.

Assuming that a skilled slave earned fourteen reales a day and accepting Harth-terré's estimate that it cost between 1.25 and 1.5 reales a day to feed a black, an owner paying the average purchase price I suggested—624 pesos—could have recovered his money in as little as seventeen months or so. There were other, minor costs to be sure, for clothing and the like, and also risks—of heavy medical expenses or, worse still, of the loss of the black through sickness or accident.[63] But for all that, the investment was sound. With good luck, the master of a skilled black could count on making almost pure profit on his slave in less than two years.

Throughout the period under study Spanish artisans continued to purchase and train blacks for their own use and for sale to colleagues and investors. More and more, however, Spanish craftsmen also taught their skills to slaves who belonged to others, and even free persons of color, under formal apprenticeship contracts. This arrangement was beneficial to all concerned. The Spaniard who wanted to own a skilled slave or two was spared the stiff cash outlay this would require in the marketplace. Instead, he could buy a likely-looking lad for a few hundred pesos or even select a candidate from among the slaves he already owned, apprentice him out to a Spanish artisan, and after a few years, enjoy the handsome wages earned by a competent journeyman. In some instances slaves were apprenticed before liberation so they would have a means of livelihood. In others, blacks were sent to learn a highly paid skill so they could purchase their freedom with a portion of their earnings. And in still others, illegitimate colored children were sent into apprenticeship by their Spanish fathers in order to have some sort of stake in the world.[64]

Many Afro-Peruvians were quick to perceive the advantages of apprenticeship and careers as craftsmen, if not for themselves, at least for their descendants. In 1605, for example, Mateo Casanga, a slave himself, managed with his master's permission to apprentice his thirteen-year-old free black son to a hatmaker for four years. Much more common were cases of free colored mothers arranging for their minor children to learn a craft. In 1581, for example, Francisca Ortiz, mulatto and widowed, apprenticed her nine-year-old son to the prominent builder Francisco de Gamarra for six years. Doubtless here, as in many other cases, the object was not only to relieve the mother of a financial burden but also to try to ensure the child a reasonably bright future. Moreover, some parents unquestionably looked to this as a way to provide for their own economic security in old age.[65]

Numbers of adult free persons of color also entered apprenticeship. Some were forced into it by the authorities, who were anxious to see this group gainfully employed and paying tribute, but many more probably did so by choice. The economic and social advantages must have been obvious to those with any knowledge of the Spanish world. In a society where educational opportunity, membership in the prestigious professions, and bureaucratic position was denied to all but the lightest and luckiest of African descent, the crafts promised financial security and some standing in the community.[66]

An examination of apprenticeship contracts for sixty-nine blacks concluded during the period under study sheds considerable light on the kind of people who sought instruction in the crafts and the circumstances that surrounded their training. Thirty-one of the sixty-nine were slaves who were apprenticed by their masters; the rest were free persons of color. Twelve of these had apprenticed themselves. The remaining twenty-six were sent into apprenticeship by others as follows: by a free mother, ten; by a judge in charge of orphans, seven; by a municipal judge, four; by free parents, two; by tax tribute commissioners, two; by a slave father, one. Most of the group, some 71 per cent, entered just four crafts: tailoring (twenty-five), shoemaking (twelve), carpentry (seven), and bricklaying (five). The other twenty entered a wide variety of trades, including metalwork, lacemaking, hatmaking, and locksmithing. Training being plainly best accomplished at an early age, the vast majority of apprentices were young: of the fifty-one who can be classified by age, twenty-six were fifteen years old or under and only eleven were over twenty-one. The length of the contract varied in rough accordance with the age of the black, the difficulty of the craft, and the amount of any previous training. Most of these agreements (sixty-one) were for four years or less, though a few ran for as long as eight years.

In general, the contracts concluded during this period involved blacks who possessed no formal training in the craft. Consequently, the question of salary was not raised under many of the agreements; the apprentice simply received instruction and eventually journeyman's status, and the craftsman in turn got the services of an increasingly competent assistant. The material wants of the apprentice, however, were invariably provided for. Typical in this regard was the 1615 agreement between the free mulatto Pedro Luis de Vivenos and Juan de Castro, a carpenter.[67] Under the terms of this contract, which was to run for two and a half years, Castro was to teach Vivenos his craft to the best of his knowledge, provide him with room, board, and medical care, furnish him with a meticulously specified amount of clothing, both during and at the termination of the contract, and equip him, at the end of his training, with the minimum number of tools necessary to practice the profession of carpentry. This contract varies only in minor details from forty-nine others in the sample.

Nineteen of the agreements, however, did involve monetary compensation, and it seems reasonable to assume that most of the blacks concerned already possessed the rudiments of their trade and were apprenticed, or apprenticed themselves, for further refinement of their skills. Even so, the sums agreed on were usually modest, amounting at best to 120 pesos a year; in most cases the apprentices received in addition the same provision for their maintenance as specified in the Vivenos contract above. In rare instances, only board in addition to salary was specified, and in one contract an apprentice agreed to work for a flat fourteen pesos a month and provide for his own support.

By and large Spanish artisans were willing to instruct both slaves and free persons of color in their crafts. In the first place, as more and more slaveholders sought training for their blacks, and with many free coloreds anxious to be taken on as apprentices, the Spanish artisan could count on a steady stream of apprentices and avoid investing his own capital in slave assistants. Moreover, in some instances skilled Spaniards could obtain valuable contracts only if they agreed to provide on-the-job instruction. Such was the case in 1650, when the contract to rebuild the Mercedarian monastery in Cuzco, destroyed by an earthquake, provided that the contractor teach the craft of stonecutting to the Africans and Indians attached to the institution.[68] In any event, it appears that save for a few men with large operations (notably in the manufacture of hats and tile) who may more properly be called entrepreneurs, the Spanish artisan class in proportion to their numbers did not possess many more slave assistants in 1650 than they had at the beginning of the colonial period, and perhaps even slightly less. The widespread apprenticeship of persons of color in large part accounts for this fact. However, as we have seen in the case of silverworking and the apparel trade, many Spanish guilds attempted to confine the skilled black to the rank of journeyman. Prompted by fear of competition, greed, and racial prejudice, these efforts were most successful in high-prestige occupations such as silversmithing and printing,[69] and in industries such as hatmaking where the trend was to large-scale operations and heavy capital investment.

On the whole the government was sympathetic to the stand of the Spanish artisans; guild regulations that excluded persons of African descent from the rank of master usually received viceregal approval. Moreover, whenever the government itself was in a position to regulate wages, white craftsmen were usually favored over blacks. We have already seen an example of this practice in the wage scales at the royal shipyards. This is far from being an isolated case. Consider, for example, Viceroy Toledo's ordinance of 1572 establishing a scale of prices on the goods and services of Cuzco's artisans, which expressly provided that Spaniards could fix higher prices than blacks, mulattoes, and Indians. Similarly, the Lima city council, in an effort to hold down building costs after the disastrous 1586 earthquake, decreed that Spanish bricklayers could charge no more than four pesos daily, and black bricklayers no more than two.[70] In addition, ostensibly to protect public health and safety, the authorities occasionally barred persons of color from all participation in certain crafts. In 1572, for example, the Lima city council forbade blacks to dispense, prepare, or recommend medicines in apothecary shops on the grounds that they confused the prescriptions of doctors and dispensed remedies laden with opium in place of "other healthful medicines."[71]

In the long run, however, many guilds discovered that their discriminatory policies were negated by forces beyond their control. For one thing, those who had skilled slaves were interested in their own profits, and guild attempts to monopolize the rank of master meant little to them. In consequence, many slaveholders, despite the protests of guilds and occasional official expressions of apprehension, allowed their skilled and trusted blacks every liberty short of freedom. Lockhart cites the example of two slave artisans who were allowed to run their own shop in Arequipa in 1550 and to share part of the returns with their respective owners, and points to another case in which a black carpenter formed a company, perhaps as the senior partner, with a Spanish counterpart. These practices continued in later decades. With the permission of their masters, skilled slaves signed contracts, opened shops, and even lived apart, as did a mulatto bricklayer who in 1610 rented his own home in Lima from no less a personage than the chief accountant of the royal treasury.[72] Needless to say, free colored artisans were equally independent in their operations.

Spanish craftsmen might have been more successful in their attempts at monopolization if they had been able to satisfy colonial demand for their products. As we have seen, however, this was frequently not the case, and colored artisans moved in to take up the slack. In these circumstances the protests of Spaniards sometimes failed to convince even the normally partisan colonial authorities. A notable example was the unsuccessful attempt of the Spanish carpenters of Lima to exclude black masters. This effort began in 1555, when the city council was petitioned to bar both free and slave blacks from using the title and setting up shop on the grounds there were already over twenty Spanish carpenters in the city with wives and children to support. The council was unimpressed and provided merely that blacks could not practice carpentry without proving their skill through examination. Twenty years later, the Spanish carpenters of Lima again turned to the council, complaining that many blacks and mulattoes who knew nothing of the craft had set up shop and were defrauding many people through their shoddy workmanship. The authorities were urged to organize the carpenters into a guild and to make provision for an examiner to screen applicants for membership. The council granted this request, and specifically forbade blacks and mulattoes to practice the trade without license from the city.

These regulations did not hamper the rise of black carpenters, and by 1590 persons of color were routinely practicing the trade on passage of the examination. Moreover, the Lima examiner could not prevent persons of color who already had the title of master from practicing in the capital. For example, in 1609 the mulatto carpenter Miguel Jerónimo testified before the city council that he had been awarded the title of master in Spain and had operated a shop there for a number of years. The council gave him a license to practice in Lima and the authority to employ the journeymen and apprentices he needed for his operations.[73]

In short, the authorities were not prepared to accede to the wishes of Spanish artisans for the exclusion of colored masters where supply could not keep up with demand, and this may have been even more true of the provincial cities of Peru than it was of the capital. In time the Spanish artisans themselves may even have realized that there was more than enough work to go around. The tailors guild of Lima, for example, made no effort to stop the operations of their black competitors, and Spanish masons and stonecutters seemingly did not object to the several lucrative contracts that went to the mulatto Francisco de Gamarra.

Although the artisan of African descent was subject to prejudice and discrimination, it is also true that relations between the races in the crafts appear to have been amicable. Indeed, perhaps in no other area of endeavor did Spaniard, African, and Indian work together so closely, on so wide a scale, and under such relatively equal terms. Spanish arti-

sans accepted apprentices of all colors simultaneously, and black artisans who came through the apprenticeship system, guided by European
techniques and taste in their work, living and working in close proximity
with their supervisors and fellows, must have been among the most
Spanish of all Afro-Peruvians.

It should also be emphasized that colored masters instructed apprentices, and not merely members of their own race but Spaniards and
Indians as well. Apparently, there was little friction. We may point, for
example, to the cases of the mulatto carpenter Mateo Roque, who in
1598 took on as an apprentice a seventeen-year-old lad from Barcelona;
and of Juan Yopo, an Indian, who was apprenticed to the mulatto
master Bartolomé Tello during the same period. Black artisans also
found themselves in the somewhat curious position of instructing slave
apprentices, as in the case of Francisco de Gamarra, mentioned many
times previously, who agreed to train Francisco Biafara in the finer
points of masonry. Similarly, Luis de Lagama, a mulatto slave later
manumitted by his mistress and the father of Diego de Lagama, a prominent housebuilder in seventeenth-century Lima, received his training
as a bricklayer from Lorenzo de la Cruz, likewise a mulatto. Occasionally, even slave artisans gave instruction. For example, Antón de Monzón, slave and bricklayer, took on a fellow slave, Gaspar Zape, as an
apprentice.[74]

Finally, a few words about the origins of Afro-Peruvian artisans. In
the beginning, colored artisans who had been trained on the Iberian
Peninsula were quite prominent in Peru. According to the sample taken
by Lockhart, they constituted approximately one-third of the artisans
of African descent, "with the rest distributed quite normally among the
African groups and creoles of the Indies." In later years, too, indeed
throughout the period under study, Peninsula-trained black artisans
continued to practice their crafts in Peru. Francisco de Gamarra, for
example, the son of a slave, had received both his training and his freedom in the Old World before arriving in Peru in 1576.[75] Increasingly,
however, the artisan ranks were swelled by blacks born in Africa, in
other American colonies, and in Peru itself. Only four of the 121 skilled
slaves in my sample, for instance, were born in Spain. The majority,
eighty-seven (or nearly 72 per cent) were born in Africa; twenty were
born either in Peru (thirteen) or in other American colonies (seven); and
the birthplaces of ten cannot be identified.

An interesting point emerges from this classification, namely, that the Spanish preference for the so-called Guinea black was apparently not carried over into the selection of slaves for training in the crafts. Of the eighty-seven African-born artisans, 48 per cent were from Senegambia and Guinea-Bissau, 18 per cent from other West African regions, and 33 per cent from Central and Southern Africa. These proportions differ very little from the proportions of the three groups in the marketplace, which stood at approximately 55, 12, and 33 per cent, respectively (see Tables 1 and 2, Chapter 2). There is even stronger evidence that the Guinea slave was not so highly esteemed in the crafts as he was in other fields in the origins of the craftsmen employed at the royal shipyards. In the years 1587-1640, as was noted, the Crown employed 377 skilled slaves at the shipyards. Of the 278 whose origins can be identified, 227 were born in Africa, and 42.7 per cent of these came from Senegambia and Guinea-Bissau, 9.7 per cent from other West African regions, and the remaining 47.6 per cent from Central and Southern Africa. In short, blacks from Central and Southern Africa, usually with the surnames Congo and Angola, were represented in the crafts in equal or greater proportion to their numbers in the market. A larger sample, analyzed on a craft-by-craft and tribe-by-tribe basis, might yield different results, but for the moment one must agree with the conclusion of Lockhart: "An even spread among the African ethnic groups shows that no one group proved to be more adept or inept at Spanish artisanry than the others."[76]

If Afro-Peruvian artisans are studied solely on the above evidence, one is left with the picture of an overwhelmingly African-born group held in bondage for the benefit of their masters and little different from their unskilled counterparts. However, an analysis of apprenticeship contracts signed during this period reveals an emerging group of black artisans whose composition was radically different in several respects. First, thirty-eight of the sixty-nine contracts (55 per cent) involved free persons of color. Second, only two of the apprentices were African-born. The great majority of the would-be artisans were not only criollos, but at least forty-seven were also of mixed blood: mulattoes, zambos, and quadroons. In short, the makeup of the unskilled and skilled components of the black labor force began to diverge markedly in the decades before 1650. The unskilled labor pool continued to be characterized by slavery and by constant fresh importation from Africa to maintain demographic stability. In the arts and crafts, however, the data of the apprenticeship contracts and much of the other information presented in this chapter argue that more and more colored artisans were free men, Peruvian-born, and of mixed blood, perhaps the most Hispanicized and advantaged of all Afro-Peruvians, and a substantial part of the growing free colored population that will be studied in more detail in later chapters.

In conclusion, it seems no exaggeration to state that the black artisan through his skill contributed quite as significantly to the colonial economy as did the black engaged in agricultural or household service. Although his numbers were smaller, the black who built the towns and the ships, who fashioned the furniture, and who made the garments and the shoes, was as vital to Peruvian development as the African who harvested sugarcane or grapes. As a group, Spanish craftsmen would no doubt have preferred to consign the skilled African to permanent journeyman status, to take the lion's share of the fruits of his labor for themselves, but in general opposing economic forces were always too strong. The labor of the skilled black was too much in demand, and his potential wages too high, for monopolization by the guild system; and once ownership of black artisans was diffused in society the occasional fulminations of Spanish craftsmen counted for little. Finally, the arts and crafts provided an ideal means for the cultural assimilation of at least a limited number of persons of color. More important, from the point of view of the Afro-Peruvian, the skilled trades allowed many black and mixed bloods to better their own lives and those of their descendants.

CHAPTER SEVEN

The Control of the African: Crime and Sedition

From the beginnings of Spanish colonization in America, the control of the African slave was of concern to both slaveholders and the authorities. The slaveholder lost a sizable investment when a black fled his service or was killed in a street brawl, and recapturing a slave or paying the fines for his misconduct involved considerable expense. From the point of view of the civil authorities, blacks were unruly and thievish in the towns, overbearing with the Indians, and, as bands of runaways, menacing to agriculture in the countryside and to trade along the highways. The very existence of a large slave population was deplored by more than one government official as a potential threat to the authority of the state. Further, the passage of time brought ever-larger numbers of free blacks, mulattoes, mestizos, and other racial mixtures, groups that in many cases were economically and socially deprived, accountable to no master, and alarming additions to an already turbulent society. To these internal threats to security was added the pressure brought to bear on the American empire by the enemies of Spain, foes who more than once attempted to gain military advantage by fomenting a slave rebellion with vague promises of freedom and a better tomorrow. For all these reasons, most Spaniards agreed on the need to keep a watchful eye on the black and brown masses of Peru, though there was much special pleading and disagreement on method.

As we saw in Chapter 2, in part official apprehension was based on religious considerations; it was feared that the Indians would be exposed to the false beliefs of the Africans, thereby hampering the work of Catholic missionaries. However, the threat of slave insurrection was also taken seriously. In 1516, for example, the government briefly suspended the importation of Africans for the express reason that the slaves, as men "without honor and without faith and thus capable of betrayals and disturbances," might become sufficiently numerous to impose on the Spanish "the same chains that they have borne."[1] Colonial demand for African labor soon caused this prohibition to be lifted, but the fears that had prompted the decree were quickly demonstrated to be valid. The first slave uprising in Spanish America, in Hispaniola in 1522, was a relatively minor affair. There followed, however, four major disturbances in the colonies in the next fifteen years, capped by an African conspiracy in Mexico in 1537, and serious consideration came to be given to the suspension of slave importation. A new element of danger was added when Spanish communities with large slave populations became subject to foreign intrusion. The French privateers were the first to hit on the idea that African slaves, if promised freedom, might assist in the looting and seizure of the islands and mainland settlements of the Caribbean area. A practical demonstration occurred in 1538, when French corsairs in league with African slaves sacked the town of Havana. In succeeding years, this incident was forgotten by neither the Spanish nor their European antagonists.[2]

These disturbances prompted considerable remedial legislation, and one of the Crown's favorite devices was to exclude certain types or groups of slaves from the Americas. Early efforts along these lines were religious in emphasis; only slaves born in the power of Christians (i.e., on the Iberian Peninsula) could go to the colonies, but, perhaps when it was realized that this measure would severely limit supply, another decree merely barred any blacks who were suspected of exposure to Islamic influence. By the 1520's the laws of exclusion were being directed more and more at blacks who might foment unrest and rebellion. One of the first groups touched by this legislation was the previously favored ladino slaves. In 1526 the Crown, holding that the ladinos were responsible for most of the disturbances in the Americas, corrupting the "pacific and obedient" blacks imported directly from Africa, decreed that they could not be taken to the New World without special license. By 1532 the tune had changed, and the Crown now blamed slave unrest on the Gelofes (Wolofs), who had acquired a reputation for insubordination and rebelliousness. Mulatto slaves became the next targets for royal ire, perhaps because many were suspected of Moorish ancestry and therefore of exposure to Islam, and in 1543 their entrance into

Spanish America was forbidden without express royal license. None of these measures was completely effective, in large part because vigorous enforcement was lacking. An even more fruitless venture was Charles V's attempt to limit the black population to a ratio of one to every three whites.[3]

During this same period the various governors and town councils of Spanish America adopted their own measures aimed at slave control, and from time to time the Crown attempted to bring some empire-wide order to this tangle of legislation. In 1535, for example, it barred all blacks from carrying weapons, and in 1542, in a decree directed to the cities of Panama and Nombre de Dios that soon received wider application, municipalities were allowed to adopt suitable measures to keep persons of color off the streets at night.[4]

Somewhere around 1545, to cap these efforts, the government issued a set of ordinances that probably codified and sanctioned much existing local law and practice. This legislation was divided into two sections, one commanding good treatment and instruction in the language and the faith, the other establishing the restrictions and precautions to be observed and enforced by slaveholders and the civil authorities. The section that dealt with the policing of the slave population reiterated the prohibition against the bearing of arms, and further stated that slaves were not to ride horses or go from one place to another without written permission. General application was given to the 1542 decree for Panama, under which blacks were forbidden to be out after dark under penalty of twenty lashes. Masters were enjoined to employ white majordomos to control their slaves, and particularly to count them every night to prevent runaways. In addition, the ordinances commanded that no one give aid or shelter to black criminals. Violation of any of the regulations carried heavy penalties.[5]

It is against this general background of concern over the African in the Americas that one must consider Peruvian legislation on the subject, since those Spaniards who flocked to the new conquest from the West Indies, Panama, and Mexico carried with them not only their slaves but also their memories of black uprisings. With the consolidation of conquest, many of these men took their places on the municipal councils (*cabildos*) of the newly created towns, and these bodies, with the assistance of the viceroy and the Audiencia and with the approval of the Crown, produced legislation relating to the colored population that equaled or exceeded in volume that emanating from Spain. It is therefore important to study the thrust of municipal law, continually supplemented by measures adopted by royal agencies of government, as directed toward the control of those of African descent.[6]

The city of Jauja, founded by Pizarro in 1533, was probably the first Peruvian municipality to legislate on the subject of African slavery. No copy of the Jauja ordinances has survived, but this legislation appears to have had great influence on the authorities of Lima, founded a few short years later, on January 18, 1535. Lima was in fact less than three months old when the cabildo began to legislate on the subject of slave control. First, a curfew for blacks was established at two hours after sundown. Unless in the company of his master, a black found in the streets after this hour was to receive 100 lashes for the first offense, to lose his genitals for the second, and to be exiled from the city for the third. The last punishment, which threatened to deprive the master of his slave's services, was intended to force slaveholders to take the curfew seriously. If a Spaniard apprehended a slave roaming free at night, he had the right to cart him off to jail, and in case of resistance, to kill him. The authorities also ruled that no slave might take up arms against a Spaniard, except in defense of his master, under penalty of death. Finally, they set a punishment of 100 lashes for any black who left the city without permission from the authorities, who took fodder or corn from the Indians (or used natives to carry these commodities), or who entered the native market (*tiangues*).[7]

In the following decades the control of the black slave continued to concern those who governed Peru, and perhaps no aspect of this problem received more attention than that of Afro-Indian relations. On this issue the home government and its colonial representatives were in the legislative vanguard, at least in part because the municipal councils of Peru were sympathetic to the conquistadores and encomenderos, men more interested in profiting from the Indian than in protecting him. Many considerations moved the Crown to action. First, the African all too often emulated his Spanish master in cowing and mistreating the Indian, and the government was determined to give substance to the superior legal status of the Indian as a free vassal of the Crown. Equally pernicious in the eyes of the authorities were the bad habits, such as gambling and drinking, that the natives allegedly picked up as a result of contact with blacks. The Crown was also grimly opposed to sexual unions between the two groups, relationships that were often characterized by rape and illegitimacy and that produced the zambo, a racial type who was difficult to assimilate into the colonial social structure. Finally, there was the danger that Africans and Indians might suppress their mutual hostility and make common cause against their Spanish overlords. To prevent these evils, the Crown consistently favored harsh penalties for Africans who mistreated the Indians and tried at the same time to hold contact between the two races to a minimum.

To this end the Crown in 1536 established 100 lashes as the standard punishment for any black who mistreated a native, except in cases involving bodily harm, where the punishment was to be determined by the gravity of the crime. In such cases, the slaveholder was responsible for all court costs; and a free person of color so convicted could even be sold into slavery if need be to meet these costs.[8] The government returned to the issue in 1541. In response to reports that African slaves coerced Indians of both sexes into their service, stole their possessions, and killed those who resisted, particularly native women reluctant to accede to their "base intentions," the Crown proposed to ban Africans from Indian pueblos. However, the administrative chaos engendered by the civil wars prevented any meaningful action, and the situation was as bad at the end of the decade as it had been at the beginning. In 1549, for example, Pedro de la Gasca, triumphant in the contest against Gonzalo Pizarro, expressed his concern about the Spanish adventurers and their black slaves who wandered about the colony oppressing the Indians. Abuses continued even around the capital, as indicated by a resolution of the Lima cabildo of the same year ordering one of the municipal magistrates to spend every Saturday in Callao hearing Indian complaints of mistreatment by Africans and Spaniards.[9]

Once the Crown had cowed the conquistadores, it moved to establish control over the native population, and Afro-Indian relations received particular attention. In general, the government frowned on mutilation as a punishment for a slave's criminal behavior, an attitude that was expressed in the 1545 ordinances concerning the control of the African. In 1551, however, this scruple was set aside in the case of blacks who impressed natives into their service. When the offender was a man and his victim an Indian woman, sexual violation was presumed, and the punishment was to be castration; otherwise, the black was to be given 100 lashes. A black woman was to get 100 lashes for her first conviction

negros hurtan plata desus amos
para enganar alas yñsputas
y las negras criollas hurtan
para seruir asus galanes es
pañoles y negros

cay micudqyn

apomaycono

Fig. 4. A black slave approaching an Indian prostitute with silver
stolen from his master

and was to have her ears cut off if there was a recurrence. Free persons of color of both sexes faced the lash on the first offense and exile on the second. Masters who allowed their slaves to lord it over the Indians in this fashion were to be fined 100 pesos.[10] In the same year, the Crown directed the Lima Audiencia to ponder its previous proposal that black slaves be barred entirely from native towns. This was soon followed with the suggestion that special constables might be appointed for this purpose, as well as to prevent general African mistreatment of the Indian. This proposal was debated in government circles into the 1560's.[11]

In the end the idea of constables was dropped in favor of an official with still wider responsibilities: the *corregidor de pueblos de indios,* who possessed broad political and judicial powers over the Indian villages in his district. The process of dividing the native areas of Peru into districts with a corregidor for each was begun during the administration of Governor Lope García de Castro (1564-69), and was greatly expanded and codified in the following decade under Viceroy Toledo.[12] One of the prime responsibilities of the *corregidor de indios* was to hold Afro-Indian contact to a minimum, both to protect the natives against the high-handed exactions of the blacks and to slow the pace of racial mixture, and a stream of legislation was issued in the 1560's and 1570's to bolster the legal position of this official. Among other measures, Indians of whatever social class were forbidden to own African slaves or to gamble with persons of color; blacks who belonged to encomenderos were forbidden to molest the native population; and Indians were given the right to arrest blacks and mulattoes who committed crimes in their villages and to take them to the corregidor for punishment.[13]

Yet with all these tools, the *corregidores de indios* were singularly unsuccessful in carrying out the Crown's Afro-Indian policy, as demonstrated by royal instructions of 1578, 1580, 1587, 1589, 1595, 1596, 1603, 1639, 1646, and 1647 reminding them of their responsibilities in this regard.[14] Part of the difficulty, according to Viceroy Enríquez, was that encomenderos and other Spaniards who had dealings with the natives customarily took their black slaves along to assist them. To forbid this practice, which was common in both Peru and Mexico, seemed unjust to the viceroy. All the same, he could not deny that despite the authorities' best efforts the natives often suffered as a result.[15] Pedro Serrano, who served as priest in the pueblo of Chilani in Chucuito province, was more explicit in his condemnation of the encomenderos.

He informed the Crown in 1609 that they were forcing Indians to serve their black slaves, and that these blacks obliged the unfortunate natives to weave large quantities of cloth for them, which they sold for handsome profits when they accompanied their masters to the cities.[16]

Worse still, if the testimony of numerous witnesses can be believed, many corregidores were negligent, if not downright malicious, in the face of these abuses. In 1607, for example, one observer lamented that the mulattoes and mestizos, so large, disorderly, and factious a group as to cause the authorities to discourage their residence in Spanish towns, had in consequence lodged themselves in the Indian villages, living there "with such insolence that there is not an Indian male who has wife, child, or sister, or possessions, that he can call his own." Far from being punished for their crimes, according to this observer, they were favored by the corregidores, priests, and native nobles, who used these castes as unsalaried employees in their own business dealings. In this fashion, everyone profited at the expense of the Indian commoner.[17] Poma de Ayala, writing in the early seventeenth century, likewise bitterly condemned the black slaves of corregidores and encomenderos, who at times raped Indian women, married and unmarried alike, and at others stole from their masters or from the Indians in order to buy sexual favors. Both their Spanish masters and the authorities winked at this state of affairs, and in Poma's view many Indian women had become little more than concubines for the slaves of corregidores, encomenderos, and even village priests. To remedy this situation, Poma advocated discouraging Afro-Indian sexual contact, even if graced by marriage, by making it punishable by exile, and urged that it be made illegal for a Spaniard to have an unmarried black man in an Indian village. Further, all persons of color should be kept in at night, and "in the countryside they should not live alone, even though free, because they are evil people."[18] Clearly, the best efforts of the Crown and its representatives were insufficient to prevent the African, often with the connivance of his master, from assuming a position in Peruvian society superior to that of the Indian, in fact if not in law.

Even more government attention was given to the control of the numerous blacks who resided in or near the Spanish cities and towns, but here, too, official zeal was forced to compromise with colonial reality. A particularly sensitive issue was the bearing of arms by persons of color. In the early years of the colony, armed blacks, most often in cloak-and-sword costume, were a common sight on the streets of Lima and other Peruvian towns. However, in 1538, perhaps in response to the royal decree of 1535, the Lima city council prohibited persons of color from carrying weapons except in the company of their masters, and eleven years later it even barred this practice, though blacks were still allowed to wear cloaks, a coveted item of wearing apparel. Presumably, other Peruvian municipalities followed Lima's example. Yet it is evident that these efforts fell short of complete success, for in succeeding decades viceroys, Audiencias, and the Lima authorities again and again forbade persons of color to carry weapons under penalties that ranged from the lash for the first offense to castration and even death for repeated violations.

To be sure, it was always necessary to make some exceptions, and even in the early seventeenth century an observer noted that certain slaves still carried arms: "Some blacks of *oidores* [members of the Audiencia] and captains and other ministers of justice are allowed to carry swords, and blacks who go to the woodlands for firewood and to the countryside for fodder are allowed a knife, as are the muleteers."[19] But the authorities found it very difficult to restrict the bearing of arms to just these cases. Many Peruvian gentlemen, seeing the armed lackeys who surrounded high government officials, thirsted to have similar escorts and prevailed on the viceroys to grant them permits to arm their slaves. Once the granting of such exemptions was begun, the practice was difficult to control, to the point where some free persons of color were also granted the privilege of bearing arms.

Even the increased danger of foreign attack did not bring about lasting reform. Indeed, it seems to have had the reverse effect. In the 1620's, for example, the Lima city council, which had so often fulminated against the possession of weapons by persons of color in the past, now asked the Crown to let municipal judges and law enforcement officers have an armed black escort, just as their royal counterparts had. In 1637 the members of the council were given the right to be accompanied by two armed blacks in the course of their duties on condition that the city made a 2,000-ducat donation to the Crown, but the council's request that the privilege be extended to minor municipal functionaries was ignored. Meanwhile, it is clear that men of influence continued to wheedle similar privileges from the viceroys, and that persons of color, both free and slave, still carried weapons, for as late as the 1650's Viceroy Salvatierra was prodded by Crown and Audiencia to try once more to disarm all blacks and mulattoes because of the "continual quarrels, disturbances, and deaths" that negligence of the prohibition had occasioned.[20]

To discourage disorder and crime, the authorities also attempted to regulate the movements, actions, and morals of the colored population, but as the repetitiveness of the legislation on the subject attests, without any great success. As we have seen, the city of Lima imposed a curfew on blacks as early as 1535, a measure confirmed by the Crown in 1551, restated by Viceroy Cañete in 1560, and enforced with some pretense at regularity during the remainder of the period under study. By day, to control theft and prostitution, as early as 1548 masters were forbidden to allow their slaves to wander about looking for work, and on several occasions shopkeepers were ordered not to buy merchandise from blacks without the written consent of the slaveholder. By the last decade of the sixteenth century, however, officials appear to have taken either a more relaxed or a more realistic view, and pulperos were allowed to accept pawned goods in payment of wares from persons of color who could properly identify themselves. Indeed, after several black women had been arrested under the 1548 vagrancy statute in 1636, the Lima city council even thought to ask the viceroy to suspend this legislation, arguing that many poor Spaniards depended on the earnings of slaves who could find no work without seeking it in the streets. The viceroy appears to have taken no action.[21]

Efforts were also made to restrict the blacks' freedom of assembly. In 1549, for example, the Lima city council forbade blacks to gather in groups, except in the religious brotherhood recently founded for them, and then only in the cathedral at specified times. This measure was allowed to lapse, and in 1574 the city heard testimony concerning the well-attended weddings, wakes, and baptisms held among the colored population, where "they eat and drink and become drunk, with the result that several are usually killed or wounded, and where they plan robberies and other crimes." In response, the cabildo banned gatherings of more than ten colored men under pain of 200 lashes and loss of the privilege of wearing a cape, if that had been granted. This measure was unrealistically harsh, and blacks were soon permitted to assemble for religious devotions and even for such secular diversions as dances, though the authorities took some care to determine the length and lo-

cation of these gatherings.[22] Since drunkenness was considered to be
the root cause of much black criminal behavior, several attempts were
made in the sixteenth century to prohibit the consumption of wine by
the colored population, but with little or no success. The usually reliable Poma de Ayala, for example, mentioned the "very great drunkards"
whom he observed among the slaves, and it seems reasonable to assume
that there was some connection between criminality, addiction to alcohol, and the miserable lives led by many Afro-Peruvians.[23]

As early as the first decade of settlement free persons of color were
numerous enough in Lima to cause official concern. For the most part,
these groups were subject to the same restrictions placed on slaves,
though penalties for violation were usually less harsh. In addition, free
coloreds were suspected of contributing to slave delinquency, usually
by conspiring with and hiding thieves and runaways in their homes, a
charge that Lockhart considers "undeniable."[24] This consideration,
which was probably of greater importance than the economic one during the early years of colonization, prompted no less than five attempts
between 1539 and 1560 to force the "many" free persons of color in
Lima to hire themselves out to, and live with, Spanish employers, or
as a minimum measure of control to register their place of residence
with the city council.

The viceroys, too, grappled with the problem of the free colored population. As we have seen, the first Marqués de Cañete thought the answer was to settle free blacks and mulattoes in the gold fields of the
remote province of Carabaya, which had the merit of both isolating
these elements and putting them to useful labor. The settlement was
denounced by some as nothing more than a potential shelter for runaway slaves, and it did not live up to official expectations in other
respects. In consequence, Cañete devoted the last years of his tenure to
the capital city. This led, eventually, to his order of October 12, 1560,
instructing the free coloreds of Lima to give up their homes and take
residence with Spanish employers within eight days; only free black
women married to Spaniards were exempted from the edict. Viceroy
Nieva issued a decree in 1563 extending this policy to the entire colony,
only to have the order set aside by the Audiencia of Charcas after an
appeal by the free coloreds of that area, and here the matter seems to
have rested for several years.[25]

With the advent of Francisco de Toledo as viceroy in 1569, the control of the colored population was again taken up in official circles. Toledo's zeal for the gainful employment of free blacks and mulattoes was in large part inspired by his wish to reduce the Indians' labor burdens. But the viceroy was also genuinely alarmed by the number of free persons of African descent, and he prodded the municipal councils of Lima and Cuzco to control this element of the population. Indeed, he framed ordinances for Cuzco in 1572 in which he tackled the problem of free blacks hiding thieves and runaways in their homes and ruled that henceforth only colored artisans could live apart; all other free persons of color were either to hire themselves out to Spanish employers within thirty days or to leave the city.

Meanwhile, in the same year Toledo's own seat of government, Lima, admitted the failure of its previous efforts by repeating—for at least the sixth time since the beginning of the colonial period—its legislation on the subject. This was followed by a proposal two years later of what amounted to a revival of Cañete's Carabaya experiment. In a petition to the Crown the Lima council branded free blacks, mulattoes, and Afro-Indians as *"gente de mal vivir"* who caused nothing but trouble among the slave population, and suggested that they be settled in suitable "remote valleys, where they may be justly governed and support themselves from their labor and live in decency." Nothing came of the idea, and after Toledo stepped down as viceroy the control of free coloreds received markedly less official attention. The subsequent decades found the Lima authorities regulating the residence and employment of free persons of color purely on a haphazard basis, usually when reports of crime and vagrancy among this element became too numerous to ignore, and a similar policy was probably followed elsewhere in Peru. In short, such legislation had its effects, at least temporarily, on some free blacks and mulattoes, but for most of them conditions of life turned on the availability of jobs and housing, not on official interference.[26]

This mass of legislation seems to suggest that the Afro-Peruvians were a pack of rebellious criminals. But this is far from being the case. Most blacks, quite to the contrary, were obedient and loyal, so much so that, in the words of Lockhart, "when Spaniards knew individual slaves really well, they gave them the kind of absolute confidence they otherwise extended only to close blood relatives." The same author mentions the 1553 case of a Spanish muleteer who had to leave his pack train and cargo to seek medical help on a journey from Arequipa to Potosí and entrusted to his senior black muleteer what amounted to his entire fortune. Seemingly, the black did not disappoint his master, and the same can be said of thousands of other slaves who earned the trust and respect of their Spanish masters. This was true especially of slave artisans and household servants, many of whom were permitted every liberty short of freedom and enjoyed very close ties with their owners.[27]

Still, some slaves (and some free persons of color) unquestionably displayed a penchant for trouble. In particular, they stole from their masters and from others, often to obtain the money for drink and gambling, and they quarreled violently, and many times fatally, with their fellows and even with Spaniards. Clearly, these vices were hardly confined to the colored element of colonial society, and most Peruvians probably did not speculate much on the subtle connections between bondage, deprivation, and black criminality. The great commentator Poma de Ayala, however, spelled out some of the most obvious conclusions. As we saw in Chapter 3, Poma had nothing but contempt for the knavery and arrogance of the criollos, and he likewise deplored the high crime rate among the slave population and urged the harshest measures to curb it. Nevertheless, Poma placed a major share of the blame squarely on the slaveholders. Many blacks, he argued, became thieves and highwaymen out of sheer need because their masters did not give them the necessities of life; other masters neither indoctrinated nor punished their slaves properly, and still others mistreated their blacks without cause—"they punish them cruelly, they give them no food, they demand much money from them, making them work without eating from morning until lunch at twelve, feeding them only once a day. . . . These are the reasons why they run away and steal. For this reason this group of masters should be justly punished, because they are the cause of the sad state of these poor souls."[28]

To be sure, gross mistreatment of the sort described by Poma cannot be blamed for every crime committed by the slave population. Indeed, there is some evidence that many black wrongdoers were intelligent and talented slaves, with considerable knowledge of the Spanish world, who turned to crime when they realized that their lives offered no hope of reward for faithful service and good conduct. For those caught in such a treadmill, the temptation to drink and gamble, to steal and run away, was very great, and some slaves could not resist. Once a slave followed this path, he became an embarrassment and an expense to his owner, and his master was soon anxious to be rid of him at any price. Thus began a vicious circle. The more the slave was shunted from one master to another, the bolder and more insubordinate he became, and the tale often ended in tragedy.

As a case in point, Lockhart mentions the experiences of Pedro Portugués, who had five masters, in Quito, Arequipa, Cuzco, and Potosí. Pedro became addicted to gambling and "would gamble the clothes off his back, then steal to gamble more"; he also ran away at least once and traveled freely about the colony by means of a forged note stating that he was on business for his master. Despite this history, Pedro's fifth owner paid a good price for him in 1550, taken in by lies about his abilities as blacksmith, butler, tailor, and cook. But Pedro had scant opportunity to demonstrate his talents. While traveling with his master in a convoy bearing royal bullion from Potosí to La Paz, Pedro was taken into custody for stealing a bar of silver and was hanged forthwith.[29]

The master of an unruly slave was likely to find himself saddled with an expense he had not bargained for, since he was held financially responsible for his slave's actions. This often meant financial settlements, in and out of court, with the aggrieved parties, besides an array of judicial fines and costs. In 1565, for example, the surgeon Juan Álvarez sold twenty-four-year-old Antón Criollo for a mere 190 pesos with the stipulation that the buyer would also pay all the costs (an estimated sixty to seventy pesos) in a lawsuit arising from Antón's unspecified misdeeds.[30] Fights between slaves, which often resulted in the death of one of the participants, could be still more costly for the master. On these occasions, settlements were frequently made out of court. In 1573, for example, Gaspar Zape, slave of Francisco Dalva, fought with and killed a slave owned by Diego Díaz. After the crime, Gaspar took refuge in the Franciscan monastery while the two masters met to make the best of a bad situation. It was finally agreed that Gaspar would be given to Díaz in compensation. In another case, this one involving a fight between two slaves named Mateo and Antón, Antón was seriously wounded. To avoid a lawsuit, Mateo's owner agreed to pay all of Antón's medical expenses and to feed him until he recovered; if the black died, the owner would then pay the slave's value as mutually agreed on by representatives of each party.[31]

The master of a troublesome slave was faced with two alternatives. He could try to reform the black through conciliation or (perhaps more frequently) through harsh punishment, such as a whipping or a term in the stocks; or he could sell the slave. As we have seen, this second course of action was not without problems: a slave with a reputation for misconduct ordinarily did not command a good price in the marketplace, and sellers who glossed over or ignored the defects of their blacks exposed themselves to the likelihood of a future lawsuit aimed at redhibition. Some masters chose the path of honesty regardless of financial sacrifice. In 1560, for example, the master of Juan Mulato sold him with the declaration that he was a drunkard and a thief who had been exiled from Cuzco as a possible murder accomplice and whose present whereabouts was unknown. Other sellers were less specific and simply labeled their blacks as "contentious liars punished by the authorities" or as "great scoundrels."[32]

Still, to judge from the quantity of surviving documentation on redhibition cases, many masters could not resist the temptation to sell unruly blacks under false pretenses and thereby achieve a higher sale price. At the same time, there were clearly cases initiated on such grounds that were not based on fact, and many did not succeed. In 1617, for example, Juan González went to court seeking a refund of the money he had paid for Gaspar Criollo. González charged that Gaspar's former owner had sold the slave knowing he was violent and disobedient, and sick besides. During the course of the trial, however, it became clear that Gaspar had taken ill after the sale, much to the distress of his new owner. González could not prove his charges of unruliness to the satisfaction of the court, and his plea was denied.[33] Whatever the merits and outcome of such cases, they were costly and time-consuming to the parties involved (the above case was not decided for three years), and burdensome to a judicial system already clogged with litigation.

Refractory slaves were vexatious not only to their masters, but also to the law enforcement agencies of Peru. Examples from the city of Lima, the focus of Peruvian slavery, will be used to illustrate these difficulties. As in other Peruvian towns of respectable size, the apprehension and trial of criminals in Lima was the primary responsibility of municipal government. Each year the city council met to elect two municipal magistrates, known as *alcaldes ordinarios*, whose jurisdiction in the first instance extended to nearly all civil and criminal offenses committed in the city and the rural areas around it, as well as to neighboring towns too small to have an independent governing body.[34] The Lima alcaldes, for example, exercised authority in Callao until the 1560's, when the press of judicial business grew so great that the port was assigned its own judge.[35] The municipal magistrates of the capital could arrest as well as try criminals, but they shared that authority with the chief constable of the city, the *alguacil mayor*. This official graced important ceremonial occasions with his presence but took little part in the rough-and-tumble of law enforcement, a task entrusted to his deputies. These men were usually called *alguaciles menores* if they served in the city, and *alguaciles del campo* if they had rural duty. Neither the constable nor his deputies drew a salary, but instead were paid more or less by the head, receiving the fines that were levied on every criminal arrested and jailed and the fees that were charged for every court order executed. It was thus in the economic interest of the alguaciles to be diligent enforcers of the law.[36]

In these respects the law enforcement system of Lima was no different than that of other important Peruvian towns. But as the seat of an Audiencia district and the capital of a viceroyalty, Lima had further complexities in its judicial-police organization. To deal with the Audiencia first, the primary function of this body was to act as the highest court of appeal in the colony. A distinction was made in its role in civil and criminal cases beginning with the administration of Viceroy Toledo, when a separate chamber of judges, called *alcaldes del crimen*, was formed to hear and decide disputes involving criminal law. In addition, the Audiencia possessed original jurisdiction in criminal cases within Lima and for a distance of five leagues around. The resulting overlap in jurisdiction was never clearly defined and was perhaps deliberately constructed as part of the divide-and-rule principle by which the Spanish Hapsburgs governed the American empire. The upshot was that both the Audiencia and the municipal government maintained their own jails and constabulary, and both jurisdictions arrested and tried criminals. The judges of the Audiencia, however, were superior in rank to the *alcaldes ordinarios* and kept tabs on them. The *alcaldes del crimen* frequently inspected the city jail, regularly heard appeals against the decisions of the city magistrates, and intervened in cases tried in municipal courts when negligence or maladministration was suspected. Further, the *alcaldes ordinarios* could not impose the death penalty without consulting the Audiencia.[37] In short, there was considerable potential for friction between the Audiencia and the municipality, and the clever masters of criminal slaves learned to exploit this fact to their own advantage.[38] Moreover, the Audiencia itself was subject to some control, for it was the viceroy who was ultimately responsible for the tranquility of the colony. In respect to law enforcement among the black population, the men who held this office played a twofold role. They intervened to correct alleged laxities on the part of the city or the Audiencia, and they mediated when the efforts of these authorities clashed with the prerogatives of the Church.

No agency of Peruvian law enforcement escaped censure during the period under study, and an examination of selected complaints and incidents sheds valuable light on the nature of a society that attempted to reconcile privilege and human bondage with the dictates of law and justice. The *alcaldes ordinarios* came in for especially severe criticism. Typical was the complaint lodged before the Crown in 1584 by Juan Ramos de Guana, a citizen of Lima. Ramos pointed to the disorder he observed among the colored population of the city, and specifically to the brawls and killings involving dangerous weapons. Blacks found it difficult to obtain the weapons of war, but kitchen knives concealed on their persons made an admirable substitute with which "to stab one another for the slightest provocation at their dances and drinking parties." Ramos found it strange that in a city where there were so many agents of the law ("hay tanta Justicia"), none of the blacks were ever punished for these offenses. Instead, in the event of a death in one of these quarrels, the slaveholders involved reached a financial settlement out of court, customarily calculated at half the appraised value of the surviving slave, who was then released on bond to commit new crimes. Ramos placed the blame for this situation squarely on the municipal magistrates, charging that since they served one-year terms almost solely for recognition and prestige, they were reluctant to offend powerful slaveholders by denying them the services of their blacks through strict enforcement of the law and instead let the colored population have their own way. Similar accusations were leveled in succeeding decades, but no serious attempts at reform were ever made. In the 1610's, for example, a minority of the city council itself charged that the *alcaldes ordinarios* were too susceptible to the pleadings of relatives and friends to control the colored population of Lima, and some forty years later

Viceroy Salvatierra, though he did not accuse the municipal magistrates directly, nevertheless noted that it was very difficult to divest blacks and mulattoes of their weapons because their masters were "powerful and privileged persons."[39]

The alguaciles were accused of a different set of offenses. The potential amount of fines to be collected from the apprehension of criminals in a city the size of Lima made many men eager to serve as deputies; and for their part, the *alguaciles mayores*, whose income depended on a percentage of these fines, were tempted to appoint an unrealistic number of deputies, which virtually ensured that they would have to support themselves through corruption and an unduly punctilious enforcement of the law. In common with the alcaldes, the constables had no desire to offend influential slaveholders, and the accusation was made more than once that alguaciles accepted bribes to overlook serious transgressions commited by blacks, though formal charges do not seem to have been filed against specific individuals. The curfew was a particularly sensitive issue between the constables and the slaveholders. The law was definite on this point—slaves were not to be allowed on the streets after the established hour—but Peruvian custom had always made an exception for those blacks who went about on their masters' orders, a practice that was viewed with sympathy by some on the city council. Naturally, the alguaciles thought differently, and they rigorously enforced the curfew even after their fee for each black apprehended was cut from four to one and a half pesos in the 1560's. Complaints against the alguaciles continued throughout the period under study, and periodic efforts were made to reduce their numbers and to curb the worst abuses. However, the root cause of much of the trouble—the dependence on fines and fees rather than a fixed salary—remained.[40]

As for the Audiencia, the judges of that body generally used their supervisory powers over the *alcaldes ordinarios* to advance the cause of justice. Nevertheless, relations between the municipal magistrates and the high court were often strained by the conflicting claims and prerogatives of each, and here slaveholders who wished to shield their blacks from punishment often found fertile ground. Indeed, in the ensuing wrangle, the fact of the crime itself was sometimes very nearly ignored. One such incident began on February 29, 1624, when the *alcalde ordinario* Don Juan de los Ríos y Berriz received a report that many blacks were playing cards in the cemetery of the cathedral. Accompanied by the *alguacil mayor*, Ríos surprised the slaves at their diversion and captured two mulattoes, Pedro de Guzmán and Juan Criollo, and one black, who tried to defend himself with a dagger. The culprits were jailed, and the alcalde was preparing his case when "some people arrived to hinder execution of the royal justice with intercessions and other means." Ríos ordered the slaves to be given 100 lashes through the city streets, basing his action on the fact that the Audiencia had previously allowed such crimes to be punished on the spot and a case prepared later. The Audiencia, contacted by one of the "people," Garci López de Morales, owner of Juan Criollo, stayed the sentence pending review, but Ríos ignored the order and prepared a brief to defend his action, taking testimony from people who lived nearby regarding the intolerable behavior of the blacks who customarily gathered in the cemetery.

Unmollified by this document, the Audiencia ordered Ríos imprisoned on March 1. At his trial, which began within the week, the city attorney produced three documents in Ríos's defense. Two were decrees issued by Viceroy Esquilache. The first, dated August 30, 1618, commanded the summary whipping of blacks found playing cards in church cemeteries. The second, issued on September 23, 1619, was directed specifically to the Lima cathedral, and was inspired by the treasurer of that institution, Don Juan de Vargas y Mendoza. In the name of the dean and the ecclesiastical cabildo, Vargas expressed concern over

the dissoluteness of the blacks who every day occupy the cemetery of this Holy Church, playing cards publicly and filling it all in groups of twenty and thirty blacks, making the Temple of God into a gambling house, from which result killings and woundings and the shedding of blood on sacred ground, and the disturbance of the church in the midst of the divine office, and robberies, for the cruets and silver of the divine worship are not safe on the altars.

To remedy the situation, the clergy, in consultation with the city, proposed to appoint a constable to patrol the area. This official was to be empowered to arrest offending blacks and give them fifty lashes on the spot. For the second offense, blacks were to be jailed and sentenced by the municipal judges. Though formalized by a decree, this plan was seemingly never carried out. The final document presented by the city attorney was a royal decree of 1621 that forbade the Audiencia to imprison *alcaldes ordinarios* without viceregal approval.

In the meantime, the owners of the other two slaves (one of them no less a personage than the current treasurer of the cathedral) had also protested the action of the municipal magistrate, and their complaints were taken under review. On March 11, the high court fined Ríos 200 pesos for his disobedience and ordered him to appear in person for reprimand. Ríos made a rambling appeal the next day, claiming that his action had been in conformance with standard practice and in the best interests of the community. The Audiencia received the appeal without comment. The city now decided to appeal to the Council of the Indies, but that body gave scant satisfaction. In 1626 the Council merely echoed the decree of 1621 (ordering the viceroy's approval of an alcalde's imprisonment) and referred Ríos's case to the viceroy and Audiencia for review.[41] In this instance, of course, the black culprits had been punished, but the treatment accorded Ríos and the demonstrated ability of slaveholders to play on the latent jealousy between high court and city could not have acted as an incentive to vigorous law enforcement.

The Audiencia and the viceroy did not always see eye to eye on the control of the slave population, perhaps in part because the oidores normally enjoyed longer tenure in the colony than the viceroys and came to identify more with local interests and customs. To illustrate, in 1618 Viceroy Esquilache informed the Crown that he had proclaimed an eight o'clock curfew[42] for blacks on threat of 100 lashes because of "some very atrocious crimes that have been committed in this city, and in particular the walls of the monastery of La Encarnación have twice been broken, and because I always understood that the blacks, being so numerous and so insolent, were the cause of these excesses." The judicial authorities having proved uncooperative, said Esquilache, he had then summoned a military company from Callao to enforce the curfew. After many exemplary punishments, the colored population had seemed sufficiently cowed, and the *alcaldes del crimen* had persuaded him to withdraw the troops. That had been done two months before, he complained, and since then the justices had "not punished a single black, and I would have the company return were it not to cause a greater sensation; all this springs from considerations and relationships that I am powerless to remedy."[43]

Esquilache was almost certainly overstating the case, for at this very time the Audiencia was once again attempting to reduce the number of *alguaciles menores*, men who were if anything overzealous in enforcing the curfew. It is entirely possible, however, that the transgressions of slaves belonging to the rich and the powerful were being ignored, a fact that the Audiencia had learned to live with but the viceroy had not. In any event, the Crown approved Esquilache's show of force in the following year, but cautioned that such demonstrations should be employed infrequently since they discredited ordinary methods of law enforcement and emboldened the blacks, "so that lacking such preventions, they will undertake outrages with even more liberty, it seeming to them that the regular justices have not the power to punish such humble people." At the same time, the government sent a blistering letter to the entire Audiencia lamenting that Esquilache's curfew had been so poorly enforced and expressing the royal dismay that the district was "so badly governed and disciplined that against some blacks, such humble people, you do not execute what can be done . . . without, owing to your lack of care and zeal for justice, it being necessary that soldiers undertake it with the noise and ostentation of war." "As persons of letters," the Crown said angrily, the members of the Audiencia understood fully "that crimes committed by omission, negligence, or lack of punishment are charged to him who could and should remedy and punish them, and does not, because of friendships and contacts from which results an equally great damage . . . since the excess grows and motivates greater effronteries and disorders." The Crown ordered a thorough investigation of the incident, with particular scrutiny directed to the relationships between the slaves involved and the oidores and their relatives and friends, with exemplary punishment for the guilty.[44]

The *alcaldes del crimen* chose to maintain a discreet silence in the face of this reprimand and to let their colleagues in the civil branch of the court defend their rectitude. This was undertaken in a letter to the Crown in 1620. In it, the civil justices noted that the entire Audiencia did not stand accused of negligence, but "so that it may not appear that we wish to throw the blame at another's door," they wanted the Crown to know that the *alcaldes del crimen* had cooperated fully with the viceroy's attempt to intimidate the colored population. Further, the crimes at La Encarnación monastery that had prompted the show of force had in fact not been committed by blacks at all, but rather by Indian employees of the institution, culprits who had been apprehended and hanged by the alcaldes. They knew of no dissimulations or failures to enforce the law that could be charged to the alcaldes, the justices stated, "but it is not news that in populous cities, such as this one, there will be crimes, and some of them cannot be ascertained or punished, and God reserves many for His judgment." It is doubtful if Esquilache was pleased by this let-well-enough-alone reasoning, but the Crown was mollified.[45]

From time to time the religious institutions of Lima were also a thorn in the side of the authorities when it came to law enforcement among the slaves, and perhaps none was more vexatious than the Holy Office of the Inquisition. Those attached to the Holy Office claimed immunity from secular prosecution in criminal cases, not only for themselves, but for their blacks as well, and used the considerable power of the institution to overawe both the municipal magistrates and the Audiencia. As the *alcaldes del crimen* put it in a letter to the Crown in 1574, "not only the officials and familiars [of the Holy Office] but all their blacks obtain exemption from the crimes they commit."[46] Continuing friction over this and other matters finally prompted the Crown to define the relationship between the Inquisition and the secular authorities. In a long decree issued in 1601, it was made clear that blacks who belonged to officials of the Holy Office did not enjoy immunity from apprehension and trial in civil courts for their crimes.[47] Thereafter, such slaves did not routinely escape punishment, as they mostly had before. In 1609, for example, a slave of the *presbítero receptor* of the Holy Office was arrested for possessing a kitchen knife and punished by the Audiencia with fifty lashes "that were given him in the royal jail of this court tied to the pole in the patio." In addition, his master paid a two-peso fine, half of the amount normally imposed in such cases. Nevertheless, some Inquisition officials still arrogantly refused to submit their slaves to the normal processes of criminal justice. In 1632, for example, the receiver-general of the Tribunal would not even allow his female slave to testify in a trial for theft in municipal court, forcing Viceroy Chinchón and the entire Audiencia to deliberate for nine hours in an effort to resolve the impasse.[48]

On occasion, blacks accused or convicted of crimes found champions among the clergy, particularly the religious orders, but the motives behind such partisanship were open to question. In an age when many young and hotblooded scions of the most prominent Peruvian families entered the clergy out of economic necessity as well as choice, these protests involved not merely words but also physical confrontation. In 1585, for example, the Audiencia ordered the expulsion of fifteen Dominican friars from the colony for seizing two blacks held in royal custody for murder and robbery and hiding them in their Lima monastery. One of the blacks was a slave of the Dominicans and the others belonged to a person who had taken sanctuary in the monastery. Appeals before the high court and the Archbishop secured pardons for all but two of the Dominicans: Father Salvador de Rivera, provincial of the order, and Father Tomás de Morales, prior of the monastery. The exiled pair no sooner got to Panama, however, than they persuaded the president of the Audiencia there to let them return to Lima. It remained for Viceroy Villar, who arrived that same year to begin his term of office, to resolve the issue. Villar decided to pardon Morales, who was old and infirm, but he believed Rivera was a dangerous man, a person of stiff pride, quality, and education, with rich relatives in practically every province in the colony, who should be sent to Spain before he caused further trouble. Villar's analysis was correct. Without viceregal permission, Rivera left Lima for Cuzco, where he used his influence to secure his election as provincial of the Dominican Order there, thinking to forestall the imposition of exile. However, Villar persuaded the Dominicans to reverse the election, and Rivera, bowing to the inevitable, left the colony for Spain.[49] Nor were other cities spared such embarrassment. Indeed, in 1635 an unnamed religious snatched a mulatto sentenced to hang for three murders from the hands of the judicial officials of Cuzco not once but twice. Neither the motive nor the fate of the cleric is known.[50]

An equally dramatic, albeit less violent, example of ecclesiastical intervention to defend condemned slaves occurred in 1621—an incident that illustrates how seriously the divide-and-rule principle undermined even the ability of the Crown to prevent potentially explosive bickering among touchy agencies charged with the control of the black population. The incident in question began when four slaves confessed (under "very light" torture) to murder and robbery; three were condemned to death and the fourth to a lesser penalty. On hearing the news of their confessions and sentencing, a Jesuit priest, Alonso Mexía, mounted the pulpit in the city plaza to declare that the slaves were innocent, and that he knew who the real culprits were. The sermon, delivered before a large audience that included many blacks, caused a sensation.

The resulting murmur among the slave population was particularly distressing to the *alcaldes del crimen*, who reported to the Crown their fears of a repercussion, "the blacks and slaves of this city being so many in number that we give them with particular care satisfaction from the wrongs that their masters and other Spaniards do them, though as a matter of policy we do not acknowledge the fact, so that they themselves recognize that in Your alcaldes they find protection and favor in all their afflictions and worries." In their letter the justices charged that similar incidents involving the Jesuits, Augustinians, and Mercedarians had occurred in the past, and that only the Dominicans were above reproach, largely because their superior had rigorously punished some lay brothers for a similar offense. Luis Enríquez, the Crown attorney in Lima, who sent a separate letter on the incident, contended that the Jesuits had become involved only because two of the blacks were owned by persons closely affiliated with their order.[51]

An outraged Crown took action in 1624. Warning the provincials of the Jesuits, Augustinians, and Mercedarians to guard against such occurrences in future, it ordered Father Mexía's provincial to administer exemplary punishment, and charged the Archbishop of Lima to punish any religious guilty of such excesses if his own superior refused to do so.[52] Father Mexía now presented his own version of the affair. In a letter to the Crown in 1626, calling himself "Your vassal and the best known religious of this kingdom," Mexía flatly denied the charges *in verbo sacerdotis*. According to the Jesuit, his sermon had been preached before the slaves had even been tortured, let alone sentenced; therefore he could not possibly have protested a ruling not yet pronounced. Further, the *alcaldes del crimen* had told the owners of the slaves the same afternoon that they would be released as innocent. Nor had he said anything inflammatory in his sermon, as Viceroy Esquilache and two oidores could verify. In any event, no blacks had been present since they were never allowed to attend sermons on Maundy Thursday so as to make room for the extraordinary numbers of Spaniards who attended. Finally, a Spaniard had confessed the crime to him shortly before fleeing the city. Mexía blamed the alcaldes' charges on a quarrel that he had had with one of them on the first Thursday of Lent over whether the plaza was to be used for public audience or for the Jesuit's sermon. Mexía had won, and bad blood had been the result.[53] The Crown was unable to cut through this tangle of charges and countercharges, and directed the viceroy to investigate the matter and dispense the appropriate exonerations and reprimands.[54] Surviving documentation contains no record of viceregal action, and the matter was probably quietly laid to rest, but the potential for serious trouble remained.

No responsible ecclesiastic attempted a legal defense of clerical involvement in such incidents. However, the Church and the Audiencia did come to blows over the question of a slave's right to religious asylum, a controversy that reached a high point in Lima during the 1630's. The quarrel began in 1634, when a quadroon and a black who had escaped jail and sought sanctuary in the cathedral were dragged out and hanged at the order of the Audiencia. The secular clergy vehemently protested the government's action. Tension between Church and state over the issue was heightened by another incident in the very next year. In the cemetery of San Marcelo, which adjoined the cathedral, a mulatto slave killed another slave with a kitchen knife and sought refuge in the cathedral, clinging to a statue of St. John the Evangelist near the high altar. Despite the remonstrances of the priests, the slave was dragged from the church and clapped into prison by the chief constable of the Audiencia. The vicar general of the diocese immediately imposed ecclesiastical censures on the *alcaldes del crimen*, but the mulatto was nevertheless sentenced to death. At the last possible moment (when the slave had already mounted the scaffold), Viceroy Chinchón intervened, granting a stay of execution. The slave was returned to jail while the viceroy and the Audiencia discussed the crisis. Unable to come to any agreement, they turned the matter over to the royal attorney, who investigated the case and concluded that the privilege of asylum was unwarranted. The Audiencia thereupon proposed that the censures against the alcaldes be lifted, and the ecclesiastical authorities agreed, provided the justices took a formal oath to obey the future commands of the Church. The dispute that followed over this ritual obscured the ultimate fate of the slave.[55] It seems fair to conclude that the involvement of the Church in the fate of condemned slaves was motivated in part by a desire for justice, but also to some degree by self-interest and concern for ecclesiastical prerogatives.

From the expressed apprehensions and the efforts of the Spanish in Peru, it is clear that disorder and crime among the colored population were of considerable concern. Unfortunately, though some sort of record was presumably prepared in most criminal cases, only a handful have survived, and in their absence it is impossible to determine the exact rate of black crime in this period. Enough data survive, however, to suggest what the most common offenses were. In the 502 cases I studied (which were scattered over the whole period 1560-1650), the charges were as follows:[56]

Running away	270	Resisting arrest	6
Theft	81	Aiding runaways	6
Assault	72	Jailbreak	4
Murder	36	Rape	2
Drunk and disorderly	14	Vandalism	1
Possession of weapons	10		

Several comments are in order. First, as this breakdown suggests (and as will be discussed in more detail in the next chapter), the runaway slave was by far the most vexatious problem for those who were called on to police the black population. Theft, assault, and murder were also major categories of crime. Curfew violations, too, seem to have been frequent, but the infraction is mentioned too casually in the records to include in the list. Second, it is important to distinguish the victims of these crimes. When blacks stole, perhaps to drink or to gamble, Spaniards or Indians were usually the victims; when they fought or killed, the victim was likely to be another person of color. Finally, there is ample evidence to indicate that blacks were frequently themselves the victims of crimes, most commonly assault and murder, at the hands of Spaniards.

In general, black criminals were punished for their offenses by the gallows, the whip (between 100 and 300 lashes), exile to Chile, or a term on the galleys. We need not linger over the first two penalties, but the others deserve a few remarks. Chile, a poor colony attractive to few settlers and often engaged in a struggle for survival against the hostile Araucanian Indians, was economically dependent on Peru for its governance. In consequence, it became to Peru what Australia was later to be for the British Empire: a dumping ground for criminals. In Chile's case, many of these criminals were black. In 1570, for example, seven free colored felons were released from the jails of Lima on condition that they volunteer for service against the Araucanians. Occasionally, owners were even allowed to sell slaves convicted of crimes to persons bound for Chile rather than yield them up for punishment in Peru. By 1614 the practice of exiling blacks to Chile had become so common that the city council of Santiago resolved that "no more blacks be imported from Peru unless the Audiencia of Lima certified that they were neither criminals nor troublemakers."[57]

Condemnation to the galleys was somewhat illusory since, as we have seen, these vessels were almost useless to the Pacific fleet. Most black criminals sentenced to the oars spent their days performing odd jobs around the royal naval facilities at Callao. Some, at least in the early seventeenth century, were transported to Cartagena to man a proposed fleet of galleys that never materialized and ended up serving in the households of royal officials there. One man worked hard over a period of years to change the situation. This was Doctor Alberto de Acuña, a member of the Audiencia. He began his effort in 1607, proposing that galley service for colored criminals be scrapped in favor of hard labor on the most dangerous sections of the Huancavelica mercury mine. Acuña argued that this would have the twofold advantage of substantially reducing the number of mita Indians assigned to the diggings and serving as a warning to potential criminals. The Crown was somewhat receptive to the idea, anxious as it was to reduce the forced labor obligations of the natives, but though Acuña lobbied for the measure into the 1620's, he could never persuade either the viceroys or a majority of his colleagues to go along. His opponents argued that the morale of the mitayos would be lowered by forced labor alongside common criminals, that the convicts would transmit their vices to the Indians, and that the cold climate of Huancavelica would be injurious to the health of the blacks. The mine operators of Huancavelica were also unenthusiastic, preferring to work their claims with docile Indians rather than with potentially dangerous convicts. Finally, the idea of galleys on the Pacific came back into official favor in the 1620's, and the viceroys argued that convicts were urgently needed to row these vessels. For all these reasons, and despite strong pressure from the Crown in the 1630's, Acuña's proposal was never adopted.[58]

Over the years there were complaints from many quarters about the quality of law enforcement among Afro-Peruvians and the efficacy of the punishments imposed. Some colonists, slaveholders in the main, deplored the harshness of the policing, and others deplored its laxness, which had reached the point where "only by a miracle is someone condemned to death in these kingdoms."[59] Of the relatively few critics who troubled to put pen to paper in search of a solution, only two advanced any sort of comprehensive program. One was a Dominican, Father Miguel de Monsalve, who was disturbed about the large number of free blacks, mulattoes, and zambos, and their lack of respect for law and religion. Monsalve's solution, which he put formally to the Crown at the beginning of the seventeenth century,[60] was to group all these free persons of color together in a separate parish in each Spanish town, where they would have their own businesses and be under a separate civil and ecclesiastical government. Where the free colored population was heavy, Monsalve advocated entrusting the rule to a Spanish governor whose salary could be paid by taxation; otherwise, the task could be assigned each year to the senior *alcalde ordinario* of the town. In either case, this man was to be assisted by a constable, who in turn would have four black assistants to ferret out criminal elements. Monsalve urged that in addition the governor himself rigorously search the free colored district on a monthly basis and confiscate any weapons he discovered.

More interesting still were the proposals made at roughly the same time by Poma de Ayala.[61] As we have seen, Poma charged that the greed and callousness of the slaveholders was a major contributing factor to black criminality, but he nevertheless advocated the harshest punishments for colored criminals and naïvely placed on Peruvian masters the responsibility for instructing their slaves in the ways of virtue and obedience. Poma felt masters who ignored potential moral and criminal defects in their blacks risked both their own souls and those of their slaves. Knavish and balky slaves must be broken, "and it is even a holy work for the service of God and of His Majesty and for the good of their souls and bodies." With regard to method, Poma recommended irons to slaveholders as the best and surest way to tame the unruly, since whippings and tarrings were useless, and threats merely provoked flight. If these harsh methods failed, and the black ran afoul of the law, Poma recommended to the authorities that black criminals be pardoned for the first offense, except in the case of thieves, who should lose an ear. For the second offense, however, Poma recommended punishment by hanging to strike fear in others or, at the very least, the wearing of irons for life.

However, Poma combined his harsh views on the subject of punishments with a surprisingly liberal proposal for their administration. The colored population, he argued, should be judged and punished by their peers. Masters should have no more authority over their slaves in criminal and civil cases than they possessed over their wives and children, and even Spanish law enforcement agencies should have no jurisdiction whenever possible. Rather, in places with as few as ten blacks there should be chosen from their number an *alcalde ordinario*, an alderman, and a notary for the administration of justice; otherwise, an alcalde, two constables, an attorney, and a crier should perform this function. In Poma's view, these officials could be either free or slave, and where possible should be elected. If the alcalde chosen was a slave, his master should allow him two days per week, perhaps Wednesdays and Fridays, to perform his duties. Ayala envisioned that these officials would mete out the punishments laid down by Spanish law, though in exceptionally grave cases the master might be informed before execution of the sentence. In the performance of their duties blacks might also be allowed to bear arms. For better or worse, the Crown does not seem to have seriously considered either of these proposals, though, as we shall see in Chapter 11, elements of Poma's program were used in the seventeenth century to collect tribute from the free colored population.

However obnoxious, the street crimes committed by blacks could be viewed by the government with a measure of equanimity. The threat of sedition and treason was another matter. Governor García de Castro was one of the first high Spanish officials to express alarm about this possibility. There were so many blacks, mulattoes, and mestizos in the land, he wrote the Crown in 1565, that "if they agree among themselves, the Spaniards here opposing them would count for nothing, and the worst of the matter is that each hour they grow in strength." Two years later, the Crown received renewed warnings on the subject, this time not only from Castro but also from Father Francisco del Corral, prior of the Augustinian monastery in Lima.[62]

In fact, there is no evidence that the colored residents of Peru ever conspired among themselves to overthrow the government, perhaps in part because (as many observers alleged) they were too divided to make common cause against the Spanish.[63] To be sure, there was an occasional disturbance in Lima, as in 1599 when a high police official was killed by a rock in what was described as a black uprising,[64] but most of these infrequent outbursts were either short-lived demonstrations against a specific grievance or spontaneous eruptions triggered by mob psychology. In 1626, for example, a large crowd of blacks, mulattoes, and other poor people, outraged at allegations that some councilmen were profiteering in the Lima meat market, marched through the streets, shouting bitter protests, and into the very room of the viceregal palace where the Audiencia was in session. The oidores placated the mob with promises to remedy the situation, but several councilmen did not show themselves in public for several days for fear of increasing the popular fury, which finally vented itself by hanging the profiteers in effigy at the Rímac bridge. Another incident occurred in 1635 when a municipal judge was supposed to distribute packed snow (used for icing drinks). So many blacks gathered that the constables and porters in assistance had to draw their swords to make their way through the crush. As a result, several blacks were wounded, and their comrades began to throw rocks, injuring the judge and one of the constables. In retaliation, four of the blacks were caught and given 200 lashes in a procession through the streets of the city.[65]

Both Africans and Indians had reason to hate the Spanish, but by and large the hostility that had developed during the conquest period continued between the two groups. Despite numerous individual friendships, sexual unions, and business contacts, most blacks could not identify with a people so thoroughly cowed by the Spanish, and many were as scornful and abusive of the natives as their white masters. For their part, most Indians preferred to have as little as possible to do with both groups, and saw scant reason to exchange white overlords for black ones. Only rarely was this pattern broken in favor of Afro-Indian cooperation, and then usually in remote areas where the realities of oppression were stronger than prejudice.

An interesting example from the beginning of the seventeenth century illustrates the point. The setting was the tropical highland province of Vilcabamba near Cuzco, where over 2,000 blacks and perhaps many more Indians were employed to work the gold deposits under typically bad labor conditions. The rugged terrain, covered with luxuriant vegetation, was ideal shelter for fugitive laborers, and in 1602 a band of runaway blacks and Indians, led by an Indian named Francisco Chichima, proved so troublesome that the governor of the area, Captain Diego de Aguilar, sent a group of Cañari Indians (faithful allies of the Spanish since the conquest) to aid in their capture. These efforts were cut short on May 20 by the rebellion of some twenty blacks on a plantation in the area, who burned the buildings of the estate, killed six faithful Indians, and almost captured their master. This action signaled a carefully planned rebellion masterminded by Chichima, and within hours the Africans of the surrounding valleys were in full revolt. A larger plan involving the blacks of Cuzco narrowly misfired, and, as it was, over 100 Spaniards were surrounded and besieged on the estate of one of their number.

The rebels thought that they had blocked any way for the Spaniards to send for help, but the *alguacil mayor* of the province, who had managed to escape their net, sent word to Aguilar, who dispatched a relief force of twelve Spaniards and some twenty Indians. Another five men subsequently joined the group, and the combined force soon slipped past the slave lines and on May 22 relieved the besieged Spaniards. At this point, the revolt collapsed. The Chichima band was pursued into the hills, and after a few isolated skirmishes, surrendered. The Spanish destroyed two storehouses of food that had been stockpiled for some two years in anticipation of the revolt, as well as crops ready for harvest. When Aguilar arrived a few days later, the Africans presented the head of Chichima as a peace offering. In his report to the Crown, Aguilar stressed the difficulties that would have been encountered if the blacks had succeeded in entrenching themselves in the rugged and thicketed hills. Another revolt of Africans and Indians occurred in the same area two years later, but the Spaniards again suppressed the outbreak with relative ease.[66]

On at least two occasions the black population figured in the crazed schemes of Spaniards to seize power. In one case, reported to the Crown in 1567, a cleric had tried to create an uprising in Arequipa. The plan was to kill the corregidor of the city, seize the ships in the harbor, come with these to Lima, and from this point burn all shipping at Callao and persuade mulattoes and mestizos to join the rebellion. In 1618 an equally insane enterprise was conceived by one Sebastián Machado, a Spaniard disappointed in a lawsuit heard by the Quito Audiencia. The angry Machado had allegedly come to Lima to mount an insurrection and had held out promises of freedom to those slaves who pledged themselves to his cause. The would-be rebel was taken into custody, found guilty of treason, and quartered.[67]

The fact is that in this whole period, blacks took up arms against their masters only on very rare occasions. But Peruvian slaveholders did not have the advantage of hindsight, and, as one observer noted, they were always fearful that the blacks would revolt.[68] In the last decades of the sixteenth century another cause for anxiety appeared: the threat of an alliance between foreign invaders and the slave population. At first, the activities of Spain's enemies were concentrated in the Atlantic, and only Peruvian communications with the mother country via Panama seemed endangered. On the Isthmus, Spanish authority outside the towns had in any case long been challenged by the bands of African marauders who lived in the nearly inaccessible interior. Indeed, in 1555 Viceroy Cañete had been compelled to conclude what amounted to an armistice with these groups before proceeding to Peru. The dangers of the situation were magnified in the 1570's, however, when Francis Drake and other English and French privateers made various incursions in the area and received help from these bands. In 1577, for example, the Spanish position on the Isthmus was so precarious that Viceroy Toledo was moved to send a relief expedition from Peru.[69] Imagine, then, the chagrin of Peruvian officialdom when "this Englishman who has now discovered this gateway of the Strait" appeared in the Pacific, heretofore a Spanish lake. The threat to commerce and the port cities was clear to all, but others, like the oidor Ramírez de Cartagena, discerned a more profound danger:

There are in this land people of condition so low and so ignorant and vicious that with very little persuasion they will embrace anything that lets them live licentiously, such as the mestizos, some Indians, blacks, mulattoes, and zambaigos, who will take for more truthful that which gives them most license, especially the blacks, who have understood that these English promise them freedom.[70]

After years of relative security, the foreign intruders, feared for so long on the Spanish Main, now seemed a very real threat to Peru as well.

In subsequent years Peruvian fears subsided somewhat, perhaps in large part because it was realized that Drake's daring feat was not the prelude to sustained raiding by English privateers. Nevertheless, the end of the colony's isolation came at precisely the time when the Peruvian slave trade expanded greatly in volume, and this influx of blacks could hardly fail to alarm those who foresaw the possibility of a renewed foreign thrust in the future. To be sure, a few high officials were confident of the loyalty of the blacks—the second Cañete even proposed to arm them in an emergency[71]—but most took a less sanguine view. The Lima city council of 1596, for example, thought slave importation ought to be limited, perhaps through an additional tax or even a ceiling, but it was unable to persuade the Crown to its view.[72]

One important official pressed for still more positive action. This was Juan Vázquez de Loaysa, artillery captain and overseer of the royal shipyards at Callao, who in 1601 urged the Crown to fortify Lima and the port city. From his thirty-six years of military experience, it seemed to him that an enemy force of 1,500 men could easily seize both cities, since the inhabitants lacked military training and the potentially treacherous blacks were so numerous. In 1615, in another letter, Vázquez claimed for Lima a slave population in excess of 25,000, and "so insolent and daring that one can truthfully say that they are the masters and the masters their servants." Only tribal animosities kept the blacks from collaborating to overthrow Spanish rule, he contended.[73] Moreover, the law enforcement agencies were helpless to control them, since many were slaves "of powerful men, and they get away with as many crimes as they attempt, and there are no notaries who dare draw up cases against them, or constables who will imprison them, both for fear of the risk they run . . . and in order not to anger their masters, to whom the slaves are necessary." Vázquez proposed a head tax to finance a citadel with a complement of 150 men to protect and patrol the capital; the application of the full force of the law against black murderers, regardless of the status of their masters, and corporal punishment for those caught with weapons in their possession (preferably the loss of nose or ears for the second and third offenses), instead of the customary twenty-five-peso fine, which punished the master rather than the slave; and a reduction in slave importation.[74] The Lima council reconsidered the problem of the colored population at roughly the same time and was not prepared to go as far as Vázquez. However, it did urge the viceroy to revoke any arms permits that had been granted to blacks and mulattoes and to assign two infantry companies to guard the city on such occasions as Holy Week, when the throngs of colored persons in the streets constituted a potential menace.[75]

In 1615 the sensation caused by the appearance of a Dutch fleet in the Pacific momentarily strengthened the position of those who had worried about the loyalty of the black population. After the crisis had passed, Viceroy Esquilache wrote the Crown that one enemy ship had captured two blacks near Arica and later released them near Paita. Interrogation had revealed an attempt to persuade the blacks to foment a slave revolt on their release, under promise that the Dutch would soon return to aid them. The same proposition had been put to some Indian fishermen. Esquilache had kept the results of the interrogation secret and had not allowed the blacks to be brought to the capital "because any rumor that is sown would arouse much anxiety, particularly where, as it happens in Lima, there are ten blacks for each Spaniard." For better defense in the future, Esquilache proposed that Callao be fortified, perhaps using African labor in the construction, a measure that was quickly seconded by the oidor Cristóbal Cacho de Santillana.[76] At the reported approach of another five enemy ships in 1618, the idea of fortifications picked up additional support from Father Diego Álvarez de Paz, provincial of the Society of Jesus. In a memorial to Esquilache, he wrote that, having resided thirty-three years in Peru, during which period he had traveled through the colony three times, and having witnessed the miserable lot of the blacks and the Indians, he knew both groups to be so oppressed as to be ripe for the sort of propaganda disseminated by the Dutch three years before. Given this state of affairs and the colonials' lack of military experience, he could see no other solution except to wall both Lima and Callao.[77]

In fact Álvarez's view was unduly pessimistic: no restiveness was reported among the slave population, and the colored militia companies that Montesclaros had reluctantly organized to meet the 1615 crisis had shown no trace of disloyalty, though care had been taken not to arm them (see Chapter 11). Whether or not the Spanish noted and were comforted by these facts, it is certain that little effective action was taken to tighten control over the blacks. In 1618, for example, when Esquilache attempted to limit the privilege of having armed black escorts to the viceroy and a selected number of high civil and ecclesiastical dignitaries,[78] his ruling aroused the instant and intense opposition of powerful men like Alonso de Lucena, the postmaster general of the colony, who claimed that right for himself and his lieutenants as accorded by Viceroy Velasco. In Lucena's case, and doubtless in others, the Crown could do no less than make the proper inquiries, and Esquilache no doubt quickly learned that the control of arms was easier to decree than to enforce.[79] Even the Lima city council, which bitterly complained in 1621 and 1622 about the large numbers of persons who went about with armed black escorts, was at the very time petitioning the Crown to secure the same privilege for themselves (a privilege for which, as we saw earlier, they were willing to pay handsomely in 1637).[80] Desire for social standing, it seems, overrode fear of danger; or perhaps Spaniards only mistrusted the slaves of others, not their own. In any event, a memorial directed to the Crown in 1623, only eight years after the Dutch threat, stated that "in this kingdom he who has wealth is a gentleman, and there are very few who do not go about with two to four armed slaves, so that in the plaza of Lima I have seen on occasion more than 2,000 armed blacks and mulattoes."[81]

Spanish fears of the colored population were heightened once again with a new Dutch threat to Lima-Callao in 1624. As Viceroy Guadal-cázar's report to the Crown of June 6 makes clear, this was something more than the simple Dutch probe of 1615. The eleven-ship Dutch fleet had planned to seize Lima "and then offer liberty to all the blacks that are in it, for which purpose they brought chests of letters of manumission with the names blank, and a large number of arms to issue and divide among them, and 800 pistols to arm as many other persons on horseback." In addition, part of the fleet, one large ship and four small ones, with 300 men, had left Lima for Pisco with the idea of fomenting a slave rebellion there. Guadalcázar also reported rumors that the Dutch had reared two sons of African kings for the specific purpose of rallying the Peruvian slaves to the cause of Holland, though these princes had apparently not accompanied the expedition. From the testimony of a prisoner from the enemy fleet, he added, the blacks captured by the Dutch, especially one Simón, were both more informative about conditions in the colony and more trusted by their captors than Spanish prisoners.[82]

Nothing came of this Dutch foray, and the colored militia of the colony again performed loyally and well during the crisis. Nevertheless, the concern of the Spanish is illustrated by a resolution of the Lima city council in the same year that called on the viceroy to restrict the activities of the Dutch then resident in the municipality, presumably men who had received special licenses from the Crown to live in Spanish America. According to the council, these Dutchmen were shamelessly currying the favor of the blacks and the Indians through drinking parties and were doubtless also disseminating propaganda designed to shake the faith of both in Crown and Church.[83] It is not known if Guadalcázar took any action to curb these mysterious Dutchmen, but he must have had the Dutch in mind when he warned his successor,

Chinchón, to handle the blacks with the greatest care. The viceroy estimated the slave population of metropolitan Lima at some 22,000, an ominous figure if things should go badly for the Spaniards in wartime, since the blacks "generally love liberty, which it may seem to them they might obtain by siding with the enemy, who are not accustomed to slaveholding."[84]

Debate concerning the control of the colored population in the event of foreign attack continued over the ten years of Chinchón's administration. None of the proposals advanced were new except in detail, and a look at just two of them is sufficient to illustrate the combination of alarm and tact that characterized Spanish attitudes toward the blacks during this often tense period. The first of these proposals, written in 1629 by Varona de Incinillas, *fiscal* of the Audiencia, revived a much-discussed issue: the possession of weapons by persons of color. Incinillas's fears and charges were familiar ones. He claimed that nearly all of Lima's 3,000 mulattoes possessed weapons by viceregal license, as did many slaves, and in consequence there were now as many persons of color with arms as Spaniards; the danger of such a situation in the event of enemy attack was clear, and the more so since the total colored population exceeded 30,000. Incinillas went on to deplore the excessive number of black household servants, sometimes as many as twenty or thirty per establishment, and maintained more for ostentation than for service. He suggested that the number of slaves per household be limited to three males and two females, and that the number employed in agriculture be reduced also where feasible. Like many before him, the *fiscal* called for the revocation of weapons permits issued to persons of color and for the rigid enforcement of the general prohibition in this regard.

More interesting than these oft-sounded alarms is the reply of the Crown. On the advice of the Council of the Indies, the government agreed to instruct the viceroy to proceed very cautiously in revoking such permits. For one thing, the conduct of the colored militia during the 1624 Dutch threat had been exemplary, so satisfactory indeed that the Crown had relieved them of their tribute obligation. In addition, it was reasoned, a blanket revocation could easily provoke among the colored population a protest more dangerous than the abuse it was designed to correct.[85] While the question was debated in Spain Viceroy Chinchón contented himself with repromulgating in 1630 Esquilache's decree on the subject of blacks and weapons,[86] and here the matter seems to have rested for the next several decades.

The second proposal of interest during this period was authored in 1634 by a private citizen of Lima, Juan Esquivel Triana, and likewise concerned a dilemma much discussed in the past: Peru's continuing demand for African labor, which necessarily increased the danger of a slave revolt. Esquivel pointed with alarm to the numerical disparity between the 3,700 Spaniards capable of bearing arms in the area (including the 500 soldiers stationed at Callao) and the 20,000 able-bodied blacks. He contended that the only reason the colored population had not seized control of the colony was the hatred slaves of different tribes bore each other. For this reason, they did not mix together

in the dances, gatherings, and religious brotherhoods that state policy has permitted them on feast days, though in marriages this distinction is not observed, wherefore unfortunately it can be affirmed that they are more masters of our lives than we of their liberty, for there is scarcely a house in which the blacks do not greatly outnumber the whites who live there. They, My Lord, are masters of the doors and therefore of the weapons during the hours of rest . . . , and the worst of the matter is an habitual impudence that has been nurtured in them from seeing themselves permitted and aided in any species of crime, because none is so unfortunate that he does not have a master who defends him as his own property, and thus few and wretched indeed are those who are punished as they deserve.

Esquivel pondered the city's danger "in the quiet of a night when confusion and fear would make destruction more certain, or in the event of another Dutch invasion." As a remedy, he proposed suspending the importation of slaves for a decade, with Indian labor used to take up the slack in the meantime. This, he asserted, would effect a near balance in the proportion of blacks and whites.[87]

Evidently the home government considered the proposal of sufficient merit to warrant viceregal consideration, but Chinchón's reply of 1636 was couched in terms of guarded contempt. After disparaging Esquivel's qualifications to comment on a subject with so many ramifications, Chinchón conceded the regrettable imbalance in the relative numbers of Spaniards and Africans, but remarked that continued slave importation was indispensable to the Peruvian economy. Moreover, care had been taken to separate Africans by "nations" in the religious brotherhoods and dances permitted them. Admittedly, there were many free mulattoes, but this was by the will of their masters; besides, the hostility between the two races was softened by feeding at the same breast and by a common upbringing, so that the mulattoes considered it a great honor to be sons of white men, "and the majority of them are of such a rustic and irrational nature that they do not aspire even to be free except for those who become ladinos." Chinchón informed the Crown that his policy had been to proceed with "disproportionate rigor" against those who punished blacks excessively, so that the Africans might know they were not without protectors, while at the same time dealing harshly with slaves who attacked Spaniards. In the event of enemy action Chinchón proposed to imprison in the galleys all blacks who were in jail at the time, as well as those who had been sentenced to terms of labor in hat factories or similar occupations. As for the rest, he stated that colored household servants were usually of the highest reliability; indeed, during the last Dutch attack, several slaves had deliberately sacrificed their own lives to save those of their masters.[88]

Despite Chinchón's confident attitude in correspondence with the Crown, he had private reservations. A relative, the Marqués de Villena, wrote Chinchón for advice on being extended the offer of a viceregal post. In reply, Chinchón expressed his own disillusionment about Peru in the strongest terms and warned Villena of the weakness of the colony in the event of enemy attack, a weakness that he attributed in part to the large colored population.[89] Chinchón was also careful to warn his successor, the Marqués de Mancera, of the potential dangers and urged the incoming viceroy to ensure by all possible means that the slave population was not driven to desperation by ill-treatment. Chinchón also confided that he had given considerable thought to the idea of one or more Protectors for the slave population, similar to those appointed for the Indians, to ensure fair treatment, but that he had not resolved the question before leaving office.[90]

Nor was the Crown entirely convinced by Chinchón's soothing assurances. In 1638 the viceroy was advised that consideration was being given to ways to minimize the dangers of a slave rebellion. In the meantime Chinchón was to bend every effort to discipline the slave population and was also to consider if it would be useful to limit the size of individual slaveholdings. To this end the viceroy was asked to send an estimate of the total number of slaves in the colony, but without calling attention to the fact through a formal census. Seemingly, the request was not complied with, and other distractions prevented further royal action beyond instructing the new viceroy, Mancera, to maintain strict vigilance with regard to the colored population.[91]

Mancera had his own ideas for the security of the colony, and these largely revolved around the fortification of Callao. In trying to justify the expense of this project, which was strongly supported by Peru's military officials, the viceroy pointed once again to the possibility of an alliance between the colored population and the enemy.[92] A note of urgency was given to the proposal in December 1640, when Portugal succeeded in throwing off sixty years of Spanish rule. Further, the swift adherence of Brazil to the Portuguese cause made Mancera doubt the loyalty of Lima's Portuguese population. The viceroy wrote the Crown in 1642 that "the Portuguese alone would not give me cause for concern, but observing the great number of blacks that there are in this city, and the affection with which they regard the Portuguese, as those white men whom they first came to know," great vigilance had been necessary. Mancera had been moved to take a censure of all Portuguese resident in Lima and Callao, and he urged that the 500-odd so enumerated be moved inland and divided up among the various towns. Though this program was approved by the Crown, many Portuguese apparently succeeded in evading the stricture. In any event, the fear of Afro-Portuguese collaboration provided Mancera with another argument for the fortification of Callao.[93] Indeed, by 1648 construction of the wall at the port town had proceeded to such a point that Mancera could minimize to his successor, Salvatierra, the dangers posed by the colored population.[94] In fact, Mancera's assertion seems to have been largely correct, and though, as we have seen, Viceroy Salvatierra did concern himself with the perennial question of blacks and weapons, Spanish fear of a slave revolt seems to have greatly subsided during the 1650's.[95]

At this point we have yet to take up the runaway problem and associated crimes, the knottiest problem of all in terms of slave control. Nevertheless, it is possible to come to some conclusions on the basis of the evidence studied thus far. First, unruly slaves did indeed cause difficulties for masters unlucky enough to own them, and misconduct was widespread enough to call forth a considerable body of legislation and a measure of official concern. However, the impact of the criminal slave on the total society appears to have been modest, and there seems little reason to suppose that the average black was any more prone to trouble than the average white. Similarly, the threat of a slave revolt appears to have been greatly exaggerated. This is not to deny that the Spanish had much to fear, surrounded as they were not only by a numerically superior slave population different in race and (partly) in culture, but also by an increasing number of free persons of color. It might also be argued that the loyalty of blacks to their white masters was never put to a severe test—that even the most serious Dutch threat to Peru in the seventeenth century did not provide a real opportunity for a slave revolt, nor the arid coast an ideal setting for prolonged guerrilla warfare against Spanish authority. Yet other factors, it seems clear, account in some part for the fact that there were no large-scale revolts of blacks against whites in this period, namely, the divisions that prevailed among the Africans themselves and the policies of the wisest Spanish administrators: an outward sanguineness, an attempt at evenhanded justice, and a considerable degree of vigilance.

CHAPTER EIGHT

The Control of the African: Cimarrones and the Santa Hermandad

Of all the crimes committed by the black slave population of Peru, few were more serious and none more widespread than flight from the master's service. The master lost a sizable investment when a runaway black made good his escape; and recapturing a runaway often involved considerable trouble and expense. Further, runaway slaves, called *cimarrones* by the Spanish, tended to band together for companionship and greater security in the countryside, and many such bands became a menace to agricultural pursuits and to trade and communication along the highways. Fortunately for the colonial authorities, coastal Peru, the heartland of African slavery, was not covered with the lush tropical vegetation that made independent runaway communities such a stubborn problem in Panama and the West Indies. Yet the runaway had little choice but to take to the bush. He had small hope of finding haven among the Indian population, where he was likely to be unwelcome as an intruder and where his black skin would give him away in any event. And seeking refuge in urban areas was almost as hopeless, since vagrants and strangers were conspicuous in the relatively small towns of Peru. All the same, for many slaves the goal was worth the risks, and in time the cimarrón problem was deemed sufficiently serious to warrant the creation of a constabulary, the Santa Hermandad, for the express purpose of controlling the slave population in the countryside and apprehending runaways.

Cimarrones were a source of concern almost from the very beginnings of Spanish Peru. As early as 1544 runaways blacks were "assaulting and killing men and robbing farms" on the outskirts of Lima and Trujillo.[1] In the following year Lorenzo de Aldana, who governed Lima in the name of Gonzalo Pizarro, took advantage of a respite in the civil wars to move against some 200 cimarrones, who had entrenched themselves in a well-organized settlement in a reedy marsh at Huara, a few miles north along the coast. The blacks had accumulated large quantities of Spanish weapons and armor and were rumored to have allies among the city's slave population. According to reports, they and their "king" planned to overthrow Spanish rule and assume governance over the Indians. Aldana was sufficiently impressed to send a 120-man force under the command of Juan de Barbarán, an old conquistador and former alcalde, to seek them out. The marsh, difficult of access in any event, had been so fortified by the cimarrones that the Spaniards were forced to dismount and fight hand-to-hand. The battle was a bloody one, since the blacks to a man refused to surrender, and before they died they took eleven Spaniards, including Barbarán, with them, and many others were wounded.[2]

No other cimarrón band thereafter even came close to threatening Spanish rule, but as Lima council records of later years attest, smaller groups of some fifteen to twenty black cimarrones continued to "go about robbing the travelers on the roads . . . and the natives," and even had "the impudence to enter the city by night and by day and to go to the farms and commit many other damages." Indeed, these groups were considerably more troublesome than the word impudence implies. One band of twenty-three men (two of them Spaniards), operating in and around Lima in 1549, was reported to be "committing many robberies and murders and other harm among the natives and other persons."[3] Alonso Borregán, a chronicler of the conquest, was among those who suffered at the hands of the cimarrones, and he gave this account of their depredations in a petition to the Council of the Indies for relief:

I beg of Your Royal Highness to grant me the lands and site of Yupiay, where I had my house and livestock and fields and created an orchard of all types of Spanish trees, which I possessed for four years without contradiction [until one night] the fugitive and thieving blacks, [who] with Martín, their leader, had repeatedly driven me out and robbed me of my cattle, . . . descended on my house and cut off the middle finger of my right hand while I fought them for six hours, and being helpless, I abandoned the house, and they robbed me of everything there was in it and of my *indios de servicio*. . . . The following day I went to the city [Lima] to complain to the authorities [and] I there submitted a statement of all that they robbed me of.[4]

In areas more sparsely settled by Spaniards than Lima, a group of fifteen or so cimarrones plainly was a much greater menace. Lockhart describes the activities of just such a band, which operated in the Piura area throughout the 1540's and much of the next decade: "They raided Indian villages, killing the men and abducting the women, and robbed Indians and others on the highways. They had brought the usual commerce of highland with coastal Indians in that area to a complete halt. Their remote base was a real settlement, with houses and fields, and they had many children, 'mulattoes,' by the Indian women they had abducted." The band was finally overtaken and defeated by a Spanish expedition.[5]

With the tightening of royal control over Peru after the civil wars, there were fewer and fewer of these potentially dangerous bands of cimarrones, even in remote parts of the colony. Nevertheless, as the figures presented in Chapters 3 and 7 demonstrate, the runaway slave remained a serious problem through the period under study. Presumably, many slaveholders kept as close watch over their blacks as possible, particularly if they suspected discontent and the chance of flight, but most slaves had to be allowed a certain mobility if they were to be useful, and the opportunities to run away were numerous. In Lima and other urban areas, where so many slaves were hired out to others or were sent out to look for work, flight could not have been difficult, but even blacks who spent their lives in relative confinement found ways to escape. For example, one female slave in Lima was said to have "jumped over the walls [of her master's home] without cause or occasion," and another, who found serving her mistress in the convent of Santa Clara too confining, slipped out among the colored construction crew at work on the building dressed in men's clothing.[6] Slaves on rural plantations also often found the opportunity to flee, even in some cases under the watchful eyes of a "captain," a black chosen from among the slave gang to look out for this sort of thing.[7] Other slaves chose to make the attempt while traveling from point to point with their master or his agent. One such was Amador Zape, who though married to a free black woman in Cuzco, was being taken to Lima to be sold. Amador managed to escape along the way, but his efforts were to no avail, and he was duly put on the block.[8]

Once a runaway was on the loose, he faced the difficult task of sustaining himself while avoiding capture. Many, having no family or friends to turn to elsewhere, were tempted to stay in the vicinity of their former places of residence and haunts, where opportunities to pilfer food and the other necessities of life were easier to come by, but this strategy also increased the chances of apprehension. Indeed, most runaways seem to have been captured within a short time after flight. Others returned voluntarily. In 1620, for example, Lázaro Mandinga was sold with assurances against all physical and moral defects but with the admission that he had fled once and had come back of his own free will. In still other cases, flight appears to have been a game, a symbolic gesture, or a means of airing a grievance. In a bill of sale of 1585 the master of Luis Criollo stated that the black had fled from fear several times, but in each case had gone "to some friends of mine to plead for him"; and in 1595 Domingo Biafara was certified to be perfect in all respects except for his habit of absenting himself "at times" for two weeks at a stretch.[9]

Other runaways, either luckier or more determined than most, succeeded in evading pursuers for years. One of these was Francisca Criolla (age forty and married), who was sold in 1645 without guarantee because "the said black woman fled from my house and service for a long time without my knowing of her whereabouts." Another was Francisco Malamba, who in 1650, after a spell of freedom of "many years," was sold immediately on his capture by the Santa Hermandad.[10] Some adventurous slaves managed to put considerable distance between themselves and their masters before they were retaken. In 1610, for example, Catalina Conga managed to get from Lima to Santa, some 175 miles away. But her feat pales in comparison with that of Josef Criollo, also of Lima, who fled all the way to Mexico, where he lived for some three years before being recaptured. In both cases the masters chose to sell the slaves at the point of capture rather than arrange for their return to Lima.[11]

As a rule the would-be runaway chose his time carefully and slipped quietly away, without violence. But there were notable exceptions. One particularly daring attempt was made on the night of September 4, 1634, when four masked slaves seized a fishing boat in Callao harbor after overpowering its two black guards. One of the guards was killed, but the other, though wounded, swam to land and sounded the alarm.

Three of the runaways were recaptured some two weeks later at Santa, but one managed to escape into the hills.[12]

As we have seen, the consequences of a slave's misdeeds often fell heavily on his master. This was all the more true in the case of a runaway, where the costs of apprehension and confinement could be sizable. Consider the case of Cristóbal de Loayza, a notary public in Pisco, who had to pay the jailer's fees for a runaway who was caught and held in jail in Ica for six weeks before he learned of her whereabouts. Some masters, like the owner of Juan Negro (age thirty-five), got out as cheaply as they could. In this case, from 1566, rather than pay the forty pesos for his slave's release, the exasperated master sold the black to a leatherworker for eight dozen dressed sheepskins of unknown value. Similarly, Antón Biafara (age twenty-seven), condemned to the galleys for four years as a runaway in 1591, was unloaded by his master for a mere 290 pesos at a time of very high slave prices.[13]

Some owners adopted a stoic, even casual, approach to the problem, and when they sold an admitted runaway trusted that the good qualities of the slave would outweigh this one defect in the minds of buyers. On occasion, this calculation was correct. In 1567 the black cobbler Juan was sold for some 660 pesos on the understanding that he had not been seen in twenty days. Similarly, Francisco Criollo (age eighteen) brought 562.5 pesos in the marketplace in 1591 despite the admission that he had fled three times before and was currently absent, though his whereabouts was known. Other masters tried still a different approach, as in 1564 when Catalina Biafara was sold to the Hospital of Santa Ana with the assurance that she would not run away for a year's time.[14]

Predictably, the sale of cimarrones generated a fair measure of lawsuits between less-than-candid sellers and frustrated buyers. To give but one example, in 1598 Luis Ramírez purchased Francisca Criolla for 430 pesos only to later discover that she was a runaway. Ramírez filed suit for a refund, but after the case dragged on for two years, he finally settled for a fifty-peso rebate. From time to time unscrupulous third parties appear to have succeeded in tricking masters and runaway slaves alike. In 1632, for example, Bartolomé de Lanza, a familiar of the Holy Office, complained that two years before he had purchased Antón Angola from a man named Don Juan de Mendoza. Antón had promptly decamped and had been gone a considerable length of time when Lanza chanced on him in the street and took him home again. No sooner was this accomplished than Lanza found himself accused of theft by one Licenciado Gutiérrez Velázquez Ovando, who claimed to have purchased Antón in 1630 from still another party. Since the case stops at this point (perhaps indicating an amicable settlement), it is impossible to determine which of the various masters was guilty of deception. It is a fair guess, however, that someone without legal title to Antón befriended him only to sell him again into servitude.[15]

In some instances, there is evidence that runaways found genuine patrons, particularly when they fled to force their masters to sell them to others. This was probably the case with Ana Angola (age twenty-six and married), who in 1640 was sold to a free mulata after having been gone from her master's service for nearly a year. Ana's new mistress immediately resold her to another free mulatto for a substantially higher price; it seems likely that both mulattoes had known of the slave's whereabouts all along. Some owners were more stubborn than Ana's and refused to be maneuvered into selling their slaves. In the same year Doña Luisa Velásquez brought suit against Luis de Aguilar y Mora, a priest stationed in the Indian town of Chilca south of Lima, charging him with retaining her slave Marcelo Criollo for some ten months in the full knowledge that the black had fled her service. More than that, when the slave made off a second time and sought haven with Aguilar, the priest had simultaneously informed the agents she had sent to fetch him back that the black had fled to the wilds and made an offer to buy Marcelo for 300 pesos. When Doña Luisa had sent her agents back to refuse the offer and bring Marcelo home, Aguilar had denied that the black was in his possession, though the Indians of the village reported that the slave was hiding in the priest's house. Aguilar's motives are difficult to divine; presumably, his sister's having been the first wife of Doña Luisa's husband, a fact that was brought out in the hearing of the case, had some bearing. At any rate, Doña Luisa succeeded in obtaining Aguilar's arrest through the ecclesiastical courts; whether she also recovered Marcelo is not recorded.[16]

Also unrecorded is what drove Marcelo to take flight in the first place. From his viewpoint, and ours, many explanations are possible. For Spaniards of the time, the reasons for slave flight were not always so obvious. Indeed, some masters professed their complete bewilderment

at the phenomenon. Others chose to regard it as merely one more man-
ifestation of the perverse nature of the black, or even specifically of
the African- or American-born black. In 1649, for example, the aggrieved purchaser of Luisa Criolla declared in his redhibition suit that
his reservations about the slave's American birth had been fully justified: during the ten weeks she had been in his possession, Luisa had
fled at least seven times and was absent at present.[17] The commentator
Poma de Ayala, despite his contempt for criollos, was sophisticated
enough to suggest a more realistic explanation:

> Their masters make tributaries of the poor blacks, with little fear of God;
> they demand monthly tribute from them at the rate of twenty pesos for the
> females and an equal amount from the males, and if they do not pay, they
> whip them to death. On seeing themselves mistreated, victims of so many
> tribulations and molestations, they flee, absenting themselves and becoming
> cimarrones, since they are unable to revolt. Their masters in this fashion do
> not comply with what God commands to avoid the suffering of the poor
> blacks of this kingdom.[18]

The truth of Poma's generalizations is amply illustrated by the 1621
case of Benito Luis Angola (age twenty-five), slave of Captain Juan
Ortíz de Zárate, a seaman of Callao. Ortíz, like many other masters,
sent Benito out to look for work where he could find it. But the day
came when the slave did not have the required amount to turn over to
Ortíz, and rather than face his master's wrath, he fled. Within three
months or so, he hooked up with a gang of cimarrones near Cañete,
and for the next several months joined with them in raids on nearby
farms and attacks on Indians along the roads. In the end, Benito and
several other members of the gang were captured, tried, and hanged.[19]
Not all blacks who ran away rather than be punished for not meeting
their masters' demands met such a tragic end. In 1645, for example, a
Spanish weaver sold Juan García Congo (age twenty-four), a journeyman of the same craft, with the declaration that Juan had fled on occasion when unable to complete the day's tasks.[20]

Separation from family or marriage partner was another major reason for slave flight. From 1573 comes the pathetic case of an eleven-
year-old runaway, Angelina Criolla, whose mistress stated that when
the child was sent out on errands she would often go instead to her
father's house and stay for several days. Angelina was sold to a resident of Guayaquil, presumably making separation from her father per-

CONZEDERACION

COMOMALTRATA·A

sus negros y negras escla / bos y los buenos esclabos lotte
ua con pasencia pora / mor de dios y no le dan de bestir y
de comer y no conze / deran q le yzo dios y murio por ellos co
mo por los españoles

Fig. 5. A Spanish slaveowner and his wife abusing their slaves

manent. In a similar case of 1625 Juan Criollo (age twelve) was declared in the bill of sale to have fled twice to his mother's house. In the same year Antón Biafara (age twenty), a journeyman cobbler in Pisco, left for Lima without permission to search for his father. In this case, Antón's master was humane enough to sell Antón to a resident of the capital for 600 pesos.[21] Black husbands and wives, owned by different masters and separated by the demands of slavery, frequently attempted reunion through flight. In 1610, for example, Isabel Criolla's new owner was alerted to the fact that she was married to a slave of the chief constable of Guayaquil and that she had twice fled to Callao, evidently with the intention of taking ship to join her husband. From time to time masters who were either kind or wise moved to end such separations by acquiring the other marriage partner. This was the happy lot of Mariana Folupa, who had run away to join her husband and was hidden by him; his owner reunited the two by purchasing Mariana in 1645.[22]

Clearly, many other reasons moved slaves to the often dangerous expedient of flight; we content ourselves with three examples. The first is that of Magdalena Criolla (age fourteen), sold in 1610 with the declaration that she had fled once to her mother, a slave of the purchaser, before a whipping. A decade earlier, María Criolla (age thirty) was sold with full assurances for the very high price of 787.5 pesos, but it was noted that she had run away in the past while suing for her liberty. A final and curious example concerns one Gabriel Angola, whose master stated that the slave had once fled for over two months to the province of Conchucos after a quarrel with a Spaniard.[23]

Many Peruvian blacks, in short, found good and sufficient reasons to run away, and their flight was of concern both to the masters involved and to the authorities. The two groups, however, approached the runaway problem with different perspectives and emphases. Most masters simply wanted to get their slaves back as quickly as possible, and with a minimum of expense and legal entanglements. The authorities, appreciating that many runaways had to steal for their living, were likewise intent on quick apprehension, but the government, mindful of experiences in Panama and the Antilles, was even more concerned to prevent the formation of bands of cimarrones in the countryside. Further, the authorities were bent on having the retrieval of runaways financed out of the pockets of their owners, whether directly or indirectly, rather than from the public coffers. Under these circumstances the slave-holders and the government, though they recognized a problem of concern to both, did not always see eye to eye on its solution.

From a very early date the authorities began to consider ways to discourage slave flight and, if possible, to capture runaways before they could band together. As early as 1535 the officials of Lima took a stern hand, providing that a slave who fled for six days was to lose his genitals, and that one who stayed away longer was to lose his life. The enforcement of this and other regulations was entrusted initially to rural constables, the first of whom, apparently, was appointed by Francisco Pizarro in 1537, with responsibility for the outskirts of Lima and the port of Callao and authority to punish most African and Indian wrongdoers on the spot (blacks involved in the death of a native were to be brought to the city for formal trial).

In the following years *alguaciles del campo* continued to be appointed regularly to patrol the outskirts of Lima, Callao, and (until corregimientos were established in Peru in the 1570's) various valleys, including Nazca, Chancay, and Ica. There were not enough of them, however, to contend with large cimarrón bands, and so these became the province of others. In 1549, for example, the Lima city council authorized the *alcalde ordinario* to gather together the men, arms, and horses necessary to apprehend gangs then plaguing the city. The council pledged to reimburse the alcalde for his expenses from municipal revenues and further provided that "if it is necessary and seems to him appropriate to inflict some punishment on the said cimarrones or on the Indians, either to repay them for their crimes or to learn of the runaways' whereabouts, or to admonish them, he may do so and execute justice on the guilty according to the ordinances of this city and as he sees fit, in order that example be given to other blacks." Such vigilante-like proceedings against runaway blacks were common in Lima during these years, and perhaps in other parts of Peru as well.[24]

Slaves and free persons of color were used whenever possible in the apprehension of runaways, primarily for their knowledge of the habits and hiding places of fleeing slaves, but also perhaps for their linguistic abilities when the escapees were bozales. This practice began very early. In 1549, for example, the Lima city council instructed two of its members to "negotiate with the black of the cobbler Medina in the manner that seems appropriate to them about capturing and bringing in black runaways, and . . . in return for his services [to] promise him that the city will free him." As it turned out, the negotiators did not have to go that far; it was agreed that the slave would merely be paid for his time, and that his master would be reimbursed in the event of death. Another black held out for more favorable terms. In exchange for information leading to the capture of certain runaways, the city agreed to apply 200 pesos toward the purchase of his freedom. Other persons of color who captured or killed cimarrones were promised the privilege of wearing a cape-and-sword costume or were given monetary rewards; usually the head of the runaway was accepted as proof of accomplishment.

Bounty payments seem to have been especially effective. These were initiated as early as 1539, when the city offered ten pesos for the capture of any black absent for more than a day, with the slaveholder responsible for payment of this reward and for all related judicial costs and fees. A decade later, the city council proposed the establishment of a permanent bounty fund, to be maintained by the slaveholders, for the capture and punishment of runaways. The council also considered it high time to codify legislation on the subject into a body of ordinances "similar to those of San Juan de Puerto Rico and Hispaniola." Accordingly, several city officials were instructed to discuss both projects with the governor of Peru, Pedro de la Gasca. The result was a slave code that, with some modification, continued in force until the end of the period under study.[25]

Formulated in consultation with the Audiencia as well as the city council, the Gasca ordinances did not simply codify existing legislation, but attempted to provide new solutions to the runaway problem and new resources with which to achieve them.[26] First, new penalties were decreed for runaway slaves. For an absence of more than three days, the offender was to receive 100 lashes and a day in the stocks. If he did not return within ten days and if there was evidence that sexual relations with a black or native woman had been his motive, his genitals were to be removed publicly; otherwise, a foot was to be cut off, with additional punishments being administered as his other crimes warranted. If a black did not return within twenty days, the death penalty was to be imposed automatically on his capture. Any master seeking to spare his slave the death penalty on the claim his slave was absent with permission would have to present legal proof to that effect within the time limits set by the judge who tried the case. A slave who fled a second time for under ten days was to be treated like a ten-day offender, and one who escaped a third time was to be executed automatically.[27]

A second set of provisions strengthened the bounty system for the recovery of slaves. Every inhabitant of the Lima area was empowered to capture runaways, and was to receive a reward of from six to twenty-five pesos, depending on the length of the cimarrón's absence. Captors had the right to kill escapees who resisted apprehension, and, as in the past, might claim their reward on presentation of the runaway's head. A new fund was established to pay the bounties, which was to be financed out of head-taxes imposed on all slaves: two pesos for each slave of ten years or older; one peso for each slave child under ten and for any babies born in future; and four pesos for every black subsequently imported into the city.[28] This duty was to be collected only once, regardless of how many times the slave changed hands thereafter. Within nine days of the promulgation of the code, all slaveholders were to pay the tax to the city clerk, who in a book reserved for the purpose was to record the date, the name and brand of the slave, and the name of his master. Future importations were subject to the same deadline and were to be processed in the same manner. To expedite collection, the clerk was to bring his records every Friday to the council meeting so that delinquent accounts could be examined and the appropriate action taken. Administration of the fund was entrusted to four men: two members of the council, including an alcalde, who were to be selected annually and were to receive all tax receipts, enter the amounts collected in an account book, and deposit the monies in a chest (*caja de los negros*) to be located in the as-yet-unbuilt quarters of the city council; and the city clerk and the corregidor of Lima,[29] who were to verify and sign each entry in the account book. Each man was to have one of the four keys that were required to open the money chest. Bounty money and judicial costs were to be paid from the fund as the occasion required, and proof of such payments entered in the account book. The clerk was to receive forty pesos a year for his services in this connection, and the other three officials twenty.

The ordinances provided that runaways had to be reported to the city clerk within twenty days. Masters who failed to meet that deadline were liable for all costs connected with capture and trial, and those who attempted to evade the requirement altogether were to be fined fifty pesos to benefit the fund. No person was to remove any chains, nose rings, stocks, or other markings placed on a slave, or hide or in any way aid a suspected cimarrón. Free blacks and mulattoes, traditionally suspected of harboring runaways, were to report to the office of the city clerk within nine days to register their names and places of residence, under penalty of 100 lashes and exile. A separate decree exempted from punishment all runaways who voluntarily surrendered themselves within twenty days after the promulgation of the ordinances, which occurred on June 1, 1549.[30]

For the next several years the bounty system, supplemented by an occasional large expedition to apprehend runaway bands, provided an apparently satisfactory solution to the cimarrón problem. Soon after Cañete became viceroy in 1555, however, he moved to strengthen the institutional arrangements for the recapture of runaways and the prevention of crime in the countryside. It was not so much the Peruvian situation that alarmed Cañete. Rather, having seen at first hand the strength of the cimarrón bands on the Isthmus on his journey to assume viceregal office, he was determined to spare Peru such disorders.[31] Focusing his efforts on the greatest concentration of slaves in the colony, Cañete in 1557 established the office of *alcalde de la Hermandad* to operate in the environs of Lima. Two men were to fill this post, which was to be financed out of head-tax revenues and to be patterned on the Spanish equivalent in Seville. The *alcaldes de la Hermandad* thus had the same duties in the rural areas that the *alcaldes ordinarios* had in the towns—the arrest and punishment of all wrongdoers—but given the large numbers of slaves in the Lima area, it was anticipated that much time would be devoted to the apprehension of runaways and other black criminals. The two outgoing *alcaldes ordinarios* of Lima were to automatically become *alcaldes de la Hermandad* for the succeeding year.[32]

Subordinate to the heads of the rural constabulary were a varying number of assistants, known as *cuadrilleros*, assigned to patrol the countryside in search of runaway slaves, to prevent the indiscriminate cutting of the region's few trees for lumber or charcoal, and to guard the crops. The first appointments were made in 1556-57, when an *alguacil del campo* was hired as *cuadrillero mayor* at a salary of 300 pesos a year. He was supposed to have six assistants, three blacks and three whites, but the proposed annual salary of 150 pesos was too low for two of the Spaniards, and they refused their posts until the pay was increased by fifty pesos. (The other white man, presumably, was not so choosy, nor were the three blacks, one of whom evidently had already been acting as a constable.) The effect of these appointments was to divide law enforcement outside the city between the unsalaried *algua-ciles del campo*, subordinate to the municipal justices and dependent on fines and bounties, and the salaried constables of the Hermandad. Otherwise, little distinction was made between their duties and rank. For example, in 1557 an *alguacil del campo* was appointed with specific authorization to recapture slaves, though the six cuadrilleros above had just been hired. In similar fashion, the *cuadrillero mayor* was sometimes also given the title of *alguacil del campo*.[33]

Cañete turned his attention specifically to the runaway in a set of ordinances he framed for Lima in 1560. Slaveholders were warned that blacks were not to be sent out on their own to seek work either within the city or on the estates outside. Rather, in order to keep track of the whereabouts of such slaves, a contract between the black and his employer was required beforehand. Slaveholders who violated the ordinance were to pay a twenty-five-peso fine for the first offense and lose the slave for the second.[34] Within three days of promulgation, masters were to provide the secretary of the Audiencia with the names of all slaves who had fled their service; failure to comply would mean confiscation of the slave if he was retaken. All subsequent runaways were likewise to be reported within three days. It was further provided that Indians might capture or kill cimarrones found in their villages and receive a reward of thirty pesos for each one brought in dead or alive. In the event the runaway was killed, his head sufficed as proof.

That a number of people were not above hiding runaways in return for their labor is indicated by the harsh penalties imposed by Cañete. Spaniards found sheltering cimarrones were to be fined 100 pesos for the first offense, and were to pay double that amount and face exile for the second. ("Exile" in most cases meant a term of forced military service in Chile.) For the same crime, an Indian noble was to have his head shorn for the first offense and to lose his high station for the second. Other Indians escaped with 200 lashes. For slaves who hid or aided runaways the penalties were 100 lashes for the initial violation, castration, and then death for later infractions, and for free persons of color the first offense brought 100 lashes and the second, death. The sale of any article to a runaway was punishable by 200 lashes and exile.[35]

The following years witnessed a slackening of legislative concern over runaways and rural crime, at least in part because so many measures were already on the books, but the 1560's and 1570's still saw a few laws framed on the subject. In 1566 the bounty system was extended to the Indian villages of northern Peru by Gregorio González de Cuenca, a member of the Lima Audiencia. Moreover, the innovation soon bore fruit, for in 1568 the Indians of Trujillo were paid 100 pesos for helping capture "some black runaways who had killed certain Spaniards and Indians, and who went about robbing and waylaying."[36] As a further step to discourage disorder in the countryside around Lima, the city council in 1571 forbade more than two blacks to gather wood outside the city together. In the next year (as we have seen in Chapter 3) the council flirted with the idea of branding known runaways on the cheek, a measure the Audiencia refused to approve.[37]

Viceroy Toledo also diverted a fraction of his formidable energies to a consideration of the cimarrón problem. Like Cañete, Toledo had the example of Panama before him, where the runaways now cooperated with the English, and he feared that a similar situation would at some point arise in Peru. Unhappy at the fact that blacks were indispensable to the coastal economy, and consequently grew in numbers "daily," Toledo endorsed the harshest of Cañete's measures to discourage runaways, including castration and the extensive use of spies to flush cimarrones from their hiding places. The viceroy reported with satisfaction that the second tactic had resulted in the capture of a band of some thirty or forty runaways, many of whom were hanged or castrated. In this case, the spies themselves were cimarrones who had been threatened with death for highway robbery if they refused to cooperate. Though Toledo confessed that more fundamental solutions to the problem were needed and promised to devise them, in fact he did no more than reiterate some standing policy. Among the ordinances he framed for Cuzco on his tour of the highlands were two articles that in routine fashion forbade free persons of color to shelter runaways, and in 1577, now back in Lima, he again outlawed the practice of permitting slaves to wander about in search of work, lodging wherever they pleased in the process. Perhaps understandably in view of the intractability of the problem, Toledo's inventiveness failed him beyond this point.[38]

Perhaps the best way to measure the effectiveness of Spanish control measures in the countryside is to study the operation of the Lima Hermandad, an institution on which Cañete had pinned his hopes and which he had endeavored to endow with the requisite authority, personnel, and revenues. Between 1549 and 1588 a total of 14,138 pesos of head-tax monies was spent on the capture of escaped slaves and the general control of the colored population on the outskirts of the capital, the larger part of it after 1557, when Cañete earmarked this revenue for the support of the Hermandad. Broken down by categories, this sum was spent as follows: 8,504 pesos for the salaries of administrators and personnel; 2,151 pesos to organize special expeditions; 1,948 pesos in bounties; 700 pesos to purchase slave cuadrilleros; 135 pesos for judicial costs; and 700 pesos for miscellaneous expenses.[39]

Spread over a span of forty years, this sum represents an average annual expenditure of some 350 pesos, a modest enough price to pay for the control of runaways. Indeed, at its best the Hermandad was both an economical and an efficient institution, able not only to thin the ranks of the cimarrones through the routine patrolling of the constables, but also to mount special expeditions of some size when necessary to break up runaway bands. Don Francisco de Ampuero, a Lima councilman who frequently accompanied these excursions, recalled one of 1561 when the forces of the Hermandad went to punish some runaways who had gathered in the Carabayllo region, "from where they came out to block the road to Chancay and committed murders and harms and robberies, as they did to the four servants of the Conde de Nieva and other people." Fifty men went with the expedition, at a cost to the head-tax fund of 300 pesos, "and we fought with the said blacks and captured and killed more than fifteen of them, and many others died of thirst while fleeing." The apprehended cimarrones were taken to Lima and executed. As a result of this and other sorties, Ampuero declared that the district had been cleared of runaways, "and the said blacks don't escape as often as they used to, nor do they gather in bands as they were accustomed to doing, and, if some black flees, later he is found and brought in by the cuadrilleros."[40]

As the figures above indicate, continued reliance was placed on the bounty system to capture runaway slaves. The nearly 2,000 pesos spent in this fashion were paid both to the cuadrilleros, who were entitled to these rewards to supplement their small salaries, and to private citizens—like one Martín de Rivera, who in 1554 captured a runaway described as a "cimarrón leader" near Maranga. Occasionally, Indians proved useful in this respect, as in 1566 when a native group held in encomienda by three Lima residents received a total of 140 pesos for their help in the apprehension of runaways. Funds from the head-tax were also used to place rewards on the heads of the most notorious escapees. In 1573, for example, fifty pesos was offered for the capture of Dominguillo Negro,

who maimed and left for dead one Blas, a slave of Francisco de Trujillo, and afterward committed certain robberies in Callao and in the countryside, and now recently has wounded Rodrigo Ortíz, taking a lance from him . . . , and there is great fear that this black, as a person now damned, will try to form a band of blacks to commit greater harm.

In this case, the *alguaciles del campo* caught and killed the violent Dominguillo and claimed the reward.[41]

Despite some unquestionable accomplishments, the Hermandad was plagued by inefficiency, corruption, and bickering during this period. In large part these difficulties stemmed from something Cañete had not foreseen, the awkwardness of a financial arrangement that made the operation of the Hermandad dependent on head-tax revenues controlled by the Lima municipal council. To say the least, the interests of the city authorities and those of the Hermandad were often at variance. In the first place, revenues that belonged to the *caja de los negros* were frequently borrowed by the city to finance other projects. This practice began in 1553, when 500 pesos was taken from the fund (over the objections of the councilman entrusted with its administration) to repair and enlarge the quarters of the city council. In the years that followed, the municipality again and again yielded to this temptation, spending nearly 2,400 pesos of head-tax revenues on everything from the water and sewage systems to the construction of the jail. In addition, an unspecified amount was withdrawn in 1576 to purchase a black and equipment for street cleaning, and still more was borrowed after the 1586 earthquake to repair the city hall. It is doubtful if the financially hard-pressed municipality ever repaid any of these loans.[42]

The head tax was collected in a negligent manner, which also contributed to the frequent sad economic state of the caja. The city made no attempt to collect the tax on slaves born in the district, but instead concentrated on the bozales who arrived at Callao. Ordinarily, private individuals or constables under the supervision of the city's majordomo or a councilman collected the tax on a percentage basis.[43] But even when these men were conscientious and able, the tax was difficult to collect. As we have seen, the dodge of landing slave cargoes on the beaches outside Callao to evade the tax was practiced often enough for the Lima authorities to take preventive measures. The first came in 1573, when ship captains were notified that they would henceforth have to show all the slaves they carried on their manifests and pay the required taxes before delivering the blacks to their owners. The order was reaffirmed in 1578 so that the head-tax revenue might "not be lost as it has been in the past," but the remedy could not have been entirely efficacious, since in 1585 the notary in charge of ships' registers at Callao was asked to keep the collection agents posted on how many slaves arrived on each vessel.

Despite all efforts, collection of the tax was a hit-and-miss thing, as indicated by the testimony during a 1588-95 suit filed by a group of merchants to abolish the tax. According to one man, whose testimony (remarkably enough) had been solicited by the city, the municipal clerk had estimated that the duty was collected on perhaps one slave in twenty. Other testimony was equally damaging.[44] Further, even the funds that Lima was fortunate enough to collect were accounted for in a careless fashion. Annual audits were not instituted until the late 1550's, but even after that head-tax revenues continued to be handled casually. In 1576, for example, the city council discovered that though there was supposed to be a chest for the deposit of the funds, "since the money was collected little by little, the past administrators had not been able to put it in the chest until the end of the year, and . . . with the passage of time, the chest had been lost." A new one was purchased.[45]

For all these reasons, the Hermandad was plagued almost from the start with financial difficulties. Even when funds were available, the salaries of the cuadrilleros were so low, and their duties so uninviting, that personnel changes were frequent. The city tried at first to keep the number of constables steady at six and to maintain some sort of racial balance, but few Spaniards were willing to sign on for a salary that rarely exceeded 200 pesos annually. Free coloreds, in contrast, were quite willing to work for as little as fifty pesos a year in some cases, and soon outnumbered the Spaniards on the force. But the savings was hardly significant enough to keep the Hermandad's coffers filled. Indeed, in 1562 the city was forced to admit the *caja de los negros* did not have the funds to respond to an alarm that a band of cimarrones had gathered in the area, and pleaded for Spanish volunteers, with the promise of reimbursement for provisions when money became available. In the following year the cuadrilleros were informed that their salaries would have to be suspended, and were given the choice of resigning or continuing their duties for such compensation as the bounties might produce. The Spaniards on the force promptly quit. For the next few years only three or four mulattoes served as cuadrilleros; they were paid the lowest of salaries or none at all.[46]

In 1565 the city council effected even greater economies, ruling that since the cuadrilleros were salaried, they ought not to receive full bounty payments on captured slaves already covered by the head tax (and for whom in consequence the caja was liable). These funds henceforth would be used to pay the judicial authorities who heard these cases. As an incentive, however, the constables were to receive four pesos for every runaway captured, a ceiling that was applied to the *alguaciles del campo* as well. This change, reasonable enough on its face, saved the city a modest amount of money: the bounties it paid to the constables of the Hermandad dwindled from a total of more than 600 pesos in the years 1551-65 (in addition to salary) to a total of only 197 in 1566-88. In 1572 the city council took the further and more drastic step of abolishing the constables' salaries altogether. (They did, however, sometimes get money thereafter for equipment and for medical treatment of wounds suffered in the line of duty.) Thus, in the space of fifteen years Cañete's idea of a salaried and reasonably honest Hermandad had for all practical purposes been destroyed.[47]

To their credit, the city authorities realized that the innovations of 1565 and 1572 would lead to a rapid decline of the rural constabulary and that alternatives would have to be found. Several things were tried out in the 1570's and 1580's. To supplement an often-small number of cuadrilleros other men, unsalaried and frequently untitled, or the alguaciles of certain areas were appointed from time to time to carry the staff of justice in the countryside. In addition, the city purchased two slaves, Pedro Galán and Francisco Jolofo, to act as cuadrilleros. Though both came relatively high on the market, the move seemed a smart one at first, for the slaves would draw no salary and claim no bounties and would cost little in upkeep. Moreover, they were wise in the ways of cimarrones and their hiding places, particularly Galán, who had been a runaway leader before turning informer and was said to be well acquainted with the countryside around Lima. But the city soon had reason to regret the decision. For one thing, the council had to pay heavy medical expenses for the wounds the slaves suffered in action, and indeed they were often too ill even to go on patrol. For another, there were many complaints about the pair, charging them with using their positions to commit various thefts and crimes, as well as with general arrogance and inefficiency. The city made numerous unsuccessful attempts to sell the two, but as late as 1598 Jolofo at least was still employed as a cuadrillero.[48]

In any case, neither of these expedients provided a sufficient number of constables to apprehend runaways, and in 1575 the Audiencia attempted to remedy the situation by appointing cuadrilleros on its own initiative. The city council, claiming that the privilege was reserved for the viceroy and the municipality, lodged a strong and successful protest against this intervention.[49] But that did not solve the problem of law enforcement in the countryside, and to attract men to serve as constables without depleting the funds of the caja, the city gave informal approval, if not official sanction, to two dubious practices. First, cuadrilleros were permitted to act as virtual free agents, negotiating directly with masters for the return of runaways for whatever price the traffic would bear. The cuadrilleros had had no such license when they were salaried; indeed in 1557 they had been fined for returning cimarrones to their masters and accepting compensation behind the backs of the authorities.[50] But by the 1570's the practice had become an open secret. Or so several witnesses alleged in the 1588 lawsuit between the merchants and the city. More, some declared that the cuadrilleros often hid their black captives in an attempt to improve their bargaining position; and one witness went so far as to charge that the constables used this tactic with the consent and even connivance of their superiors.

Second, and worse still, municipal justices who tried runaway cases forced even those masters who had paid the head tax on their slaves to reimburse the cuadrilleros before the captured blacks were released. One slaveholder who testified in the 1588 trial declared that he had always paid the head tax, and that when slaves fled his service he had always notified the constables to capture them,

and he has come for them and asked the judicial authorities for them, and the authorities have said to this witness that the imprisoned blacks will be returned to him and that this witness satisfy the said constables. [Accordingly] this witness, in order to free his blacks, bargained with the constables and paid them, and he did the same thing when the said constables brought the slaves to the home of this witness, because [he] told them not to carry them to the jail and that he would satisfy them in order to avoid costs, and this witness understands that the other slaveholders have done the same thing.

Curiously, the Audiencia made no sustained effort to enforce a stricter interpretation of the head-tax ordinances, though the complaints of slaveholders sometimes led to a moderation of the fees and fines imposed.[51]

In this suit, the city maintained that if the head tax had been paid and the conditions of the ordinances met, runaways were returned free of charge. However, an examination of municipal records reveals that no attempt was made to inform slaveholders of their rights unless the point was pressed. In 1572, for example, the head-tax regulations were re-proclaimed only after the city attorney warned that many slaveholders who had paid the duty were up in arms over the fees demanded by the constables. In 1580 Toledo was also moved to inquire by what right the municipality collected the head tax. The city council explained the matter and again promulgated the relevant ordinances, stressing that runaways had to be reported within three days. Toledo, for his part, promised new legislation, but this never materialized. Perhaps influenced by Toledo's skepticism, the Audiencia suspended collection of the head tax in 1582 pending a complete accounting, but the city, successfully appealing the decision, carried on until the merchants took legal action six years later.[52]

While the rural constables eked out a living as best they could, the office that was supposed to control and coordinate their activities stood in legal limbo. Cañete, it will be recalled, had provided that the two outgoing *alcaldes ordinarios* were automatically to become *alcaldes de la Hermandad* the next year. However, for unexplained reasons, Cañete violated his own ruling in 1560 by naming a Lima councilman to the post. The city protested this infringement of its electoral prerogatives, and the result was a dispute with the viceroy that dragged on until 1566, when the appointment of an *alcalde de la Hermandad* was suspended pending royal review of the case. Only principle was involved in this wrangle, since the office carried no salary, slim judicial fees, and great responsibility without the resources to back it up.[53] The city council named *alcaldes de la Hermandad* in the years 1571-75 to lead expeditions against runaway bands in the area, though it had no legal authority to do so, but thereafter the office was once again allowed to lapse. Now when military excursions against large groups of cimarrones were needed, they were led by members of the Lima city council and financed by head-tax revenues; and the cuadrilleros maintained their routine patrols under the supervision of the *alcaldes ordinarios*. For all practical purposes, the Hermandad had ceased to exist.[54]

Toward the end of the 1580's, Viceroy Villar made an attempt to revive the rural constabulary along the lines laid down by Cañete thirty years earlier. Responding to reports that runaways were committing numerous crimes as far away as Cañete and Chancay and were beginning to band together, Villar reestablished the office of *alcalde de la Hermandad* in 1586 as a viceregal appointment. During this same period, the Lima city council was petitioning the Crown for recognition of its right to elect this official, but the municipality made no objection to Villar's appointment. In large part, this newfound harmony between city and viceroy over the Hermandad was due to Villar's plans for strengthening the organization, first by guaranteeing his appointee a salary of 800 pesos a year through membership in the viceregal guard and, more importantly, by expanding the cuadrillero force to a sergeant and twelve assistants, all salaried. To provide the necessary revenue, the head tax was to be raised by a half peso, to four and a half per slave.[55]

If the city was gratified by Villar's proposals, however, others were not. The head tax had long been resented by the Spanish merchants and traders, who now complained that the rate was too high, and that besides, the cimarrón menace, which had given rise to it in the 1540's, had largely subsided. Twice in the 1560's and again in 1589 the powerful merchant guild of Seville had used its influence at court to prompt royal inquiries concerning the legitimacy and utility of the tax,[56] and before the last request for information could be answered the merchants of Lima took matters into their own hands and (as we have seen) in 1588 filed suit against the city for abolition of the duty. By the time the case was finally adjudicated, Villar had been succeeded by the second Marqués de Cañete, and his project long since abandoned. As for the city, it saw its right to collect the revenue upheld by the Audiencia in 1595 and then confirmed by the Crown two years later, though this victory did not imply approval of its administration of the funds.[57] Collection of the head tax, meanwhile, was virtually suspended during the early years of the suit, leaving Villar's appointee as *alcalde de la Hermandad* with few constables to command, and the viceroy attempted no new initiatives.

By the account of Cañete's biographer, at least, Villar's successor found himself confronted with a deteriorating situation:

Around the city of Los Reyes, among the woods, marshes, and canefields there were a large number of black runaways who went about pillaging, robbing, and assaulting to such an extent that robberies and deaths were commonplace, and one could not go outside the city for a league without much risk, and since there were no *alcaldes de la Hermandad* in the cities, towns, and villages of the kingdom, these crimes were not prosecuted or punished, nor did the municipal justices take steps to punish these delinquents . . . , and the unfortunate natives, being people without recourse, endured it, and had no security in their wives, lives, residences, or fortunes.

On the other side of the Rímac River and bridge of the city of Los Reyes, called San Lázaro, were some settlements and shacks, in which lived newly arrived Indians who had fled from their settlements [*reducciones*], and who lived without religious instruction and as lawless people, persecuted by the mestizos, mulattoes, blacks, and zambaigos, who mistreated, robbed, and violently made use of them, and they were unsafe in their own houses, and many other offenses against God were committed.[58]

Contemplating these excesses around Lima and in other parts of Peru, Cañete ordered the establishment of the Hermandad colony-wide in 1590. Two years later he proudly reported that thanks to this measure, many "black and mulatto cimarrones" had been brought to justice.[59] The Crown approved the action and, responding to a petition from the city of Cuzco, declared the Hermandad a municipal institution with the same authority and prerogatives as its counterparts in Spain.[60] The viceregal capital represented a special case, however, and Cañete's actions there were intended to be temporary ones subject to an agreement between the municipality and the Crown on the status of the Hermandad. The viceroy reappointed Villar's choice to head the rural constabulary.

The new office holder promptly appealed to Cañete to meet the cimarrón menace by assigning some salary to the cuadrilleros named by his predecessor. Cañete, mindful that the head tax was under litigation, first wisely attempted in 1591 to bring the city and the merchants to agreement by cutting the duty on slaves in half, to two pesos per head.

When this effort at compromise failed, the viceroy called into play the royal authority he had been granted to investigate the head tax, appointing a Lima councilman to audit the head-tax records and giving him permission to collect the duty despite the lawsuit.

In the end, as noted, the city successfully reclaimed the right to appoint its own collectors, but the short-term effect of Cañete's action was to keep funds flowing in and out of the caja (including bounties to the cuadrilleros and a loan of 1,500 pesos to the city that had nothing to do with runaways). Furthermore, in 1594 the viceroy decided that the Lima Hermandad would consist of a sergeant and six assistants. This was half the number envisioned by Villar, but perhaps more realistic since all were to be salaried. In the same year Cañete rounded out his efforts to control runaways with a few ordinances on the subject in the nearly 250 he promulgated for the governance of Lima, but these regulations merely echoed those issued by his father thirty-four years before.[61]

Withal, the dispute between the city of Lima and the royal authorities over who was to select the *alcalde de la Hermandad* was still to be resolved. Between 1574 and 1592 the city appealed to the Crown on three occasions to affirm the municipal council's right to elect the head of the rural constabulary.[62] The Crown refused to commit itself, and shortly before Cañete left office in 1596 he attempted to establish an interim solution by ruling that the municipality could name an alcalde on an annual basis provided it did not choose a member of the city council. Lima accepted this compromise, which was ultimately given royal approval, and for the next several decades, with rare exceptions, the head of the Hermandad was regularly selected by the council from among the most prominent citizens.[63]

With the head tax and selection of the alcalde now apparently under municipal control, steps were taken to increase the effectiveness and standing of the Hermandad. In 1598 the number of constables was doubled after the city complained to Viceroy Velasco that the six cuadrilleros then employed were more interested in arresting blacks within the city, so as to return them to their masters at exorbitant fees behind the backs of the authorities, than in patrolling the countryside, with the result that none were available when emergencies arose. The municipality proposed the appointment of six unsalaried constables, who would serve in the city and make their living from fines, to supplement the salaried men, who should be compelled to patrol the rural areas. Velasco agreed to the increased staff, but insisted that all the constables be salaried. Despite the dismal experiences of the past, the city also reconciled itself to buying slaves to serve as cuadrilleros, principally because of their contacts among the slave population. Thus, one Pedro Angola was acquired in 1599 after the information he provided led to the break-up of a runaway settlement. Finally, in 1602 Viceroy Velasco attempted to increase the prestige of the Lima Hermandad by extending the alcalde's authority to "the corregimientos and districts of the villas of Cañete and Arnedo," "the district of the corregimiento of Ica," and "the districts of the corregimientos of the provinces of Huaylas, Cajatambo, Jauja, and Casma." With this broadened jurisdiction, the head of the Lima Hermandad became—in theory, if not in practice—a provincial-level official, an elevation in status that was reflected in his new title, *alcalde provincial*.[64]

The city had little time to savor its triumph, for almost from the start its authority over the Hermandad was whittled away. At the end of the process, some thirty years later, the Lima Hermandad had been transformed into a proprietary office whose finances were controlled by the Crown. The groundwork for the first step of this metamorphosis was laid in 1599, with the death of the longtime sergeant of the constabulary. The city then proceeded to choose a new man annually, usually from among the cuadrilleros or *alguaciles del campo*, but the selection was accompanied by so much wrangling and favoritism that in 1606 the Audiencia intervened and claimed the authority to name all the personnel of the Hermandad, sergeant and constables alike. The city's efforts to reverse the decision were fruitless.[65] The lessons of the 1588-95 lawsuit, an action that had been won in spite of unrefuted charges of municipal maladministration, were also lost on the city authorities. In 1598, a scant three years after the legal victory over the merchants, it was disclosed that a councilman who had administered the head tax had appropriated a large sum for his personal use. (The money was eventually repaid, but not until 1603.) To correct such abuses, in 1600 the majordomo of the city was made responsible for the collection of the tax, 6 per cent of which he was to keep as compensation, though trustees of the caja were to continue to oversee the accounting. The very next year it was learned that the majordomo had attempted to pay the constables in cheap clothing instead of silver, and the administration of the head tax was assigned to the city clerk, who was to be paid 7 per cent of all revenue collected. Meanwhile, the chest designated to hold the proceeds had been misplaced again, and a new one was purchased, with keys going to the clerk and the other trustees. However, attempts at reform from within had come too late. In 1605 Viceroy Monterrey ordered the *alcalde de la Hermandad* to seize the keys to the chest and to remove the collectors and trustees appointed by the city. The city successfully appealed this decision, but in 1608 the new viceroy, the Marqués de Montesclaros, again removed collection of the head tax from municipal control. Thereafter, the tax was collected by a viceregal appointee, and all expenditures had to be authorized by the viceroy.[66]

The next decade brought a bid to make the capture of runaways a matter of private enterprise, a job for professional slavecatchers, along the lines of the *rancheadores* of Cuba. Specifically, in 1617 and again in 1619, Captain Pedro López de Lara, a former head of the Hermandad, proposed that slaveholders pay him a peso a year for each black, with the understanding that he would either return a runaway to his owner within a certain time limit or pay the assessed value of the slave. Viceroy Esquilache was interested enough to solicit the opinions of the archbishop, the ecclesiastical cabildo, and several monasteries, but the city, perhaps with an eye to the reassertion of its lost jurisdiction over the head-tax revenues, fought successfully to defeat the proposal. In return López was re-elected *alcalde de la Hermandad* in 1620. After a final, futile effort to revive interest in his scheme in 1622, he let the matter drop.[67]

Meanwhile, the city's petitions to the Audiencia of 1622-23 to regain control of the head tax had the unintended effect of setting in motion a chain of events that led to a royal takeover of the revenue. The *fiscal* of the Audiencia, Luis Enríquez, was sufficiently moved by the city's contentions to investigate the question. This led to a 1623 letter to the Crown in which he alleged there were serious irregularities in the collection of the head tax. According to Enríquez, the collectors appointed by the viceroys received a third of the revenue as their commission, and as a result the current appointee was paying the caja only 1,000 pesos annually. Moreover, a talk with a former collector had revealed that he had pocketed a surplus of 5,000 to 6,000 pesos. Enríquez explained that this would be easy enough to do by falsifying the import records, and that he had called on the viceroy to review the history of the tax and produce a record of its administration for the Crown. This demand implied—and probably with good cause—that the viceroys had used the post as a form of patronage. The *fiscal* suggested that the royal treasury officials at Callao administer the revenue, and that any surplus pass into the coffers of the Crown.[68]

The home government was sufficiently interested to order Viceroy Guadalcázar in 1626 to make a full report of the matter. Guadalcázar framed a soothing reply two years later, assuring the Crown that the viceregal appointees who collected the revenue were "always" bonded and subject to audit, and that no funds were disbursed without authorization. Since the audits were made on the basis of ships' registers, there was no chance of fraud. The viceroy advised against placing the revenue under the administration of the treasury officials since it did not properly belong to the Crown, and its collection would distract from more important duties. In 1630 the home government agreed with the viceregal analysis and ordered the system to be left as it was.[69]

Thanks to the accounts of the head-tax revenue Guadalcázar forwarded in his letter of 1628, we have considerable detail on the size and budget of the Hermandad at this juncture. The staff consisted of eight constables, who made 250 pesos a year, a corporal who made 337.5, and a sergeant who made 450. Their superior, the alcalde, though unsalaried, had an expense account of 400 pesos, making for annual expenditures of 3,187.5 pesos. In the years 1623-27, the period covered in these accounts, 14,843 pesos had been collected from the importation of 4,750 slaves. Subtracting the collector's commission of 10 per cent from this, there remained a net total of about 13,360 pesos, or an average of about 2,670 pesos a year. The *caja de los negros* thus operated at an annual loss of about 517 pesos in this period, and it was doubtless this fact that made the Crown go along with Guadalcázar's suggestion to leave well enough alone.[70]

Still, the home government was ever desperate for additional revenue, and if the head tax itself promised no rewards, the position of collector with its lucrative commission did. Accordingly, the Crown put the office up for sale in 1633. In return for a lump-sum payment, the titleholder was to keep one-third of the revenue collected and deposit the rest with the *caja de los negros*. Two bids were received. One came from an unnamed individual, who offered 3,000 pesos, the other from the *alcalde de la Hermandad*, who claimed the collection of the head tax was a prerogative of his position but offered 8,000 pesos anyway, in case his claim was denied. Viceroy Chinchón suspended the sale until the Crown could be consulted, arguing that if the office was sold the buyer would recover his purchase price illegally, by negotiating directly with the slave merchants or by defrauding the constables of a percentage of their salaries. In the meantime, the accountant of the royal treasury in Lima, Hernando de Valencia, had written the Crown hinting at scandals in the collection of the head tax and urging an audit.[71] From the Crown's response in 1635, it is quite clear that considerable thought was given to the letters of both Chinchón and Valencia (and to other reports that have not come to light). In a decree to the viceroy, the Crown said it had received information indicating that the head tax in fact produced large revenue surpluses, even after the expenses of the Hermandad had been paid, surpluses that reverted to no known agency. The decree went on in effect to accuse the collector Chinchón had appointed of corruption, then ordered major changes: the collection of the tax under the administration of the royal treasury officials, who would also supervise all disbursements with viceregal authorization; the reversion of any surplus revenues to the Crown, with shipment to Spain under separate account; and the submission of the records of collection to routine audits by the Tribunal of Accounts. In an acid reply Chinchón could not resist minimizing the importance of the revenue and denied that any member of his entourage had ever been charged with its collection. Having vented his feelings, he then bowed to the royal command. Thereafter, the tax was collected by a man appointed by the treasury officials for a fee of 10 per cent.[72]

Beyond all this, the Hermandad itself was also effectively brought under royal control at this time. In 1633 the Crown broke the decades-old understanding with the city of Lima on the election of the alcalde and sold the office for the benefit of the royal treasury. The increased prestige of the post was well reflected in the purchase price of 50,000 pesos paid by Don Diego de Ayala y Contreras, a former *alcalde ordinario* and a prominent landowner. For this princely sum, the new proprietary *alcalde provincial* of the Hermandad enjoyed the privilege of a seat on the municipal council, received a handsome expense account from the head tax, as well as a percentage of all the fines levied in the cases he heard, and even had the right to erect his own jail facilities, if he so chose. The real attraction of the post, however, was its prestige, not its financial rewards.[73] The transaction was clouded for a few years by the vigorous protests of the city of Lima, which were seconded by Viceroy Chinchón, and by Ayala's inability in 1636 to make his scheduled payments. Chinchón appointed an interim alcalde, but Ayala reclaimed the office in the same year, and a royal decree of 1637 firmly rejected colonial complaints. In the meantime, in 1635 the Crown ordered the sale of the office of *alcalde provincial* in cities and towns throughout Spanish America, at the discretion of the viceroy, the Audiencia, and the various governors or corregidores, but there is no record of such sales in other parts of Peru.[74]

The transformation of the Hermandad into an organization dominated by a proprietary officeholder coincided with a sharp increase in cimarrón activity in the area around the capital. The appearance of large bands, more highly organized and bolder than before, may well be linked to the fact that the black population of Peru reached record numbers in the 1630's, but whatever the cause, it is certain that the Hermandad had serious problems to contend with in this period. One major incident occurred in 1631, when a large group of galley slaves fled the port of Callao, gathered in the hills around Lima with other runaways, and resisted all attempts to encircle them. Fortunately for the alarmed Spanish authorities, a free mulatto soldier, Juan de Valladolid Mogorón, saw a chance to advance himself by turning informer and leading the forces of the Hermandad to the band's hideout, where the runaways were routed after a pitched battle. In the next year, the corregidor of Cañete reported the discovery and dispersal of a runaway settlement of about forty blacks, of whom only eighteen were captured.[75]

These incidents did not always reflect well on the capabilities of the Hermandad. This was notably true in the case of one of the most troublesome of the runaway gangs, composed of about thirty cimarrones, which staved off pursuers in one way or another for half a year. On November 8, 1633, this gang, which operated out of the rugged territory called La Cieneguilla, some nine leagues from Lima, ambushed a merchant convoy and carried off thirty-six loaded mules and a female slave; and less than two weeks later the newly appointed corregidor of Huarochirí and his wife narrowly escaped capture by the same gang. Since at the time Ayala and the viceroy were still at odds over the purchase of the office of *alcalde provincial* Chinchón himself took a hand, sending a force on December 5 under a subordinate officer of the Hermandad to clear the area. The expedition returned empty-handed. More, its members were jailed in disgrace shortly thereafter, when word leaked out that they had traded the runaways their freedom for a considerable amount of stolen merchandise. Another expedition, launched on April 2 of the following year, had no greater success, and one of its members was drowned besides. A third was organized on April 24, after a colored spy promised to lead it to the cimarrón camp. But, despite a stealthy night march, the band decamped before the Spanish arrived, and only a single runaway was captured. Finally, in May, the corregidor of Huarochirí, with a band of Indians, succeeded in taking part of the gang and sent six runaway heads to Lima along with twelve live female fugitives. Never again during the period under study was the Lima Hermandad quite so openly ineffective. Nevertheless, in 1640, despite years of supposedly vigilant patrols on the outskirts of the capital, it was necessary to mount a very large special expedition to suppress "the troops of black runaways who were going about the roads and farms of the countryside" committing numerous robberies.[76]

In general, other areas of Peru do not seem to have suffered much from the activities of cimarrón bands. One of the most spectacular incidents, however, occurred near San Miguel de Piura in 1638, when a band of runaways surprised the *alcalde provincial* of that city and his assistant, cut off their heads, and burned the bodies.[77]

With the proliferation of working farms on the outskirts of Lima and the spread of the city itself, the Hermandad was increasingly concerned with aspects of law enforcement that were only marginally related, if at all, to the crime of flight. Ayala soon discovered that the 50,000 pesos he had paid had not bought him enough authority and prestige to intimidate powerful slaveholders and other government agencies. Two examples will illustrate these difficulties. The first dates from 1635 when Fernando Felis de Porras decided to sell his slave Gregorio Criollo (age fifteen) after the boy's numerous scrapes with the law had cost Porras forty-two pesos in a single month. Gregorio was to be shipped by muleback to Huancavelica for sale, presumably on the theory that he would fetch a higher price where his escapades were unknown. With Gregorio in shackles, the caravan left Lima, guarded by a Spanish assistant and an Indian, and was promptly ambushed by a band of armed blacks. Leading this group was Gregorio's father, a Jesuit-owned slave named Ignacio de Jesús, who was bent on keeping his son from being sold outside the city. Knocking the Spaniard off his horse with a rock and wounding the Indian, Gregorio's rescuers took the boy to a nearby estate, where his shackles were removed and pawned that same night for food at a pulpería. However, when one of the gang was discovered smuggling Gregorio into the house of his master, the boy was seized and returned to the bakery where he had lately been apprenticed. Porras complained to the Hermandad, an investigation was made, and several blacks were arrested, though no further mention of Ignacio de Jesús appears in the record. At this juncture some powerful but unnamed person must have intervened in the case. Over the protests of Ayala, the black suspects were released on bail, and apparently no punishments were ever meted out for the crime. Furthermore, the Hermandad collected no fees for its services.[78]

The second incident that points up the difficulties Ayala encountered began on the evening of July 22, 1636 (the feast day of Saint Mary Magdalene, and therefore a holiday), and involved the slaves of the Jesuit estate of Bocanegra near Callao. Despite the Jesuits' reputation for discipline, the blacks of Bocanegra were particularly intractable. Four years earlier, a band of them had been strongly suspected of robbing and drowning an Indian, and shortly thereafter one of their number killed a Jesuit who attempted to punish him for running away.[79] On the holiday in question, most of the slaves had gone to seek diversion in Callao or Lima. On the way back several got into a fight with the blacks of a neighboring estate belonging to Pedro Sánchez de Aguilar, and one was wounded. Summoning comrades, the Bocanegra group sought revenge the same night. In the words of Sánchez:

At approximately 8:30 last night, this witness was at home on his farm with his wife and children, and there arrived what appeared to be more than forty blacks, more or less, though since it was night and dark, [Sánchez] did not count them nor could he recognize any of them, except that he heard Gonzalillo Angola and Francisco Cocoli and one Mateo mentioned by name. This witness recognized the last-named because he was their captain and leader, and he knows that all the said blacks are slaves of the fathers of the Company, from the chácara of Bocanegra. And, as soon as all the said blacks arrived at the house of this witness with swords, knives, and cutlasses, and carrying rocks and sticks . . . and riotously [shouting insults], this witness told them to stop, and the said blacks replied that there was no need to stop because they were going to kill this witness and his wife and children and all the blacks of his farm. With this, they threw many stones at this witness's blacks and at his children and at his majordomo, so that they were obliged to go inside the house, fleeing from the said blacks so that they would not be killed. And this witness and all his blacks after him locked themselves in. [The Boca-negra slaves] upon his retreat entered all of the houses of this witness's blacks and robbed their blankets and clothing [and] something even worse would have occurred except for the fact that many people were attracted by the commotion, including a Jesuit father and his majordomo, who quieted the blacks and led them away. And this witness was awake all night on his farm for fear that the blacks would return. . . . Later, Brother Cardoso [a Jesuit], having come to speak with this witness, told him that not even the Duke of Alba or the Constable of Castile would be able to control their blacks.

Sánchez's complaint to the Hermandad produced an investigation, and the resulting depositions by the slaves are models of arrogant evasive-ness. The Jesuits stoutly defended their charges, and in response to a plea from the Society that the services of the arrested slaves were des-perately needed, the Audiencia ordered their release under bond. Sev-eral days later, the Jesuits induced Sánchez to withdraw his complaint. The chagrin of the *alcalde provincial* can well be imagined.[80]

Ayala was as insistent on the recognition of his privileges as he was conscientious in the performance of his duties, and the lack of coopera-tion displayed by other government agencies infuriated him. As early as 1637 he appealed to the Council of the Indies against both the crim-inal branch of the Audiencia and the Holy Office. Noting that Viceroy Chinchón had ruled that in no case was there to be a reduction of the fines due the cuadrilleros for their services, Ayala charged that the *al-caldes del crimen* had nevertheless allowed such reductions in appeals made on the flimsiest grounds, had freed the black culprits on bond in the interval, and had so spun out the determination of cases as to ne-gate the viceregal intent and hamstring the operation of the Herman-dad.[81] In Ayala's view the Holy Office was even more high-handed, intervening on the shallowest of pretexts on behalf of slaves who be-longed to its officials or clients, and demanding the instant release of both the culprit and the case prepared against him, with never a thought of reward for the cuadrillero. Ayala reminded the Crown that the value of his office might easily decline if the erosion of its prerogatives and authority was allowed to continue. The government was sufficiently moved to issue a 1638 decree, addressed to the viceroy and the Audiencia, ordering them to see to it that the jurisdiction of the Hermandad was respected, and stressing the Crown's financial stake in the matter. This expression of the royal will had so little effect that Ayala went to Spain in 1646 to press his case. He died there two years later, having obtained little satisfaction.[82]

Worse than these jurisdictional conflicts was the Hermandad's financial crisis after the Portuguese revolt of 1640 brought the cessation of the slave trade. According to the records for 1636-48, the structure of the Hermandad changed but little during the first years of Ayala's proprietary control. The day-to-day routine of the constabulary was in the hands of a sergeant and a corporal who commanded anywhere from four to eight cuadrilleros at a given time. Ayala received 400 pesos a year for expenses, and the sergeant, corporal, and constables drew annual salaries of 400, 300, and 200-225 pesos, respectively. The head tax, now called the *avería de los negros bozales*, also paid the salary of an official titled the *alguacil del gobierno*, who commanded the city's colored militia, and a pension to the family of a cuadrillero killed in the line of duty. These sums disbursed, the balance of the revenue, minus the collector's commission and expenses for special expeditions, was sent to Spain on an annual basis.

Expressed in whole pesos, the total amount expended in the 1636-48 period was 20,205 pesos, paid out as follows:

Purpose	Total	Purpose	Total
Expense account, *alcalde provincial*	4,358	Pension payments	1,134
Salary, sergeant	1,393	Expenses for special expeditions	550
Salary, corporal	900	Commissions to collectors	1,120
Salary, constables	4,123	Remitted to Spain as royal revenue	5,892
Salary, *alguacil del gobierno*	735		

These figures become more meaningful when it is realized that less than 6,000 pesos of this total was disbursed after 1640, for the simple reason that the suspension of the slave trade brought a severe financial crimp. The first to feel it, obviously, were the constables. The Crown was never a prompt paymaster, e.g., wages owed for 1637-38 were not paid until 1646, and after 1640 the constables were unsalaried, dependent on fines alone. Even the posts of sergeant and corporal were affected, since the assigned salaries had never been very attractive and now could not be paid until some unspecified future date. The situation led to a decline in the number and quality of personnel, probably inviting a return to the abuses of the sixteenth century. It will be noted, however, that the Crown made a tidy profit from the head tax before the collapse of the slave trade, and thereby refuted Chinchón's prediction.[83]

From what we have seen here and in the preceding chapter, we can conclude that there was unquestionably a fair measure of crime and unrest among the colored population of Peru, but that these phenomena were frequently and perhaps understandably exaggerated by the Spanish. The African and his American-born descendants had not chosen enslavement, a fate that most Spanish contemporaries admitted was unenviable. Moreover, the color line prevented complete assimilation even when the legal impediment of bondage was removed. The Spaniard had reason to fear the person of color, particularly during the critical half-century after 1600, when increased slave importation coincided with the shattering of the comforting notion that Peru was invulnerable to foreign attack. In consequence, criminality and turbulence among the colored population were taken very seriously. The luxury of hindsight permits us to see what was less than clear to outraged slaveholders and worried bureaucrats: the black slave and the free person of color were not all that prone to crime, and their transgressions, however painful to victims and to masters, were kept within acceptable limits by the agencies of law enforcement. Further, however little love Afro-Peruvians had for the Spanish, they seem to have plotted few acts of rebellion and did not flock to the standards of foreign invaders.

The runaway problem is more difficult to evaluate. When Spanish Peruvians thought of cimarrones, the grave difficulties they presented in Panama and the West Indies tended to blow the local situation out of proportion. To be sure, many slaves did take flight in Peru, and their tendency to band together in relatively isolated areas made them a considerable nuisance from time to time. The Indians in particular seem to have suffered at their hands. Yet, there is overwhelming evidence that most runaways were captured soon rather than late, albeit at some expense and inconvenience to the slaveholder. One is tempted to say that the principal difficulty with runaways, at least in the Lima area, was that Spanish efforts to control them were hampered by a tendency toward overbureaucratization compounded by maladministration. It seems clear that a modest number of full-time slavecatchers of whatever title, adequately compensated for their labors by whatever means, would have been sufficient to contain the cimarrones under normal circumstances; and that the now-and-then threat of the larger bands could have been met by organizing special expeditions as the situation required. That is, the methods of the 1540's would have served equally well until at least 1600, and in fact runaways were most often apprehended by precisely these methods, with the slaveholders footing the bill. But official eyes were often blinded by the issue of the head tax, a duty that gave the city more revenue than was needed to control runaways had it not been inefficiently collected, badly accounted for, and frequently diverted to other uses over the years. Meanwhile, the municipality and the viceroys tinkered with the notion of the Hermandad, another layer of law enforcement and justice that was scarcely justified by the circumstances for decades. By the 1630's the growth of the slave population may well have made the Hermandad a necessity, but by this date scandal and the Crown's search for additional revenue had transformed the rural constabulary into a proprietary institution. It was perhaps a change for the better in terms of efficiency, but one that was prompted as much by a desire to fill the royal coffers as by considerations of public tranquility.

CHAPTER NINE

Physical and Spiritual Concerns

At first glance, Spain during the fifteenth and sixteenth centuries presents the historian with the curious spectacle of a nation that simultaneously pressed with Draconian determination for cultural unity at home while creating an American empire marked by conspicuous diversity. As Jews, Moors, and suspected Protestants were expelled from the Peninsula or hounded into conformity, Amerindians and Africans became the building blocks of the New World possessions. The apparent paradox between Spanish policies at home and abroad, however, is largely resolved when we realize that the Crown's intolerance of dissent did not extend much beyond the question of religion. Apart from the possible influence of Islam, a threat that was not taken seriously, nothing seemed to prevent the smooth incorporation of the black man into the workings of the American empire. The African would be a separate, black, Christian component of the corporate structure of American society. Good treatment would reward his exertions and in time, supplemented by Catholicism, obviate the need for more than routine vigilance.

In this connection, the attitudes and policies of the Crown are nowhere better expressed than in the 1545 ordinances adopted for the governance of the African population in the New World.[1] In part, these regulations concerned themselves with the control of the slave, primarily as a potential rebel, but the basic thrust of the code was positive. The slave was to be provided with decent food and clothing, and punishment was to be inflicted only for just cause. Above all, the African was to be Christianized and, to that end, taught the Spanish language. The Crown saw no need to mince words: good treatment and indoctrination in the Faith were in order not merely in an effort to keep the African reasonably contented but also in recognition of his essential humanity. Yet this was not to say—and the code explicitly denied it—that the African was the equal of the Spaniard, and no extended justification of his enslavement was deemed necessary. Even among the religious this attitude changed but little in succeeding decades. The Jesuit Sandoval himself, as ardent a champion of the black slave as any, conceded the inferiority of the African and reluctantly agreed with Aristotle that some men seemed to have been born to serve their superiors. Several of Sandoval's co-religionists in seventeenth-century Peru shared his doubts about the morality of the slave trade, so much so that their acceptance of the institution of slavery itself was shaken or destroyed, but they too stopped well short of advocating the equality of the races, except before God. The Peruvian Jesuits, along with many other religious, contented themselves with carrying out the 1545 strictures with their own slaves and urging the lay population to do likewise.[2]

In short, the most enlightened of Peruvian masters realized that the slave was not "a mere piece of property to be used at the owner's absolute will, but a person who, through insurmountable odds, had been placed in a situation which was against the laws of nature. He had certain inalienable rights, among them life, health, bodily integrity, and at least a minimum of human development. And the slaveowner was justly obligated to respect those rights."[3] It is difficult, however, to determine the extent to which these lofty precepts were reflected in reality. What is clear is that many informed observers despaired of the lot of the African slave. Concerned men like Sandoval have left us a grim picture of conditions under slavery. By his account, the typical African, whether agricultural laborer or household servant, toiled from dawn to dusk, went about almost naked unless he worked on Sundays and feast days to obtain money for clothing, was miserably fed, received no medical attention, and was harshly, even sadistically, punished for the most frivolous reasons. Sandoval quotes (and supports) the observation of an acquaintance that the Christians punished their slaves more in a week than the Moors did in a year. The good Jesuit speaks of masters who freed sick slaves to avoid medical and burial expenses; if the black recovered, he was to return to service; if he died, burial expenses fell on the slave's confraternity and, failing that, on his relatives or on members of his "caste." And this treatment, he alleged, was accorded even to ladinos who had grown old in the service of the same master. Sandoval also mentions blacks who were beaten to death, and others who were so terrified after the beating that they did not ask for medical attention and died of infection, their wounds full of maggots.[4]

Sandoval's picture might be discounted as an affecting but over-drawn one, as the product of an excess of indignation over the patent immorality of the slave trade, if it were not backed up by Poma de Ayala's version. At the end of his account of injustices and cruelties, interspersed with suggestions for reform, Poma could only counsel patience to the black slave:

Know, my brothers, as a certain thing that Our Lord Jesus Christ endured many tribulations . . . for your good, you who are sinners and poor devils. Bear all with saintly patience. . . . On hearing your tearful voices, the Lord will send comfort for your hearts; He will promise you and reward you with that gift of the crown of Heaven, better than all the gold . . . , precious stones and jewels that can be named or even imagined, so much so that the angels of Heaven . . . do not venture to describe it, a hundred times more resplendent than the sun. In Heaven we will gather together forever, as God promised us.[5]

The combined testimony of Sandoval and Poma, though it cannot be lightly dismissed, still fails to convince entirely, and thereby illustrates the difficulty of making valid generalizations about even the most mundane details of day-to-day life under slavery. Many masters, for example, addressed their adult slaves, both male and female, by the diminutive forms of their Christian names (e.g., Antonillo). Was this a mark of affection or simply a reminder of subservience, in a society that accepted the branding of blacks as a sign of ownership? Even contemporaries appear to have wavered in their evaluations of the slave's lot. Viceroy Chinchón, for example, could assure the Crown that the blacks and mulattoes were reasonably content and loyal, but he also gave thought to the appointment of a Protector to "dulcify the condition of their servitude."[6] It is with these caveats in mind that we now turn our attention to some aspects of slave life.

Beginning at the most basic level—food—corn was the staple of the black man's diet, as it was of the Indian's and the Spaniard's. If we may believe one seventeenth-century observer, it could be prepared in countless, tasty ways. And from corn, too, came the ubiquitous chicha, consumed in vast quantities by African and Indian alike. In addition, blacks seem to have been given relatively abundant amounts of bread, fish, plantains, and sweet potatoes, along with small servings of meat— all of the cheapest possible variety. In an age still exploring the properties of tobacco, blacks were provided with quantities of this plant to chew and also with rum on occasion. The variety and abundance of the black's diet obviously varied with the liberality and economic standing of the master, but doubtless as a group the apprentices and journeymen attached to craftsmen were the best-fed element of the African population. The terms of their contracts usually included board at the artisan's table, and it is reasonable to assume that the fare was essentially the same for all.[7]

It is unclear whether there were significant differences in the diets of urban and rural slaves, since we have few surviving records on this point from private urban owners, and the expense accounts we have of the Peruvian plantations probably do not reflect their self-sufficiency in food and the like. At any rate, one authority estimates the cost of an urban slave's daily board at between 1.25 and 1.5 reales. This estimate may be on the generous side, since the Crown, the Inquisition, and the city of Lima usually set the cost per slave at one *real* a day. In 1573, for example, the Lima city council, periodically terrified at the thought of losing its investment in blacks and most reluctant to bear the expenses of slaveholding, estimated the annual cost of feeding the thirteen municipal slaves at 600 pesos a year, i.e., slightly more than one *real* per day each. At that time, the slaves presumably were allotted three pounds of bread and two pounds of meat or of the cheapest fish per day, as provided by a decision of 1563. Similarly, the blacks employed in the construction of the quarters of the Holy Office in Lima were fed at a cost of one *real* per day, largely on bread and fish with smaller amounts of meat and potatoes, supplemented by rum, chicha, and tobacco.[8]

Two examples will give a rough idea of food costs for slaves in the countryside. The first is based on the records of an estate in the Mala Valley, operated as a partnership from 1616 to 1620 for the production of wheat and alfalfa and the raising of cattle and worked by eleven blacks. During this period a calf or a young bull was slaughtered every five or six weeks to feed the slaves, to which diet was added corn and bread on a regular basis, fish every Friday and Saturday, and beans, eggs, plantains, honey, and tobacco on rare occasion. Apart from the meat, the cost of which the owners did not estimate in their records, the total food bill for the eleven slaves during a twelve-month period in 1619-20 came to only some 350 pesos, or a little over 7.5 reales daily for the entire gang. Even if the cost of the beef is added to this figure, the total cost per slave per day could not have exceeded one *real* by much. The 1637-39 accounts kept by the administrator of the Lima chácara of Captain Lorenzo Pérez de Noguera are considerably more precise. The estate was worked by sixteen blacks whose combined weekly ration cost sixty-five reales, broken down as follows: mutton (ten reales); one and a half *fanegas* (bushels) of wheat (thirty reales); one fanega of corn (twenty reales); and fees for grinding wheat and corn (five reales). Some twenty-four pesos were also spent in this period for beans, but in essence the blacks were being fed at a cost of about four reales each per week, or considerably less than a *real* per day. In both cases, and particularly in that of Pérez, it seems reasonable to assume the blacks supplemented their diets with produce from garden plots.[9]

The gloomy picture painted by Sandoval and Poma of the slave's existence may come close to the mark on the question of clothing. This was hardly a major expense for slaveowners, but it was one most were tempted to economize on. As a result, the clothing worn by the average slave often barely met the requirements imposed by modesty and the climate. If the municipal slaves of Lima can be taken as examples of Peruvian practice in the urban areas, then blacks seem to have worn their clothes until the last shred fell off their backs. For example, between 1565 and 1574, during the construction of the municipal water system, an arduous and messy task, clothing was purchased for the black workers only six times, once after an interval of nearly two years and usually after a report by the overseer of the project that the slaves were "naked." The twelve to thirteen slaves the city possessed over this period cost about 100 pesos to outfit in clothing "of the most reasonable price and quality that can be had." According to the most detailed records on the subject, the city bought thirteen outfits in 1574, consisting of ponchos, breeches, and shirts, for a total of 117 pesos. The bulk of this amount, sixty-three and a half pesos, was spent on cheap woolen cloth (*sayal*); the rest went for shirts (thirteen at two pesos each), for thread (three and a half pesos), and for the tailor's fees on the ponchos and breeches (twenty-four pesos).[10]

There were doubtless exceptions to this rule of cheeseparing. Slaves whose masters dressed them in liveries for reasons of social prestige may have cut fine figures, and the blacks of the Jesuits, we are told, were "abundantly provided with the clothing proper to each season," but most slaveholders probably tried to replace clothing only when absolutely necessary and then as cheaply as possible.

The market for low-cost clothing for slaves eventually enticed trade from as far away as Quito, which shipped cheap leather shoes (worth approximately four reales the pair) to Lima to be worn by blacks. Likewise, the province of Guayras found a market in the capital for its crude colored textiles and blankets. Indeed, there seems to have been a street of ready-made clothing shops in Lima that catered specifically to the needs of the black population.[11]

The amounts spent on slave clothing were equally stingy in the rural areas. Between 1619 and 1620, for example, the Mala Valley partnership spent only thirty-five pesos all told on clothing and bedding for its eleven slaves: thirty for seven outfits of coarse wool for the men, and five for two blankets and a cloak. The slaves of the Pérez Noguera chácara were treated more generously. Both men and women received new outfits every year: woolen suits for the men (at four and a half pesos each), skirts and blouses for the women (six and a half to seven), undershirts for both (two to two and a half), and certain unspecified garments for the children. For the years 1637-38 the total outlay came to 213 pesos.[12]

On another important element of slave life, housing, we have only the skimpiest of information. Whenever possible, in both town and countryside, all but the most trusted black household servants were lodged apart from the main house. Generally each slave or slave family, as the case may be, had a small rude hut, called a *rancho*. Groups of these ranchos, according to one seventeenth-century account, were to be found behind every house in Lima, located in the corrals, "which serve as a place for the livestock and the poultry and all the other service of the house."[13]

As the fragmentary evidence on mortality rates and the laments of slaveholders presented in Chapter 3 indicate, poor diet and living conditions, combined with hard labor, assured many blacks an early grave. In addition, the African seems to have been little more immune to the common European diseases than the Indian. In 1589, for example, an epidemic of smallpox, measles, and severe colds combined, which originated in Trujillo and spread over much of the colony, struck with particular force among the colored population. Viceroy Cañete reported that 6,000 persons died in Lima alone before the epidemic ran its course, "and the majority were creoles [i.e., probably mestizos] and blacks." Another outbreak of smallpox in 1606 was reported to be particularly prevalent among the "common people and slaves."[14]

Though disease plainly took a heavy toll, for Peru at least there is little evidence to support Sandoval's charges of slaveholder callousness about providing medical care. To be sure, such references would be rare in any event, for few masters would admit to withholding medical assistance or to leaving aged and infirm slaves to their own devices, but much indirect evidence supports a contrary assertion. As we have seen in Chapter 4, a sample of plantation inventories reveals that a substantial minority of rural blacks were age thirty-six or older, and an impressive number were over the age of forty-five. There is no good reason to ascribe this longevity in any great degree to the quality of medical care; but at the same time one cannot help concluding that even the most selfish or indifferent masters would have had second thoughts about allowing expensive blacks to die of an unattended illness. In addition, old or seriously ill slaves who were abandoned presumably were able to turn to one of the religious orders or to the Confraternity of the Prisons and Charity for medical aid.

Among the institutions, the Society of Jesus stands out for the care given to old and sick slaves. By the early seventeenth century each Jesuit hacienda was able to take care of emergencies and mild cases at its own small infirmary and to refer serious cases to the Jesuit hospital in Lima, located across the street from the College of San Pablo. According to Luis Martín, "In the hospital the Negro slaves received the same basic treatment accorded the Jesuits themselves when ill. Comfortable beds with clean sheets were provided, and food was carefully cooked according to the needs of the patients. A Jesuit brother was assigned as a nurse to wait on them, and one or two fathers were charged to visit and comfort them." On a visit in 1648, the provincial of the Order pronounced himself satisfied on the whole with the administration of the hospital, though he thought that a good doctor should always be available and that no expense should be spared with regard to medicine—measures justified not merely by justice and charity but also by the principles of sound economics. In addition, the Jesuits provided their women slaves with midwives, and frequently became godfathers of the offspring, "thus becoming *compadres* of their own slaves."[15]

Few other slaveholders, institutions or otherwise, matched the Jesuits in this regard, but most, by the lights of the age, did what they could. Initially, the city of Lima cared for its blacks on an ad hoc basis. For example, in 1550, when the municipal authorities still operated the central meat market, fifty pesos was spent for the care of a worker, Pedro Negro, who had lost his genitals. After some haggling, the city in 1571 paid the pharmacist Bartolomé Alba twenty-five pesos for the medicines used to treat the various ills of the slaves employed in the construction of the city water system. The next year the municipality decided to economize by contracting a physician to care for the health of its blacks for a flat fee, and finally engaged a doctor in 1573 for thirty pesos a year. The city also negotiated with a barber to perform simpler medical procedures, such as bleeding, for ten pesos a year. Neither contract covered the costs of medicines. The contracting physician soon died, and the city managed to economize still further by hiring a successor for twenty-five pesos a year.[16]

In the urban areas, similar arrangements may have been made by slaveholders with large black staffs, but those with few blacks no doubt simply summoned a physician as needed and bargained over the fee when the crisis had passed. In the Lima area, however, even the best-intentioned master had difficulty procuring adequate medical care for his slaves, since (unlike the Indian) the black had no access to a hospital specially designated for his care. For much of the period under study, slaveholders relied on the Hospital of San Andrés, a charity institution for impoverished Spaniards, but in 1640 the crush became so bad that the institution was having difficulty in serving even its Spanish clients. The hospital officials charged that this situation arose mostly because judges of the Audiencia and other government officials had abused the privilege of sending their blacks to San Andrés for care. In response, the Crown ordered that henceforth no blacks were to be admitted even if their masters offered alms to cover the necessary expenses. It did not suggest any alternative, nor does any move seem to have been made to provide for another facility.[17]

In the rural areas, even quite near Lima, the provision of adequate medical care was often more difficult still. In the 1590's, for example, two black hatmakers attached to the woolen mill of Poyor in the corregimiento of Santa were taken sick and had to be laboriously packed by mule to Huaráz and back for treatment; one died anyway, apparently of measles.[18] What little evidence there is on the Pérez Noguera chácara in the Lima area indicates that slaves who sickened had only a slightly better-than-even chance of recovery. Ten blacks took sick between August 1637 and October 1638, eight of them with what was diagnosed as smallpox. Only four of these survived the rigors of that dread disease. In this year 112.5 pesos was spent for medicines, bleedings, special foods, and physicians' fees, plus another twenty-five for burial costs and death certificates. On half of the six occasions when expert opinion was consulted, a friar (possibly the parish priest) was summoned and received a fee; a doctor was called in to deal with the smallpox attack and with two other emergencies. As will be recalled, this chácara had a staff of sixteen blacks; accordingly, in this one year alone it lost 25 per cent of its personnel. If a similar mortality rate prevailed on other Peruvian plantations, it is easy to see why the cessation of the slave trade after 1640 provoked such anguished outcries from agriculturalists.

Finally, the slaveowner might have additional medical expenses arising in the brawls and quarrels of his slaves. Besides caring for his own property, he was sometimes obliged to pay the medical expenses of the aggrieved party. These could be humiliatingly costly, as witness the case of Catalina de Herrera, no doubt a woman of very modest means, who was imprisoned for her inability to pay the sixty-three pesos that had been spent caring for a black her slave had wounded. The unfortunate woman was among those ordered released by Viceroy Toledo to celebrate the news of Philip II's coronation as king of Porugal in 1580, and the Crown paid the physician's bill.[19]

From all evidence the extraordinarily gloomy picture of slave existence drawn by Sandoval and Poma seems to have been true for only a minority of Afro-Peruvians. Even so, the lot of the slave was scarcely enviable at this most basic level of human wants, and beyond these the threat of pain must have seemed as vivid as the anticipation of some simple pleasure. Most masters claimed, and vigorously exercised, the right of corporal punishment over their blacks, though it must be borne in mind that even free men were harshly punished during this era. In this regard, as in so many others, the Jesuits attempted a policy of enlightened moderation, at least among the slaves who were attached to the College of San Pablo. The administrators of the college were reminded more than once by their superiors that "delinquents should not be kept in jail and stocks more than a week, nor punished with more than fifty lashes, even if the fault was grave, nor should they ever be hurt or harmed in their limbs. If a slave was guilty of serious crimes, he should be sold or given away, but never condemned to capital punishment while under the ownership of the college." The intentions and practices of private individuals are more difficult to evaluate, but it appears that the lurid drawings illustrating Poma's text do not exaggerate. Corporal punishment, primarily whipping, was at the very base of relationships between master and slave, perhaps so much so as to be accepted as routine. As Viceroy Chinchón wrote the Crown, short of the death penalty, it was difficult to devise punishments for crimes committed by blacks; a specified number of lashes was useless since the slaves were "so accustomed to receiving them at the hands of their masters."[20]

Clearly, when the power to inflict corporal punishment on members of a supposedly inferior race is widely diffused in a society, there are bound to be abuses, whether inspired by anger, carelessness, or sadism. Colonial Peru was no exception. The problem was compounded by the fact that a Spaniard rarely paid with his own life for killing his slave or even a free person of color. In 1555, for example, the blacksmith Juan Macias was fined a mere 100 pesos for beating a slave to death. Another Spaniard, who fatally stabbed a mulatto youth he found in bed with one of his female blacks, likewise got off with his life.[21]

It may well be that the very lightness of the penalties, commonly no more than a fine of 300 pesos or so, encouraged whites to violence and brutality.[22] Nevertheless, Spaniards who killed or maimed blacks were usually brought to account in some way. Even so high a personage as the royal factor for Lima, Don Francisco Manrique de Lara, was prosecuted for the death of one of his slaves,[23] and though many blacks who were severely treated by Spaniards may have suffered in silence, others did not hesitate to complain to the authorities with some success.[24] Occasionally, slaveowners may have brought pressure to bear to forestall judicial action. In 1568, for example, it was rumored that the royal attorney before the Audiencia had deliberately delayed disposition of a case involving a master who had whipped and burned a slave to death on an estate near Lima.[25] But such isolated incidents of sadism, whether discovered and punished or not, should not blind us to the fact that a slave represented a considerable capital investment to his master. However common the lash, it seems unlikely that any but the most disturbed slaveholders indulged in extreme forms of corporal punishment.

This question aside, there is no denying that at best the life of most blacks was hard and monotonous. If there was messy, disagreeable work to be done, it was the African (or the Indian) who performed it, and by and large material comfort was not his reward. His diversions were few and in the main unedifying. At least in Lima and other Peruvian towns of some size, most blacks might take part in the religious festivals that punctuated the year, and some might be drawn even closer to the Church for solace and instruction. Many others, however, turned to more secular and often conspicuous diversions, such as music and dancing, to the frequent discomfort, scandal, and even fear of the respectable classes. In 1563, for example, the Lima city council felt forced to respond to numerous complaints about slaves dancing wildly through the streets on holidays to the beating of drums, blocking traffic and frightening the horses, and ordered all such dances thereafter to be confined to the main square of the city and the plaza of Nicolás de Ribera, el Mozo.[26] Despite this legislation and the best efforts of Viceroy Cañete and others, the musical amusements of blacks were rarely so neatly confined during succeeding decades. For instance, around the turn of the seventeenth century, one observer noted that there were numerous dances staged in *corrales* occupied by blacks, which were attended by large numbers of people, and remarked on the dancing and singing by slaves, persistently accompanied by drums, "through all the plazas and streets."[27] The authorities and various commentators alike deplored the sexual promiscuity of at least a minority of the black population, and occasionally the Holy Office was moved to take action, as in the case of one Leonor Negra, a married woman, who was given 100 lashes and exiled from Callao for three years for daring to declare that mere fornication appeared no sin to her.[28] When informed that slaves in the municipal jail were practicing—to the titillated horror of passersby—what Leonor had no more than advocated, the Lima authorities could think of nothing else to do but to order certain alterations so as to block the view from the public.[29] Still other slaves, as we have seen in the section on control, preferred to spend feast days and other moments of leisure far from the word of God, wandering the streets of Callao and Lima, and gambling, swearing, and quarreling with one another. And, all too often, theft supported this profitless leisure—at least as far as the authorities were concerned. The civilian population, meanwhile, largely ignored the problem unless their own convenience or property was threatened.

The black man, and particularly the slave, may have been at or near the bottom of society, and many were ignorant, despised, and sunk in vices, but these tendencies were in part counterbalanced by the efforts of Crown and Church at Christianization. The Spaniards, as John Phelan observes, though rigidly opposed to doctrinal innovation during this period, were "externally flexible in providing some place for all races inside the framework of their religion." In the American colonies, Peru included, it was envisioned that the Spaniards would be the "head of the body social, so to speak, and the Indians and Negroes . . . the arms and legs."[30] To have attempted less than the Christianization of the African and his descendants would have destroyed the moral underpinnings of the slave trade; and fortunately the racial trichotomy the Spanish Crown attempted to maintain within its American possessions, at least theoretically neo-medieval and corporate in nature, discouraged the tendencies toward egalitarianism and individualism that would make almost a nonhuman being of the black man in Anglo-America. In any case, the teachings and influence of organized religion were early recognized as a useful tool to control the colored population.

For all these reasons, the Crown and its officials took their obligation to Christianize the African with consistent seriousness. As early as 1544 a royal decree deplored the fact that many slaveholders forced their blacks to work on Sundays and on the feast days of the Church; the authorities were commanded to ensure that the slaves heard Mass on those occasions in common with the rest of the population. The next year, in a series of ordinances the Crown took several steps to further the Christianization of the African. Spanish agriculturalists were to instruct their majordomos to see to it that their estates contained a structure to serve as a church, with an altar and the appropriate religious images. Here, each morning before going to work in the fields, the slaves were to come to pray and commend themselves to God. Mass was to be held in the church on Sundays and holy days, and on these occasions the blacks were to return for religious instruction after the morning meal. These instructions were to be obeyed under penalty of a thirty-peso fine for each violation. (The question of where the necessary number of priests was to come from was left unanswered, however.) In addition, slaveholders were to be sure that newly purchased slaves were both baptized and taught the Spanish language within six months after purchase, since "all blacks by inclination want to become Christians and are easy to convert." Failure to comply was to cost the slaveholder a third of the assessed value of the black, and subsequent violations were to bring first a fine amounting to half the slave's value and then confiscation of the African.[31]

The passage of time did not diminish one whit the conviction of most Spanish officials that the Christianization of the African was altogether desirable—both as a worthy end in itself and as an effective control device. Viceroy Toledo, surveying a kingdom "so loaded with slaves, and with the expectation that each day there will be more," thought "one of the restraints that can be put on them for the security of the said kingdom, in addition to those already placed on them, would be that the blacks become Christians, understanding the teachings that they receive." Indeed, under the Toledo regime, it was specified that on Sundays and holy days the chaplains of the jails were to gather together the black, mulatto, and Indian prisoners of both sexes before Mass and explain to them

the orations, commandments, and charitable works of the Church, declaring to them the obligation that as Christians they have to fulfill them, and the reward that is given to those who comply, and the punishment that is threatened those who do the contrary, in clear words that all may understand as befits their inability and weakness, so that by being imprisoned they will not lack doctrine and instruction which is important for the salvation of their souls.

Other officials stressed the important role of godfathers, fixtures even of adult baptisms at this date, in inspiring the sentiments of "obedience, respect, and love" in the minds of slaves.[32]

But royal intentions on the Christianization of the African were easier to formulate than to accomplish, and the best missionaries were painfully aware of the difficulties. Sandoval saw some grounds for optimism, writing of the Angolans in general, for example, that "these people are very docile, and it appears that they will come very easily to our Holy Faith, toward which end the fact that they do not have idols, as they say they do not, will help them much, and also the belief, as they believe, in a God that is in heaven, whom they call Zambian-pungo. All speak a common language, though with some variety."[33] However, the bulk of Sandoval's work stresses the obstacles to prose-lytism, and not least of these was the enormous problem of communi-cation with a people who spoke a bewildering number of languages and dialects. Although his fellow Jesuits in Lima made considerable progress in mastering the so-called "language of Angola" for mission-ary purposes, as we shall see, the blunt fact was that those who labored among the bozales had to content themselves with slow, painful prog-ress, often with the aid of an interpreter. As Sandoval himself admitted, the conscientious missionary required a fund of endless patience in order that the slave might grasp the abstractions essential to member-ship in the Christian faith.

In Sandoval's view, far greater than cultural and linguistic differ-ences as barriers to conversion were the attitudes held by many Spanish slaveholders toward the Christianization of their blacks, attitudes to which they clung so tenaciously that the good Jesuit thought he dis-cerned the Devil's perverse influence. If there was one thing Spanish masters were convinced of, he asserted, it was that their slaves were less valuable the moment they had been instructed in the Christian faith and baptized: this began the process by which the naïve and docile bozal, frightened and newly arrived from Africa, was transformed into the sly, lazy, and impudent ladino. Sandoval assures us that evidence of an African's knowledge of Christian precepts identified him as a ladino and therefore lowered his sale price, an assertion that is partially confirmed by the analysis of transactions in the Lima slave market pre-sented in Chapter 3. Accordingly, said Sandoval, slaveowners, seeking to keep the value of their blacks high, not only did nothing to facilitate the Christianization of their slaves, but impeded the process by all pos-sible means. Such masters denied the priests access to their blacks, even hid them on occasion, and tried to persuade the Africans that baptism was a harmful thing.

However, this selfish denial of the benefits of Christianity could be respectably cloaked in the widely held belief that the African was an uncomprehending and thoroughly inferior being—as Sandoval well knew. Some of the most bitter passages in his writings deplore the fact that many slaveowners believed, or claimed to believe, that the Christianization of the African was a waste of time. Admittedly, Sandoval's views were advanced for his day. He advocated that slaves receive the Eucharist, a sacrament the Indians of Peru only rarely received; he deplored the tendency of the missionary effort to ignore the African and favor the Indian; and he, along with other enlightened Spaniards, stressed the mutual responsibility of servant and master. The slave was bound to serve his master, whether the master was good or bad, for the Lord would in any case reward his loyalty and patience. At the same time, the master was obliged to treat his slaves as he himself would wish to be treated and to look out for their material and spiritual welfare, since he too would be judged by his deeds.

Indeed, Sandoval seems to have had several sharp clashes with the Holy Office concerning the quality of spiritual care given the African, but there is little evidence that his missionary zeal made him portray less than faithfully the contempt of many Spanish for the spiritual capacity of the African. And for these men, to baptize the Africans was "profitless, to hear their confessions laughable, and to expect them to take communion blasphemy," an attitude directed not merely at the bozal, but applied with equal force to the ladino. Sandoval himself admitted the inferiority of the African and knew from experience that the black slave was slow to respond to the doctrinal subtleties of the Church, but in his view this slowness called for greater patience and care in teaching. Instead, many Spanish slaveowners attempted to use these facts as a pretext to deny their blacks all contact with Christian doctrine, and the effect was to confirm their view that the African was no better than an ignorant brute. Sandoval accused the slaveholders of refusing to send for a priest even when a black was on the point of death. This attitude had obliged Sandoval to request the physicians of the city to inform him when a slaveowner summoned them, but the Jesuit reported that this device did not always prove successful, since some masters still refused him admittance. The result of all this, Sandoval declared, was that blacks who had been in Spanish America for twenty years could not even make the sign of the cross.

As an illustration of Sandoval's generalizations, let us take the case of Bartolomé Sánchez, a slaveholder and resident of Peru for some eighteen years, who was hauled before the archepiscopal court of Lima in 1617 on charges that he refused to let the slaves on his chácara hear Mass on Sundays and feast days. The ecclesiastical attorney who filed the charges went on to accuse Sánchez of forcing his blacks to work on these occasions and of whipping those who came to Lima to religious services anyway. Testimony taken from two of his slaves confirmed the accusations, though both stated that the farm currently leased by their master was so near the road that they were no longer forced to work on Sundays, since too many people passed by and might see it. They were, however, still forbidden to hear Mass. Sánchez denied the charges, and though the case was ordered formally taken up by the court, here matters seem to have remained. It may be that the ecclesiastical authorities contented themselves with a promise of more Christian behavior from Sánchez in future.[34]

Whether more than a minority of slaveholders carried things this far, a large number certainly shared the prejudices deplored by Sandoval. This appears to have been sufficient, however, when combined with the inherent linguistic and cultural difficulties faced by the missionary effort among the Africans, to dampen the enthusiasm of most of the secular clergy for proselytism. As a result, correspondence between the Crown and the Peruvian ecclesiastical authorities on the conversion of the black man very quickly assumed a circular form that has since come to be termed buckpassing.

In the early decades of Spanish Peru, when the black population was relatively small, there were either enough priests around to permit the more or less automatic incorporation of the slaves into the Church or else the uninitiated were too few and too scattered to attract much official notice. As the years passed, however, it became increasingly obvious that the conversion of blacks had to be systematized. The Crown first broached the subject to the Archbishop of Lima in a letter of 1569, expressing its concern over reports that the Christianization of Peru's slave population was being scandalously neglected: many blacks, it seemed, even after years of service under one master had not yet been baptized and knew nothing of Christian doctrine. Clearly, the ordinances of 1545 had been forgotten or ignored. The Crown mentioned that the government was considering prohibiting the sale of any slave who had served for a specified length of time without proof of baptism, a measure that would have made virtually all blacks who were not bozales unmarketable. In the meantime the Archbishop was urged to apply the same diligence to converting the African as to converting the Indian. The Archbishop reported back in 1572 that better progress was now being made and claimed the chief obstacle to complete suc-

cess was that so many of the blacks were scattered in numerous plantations outside the city.[35] Debatable though the prelate's optimism may
have been, his reply appears to have satisfied the Crown, perhaps in
part because Viceroy Toledo during these same years was promising
fundamental solutions to the entire problem of the African population.
In any event little more was said on the subject for several decades.

With the mushrooming number of bozales in the 1580's and 1590's,
however, the secular clergy were finally pushed to voice their continuing frustration. In a petition to the Archbishop in 1593 the priests of
Lima complained that the bozales who were arriving constantly from
Africa had not been baptized before departure, and that once in Peru
they steadfastly refused to admit their heathen status for fear of losing
face with their Hispanicized co-workers, the ladinos. The result was
that many unbaptized Africans improperly received the rites of the
Church throughout their lives and usually did not confess to this status
until the hour of death. The Archbishop was urged to remedy the situation, preferably by requesting the Crown to forbid the embarkation
of any slaves from the African coast who had not been properly baptized.[36]

There was certainly a basis in fact for the complaints of the Lima
clergy. As the similar laments of the Jesuits in Cartagena so eloquently
testify (see Chapter 2), the sacrament of baptism was only perfunctorily
administered, if at all, to the African captives. What the Lima priests
did not explain, however, was why the negligence of their colleagues
in Africa excused them from performing their own duties, why they
did not (as Sandoval was to later urge on his brother Jesuits) patiently
seek to determine the validity of the baptism of each bozal. Untroubled,
apparently, by the inconsistency, the Archbishop obligingly forwarded
these complaints to the Crown on May 13, 1593. This brought the
home government to make a start at reform. In 1595 the Council of
the Indies recommended that its counterpart for Portugal order that
all blacks departing the coast of Africa be properly baptized and carry
certification of the fact. Rather than act hastily on this advice, the
Crown instead convoked a panel of lawyers in Lisbon to consider the
matter. The Council of Portugal, which was invited to express an opinion as well, likewise refused to plunge headlong into reform. Wary,
perhaps, of acknowledging past guilt, the Council simply recommended
that the entire question, along with the documents accumulated thus
far, be referred to the Lisbon convocation. The Crown agreed, but if

the lawyers reached any firm decision it has not come to light. At any rate it is plain that no reforms were effected on the African coast during the period of Luso-Spanish union. Indeed, despite the best efforts of Sandoval and his colleagues in Cartagena, so few baptized bozales were sold in the Lima slave market that most notaries who prepared bills of sale automatically assumed all new arrivals were pagans.

The Crown appears to have let the matter rest again until 1603, when Viceroy Monterrey was queried about the truth of the reports of various prelates that the bulk of the blacks of Peru, who numbered 20,000 in Lima alone, were without religious instruction. Only the Jesuits, it seemed, even tried to instruct them in the Faith, working among them on feast days when their masters allowed them free time. But this system had proved less than successful, by all accounts. The slaves were tired after their labors and, despite the Society's best efforts to attract them, preferred dances and drunken orgies to religious instruction. As a result of this widespread indifference to the conversion of the African, few blacks ever went to confession, and fewer still took communion. The viceroy was requested to see if the situation could perhaps be remedied by making three or four priests responsible for the spiritual welfare of the predominantly African areas of Lima, as was the case with the Indians, an arrangement that might be extended to other towns with large slave populations as well. The Crown suggested that the ecclesiastical personnel could be supported by obliging slaveholders to pay half a peso a year for each slave.[37]

Monterrey died in 1606, and it was left to the Audiencia to respond to the Crown. When it did so, it was in strongly negative terms. The slave population of Lima had been greatly exaggerated to the Crown, the oidores contended; according to the census taken in 1600, there were only some 6,600 persons of color in the city, and they were well served by the existing parish organization and the members of the Orders. Moreover, though a few slaveholders were indeed indifferent to the spiritual lives of their bliacks, the vast majority were not. Finally, the proposed half-peso levy to expand the ecclesiastical establishment would be resented by the slaveowners, who believed that their obligation to support the Church was already sufficiently fulfilled through the payment of the tithe and "other obventions and ecclesiastical taxes." The Crown yielded to these arguments and dropped the matter.[38]

Another attempt at reform was a quarter-century in coming. This time the source was the Archbishop of Lima himself. In a 1632 letter to the Crown the prelate asserted that the African population of the area was woefully ignorant of the Faith, particularly those unfortunates who worked on the outlying plantations, and revived the notion of assigning a priest in each parish to care exclusively for the spiritual welfare of the blacks. The Crown's response was to ask Viceroy Chinchón for his opinion of the idea.[39] Chinchón thereupon turned to the Archbishop, asking for precise information on the number of parishioners involved and the number of additional churches and priests that would be required. The Archbishop complied, forwarding to Chinchón summaries of parish records for Lima that showed a current colored population of over 14,000 persons (see Appendix A). The parish priests at his disposal were already overburdened, he noted, and additional personnel were desperately needed if the coloreds of the capital were to be instructed in the Faith. Though he recognized that funds to support additional clerics would be difficult to obtain, he told Chinchón, Potosí had two priests exclusively for the black population and surely Lima could do as much. The Archbishop also sent Chinchón detailed proposals for additional parish churches.

On the basis of this exchange Chinchón wrote the Crown giving very guarded support to the proposal but stressing at the same time the expense that would be involved, given the prevailing high cost of construction materials and wages.[40] As Chinchón had perhaps realized, mention of additional expenses was enough to chill the enthusiasm of the war-weary and financially embarrassed home government. In 1637 the Crown sent a decree to the Archbishop that all but killed the original proposal. In consultation with Chinchón the Archbishop was to try to assign one cleric to deal almost exclusively with the African population of Lima, though this measure was not to excuse any parish priest from his own responsibilities in serving his black parishioners. All projects for new ecclesiastical construction and any proposals that would obligate the citizenry or the Crown to additional financial support were to be put aside for the moment.[41] It is not known what further action Chinchón and the Archbishop took between them, but during the remainder of our period no further proposals on the subject were made at the highest levels of government.

As this chronicle of intermittent and largely ineffectual concern over the performance of the secular clergy makes clear, the parish priests as a group made no systematic and sustained attempt to Christianize the blacks. Still, the case of the priest Don Francisco de Godoy tells us that there were exceptions. A harsher critic of the clergy's efforts among the blacks could scarcely have been found. In a very gloomy letter to the Crown in 1652 Godoy deplored the fact that religious instruction was not provided to the Indians and Africans on a regular basis, and pronounced himself appalled at their ignorance of even the simplest articles of faith. Indeed, he was moved to tears, he said, at the thought that "Christ has died for them and they know Him not."[42] Godoy had himself worked hard and long among the black and brown population during his years of service in Lima, moving beyond his own pulpit to preach on estates in the countryside and at black baptisms, weddings, and funerals. By his report slave funerals were especially well attended, and he had often appeared at two or three in a single day. His example, perhaps because of its very rarity, had won the enthusiastic praise of both his fellow priests and the Mendicant Orders, and had led to his appointment to the bishopric of Ayacucho (Guamanga).[43]

For areas outside Lima, the evidence on the work of the parish priests is altogether ambiguous. On the one hand, there is the 1625 letter of a Jesuit deploring the scandalous idolatries and superstitions he found rampant among the African populations of Trujillo and Pisco (a report that obviously must be measured against his admitted objective, to secure royal permission for Jesuit establishments in those areas).[44] On the other hand, there is the report of the usually reliable Vázquez de Espinosa that in all the vineyards of the Pisco Valley "there are chapels ... for the service contingent and in particular for the Negro slaves; every ranch has a village made up of them for them to hear Mass and so many of these priests in attendance at Pisco get very good salaries for going to say Mass at the ranches on feast days."[45] In addition, during the 1630's at least, the Archbishop of Lima seems to have taken an active interest in the spiritual welfare of the inhabitants of the south coast, for in 1632 he ordered Licenciado Gerónimo Santa Cruz y Padilla to visit all the agricultural valleys between Cañete and Nazca. During the course of this tour the priest confirmed 1,947 baptisms, over half of them (1,067) for persons of color.[46]

The uneven performance of the secular clergy among the black population can perhaps be ascribed in large part to their having to make their spiritual ministrations pay. For men of notoriously lower caliber than the members of the Holy Orders, the situation almost invited abuses. The Crown made feeble attempts to provide some spiritual care for the slaves free of charge, but largely to no avail. As late as the 1620's, for example, Luis Enríquez, Crown attorney before the Lima Audiencia, accused the secular clergy of charging fees for the Masses they said in their rounds among the slave population on the outskirts of the city. Enríquez requested a decree from the Crown, similar to one recently issued for New Granada, reaffirming that clerics were to receive only the necessary food during such visits. The home government directed Enríquez to seek action from the viceroy in the matter, thereby tacitly acknowledging the blunt fact that fees had come to be attached to most of the sacramental duties the secular clergy performed among the blacks. Indeed, tariffs for at least some church services were differentiated on an ethnic basis in Peru at least as early as 1583, and the practice was full blown by the seventeenth century.[47]

In effect, then, the spiritual welfare of the individual slave, barring contact with a dedicated secular priest like Godoy or with a member of the Orders, was largely dependent on the whim of his master, and here the record is likewise spotty. Some masters calmly listed unbaptized slaves in their wills,[48] and numbers of others may have been indifferent to whether their blacks were Christians. But many seem to have been as scrupulous of the salvation of their slaves as they were of their own. Many Peruvian plantations boasted a chapel for religious worship, though these structures and the ornaments they contained were often in an alarming state of disrepair and decrepitude,[49] and even in rural Peru the quality of spiritual care given blacks was often quite good. The practice Espinoza noted in the Pisco Valley in the seventeenth century was widely employed elsewhere: a priest was paid to make the circuit from plantation to plantation, ministering to the blacks. A similar arrangement is mentioned in a 1600 lease of a vineyard in the Chunchanga Valley near Ica, and some twenty years later the agriculturalists of the Mala Valley near Lima also employed a circuit priest.[50]

Under this happy arrangement, the priest probably earned a good salary in the aggregate while the individual agriculturalist had to contribute very little. In the Mala Valley, for instance, Father Don Julián de la Rua was paid ten pesos by the majordomo of the estate mentioned previously "because he was present in the valley all during Lent of this year of 1620 to say Mass and confess and instruct the blacks and thus he was paid by all those of the valley." Occasionally, the same major-domo paid the priest to administer sacraments over and above those provided for in the cost-sharing arrangement made with the other landowners. The majordomo of the Pérez Noguera chácara near Lima was so solicitous of the spiritual welfare of his black workers that during Lent of 1639 he purchased a letter of indulgence for each of the fourteen adult slaves at a total of five pesos.[51] In Lima the Confraternity of the Prisons and Charity was very active among the poor—the blacks and mulattoes as well as the Spaniards and Indians. Called the Confraternity of the Saints Peter and Paul, this organization provided the indigent who had been jailed for one reason or another with rations, legal assistance, and medical care, and with "preachers and persons to pray with them at night and teach them Christian doctrine."[52]

The secular clergy plainly did not neglect the colored population entirely, especially when the financial advantage was clear, but their efforts were insignificant next to those of the religious orders. The Dominicans and Augustinians both played a substantial role—that of the Dominicans is perhaps best exemplified by San Martín de Porres, a lay brother of the order,[53] and that of the Augustinians by their religious establishment in the Triana district on the outskirts of Lima "for the good of the poor and the slaves belonging to the neighboring farms and estates, and for the workers who go out into the country in that direction on the Malambo road."[54] The Jesuits, however, were by far the most zealous of all in this respect. Indeed, they saw this work as their clear duty. As Alonso de Sandoval, mentioned many times in these pages, observed, since the African had been imported to make up for the shortage of Indians available to serve the Spaniards, that fact alone imposed an obligation on the Spaniards to show equal concern for the spiritual welfare of both servile groups. The Society's effort began from the moment the first eight Jesuits set foot on Peruvian soil in 1568. One of their number, Father Luis López, started work almost immediately among the blacks of Lima. Similarly, when members of the Society first entered the Trujillo area in 1618, one of their foremost concerns was to assemble the Africans and Indians for religious instruction. In this instance, as in so many others, their effectiveness was not entirely pleasing to colleagues and rivals of less zeal, but as one Jesuit put it, "Many were happy to see us, and others, if they were not pleased, were ashamed and kept quiet."[55]

The Jesuit approach to proselytism among the Africans was stamped

PRIMERA HISTORIA
CRISTIANONEG

gra qʒaten deneegros boza
destos salio elbienaue

les deguinea t
racados ṗ̃ bues

Fig. 6. Two Afro-Peruvians at their devotions

with their characteristic care, and they soon perceived the need for at least some grounding in the so-called "language of Angola," a point that Sandoval was later to stress heavily. Serious consideration was given to the establishment of courses in the African languages at the College of San Pablo in Lima and to the printing of a simple dictionary and grammar, along with the guide for confessors that had already been prepared in the language of the slaves (the so-called language of Angola) at that institution. These ambitious projects evidently did not reach full fruition, but

in 1629 San Pablo was using and distributing, even to the furthest ends of the viceroyalty, prayer leaflets, catechisms, and instructions printed in Lima in the language of the slaves. In 1630, fourteen hundred and forty copies of a simple grammar came off the press, and the Jesuits of San Pablo were furnished with the essential tools to begin the systematic study of the "language of Angola." For these linguistic publications in the African language, the Jesuits of San Pablo did not produce an original work as in the case of Quechua, but rather used a work edited in Portugal by Mateo Cardoso, a Jesuit theologian born in Lisbon, adapting it to the needs of America.[56]

Sandoval's *De instauranda* was received with enthusiasm by the Jesuits of seventeenth-century Lima. Widely circulated in the colony, the work was avidly read for its information on African life and culture by those who wished to profit from the author's many years of missionary labor among arriving slave cargoes. By this date, however, the Jesuits of Lima themselves had accumulated a goodly store of proselytizing techniques, which they practiced to great effect among the blacks of the area. Many members of the Society were celebrated preachers, relying on their great oratorical powers to attract and hold the attention of large numbers of blacks. Father López was one of these. He succeeded in drawing as many as 2,000 slaves to San Pablo on Sundays for a weekly religion class, and he used the accumulated prestige and good will to gain acceptance "as peacemaker and counselor in the slaves' quarters." Father Piñas, a favorite preacher of Viceroy Toledo, made it his custom on Sundays and feast days to go to the main square of Lima, mount a stone bench, and proclaim the gospel to the blacks who gathered around him. Another Jesuit, Father Portillo, known as the Trumpet of God for his stentorian voice, was capable (it was said) of striking fear into the heart of the most recalcitrant black as he recounted the punishments of Hell; and his colleague Father González acquired such a reputation that masters supposedly had merely to mention his name to quiet restless slaves.

The Jesuits also made good use of the pomp and ceremony of the Church, depending on processions with multicolored standards, garlands, incense, and especially music to attract the blacks. Dialogues with a Christian message were set to music for use among the slaves, and in the seventeenth century the College of San Pablo had a fine band of black musicians,

accomplished players of clarinets and *chirimias*, the Spanish version of the Scottish bagpipe. These Negro musicians performed at the festivities organized by the sodalities and became so famous that they were in great demand even outside the college. Besides clarinets and bagpipes, one could listen at San Pablo to trumpets, drum, flutes, and to the more delicate music of string instruments like guitars, lutes, and *rabeles*.[57]

Still, the inducements, whether oratorical, visual, or musical, were never allowed to obscure the point of the exercise: Christianization. By the seventeenth century the practice of holding weekly classes in religion was thoroughly established in Lima, and the Jesuits had a large congregation of blacks who met every Sunday afternoon for a spiritual reading followed by a sermon. Many slaves could not attend these sessions, since their masters gathered in a similar congregation at San Pablo, leaving their blacks outside to hold their horses. Appreciating the situation, the Jesuits would send one of their number out to preach to the slaves, so that they might not on their masters' account be deprived of good doctrine and instruction. Like the other congregations, the black congregation had a festival and communion every month, at which time the Holy Sacrament was "exposed with remarkable lavishness of elaborate decoration." These Jesuit gatherings seem to have become fairly specialized by mid-century. The Church of Nuestra Señora de los Desamparados, for example, had a congregation of black and mulatto women who met for devotions every Wednesday and for communion every fourth Sunday.[58]

The Jesuits well appreciated that many slaves had neither the leisure nor the inclination for such systematic instruction. Accordingly, lay helpers were soon recruited from among the various African groups to catechize among their fellows as the opportunity arose. In addition, members of the Society would go every day to the main plaza to work among the blacks who gathered there to hire out as day laborers. And at the Friday fish market, where some blacks unloaded the catch brought up from Callao and others shopped for their masters, "every week, in the middle of that confusion, appeared the preachers of San Pablo, bell in hand, and for a while transactions were suspended and a short sermon delivered." The general public market, the hospitals and jails, and the mint were likewise regularly visited. The textile mills and workshops, where conditions were notably harsh and the blacks were treated as virtual prisoners, were of particular concern. At least once a week a Jesuit father, often accompanied by students at San Pablo, would go to the mills, many of which were in the San Lázaro district, to console and catechize the slaves "in order that they may patiently bear the heavy labor that there weighs them down." In addition, at Lent each year a member of the Society was sent to make sure that these blacks confessed and took communion, "since most of them are imprisoned and cannot come to confess and take communion in the church."

One aspect of Catholicism to which some Africans responded with apparent enthusiasm was the religious brotherhood, or sodality (*cofradía*). These brotherhoods, each of which was devoted to a particular patron saint, arranged to have Masses said for the souls of their members, living and dead, took part in the appropriate religious processions and festivities, and no doubt gave those blacks and mulattoes who were fortunate enough to belong some sense of spiritual well-being and standing in the larger community. For the Church, the brotherhoods were a source of modest income. In Lima the first religious brotherhood for the black population was established in the 1540's, an affiliate of the Spanish one devoted to the Most Holy Sacrament. Others followed as the number of Africans grew.[59]

The authorities were always rather suspicious of the colored sodalities. As early as 1549 the Lima municipal council complained that the meetings of the black confraternity were no more than planning sessions for crimes and robberies and an excuse for drunkenness.[60] In later years concern continued to be voiced intermittently that members of black sodalities gathered only to plan crimes or to hatch rebellions. In 1591, indeed, the Council of the Indies, in a document designed primarily to block the organization of colored militia in Peru, ventured to remind the Crown that even the cofradías of blacks and mulattoes, composed of "such ignorant people toward a pious goal," had in the past caused scandals and unrest, though the nature of these disturbances was not specified. Later, in 1602, the Crown prohibited any meeting of the African and Indian sodalities without the prelate of the sponsoring religious house or his appointed surrogate in attendance.[61]

For all that, the African confraternities appear to have been harmless enough. In fact the Lima city council, so critical of the slave cofradía in 1549, some forty years later ordered the black and mulatto sodalities of the city to perform their dances on the occasion of the feast day of the Most Holy Sacrament—"as they are obliged to and as they have been accustomed to do in past years."[62] The Crown's decree of 1602 on the black confraternity meetings led to an inquiry the next year on the number of such brotherhoods in Lima. The replies of the Dominicans and the Jesuits have survived. The Dominicans reported they had two African brotherhoods, one for mulattoes and the other for *negros congos*. The Jesuits reported one, and set forth in some detail what the group was all about. Its principal purpose was to provide religious instruction to its approximately 100 black members each Sunday and "to bring order to their lives and customs, teaching them how to live in a Christian manner." On the many feast days of the year, the members met in the church and then went to feed the poor in the jails or to serve the sick in the hospitals, always accompanied by a priest. The brotherhood relied on alms to support these charities and to obtain the wax used for processions and burials, the collection of which was entered with great care in an account book. One day each year all the members gathered to confess and take communion (though some did so more often). In addition, two meetings were held annually for the election of majordomos and other officials; these meetings, the Jesuits reported, were always orderly and held under the supervision of a priest.[63]

By 1619, according to a report sent to the Crown by the Archbishop of Lima, there were fifteen sodalities for blacks and mulattoes in the capital (see Table 3). In addition, the Dominican and Franciscan monasteries in Callao sponsored brotherhoods for Afro-Peruvians, the first an organization for mulattoes and the second one for blacks. No other Spanish town in the diocese, which at this date did not include the districts of Trujillo and Cuzco, had enough blacks to support a confraternity. Though most of the cofradías were poor and without fixed income, only two—the brotherhood of San Bartolomé in Santa Ana parish and the brotherhood of Los Remedios in San Marcelo parish—complained of lack of attendance and indifference on the part of members. Against this, the Franciscan-sponsored brotherhood of Los Reyes,

TABLE 3
Afro-Peruvian Religious Brotherhoods in Lima, 1619

Sponsor	Patron	Estimated annual alms (pesos)
	BLACKS ONLY	
Franciscans	Nuestra Señora de los Reyes	1,000
Dominicans	Nuestra Señora del Rosario	250-300
Augustinians	Nuestra Señora de Guadalupe	50
Jesuits	El Salvador	50
Mercedarians	Nuestra Señora de Agua Santa	40
Mercedarians	Nuestra Señora de Loreto	40
	MULATTOES ONLY	
Dominicans	Nuestra Señora del Rosario	400
Santa Ana parish	San Juan Bautista	60
Franciscans	San Juan de Buenaventura	40-50
	BLACKS AND MULATTOES COMBINED	
San Marcelo parish	San Antón	300
Cathedral parish	Nuestra Señora de la Antigua	100
San Sebastián parish	Nuestra Señora de la Victoria	100
Mercedarians	Santa Justa y Rufina	60
San Marcelo parish	Nuestra Señora de los Remedios	30-40
Santa Ana parish	San Bartolomé	30-40

SOURCE: AGIL 301, "Relación de las ciudades, villas, y lugares . . . parrochias y doctrinas que hay en este Arzobispado de Lima, de españoles y de indios, y de las personas que las sirven . . . ," April 20, 1619.

composed of Africans of different ethnic groups, was noted for the splendor of its ceremonies and was described as one of the best-served and richest confraternities in the city. The total membership of the colored sodalities was not given.

As is suggested by the Dominicans' report of a confraternity for *negros congos* and by the membership classifications in Table 3, the black sodalities were structured to some extent along either "tribal" or "racial" lines. That is, some were composed of members of a certain African ethnic group, and others drew a distinction between "pure" blacks and persons of color with some admixture of white blood, the mulattoes (or *pardos*, to employ a euphemism that gained currency in the seventeenth century). Organizing cofradías along African ethnic lines was particularly favored in the sixteenth century. It is not clear whether this policy was merely an ecclesiastical extension of the civil divide-and-rule principle or a practice dictated by the linguistic and cultural difficulties encountered by the missionaries. It may also be that the ethnic distinctions were not as hard and fast over time as surviving documentation would lead us to believe. At any rate, the researches of Emilio Harth-terré and Alberto Márquez Abanto indicate that many black sodalities had an ethnic focus in the sixteenth century: the brotherhood of Nuestra Señora del Socorro in the church of San Francisco de Paula was for Angolans (Malambas), that of Nuestra Señora de la Antigua in the Cathedral for criollos, and so forth.[64] During the seventeenth century, as Africans of different ethnic backgrounds intermarried and as the process of race mixture produced a multiplicity of "castes," the division of sodalities along tribal lines waned, only to be replaced by new standards of discrimination. The experience of the Jesuit-sponsored brotherhood well illustrates this development. From the time it was organized (at some point before the end of the sixteenth century) until the 1630's the sodality was apparently open to all blacks. By 1650, however, it had split into three distinct organizations. The first split was at the insistence of the Peruvian-born blacks, ladinos who had mastered the Spanish language and customs and wished to be separate from the rude bozales. That accomplished, the ladino confraternity split once again, this time divided by tensions between the "pure" black criollos and the mulattoes.[65] The Jesuit experience may well have been shared by other black sodalities before mid-century. In any event, as the table shows, as early as 1619 a distinction was made between blacks and mulattoes in nine of the fifteen cases. Eight of these were sodalities organized by the religious orders, whose own great prestige perhaps attached in some measure to their black charges. Unfortunately, at this date the balance between African ethnicity, cultural traits acquired in America, and considerations based on race mixture in these divisions is not clear.

Finally, we must note that if the total membership of the Jesuit confraternity reported to the Crown in 1603 was typical, i.e., some 100 persons of color per sodality, then only a slim minority of the African population of Lima, much less of the colony, belonged to such organizations. Indeed, it seems clear that membership in a religious brotherhood was restricted to what may be loosely termed the colored elite, whether free or slave. Sodalities were urban institutions, and they functioned best when composed of blacks who were in a relatively favored position in society: artisans, small merchants and peddlers, household servants, and the like. These were the persons of color who had the leisure time and the economic resources necessary for active participation in the affairs of the confraternity, and the majority were perhaps both ladinos and criollos. Most of the rest of the Afro-Peruvians had more tenuous ties to the Church: perhaps as a member of one of the informal congregations similar to that organized by the Jesuits in Lima, perhaps as the parishioner of a devoted priest, whether in city or country, or perhaps most frequently of all, as no more than a chance participant when a priest conducted a prayer on his rounds or when a religious processional passed, with formal contact reduced to occasional communion and to the last rites of the Church.

Indeed, the lives of many in Peru were so lightly touched by the Church, and not merely Africans but also Indians and Spaniards, as to create a subculture marked by heresy and superstition. The authorities, and particularly the Inquisition, did what they could to keep this undergrowth in check, striking intermittently at the most flagrant contraventions of Christian decency and doctrine. The simplest cases were those that at least paid Christianity the compliment of perverting or challenging it. There was, for example, the 1560 case of Luis Solano, son of a Spaniard and a black woman, who, along with Lope de la Peña, described as a Moor from Guadalajara, was convicted by the Holy Office of practicing and spreading Muhammadanism in Cuzco. Solano was executed, and Peña was sentenced to life imprisonment. We also have the example of Hernando Maravilla, slave of Doña Antonia Nabía (wife of a former oidor of the Audiencia of Chile), who was accused in the 1580's of openly proclaiming his repudiation of Christianity and his belief that marriage was sanctioned by the Devil, to whose cause he was pledged. Hernando, a native of Lima, was returned to that city for questioning. He confessed to having spoken these words in anger (more than once) in the belief that his mistress had frustrated his proposed marriage; he also confessed that he had been whipped twice already by the Chilean authorities. After due deliberation, the inquisitors decided that Hernando should be whipped 200 times through the streets of Lima, with a gag in his mouth, and be subjected to the same punishment again on his return to Santiago.[66]

Spanish churchmen periodically raised alarms about the pagan practices and superstitions among Afro-Peruvians. However, those writers who commented on the issue during our period were so contemptuous of what they saw that their remarks reveal very little. For example, one seventeenth-century observer (who was in any case sharply critical of the moral tone of Peruvian society) charged that "the blacks and Indians are more barbarous now than before they came into contact with the Spaniards, because then they had no one to show them the way, and now they are sorcerers and full of superstitions; they are devotees of the Devil whom the Indians call *supay*. . . . The blacks give themselves over to knaveries and are so stubborn that the Devil himself would be unable to manage them."[67] In short, it is difficult to say to what extent African religious beliefs survived. The scant available evidence argues that most non-Christian practices of Peruvian blacks during this period were at the level of superstitions, informed not only by their own traditions and the abundant superstitions of the Spaniards themselves, but also by the remnants of the native religion.

For example, as early as 1547 a black slave prevailed on an Indian sorcerer to help kill his master, a Spanish surgeon, who had mistreated him. To this end the sorcerer cast a spell on bits of wool from the surgeon's pillow, which were placed under his saddle and mattress, and another on some grains of sand, which were sprinkled about where the master would step on them. In addition, the Indian had a conference with the Devil, at which time the master's shadow appeared and was given a potion that guaranteed death within three months. The testimony of the principals involved was evasive, but it appears the surgeon's food may have been drugged as well. At any rate he did indeed fall desperately ill. In the meantime, however, the slave made the mistake of trying to force his way into the home of an Indian noblewoman while drunk, and after being severely beaten for the offense by her retainers, was unwise enough to threaten to cast a spell on her. This proved to be his undoing, for word of the threat reached the Spanish authorities, who conducted a meticulous investigation of the case. In the process, another case came to light, this one involving an Indian sorceress who was accused of casting spells on Don Francisco de Ampuero, one of the most prominent of the conquistadores and a member of the Lima cabildo, at the behest of his wife, Doña Inés Yupanqui, daughter of the Inca Huayna Capac and sister of Atahualpa. The inquiry led to the execution of three of the conspirators; the black was garrotted after red-hot pincers had been applied to various parts of his body, the sorcerer was flayed alive, and the sorceress was burned at the stake. Doña Inés was too exalted a personage to bring to justice, particularly since the whole affair occurred during the chaos of the Gonzalo Pizarro rebellion, and was left to the tender mercies of her husband. The Spanish surgeon recovered.[68]

Black practitioners of the art of witchcraft were no less in evidence. The earliest case we know of is that of Beatriz Negra, a slave of Arequipa, who in the 1570's was brought before the Audiencia of Lima as a sorceress and "convoker of demons." Though condemned to no more than perpetual exile from Arequipa, Beatriz seems to have been a woman of resources or at least tenacity, for she appealed the sentence. Unfortunately, we know no more than that she was forbidden to leave Lima while her appeal went forward, for here the record ends. Lima seems to have supplied other areas with a fair share of their black sorcerers. A case tried before the Inquisition of Cartagena in 1613, for example, involved a mulatto born in Lima, Juan Lorenzo, the slave of an Augustinian friar. Some twenty-six years old at the time, Lorenzo was described as a "heretical witch and fortuneteller." Again in the 1630's, while investigating another sect of witches active in the Cartagena area, the Holy Office turned up one Ana María, a quadroon who had been born in Lima.[69]

Many, if not most, Spaniards assumed (correctly or not) that those blacks who were not sorcerers themselves at least knew others who were. We read, for example, of the curious case of Father Juan de Luna, who had been appointed to the deanship of the cathedral at Popayán, but who had chanced upon the party of Viceroy Toledo in Panama as Toledo was proceeding to Peru to assume office and been taken on as the viceroy's chaplain. Luna was dismissed in 1571 for taking a bribe and for theft during the viceroy's inspection tour of the interior provinces, and thinking to restore himself to Toledo's good graces through witchcraft, began casting about for a sorcerer. Among those he approached in his search was Juana de Ontiveros, a free mulata who had sold pastries for a living during most of her forty years' residence in Cuzco. Juana evidently knew a harebrained scheme when she saw one and refused to have anything to do with Luna. Her judgment was confirmed when he was arrested after an incredible series of blunders revolving around his efforts to obtain certain unmentionable items of the viceroy's for the purpose of casting the spell. During the subsequent investigation, though Juana denied all knowledge of the supernatural, the testimony of other witnesses strongly hinted that she was well acquainted with the practitioners of witchcraft in Cuzco. The authorities, however, seem to have been so concerned with the disposition of Luna, who was turned over to the Church for punishment, that possible accomplices were apparently ignored or forgotten.[70]

To complete our discussion of slave life, we turn now to the subject of marriage and the family, and here too the Church played an important role. In both civil and canon law, slaves had the right to marry, even without their master's permission; slave wives were protected against the importunings of their masters; and slaveholders were forbidden to separate black families by unreasonable distances or circumstances that made married life impossible.[71] Though the Crown did not actively promote the principle of marriage among African slaves in the Americas, it was certainly aware that a roughly equal ratio between the sexes would help allay slave discontent and also reduce sexual contacts between African men and Indian women. As we have seen, as early as 1524 the Crown decreed that a third of all slave cargoes from Africa must be female. The realities of American demand reinforced this legislation, and as the sample taken from notarial records indicates, females accounted for 34.5 per cent of the bozales sold in the Lima slave market between 1560 and 1650. If all slaves are included, the figure rises to nearly 40 per cent. Further, in all of the censuses taken in Lima during this period the number of black females equaled or exceeded the number of black males (see Appendix A). Both imperial law and the actual ratio between the sexes in Peru, then, seemed to favor slave marriages.

Blacks who wished to marry found a consistent champion in the Peruvian Church. Ecclesiastical councils held in Lima twice declared that slaveholders were not to oppose slave marriages or divide black families, first in 1567-68 and again in 1582-83; and these same principles were reaffirmed still later, in 1629, for the bishopric of Ayacucho.[72] Public opinion was another matter, though the most enlightened colonists went along with the stand taken by Crown and Church. Poma de Ayala, for example, declared that slave marriages were in the interests of all concerned—God, king, masters, and the blacks themselves—and he was in favor of excommunication and other severe penalties for slaveowners who interfered with conjugal rights or separated families through sale. Poma expounded at some length on the subject: married blacks should if possible live under the same roof, but if ownership by different masters prevented this, then man and wife should either be allowed to pass the nights together or at least be given two evenings off per week by their owners; similarly, slaves married to free persons should be given eight free evenings a month; and children, far from being separated from their parents, should be allowed to perform the domestic chores their fathers and mothers had no time for, should be taught to read and write, and should be instructed in the Faith "in order that they be Christian, orderly, and honorable."

The implication of all this is that these precepts were not being followed in the Peru of Poma's day, a reading that is confirmed by Alonso de Sandoval. In Sandoval's harsh view, slaveholders had no objections to sexual intercourse between slaves, since the resulting offspring supplemented their human property. Indeed, moral considerations had so little force that many black women were forced into prostitution to earn the inordinately high sums their masters demanded. However, slaveowners took an altogether different view of marriage, Sandoval charged. Wedlock among slaves was inconvenient, since the partners and any children they produced could not be transferred from one place to another or sold without taking family ties into consideration. Consequently, in defiance of the law masters discouraged marriage by threats and whippings, often denied married couples conjugal rights, and presented their children for sale as the products of illicit unions.[73]

As Sandoval's remarks make clear, the will and consent of the master were often more important than the law when it came to slave marriages. But the whole economic design of slavery also played a vital role, particularly in the rural areas where the emphasis was on males fit for agricultural service. Here, the opportunities for married life were minimal whatever the attitude of the master. In 1622, for example, Juan Rodríguez Acevedo operated his leased chácara in Herbay with a force of twenty-four male and four female blacks; only one of the twenty-eight slaves, a female, was married, and her husband was in Lima. In 1647 the hacienda of Acaray in the Guaura Valley depended on a labor force of twenty-one adult slaves, including nineteen men. Three of the men were married, one evidently to a woman on another plantation, but only two children were in evidence, both boys, ages ten and eight, respectively. The Pérez Noguera chácara near Lima, so admirably operated in many other respects and where a secular priest was at hand to minister to the slaves, does not seem to have even countenanced matrimony. In 1639 it had seventeen blacks, ten adult males, four women, and three children. None of the slaves were reported as being married, and two of the offspring were referred to as mulattoes.[74]

It is possible, however, to find happier examples. In 1576 the sugar plantation of Andahuasi in the Chancay Valley was worked by twelve black males, of whom seven were married, three to slaves and the others to Indians. On the San José de Quipico plantation in Chircay, with a large slave population of 104 in 1636 (including eight children), fourteen female slaves in a total of seventeen were married to males of the plantation, and another was widowed. Two other males were also married, one to a woman in Lima and the other to an Indian woman. Among Peruvian agricultural holdings, the vineyard of Hernando de la Concha in the valley of Guayuri de Ordás near Ica seems to have been unfortunately rare. In 1625 it was populated by twenty-five males, ten females, and fourteen children ranging in age from one to twelve years. A later inventory, in 1632, revealed one widower and seven slave couples with a total of nine children among them, nineteen single male slaves, and two single females.[75] Clearly, the preponderance of black males in the Peruvian countryside not only sharply limited the opportunities for slave marriage, but also meant that the slave population did not reproduce itself.

If Lima is at all representative, the situation was scarcely better in the cities and towns of Peru. I use here the sample of 6,890 slaves of both sexes and all ages sold in the Lima market between 1560 and 1650. All bozales must be subtracted from this total, since such slaves were usually not even baptized on arrival, much less sold as husband-and-wife teams married within the Christian church. All blacks under the age of eighteen may likewise be deducted. This leaves a total of 2,192 black males and 1,696 females, of whom 122 and 161, or 5.5 and 9.5 per cent, respectively, were listed as married. (These figures are close to accurate, for the marital status of the slave was almost always included in the bill of sale to forestall legal problems, e.g., redhibition.) Over and above this there were sixty-seven slave families in the sample that were sold as units. Even then the percentages are still unimpressive, and particularly so when contrasted with the 321 women (19 per cent of the female total) who were sold either as mothers or as pregnant but with no mention of marriage.

Some may object—and perhaps with some justification—that these figures represent the relationship between the institutions of slavery and marriage in the most unfavorable light, since the great majority of blacks who changed hands were in the sixteen to twenty-five age bracket; within this group, slaves aged eighteen or older had the best years of their lives before them during which to marry and may have been permitted by their masters to do so at (say) age twenty-seven, when their resale was no longer contemplated and their marital status was therefore no longer a complicating factor in terms of market value. However, among the numerous and scattered wills of urban slaveholders I examined, which more often than not list only the names of the slaves and not their ages, the incidence of marriage is not perceptibly higher. Further, even if it is argued that most masters effectively shut off their blacks from marriage before the age of twenty, and all slaves below that age are deducted from the sample, the percentages do not change much: 5.8 per cent among the males (117 of 2,021) and 9.85 per cent among the females (156 of 1,583). In the older age groups, the percentage of married slaves increases only modestly. Among the 766 male blacks aged twenty-six to thirty-five, for example, only ninety-nine (13 per cent) were married; and among women in this age group, ninety-seven of 583, or 16.6 per cent, were married. Thus, even these figures lend credence to the gloomy picture painted by Sandoval and make it easy to see why illegitimate birth was generally assumed for American-born persons of color.

What is less than clear in all this is the reasons the slaveowners opposed slave marriages, or at least failed to promote them. Few people in colonial society cared to challenge the views of Crown and Church openly and directly. The city of Lima came closest in bringing a bitter complaint before the 1582-83 ecclesiastical council to the effect that slaves all too frequently married without the consent of their masters, a practice that created endless complications if their masters wished to sell them later. Further, the city charged that the activities of married slaves who belonged to different masters were scandalizing the community: husbands had formed the habit of going to their wives' residences "at various indecent times and hours" for sexual purposes, and if the doors were not opened to them they did not hesitate to force their way through the windows.[76]

The assembled churchmen were unmoved by these laments, and with good reason. It is true, as we shall see, that married blacks could not be sold or moved about with quite the same flexibility as their unmarried counterparts, but the claim that marriage lowered the value of slaves is apparently without foundation. An analysis of married blacks who changed hands in the Lima slave market between 1560 and 1650 reveals that marital status had little or nothing to do with slave prices. Indeed, in many instances single blacks sold for less than married ones. In a group of thirty-nine female (ladina) slaves, aged twenty-six to thirty-five, sold in 1650, for example, the twelve who were married brought an average of 574 pesos as against an average of 548 pesos for the others. As for the offspring of black marriages, only moral pressure prevented their sale by the master at any age. At the same time, as a rule not even illegitimate children were sold separately from their mothers because of the care they required; there was in fact little market for slaves who were not at least in their teens. More often than not, black husbands and wives belonged to different masters, and provisions for housing in the crowded urban areas posed some difficulties. Yet, as we have seen, even in the towns slaves tended to live in their own huts apart from the main residence, and these were surely far enough away to spare the owner's modesty when husband and wife bedded together.[77] It might even be argued that the improved morale of a slave as a result of marriage and family life, not to mention the service of God, was well worth any accompanying sacrifices this required of his owner, but the Peruvian slaveholders clearly did not weigh the question in this light in the period under study.

The simple fact is that most masters brought a variety of weapons to bear to thwart the marriages of their slaves. These ranged from threats and whippings to virtual imprisonment and even sale outside the area. More effective than these, perhaps, was ensuring that the slave remained ignorant of his rights in this regard. It is worth looking at a few examples of clashes between masters and slaves over the issue of marriage. Suardo records the particularly touching case of a slave couple who had married without first asking their owners' permission. After the ceremony the groom went to his bride's master, a pulpero, to seek his blessing. As the slave knelt to kiss the man's hand, presumably a customary act in such cases, the pulpero snatched up a club and hit him twice on the head. The slave died soon after. Suardo tells us the pulpero sought refuge in the Dominican monastery, but does not say what his ultimate fate was.[78] Few masters were as violent in their opposition to slave marriage as this, but many were as unyielding. Often the slaves involved vented their anger in one way or another. The reader will recall the wild response of Hernando Maravilla, who renounced what may have been a tenuous belief in Christianity in favor of the Devil, for which public declaration he was subsequently punished by the Lima Holy Office. Many other slaves may have worked off their frustration through petty crimes and mischiefmaking. Still others fled their master's service temporarily and married without permission, accepting the risk of punishment on their return. Such was the case with María Angola, whose owner sold her with the declaration that she had once disappeared for a month to marry.[79]

The shrewdest and most resourceful blacks appealed to the ecclesiastical courts for the assistance that was rightfully theirs under the law. In 1636, for example, Antón Bran, a free mulatto, stated to the diocesan court of Lima that he had obtained the necessary license to marry Ana Bran, a slave of Doña Isabel de las Casas, but that Doña Isabel had hidden Ana to prevent the marriage. Antón received a court order commanding Doña Isabel to release Ana, but she ignored it. When a second one was issued, which carried the threat of excommunication, Doña Isabel contended that she had only kept Ana under lock and key to prevent her flight, that she had not succeeded in doing so, and that Antón knew of his bride-to-be's whereabouts and had taken legal action in an effort to obtain her freedom. This argument did not serve, and Antón obtained a third writ, which ordered that Ana be brought to the archiepiscopal jail to resolve the issue. Instead, a new petition was now filed by Gaspar Jiménez, who had just purchased Ana: he had permitted the couple to marry, and was asking the court for assurances that Ana would return to work. This the court agreed to guarantee, but it also enjoined Jiménez from interfering with the married life of the couple.

It should also be mentioned that a slave's wish to marry was sometimes frustrated for reasons other than the master's opposition. In 1619, for example, Pascual de Navamuel, black slave of Don Álvaro de los Ríos, informed the ecclesiastical judges that for many days he had attempted to marry the free mulata Ursula de Vergara, but that the bride's mother (also free) and other persons had frustrated his efforts. The court agreed to take formal testimony of Ursula's wishes in the matter, but several days later Pascual again petitioned the judges to the effect that her mother had arranged for his imprisonment by the Audiencia on trumped-up charges, and that the wedding was as far away as ever. Pascual pleaded that Ursula be removed from her mother's keeping and her true feelings ascertained, and, probably to his consternation, when this was done the young woman declared to the governess of the Reco-gimiento de Divorcio that she had accepted Pascual's proposal but had now changed her mind. Ursula was remanded to the care of her employer, and, presumably, Pascual was eventually released from jail.[80]

Though slave marriages were impeded and comparatively infrequent, they were common enough for the documents to record cases of widowed slaves who remarried.[81] For slaves lucky enough to obtain the consent of their masters, the mechanics of marriage were very similar to those that prevailed for free persons. Licenses to marry were granted by the ecclesiastical authorities, ordinarily by the vicar general of the archdiocese, on presentation of testimony showing that both parties were single and free in all other respects to contract matrimony. The license also stipulated the site for the ceremony, usually the parish church where one or both of the slaves were parishioners. Fortunately, 289 licenses for slave couples married in Lima between 1600 and 1650 have been preserved, so that even with what is clearly only a fraction of the licenses issued, we can say something about the kind of slave who did marry in Peru.[82]

First, the black who was allowed to wed tended to be owned by a master of high social status or by an institution subject to public scrutiny and with an example to set. A cursory examination of the Lima licenses reveals the following ownership for 282, or almost half, of the slaves involved: persons bearing the title Don or Doña (174); government officials and members of the Lima cabildo (33); religious orders and convents (31); military officers (21); members of the secular clergy (18); and prominent merchants (5). It is likely that many more of the slaveowners involved were people of wealth and social pretensions, though they cannot be so identified failing a title or honorific designation. The occupations of the blacks are not given in the licenses, but the majority may have been household servants, in a position to ingratiate themselves with their masters, or (in the case of men) artisans, who were customarily allowed a large measure of freedom. Still, only seventeen of the 122 married black males in the sample taken from notarial records (14 per cent) were identified as skilled workers, not an impressive proportion.

Second, the marriage licenses indicate that Peruvian blacks showed some preference for marriage within their African ethnic group, a tendency that fitted well with the Spanish policy of segregating coloreds along these lines in the confraternities and at social gatherings. Of the 280 unions in which both partners were slaves, 156 (54 per cent) were between members of the same ethnic group, and sixty others between people from roughly the same area of the African coast. Only a handful of these licenses involved marriages between free and slave blacks; similar unions, as well as marriages between Africans and Indians, are also mentioned in notarial records. The implications of both will be discussed in the next two chapters.

Legal union did not by any means assure a slave couple's future together, especially since most married blacks (assuming those of Lima were representative) did not belong to the same master. Indeed, being the common property of a slaveholder was no guarantee either, for one or other partner could be sold.[83] The intent in such cases was not necessarily malicious. The master may simply have been pressed for cash, for example. And if a tolerant purchaser was found the married life of the slave couple may have changed very little in the transaction. Such sales were certainly not illegal unless man and wife were separated by such a distance or for so long a period of time that their married life became a mockery. Yet more than one master was able to defy the law, perhaps because the slave involved did not know his rights, for there were blacks sold in Lima who were legally tied to mates in places as far away as Trujillo, Panama, Quito, and Ayacucho.[84] Against this, there were also cases of slave couples being united by a generous master through purchase; of the 5,753 transactions I examined for the years 1560-1650, thirty-three were entered into for the express purpose of unifying slave husbands and wives. Further, as we have seen, there were also in this group sixty-seven couples who were sold as a unit to keep the family together. Additional references to such acts of generosity are scattered through other documentation I studied.[85]

A fair share of blacks had recourse to the ecclesiastical courts, some seeking reunion with a mate, others seeking to avert the de facto dissolution of a marriage. Turning to cases of the first type,[86] we find that on occasion a master even initiated his slave's court action, sometimes out of pure benevolence, sometimes not. In 1637, for example, Gerónimo de Guzmán, a seaman of Callao, charged on behalf of his slave Gaspar Angola that another Callao sailor, Pedro Rodríguez Canastas, was deliberately hiding Gaspar's wife, Ana, despite an earlier ecclesiastical order to present her. At the subsequent hearing before the court witnesses testified that Guzmán had agreed to buy Ana but that Rodrí-guez had backed out at the last minute and had sent her for sale to Trujillo. Rodríguez was ordered to present Ana to the court within forty days or face excommunication. When Rodríguez was not forth-coming, this penalty was duly imposed. Evidently prodded by this, he made a formal reply to the charges about a month later. By his account, his wife could not control Ana while he was at sea, and the slave had run away twice. In consequence he had had to pay dearly for her ap-prehension. Since he was a poor man and knew nothing of her mar-riage, he had sent Ana to Trujillo lest she cause him further trouble, but his agent had died along the way. As a result, Ana had been sold by mistake as intestate property and was now in Cajamarca. He had agreed to sell her to Guzmán if Guzmán would retrieve her at his own cost, but this arrangement had fallen through. Rodríguez concluded his statement by pleading that he was too poor to pay for Ana's return, that he had not known of her marital status, and that with the elapse of so much time her whereabouts was uncertain in any event. Guzmán promptly contradicted Rodríguez's story, stating that Rodríguez knew full well of Ana's marriage, since Gaspar had been admitted into his home for conjugal rights every Saturday night, that Ana had been ob-viously pregnant when sent to Trujillo and then to Cajamarca for sale, and that his own attempt to buy her had not succeeded only because Rodríguez believed he could get a better price outside Lima. Unfor-tunately, at this stage, documentation of the case ends, suggesting that an out-of-court settlement was arranged—by which Rodríguez in all likelihood escaped ecclesiastical censure and fine.

In other cases in which a master took a hand the intentions were decidedly more ambiguous. In 1644, for example, the secular priest Gerónimo de Orellana Garrido, owner of Isabel Criolla, requested the archepiscopal court to order her husband Gregorio de Maridueñas, a free mulatto tailor, to take her back into his household and resume their married life. Orellana stated that the couple had lived apart for over four years despite his efforts to reconcile them and even though no divorce decree had ever been granted to permit such a state. Mari-dueñas, in reply, began by pleading that because of Isabel's slave status, cohabitation was difficult unless fixed times were set by the court. Warming to his task, he went on to declare that since his wife led such a "loose and depraved life," it was unfair to compel him to pay Orellana the equivalent of her wages, at the expense of his own food and clothing; that even her master had been forced to put shackles on her and confine her more than once to a bakery; and further, that Isabel had a harsh and fearful personality, having threatened to kill him several times. In short, the tailor wanted the order to take her back into his house quashed. The archepiscopal attorney took a dim view of all this, charging that the pleas of Maridueñas were frivolous and unfounded, that Isabel was an honest and respected person, and that her husband should lead a married life with her "at least on Saturday nights as laid down by synodal decisions and during all the rest of the time that her master will permit." The court ordered Maridueñas to comply with this request. His appeal to the episcopal court of Ayacucho, standard procedure at the time, was turned down. One would have to guess that Isabel's owner, Orellana, heaved a vast sigh of relief when she finally departed his hearth.

In a somewhat similar case of 1625, Bachiller Antonio Jaime Trevejo charged that eight years before he had purchased Juan Samaná, a mulatto tailor, only to be bitterly disappointed. Juan had refused to reside with him, had paid wages only reluctantly though he was a master and had journeymen in his employ, and had married only to avoid sale (presumably outside the city where his recalcitrance was unknown). To top it all Juan had cost him more than 250 pesos in fines during this period of ownership. Trevejo, petitioning for relief, asked the court to compel the owner of Juan's wife either to buy Juan from him or to sell him the wife. Presumably, he thought that single ownership would lead to greater control over the pair. Surprisingly, the vicar general concurred and ordered that the transaction be made within three days.

In instances where blacks themselves took the legal initiative, the circumstances were usually more moving. In 1640, for example, Antón Bran, owned by José Núñez del Prado, appealed to the archepiscopal court to be reunited with his wife in Panama. According to Antón, his former owner had brought him to Callao on the pretext that his absence from the Isthmus would only be temporary, and then had sold him in Callao without telling the purchaser of his marital status. Núñez, when informed of his slave's petition, used his experience as a lawyer before the Audiencia to reply not only that Antón's story was false, but indeed that without his permission the slave "had no person" for legal actions. Furthermore, he declared, no one, Antón included, had mentioned a wife in Panama, and nothing of the sort was mentioned in the bill of sale. In reply, Antón admitted his lack of legal rights with regard to "some contract or another profane matter," but declared that marriage was different, and pointed out that the silence in the bill of sale did not necessarily make his story less true. The court permitted Antón to bring witnesses to testify to his marriage, and he succeeded in getting several mariners to step forward. On the basis of their sworn statements, the court ordered Antón returned to Panama on the next boat. Núñez was granted a copy of the proceedings with which to secure a refund of the purchase price.[87]

A more conventional case of 1647 involved the complaint of the slave Antón Bran that his wife's owner, a swordmaker, was preventing the pair from leading a married life. Antón obtained a court order for the master to desist, only to return with the statement that the order, far from producing a positive effect, had merely led the swordmaker to exclude him more harshly than before from contact with Mariana. A new court order brought a reply from the master that he had kept Antón away because he mistreated his wife. Moreover, said the owner, he could not immediately comply with the ruling because the woman, Mariana, had run away. Antón responded that neither statement was true, and the court again ordered the master to desist from further harassment, at which point documentation of the case ends.

As a final example of cases of this sort, we may cite one from 1634, which began with a petition to the court from Juan Bernardo de Argote requesting permission to take his slave Diego Angola to Cajamarca for service. Argote stated that he had been granted a license to do so, but that it had been withdrawn when it was learned Diego was married. Argote offered to post bond for the return of the slave or even to buy his wife if necessary. Seemingly, the court dragged its heels, for there is no record of a reply before the filing of a second petition a year later, this one by María Balanta, Diego's wife. She charged that Argote had taken her husband from Lima for four months (presumably with license to do so) but had returned without him, and requested the court to compel Argote to produce Diego. This petition was filed several times before the court ordered the master to respond. When he did so, it was to state that Diego was resident on his holdings in the country and would be returned before the expiration of the one-year license he had, which permitted him to use the black in this way. Argote also renewed his request to be allowed to buy María. Since María does not seem to have petitioned the court for further action, the couple were presumably reunited.

Virtually all the petitions the court received seeking to prevent the break-up of couples seem to have been filed by the blacks themselves. Such cases fall roughly into two types: those that sought to prevent the permanent separation of a black couple through sale of one of the partners by the master and those that sought to prevent even the temporary absence of one of the mates through extended service to the slaveholder elsewhere. In both situations the ecclesiastical judges tried to strike a reasonable balance between the interests of master and slave. Let us first examine a few cases where permanent separation through sale was contemplated or feared. In 1621 an action was brought by Francisca Bran to contest the sale of her husband, Pedro, in Arica. Francisca secured a restraining order, which Pedro's owner, Doña Isabel Vilicia, ignored. Her excommunication followed. Under this prod she then told the court that she had sent Pedro off to Arica for sale in great haste because his conduct in Lima had been so bad as to endanger his life and to send him to jail three times. Her intentions had not been malicious, she claimed, and Pedro was in fact in the keeping of her brother in the southern port. The vicar general agreed to lift the excommunication if Doña Isabel returned Pedro to Lima within four months or else paid the 100 pesos the court would need to arrange for his transportation. Doña Isabel, after deciding against an appeal to Ayacucho, asked for and got a four-month extension.

In a less complicated case of 1642 the slave Francisco Folupo had successfully blocked an effort to send his wife, Juana, for sale to Pisco from Lima. The Spaniard involved had claimed that he was merely an agent for Juana's legal owner, and that what was at issue was a change of residence, not a sale, but the court had not believed the story. Francisco now came before the court to assert that the so-called agent in his frustration had viciously beaten Juana on her return to Lima and would have killed her if the authorities had not intervened. Francisco petitioned the court to order Juana sold to another master, but it merely commanded her owner to keep her in Lima and treat her well. In another attempt at sale that misfired, the mulatto Juan Jaraba, slave of Doña Clara de Ayala, was sent from Panama to Lima for sale in the care of an agent. However, Juan married soon after his arrival, and when Doña Clara changed her mind and asked that he be returned to Panama, his new wife petitioned the ecclesiastical authorities to block the move. This was done despite the pleas of Doña Clara's agent that Juan's services were badly needed in Panama, his contention that the mulatto had married only to avoid being sent back, and his promise to send for the wife.

On the whole, it appears that slave couples could be separated by distance through sale only if the blacks were ignorant of the law or if the master moved very quickly. In the second case, the unwary purchaser was sometimes left with the responsibility for reunification. In 1642, for example, the free black Isabel Bran was unable to prevent the removal of her slave husband, Antón, to Pisco by Pedro de Garate, executor of the estate of Antón's dead master. When the court ordered the slave returned to Lima, Garate replied that Antón had been sold, and that it was up to his new owner, Domingo de Busturia, to fulfill the court's order. The ecclesiastical judge yielded when Garate presented proof of sale, and word was sent to Busturia to return Antón. The new master, pleading that his affairs were in disorder owing to his move from Lima to Pisco, requested permission to keep Antón there for a year. He was allowed six months instead, but managed to retain the services of the black longer despite the pleas of Isabel for his return. In this case the position of the wife was weakened by a subsidiary dispute over her status as a free woman, and available documentation does not make the outcome clear.

Masters were much more successful when it came to separating married slaves for limited periods of service elsewhere, though sometimes bond had to be posted to obtain ecclesiastical license. In 1618, for example, the slave Agustín Angola protested the proposed transfer of his wife, the criolla Cosma Damiana, to serve indefinitely on her master's estate some sixty leagues from Lima, and this in face of an offer by Agustín's master to purchase her and prevent the separation. That this was indeed the intention of the woman's master, Hernando de la Concha, was demonstrated when he sought and obtained a one-year license from the ecclesiastical court to take Cosma from the city. Agustín again protested the action, claiming that masters had never honored their sureties to return such blacks in the past, and that outside of Lima it was easy to do what one wished with slaves. This appeal produced results and Concha was ordered to sell Cosma to the owner of Agustín, thus preventing separation of the couple. Now it was Concha's turn to appeal, and he won the right to take Cosma to his rural holdings for a year before selling her. Similarly, in 1627 Pedro de Mendoza was allowed to take the married slave María Bañol on business to Quito for a year over the protests of her husband, who claimed that his master would buy María. In this case the court probably took into account that the slave woman was the nursemaid of Mendoza's infant child, that his request for a license was filed at the proper time, and that he had posted bond for María's return. In 1643 Lorenzo Chacón de los Ríos was permitted to take Gracia Malemba to Arequipa for a year, where he was in charge of building the cathedral. The action had been contested by both her husband, who complained that they had been married only two months, and his master, who pleaded that the slave would surely run away to follow his wife, in which case he stood to lose 2,000 pesos since the black was a wax chandler. In 1648 Juan de Nolete was allowed to send Pedro Bran to Potosí for six months. The court evidently believed Nolete's allegations that Pedro was married "only verbally" to avoid the journey and that even this ceremony had taken place without his consent. In this case as well the black was a wax chandler, and according to Nolete, was vital to his merchandising operations. In a curious case of 1640 the slave Luis Bañol petitioned to prevent the return of his wife, María, to her owner, Pedro González, a notary public in Guauray. González's agent in Lima, in reply, charged that María had been sent to the capital in the first place to serve González's two daughters, who were nuns in the Santa Clara convent. Instead, she had run away, and when apprehended three months later, was found to be married. The agent argued that González urgently needed and was entitled to the slave's services but coupled with this an offer to post bond guaranteeing María's return to Lima within two years. The court acceded to this request but reduced the separation time to six months.

It is impossible to say how extensive a role the ecclesiastical courts played in disputes that in their essence involved conflicts between marriage rights and property rights. About the most one can say is that the ecclesiastical judges did a fair job of reconciling the two principles in those cases that were brought to their attention, and that the slave population benefited to the extent that the courts were able to enforce the Church's jurisdiction.

The ties between parents and children, under slavery, were every bit as fragile as the ties between man and wife. Children born of blacks, whether legitimate or illegitimate, automatically assumed their mother's status; if she was a slave, then her offspring became slaves as well, even if the father was white and free. That is, the children of female slaves, married and unmarried alike, became the property of the mother's master, to be disposed of as his own conscience dictated and the pressure of public opinion allowed. Slavery worked to make the family unit strongly matriarchal in tone. The slave father may have loved and been loved by his children, but usually he belonged to another master, his visits (however frequent) were precisely that, and beyond affection there was little he could give his children. In rare cases a slave father accumulated the money to manumit one of his children, and even once in a while arranged an apprenticeship contract for him as well. But by and large the mother was all-important: the children inherited her status, were reared by her, and were usually sold along with her. Further, as we shall see when we come to discuss the free person of color, the slave mother was much more important than the father in obtaining freedom for her children, and circumstances also operated among free persons of color to emphasize the role of the woman.

In general, black children were not sold until they were in their late teens. Of the 4,595 ladino slaves who changed hands in the Lima market between 1560 and 1650, only 465 were under fifteen and only sixty-eight under eight. Unfortunately, in most instances it cannot be determined if the child was legitimate or illegitimate or if the seller also owned the mother. In any event, with all due credit to Spanish humanity for the infrequency of such occurrences, it must also be said that the sale of children of tender age made very little sense. They could not be sold for much, since they cost far more to care for than they could possibly earn. Accordingly, it was not only humane but reasonable that they be entrusted to their mothers. During these formative years boys might be apprenticed to a trade and girls instructed in household duties. Once a young black had mastered these skills, or even if he had only demonstrated a capacity for hard work, sale was then something to be contemplated. Thus, though many masters may have been concerned about fragmenting a slave family, particularly if the children were legitimate, the fact remains that market value was also a decisive factor. Young blacks were kept with their mothers until some time in their teens at least in part because no one wished to buy them.

This is not to say that notarial records do not contain impressive examples of stability among slave families. In 1625, for example, María Antonia, a widow, sold Dominga Criolla (age twenty-four), along with her infant mulatto son, for 450 pesos, noting in the bill of sale that Dominga was "the daughter of Isabel Bran, also a slave of mine." The buyer resold the pair to María Antonia a few months later. We may conclude that María had had no intention of disturbing the pattern of family life among her blacks, but had merely arranged a kind of "loan," putting the slaves up as security. Probably, the slaves did not even change residence. We read also of the 1575 sale of Mateo and Beatriz Bran, a married couple described as "old" in the notarial document, along with their son Bartolomé (age twenty), indicating family stability for at least two decades. Similarly, Marcela Criolla (age twenty-two), sold to the convent of Santa Clara in 1650, was declared by her mistress to have been "born in my home and the daughter of Isabel Lucumi, my slave." Sale might also unite rather than divide mother and child, as in the case of Magdalena Criolla (age fourteen), purchased in 1610 by Martín Díaz de Contreras, secretary of the Holy Office and owner of the mother.[88]

These examples, of course, portray black family life under slavery in the most flattering light. Children undeniably changed hands, and some transactions are clearly indefensible on the basis of the reported facts. On its face, for example, the sale in 1590 of an unnamed criolla (age four) by Blas de los Ríos, who also owned Francisco and Magdalena Biafara, her parents, seems altogether heartless, as does that of nine-year-old Antonio Criollo, "born and brought up in our home and the son of Francisco Angola and of María Angola, our slaves." A third example is the case of Susana Negra (age thirty-five, pregnant, and married), who was sold to Francisco Hernández de los Palacios in 1570 along with her children, María, Antón, and Mayor (ages nine, six, and three, respectively). Within the year, Hernández resold Susana, María, and Mayor, to the College of San Pablo, but the fate of six-year-old Antón is unknown.[89] Apparent hardheartedness with regard to slave children took many forms. In 1595 the master of eight-year-old María Criolla sold her with the declaration that she was the daughter of Catalina Bañol, "who used to be a slave of mine and who now belongs to Juan de Montalbán." In 1630 María Bañol was sold together with her two-month-old mulatto daughter Sabina with the stipulation that the child was to be cared for by her mother for two years but was then to be at the disposal of the seller. Finally, in 1650 Doña Ana María de Guzmán sold Juana Criolla (age twenty-four), but claimed for herself possession of Juana's child if she should bear one.[90]

In some cases, it is clear that hardship, economic or otherwise, forced the sale of slave children. In 1650, for example, Doña Agustina de Segura, recently widowed and burdened with pressing debts left by her husband, was forced to sell Francisco Gabriel and Juan Criollo (ages seven and four, respectively), children of two of her female slaves. She apparently retained the mothers, perhaps because of their earning power. Francisco de Toledo y Mendoza sold Juana Criolla, only four months old and daughter of his slave María Angola, for a mere eighteen pesos in 1625 "because she is so tiny and I do not have the means to raise her." And in 1640 the widow Doña Luisa Álvarez reluctantly sold the four children of Elena Criolla on the slave's death, evidently considering the task of bringing them up beyond her energies or resources.[91]

It should also be stressed that we are dealing here with an age in which even free children of the lower classes were expected to make their way in life early (as demonstrated by the apprenticeship contracts studied in Chapter 6), and slaves were no exceptions to the rule. For this reason, neither the masters nor society in general saw anything immoral about the sale of slave children in their early teens or even younger. One example of such routine transactions should suffice: the 1640 sale of Felipe Criollo (age eleven) by Francisco Pérez Cavallero, who also owned the mother María Mandinga, and who sold Felipe with no assurances as to his physical or moral state "because he is yet a boy."[92] Some of these transfers of ownership seem to have been made to the advantage of the children involved, and often deliberately so, however painful they may have been in the short run. In 1630, for example, six-year-old Juan Criollo was sold by his mistress, a single woman of modest circumstances, to a prominent member of the secular clergy of Lima, perhaps guaranteeing the child some rudimentary education. Young Beatriz Criolla, separated from her mother at age ten, went to a nun of La Encarnación. Convent service at such a tender age held the possibility of some schooling, and perhaps even eventual membership in the convent as a lay sister; at worst Beatriz could expect an easier life than that enjoyed by most household servants. Somewhat less promising was the future of Santiago Criollo (age eight), who was sold in 1650 to Maestre de Campo Don Eugenio de Segura; endless drudgery as an orderly may have been the lad's fate, but with luck service to a prominent military officer might bring freedom at manhood, easy entrance into the prestigious colored militia units, and the possibility of socoeconomic advancement.[93]

In general the life of the Peruvian slave in the sixteenth and seventeenth centuries can best be described as bleak and monotonous. From the most mundane details of his daily work and leisure to the quality of his spiritual and personal life, the dominant note was not grinding hardship and misery but drabness and indifference. Society meant him neither well nor ill. In return for his labor, which was often taxing but rarely killing, he was indifferently fed, clothed, housed, and looked after. Haphazardly disciplined and catechized, the Afro-Peruvian was permitted sexual gratification on occasion and often allowed the substance and, in a limited way, even the form of marriage and family life. In short, there was usually as little to be thankful for as to rage against.

The Free Person of Color:
Manumission

The African in bondage is both more dramatic and easier to study than his free and often racially mixed brother. Both in the mass and individually, the slave was recorded many times: in documents of importation, in bills of sale, in wills of masters, in letters of manumission. The free colored is a more elusive subject for study. Frequently at the bottom of the social and economic scale, he aroused only intermittent government concern, was often mentioned only in the most general terms in the accounts of travelers, and rarely participated in the types of activities that generated official records. His very existence, not to mention individuality, is difficult for the historian to uncover. Further, an ambitious person of African descent seems to have made every effort to hide his racial origins, and his saga, barring archival research of the most painstaking sort, is lost to us.

Accordingly, like most historians I have chosen to concentrate on the slave in this study. Yet I cannot simply ignore the question of the free person of color, for if we are to understand the development and civilization of Spanish America we plainly need to understand how thousands of slaves secured, not merely their freedom, but also, despite many legal restrictions and much opposition from the dominant white society, a better life for themselves and their descendants. What follows is an attempt to probe, to add monographic detail and insight to this problem for colonial Peru. More specifically, we shall look at the origins, size, legal and real status, opportunities, and degree of assimilation of the free colored population for the period to 1650.[1]

The presence of free blacks and mulattoes in Peru dates from the earliest days of the conquest. As noted in Chapter 1, certain blacks who had come to the New World as slaves distinguished themselves through military prowess or faithful service, and profited by the free-and-easy atmosphere of the conquest period to gain their freedom. Many more of those first on the scene, however, came to Peru from the Peninsula as free persons, a good number as part of the entourage that surrounded all prominent conquistadores and high government officials. Others migrated on their own to establish themselves as colonists. In 1561, for example, Francisca Mulata requested and received license from the Crown to go to Peru after being summoned there by her father, whose racial background is unclear.[2] By all these means, free persons of color quickly became an important group in the new colony, particularly along the coast; indeed, they were numerous enough to be considered a serious problem in Lima as early as 1538.[3]

However, as the exuberance and liberality of the conquest period waned and the Spanish Crown addressed itself to the hard task of building a society in America, the processes of manumission, like other aspects of colonial society, were brought under stricter control. As Magnus Mörner reminds us, Spain, in common with most nations of Europe in this period, desired to "regulate every part of society by means of legislation," and in the Spanish case such legislation was both casuistic and particularistic, "a series of administrative decisions arrived at in certain cases and with regard to local jurisdictions."[4] Generalizations on the Crown's intentions for either the American colonies in general or Peru in particular are therefore difficult to formulate. Let us say simply that by and large an effort was made to take legislation framed for the Peninsula and modify it in accordance with New World realities. For the black population, both free and slave, specifically, the model was the famous *Las Siete Partidas*, drawn up in the thirteenth century at the order of Alfonso the Wise.

The *Siete Partidas* was more a statement of legal and moral principles than a compilation of specific legislation.[5] Thus, it was not that a body of existing Spanish slave legislation was snipped out of the *Partidas* and applied to America, but rather that the principles embodied therein guided Spanish lawmakers in their task. The *Partidas* viewed slavery as a necessary evil, as a transitory condition that did not alter or diminish the nature of the slave, and proclaimed liberty one of the greatest of human possessions. In this light, the document not only declared that freedom was a legitimate goal for the slave, but also stated that society should aid those in bondage; masters who manumitted their slaves performed a service to God, as did interested third parties who liberated the enslaved with gift money.[6]

Thanks to this precept, slaves' claims to freedom became privileged cases in royal courts of law. If black slaves "should publicly demand their liberty," the Crown told the Audiencias of Spanish America in 1540, "they should be heard and justice done to them, and care be taken that they should not on that account . . . be maltreated by their Masters."[7] Further, as the Spanish Crown and various agencies of local government slowly defined the status of the black man in America, the strictures of the *Partidas* were not only adhered to, but even expanded to favor the achievement of free status. As the institution of slavery evolved in Spanish America, the paths to freedom took three forms: manumission by the master, various types of purchase, and (indirectly but vitally) the continuing process of racial mixture. We will examine these three paths in turn.[8]

Voluntary manumission by the master was a fixture of slavery throughout the period under study. In its simplest form freedom was granted to the slave in the master's last will and testament or in a letter of manumission while the master still lived. Either way it was customary to stress the Christian love and charity that motivated the act. Many times such documents also mentioned the long and faithful service that freedom now rewarded. For example, Juan del Corral, a prominent Lima builder, provided for the freedom of his slave Luisa Berbesi at his death in gratitude for the "fidelity and love" she had displayed while nursing him through several severe illnesses; Dominga Conga, age forty-five, was freed not only for the service of God, but also for her faithful service and success in bringing up five children; and the mistress of Gaspar Biafara carefully mentioned his thirty years of service in her letter of manumission in 1605.[9] In the case of slave mothers, the practice of manumission varied from master to master, perhaps prompted by circumstances that are not reflected in the legal formulae of surviving documentation. Some mothers were freed along with their children, as in the case of Ana Criolla and her two-year-old daughter, liberated by testament in 1650.[10] In other instances slave children were freed to reward the parents for their service, but the adults themselves remained in bondage.[11] Occasionally, one even finds the reverse: a mother freed and her child held in slavery. In 1616, for example, a female slave was manumitted in reward for the "care, fondness, love, and felicity" she had shown in service, but her nine-month-old son was to be given liberty only on payment of 100 pesos by his mother or some other interested party.[12]

Clearly, manumission was not an act of generosity when the blacks concerned were aged or infirm with no one to fall back on for assistance. On the contrary, some observers (Sandoval included) accused selfish masters of freeing such slaves to avoid the cost of supporting them. The frequency of these cases is impossible to determine, since slaveholders rarely confessed to such actions, but by all evidence few masters were that hardhearted.[13] Indeed, the very selectivity with which many slaveholders freed blacks in their wills indicates a realization that liberty was a cruel illusion for slaves who were aged, incapacitated, or simply naïve to the point of incompetency. In 1637, for example, Esteban González provided in his will for the freeing of two of the thirteen adult blacks who worked his sugar plantation, but specifically excluded Lucás de Mendoza, who was "old and blind," and Ignacio Mulato, whose hands were missing. Other masters willed their aged slaves both freedom and a small bequest, as in the case of Francisca Conga (*vieja*), who received 500 pesos along with manumission in 1640. The more pathetic case of Ursula Criolla is mentioned in the 1630 will of Isabel Pérez, which specified that the black, who had been previously freed and was now so sick that movement was impossible, be given 100 pesos. More, the dead woman had also ordered the manumission of her ex-slave's three children, two small boys and a daughter who was serving a nun in the convent of Concepción, and left the girl 100 pesos as well. Still other masters who manumitted slaves of uncertain capacity in their wills urged relatives and friends to look out for the welfare of the blacks. This was the case with Doña Juana Ravanal, who set Isabel Biafara free with a new set of clothes and requested her heirs to place the black in a situation that would permit her to lead a "good and Christian" life.[14]

Many slaveholders, recognizing that a simple declaration of freedom would work a hardship on certain blacks, hedged their manumissions with conditions designed to provide for their welfare and support. In 1625, for example, Isabel Folupa, judged to be over sixty, and Augustina Mulata, age four and cryptically described as the "daughter of a slave of mine" (perhaps an illegitimate child), were both freed by their master on specific terms. Isabel had to raise the child and to pay for the saying of one Mass per month for the soul of the master. In addition, if she so chose she could live in the house of a certain Spanish hatmaker for the rest of her days for whatever assistance she and the girl cared to provide. Augustina on her part was obligated when grown to care for Isabel and could not under any circumstances abandon the woman who had looked after her during her youth.[15] Pedro de Saavedra y Aguilera, an alderman of Guánuco, was equally meticulous in arranging the future of a black slave girl named Pascuala. The girl, who was eight years old when freed by his will, was to be cared for by an Indian woman in his service until the age of twelve, after which she was to be sent to the care of his sister in the Encarnación convent of Lima for four years to be taught good habits and Christian doctrine. The sister was further charged to look out for the girl after this period, preferably by persuading Pascuala to continue to serve the convent.[16] Other masters also looked to religion as a means of ensuring that ex-slaves walked a straight and narrow path. In 1592, for example, Catalina Mulata (age fourteen) was willed her freedom and 200 pesos for her dowry on condition that she serve the Casa de la Caridad in Lima for a year, in the course of which service, it was hoped, she would learn good habits and Christian doctrine. In 1610 Juana Bañol (age eight) was freed by her mistress provided she became a servant of the convent of Nuestra Señora de la Limpia Concepción in Lima until old enough to become a lay sister; at that time Juana was either to pledge herself to a religious life or to serve another four years. In 1640 Doña Felipe Velásquez tried to provide for Isabel Mulata, pregnant and unskilled, by willing her to her son, a member of the secular clergy; he was to give her her freedom in eight years, or earlier if she married or attached herself to a religious order.[17] Finally, there is the unusual case of José de la Compasión, child of Mariana Angola. Mariana had been donated to the convent of Encarnación to serve three of the nuns, but tiring of the monastic routine, she had run away, had become pregnant, and not only had refused to return to service but had consigned her newborn child to the care of the nuns. When the boy reached the age of four, the nuns decided to free him on two conditions: that he assist at every festival honoring Nuestra Señora de la Encarnación for the rest of his life, and that he serve one of the three nuns until he came of age (the other two nuns waived all claims to the boy).[18]

Others who wanted to free boys in their service took care to see that they were first equipped with some skill. In 1635, for example, Antonia

González, a free black woman of very modest means, decreed the following fate for her slave Gracia Negra and Gracia's four small children: the mother and her infant son were to be sold to pay for the other testamentary provisions; Gracia's daughter (age five) was willed to the Descalzas convent; and her other two sons (ages seven and three) were entrusted to a male friend to be apprenticed out at the age of twelve and freed at his death. In 1650 Doña Beatriz de Rivas made similar arrangements for three-year-old Pascual Mulato (who may have been the illegitimate son of her dead husband). Pascual was to be taken in charge by either her niece or her sister for religious instruction and eventual apprenticeship, and at the age of twenty was to receive his letter of manumission and 200 pesos.[19]

In other instances of conditional manumission at the owner's death, the master tried to balance the interests of the blacks against those of dependent relatives and friends. An Indian woman, for example, freed two female slaves (both twenty-five) on condition that one serve an aged friend of hers for six years and the other (along with her two small children) serve another friend for ten.[20] A clergyman in 1645 willed a female friend three adult male slaves, one of them a bricklayer, to serve her for the rest of her days, after which they were to be free. By the 1615 will of Isabel Cataño, a free mulata, an eight-month-old goddaughter acquired the future services of Francisca Negra (age three months). Both were to be cared for by a friend, and Francisca was to be free on the death of her mistress. In that day and age, when early death was common enough, Francisca's chances of freedom were not so dim as they may seem.[21] Some masters who bestowed manumission contingent on an additional period of labor did so in a tight-fisted way. A notable example was Don Pedro Ysasaga, an important encomendero and member of a prominent officeholding family. He set out in his will that Francisca Biafara was to be freed as a reward for her efforts in raising his nephew; but he also provided that she must continue to serve the nephew for six more years and explicitly stated that she was to earn nothing for this service beyond the normal sustenance. Her four children, moreover, were passed to the nephew as slaves.[22] Equally ungenerous were the terms of freedom for Magdalena Mulata, who was promised liberty at the age of thirty-five on condition that she serve the daughter of her mistress for fifteen years thereafter; Magdalena in fact worked for twelve more years and then paid

250 pesos to get her freedom three years early. As this suggests, the beneficiaries did not always hold the blacks to their years of service. The new master of Francisco Caboverde, in deference to the black's age, waived the two years of service Francisco was to put in prior to gaining his freedom and manumitted the slave immediately.[23]

In some cases of conditional manumission, it was the interests of the slaveholders themselves that were served. Slaves were freed, for example, on condition that they continue to work for their former masters for a certain period of time each day. Or a slave owned by a three-man partnership (say) might become one-third free on manumission by one partner, in which case he divided his time between his own occupations and continuing service to the partnership.[24] Further, intelligent and restless slaves were sometimes placated by being given conditional freedom in return for continued service for a specified period of time. In 1605, for example, María de Cevallos, a slave born in Lima, was freed by her master on condition that she serve him for an additional four years.[25] In general such extensions of slave status did not exceed six years. At other times, elderly slaveholders gave their slaves letters of manumission that were to take effect on their deaths, thereby at once assuring themselves of service during their remaining years and giving the slaves something more concrete than a mere promise.[26] The conditions of the agreement might even be altered, as in the case of Isabel Criolla, whose master had originally asked that she serve him five more years and pay 250 pesos for her freedom, but was persuaded after two years to manumit her and relinquish his demand for monetary compensation.[27]

When it came to freedom by purchase, Peruvian practice deviated from the provisions of the *Siete Partidas*, which sanctioned the purchase of freedom by gift money, but barred slaves from owning property (*peculium*).[28] In Spanish America the slave's right to peculium was unobtrusively, and perhaps unconsciously, restored. As early as 1526 royal officials were ordered to study the feasibility of establishing a scale of prices, depending on the age and condition of the slave, for blacks to use in buying their freedom.[29] It is quite possible, however, that the Crown had nothing more than gift money in mind, and certainly such price scales were never established for the American empire as a whole. In any event, soon after the colony was founded, we find slaves purchasing their freedom, and often with sums that they must have accumulated themselves. Indeed, available evidence indicates that the purchase of freedom by the slave—whether with earnings, gift-money, or loans—was more important than voluntary manumission in all its forms in the creation and development of the colony's free colored population, a phenomenon noted by Lockhart for the earliest decades of Spanish Peru.[30]

During the period under study the arrangements made by slaves to purchase their freedom were individualistic and informal. At this stage blacks had no clear-cut right to buy liberation, nor were slaveholders obliged to set a just price for the privilege.* For example, the mistress of Isabel Godiño (age thirty) agreed to liberate the slave on her death but not before, even though Isabel offered to purchase her freedom.[31] Ordinarily, however, master and slave agreed on the slave's worth, perhaps with the aid of an appraisal by a distinterested third party, and the owner then swore not only that the black could have his freedom if this sum was paid, but also that the slave could never be sold for more than this amount. All subsequent buyers of the slave were then obliged to agree to these conditions. This agreement might be reached while the master was still alive, or it might be embodied as an act of generosity in his will. In 1583, for example, Beatriz Zape (married, pregnant, and with two small children) persuaded her master to free her in return for an initial payment of 500 pesos in cash and the promise of 200 more plus three years' additional service. In a will of 1620 the merchant Francisco Hernández Irola provided that four of his slaves, of different sexes and ages, might purchase their freedom for amounts that ranged from 100 to 400 pesos.[32]

The prices slaves were required to pay for liberty varied sharply from master to master, unless the blacks were shrewd enough to secure an impartial appraisal. In 1593, for example, María Criolla had to pay 787.5 pesos for a letter of manumission. Admittedly, this was a period of high prices, but in some cases it was clearly just a matter of what the

---

* At some point after 1650 the purchase of freedom by blacks became institutionalized, at least in some areas of Spanish America. The famous *coartación* system of Cuba provides the most spectacular example. Under this system, which was eventually accepted and codified by the Spanish Crown in the 18th century, a slave had the right to demand that his value be publicly declared by a court of law, and he was then permitted to pay this amount off in several installments. Once a slave became *coartado*, he also acquired the right to change masters at will provided he could find a purchaser who was willing to accept his status. For more detail, see Klein, *Slavery in the Americas*, pp. 78, 196-97; and Bowser, *Neither Slave Nor Free*.

traffic would bear. In 1615, when prices for blacks were considerably lower than they were when María bought her freedom, the clothier Antón Bran was forced to pay 1,000 pesos (half on credit) for the liberty of his wife, Isabel. Similarly, Doña María Valverde was paid 800 pesos in the same year by her sister nuns at the convent of Encarnación to free Isabel Cepeda in reward for her faithful service.[33] Other masters, however, were prepared to be reasonably generous in this respect. In 1585, when slave prices were also very high, the mistress of forty-year-old Marta Berbesi stipulated in her will that the slave could have her freedom for only fifty pesos; and in 1615 another master provided in his will for a reduction in the amount his slave Fabiana Criolla (age fifty-five) had to pay for her freedom, lowering the figure from 200 to 150 pesos. As a final example of generosity, the owner of a mulata named Ursula de Vergara, whose age is not recorded, sold her in 1619 for 270 pesos on condition that she was to be set free if she could raise this sum and with the further proviso that the amount was to be reduced by twenty-five pesos for each year of service to her new master. A year later the slave's free mulata mother persuaded a Spaniard to loan her the requisite amount.[34]

Ordinarily, cash was used to purchase freedom, and its accumulation must have frequently been painful, but some owners accepted other arrangements. In 1610 the master of Gaspar Bañol liberated him after seventeen years' service, citing all of the usual pious reasons; more to the point, however, was the fact that Gaspar had constructed some houses for his master in Lima. In 1620 Francisco de Funes Bonilla, apparently free and taken for white, liberated his mulata wife by giving her owner in exchange eighteen-year-old Gracia Biafara, valued at 650 pesos, plus 100 pesos in cash.[35]

The tradition of donating money as gifts or charity for manumission was carried from Spain to Peru. In 1616, for example, Asencio Pérez de Longarte, an agriculturalist with holdings near Arica, willed 300 pesos toward the purchase of liberty for two daughters of his slaves. In 1625 Ana López, whose mother had already paid 300 of the 500 pesos required for her liberty, was given the other 200 pesos as a wedding gift by her mistress's mother. Blacks also relied on godparents to free them, and these ties were almost certainly sometimes chosen by parents with this purpose in mind. This was perhaps the case with six-month-old Pedro Mulato, who was liberated by his godfather, Gregorio Pérez, in 1625, but whose mother remained in bondage.[36]

In other instances purchase money was borrowed. In 1645, for example, the mulata María Criolla, who had been donated to the Concepción convent in Lima, bought her liberty with borrowed money. In the same year the free mulatto Juan de Guarnido freed Juana de Santa Cruz for 200 pesos, the amount specified in her deceased master's will; and Juana persuaded a Spaniard to put up a like amount to purchase the liberty of one of her three children from the dead man's estate. The other two children, whose freedom by purchase for the same sum was also provided for in the master's will, seem to have remained in bondage.[37] Some acts of liberation may have been inspired by affairs of the heart, as in the case of Augustina Criolla (age twenty-six), whose liberty was purchased by Manuel de Rivera for 600 pesos. In still other cases the reason is neither given nor easy to infer. In 1650, for example, Doña Ambrosia de Castro paid 550 pesos to free Clara Bran, the wife of Pedro Badillo, himself a slave of the Hospital of San Andrés.[38]

Obviously, the right to purchase freedom, failing the assistance of an outside party, would have been meaningless if masters had not permitted slaves to accumulate the sum in various ways. Fortunately, many slaveowners were generous in this respect. To take an example or two from the seventeenth century, Gaspar Mandinga by the terms of his master's will was required to work three days a week on the estate of the heirs, but the rest of his time was his own, and he eventually accumulated the 200 pesos with which to purchase his freedom.[39] The master of Polonia Negra, whose two free mulatto sons had already paid 330 pesos of the 630 required to liberate her, agreed that if she worked in his household until noon each day and slept there at night she could have the rest of the day to herself to earn the balance of her freedom money. Black artisans were sometimes allowed to apply a portion of their daily wages toward their liberation, and the same practice no doubt prevailed in other occupations. In addition some masters apprenticed slaves so they would have a skill that would enable them to purchase their liberty. This was explicitly the case with Domingo Congo (age sixteen and a tailor's apprentice), whose master willed him to a niece in 1635 with the understanding that she would retain the lad for five years, then place him with another master craftsman so he could accumulate the 400 pesos he needed to buy his freedom.[40]

As the previously cited case of Polonia Negra indicates, the desire to secure a family member's freedom ran deep in the Peruvian black community. Occasionally, one slave contrived to raise enough money to free another, as in 1640, when María Ramos paid her mistress seventy pesos to free her four-month-old daughter, Inés. Similarly, in 1595 Juana Bioho purchased the liberty of her niece Lorenza; together with the mother, Damiana, all three were the property of a single master.[41] As a rule, however, the release from slavery was the work of a free black. Free husbands or wives paid to manumit their mates; free parents paid to manumit their children;[42] and grown children paid to manumit their parents. Most often a free parent liberated his children when they were small, but this was not always the case. In 1645, for example, Luis Manuel was age forty-two when his father freed him for 300 pesos. Similarly, Juliana Criolla, who was also liberated by her free father for 300 pesos, was twenty-eight and pregnant at the time.[43]

From time to time a free person would liberate some adult relative outside the immediate family, a niece, perhaps, as in the case of the mulata Francisca Bastida (age twenty-six), who was freed by her aunt for 600 pesos. There was probably an even more distant relationship in the case of María Terranova, freed by her "relatives" (*parientes*) in 1650 for 400 pesos.[44] Slave adults were also helped by friends, god-parents, and others in the black community, and even (though perhaps only indirectly) by ties to religious brotherhoods. In 1625, for example, María Bañol (age forty-four) was liberated by a free black woman of the same name for 330 pesos, and in 1640 the free mulata Luisa Bañol paid 400 pesos for the release of her goddaughter, Magdalena Bañol (age thirty-five).[45] In the letters of manumission for Catalina Bran (age forty-four) and her seven-year-old son, who were freed by Gaspar and Antón Bran for 530 pesos, the two men were careful to identify themselves as officers of the confraternity of Nuestra Señora de los Reyes, though it is not clear if the funds of that organization were used in the transaction.[46]

In Peru as in other Spanish American colonies, race mixture played an important role in the development of a substantial free colored population. Spain would have wished it otherwise. If the Crown had had its way, the Americas would have been populated by three distinct racial estates: the European, the Indian, and the African. Spanish officialdom could tolerate, and even heartily approve, the occasional marriage of a conquistador with an Inca or Aztec princess, but neither the

Crown nor the Church was prepared to go beyond that. In their eyes and in the view of society at large race mixture produced types who combined the worst defects and vices of both parents. Indeed, so strong was the prejudice that this view tended to become something of a self-fulfilling prophecy. We would not predict much future for the racial "castes," for example, when we find the Crown attorney before the Audiencia confiding to the home government in 1576 that he despaired of their ever being transformed into useful members of the community.[47] The pressures of Crown, Church, and society, however, did not prevent Spaniard, African, and Indian from sexual contact over the years, producing a bewildering variety of racial mixtures and bringing into being a large class of free "blacks."[48]

Civil and ecclesiastical authorities were fiercely opposed in particular to sexual unions between Africans and Indians. The Church feared that the African would reinforce the Indian's attachment to paganism, and perhaps even infect him with the infidelity of Islam. The Crown not only shared this apprehension, but appreciated as well that the Indian's status as a free vassal was largely illusory. For all practical purposes the natives of Peru were second-class citizens, and intimacy with Africans served only to worsen this situation. Accordingly, as we have seen in Chapter 7, time and time again during the sixteenth and seventeenth centuries the Crown demanded that the Indians be segregated from the Afro-caste population.[49] The wearisome reiteration of these injunctions casts doubt on their effectiveness, though various viceroys periodically assured the Crown that they were bending every effort to carry out its orders. Viceroy Villar, for one, informed the government that he had disembarked at the northern port of Paita to assume his duties and had journeyed to Lima by land, exerting himself along the way during much of 1585 to cleanse the Indian villages of everyone except the natives themselves. Over forty years later Viceroy Guadalcázar advised the Crown of his own vigorous efforts to the same end.[50]

But the simple fact is, whether pushed vigorously or not, the Crown's program of segregating the two groups was a futile dream. Lima and the other urban centers of Peru soon possessed sizable Indian populations, natives drawn in by the exigencies of the mita and economic lure or hardship, and contact with the black man was inevitable. Even the Indians living in their own outlying villages could not be sealed off completely, since they too served as mitayos and were likely to meet

Fig. 7. A Spanish corregidor and his mulatto and mestizo underlings
being served by Indians

the blacks of the Peruvian countryside. Indeed, in the 1580's and 1590's Viceroys Villar and Cañete charged that the Crown's own chosen officials for the governance of the rural Indian population, the *corregidores de indios*, were in large part responsible for the Afro-Indian contact so dreaded in Spain. Allegedly, these men often brought mulatto or zambo underlings to assist them, sometimes even putting them in charge of the craft industries that belonged to Indian communities. Further the negligence and indifference of the corregidores and their mixed-blood assistants permitted still more persons of African descent to wander about the native districts at will.[51]

Not all colonial officials were convinced in any event of the desirability of segregation. No less a personage than Viceroy Toledo argued against it in a long and moving passage to the Crown. Toledo believed that the policy had been a sound one in the turbulent early years of the colony, but held that with the restoration of order and with honest officials, abuses committed against the Indian could now be speedily punished. The effect of the Crown's policy was to wall off the Indian in his remote village from all contact with Spanish society and to breed divisions and mistrust between the races. According to the ecclesiastics he had consulted, Toledo reported, the natives who had had close contact with Spanish and African Peruvians tended to be "more malicious than the other Indians, but at least they have more faith and knowledge of God and of their sins." Toledo condemned the mestizo and mulatto vagabonds who wandered among the Indians, but saw no reason why respectable, married householders from these two groups should not be given land and encouraged to settle in the Indian villages, "for the greatest danger this land faces with regard to the natives is the little love that they bear our nation." The Crown would have none of this proposal, and good civil servant that he was, Toledo resignedly obeyed his instructions.[52]

Even Viceroy Villar, who had boasted to the Crown in 1585 of his diligence in pushing Afro-Indian segregation, changed his tune in 1590 to the extent of advocating that only free blacks and mulattoes be expelled from native villages unless good reasons were advanced that they remain. To exclude all zambos would be cruel, he explained, since many were the legitimate heirs to property that was of little or no interest to others, and so could not be sold; expulsion therefore also meant the arbitrary confiscation of what little worldly possesions these Afro-Indians had managed to accumulate. Some forty years later Captain Andrés de Deza, majordomo of the city of León de Huánuco, likewise pleaded with the government to relax its stand on the segregation of the Indian, and once again the Council of the Indies rejected all thought of change.[53]

The policies of the Spanish Crown may have encouraged the Indian to become an alien in his own land, but they could not stop the proliferation of the zambos, men who were regarded in the words of one contemporary as the "worst and basest people that those regions hold."[54] Most zambos were the offspring of African men (often slaves) and Indian women, and as such were assured by law of the mother's free status. But freedom was one of the few advantages they possessed.[55] The zambo (in this discussion I use the term exclusively for the usual parentage, a black father and Indian mother) was caught in an awkward position. There was some temptation for him to identify with his mother, to attempt to be accepted in her village, to work part of the lands that belonged to her family, in short, to become an Indian. However, one is hard put to believe that any but the best-connected or shrewdest zambos managed to live on equal terms in the native villages. Further, the real social standing of the Indian, as distinct from his legal condition, was generally inferior even to that of the slave. Among other things, if the zambo attempted to pass himself off as an Indian, he risked being subjected to the various tribute and labor demands of the Spanish, obligations that he might otherwise avoid.[56] Yet those Afro-Indians who turned away from whatever security and acceptance were offered by village life were then forced to make their way in the larger Spanish world as members of an inferior racial group. In any event many zambos were born in the urban centers, the offspring of Indians who had abandoned village life, and for them there was no alternative but to adapt themselves as best they could to Spanish ways. Whatever road the zambo took, as the product of the two most despised racial groups in Spanish America, he faced an unenviable future.

The fate of the mulatto and of the still lighter products of Afro-Spanish sexual unions was in many instances somewhat more pleasant. Despite the frequently stated, almost ritualistic alarm of the Crown and its representatives, sexual contact between Spanish men and African women was widespread and persistent throughout the colonial period.[57] One seventeenth-century observer noted maliciously that the Spanish men of Peru seemed to prefer black women over their own, and ascribed the tendency to the fact that most of them had been suckled by African wet nurses.[58] Whatever the reason, the black women of the colony, and particularly the mulatas, seem to have held an overpowering attraction for the Spanish, and even the Indian, male—they were the cause of countless crimes of passion, for example—and the inevitable result was the creation of a large mulatto group. As Ricardo Palma says, of the ethnic composition of the Peruvian population, "Él que no tiene de Inga tiene de Mandinga" (he who is not descended from an Inga, i.e., Inca, is descended from a Mandinga).[59]

Since the Afro-Peruvians assumed their mother's status (here again, as in the case of the zambo, I deal in this discussion only with the product of the usual kind of union, that is, where the Spanish blood was the father's), they were often born slaves, and the majority remained so throughout their lives. A number, however, were freed by their fathers—enough for the Crown to capitulate in 1563 to the realities of race mixture between Spaniard and African by decreeing that the Spanish father of a child put up for sale by the mother's owner be given preference if it was his intent to free the child.[60] This decree merely sanctioned Peruvian practice, since from the earliest days of the conquest compassionate Spanish fathers freed their slave mulatto children and provided for them.

A white father who wanted to recognize and free his colored offspring could do so either by letter of manumission or by provision in his will. If the child was the slave of another, a letter of manumission usually required the payment of cash, but there were exceptions. One father secured the liberation of his child in return for past favors (*buenos servicios*), and another freed his two-year-old son by giving the owner a four-year-old slave plus forty pesos. Most masters appear to have cheerfully accepted money in exchange for the fertility of their female blacks, but at least one Spanish father threatened to sue before he was able to liberate his two-year-old mulatto son for 140 pesos.[61]

Mention of earlier liberation or the act itself was usually discussed with more frankness in wills than in open society, perhaps because imminent death was contemplated. The Portuguese Benito Rodrigues recognized his daughter Clemencia (age six months) in his will and admitted that she had been conceived in the slave of another. Clemencia, who was already free, was willed 300 pesos and entrusted to a friend, who was to use the money for her upbringing and place her in the service of a convent at the proper age. The Spaniard Pedro de Figueroa declared in his will that he had purchased a mulatto lad named Nicolás as his probable son, and had taught the child carpentry. But Nicolás had proved a disappointment. He had somehow managed to obligate his father for many pesos in unspecified ways and besides, declared the outraged Figueroa, who disinherited his offspring, "on various occasions he has been disrespectful to me" ("me ha perdido en diferentes veces el respeto").[62]

In some instances the families of a dead man freed the product of his indiscretion on the basis of details that could have been provided only in a will or a death-bed confession. In a letter of manumission of 1585, for example, the mother of Nicolás de Acevedo freed the mulatto boy Lucás de Acevedo because her son before his death had confessed to being the father and had begged her to use his share of his own father's estate to buy the child's freedom. The mother of Acevedo in fact purchased the slave woman as well, but freed only the boy.[63] In a testamentary declaration that may have been exceedingly painful, the Spanish widow of an artisan stated that she wished to free Isabel Mulata (age eight), who she knew to be her dead husband's daughter by her slave Francisca Jolofa.[64]

Other Spanish men freed colored children but refused to acknowledge them as their offspring. In 1600, for example, Melchior de Sintra, a resident of Lima, manumitted María Mulata (age five) "for reasons that move me." The child, along with her mother, was conveniently out of sight in Ica. In a like case of 1615 a six-month-old mulatto boy was conditionally freed by the cleric Doctor Bernardo Cavero, who had packed the pregnant slave mother off to Panama to join the household service of a friend. Cavero stipulated that the boy must first serve the son of the friend for twenty years, during which time he was to be taught "good habits and some office."[65] Others, similarly embarrassed but with even less nerve, preferred to remain anonymous in the liberation process. For example, the mulata Francisca Rodríguez and her one-month-old quadroon son were freed in 1630 on payment of 900 pesos by an unnamed third party to their master.[66]

There were still other variations in the manumission of Afro-Spaniards. Occasionally, when a slave mother failed to persuade the Spanish father to liberate their child, she was able to prevail on another, more charitable patron, such as the godfather, to do so. At other times, such a child was freed simply at the intercession of "some persons," as one letter of manumission put it. Slave children of startlingly Caucasian appearance were particularly favored in this respect. In 1610, for example, Felipe Mulato, age four and seemingly "the son of a Spaniard," was liberated by Captain Juan de Fiancas for the boy's appraised value —177 pesos—as determined by the *alcalde ordinario*. Likewise, in 1635 Don Pedro Ramírez de Valdés and his wife freed the eighteen-month-old son of their slave María Mulata because he was "white and blonde and had a Roman nose."[67]

In their efforts to attain freedom, some slaves simply misunderstood their masters' intentions. Others were deliberately deceived. No more than confusion was involved, for example, in the case of Juana Mulata, who claimed that she was the illegitimate child of her dead master, and that he had freed her in his will on condition she serve his wife and daughter during their lifetimes. The wife having waived such service, and the daughter having died, Juana claimed that she was now relieved of her obligation. Unfortunately, she was mistaken about the will; her dead father had made no mention of her liberation, though her service to his family had indeed been provided for. Juana's claim was disallowed, and she was seized and sold by the man's creditors.

Though a letter of manumission could not be revoked, slaveowners could and often did change their wills as they liked in their lifetimes—no doubt to the confusion and disappointment of many blacks. The most spectacular example, among hundreds of such testamentary revisions, involved one Luis de Morales. In 1625, when Morales recorded his first will, he owned eleven slaves of all ages. In this document he freed two slaves outright and permitted five more, two women and their three children, to purchase their liberty for various amounts. In a codicil drawn up in early 1629 Morales revoked the privilege of purchase for one of the women, Juana Criolla, who by this date had four children. Three days later he added a second codicil, permitting another slave woman, who originally was supposed to be sold as part of his estate, to purchase her freedom at his death. A third codicil followed several months later. In it Morales again bestowed on Juana Criolla and her children the right to buy their freedom. In addition he provided for the release of two other slaves, Francisco Criollo (age eight when the original will was signed) and Pedro Criollo (acquired since

1625 and a tailor), who were to serve a relative for the rest of her days and then go free. In a fourth and final revision, dated August 25, 1629, Morales changed his mind again and willed Francisco and Pedro to the same relative unconditionally as her property.[68] Blacks who dreamed of relief from bondage and who served masters such as Morales can only be pitied.

On the positive side, the colonial courts usually ruled favorably when a slave had not written evidence of the master's wishes but could marshal other proof in support of the claim. One successful suit of the sort was brought by the blacks Juana Navarro (age sixty) and her son Lorenzo, who had been purchased in 1590 by Bachiller Álvaro Sánchez Navarro in Guatemala and taken to Cuzco, where their master served as a canon of the cathedral. When Sánchez died intestate twelve years later, the two slaves appealed for their liberty as their master had promised them "many different times." The corroborating testimony of various highly placed clerics and other associates of Navarro persuaded the court to reject the argument of the public defender of intestate property, who contended that the fact Sánchez had listed the two slaves along with his other property indicated he never had any intention of freeing them.[69]

In a second case, the slave Ana Flores defied her master, Pedro Díaz Flores, and in 1623 successfully appealed to the ecclesiastical court of Lima to appoint a guardian for her two mulata daughters, Jusepa and Damiana, while a suit for their freedom went forward. According to the guardian, all three had been the slaves of Díaz's aunt, María de Riceda, who had given the two girls their freedom on her death, with the further provision that they were to enter the convent of Santíssima Trinidad under the care of her niece. However, since Jusepa and Damiana were only seven and five when she died, they passed instead to the care of Díaz, who (it was alleged) treated them as slaves and planned to sell them. The guardian proposed that the girls, now of an age to do so, be allowed to enter the convent, and that their freedom be formally declared at this time. Díaz replied to all this that his aunt, who had apparently died intestate, had told him many times that all three blacks must be sold to pay her debts, with the balance being used to establish a chaplaincy; he argued further that the mere fact his aunt had treated the slaves "with charity" did not imply a guarantee of freedom. As in the previous case, the court found the testimony of witnesses presented by the guardian convincing, and the two mulatas won their freedom.[70]

As a third and last example, let us consider a suit filed in 1647 by the mulata Juana de Bolívar against Don Joseph de Bolívar, an accountant of the royal treasury and member of the Order of Santiago. According to Juana, she had been freed in Cartagena many years before on the death of Don Joseph's mother-in-law. However, she was only six months old at the time and was not informed of the fact until much later, at which time she chose to remain in the service of the accountant anyway. But now she had children and was growing old, and found that she was being treated badly. She was prompted therefore to sue for her own freedom and that of her children, though she had no written record of her former mistress's action. Unfortunately, the Audiencia's disposition of the case is unknown, for the only record that survives is the opinion of the Crown attorney. It is likely, however, that she was freed, since the attorney noted that the witnesses she presented were credible and Don Joseph's counterarguments weak. In support of his case, he insisted his mother-in-law's estate had been so burdened with debts that if Juana had been set free they could not have been paid; yet he refused to produce either his mother-in-law's will or an inventory of her possessions, claiming that these had been left behind in Tierra Firme. The *fiscal* acidly observed in his written opinion that a person of Don Joseph's knowledge was hardly likely to be unaware of the importance of such documents, and noted further that the accountant was both unwilling to send for the papers and unable to refute the testimony of witnesses that his mother-in-law was a rich woman on her death.[71]

Occasionally, the inheritance laws conflicted with the desire of masters to free their slaves. A poignant case from the 1620's concerns the attempt of Doña Francisca de Mingolla to free Francisca Mulata and her baby girl. Shortly before her death, Doña Francisca manumitted the two largely on the "persuasions" of her slave Dominga Bran, mother and grandmother of the pair, who, as Doña Francisca declared, had served her for more than twenty-eight years and who had punctually turned over her wages, amounting to more than 4,000 pesos. By this act, however, Doña Francisca so reduced the value of her estate that her legitimate son would not inherit the fifth he was entitled to under the law. Realizing this, Doña Francisca revoked the letter of manumission, which was not to take effect until her death in any event, and in her will provided merely for the freeing of the baby. A codicil dated less than two weeks later was harsher still, committing the girl to remain in bondage to the son until she reached the age of majority. When Doña Francisca died the interests of heir and slaves clashed and were left for the Audiencia to resolve. This body determined that Doña Francisca had neither the right to free the two blacks, since this reduced the value of her possessions to her child below the legal minimum, nor the right to revoke the letter of manumission, since this document was irrevocable. By way of compromise, the Audiencia ordered that the value of the two slaves be determined by two persons, one nominated by each party to the suit; and that whatever the amount left over after the fifth of Doña Francisca's estate was calculated would then represent the figure the slaves might pay to the son to obtain their freedom, less 100 pesos for the time the child would have to serve him; her mother was also to remain in his service, but without compensation, until she was able to buy her freedom.[72]

In certain cases slaves either misunderstood the law or believed that it could be twisted to their advantage. In 1601, for example, Doña Ana de Cáceres provided in her will that Juana Criolla might secure her freedom from future owners for 300 pesos and at her urging her niece and heir contributed a third of the sum to this end. In the next two years the slave changed hands four times, and at the end of the process, since part of her liberation money had been paid, she began to style herself a free woman and to claim the same status for her newborn mulatto son. Indeed, from the time the child, Juan, was born in 1603, Juana's legal actions effectively blocked his outright sale, so that though he was separated from her at the age of six months by legal sale, he was in fact merely held in deposit until 1623. By that time Juan was old enough to fight for his own freedom through the courts, only to lose and become the unwilling slave of the man who had inherited him some twenty years before.[73]

Other blacks were frustrated in their efforts to buy freedom, at least momentarily, by a misunderstanding of the amount required or by the trickery of unscrupulous slaveholders. In 1644, for example, Hernando Lucumi complained to the ecclesiastical court that the master of his wife, María Terranova, refused to free her for less than 300 pesos, even though her former mistress had granted her the testamentary right to pay only 200. When the dead woman's will was examined, however, Hernando was found to be in error and María's master won the case.[74] In 1600 the slave Catalina de Caboverde stated that she had paid 300 pesos to free her daughter only to have the master refuse to sign a letter of manumission. Catalina initiated legal action, but dropped the suit when the master agreed to sell the daughter to another for an equal amount under formal provision that the daughter's liberty might be purchased for this amount.[75] In an interesting case of the 1590's, a Spaniard named Francisco Martínez, feigning sympathy for the plight of the slave Isabel Martín, agreed to purchase her entirely on credit if her free mulata daughter, Isabel de la Rosa, would make the stipulated payments. Once the debt was paid off, the mother was to be free. The daughter agreed and paid the 410-peso price cited in the bill of sale in a year, only to have Martínez then insist on payment of another 410 pesos to himself. In this instance, mother and daughter were too wise to be deceived, took Martínez to court, and won.[76]

Some disputes over the purchase of freedom are difficult to evaluate. In 1614, for example, the master of the mulatto cobbler Juan Ruiz de Avendaño died intestate, and Ruiz claimed his liberty. He argued that he had always faithfully served his master, Alonso Ruiz Bonifacio, giving him at times sums as large as 800 pesos earned from shoemaking. Moreover, said Juan, his Indian wife had given his master 600 pesos for the mulatto's liberation. The master, on his part, had declared many times that Juan was to be free on his death and had let him practice his craft as though free in return for two reales a day. Unfortunately, Ruiz Bonifacio had been suddenly stricken on his remote estate in the corregimiento of Cajamarca and had died before he could formalize all this in a will. The heirs of the master disputed these claims. They argued five points in rebuttal, to wit: relations between master and cobbler had become so strained that Ruiz Bonifacio, after attempting to sell the slave several times, had sent him away to live on his own in return for the daily two-*real* payment Juan spoke of; the wife of the mulatto was too poor to have paid the alleged sum; since Ruiz Bonifacio had died intestate the presumption was in favor of continued enslavement; the cobbler actually belonged to the father of Ruiz Bonifacio, who merely administered the estate for the rest of the heirs and who therefore could not have freed the slave in any event; and, finally, the mulatto had demonstrated his lack of credibility by running away from the heirs before initiating the suit. In its decision a year later, the Audiencia ruled that the slave had not proved his case, and appeals were seemingly to no avail.[77]

Another complex and questionable case from the same period involved the efforts of Juan Ramos, a free mulatto tailor, to liberate his wife, Isabel Bañol, the slave of Bachiller Francisco Díaz de Arroyo. According to Ramos, when he had married Isabel some fifteen years earlier her master had agreed before the ceremony that the bride could have her liberty for 300 pesos. After the sacrament, however, Díaz had changed his mind, sent Isabel to Guamanga, and sold her to a muleteer for 600 pesos with the proviso that she was to be returned to Lima at his request. In fact Isabel came back to the capital several years later, but Díaz still attempted to block any married life between Juan and Isabel, in defiance of ecclesiastical censures, and once used his power to have Juan jailed for six months. Isabel changed hands several times after her return to Lima, though (according to Ramos) Díaz always managed to retain ultimate control over her destiny. Finally, in 1618 the frustrated husband appealed anew to the church courts when he learned that Isabel was in danger of being sent for sale to Chile. Ramos also charged that Díaz had managed once again to secure his imprisonment on false charges and, on another occasion, had paid some black ruffians to assault him. The surviving record of the suit extends over nearly a year, and for much of this time Isabel languished in jail, allegedly because no one could prove ownership to the satisfaction of the authorities and yet they could not determine the validity of Ramos's account.

Díaz, when he at last consented to answer the claims against him, also presented a reasonable case. According to his story, Isabel had never been his property, but was rather his father's slave. The trouble had all started some seventeen years before, when Juan took Isabel out of his father's house every night "to sleep," to the scandal of the neighborhood. His father had then forced them to marry, and at this point Ramos had proposed to buy Isabel's freedom. The father, though a poor man, had agreed, but Juan had vacillated for five months and Isabel had tried to run away. In fact she had been caught with one foot out of the window and had had to be shackled. At this point, Juan had entered the scene to demand her release at sword's point, and had wounded another black of the household. For this offense he was condemned to serve two years in the galleys. Díaz's father then sold Isabel in Guamanga, and when this news reached Ramos he escaped from the galleys, returned to Lima, and assaulted Isabel's former master, wounding him severely. Ramos had then fled Lima and had stayed away until the death of the father, at which time he had sent word to Isabel to flee and join him. At the close of this presentation, Díaz demanded that the suit be quashed. Ramos charged in return that legal documents would prove Isabel did in fact belong to Díaz, but he glossed over the rest of Díaz's points, attributing his own behavior to frustration over his marital state. Unfortunately, at this point, the documentation ends, and one is left to guess at the decision of the ecclesiastical judges.[78]

The very fact that many mulattoes were freed by their Spanish fathers encouraged others to sue for liberty, basing their claims on the alleged intentions of their dead or missing parents. We take here two examples. The first, which dates from the 1590's, concerns the efforts of the mulatto Juan Calvo (age thirty-seven) to claim his liberty on the death of his master of the same name. The mulatto insisted he was the natural son of the Spaniard by his slave, María Jolofa, and called on several witnesses to verify his resemblance to the master, to attest to the fact that the relationship between the Spaniard and the slave had been so notorious the Archbishop of Lima himself had attempted to break it off, and to affirm that his father had recognized him as his natural son until the very end of his life, when senility had overtaken him. The mulatto Calvo also pointed to the financial assistance he had given to his father in his old age (the charity of a good son and not the wages of a slave), to the fact that the Spaniard's legitimate sons had always recognized his status, and to his own marriage to a free woman. The legitimate children of the Spaniard denied most of this story and scored very telling points: the mulatto had been purchased in Panama along with his slave mother by the Spaniard Calvo and both had been taken thereafter to Lima; the money paid by the mulatto (a fisherman) to the Spaniard Calvo in fact represented wages, not charity; and there had been no mention of natural children in their father's will. In 1597 the mulatto lost his case and was sold by the heirs. At this he went into hiding for a while, then pushed his appeal until 1604, when the Audiencia confirmed its earlier decision. Juan's new master now sued the slave's bondsman for the amount of wages the slave could have earned in this interval, a legal action that went against him in 1608. Evidently the mulatto Calvo remained a slave, but his story illustrates the difficulties encountered by a slaveholder when a black was determined to fight for his freedom.[79]

The second example concerns the legal action initiated against the Society of Jesus in 1655 by the mulatto Juan Hernández del Corro, who claimed liberty on the basis of a 1625 letter of manumission granted to an eight-month-old child. The story presented by Hernández and his witnesses, as the case passed slowly from *alcalde ordinario* to Audiencia to the archdiocesan court, was as follows. He was the "nephew," i.e., the illegitimate child, of a Mercedarian priest, Father Antonio Hernández, and had been freed as an infant in Guayaquil, where the priest lived. He had then been sent to Lima to be brought up by the cleric's mother, and there, at the age of five, he had been kidnaped one day on the way to school. His abductors changed his name to Jusepe, and sold him into slavery. He had wound up in the hands of Don Francisco Dávila, a canon of the Lima cathedral, and a slave he had remained, willed on Dávila's death to the Jesuits. At this point his mother came from Ecuador in search of her long-lost son, recognized him as the slave held by the Society (thereby reinforcing his tale, hitherto unsupported), and thus the suit. As developed by his witnesses, Juan's story had a number of inconsistencies, which need not be gone into here, but practically all the witnesses agreed that Juan was the "son of a friar." Indeed, the mulatto's story was convincing enough to persuade the *alcalde ordinario*, with prodding from the Audiencia, to grant Juan temporary liberty until Dávila's estate could be settled and the Jesuits had had time to reply. The case presented by the Society was convincing, if not touching. Three documents were involved. The first was a 1639 bill of sale in which one Licenciado Don Diego Gatica purchased for 127 pesos a seven-year-old boy, Joseph Mulato, described by the sellers as "born in our home, a native of the city of Guatemala, son of Isabel Mulata, who was our slave and who we later sold in Realejo." The following year, as certified by another bill of sale, Gatica turned around and sold the lad for the very handsome (and somewhat suspicious) price of 660 pesos to Dávila. Finally, the Jesuits presented the will of Dávila, who left Joseph to the Jesuits. Dated in 1647, the year of his death, the testament described Joseph as a native of Nicaragua who had been in Dávila's possession "since his teeth changed." Clearly, as the judges noted, the two bills of sale above dealt with a younger slave than the babe liberated in the letter of manumission of 1625. Ultimately, the documents in the hands of the Jesuits were more convincing than Juan's story. He may indeed have been the son of a cleric, but in 1659 the Society's right of ownership was finally confirmed.[80]

Finally, the sexual attraction that the colored woman held for the Spaniard could impede rather than promote liberation if the jealousy of white wives was sufficiently aroused. The saga of Inés Mulata illustrates this point, and we learn of it through a legal action initiated by her free mother, Lucrecia Folupa, in 1646. By Lucrecia's account, which is partially confirmed by various notarial documents entered as evidence, approximately a year earlier Doña Leonor de Bullones, suspecting that her husband (now dead) was having sexual relations with their slave Inés, persuaded him to get rid of her. He thereupon sold Inés (then some three to four months pregnant) to Juan Rodríguez Lozano with the understanding that if she was returned to Lima both the slave and the purchase price of 500 pesos would have to be returned. Rodríguez quickly sold Inés to Bachiller Juan Zapata de Henão under the same terms. At roughly this time Inés's mother, Lucrecia, offered to buy her daughter's freedom and was rebuffed. Instead, Zapata sold Inés to the Marqués de Vaides, governor of Chile, on condition that he win the suit Lucrecia had filed against Zapata to force him to let her purchase her child's freedom. Vaides seems to have taken Inés to Chile, but to have sent her back to Lima soon after to serve his wife. At this point, Doña Leonor, who must have truly hated Inés, reminded Rodríguez of the terms of sale, and he in turn sued Zapata for the return of the slave and the purchase price. Lucrecia, in the meantime, fearing that her daughter would be sold outside the city again, petitioned the court to compel the master of Inés, whoever that turned out to be in the judges' determination, to free the slave for the stated 500 pesos. Lucrecia was successful in her effort to have Inés held in the custody of one Don Miguel de Meneses until the case was settled, and he now offered to pay Doña Leonor or Rodríguez the 500 pesos if either would sign a letter of manumission. As it turned out neither could have obliged, for in 1647 the church court awarded Zapata possession of Inés, and as far as we know she remained in bondage.[81]

Before we leave the subject of manumission there are several important points to be considered. First, there is the question of the frequency

TABLE 4

Manumissions of Peruvian Slaves by Age, Sex, and Type,
1560-1650

Age of slave	Sex		Unconditional	Future service	Other obligations	By full payment at manumission	By future payment after manumission
	Males	Females					
Over 45	8	21	15	2	1	10	2
36-45	6	22	9	1	—	16	1
26-35	9	24	7	6	—	19	1
16-25	2	19	5	4	—	10	3
8-15	9	27	16	13	—	5	3
Under 8	54	30	37	8	1	37	2
Unknown	18	71	19	21	3	32	16
TOTAL	106	214	108	55	5	129	28

SOURCE: Notarial records cited in Bibliography.
    NOTE: The number of individuals does not correspond to the totals under "terms of liberation" because some slaves fell into more than one category, e.g., "future service" and "by full payment at manumission."

of the various types of manumission and of the sex and age of the slaves involved. My own findings, as presented in Table 4, suggest that the principal beneficiaries of manumission were women and children, who compose 82 per cent of the cases in the sample, and that adult males in the prime of life (sixteen to thirty-five) were the least favored (3 per cent). This means that in the early decades of colonization the adult free black population of the colony must have been heavily female, and that a rough balance between the sexes was only slowly achieved as new generations of freeborn males attained manhood. These figures also reveal that, as in the first years of Spanish Peru, various forms of purchase constituted the most important path to liberty, followed rather closely by unconditional manumission by the slaveholder. The importance of race mixture as a factor in liberation is underscored by this sample as well: 115 of the 320 freed slaves, or nearly 36 per cent, were identified in the notarial documents as mulatto, zambo, quadroon, or otherwise racially mixed.[82]

Further, there is considerable evidence that manumission benefited the urban slave more than the rural slave. Though the wills of agriculturalists are amply represented in the above sample, none of the blacks involved were freed voluntarily and unconditionally. In fact, only one rural slave figures among the 320: Gaspar Mandinga, who managed to purchase his freedom (and whose case was discussed on p. 281). Other documentation of the period tells the same story. A rare exception was Asencio Pérez de Longarte, who owned a chácara near Arica. On his deathbed in 1616 Pérez granted conditional manumission to two blacks who worked his lands; one was to be liberated after five more years of service and the second after ten. But Lorenzo Pérez Noguera, who was more solicitous than most in his provisions for the blacks of his chácara, was much more typical of Peruvian practice in this regard. In his will of 1637 Pérez freed only one slave, a man who had assisted him in his mercantile operations; the sixteen blacks on his rural estate were listed as mere property.[83]

The indifference of masters to the fate of rural slaves is largely explained by the fact that Peruvian agriculturalists, like their counterparts elsewhere in Spanish America, preferred to live in towns, leaving the management of their estates to foremen. In consequence, they did not know their rural slaves well, if at all, and rarely gave thought to freeing them voluntarily.[84] As for the purchase of freedom, it was next to impossible for the rural slave to accumulate the necessary cash, for at the very seasons when the nearby plantations might have needed additional hands, he was employed at home. In off-seasons, there was no demand for labor anywhere within reasonable distance. Many rural slaves were granted garden plots, which they worked on Sundays and on the many religious holidays, but though they could trade surplus produce for different commodities, they were rarely able to sell it, since most of their fellow workers had similar plots and little cash. Even race mixture did not favor the rural slave. It seems unnecessary to belabor the fact that planters and foremen indulged themselves sexually among their black female charges, and some of the offspring were freed. However, the inventories of Peruvian agricultural holdings indicate that many more remained in bondage. At the same time, in rural areas where there were some numbers of Indians, slaves were sometimes allowed to marry native women, and presumably their zambo children were free.[85]

In fact, even if a rural slave did gain freedom, his prospects for achieving a substantially better life were dim. Most adults knew nothing but agricultural work, and to acquire a skill late in life must have been difficult. The majority no doubt continued agricultural pursuits as free laborers or squatted on a small parcel of unclaimed land to lead a marginal existence.[86] Obviously, an emancipated rural slave who possessed some skill had a better time of it, and freed infants might be sent at the appropriate time to the nearest town for apprenticeship in some craft if anyone around them was aware that this could be arranged.

For the urban slave, the possibilities and conditions of manumission were far better. Urban slavery above all else meant household service, and this in turn provided an opportunity to be close to the master on a daily basis and to win his favor over the years. Since household service was largely woman's work, this fact may account for the high percentage of females in my sample. A fair proportion of the urban blacks, moreover, were skilled, wage-earning slaves with a chance, at least, of persuading their masters to apply a portion of their earnings toward the purchase of freedom, or of otherwise accumulating cash. Even the unskilled could hope to earn money in towns. A laundress, for example, who was permitted to work part-time on her own account doubtless found no lack of customers. Finally, slaves in the cities were in a much better position than their isolated rural counterparts to learn of the Spanish world and its ways. As we saw in Chapter 6, urban slaves with free male children often knew of the demand for artisans and arranged apprenticeships for their sons, thereby assuring them a better future than their own. Many rural slaves in similar circumstances probably condemned their children to the unrewarding life of an agricultural laborer through simple ignorance of the alternatives.

Throughout the period under study manumission and (occasionally) flight contributed to the numbers of free Afro-Peruvians, but as time went on these two factors had less and less part in the growth of the free colored population. Manumitted blacks passed their own freedom on to their children, and Spaniards and free colored women produced offspring whose liberty was not in question. These generations in turn mingled with Europeans, Indians, and various castes to produce an ever-larger and more bewildering variety of free "blacks." Free coloreds, "an important class of people" as early as the beginning of the Peruvian civil wars, continued to be a highly visible part of the colony, and were concentrated, along with their slave brothers, primarily along the coast.[87] It is impossible to state precisely the number of free persons of color in Peru during this interval, not only because those of light hue found it in their interest to "pass" as Spanish, but also because most censuses made no distinction between free coloreds and slaves. However, it is safe to say a sizable minority of the colored population of Peru enjoyed this status. In 1586, for example, the city of Lima had an estimated population of 4,000 blacks, mulattoes, and zambos, of whom 932, or nearly a quarter, were free.[88] In later years official figures indicated both a relative and an absolute decline in the number of free persons of color. In a 1611 census aimed at adding the free blacks of Lima and Callao to the tax rolls, for example, only 630 persons were counted, whereas in a census made three year later, Lima alone had 11,130 persons of African descent.[89] The relative decline in the numbers of free persons of color is, of course, explained by the dramatic increase in the slave trade during this period, and the absolute decline by the purpose of the 1611 census, tribute collection, an obligation resented by many free coloreds and escaped by avoiding enumeration. Every other type of documentary evidence indicates that free Afro-Peruvians grew rather than declined in numbers in the seventeenth century, and it seems reasonable to assume that by 1650 approximately 10 per cent of Peru's colored population was free, or perhaps 3,000 of an estimated total of 30,000 (see Appendix A). But liberty, greatly prized and frequently achieved at considerable sacrifice, in turn presented a new set of challenges. The Afro-Peruvian had now to make his way in an often hostile world as a free person, where dependency was more subtle but no less real. It is to these challenges that we now turn.

CHAPTER ELEVEN

The Free Person of Color: Acceptance and Advancement

The Spanish community of Peru regarded the free person of African descent with marked ambivalence. Color prejudice and presumed illegitimacy doomed most free Afro-Peruvians to the ranks of the disadvantaged, and it was easy for Spaniards to characterize them in the mass as "a band of troublemakers, abetting runaway slaves, covering up thefts, fomenting unrest." Yet day-to-day experience was studded with examples indicating that free coloreds were "an industrious and useful class of people who seized every opportunity given them, and did much to build up the country for themselves and the Spaniards."[1] In short, the free person of color presented a "double image" to the Spanish, an image that was reflected in Peruvian law and reality. In law, the free person of color was closely identified with the slave, and most restrictions and reminders of inferior status were applied to both, though the free man was sometimes penalized less heavily for violations. In his free status, the person of color also assumed many of the burdens expected of the Indian and the Spaniard: like the Indian, he was obliged to pay tribute and was not supposed to be idle; like the Spaniard, he was expected to defend the state by serving in the militia and was subject to the supervision of the Holy Office. In addition, free coloreds of mixed blood and illegitimate birth had to deal with a peculiar prejudice faced by neither white nor brown nor black. Remarkably, many free Afro-Peruvians gained modest fortune and acceptance in the face of these odds, and even turned obligations into advantages, but racial cohesion and identity were lost in the process.

The payment of tribute was particularly resented by free persons of color, both because it confirmed their inferior status and because it was coupled to employment and housing regulations that seriously circumscribed their freedom. The Crown, however, took a different point of view. Zambos were nominally obliged to pay tribute as early as 1572, at least partly in an effort to cut the rate of sexual promiscuity among Indian women who thought that children fathered by non-Indians would be exempt from this tax. Doubts about the legality of zambo tribute payments persisted as late as 1580, however, and it was not until the 1590's that their obligation was confirmed.[2] Meanwhile, in 1574 the Crown extended the payment of tribute to free blacks and mulattoes. In justification of this action, it was noted that those of African descent who had come to America as slaves and who had profited by the richness of the region to free themselves and to accumulate modest fortunes should express their gratitude for the peace, justice, and freedom they enjoyed by paying a small annual tax, the more so since tribute payment was also an African custom. Though Viceroy Toledo, renowned for his administrative abilities, governed at the time, this decree had still to be implemented two years later. When the Crown attorney of the Audiencia ascribed this failure in major part to the fact that many free persons of color seemingly had no fixed residence or visible means of support, the Crown moved to remedy the situation. In 1577 free blacks and mulattoes were ordered to live with and work for an employer, who would then pay their tribute and deduct it from their wages. Once all had complied, the viceroy was to order the registration of the free coloreds in each district, specifying their names and their employers—with whom they were to stay unless the authorities said otherwise.[3] These measures fitted perfectly with Toledo's desire to force idle free coloreds into the work force to reduce the burden of the mita, but even armed with this new authority he apparently made little effort to collect the tribute—perhaps out of discouragement at the failure of his earlier schemes to find an alternative to forced Indian labor. His subordinates in the government were scarcely more active, and as a result the free coloreds of Peru gained a reprieve of nearly two decades in the collection of tribute.[4]

On assuming office in 1596, Viceroy Velasco tried to systematize the collection of this revenue. The free coloreds of Arequipa appear to have been the first targets of this effort. In the first year of his tenure Velasco ordered the treasury officials there to make a census of the free persons of color and to collect one *peso ensayado* annually from each in tribute.

The count revealed exactly forty persons, and the appropriate amount was duly collected for 1596-97. Thereafter, the treasury officials appointed from among the colored population an *alcalde de los mulatos* to be in charge of tribute collection or paid the constable of Arequipa a commission to perform this service. Occasionally in the early years a full *peso ensayado* was not collected in every case on the plea of poverty. By 1650 the free coloreds of Arequipa had contributed at least 2,510 pesos (of eight reales) to the royal treasury.[5] Tribute was also collected from those of African descent in the Ica district on the south coast in 1596, but no collections seem to have been made in subsequent years.[6]

Velasco made no attempt to collect tribute in Trujillo until 1604. In that year the local treasury officials were instructed to levy four pesos (of eight reales) on each free colored male and two pesos on each female. It was provided that a trustworthy person might be appointed to collect the tribute for a commission of 6 per cent. A census taken in 1605 revealed that Trujillo, Santa, Saña, and Chiclayo between them had fifty free men of color and fifty-five women. In the period 1604-8, 1,240 pesos in tribute was collected, and another 700 was carried on the books as owed by people who had presumably died or fled the district. Indeed, it soon became obvious to the treasury officials that free persons of color were fleeing the area rather than pay tribute. In the period 1608-11 only thirty-two men and twenty-six women paid the tax and only some 395 pesos was collected; almost as much again, 302 pesos, was owed by coloreds who could not be located. Few of the Trujillo treasury records for the subsequent years have survived; but those for 1625-29 show that over 415 pesos was collected, and for 1627 we have the estimate of treasury officials of an expected annual tribute from persons of color of approximately 130 pesos.[7] The free colored population of Arica was not obliged to pay tribute until 1609, and to 1645 some 1,576 pesos had been collected.[8]

More than any others, the free persons of color of Lima resisted the Crown's efforts to bring them into the tribute system. One of Velasco's predecessors, Viceroy Villar, claimed to have made a start in this direction by having a census taken for this purpose, and one collection was made in 1595. Velasco himself let the matter ride for several years, though a small collection was made in 1603, but in 1604 he took steps to place the system on a firm footing.[9] At that time he ordered all free persons of color between the ages of eighteen and fifty to pay tribute at an annual rate of four pesos for men and two pesos for women. Collection was entrusted to the corregidor of the Indian district of Santiago del Cercado, who was empowered to appoint a deputy to handle the task for either a salary of 300 pesos a year or 6 per cent of the receipts, as he chose.[10]

The first corregidor to get the assignment, Don José de Rivera, collected a substantial amount of money between 1604 and 1606, but he still owed much of it to the Crown as late as 1611. Worse, collection had aroused so much hostility among the free colored population that his successor, Domingo de Luna, flatly refused to make the attempt, alleging that previous agents had been set upon with knives and other weapons. Luna stood fast until 1609, when the Audiencia relieved him of the obligation.[11] However, the then viceroy, Montesclaros, was determined to collect the tribute in one way or another. In 1610 he ordered a new census of the free colored population of Lima, which revealed 410 persons of color (in a total of 630) who were liable for tribute under the age limits previously established by Velasco.* Several free coloreds chose to resist this new effort to collect tribute, especially some quadroons who claimed exemption by virtue of their Spanish blood, and there were a number of lawsuits and arrests. Nevertheless, Montesclaros plunged ahead, and by 1612 could report to a suitably grateful Crown that tribute collection in Lima had been farmed out for 650 pesos.[12]

His success was only temporary, however, for in 1613, after two years of collections,[13] the initial contract expired, and the treasury officials claimed that another contractor could not be found. In consequence, no further tribute was received from the colored population for the next several years. (The Crown suffered no loss, however, for the treasury officials were made personally responsible for the 650 pesos lost annually in the interim.[14]) In 1619 the Crown ordered that the situation be remedied, but by this time Viceroy Esquilache had already con-

---

* As we saw in Chapter 10, this figure is too low for the simple reason that many of African descent, especially quadroons, escaped enumeration by "passing" as white. This was easy to do, according to Poma de Ayala, because quadroons, whether mulattoes or zambos (and their descendants even more), could scarcely be distinguished from the "pure Castilian race." Only their ears, in his opinion, gave their ancestry away. *Nueva corónica* (1936), p. 710. On the subject of "passing" in colonial Spanish America in general, see Mörner, *Race Mixture*, pp. 68-70; and my paper in *Neither Slave Nor Free*.

sulted with the Audiencia and the treasury officials and taken action. Quadroons, who had most resolutely resisted paying the tribute, were now exempted, and future contractors were given sufficient judicial authority (presumably the power to arrest or confiscate) to enforce collection, though the persons involved had the right to appeal to the Audiencia. Under these terms a three-year contract was concluded for 1619-21 guaranteeing the Crown an annual payment of 650 pesos.[15]

This agreement was honored,[16] but the contractors seem to have abused their judicial authority. As Esquilache confided to his successor, the tribute of free persons of color in most of Peru was "of little substance but causes a great uproar"; and in Lima, where "it is worth something," attempts at enforcement had provoked such a flood of complaints that he had been led to appoint Doctor Juan de la Celda to hear them before further action was taken.[17] Indeed, so great was the volume of protest against the contractors that the Audiencia in 1621 suggested making tribute a semi-voluntary contribution, to be funneled through the confraternities (a suggestion prompted no doubt by the handsome contribution of 557 pesos the free blacks, mulattoes, and zambos gave to the Crown that year in response to the government's appeal for a *donativo*).[18] In 1626 the authorities in Madrid referred the proposal back to the viceroy and the Audiencia for consideration,[19] and there the matter ended. At some point in the late 1620's, it was decided to organize the free mulattoes of Lima into a guild, which would be responsible for the collection of tribute, the recruitment of the colored militia companies, and the collection of special contributions for various religious and civic festivities.[20] As it turned out, the guild showed itself quite willing, in January and February of 1631, to participate on a lavish scale in the celebrations honoring the birth of Baltasar Carlos, heir to the Spanish throne,[21] but it was either unwilling or unable to collect tribute from its members. Nor could the treasury officials find a new contractor to do the job. As a result, the tribute of the free colored population of Lima went uncollected through the end of our period.[22]

The home government and its representatives continued to press for the payment of tribute by the free colored population of Lima from time to time, but not too hard. This was thanks in good part to the intercession of the colored militia units. In 1627 these forces, which had performed extremely well against the Dutch threat on several oc-

casions, petitioned the Crown to lift the tribute requirement as a reward. They were backed in their request by the Audiencia and the
Crown attorney, who argued that the revenue involved was not worth
the general ill-will payment of tribute aroused and urged that the colored community as a whole be freed of the obligation.[23] The Crown
was not prepared to go this far, but in 1631 it did exempt all free
women of color and all men who had served or who were currently
serving in the militia from the tax.[24] Once these elements were subtracted from the already small number of colored persons in the capital who had not managed in one way or another to avoid the tribute
rolls, the revenue was obviously too small to make collecting it worth
the bother. Further, the free coloreds of Piura and Paita used the example of Lima as an excuse to be relieved of their tribute obligations as
well. Indeed, with all these exemptions, the wonder is that the tax was
collected anywhere in Peru in the 1640's and 1650's.

The requirements that free persons of color hire themselves out to
and reside with Spaniards were also haphazardly enforced. To deal
with the question of employment first, Peruvian notarial records indicate that from time to time the municipal authorities or those responsible for tribute collection would round up idle free coloreds and contract them to Spanish employers, usually for a year's time and apparently never on a systematic basis. Yet it should be stressed at the same
time that this requirement, though closely related to tribute collection,
was adopted before the imposition of that tax and was often enforced
for a variety of other reasons: the elimination of prostitution and vagrancy, the necessity of providing for orphaned free coloreds who were
minors, the jealousy of Spanish artisans, and the periodic official concern for keeping tabs on free Afro-Peruvians. In 1574, for example,
two mulatas named Catalina and Magdalena de Santa Cruz, the first
a young adult and the second a fourteen-year-old, were held in the
public jail until they agreed to hire themselves out; and in the same
year the authorities took a ten-year-old girl away from her mother,
Antonia Descate, a free black woman from Panama of unsavory reputation, lest the child "lose her virtue." The girl was placed with a distant relative for four years, during which time she was to be fed, clothed,
instructed in good habits, and paid twelve pesos a year. Similarly, in
1575 the authorities placed Francisca Mulata, a six-year-old orphan,
with a Spanish mistress who agreed to look after the child for ten years

and to pay her a modest wage.[25] Lockhart cites the case of Juan de Fregenal, the ex-slave of a notary public of Lima and a mason by profession. Fregenal was liberated around 1547 and thereafter achieved considerable success, but his life may have been typical of many free coloreds in that he was plagued by the requirement of taking residence with a Spanish employer. "Three times he entered the pay of Spaniards, once specifically saying he did so to meet the legal requirements. It appears probable that Fregenal worked only part-time for his employers, and with his legal position thus assured, continued his independent activity."[26]

As might be expected, the authorities themselves took advantage of the employment requirement to press free persons of color into certain unpleasant tasks. In 1555, for example, the Lima councilmen took note of the fact that the city streets were extraordinarily filthy, and that they had no funds to remedy the situation. Then someone thought of using the "idle" and "prejudicial" free coloreds for the task. A free man of color named Francisco Hernández, a "well-known family man and property owner," was thereupon appointed to supervise the work on a permanent basis, and was given a staff of office and the necessary authority to compel his fellows to serve as the streetsweepers of the city. Hernández was also empowered to use any black criminals jailed by the municipality for the job. Similarly, in 1572 and again in 1578, when emergency repairs had to be made on the dikes and cutwaters of the Rímac, the city authorized those in charge to force members of the free colored population to work without compensation. During the 1589 epidemic it was likewise proposed to make free blacks and mulattoes care for the sick.[27]

As for the residence requirement, that too was evaded with some impunity. To be sure, some free Afro-Peruvians did live with Spaniards, perhaps because they could not find or afford housing or wanted to save money. We note, for example, the case of Diego Rodríguez, a free black tailor, who lived in the home of Don Dionisio Manrique, a member of the Lima Audiencia.[28] Nevertheless, hundreds of rental contracts in notarial records testify that free coloreds in Lima (and doubtless elsewhere in Peru as well) successfully defied the attempts to make them live with Spaniards. Moreover, the authorities probably made little effort to enforce the requirement among those who had the resources to secure their own housing. To cite a few examples, in 1605 the free mulatto Diego de Sá rented "a small dwelling" in Lima for five pesos a month; in 1615 the married couple Juan de Herrera and Ursula Rodríguez, also mulattoes, rented a house in the San Lázaro district for a year for the sum of 114 pesos; and in 1640 the free coloreds María Bañol and Leonor Bañol leased "a small house with a room adjoining" for seven pesos a month.[29] Many free colored artisans, like their associates of other hues, chose to stay in the same structure where they practiced their trade and others to keep separate lodgings, but few chose to live under the eyes of Spaniards.[30]

Though the free person of color was under the same curfew laws and the same injunctions against bearing arms as the slave, this did not prevent the authorities from imposing military service on him in time of emergency, a duty that some free Afro-Peruvians managed to turn to their own advantage.* It was with some trepidation that Viceroy Montesclaros organized the first colored militia in 1615 to help meet the threat of a Dutch fleet along the coast; but once the decision was made, the program moved along smartly and before long Lima had three companies of mulattoes and two of free blacks, who played a "necessary and important" role in the total defense effort.[31] It was not, however, a military role strictly speaking, for the Spanish authorities did not trust the colored militia and were careful to assign them to support duties. During the alarm created by the Dutch in 1615, for example, they dug trenches for the defense of Callao and hauled supplies, operations that consumed nine days. In 1618, on word that another Dutch fleet (which failed to materialize) was approaching, the colored companies were sent to Callao to guard the royal customhouse and perform the night patrol. During the serious intrusion of the Dutch in 1624 the Afro-Peruvians first went to the nearby port of Surco to erect fortifications and were then ordered back to Callao, where they were held in readiness for an assault that never came. As we have seen, these

---

* Occasionally, free blacks and mulattoes served as regular soldiers in various military expeditions, and notably in the campaign against the Araucanians in Chile, an undertaking that attracted few recruits. Most of those involved in the Chilean effort were convicted criminals who chose this duty (perhaps with some prompting) to shorten their sentences. This was apparently the aim of the group of seven free blacks and mulattoes who were released from the jails of Lima in 1570 for service in Chile and given 490 pesos for equipment and expenses. Two free mulatto soldiers also accompanied the 1579 expedition of Pedro de Sarmiento y Gamboa to the Strait of Magellan. AGIC 1686, expenditures for 1570: 103-4; AGIC 1689, "Data de hacienda real hecha para los gastos de la guerra y munición y jornada del estrecho [de Magallanes] del cargo del tesorero Pedro de Vega."

demonstrations of loyalty persuaded the Crown to exempt the colored militiamen of Lima from tribute payment. The free black and mulatto militiamen of Piura and Paita in northern Peru, who were activated in 1624, and who regularly hauled the royal revenues down to Lima for a reduced rate, were granted a similar exemption in 1641.[32]

An emergency of the magnitude of that of 1624 did not occur again during the period under study. In later years the colored militia, their strength now up to six companies, were chiefly occupied in modifying the Callao fortifications, and in 1645 they assisted in the preparation of an expedition sent to Chile in response to the brief Dutch occupation of Valdivia. The Afro-Peruvian companies were ordinarily commanded by salaried Spaniards, usually captains (or occasionally sergeants), who drew only a soldier's pay of some twenty to twenty-two and a half pesos a month. But at least one man from the ranks, a free mulatto named Juan de Valladolid Mogorón, attained high military position. Valladolid began his military service in 1631, and nine years later was appointed corporal of the colored companies. In 1642, in recognition of his services, Viceroy Mancera appointed him adjutant of the Afro-Peruvian militia, and three years later, he was allowed to exercise the authority of a lieutenant. Valladolid went to Spain in 1653 to petition the Crown to reward him with the title of Maestre de Campo. The king instructed the viceroy to grant this request if circumstances did not prevent it, but no record remains to tell us what the viceroy's decision was.[33]

The government exhibited proper concern for the spiritual welfare of the free person of color. Decrees were sent periodically from Spain ordering the indoctrination of free blacks and mulattoes in the principles of Christianity so they could lead orderly and upright lives,[34] and many free Afro-Peruvians did indeed become very attached to Catholicism. Yet the Church too was capable of patent discrimination. In 1614, for example, a synod convoked by the Archbishop of Lima ruled that no blacks or mulattoes were to be buried in the cathedral. The Crown attorney before the Audiencia deplored the possible effects of this harsh measure on the religious sentiments of the Afro-Peruvians, arguing that some of them "merited this and other honors," but there is no evidence that the ruling was reversed. In the same year the Lima city council prohibited the use of coffins by those of African ancestry as a grave affront to the superior status of the Spanish, and the Church apparently made no protest.[35]

This was but one of the many petty and galling ways in which the secular authorities sought to regulate the lives of the free persons of color. Free black women in particular were the objects of numerous attempts at sumptuary legislation, perhaps because of the Spanish male's interest in them. At least as early as 1574 the Crown approved ordinances for the city of Panama, which were widely imitated along the Pacific coast, enjoining black women, whether slave or free, from using silk, pearls, gold, or mantillas in any form as wearing apparel.[36] Perhaps the most annoying aspect of the sumptuary laws against the colored population was their haphazard enforcement. In 1580, for example, the black woman María Becas had her jewels seized and sold by the municipal authorities; the third that belonged to the Crown under the law amounted to the magnificent sum of twenty-four pesos.[37]

Such incidents must have been painful to the individuals involved, but they did very little to solve what the Spanish perceived as a problem. In 1622, for example, some forty years later, the Lima city council passed a resolution urging the viceroy to reconfirm the existing sumptuary legislation, which barred black and mulatto women from wearing silk and ornaments of gold and silver; prohibited even those married to Spaniards from wearing anything more luxurious than woolen garments; and forebade colored women to bring rugs or cushions to sit on in church, or to have any sort of dais at home. Fines for violations were evidently severe.[38] The viceroy's action, if any, is unknown, but it could not have been forceful, since we find the Crown attorney complaining in 1629 that the mulatas paid no heed to the sumptuary laws, dressing ostentatiously and scandalizing their betters by bringing prayer rugs to church. Perhaps in reaction to this complaint, Viceroy Chinchón proclaimed the existing sumptuary legislation once again in 1631, and this time the prohibitions extended to slippers ornamented with silver bells and to canopied beds. The presumption was that such fripperies were the fruits of prostitution, and the women who favored them were therefore directed to seek honorable employment.[39] Whether there was in fact any connection between that occupation and garish clothes, there were enough free colored women so engaged to cause a contemporary to remark that many Spanish adventurers in the capital, who lived only for "disturbances and riots," were able to maintain an outward show of elegance because of the funds they received from colored paramours in return for a gallant escort by day and by night.[40]

In official eyes and in the eyes of society at large, the free Afro-Peruvian's color and presumed illegitimacy marked him as an inferior creature,[41] and therefore, the reasoning went, it was useless to educate him. The free person of color was thus caught in a vicious circle, for without an education he was indeed inferior. There were, to be sure, enlightened men who believed that those of African descent should be educated. In 1577, for example, the Bishop of Cuzco even proposed that the University at Lima be opened to those of the racially mixed population who seemed likely to profit by the experience. This suggestion was ignored, and the universities of Spanish America were officially closed to all persons of color, with such exclusions usually worded in a "casual, mechanical way, as if the problem might not arise."[42] The same attitude prevailed at the secondary level, as in the case of the Colegio Real de San Felipe y San Marcos in Lima, founded to educate the sons of the leading conquistadores. From this school, all those of African descent were excluded, along with the offspring of other "unworthy people and infamous men punished by the Holy Office."[43]

There were exceptions to this policy of exclusion, but some were pathetic and others did not endure. For example, the orphanage of Our Lady of Atocha, founded in Lima in 1603, was not permitted to accept blacks, mulattoes, or zambos knowingly, but neither could it turn away infants of such descent left at its portals, for this would be inhumane. Rather, these children were to be taken in subject to certain involuntary obligations. Beginning at age seven boys were to be instructed in reading, writing, and "other virtues"; were then at age fourteen to begin helping in the operations of the orphanage; and, finally, at age twenty were to be placed in some gainful employment at the discretion of the municipal authorities. From the age of nine on, girls were to be hired out as convent servants. Until they reached the age of twelve, their wages were to go to the orphanage in compensation for expenses incurred. Thereafter, if they did not go into the Church as lay sisters, their wages were to be their own, and the administrators of the orphanage were to look out for their "remedy and advantage," that is, find them a husband.[44]

The Jesuits attempted to keep their College of San Pablo open to all races initially, and apparently succeeded in doing so for several decades. As Luis Martín, who has studied this question closely, puts it: "White boys from the best families of Lima, tracing their ancestors back to the founders of the city, freely mixed in studies and play, under the eyes of the Jesuits, with all shades of mestizos, and with youngsters whose flat noses, protruding lips, and kinky hair were the unmistakable seal of the Negro." But the Society discovered that colonial Peru was not post-Renaissance Italy. The *gente decente* of Lima, "who naturally did not see any major objection to occasionally bedding down with an attractive slave-girl," and who may have moved heaven and earth to make an exception for their own colored offspring, nevertheless forced the College to adopt the policy of admitting only those of ostensibly pure Spanish ancestry. This rule was first stated in 1648, but it may have been followed in practice at a considerably earlier date.[45]

The home government on at least one occasion, in a decree of 1607, suggested the desirability of some form of vocational training for the colored population. In a reply two years later, Viceroy Montesclaros promised to implement the proposal in all possible ways, but the only specific measure he mentioned was the continuation of a program instituted by his predecessor, Don Luis de Velasco. Under this plan, orphaned boys of all racial mixtures in each of the parishes of Lima were assigned teachers (who were paid from unassigned Indian tributes) to instruct them in reading, writing, and elementary arithmetic. The program is not mentioned in subsequent documentation, and there is no way of measuring its success.[46]

Lack of a university education and skin of too dark a hue combined to close the professions to the free Afro-Peruvian, just as his color and presumed bastardy generally combined to deny him public office and grants of Indian tribute and labor, as stated by a royal decree of 1549.[47] However, when the Crown began selling minor positions in the colonial bureaucracy in the late sixteenth century, some free coloreds with money, skill, and connections were able to overcome the weight of their ancestry. In 1619, the mulatto son of a former doorkeeper of the criminal branch of the Audiencia, Juan Ochoa, bought the same position for the civil bench of that body. However, his success was short-lived, for the tribunal accepted the appointment, but speedily wrote the home government that they regarded the situation as "indecent" since Ochoa's mulata mother and black grandmother were both well known in Lima. In response the Crown ordered Ochoa relieved of the office and instructed the Audiencia to disregard similar mistaken royal appointments in the future. Scarcely had this incident passed when the

Crown was forced to admit that some mulattoes had managed to purchase notaryships despite the biographical information required of all
potential officeholders. In 1621 it ordered that greater care be exercised
with regard to the question of race, and that if by chance a person of
African descent still managed to obtain an appointment, the Audiencia
was to prevent him from exercising the office.[48]

These safeguards were not always effective against mulattoes with
talent and influential friends, and still less so against quadroons. Two
examples will illustrate the point. The first concerns Alonso Sánchez de
Figueroa, a mulatto born in Badajoz and the son of a Spanish bachiller.
Sánchez served as a scribe in a notary's office in Seville before coming
to Peru, where his former Badajoz connections soon stood him in good
stead. Among them was Pedro Pérez Landero, the head notary of a
government mission sent to inspect the colony in the 1630's, who made
Sánchez his chief clerk. Soon after, Sánchez moved to purchase the
title of notary through agents in Spain for some 100 ducats of his
savings. His friend Pérez, called upon to make a statement of Sánchez's
competence, testified that the mulatto's script was legible and finely
formed, and that he was entirely trustworthy and completely in command of the various legal formulae used in the documents of the time.
Pérez also declared that Sánchez had accumulated capital amounting
to some 600 pesos. Another old friend from Badajoz who testified on
Sánchez's behalf was Antonio Fernández de la Cruz, chief clerk of the
Lima city council. Nevertheless, the members of the Audiencia refused
to confirm the appointment because of Sánchez's race and in 1637 appealed to Spain for a decision in accordance with their general instructions. As we shall see in the next case, there is evidence that the appointment was eventually confirmed.[49]

That case, which came up scarcely two years later, involved the sale
of the office of solicitor to the Audiencia (*procurador*) by its current
holder, Alonso de Castro, to a notary named José Núñez de Prado,
an action that Castro's colleagues immediately protested on the grounds
Núñez was a mulatto. Viceroy Chinchón, asked to intercede, turned
for legal counsel to a professor of law at San Marcos, who advised him
to confirm the sale, pointing out that Núñez was not really a mulatto
but a quadroon, that he was a person of unquestioned ability, and that
he had paid twice as much for the office (6,000 pesos) as any previous
holder. The professor also pointed out that a similar case involving a

notaryship—presumably the Sánchez case—had recently been appealed to Spain, where the mulatto candidate had won a favorable decision. The viceroy accepted this recommendation and advised the Crown to confirm the appointment, with what success we do not know.[50]

Public office was one thing, and service in the Church quite another. Perhaps more than the issue of race itself, the shadow of illegitimacy barred those of African descent from the priesthood. The Crown, for example, feared that the public would be scandalized to see "such unworthy people so highly placed."[51] To be sure, San Martín de Porres is an exception to this rule, but an exceedingly rare one. Whatever his saintly qualities, and one author assures us that these included extreme humility, it was perhaps his education in Ecuador and the status of his father ("of the bluest and purest Castilian blood, a native of Burgos, and a very important person") that guaranteed San Martín's acceptance first as a Dominican oblate (1601) and then as a lay brother.[52]

Though many Spanish fathers, like San Martín's, concerned themselves with the fate of their colored offspring, this was not generally true; relationships between Spanish men and African women tended to be relatively casual affairs.[53] Further, even among those fathers who took an interest, the degree of concern, and sometimes indeed the ability to help, varied markedly. One father who equaled San Martín's in his compassion for his natural child was the Peruvian conquistador Domingo de Destre, who recognized a son named Miguel born to the slave Ana Negra, purchased the boy's freedom, and at death bequeathed him a farm on the outskirts of Lima. A more pathetic case was that of the glassmaker Pedro de la Barrera, who made his will in 1630 and died in the knowledge of his bankruptcy. Barrera confessed that he had sired a child by his slave Juana Bautista, whom he had been forced to mortgage for 300 pesos. The most he could do for her on his deathbed was to grant her the right to freedom if this amount was paid. The child, an eight-year-old boy named Salvador, was freed outright and had to take what comfort he could from his father's testamentary declaration that at the time he had been conceived Barrera had "owed no pesos to anyone and was rich with much capital."[54]

For a middling example of the fate of free colored children sired by white fathers we take the mulatto son of Juan Antonio. The case began in 1602, when Antonio, who described himself as a simple farmer, departed the Duchy of Savoy bound first for Mexico and then for Peru.

He left a wife and child behind in Savoy, but this did not prevent him from having a son in Peru by the slave María Angola in 1607. By this time Antonio was making some money by working lands leased from various religious orders, and he was able to buy the freedom of the child, named Andrés, almost immediately after his birth for ninety pesos. Antonio also arranged to pay María's owner eight pesos a month for the child's upkeep (not including clothing) so she could raise him and also (it was understood) spend considerable time at Antonio's residence. The Savoyard, who had added the more aristocratic "de los Reyes" to his name by this point, managed to evade deportation as a foreigner in 1612, and at approximately the same time by word and deed he recognized Andrés as his son. Andrés came to live with his father, and the slave mother was left to recede into the background; presumably, Antonio's growing respectability in the community precluded such a liaison. Relations between father and son were harmonious until 1621, when Antonio saw a chance to marry again (his Italian wife had died) and secure a considerable dowry. His new bride, born Ana Sánchez de Vergara, deeply resented the presence of the mulatto lad, which led to such bitter quarrels that Andrés, to his father's sorrow, left for Panama to become a carpenter's apprentice. For the next eighteen years, there was no contact between father and son, and during this interval Andrés had little luck on his own. He could make no money at carpentry and had married a mulata, thereby advancing not at all on the socio-racial scale. His father, in contrast, had done very well, and on his death in 1639 left an estate valued at 70,000 pesos, which included a large farm, a ship, and twenty black slaves. The entire estate went to Doña Ana, who promptly remarried, but Andrés learned of his father's death and hurried to Lima to claim his inheritance. Doña Ana evidently felt that she had to take him into her household, but by 1643 his presence had grown irksome. His "stepmother" then played her trump card. Andrés did not know that he was free, and Doña Ana, who had the letter of manumission in her possession, threatened to enslave him unless he waived all rights to his father's estate in return for 400 pesos. Andrés yielded, but later brought suit for 10,000 pesos as his rightful share of his father's possessions. In 1644 he was awarded 1,000 pesos. Dissatisfied with this verdict, he then appealed to the Council of the Indies, which refused to consider the case.[55]

As the last two cases make clear, even the patronage and love of a white father could not guarantee the free person of color the socio-economic success that would have truly liberated him, and failing this, it was difficult in the extreme for him to compete with Spaniards in a colony whose very name lured many with the cruel illusion of instant wealth and success. On balance, and despite the bad luck of the carpenter Andrés, free colored artisans probably had the easiest time of it. The mason Juan de Fregenal, who was mentioned earlier in the discussion of employment requirements, had a certain success. After gaining his freedom in 1547, he used his earnings as a mason to branch out into real estate and truck gardening, and his ventures proved profitable enough to allow him to settle a dowry of 400 pesos on his daughter in 1550. By the end of that decade Fregenal "was a fixture in Lima, a man of some wealth, one of the few Negroes who could make a signature (though crudely), and to whose name the Spanish secretaries did not studiously attach the affix 'free Negro.' "[56]

As we have seen in Chapter 6, many Afro-Peruvians, like Fregenal, recognized the potential of the crafts as a career, and despite increasing socioeconomic stratification in later decades, a number of free persons of color led satisfying lives as artisans. For their unskilled brothers, the story was often a less happy one. Adult slaves without a trade who secured their freedom, along with persons of color freed as children but not apprenticed or otherwise provided for, tended to follow the same livelihoods as those in bondage. Women were particularly disadvantaged, since there was little place for them in the skilled trades, but the unskilled of both sexes became servants or agricultural laborers, often in the employ of their former masters, or turned their hands to petty vending and merchandising of various products, along with the loaning of small sums of money, usually to members of the colored community.

Many of those who prospered in such enterprises plowed their profits into land or houses, and into inheritances for children and relatives. For example, the free coloreds Viceroy Cañete had sent into the highlands to mine gold at Carabaya stayed on in the area, but eventually turned to agriculture, buying their own land and in some cases hiring Indian labor, in defiance of royal prohibitions. Free blacks were equally eager to acquire land in the urban areas. In 1595 the free mulata Isabel Jiménez (a native of Trujillo) listed in her will a lot purchased in Lima for 225 pesos some eight months before. Isabel, who was married and who, like many other free blacks, loaned very small amounts of money to others, found little else except some corn to list in her estate, which was bequeathed to her father in Trujillo.[57] Other free persons of color became landlords as well, as in the case of Cristóbal Méndez, who in 1590 rented some houses he owned in the San Sebastián district for a year for eighty-one pesos. In this respect, some blacks overreached themselves. This was true, for example, of Francisco Hernández, a mulatto fisherman, who purchased a lot and house in Lima, already mortgaged to the convent of Santa Clara, for the sum of 2,275 pesos. Unable to meet the mortgage payments out of his earnings, Hernández was forced to default, wound up in jail, ill, and saw his wife left without means of support.[58] In 1615 the free mulata Ana de Guadalupe, a native of Santo Domingo and one of the rare free persons of color able to name both of her parents in her will, had little more to leave than 100 pesos loaned to a black in Pisco and a slave, María Bran, whom she had brought to her husband in dowry. She willed these few possessions to her confraternity, the Dominican-sponsored Nuestra Señora del Rosario, but in a later codicil granted the slave her freedom and left the rest of her estate to her husband.[59]

Free coloreds were especially prominent in the vending and merchandising of a variety of articles and services, and some achieved a degree of success. A free black woman named Catalina de Zorita, for example, owned a bakery and confectionary in Lima in the 1540's and 1550's that was staffed by ten slaves and probably worth several thousand pesos. Catalina, perhaps married to a Spaniard herself, arranged for the marriage of her daughter to a white, accompanied by a handsome dowry, and she was rarely reminded of her color to her face.[60] Francisco de Marchena, one of the most prominent free mulattoes of the early colonial period and a slaveholder himself, petitioned the Lima city council in 1576 for permission to build an inn two leagues outside the city on the road to Cuzco and Potosí, where provisions for travelers and pasture for their horses and mules were scarce. He also asked to be given the use of encomienda Indians to serve in the establishment, in accordance with established practice. In response to the first request the council granted Marchena a license to operate the inn for four years without payment of fees. On the second, he was told that the municipal magistrate in charge of assigning Indian labor would consider his request after construction of the inn had begun.[61]

Free coloreds operated both inns and pulperías throughout the period under study. Some plainly ran these businesses on a shoestring. For example, one mulata, Micaela de Vergara, left barely enough wine on her death to pay for the liquidation of her pulpería and for the care of her two illegitimate children, ages four years and three months, respectively. Much more successful was another free mulata, Magdalena de la Paz, whose free mother lived in Guatemala. Within five years of her own arrival from Seville, Magdalena established a thriving business selling wine, lard, cheese, and other provisions in Chile, Panama, and the highland provinces through various shipmasters and muleteers. She also leased and operated a pulpería in Lima. The bulk of this estate was left to a sister who still resided in Andalusia.[62] Some free persons of color seem to have been engaged in several different enterprises at once, as in the case of Isabel de la Rosa (age twenty-two), who was at pains to mention "her house . . . and her businesses and profits and monies and capital" in a lawsuit that in part concerned her credit.[63]

In most cases, however, there was very little to show for a lifetime of labor. On the whole, free persons of color were as low in the economic scale as they were in the social scale. Most started life with little money and ended it in the same state, with only a few possessions to pass on to their heirs. The free black Martín de Rivadeneira declared in his will of 1640, for example, that he had possessed no worldly goods on the occasion of his marriage, and that he now had a female slave and her ten-year-old child, a horse, his clothing, and 1,300 pesos, which had been loaned to his confraternity of Nuestra Señora de los Reyes for the purchase of a lot and fourteen doors. At the end of her life the free mulata Francisca Ángel could point to little more than her female slave María Mandinga; and in 1573 Ana de Guerra, who noted that she was of Wolof extraction, stated that she and her husband owned a slave, 100 pesos, two horses, and some household effects.[64]

Clearly, modest wealth made for small dowries and inheritances, and thus perpetuated the cycle of economic weakness. In 1643, for example, the free mulatto José de Acuña, married to a slave, inherited the sum of 280 pesos from the estate of his free mother; his father, it appears, remained to the end of his days a slave of the Jesuits.[65] In 1578 the free mulata Ana Pinto (born in Portugal) made small bequests to three black friends and left the rest of her estate—a house—to her son, Blas Hernández, a resident of Potosí. A decade later María de Vargas, also a mulata, willed to her two minor daughters the sum of 180 pesos (to be administered by her sister) plus a modest amount of clothing and household effects.[66]

In many cases, misfortune, bad management, or religiosity dissipated such modest amounts of capital as were accumulated. In her will of 1565, for example, Francisca Rodríguez (mulata and widowed) observed that she had brought a dowry of 1,000 pesos to her penniless husband, and nothing was left now but a slave—who was to be sold to pay for such pitiful bequests as the grant of twelve pesos to her daughter-in-law "in order that she may purchase a skirt." In the same year the mulata Isabel Brava, who had been born in Spain and knew the name of her Spanish father, stated that she had brought the very handsome dowry of 2,500 *pesos ensayados* to her husband (race unspecified), and that he had had no possessions at the time. All that was left was 300 pesos and various personal effects, the whole of which she willed to the Franciscan monastery. Similarly, in 1578 the free woman of color Catalina de Ysasaga (born on Cape Verde) willed her slave to the Indian hospital, "because since I have lived in this city I have dealt with Indians, and for the discharge of my conscience," and left her home to the Augustinian monastery; her personal possessions and some 100 pesos in cash were set aside to pay for her burial.[67] As we have seen in Chapter 9, the Church did not appeal to all Afro-Peruvians, but so many free coloreds were moved to squander their capital on lavish funerals that in 1633 the Lima city council felt compelled to set limits in this regard lest Spaniards bankrupt themselves through imitation.[68]

In the beginning, as Lockhart makes clear, free persons of color exhibited a high degree of solidarity: "Free Negroes formed a coherent group or community, much like the Basques or foreigners, but even more tightly knit. Negroes married within the community, had their closest friends and worst enemies within it, loaned each other money, and preferred to do all kinds of business with each other."[69] To some extent this cohesiveness lasted throughout the colonial period. Many Afro-Peruvians continued to identify themselves as free persons of color and derived a sense of community and even satisfaction from that fact. Further, many free coloreds had close ties with slaves—whether friends or family—a fact that reinforced the Spanish tendency to lump all those of African descent together. Indeed, some Spaniards worried about the separateness of free Afro-Peruvians. One was Father José Tiruel, rector of the Jesuit colegio in Cuzco, who in 1585 expressed to the Crown his dismay at the growing numbers of free blacks, mulattoes, and "many other mixtures of peoples." Most of them, he said, were illegitimate and reared in the presence of vice and licentiousness; tended to make common cause with the Indian in his superstitions and drunkenness; and "in a whole year, except in rare cases, . . . never hear a Mass or a sermon, and thus . . . do not know the law of God." Tiruel warned of the dangers, including insurrection, if this group was permitted to diverge so radically in culture and belief.[70]

As it turned out Tiruel's worst fears were not realized, perhaps because his main concern, the divergence of this group, did not come to pass. Though Church and state often made no great attempt to assimilate those of African descent, free persons of color became more and more Spanish almost by default. There was no other cultural example to order their existence, except that of the despised Indian. Use of the Spanish language was inevitable, if only because it served as the common tongue, and few outstanding differences in dress, housing, or diet separated black from white, however sharp the contrast in the quality of their lives. Indeed, the process of race mixture ensured that many free Afro-Peruvians *were* Spanish, at least in part. Further, the overwhelming preponderance of evidence in surviving documentation, pinpoint in nature but impressive in its constant reiteration, argues that it was the racially mixed who moved upward in Spanish society. This was perhaps because of the paradoxical nature of Spanish racial attitudes: race mixture was regarded with contempt, but the white blood in a mulatto made him more acceptable than a black man. As the process of race mixture in Peru continued and, with it, the almost morbid fascination of society with racial classification, free coloreds came to share this fascination, and to see in it the advancement or frustration of their own ambitions and those of their children. Intelligent free Afro-Peruvians who had accumulated modest fortunes were quick to see that racial solidarity was all very well, but that "whitening" and "passing," culturally if not racially, was the key to socioeconomic advancement. Any sense of community the free coloreds possessed was constantly eroded by their recognition of the value of having ties to those who were lighter or wealthier or better connected than themselves.

Torn by values and ambitions imposed on them by the larger society, many free coloreds were anxious to forget their racial origins or at least to whiten themselves as much as possible. As we saw in Chapter 9, the Jesuit-sponsored confraternity for Afro-Peruvians fragmented on precisely the question of racial and cultural whiteness. Moreover, even free persons who were not of mixed ancestry affected, and perhaps believed in, Spanish ways. Whether they also appreciated the supreme irony of their situation is an open question. One can only speculate, for example, on the feelings of Antón Calderón, a black man of the Soso "caste," who confessed in his will that he did not remember his parents "because I came from Guinea while very young." Antón seems to have lived in two worlds. As "head of the bench of Soso people" (*caporal del banco de gente zoza*) within the Dominican confraternity of Nuestra Señora del Rosario "*de los morenos*," he was reminded of an African past even as he sought in that confraternity an identification with things Spanish. Antón had paid 100 pesos for a burial plot outside the chapel of his confraternity, but in his will requested a resting place within. He owned three slaves. One, Clara Criolla (age ten), he freed outright; but her mother, Isabel Folupa, was only to have her freedom in eight years, and then on condition that she pay four pesos a month over the whole period for Masses for the repose of Antón's soul. The third slave was to be freed if she or a benefactor paid 250 pesos to his executor; otherwise she was to be sold to pay for his burial expenses, bequests, and debts. Antón left a few personal possessions to the child Clara, but his horse and mule were to be sold and the proceeds given to the Dominicans for Masses.[71]

As with the Spanish, deep religious sentiments appear to have been more common among colored women than men, and when words were matched with deeds it is difficult to doubt the sincerity of these convictions. From her pathetic estate, which consisted of nothing more than a female slave, the mulata Francisca Rodríguez willed fifteen pesos to the construction of the church of San Sebastián, and eight pesos each to the Mercedarian Order, the chapel of the municipal jail, the Indian hospital, and the confraternity of La Caridad; the total exceeded the amounts left to her daughter and daughter-in-law combined. The much more prosperous Magdalena de la Paz bequeathed no less than 430 pesos to various churches, hospitals, and convents; 200 went to the convent of Santa Paula in Seville, where Magdalena had been born.[72]

We close with a labor contract of 1600 between Juan Tacuri, an Indian of Huaylas, and the free black María de Angulo, in which Juan agreed to serve María for a year in return for the usual room, board, and clothing; twenty pesos; and instruction "in the things of Our Holy Catholic Faith."[73] It is to be doubted that either of the parties understood the significance of the historical process to which they were tied, and with whose consequences we still live.

CHAPTER TWELVE

Conclusion

In the early colonial period the Africans who came to Peru were regarded by their Spanish overlords as of marginal and transitory importance to the endeavor of conquest and colonization. The Spanish conquerors, accustomed as they were to centuries of slavery, took African slaves along to the new territory without a second thought to serve as useful and trustworthy subordinates, but only until the point of the exercise, the conquest of a numerous Indian population, was accomplished. Thereafter, the black man would be no more than a curiosity, a symbol of material success, just as he was in the courts of Renaissance Italy. But the African was destined to play a much greater role in the development of colonial Peru. The Peruvian conquistadores, like their compatriots in other parts of the New World, prevailed over the Indians only to witness the dismaying decline of the native population, particularly along the Peruvian coast.

For a time, and with the grudging consent of the Crown, Indian labor from the sierra was forced under the mita system both to serve the needs of the expanding agricultural economy of the coast and to exploit the rich highland mines. But by the 1560's it was becoming increasingly clear that the shrinking native labor supply could not meet the demands of both coastal agriculture and highland mining, where falling yields indicated the need of a vastly enlarged work force if royal revenues were to remain constant. In the 1570's it became the distasteful responsibility of Viceroy Francisco de Toledo to allocate the manpower resources of Peru in a way calculated to ensure the continued prosperity of the colony. Toledo began his tenure with the belief that he could limit the extent of African slavery in the colony and at the same time ease the burden of the mita on the Indian, but he ended his term with the knowledge that the scope of both institutions would inevitably increase.

By the time Toledo stepped down as viceroy of Peru, the basic pattern of labor allocation in the colony had been established. Forced Indian labor was increasingly relied on to develop the highlands, and particularly to meet the imperious needs of the mines. At the same time, since the human reserves of the sierra could be stretched only so far, Toledo's successors, with the approval of the Crown, steadily restricted the use of forced Indian labor in the agricultural areas and cities of the Peruvian coast. As the inhabitants of the coast came to appreciate the thrust of government policy the demand for blacks increased dramatically, so much so that a greatly expanded slave trade only slowly brought about a diminution of slave prices in the Peruvian market. In less than fifty years of Spanish rule, the goal of economic development had interacted with the demographic and topographic realities of the colony to transform the black slave into a necessity.

As it happened, the intellectual climate of the time was such that the resulting expansion of the Atlantic slave trade was accepted with complacency. African slavery had been regarded as normal for centuries, and so, too, was the trade in blacks, whether in Arab or Iberian hands. Further, though the slave traffic to Spanish America increased markedly after the middle of the sixteenth century, the rate of increase was slow enough to numb most observers to the horrible fact that the slave trade had become a large-scale enterprise marked by the most flagrant contraventions of the law of nations and Christian morality. The Indian's great champion, Bartolomé de las Casas, who had called for the importation of Africans to spare his native charges, later repented his solution. But he was one of the last Iberians to realize, and shrink back from, the moral implications of widespread use of African labor in the Americas. Those who came after him, even among the religious, had fewer, if any, qualms.

Rather, as the slave trade expanded the Spanish and the Portuguese took increasing comfort in the notion of the inherent inferiority of the African. On this score, it is difficult to strike a balance between genuine belief and the cynical taking of ideological refuge, but there is no disputing the fact that the idea of African inferiority, always vaguely present in the European mind, was given impetus by colonial need for labor.

Further, the notion was given spurious sanction by the ideal of bringing Christianity to the heathen, an aim so indubitably blessed that even the harshest critics of the trade did not question the fundamental correctness of African enslavement under the proper circumstances.

If the steady growth of the African slave trade to Spanish America occasioned few moral reservations, it is nevertheless true that imperial interests caused the Spanish Crown to consider American demand for black labor with mixed emotions. In the first palmy decades after the conquest of the Incas and the Aztecs, the concessions made to Portugal in Africa had been all but forgotten. Even after the demographic catastrophe of the West Indies forced the authorization of direct trade in slaves between Portuguese Africa and Spanish America, this commerce was of minor importance for many years, and was carefully regulated and profitably taxed by the Crown. The American labor crisis of the late sixteenth century, which called for a drastic increase in slave importation to the mainland, was another matter. Fortunately for the American colonists, at almost precisely this point dynastic union brought the Portuguese empire under the indirect control of the Spanish Crown, thereby ensuring that the Portuguese possessions in Africa yielded up more of their inhabitants for the benefit of the Spanish American empire. However, unrestricted commerce in blacks between the two regions was unthinkable to Spanish officials, in large part because the Portuguese merchants who dominated the slave trade demanded payment for their human merchandise in American silver, a commodity that Spain wished to monopolize for the benefit of her own nationals. Therefore, even after the two empires were united in the person of the Spanish king, an expanded Atlantic slave trade was viewed as a necessary evil, as a commerce to be restricted to the bare minimum of blacks necessary for American prosperity.

During most of the period of Luso-Spanish union the government attempted to regulate the slave trade to the American colonies by means of a monopoly contract (asiento), an arrangement in which the holder acted as the Crown's intermediary, selling a specified number of permits to import slaves to the merchants. The Crown, however, effectively scuttled its own efforts, for in its desire to limit the amount of silver that fell into the hands of the Portuguese—who held all the asientos and controlled the sources of slave supply in Africa—it consistently underestimated the American demand for blacks. The result was widespread smuggling of slaves, which legislation and investigation were never able to suppress. If we are to believe the claims of enraged Spanish merchants and bureaucrats, the Portuguese slave traders also took advantage of Spain's growing commercial weakness and stretched their profits through the sale of other contraband. True or not, there is no denying that the Portuguese slavers who operated during the asiento period managed to haul several hundred thousand African slaves across the Atlantic to Spanish America in response to the colonial demand.

Slave traffic along the Pacific coast to Peru was also dominated by Portuguese traders, men who were often tied by family and friendship as well as by nationality to their colleagues who plied the Atlantic. Armed with Peruvian silver, merchants like Manuel Bautista Pérez made their fortunes and spent their lives haggling over the price of human flesh. It would be easy to dismiss these men, whether based in Atlantic or Pacific, with contempt. By modern standards, every aspect of their operations was sordid, from the procurement of slaves on the West African coast to their final sale in America. But these men were products of their time and must be so judged. If the slave merchants destroyed any lingering hopes of a benign relationship between European and African for centuries, it must be kept in mind that this destruction was condoned, even ordered, by their nation states. Moreover, though some slavers were undoubtedly callous toward their black merchandise, others were kind, at least within the limits of the curious relationship between possessor and possessed that few questioned at the time. Whatever their virtues or failings, most were envied and even honored for their acumen, daring, and wealth. Slave merchants performed a function that society regarded as both legitimate and essential; they helped sustain the structure of the Spanish American empire, and if they deserve our moral censure, then so do their customers and the Crown.

Along the Peruvian coast and even in certain areas of the highlands the black man became steadily more important to the economy in the decades after 1580, a development that sharply reduced the need for forced Indian labor. The mita remained a heavy burden on the native population, but Spanish demands for manpower would have been more onerous still without those thousands of blacks in the rural and urban areas of Peru who performed a host of menial and often disagreeable tasks. Indeed, the Spanish Crown was slow to abandon the notion that African manpower could be used to reduce still further, and perhaps even eliminate, the need for forced Indian labor. But the government never quite possessed the courage of its convictions. It was relatively easy to curtail the use of the mita in agricultural enterprises and urban occupations along the coast, which produced little direct revenue for the Crown, and where a very real shortage of Indians gave added force to royal injunctions that African labor be used instead. The mining operations of the highlands, however, were another matter. Locked in an increasingly desperate struggle to preserve the primacy of Spain among European powers, the Crown could ill afford to lose the lucrative revenues in silver that contributed so greatly to its strength. Yet the production of this wealth was dependent on the mining mita, an institution whose oppressiveness could not be ignored. The Crown never resolved the dilemma. On more than one occasion the Spanish kings and their advisers tinkered with various schemes to employ Africans, both slave and free, in the silver mines, but nothing came of these projects. State revenues were always felt to be too precious to be diverted toward this end, and the Crown could never bring itself to compel the colonial mining interests to make the transition to black labor for fear of disrupting the industry. In Peru, as elsewhere in the American empire, the concern of the government for the welfare of the native population was diluted by economic and demographic realities. The African and the Indian both found their place in the economy, but this was due at least as much to the failures of royal labor policy as to its successes.

It is difficult to underestimate the contribution of black labor to the Peruvian economy. African slaves played an important role in agricultural production along the Peruvian coast, and that role may in fact have been underestimated in these pages, since extant documentation is to a certain extent biased in favor of the cities and towns of the colony. Nevertheless, it should be stressed that African slavery in Peru was first and foremost an urban institution centered in Lima, a city with the largest concentration of blacks in the Western Hemisphere in this period with the possible exception of Mexico City. This fact operated in many ways to give a stamp of benignity to Peruvian slavery that extended even to the question of labor. Obviously, society expected the slave to benefit very little, if at all, from his exertions, and most Afro-Peruvians spent their days in the performance of essential but unrewarding tasks, laboring at occupations that offered little hope of advancement even if freedom was achieved. This state of affairs was particularly true of the rural areas, but in the cities there was some demand for skilled and semi-skilled blacks—artisans who were much more versed in Spanish ways than their unskilled fellows of country or village and who were much more aware of the opportunities for freedom and advancement available to them.

Colored artisans were prominent in Peru from a very early date, and though many Spanish craft guilds attempted to freeze skilled blacks at the journeyman level, colonial demand for their services usually frustrated this intention. To be sure, many skilled blacks worked under the close supervision of the white craftsmen who had trained them, but as the apprenticeship system continued to operate in Peru, more and more colored artisans were owned by masters who were interested primarily in their slaves' wages, not in the preservation of Spanish dominance in the crafts. Many slaveholders permitted their skilled blacks to live and work more or less as they chose in return for a share of their earnings, and numbers of colored artisans managed to obtain their freedom in exchange for substantial monetary compensation. Though the skilled blacks represented only a small proportion of the Afro-Peruvian population, they made a significant contribution to the development of the colony. Of equal importance, as the most advantaged and probably the most Hispanicized of the Afro-Peruvians, they provided inspiration and example to other blacks who sought a better future for themselves or for their children.

By and large Peruvian slavery was a profitable institution for Spanish masters, but too much should not be made of this fact. First and foremost slavery in Peru was an economic necessity, but it soon became almost as firmly entrenched in the social sphere as it was in the economy. That is, most Peruvian slaveholders, though they expected to make money or at least to receive their money's worth from the ownership of blacks, did not stop to consider whether their capital could have been invested at a higher rate of return elsewhere. The labor situation in Peru militated against such considerations, and social convention still more so: respectable people were expected to hold slaves. In short slavery was a form of investment, but beyond that it was an unquestioned fact of life and not far short of a social responsibility.

On an individual basis, relations between masters and slaves in Peru were often marked by trust, respect, and even love. In the mass, however, Afro-Peruvians were regarded by many Spaniards as a pack of actual or potential criminals and rebels whose activities had to be carefully regulated to ensure public order and the authority of the state. Spanish fear of the growing Afro-Peruvian population intensified when first the English and then the Dutch demonstrated that Peru was not invulnerable to attack, and that they were prepared to enlist the help of the blacks in their struggle for military advantage. In point of fact criminal activity was probably no more common among Afro-Peruvians than among lower-class Spaniards (though policing the blacks caused endless squabbles among the civil and ecclesiastical agencies, largely because masters persistently intervened to secure lenient treatment for their errant slaves). With few exceptions and despite Spanish anxiety, Afro-Peruvians do not appear to have been sufficiently unhappy with their lot to rebel, and the free coloreds served well during the two serious Dutch threats to the colony in the seventeenth century. It may well be, of course, that the Afro-Peruvians were wise enough to see that a Dutch victory would mean merely the exchange of one master for another, and to settle for the Spanish as a known evil. In any event, and whether we credit the benignity of Peruvian slavery, the sagacity of those who ruled the colony, or the hatred that many Africans of different groups and cultures held for each other, the fact remains that Spanish sovereignty in Peru was never seriously threatened by black insurrection.

In Peru, as elsewhere in Spanish America, flight rather than rebellion was far and away the most common form of slave protest. Indeed, runaway slaves perhaps posed more difficulties for Peruvian law enforcement than all other types of black criminals combined. At any rate the creation of a special institution, the Santa Hermandad, for their apprehension suggests the extent of the problem. For some slaves flight was little more than a symbolic gesture, a confession of despair, and many returned voluntarily or were easily apprehended. Other runaways were more determined, and many banded together in the countryside for companionship and support. In the main these bands were not so much concerned with overthrowing Spanish authority as escaping it, though many slaves were willing to take up arms to resist capture. However, unlike Panama or eastern Mexico, the Peruvian coast afforded little shelter for runaway communities. Consequently, most bands of Peruvian *cimarrones* were small, constantly shifting in both membership and base of operations, and usually forced to resort to robbery to acquire the necessities of life. Such bands were troublesome, but the Hermandad, though hardly a model of efficiency, managed to keep them more or less under control and to maintain a measure of tranquility in the rural areas.

The relatively low level of unrest among Afro-Peruvians may stem in large part from the fact that even in the rural areas conditions under slavery, though often bleak, were rarely grindingly harsh. More often than not black slaves were indifferently fed, clothed, and housed; the medical care was poor; and the threat of the lash was always present. We must remember, however, that this was an age more reconciled to human suffering than our own, and many Afro-Peruvians must have observed that poor whites and mestizos, not to mention the Indians, led equally dismal lives. Further, the Spanish government was officially committed to the semiassimilation of the black population; Afro-Peruvians were to become as Spanish as their color and their degraded secular status would permit. Individual masters and the Church were to be the chief assimilative agents, but with the notable exception of the Society of Jesus, it cannot be said that either approached the task with any marked degree of enthusiasm. Nevertheless, some persons of color were afforded the solace of religion, and others perhaps took comfort in fragments of their African faiths or, like many Spaniards and Indians, fell back on superstitions and witchcraft. To its credit the Church consistently defended the right of the slave to marriage and family life, though slaveholder opposition everywhere and sexual imbalance in the rural areas often made a mockery of these rights and encouraged promiscuity and illegitimate offspring. In short most slaves led a gloomy but not intolerable existence. In this respect Peruvian practice seems to have faithfully mirrored conditions elsewhere in Spanish America, though the distinction between rural and urban areas must be constantly borne in mind.

For the black man there was always the hope of liberation, a goal achieved by a sufficient number of Afro-Peruvians to keep the promise bright in the hearts of most. Some Afro-Peruvians were manumitted by their masters. A spirit of Christian charity and gratitude for faithful service were the most commonly cited reasons for such acts, though some slaveholders may have seen selected manumissions as a useful means of allaying slave discontent. Other slaves were able to purchase their freedom, either with their own earnings or with gift money provided by family, friends, or patrons. Race mixture, the widespread sexual mingling of African, Indian, and Spaniard, played an important role in creating and sustaining a class of free Afro-Peruvians. Spanish males often freed the children they had fathered by slave women; and African males, in imitation of their overlords, sired numerous offspring by Indian women, zambos who were automatically free. It is clear that women and small children were the chief beneficiaries of all forms of manumission, and that adult males of working age were rarely freed, perhaps a reflection of the critical labor situation which prevailed in Peru during most of this period. It is clear also that freedom was a goal most realistically aspired to by urban slaves, blacks who were close to their masters, who had some earning power, and who were aware of their opportunities and privileges. Rural slaves were unlikely to be liberated by masters who scarcely knew them, and in the countryside it was difficult to accumulate the capital to purchase manumission. When it came to liberation, as in so many other aspects of life, urban blacks had a distinct advantage over their rural counterparts.

If the achievement of freedom was a hard task for the Afro-Peruvian, acceptance and advancement were usually more difficult still. Most of the restrictions that applied to the slave population applied also to the free coloreds, and the Crown further presumed to regulate the employment, place of residence, and even the wearing apparel of this group. Further, freedom brought new obligations in the form of tribute payment and militia duty, though the one was often evaded and the other brought some prestige to those who saw service. The free person of color found the burden of slavery lifted, but the weights of color prejudice and presumed bastardy remained. The free coloreds who stood the best chance of overcoming these handicaps were those who had acquired a skill or those whose white fathers managed to give them some advantage. But most free persons of color were unskilled and born into near-poverty, and all too often they remained at or near the bottom of the socioeconomic scale.

Yet over the long haul widespread disadvantage did not serve to create cohesiveness among free Afro-Peruvians. In urban areas, where the great majority of the free coloreds were concentrated, even housing patterns militated against a sense of community. Many free Afro-Peruvians in Lima, for example, were forced to live in the homes of Spaniards, either because of government pressure or because of economic necessity, and others took cheap housing wherever they could find it. As a result some areas of the capital contained more persons of color than others, but the city had nothing approaching a black ghetto, which might have reinforced a sense of separateness. More important, perceptive free persons of color realized that the key to their advancement consisted of their ability to move in the world as Spaniards with dark skins. Spanish culture was therefore the model for most free Afro-Peruvians; emphasis on an African past and identification with the slave population were profitless. Further, many free Afro-Peruvians perceived the peculiar anomaly of Spanish racial attitudes, the officially proclaimed dread of racial mixture that went hand in hand with a greater social acceptance of the mulatto and quadroon than of the "pure" black. In consequence, free Afro-Peruvians attempted to "whiten" themselves culturally and, if possible, to "whiten" their descendants biologically or at least socially through education, the right marriages, and the painful accumulation of property and place within the community.

Thus, under slavery a group of free persons of color existed in Peru whose numbers were swelled century by century through manumission and reproduction and whose strength in relation to the slave population steadily increased. At the twilight of the colonial period in 1792, when Afro-Peruvians accounted for over 7.5 per cent of Peru's population of some 1,076,000 people, free persons of color slightly outnumbered their fellows who remained in slavery.[1] But this same free Afro-Peruvian community was constantly splintered and diminished by those who succeeded in moving into the larger Spanish world. And even those who were forced to remain within the colored community by fiat of social classification could not fail to become more or less Spanish in mentality and outlook, often by dint of much conscious striving. The ambitious person of color simply could not afford the luxury of black solidarity when the rewards for partial assimilation, however illusory or long in coming, seemed so great. For the same reason the bulk of the free Afro-Peruvian population did not hanker for social revolution, and indeed may have constituted one of the most conservative elements of colonial society. In the 1780's, the free colored militia provided most of the troops that suppressed the Túpac Amarú rebellion —the greatest outburst of Indian protest against the Spanish colonial system in centuries—and thirty years later the same units made loyal soldiers for the Crown during the independence struggles.[2] However narrow the tolerances and steep the ascent, the free person of color preferred to make his way within the existing structure of society.

In short, though slavery persisted in Peru for another 200 years or so after 1650, sustained as before by the constant importation of new blacks, by the middle of the seventeenth century the social attitudes that made for the assimilation and near-disappearance of the Afro-Peruvian after abolition had been firmly established.[*] Spanish society did not bother to conceal its contempt for the person of color, whether free or slave, but the Afro-Peruvian and his descendants were also allowed, slowly and painfully, generation by generation, to lay to rest the burden of race.

---

[*] According to the 1876 census of Peru, there were only 44,224 persons of color in a total population of 2,704,998 (1.94 per cent), and by 1940, evidently the last census in which such racial distinctions were made, the percentage had fallen to 0.47: 29,054 Afro-Peruvians in a total of 7,023,111 inhabitants. The remainder of the descendants of Peru's once-numerous colored population had joined the ranks of the nation's "mestizos." Romero, "Slave Trade," p. 378; Mário C. Vázquez, "Immigration," pp. 83-87, 91-95.

Appendixes

The Colored Population of Lima

One of the most difficult aspects of this work has been to find trustworthy statistics on the colored population, and especially for the first half of the sixteenth century. I have used the Lima head-tax revenues to make a crude estimate for 1554.

In 1549, to finance the policing of the black population and the apprehension of runaways, the municipality was permitted to collect a tax of two pesos on each African slave of ten or more years who was then in Lima, and a tax of one peso for younger blacks. All slaves imported into the capital in the future were subject to a four-peso head tax. Masters of slaves then living within municipal boundaries were given nine days to register their blacks and pay the tax, and in the beginning some effort was made to collect this revenue. In 1554, desperate for money to suppress the Hernández Girón rebellion, the Crown borrowed 2,951 pesos from head-tax coffers, and a year earlier the city tapped the fund for 500 pesos to repair the city hall, a sum that was probably never repaid. In addition, between 1549 and 1554 slightly over 126 pesos of this revenue was used to apprehend runaway slaves, and another 460 was disbursed as compensation to the administrators of the tax. From these figures it appears that some 4,036 pesos was paid into the fund between 1549 and 1554. (See AGI, Contaduría 1680, list of money borrowed by the Crown in 1554; and Chapter 8, pp. 187ff, for more details concerning the tax.)

With this total to work with, the problem becomes one of interpretation, and only arbitrary assumptions are possible. I assume here that half of the head-tax revenue came from slave importations during this five-year period for a total of roughly 505 Africans, and that the remainder of the sum came from blacks resident in Lima in 1549. Given the low rate of slave reproduction, I put the number of children under ten, taxed at one peso apiece, at fifty, and divide the remaining 1,968 pesos by the tax rate of two pesos a head for a total of 984 slaves. The results so obtained are summarized as follows:

Slaves imported, 1549-54	505
Slaves ten years of age or older as of 1549	984
Slaves younger than ten as of 1549	50
Approximate total slave population of Lima, 1554	1,539

If anything, this figure is low, but I have made an effort to keep in mind the high rate of slave mortality, the low rate of reproduction, and the possibility that mercantile confidence in the credit of many of the principal colonists may have been undermined by the prolonged strife of the Gonzalo Pizarro rebellion, thereby cutting the volume of the slave trade. In any event an estimated importation of 505 Africans between 1549 and 1555 does not appear unreasonable, and a mass of pinpoint evidence argues that a figure of 1,500 for the colored population of Lima in 1554 is conservative. We may carry this exercise in arbitrary assumptions one step further and postulate that approximately half of the African population of Peru was clustered in the capital, with the balance concentrated mainly along the coast. If this is true, then the number of blacks in the colony as of 1554 would have been some 3,000.

After 1554 the head-tax revenue is useless as an estimate of demographic trends. Until the Crown appropriated the revenue for its own purposes in the seventeenth century, the city collected the impost in the most slipshod fashion. In any case in 1964 I was assured by the personnel of the Lima Municipal Archive that the records of collection had disappeared. Fortunately, population figures from other sources become more plentiful for the late-sixteenth and seventeenth centuries. Available demographic information for regions other than the Lima area is scattered and has been included where appropriate in the text. Statistics and estimates for the viceregal capital are relatively more numerous and, though discussed in various chapters, will be analyzed in more detail here. This information comes from three sources: various chroniclers and observers; enumerations presented by ecclesiastical authorities, which usually were based on parish records; and censuses taken by the civil authorities for various reasons. Data from the last source are scarcer than might be supposed, since the Crown received no revenue from the slave once debarkation duties were collected. Hence, there was no need to determine the number of coloreds in the capital with any frequency, except for the sporadic efforts made to collect tribute from free persons of color. The limited amount of demographic data on this group, both for Lima and other Peruvian towns, is presented in Chapters 10 and 11.

The bulk of the information supplied by chroniclers and observers is vague (e.g., that the Limeños possessed "many" or "numerous" blacks), and when approximate numbers are stated, even careful writers, viewing a city whose population was heavily African, tended to exaggerate the number of persons of color. In the 1570's, for example, Juan López de Velasco, in his *Geografía* (pp. 463-64), put the black population of Lima at 12,000. Antonio de Herrera, in his *Historia* (I: 42), gave the figure of 20,000 for the end of the six-teenth century. In the early part of the seventeenth-century, the anonymous chronicler edited by Boleslao Lewin (*Descripción*, p. 40) estimated that there were 40,000 Africans in Lima; and Antonio Vásquez de Espinosa, in his *Compendium* (p. 428), which chronicles his travels in Spanish America be-tween 1612 and 1621, gave a figure of 50,000. For the mid-seventeenth cen-tury, the observers cited by Ángel Rosenblat, *La población indígena* (I: 225-27), tended to put the number of coloreds in the capital of Peru at 30,000.

Ordinarily, the estimates of civil and ecclesiastical authorities were more exact. The first available calculation, made by Juan Canelas Albarrán in 1586, put the black and colored population of Lima at 4,000, of whom 932 were free, in a total population of 30,000 (Biblioteca Nacional [Madrid], ms. 3178: 9v). The Canelas survey made at the order of Doctor Alonso Criado de Cas-tilla, a member of the Lima Audiencia, took in all the territory from Panama to Chile. The object was to determine the number of tribute-paying Indians, and except for Lima, no numerical distinctions were made between Spaniards, Africans, and the racial mixes. The number of blacks in Lima seems low, despite the sluggishness of the Peruvian slave trade before the 1580's, and the figure for the total population, in comparison with later censuses, seems high. For example, Viceroy Cañete reported to the Crown (Levillier, *Gober-nantes del Perú*, 12: 89) that the terrible epidemics of smallpox and measles of 1588-89 killed 6,000 people in Lima, including many blacks, yet the 1593 census given below showed a substantially higher figure for the slave popula-tion than Canelas's, and a substantially lower figure for the total population. The same holds true when his figures are compared with those of the 1614 census, which also follows. One must conclude that his count was approxi-mate at best.

The next estimate of the African population was provided in a letter from the Archbishop of Lima to the Crown on May 8, 1593 (AGI, Patronato 248.28). Taken from parish records, the number of blacks and mulattoes was set at 6,690 in a total population of 12,790 as follows:

Lima parishes	Blacks/mulattoes	Remainder of population
Cathedral parish (mulattoes: 210)	3,980	4,790
Parish of Santa Ana	1,500	500
Parish of San Sebastián	1,210	810
TOTAL	6,690	6,100

There seems to be little reason to doubt the rough accuracy of these figures, even though they were submitted in an effort to obtain additional parish priests to care for the spiritual welfare of the colored population.

Military considerations inspired a new count of Lima's population in about 1600, as the document's title frankly declared: "General Summation of All the People, Arms, and Horses" (AGIL 34). The following totals were recorded:

Category	Men	Women	Total
Spaniards	3,949	3,244	7,193
Blacks and mulattoes	3,203	3,428	6,621
Indians	306	132	438
TOTAL	7,458	6,804	14,262

Two points need to be made concerning this census. First, colored women were more numerous than men, though some historians have made much of the scarcity of women as a factor in the low rate of slave procreation. Second, it is also clear from this and the data that follow that sexual imbalance had little to do with the low incidence of colored marriages in the urban areas as reported in Chapter 9.

The next census, ordered in 1614 by Montesclaros, revealed the following:

Category	Men	Women	Total
Spaniards	6,165	5,702	11,867
Blacks	4,529	5,857	10,386
Indians	1,116	862	1,978
Mulattoes	326	418	744
Mestizos	97	95	192
TOTAL	12,233	12,934	25,167

This census (which is printed in Vargas Ugarte, *Biblioteca Peruana*, 1: 292-93; and in Salinas y Córdova, *Memorial*, p. 245) is interesting on several counts. First, we see here an even greater predominance of colored women over men than in 1600. Second, the number of mulattoes and mestizos is impossibly low, indicating that many members of these two groups were "passing" as Spaniards. Third, though the number of Indians is up sharply from the 1600 count, this is only because the natives, concentrated in their own district called the Cercado, were not considered a part of Lima proper in many censuses (see Escobar Gamboa and Cook). Finally, this census, like others, fails to mention a not inconsiderable number of Oriental slaves, usually called *esclavos chinos*, who found their way to Lima via trade with Mexico and Manila. The Crown frowned on this traffic in Asian slaves, but notarial records show that many of them were sold on the Lima market anyway, suggesting that royal efforts to ban such commerce met with little success.

An ecclesiastical enumeration was submitted by the Archbishop of Lima five years later, in 1619, which gave the following for Lima (AGIL 301):

Parish	Spanish/mestizos Men	Spanish/mestizos Women	Blacks Men	Blacks Women	Mulattoes Men	Mulattoes Women	Indians Men	Indians Women
Cathedral	3,563	2,069	4,260	3,604	251	370	543	352
Santa Ana	1,129	816	962	1,062	97	101	109	211
San Sebastián	574	783	489	674	110[a]	141[a]	63	58
San Marcelo	462	310	424	522	52	34	40	30
TOTAL	5,728	3,978	6,135	5,862	510	656	755	651

[a] The mulatto count for San Sebastián parish was made without distinction as to sex; I have divided the total, 251, roughly in accordance with the sexual distribution found in the other parishes, i.e., 44 per cent men and 56 per cent women.

Note the total population here of 24,275 as compared to the 30,000 figure Canelas calculated for 1586.

The final estimate that has come to light for Lima during the period was the one the Archbishop of Lima submitted to Viceroy Chinchón and also forwarded in a letter to the Crown in 1636 (AGIL 47). As in 1593, the figures were prepared with a view to bringing in additional parish priests to work exclusively among the colored population. The following figures were submitted:

Category	Men	Women	Total
Blacks	6,544	7,076	13,620
Spaniards	5,109	5,649	10,758
Indians	812	614	1,426
Mulattoes	276	585	861
Mestizos	142	235	377
Chinese	22	—	22
TOTAL	12,905	14,159	27,064

To these numbers must be added 330 religious for a total population of 27,394 people.

Though this count indicated the mulatto population declined between 1619 and 1636, this was surely not the case. Rather the 1636 estimate reflects the efforts of the free coloreds to avoid the payment of tribute. As in previous censuses, the above figures are no doubt based on the records of Lima's four parishes and do not include many persons of color who worked the chácaras on the outskirts of the capital. It therefore seems reasonable to assign to metropolitan Lima a total colored population of some 20,000 persons as of 1640. If we further assume, somewhat arbitrarily, that two-thirds of the persons of color in the colony were concentrated in Lima, then Peru had somewhere in the neighborhood of 30,000 persons of African descent in 1640.

⊷⧉⊶

Lima Slave Prices, 1560-1650

The graphs and tables of Lima slave prices reproduced in this appendix, and extensively referred to in Chapter 3, are based on an examination of 273 registers of notaries active in the city in the sixteenth and seventeenth centuries (see list in Bibliography, pp. 420-21). A sample of slave prices was taken for five-year intervals beginning with the year 1560, except in the case of certain periods in the sixteenth century (e.g., 1564-66) when the paucity of surviving documentation argued for an examination of notarial registers on both sides of the key year in order to obtain a larger number of slave transactions. When this device was employed, the variation in slave prices from year to year was not great enough to distort the composite average to any significant degree. As a further test of representativeness, I took two separate samples for each interval in the period: one in the summer of 1968, the other in the summer of 1969. The results of the two were compared, and the graphed prices are presumed to be accurate within a range of ±30 pesos for any given interval, with perhaps a slightly greater margin of error for the period before 1580. A total of 5,753 transactions involving 6,890 slaves were studied. These break down by intervals as follows:

Interval	Transactions	Slaves	Interval	Transactions	Slaves
1560-62	210	276	1605	297	360
1564-66	225	239	1610	275	318
1568-73	241	259	1615	278	298
1575-77	205	211	1620	514	650
1578-79	122	129	1625	407	551
1580-82	119	132	1630	414	519
1585	256	269	1635	426	636
1589-91	276	301	1640	386	468
1595	355	425	1645	243	271
1600	261	310	1650	243	268
				5,753	6,890

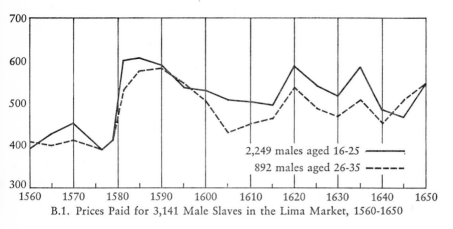

B.1. Prices Paid for 3,141 Male Slaves in the Lima Market, 1560-1650

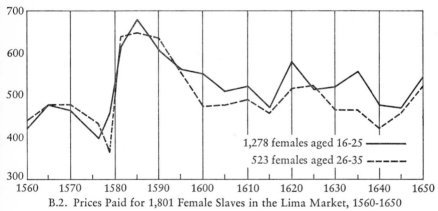

B.2. Prices Paid for 1,801 Female Slaves in the Lima Market, 1560-1650

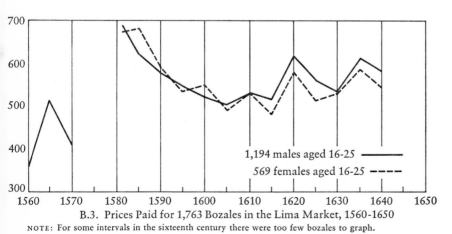

B.3. Prices Paid for 1,763 Bozales in the Lima Market, 1560-1650

NOTE: For some intervals in the sixteenth century there were too few bozales to graph.

TABLE B.1. *Average Price of Slaves Aged 8-15 Sold in the Lima Market, 1585-1645 (pesos of 8 reales)*

	Bozales		Ladinos/Criollos		All slaves 8–15	
Year	Males (149)	Females (124)	Males (117)	Females (63)	Males (341)	Females (226)
1585	—	529.5	—	—	—	466
1589-91	461	541	299	—	429	540
1595	442	495	395	337.5	429	476
1600	457	508	315	—	398	503
1605	423	454	331	530	373	462
1610	499	—	380	306	430	411
1615	430	—	311	260	366	270
1620	470	526	380	410	424	497
1625	443	422	267	301	378	394
1630	441	460	264	282	371	380
1635	464	516	251	220	384	458
1640	437	410	228	276	298	312
1645	—	—	—	342	—	336

NOTE: The vast majority of the slaves not specifically identified as bozales or ladinos/criollos appear to have been African–born, but the extent of their acculturation was not given in the bill of sale. Occasionally, the term *entre bozal y ladino* was used in these documents to designate slaves who had partly accustomed themselves to Spanish ways, but there are too few cases to put in a separate category. In general, it is clear from this table and the ones that follow that even if all blacks of uncertain category were presumed to be ladinos/criollos, the results would be the same: bozales almost always brought higher prices. Observe, however, that this is truer of males than of females, perhaps because the latter were mostly household servants and performed tasks that made a certain degree of acculturation desirable.

TABLE B.2. *Average Price of Slaves Aged 16-25 Sold in the Lima Market, 1560-1650 (pesos of 8 reales)*

	Bozales		Ladinos/Criollos		All slaves 16–25	
Year	Males (1,194)	Females (569)	Males (385)	Females (282)	Males (2,249)	Females (1,278)
1560-62	355	403	385	409	394	416
1564-66	515	—	395	546	427	479
1568-73	409	414	484	465	454	463
1575-77	—	431	377	375	386	397
1578-79	—	—	367	474	412	456
1580-82	690	672	510	694	604	614
1585	627	684	625	648	609	681
1589-91	583	581	586	644	588	605
1595	550	537	557	727	537	563
1600	522	554	555	473	532	553
1605	507	493	574	580	506	507
1610	534	534	438	559	504	519
1615	518	483	444	462	494	473
1620	620	583	479	566	588	584
1625	561	513	487	472	543	510
1630	539	537	454	509	516	516
1635	617	593	425	462	585	558
1640	580	546	363	438	484	471
1645	—	—	417	451	468	471
1650	687.5	—	522	541	550	543

TABLE B.3. *Average Price of Slaves Aged 26-35 Sold in the Lima Market, 1560-1650 (pesos of 8 reales)*

Year	Bozales Males (154)	Bozales Females (67)	Ladinos/Criollos Males (235)	Ladinos/Criollos Females (193)	All slaves 26–35 Males (892)	All slaves 26–35 Females (523)
1560-62	—	—	439	471	410	436
1564-66	321	—	373	539	401	480
1568-73	458	—	454	449	412	477
1575-77	—	—	435	544	386	429
1578-79	406	—	419	444	412	364
1580-82	708	—	573	641	533	638
1585	—	637	547	689	576	648
1589-91	591	569	649	664	581	634
1595	519	562	569	572	546	557
1600	579	542	478	511	504	471
1605	458	510	443	475	430	479
1610	550	552	462	585	454	490
1615	516	513	462	521	465	457
1620	599	606	547	518	543	516
1625	506	490	558	566	490	521
1630	513	533	401	455	469	462
1635	595	588	472	455	508	465
1640	575	—	397	443	447	417
1645	—	—	460	443	483	461
1650	—	—	504	548	552	524

TABLE B.4. *Average Price of Prime Slaves Sold With or Without Guarantees in the Lima Market, 1560-1650 (pesos of 8 reales)*

Year	Slaves sold with guarantees against defects Males 16–25 (706)	Males 26–35 (459)	Females 16–25 (526)	Females 26–35 (309)	Slaves sold without guarantees and/or with specific defects Males 16–25 (349)	Males 26–35 (249)	Females 16–25 (183)	Females 26–35 (131)
1560-62	397	406	392	438	395	432	444	—
1564-66	453	386	466	520	410	377	468	353
1568-73	481	427	476	460	356	354	418	379
1575-77	413	383	433	509	349	367	350	346
1578-79	428	464	451	—	370	298	500	439
1580-82	586	560	663	729	481	524	541	581
1585	618	581	717	665	556	550	606	598
1589-91	625	614	623	645	503	554	606	577
1595	560	570	630	560	521	528	622	514.5
1600	553	480	563	468	501	441	484	386
1605	529	424	543	483	458	392	466	478
1610	516	467	528	496	443	414	469	443
1615	494	482	481	435	418	356	398	424
1620	534	531	588	491	457	495	527	470
1625	496	478	506	525	442	454	425	—
1630	506	410	508	474	403	401	477	319
1635	484	467	498	474	444	426	473	371
1640	441	465	466	439	347	376	386	372
1645	496	523	490	498	445	453	455	426
1650	589	614	543	605	520	505	544	474

African Ethnic Names

Nomenclature of the period	Modern name of ethnic or cultural group(s)	Geographical location
Alonga (Longo)	Bakongo subgroup of Sorongo	Central and southern Africa
Anchico	Tio or Teke	Southern Congo-Brazzaville
Arara (Arda)	Fon, Gun, and related peoples; also Ardra?	Coastal Dahomey
Bañol	Banyun	Guinea-Buissau
Berbesi	Serer	Senegal
Biafara	Biafada	Guinea-Buissau
Bioho	Bissago	Guinea-Buissau
Bleblo	Bobo?	Windward Coast
Bran	Bram, Gola, Burama	Guinea-Buissau
Caravali	Ibo or Ijo; or possibly Efik, Ibibio, or Moko	Eastern Nigeria
Casanga	Kassanga	Casamance and Guinea-Buissau
Cocoli	Kotokoli, Tem	Bight of Benin
Congo	Bakongo and peoples from same area	Lower Congo River Basin
Fula	Fulbe	Hinterland of the Senegambia
Jolofo (Gelofe)	Wolof	Senegal
Mandinga	Malinke	Gambia Valley
Mozambique	——	Southeastern Africa generally
Nalu	——	Guinea-Buissau
Soso	Susu	Guinea-Conakry
Terranova	——	East Guinea coast generally?
Zape	Landuma, Baga, Temne, and related peoples	Coastal Sierra Leone

Much of the above information is drawn from Curtin, *Atlantic Slave Trade*; and Sandoval, *De instauranda*.

Glossary

Alcabala. Sales tax.

Alcalde de la Hermandad. Peace officer and magistrate who headed the *Santa Hermandad,* q.v.

Alcalde del crimen. Judge of the criminal branch of the *Audiencia,* q.v.

Alcalde ordinario. Municipal magistrate.

Alguacil del campo. Deputy constable in the rural areas.

Alguacil mayor. Chief constable.

Alguacil menor. Deputy constable.

Almojarifazgo. Customs duty.

Asentista. Holder of an *asiento,* q.v.

Asesor. Legal adviser.

Asiento. Long-term contract granted by the Crown to a company or individual giving a monopoly on sale of slave licenses.

Audiencia. High court of justice and governing body under the viceroy within the area of its jurisdiction.

Avenças. Agreements for slave exportation concluded between Portuguese revenue collectors for West Africa and slave traders.

Avería. Export-import tax to defray the costs of the armed escort for the merchant fleet plying the Seville-Spanish America route.

Avería de los negros bozales. Term used for the head tax collected on slaves imported into Lima.

Botija. Wine jug.

Bozal. Slave newly arrived from Africa, presumably with no knowledge of the Spanish language, religion, or customs.

Cabildo. Municipal council.

Cacique. Indian chief or local ruler.

Carbonería. Charcoal-making plant.

Carbonero. Charcoal-maker.

Carta de alquiler. Employment contract; rental agreement.

Carta de dote. Dowry contract.

Chácara. Truck garden, small farm.

Chasquis. Indian mail couriers.

Cimarrón. Runaway slave.

Cofradía. Religious brotherhood.

Corregidor de indios. Royal official in charge of an Indian district with authority similar to a governor.

Corregimiento. Indian district.

Criollo. As used in this book, slave born under Spanish or Portuguese masters; often modified to indicate area or town of birth, e.g., Criollo de Lima.

Cuadrilleros. Law officers charged with the apprehension of runaway slaves.

Derecho de unión de armas. Sales tax imposed to support the galleons that protected the transatlantic trade route.

Encomendero. Possessor of an *encomienda,* q.v.

Encomienda. Grant of Indian labor and tribute, later modified to include tribute payments only; area of the Indians granted.

Esclavos Gelofes (Wolofs). African ethnic group alleged to be Islamic and insubordinate.

Fe de entrada (fes). Official certification that a slave was legally imported under the *asiento* (q.v.) with the proper duties paid.

Feria de los negros. Slave sale.

Fiador. Bondsman.

Forastero. Indian who abandoned his traditional land and village.

Grumete. Cabin boy.

Juro. Government bond secured by a specific revenue.

Ladino. Slave of African descent but with some knowledge of the Spanish language and customs.

Lançados. See *tangomaos.*

Limeño. Resident of Lima.

Mestizo. Person of mixed white and Indian ancestry.

Mita (repartimiento). System of forced Indian labor for wages.

Mitayo. Indian who performed *mita* (q.v.) service.

Mochileros. Black or mulatto agents who procured slaves for the *tangomao* (q.v.) middlemen of Guinea.

Njimbu. See *zimbo.*

Obraje. Textile mill.

Oidor. Judge of the *Audiencia,* q.v.

Panos. Palm-leaf cloth used as a medium of exchange for slaves in Angola.

Pardo. Mulatto.

Peso. See Author's Note, pp. xiii-xiv.

Pombeiros (pumbeiros). Black or mulatto agents who procured slaves for the Portuguese in Angola.

Probanza. Proof of services.

Pulpería. Small shop combining functions of grocery store, delicatessen, and tavern.

Pulpero. Operator of a *pulpería.*

Regidor. Town councilman.

Repartimiento. See *mita.*

Santa Hermandad. Rural constabulary.

Sayal. Coarse woolen cloth.

Tacha. Physical or moral blemish of a slave.

Tangomaos. Adventurers who controlled much of the barter and procurement of slaves in the Guinea area; also called *lançados.*

Tiangues. Native market.

Tienda. Shop, store.

Tumbeiros. Literally, "coffins"; term applied to the slave ships of the period.

Villa. A municipal corporation one step below the city; many Spanish communities in Peru were organized as *villas.*

Yanaconas. Indian servant class since Inca times, without village ties and not subject to the *encomienda* and *mita* (q.v.) systems.

Zambaigo. Person of mixed African and Indian blood; term came to be shortened to *zambo.*

Zimbo (njimbu). Cowrie shell used as medium of exchange for slaves in Angola.

Notes

Notes

In the Notes I have abbreviated *legajos* (bundles of papers) and *pliegos* (sheets of paper folded four ways and numbered on each side) leg. and pl., respectively; and I have treated folios exactly as I have treated pages, so that all numbers following a colon are pages or folios as the case may be. Rather than list the essentially meaningless names of individual notaries over and over in citing documents in their records, I have assigned each of them a number, based on the order in which they are listed in the Bibliography, pp. 420-21. Accordingly, a note reading SN 13 (1565): 45r, refers to fol. 45r in the records of the notary Juan Tomino García for the year 1565. As the SN indicates, these records are housed in the Sección Notarial of the Archivo Nacional del Perú in Lima. Most works are cited in short form here; complete authors' names, titles, and publication data are given in the Bibliography. Other abbreviations used in these Notes are:

AGI	Archivo General de Indias (Seville)
AGIC	AGI, Contaduría
AGIJ	AGI, Justicia
AGIL	AGI, Audiencia de Lima
AHU	Arquivo Histórico Ultramarino (Lisbon)
ANP	Archivo Nacional del Perú
CDII	*Colección de documentos inéditos . . . Indias*
CDIU	*Colección de documentos inéditos . . . Ultramar*
Concurso/ Pérez	ANP, Tribunal de la Inquisición, "Concurso de acreedores de Don Manuel Bautista Pérez, mercador de negros" *(legajos)*. Similarly, Concurso/Silva for the records on Domingo de Silva.
DGG	"Data de los gastos de la guerra"
LCL	*Libros de cabildos de Lima*
RA/PC	Archivo Nacional del Perú, Real Audiencia and Procedimientos Civiles section
RANP	*Revista del Archivo Nacional del Perú*

CHAPTER ONE

1. The latest and most reliable estimates of the volume of the African slave trade to Europe and America are contained in Curtin, *The Atlantic Slave Trade.* As summarized on p. 268, these estimates for the years 1451-1870 place the number of slaves imported at 9,566,100, of whom 1,552,100 were destined for Spanish America.

2. I rely here on Vicenta Cortés, *La esclavitud en Valencia durante el reinado de los Reyes Católicos,* and on the studies of Charles Verlinden, esp. *L'esclavage dans l'Europe médiévale, 1: Péninsule Ibérique-France.* Much information from Verlinden's researches is summarized in David Brion Davis, *The Problem of Slavery in Western Culture,* pp. 29-61, 91-121 *passim.* On Spain and the trans-Saharan trade in African slaves, see Antonio Rumeu de Armas, *España en el Africa Atlántica,* 1: 163-66.

3. Pike, *Aristocrats,* p. 174.

4. I follow here the conservative estimate of Curtin, pp. 15-21, who thinks that some 50,000 slaves were transported from Africa to Europe during the entire period of the trade. It should be noted, however, that other careful scholars argue for higher figures. For example, Boxer, *Portuguese Seaborne Empire,* p. 31, states that in West Africa "something like 150,000 Negro slaves were probably secured by the Portuguese between 1450 and 1500."

5. Blake, pp. 41-56; Parry, *Spanish Seaborne Empire,* pp. 46-47.

6. On the introduction of African slavery in America, see Instructions to Nicolás de Ovando, gov. of the Indies, Granada, 16 Sept 1501, in *CDII,* 31: 23; Herrera (1934), 1: 142; and Lamb, p. 178. According to Ortiz Fernández, *Hampa afro-cubana,* p. 65, the license rule was applied to blacks in 1513, at which time a head fee of 2 ducats was imposed along with customs duties of 7 reales.

7. Sauer, pp. 200-207; Pike, *Enterprise,* pp. 57-59.

8. On African slavery in Panama in the early 16th century, see Castillero C.; Mellafe, *Introducción,* pp. 27-30; Meléndez Chaverri, p. 388; Herrera (1934), 6: 93, 8: 106; and Saco, p. 177.

9. W. H. Prescott, *History of the Conquest of Peru,* remains the most useful account of the exploits of Pizarro and his associates. See also Meza Villalobos, pp. 17-18; Mellafe, *Diego de Almagro,* pp. 35-36, 83ff; and Góngora. On the blacks accompanying him, see J. T. Medina, *Descubrimiento,* 2: 384-89; and Herrera (1934), 7: 447-48. At least one black was less faithful to the Spanish. In 1528 he escaped from one of the vessels along the Ecuadorian coast, swam ashore, and ingratiated himself into an Indian community, which he subsequently organized into bitter opposition to the Spanish. It was not until his death in 1535 that 2 Spanish friars were able to pacify the area. See Murphy, p. 16.

10. Slave licenses issued during the conquest and civil war periods in Peru are generally in chronological order in the registers in AGIL 565-67, 578, and scattered permits are also in AGIL 1628. The registers of 565 for the years

1529-38 have been published as *Cedulario del Perú*, by Porras Barrenechea. On the movement of African slaves from Seville to America, see Pike, *Aristocrats*, pp. 174-76. A few so-called *esclavos blancos* were also imported during this period, the majority Moorish and Morisco slaves. See Lockhart, pp. 196-98, for an excellent discussion of this group.

11. Porras Barrenechea, 2: 157-58, 228-29.

12. Lockhart, pp. 172-76, states that "not all Negroes in Peru came directly from Africa. A significant minority were born in Spain and Portugal." But his evidence is not entirely convincing. He bases his opinion on a sample of notarial registers for Lima and Arequipa during the years 1548-60, which revealed the approximate origins of 256 Afro-Peruvians. Of this number, 49 were called creoles, that is, born in Spain, Portugal, Spanish America, or the various islands off the coast of Africa where the Portuguese and Spanish were established. Lockhart correctly asserts that "Though much is hidden behind the all-inclusive term 'creole,' it appears that very few Negros *born* in other parts of the Indies ever reached Peru" (italics mine). What we do not know, however, is how many of the other 207 slaves in the sample were *bozales*, i.e., new arrivals from Africa, as distinct from *ladinos*, slaves of some experience in the Indies who presumably spoke Spanish. This distinction is crucial, since it would have been perfectly logical for black slaves whose surnames identified their African origin to have been taken first to (say) Hispaniola and to have served there for a number of years before coming to Peru. That is, it is not enough to separate the creoles from the African-born; one must also divide the second category into those sold as bozales in a given colony, which implies direct importation from Africa, and those sold as ladinos. The ladinos may well have preserved the surname that indicated African birth, but this does not prove direct importation from that continent to Peru or any other colony.

Further, it is difficult to believe that the volume of the slave trade between Africa and Peru before 1560 was sufficiently high to have made bozales preponderant in the colony. My own samplings of slaves sold in Lima during 1560-62 show a total of 70 bozales among 276 blacks offered for sale; the sample for 1564-66 yields 23 bozales out of a total of 239 slaves. By this date, of course (and as Lockhart indicates), a generation of Peruvian-born blacks would have reached salable age, perhaps reducing a still-modest demand for slaves and therefore momentarily cutting direct importation from Africa.

13. AGI Patronato 28.57, "Viaje de don Pedro de Alvarado al Perú, 1532" (*sic*); Saco, p. 165.

14. AGI Charcas 44. See also Saco, p. 166; Díaz Soler (1953), pp. 47-50; and Larrazábal Blanco, pp. 35-36. As early as 1526, no doubt in response to a similar exodus to Mexico, the Crown forbade Spaniards to leave the Antilles for the mainland under pain of death, but the decree could not be enforced. See Ortiz Fernández, *Hampa afro-cubana*, p. 4.

15. Levillier, 2: 404-5; Lockhart, pp. 171-72.

16. Mellafe, *Introducción*, pp. 42-50.

17. *Ibid.*, pp. 33-34.

18. Lockhart, pp. 199-205.

19. See *ibid.*, pp. 205-20, for a good account of Indian tribute and labor obligations under the encomienda in the early decades of Spanish Peru.

20. AGIL 205, where there are two documents on African participation during the Inca revolt. The first concerns the proof of the services of one Martín González de Pedraza, who claimed to have led a force of blacks on foraging expeditions from Lima when the city was under siege by Manco's forces. González also claimed to have commanded a group of blacks on a similar mission in the Cuzco area in 1537 during the civil war between Pizarro and Almagro. The second document was presented by the natives of the Atunxauxa region, who stated that they contributed provisions to the "many" blacks on the relief expedition Pizarro sent to lift the Inca siege of Cuzco.

21. For example, at a 1535 meeting of the Lima city council cryptic mention was made of an existing ordinance, never enforced, that "for certain reasons" barred blacks from entering the colony. The council members, appreciating that the Indian population was in revolt and that blacks were needed for service, suspended the ordinance until such time as the move was warranted. I have found no other reference to date the origin of this regulation, but it was never reinstated. *LCL*, 1: 24.

22. Lockhart, pp. 53, 171-72, 181. A minor incentive for investment in blacks was the fact that the Crown routinely exempted from seizure for debt a varying number of slaves possessed by conquistadores, in addition to such equipment as arms, horses, and bedding. The intent of such exemptions was to stimulate the pace of American conquest. In later years similar legislation was applied to such key industries as mining and sugar cultivation to prevent undue disruption of operations. See Porras Barrenechea, 1: 177-78, 2: 366; Encinas, 2: 99; AGIL 569.13: 147, decree of 3 Aug 1570; and AGIL 579.4: 131-151, decree of 3 Dec 1576, with references to earlier legislation of 1529 and 1572.

23. Clemence, *Harkness Calendar*, p. 97; Barriga, *Mercedarios*, 2: 184-88; AGIC 1680, "Cargo de los pesos de oro que recibió . . . de los depósitos y emprestidos para los gastos de la guerra que se hizo contra Francisco Hernández Girón . . . ," entry of 14 Feb 1554.

24. Lockhart, p. 181; AGIL 1621, proof of services of Juan de Pancorvo, Cuzco (1541). Also valuable in this respect are the wills edited by Urteaga; see his "Conquistador," "Don Diego," and "Cristóbal de Burgos."

25. On these events, see Prescott; and Means, pp. 78-102.

26. Lockhart, p. 172.

27. Levillier, 1: 33-34. See also Herrera (1934), 14: 211; and Angulo, p. 109.

28. Herrera (1934), 16: 15-18. According to Gutiérrez de Santa Clara, 2: 177-78, a reconnaissance party sent by Pizarro before the battle apprehended and hanged one Rafael Vela, alleged to be a mulatto relative of the viceroy.

29. AGIJ 451, "Residencia tomada de los Licenciados Diego Vázquez de Cepeda, Pedro Ortiz de Zárate, Alonso Álvarez, y Lisón de Tejada, oidores de esta real audiencia, por el Licenciado Pedro de la Gasca, presidente [de la]

misma audiencia [1549]": 268v-269r, 319v, 399r, 455v, 1765. See also Angulo, pp. 110-11. Herrera (1726), década 7: 59, disapprovingly notes that blacks and Indians engaged in a similar massacre after the battle of Chupas.

30. AGIC 1679-80, which contain a number of documents relating to an audit of the expenditures made to equip the royal army. None of these documents is numbered, making a more complete citation impossible. On the black artisan class in this early period, see Lockhart, pp. 182-84, 193-96; and the discussion in Chapter 6, following, pp. 125-46.

31. On the practice under Pizarro, see AGIJ 451, the case cited in note 29 above, fol. 285r. For examples of blacks auctioned for the benefit of the Crown, see various accounts in AGIC 1680.

32. Mellafe, *Introducción*, p. 42.

33. The quotation comes from Herrera (1934), 17: 402, who sets the number of blacks at 250. Garcilaso de la Vega, 3: 131-32, 171, closely parallels Herrera's account but assigns a higher figure. In AGIL 1633, a copy of a letter written to the Crown by a judge of the Lima Audiencia on 25 Oct 1554 puts the number of blacks serving with Hernández at 200.

34. AGIC 1680, list of expenditures made by the treasurer Sancho de Ugarte, 3 and 25 June 1554; Saco, pp. 207-8; Biblioteca Nacional (Madrid), mss. 2010, tomo 4, año de 1610, fols. 148v-49r, "Memorial de los pretensores . . . ," which contains an old proof of services of Francisco de Trigueros, who served at the time with his "person, arms, horse, and slaves."

35. See the examples provided by Lohmann Villena, *RANP* 16: 88, 193-94; and Clemence, *Harkness Calendar*, pp. 1-92 *passim*.

36. The associate died in the middle of his dealings, leaving the bulk of the goods to be sold at auction. See AGIL 566.4: 309v-10r, decree of 4 Apr 1542, on the recovery of the proceeds.

37. Bertram Lee, pp. 228-29. From the will of the viceroy's brother printed therein, it is clear that the 60 slaves requested by Núñez Vela had arrived by 1546, but both these and the other blacks who belonged to the pair were scattered and dispersed among their enemies. See also AGIL 566.6: 291v-93v; AGIJ 451, "Residencia" (as in note 29): 138; Gutiérrez de Santa Clara, 1: 362-63.

38. Lockhart, pp. 83-84.

39. *Ibid.*, pp. 176-78.

40. Clemence, *Harkness Calendar*, pp. 1-92 *passim*; Lohmann Villena, "Indice," *passim*. Clemence, p. 9, records a 1533 transaction that involved "100 branded slaves," but it is unclear if they were Africans or Indians.

41. Levillier, 2: 31; Lockhart, p. 179. Scattered data I gathered in AGIC 1680 on slaves bought and sold by the Crown during the 1550's, including blacks who had formerly belonged to the partisans of Gonzalo Pizarro, are in rough agreement with Lockhart's findings for that decade.

42. Lewin, *Descripción*, p. 40.

43. The debate over Spanish title to the American possessions and the Crown's responsibility to the native inhabitants has been explored by several

writers, among them Lewis Hanke and Silvio Zavala. Parry, *Spanish Seaborne Empire*, pp. 389-90, provides a good bibliography of the subject.

44. See Haring, pp. 55-59, for a discussion of the events that led to the promulgation of the New Laws, their reception in the American colonies, and their subsequent modification.

45. Lockhart, pp. 199-205. However, the notarial records of the period make clear that in subsequent years the continuing conflicts with the Araucanians in Chile provided Peru with a trickle of Indian slaves captured in supposedly just wars. See also Mellafe, *Introducción*, pp. 122-31.

46. My discussion of Indian tribute and labor in Peru during this period is based mainly on Rowe, "The Incas," pp. 159-61; Lockhart, pp. 205-8, 217, 219, 229-30; Belaúnde Guinassi; Basadre, pp. 325-64; and Wiedner. For a good survey of the origins and spread of the encomienda system throughout Spanish America, based on the latest research, see Parry, *Spanish Seaborne Empire*.

47. Lockhart, p. 185.

48. Levillier, 1: 90-91, Núñez Vela to Crown, 15 Feb 1544.

49. AGIJ 451, "Residencia" (as in note 29 above). The colonists' argument against the employment of African slaves comes from a document (ca. 1545-46) entered as testimony: "Instrucción de lo que se ha de suplicar a Su Majestad por los procuradores de los reinos y provincias del Perú es lo siguiente," fol. 725v.

50. Biblioteca Nacional (Lima), ms. A127, "Correspondencia de Pedro de la Gasca (1547-1549): Copied under the superintendence of Don Pascual de Gayangos from the originals in the archives of the Counts of Cancelada, 1860," letter to the President of the Council of the Indies, Cuzco, 3 May 1548; Archivo Histórico Nacional (Madrid), Sección de Diversos, Documentos de Indias, doc. no. 77, Gasca letter to same, ca. 1548-49.

51. AGIL 118, Cáceres to Crown, Lima, 20 Feb 1551.

52. Levillier, 2: 425.

53. AGIL 118, "Relación por el señor secretario Francisco de Eraso sacada de las dos que yo dí al virrey don Antonio de Mendoza. . . ." An undated copy; the original was probably prepared in 1552.

54. My information on this investigation comes from Mellafe, *Introducción*, pp. 60-65, 257-59.

55. Soria's calculated maintenance cost of 647 pesos broke down this way: 12 per cent interest on purchase price of slave couple, 96 pesos; food, 202 pesos; insurance against death or sickness, 56 pesos, and against runaways, 37 pesos; salaries of a Spanish foreman and two assistants, 117 pesos; tools and equipment, 100 pesos; clothing and other maintenance, 24 pesos; and 2 per cent charge at the mint on the ore the slave couple extracted. These figures are clearly inflated. The Crown could have purchased blacks for cash and eliminated interest expense. The insurance that Soria regarded as commonplace in Spain was never written on a large scale in Peru, and the salaries paid to Spanish personnel probably would not have varied regardless of the labor employed.

In addition, the mint charges went to the Crown and therefore cannot be regarded as expenses in a strict sense.

56. Levillier, 1: 291, 317-18, Cañete to Crown, 15 Sept 1556 and 8 Dec 1557.

57. AGIC 1680, list of expenditures for 1557, entry of 30 Oct. These 16 blacks were probably freed from Lima jails on condition that they colonize in Carabaya.

58. Lockhart, p. 192; López de Velasco, p. 487.

59. Lockhart, pp. 31, 199-200, 207-8, 219-20.

60. Von Hagen, pp. 300-302, 308, 320-21, 323-27, 330, 346-50.

61. In addition to Von Hagen, this paragraph relies on Rowe, "Inca Culture," pp. 184-85; Kubler, pp. 334-40; Noble Cook; Dobyns, "Outline"; and Crosby. The population estimates in the text are for the approximate equivalent of modern Ecuador, Peru, and Bolivia. In recent years, there has been a tendency to assign a higher figure for the pre-conquest population of this area (30-37 million)—thereby postulating a sharper decline but one that perhaps reached its nadir by 1650—and to question the relation between these demographic trends and the advent of the Spanish. See Dobyns, "Estimating"; and Smith. See also Spalding, pp. 60-62.

62. Konetzke, 1: 402-3, decree of 14 Nov 1563.

63. Levillier, 3: 248, García de Castro to Council of the Indies, 2 Apr 1567.

64. AGIL 123, Francisco Núñez to Crown, 12 Nov 1574.

65. Lockhart, p. 31; Levillier, 1: 293, 403-4.

66. Konetzke, 1: 422, decree of 20 Apr 1567. In that very year the Indians of the pueblo of Chuschi, in Vilcas province, complained that their encomendero had permitted some of his African slaves to usurp village lands. See Ramón et al. I am indebted to Billy Jean Isbell for this reference.

67. Rowe, "The Incas," pp. 172-76. On early conditions in the Peruvian mines, see Lockhart, pp. 186, 208, 219-20. According to him, a few blacks were employed in a supervisory capacity in the extraction of silver, but Indians constituted the bulk of the labor force.

68. Levillier, 1: 529, 539-40, Nieva to Crown, 30 Aug and 10 Sept 1563.

69. *Ibid.*, 3: 346-47, 429-30, Toledo to Crown, 8 Feb and 10 June 1570.

70. *Ibid.*, 7: 61-64, document of 3 Aug 1571.

71. Konetzke, 1: 482-83, decree of 27 Apr 1574. Initially Toledo was a strong proponent of this measure and even advocated that mestizos be subject to tribute. See the Crown's letter to him on this proposal in AGIL 570.14: 118v-19r, 27 Feb 1575.

72. Levillier, 7: 287-88, Licenciado Ramírez de Cartagena to Crown, 6 May 1576.

73. Konetzke, 1: 502-3, decree of 29 Apr 1577.

74. Levillier, 3: 449, Toledo to president, Council of the Indies, undated (1571?).

75. For details, see Rowe, "The Incas," pp. 172-76.

76. Levillier, 6: 235-36, Toledo to Crown, 9 Apr 1580.

CHAPTER TWO

1. The phenomenon of native population decline has been most closely studied for Mexico in the monographs of Woodrow Borah, Sherburne F. Cook, and Lesley Byrd Simpson. On the rest of Spanish America, see Mörner, *Race Mixture*, pp. 31-33; and West, pp. 80-83.

2. The quotation and the accompanying information come from Baudet, pp. 17-18, 29.

3. Davis, pp. 63-64 (note 2), 97-98, 236, 281, 451-52, discusses the legend of Ham's curse and its underlying inconsistencies. Not the least of these are the confused relationship between Ham and Canaan and the fact that the Biblical account of the curse contains no mention of blackness. Defenders of African slavery were either unaware of or brushed aside such difficulties. No less a personage than the Franciscan Juan de Torquemada, writing in the 17th century, affirmed his belief in the curse (2: 569).

4. See Davis, pp. 167-96, for the quotation and for a good summary of both rationalizations and doubts on the Peninsula about the institution of African slavery. Also useful is Saraiva.

5. For an extended discussion of these points, see Davis, pp. 48-54, 167-96, 223ff, 447ff; Hoetink; and Dodge, a critique of the Hoetink work.

6. The decree cited, issued in about 1545, is in Konetzke, 1: 237. On the corporate nature of colonial Spanish American society, see Phelan, pp. 56-58.

7. The importation of Wolofs was forbidden by a decree of 1532. As early as 1506 Berber and Moorish slaves were also excluded from America because of suspected membership in the Islamic faith, and the prohibition against importing Berbers was restated in 1531. The ineffectiveness of this exclusion may be gauged by the fact that in 1543, and again in 1550 and 1578, the government felt compelled to order the expulsion of all Berbers and Moors from America, and Wolofs were still being offered for sale in Lima in the 17th century. See my Tables 1 and 2 (pp. 40ff); and the following sources: *CDIU*, 10: 103-4, 141-42; Herrera (1934), 1: 175; Ortiz Fernández, *Hampa afro-cubana*, p. 343n; and Encinas, 4: 383.

8. On the issuance of slave licenses to pay government debts, see Otte and Ruiz-Burruecos, pp. 20-21; and Scelle, 1: 337.

9. For examples of early speculation in slave licenses, see Pike, *Enterprise*, pp. 56-57.

10. Between 1538 and 1601, for example, 999 such permits were granted for Peru, of which 535 went to government officials, 379 to the clergy, and the remaining 85 to private individuals. These licenses are recorded in the *cédula* registers of AGIL 565-69, 578-82, and 1628 (*papeles por agregar*). No fee was generally charged for these permits on the assumption the blacks would be used as household servants or as subordinate members of the individual's retinue. Until the 1550's viceroys customarily received 12 permits as a perquisite of their high office, *oidores* 4, and treasury officials 3; and the Archbishop of Lima was given 6, bishops 4 (but occasionally more), and secular clergy 2.

Members of the Orders, pledged to poverty, did not receive such largess, but on occasion the Order itself was allowed to import a specified number of black artisans to assist in construction projects. For examples, see AGIL 566.5: 21r-22r; 566.6: 168r. During the 1560's oidores, treasury officials, Holy Office inquisitors, and corregidores and governors of important districts were all allowed 3, the more important clerks of the government were permitted 2, and the number allowed viceroys was upped to 20. The integrity of the secular clergy was such that from 1549 they were forced to swear that all slaves imported were for their own service and were not the property of others or carried for purposes of resale. (The first permit with this requirement is to be found in AGIL 566.6: 77v.) In time such permits became so routine that their issuance fell to the Casa de la Contratación (the body that oversaw colonial trade), which assumed responsibility for all licenses issued to the secular clergy after 1572 and for all licenses issued to government officials after 1601. There is no way to judge how many of these permits were actually used.

11. Otte and Ruiz-Burruecos, pp. 10-12.

12. See *ibid.*, pp. 11-12; Encinas, 4: 398-401; AGIJ 432 (1560), "Iñigo de Bocanegra . . . con el fiscal de Su Majestad sobre que pide se le dé testimonio si había habido declaración de la tasa y pragmática de los esclavos." In Peru, no black was to be sold for more than 150 ducats under the price ceilings, with the exception of the favored Guinea slaves who might be sold for 170. The weight of royal taxation can be appreciated by noting that the 30-ducat license fee represented 20 per cent of the maximum sale price.

13. On Spanish merchants in the slave trade, see Pike, *Aristocrats*, pp. 104-8, 122; on increasing Portuguese control, see Otte and Ruiz-Burruecos, pp. 6-15.

14. This discussion is based on Otte and Ruiz-Burruecos, pp. 15-31; Scelle, 1: 317-38, 790-98; Mauro, pp. 157-81; and Garcia, pp. 24-27.

15. Between 1581 and 1594, the government issued licenses for the importation of 17,383 slaves into Spanish America, or an annual average of about 1,242 blacks. Garcia, pp. 23, 35n.

16. The discussion of the slave trade asientos in this period is based largely on Scelle, 1: 347-469; Garcia, pp. 29-195; Molinari, appendix; and my own unpublished paper on the 1615-22 asiento held by Antonio Fernandes d'Elvas.

17. In addition to the license fee, slave traders were required to pay export duties (*aduanilla*) on their cargoes, and also, after 1552, the *avería*, a duty on imports and exports to defray the cost of the armed escort for the annual merchant convoys from Seville to Spanish America. Prior to dynastic union, the customs duty was ordinarily incorporated into the price of the slave license. After that, it became a separate tax of 2.5 pesos levied on each license and payable prior to departure from the Peninsula. However, Veitia Linage, p. 385, states that at some point before 1640 the duty, increased to nearly 4 pesos per slave, could be paid in America. Slave ships in fact rarely sailed with the merchant convoys, even if the blacks were obtained at the Lisbon slave mart rather than on the African coast, owing to the complications involved in transporting them to Seville or Cadiz and then waiting for the frequently delayed fleet to

sail. Nevertheless, the Crown compelled the slave trade to pay the avería in support of the operation of the convoy. On that tax and the convoys in general, see Parry, *Spanish Seaborne Empire*, pp. 117-35, 237-71; and Huguette and Pierre Chaunu, 1: 169-244.

18. An asiento concluded with João Rodrigues Coutinho in 1601 and renegotiated in 1605 with his brother Gonzalo Vaez Coutinho is the most specific on the destination of the slaves involved. It provided that 2,000 of the 3,500 blacks to be exported every year go to the following regions: Hispaniola, Cuba, and Puerto Rico (600); Mexico (700); Honduras (200); and Santa Marta, Río de la Hacha, Cumaná, and Venezuela (500). See Molinari, pp. 169-71, 195-96.

19. For a general discussion of the juros, see Elliott, pp. 198-99. On their connection with the slave trade, see Scelle, 1: 268ff.

20. Parry, *Spanish Seaborne Empire*, pp. 229-63, provides a good discussion of the increasing difficulties legal commerce experienced under the convoy system during these critical years. Though the extent to which Portuguese merchants dabbled in merchandise as well as slaves is difficult to determine, I must disagree with Curtin, pp. 21-22, who asserts that the economic advantage of the asentistas "was in pretending to carry more slaves than they actually did, leaving room to fill out the cargo with other goods. For this reason, delivery figures are likely to be inflated through the corruption of American customs-house officers, even though the official returns (where they exist) show that deliveries were not up to the contract stipulation. A calculation of Spanish American slave imports based on a simple addition of the quantities mentioned by each asiento in turn would therefore give a greatly inflated figure."

Curtin relies too heavily, I think, on 18th-century evidence that cannot be extrapolated for the earlier period. Until 1640 the asentista was not the principal importer of slaves but rather an agent for the sale of licenses, and it was to his advantage to sell every permit allowed by his contract. Further, though the slave traders dealt in contraband merchandise, the substantial profits to be made in Africans should not be ignored. The evidence is overwhelming that most slave merchants, far from carrying fewer blacks than allowed by their licenses, smuggled in many, many more, and relied on bribery and forgery to hide their transgressions. The number of licenses stipulated in the asientos, at least until 1640, can therefore be taken to equal the minimum number of slaves imported in any given year, a figure that Curtin (pp. 22-23) accepts for different reasons. The actual number imported in a normal year was certainly considerably higher.

21. The Seville merchant guild itself had negotiated with the Crown for an asiento in 1590, and a tentative contract had even been drawn up. The scheme was evidently designed to supply slaves to Spanish America while protecting Spanish commercial monopoly, but for unknown reasons the project fell through. See Scelle, 1: 341-43, 799-809; and Garcia, p. 28.

22. All aliens resident in Spanish America at the time the decree was issued were required to supply proof that these conditions had been met or face ex-

pulsion. See Council of the Indies to Audiencia of Santo Domingo, 22 Apr 1609, in AGI, Santo Domingo, 100. An earlier decree of 1596, reaffirmed in 1614, prohibited the Portuguese subjects of the Hapsburgs from claiming Spanish nationality. Scelle, 1: 318.

23. The foregoing discussion is based on various documents in the Biblioteca Nacional (Lisbon), Collecção Pombalina, códice 249, and in AGI, Indiferente 2829. See also Scelle, 1: 407-22; Huguette and Pierre Chaunu, 1: 154-57, 162-63; 8.1: 351-441; and Garcia, pp. 65-109.

24. The low estimate is from Curtin, pp. 106-7, a figure that I think conservative for the reasons stated in note 20, above. The high estimate is from Mellafe, *Esclavitud*, pp. 58-59. However, his method of calculation is purely arbitrary. Relying primarily on Scelle, Mellafe estimates that 1,207 slave ships entered Spanish American ports in this period and granting them an average size of 118 nautical tons, concludes the total tonnage was 142,426. He then presumably uses the figure assumed by the Spanish government, three slaves per nautical ton (*ibid.*, p. 40), to obtain 427,278 slaves, which he reduces to 350,000 by assuming a mortality rate on the Atlantic crossing of something over 15 per cent. Curiously, Mellafe also acknowledges that slave traders in practice sometimes carried as many as 7 blacks per nautical ton, but he seemingly backs away from the enormous total figure implied by this assertion. Huguette and Pierre Chaunu, 5: 70-73, 138-41, 156-57, 188-89, 208-9, 218-19; 6.1: 394-403; and 7: 72-73, 78-79, provide a general view of the volume of the Spanish American slave trade in this period, expressed in tables and graphs, and relied on by Curtin. See also Garcia, pp. 151-53.

25. Alonso de Sandoval, a Jesuit priest who worked among the slaves arriving at Cartagena in the early 17th century, can hardly praise the Guinea slave too highly. His opinions of the various African tribes, gained through his own experience and through many conversations with slave traders and buyers, are set forth at great length and with much precision in his classic work (pp. 64-97). On the African origins of the slaves exported to Spanish America, as well as their alleged characteristics and traits, see also Ortiz Fernández, *Hampa afro-cubana*, pp. 57-62; Mauro, pp. 152-56; and Aguirre Beltrán, *Población*, pp. 95-150. On the trickle of slaves from Morocco to Spanish America, see Huguette and Pierre Chaunu, 8.1: 332-34; and Chaunu, "Maroc."

26. Mauro, p. 155; Rodney, "Portuguese Attempts," pp. 309, 314-15.

27. During this period the Portuguese government attempted to force slave merchants who traded in Guinea to pay the duties necessary to support the governance of the Cape Verde Islands, whose inhabitants had been stripped of the exclusive right to barter for slaves on the mainland early in the 16th century. The attempt proved futile, aroused much bitterness among all parties, and served to reduce sharply the value of the Guinea contract, since the holder was responsible for this support regardless of evasion by slave merchants. My account of Guinea relies on various AHU documents, in caixas 1 for both Cape Verde and Angola; and on Rodney, "Portuguese Attempts," pp. 307-14, 319; Blake, pp. 138-92; Mauro, p. 161; Correia Lopes, pp. 56-58; Senna Barcellos,

1: 153-58, 203, 209, 221-25, 244-45; Galvão and Selvagem, 1: 77-79, 81, 375-77; and Andrade e Silva, 2: 127-29.

28. On São Tomé, see Curtin, pp. 99-119 *passim*; Aguirre Beltrán, *Población*, pp. 129-36; Scelle, 1: 336; Otte and Ruiz-Burruecos, p. 21; Mauro, p. 175; and Correia Lopes, pp. 66-76. On the Portuguese shift from São Tomé to Angola, see Birmingham, pp. 6-13.

29. Quoted in Boxer, *Golden Age*, p. 4. On the characteristics of the Bantu peoples, see Boxer, *Salvador de Sá*, pp. 225-28; and Sandoval, p. 96.

30. Huguette and Pierre Chaunu, 6: 398-403. These percentages do not include slaving vessels with multiple destinations. See also Garcia, pp. 132 (n3), 182-85.

31. Rodney, "Portuguese Attempts," pp. 307-14, 319; Boxer, *Salvador de Sá*, p. 225. Boxer's estimates in *Portuguese Seaborne Empire*, p. 103, are higher still: "The available evidence indicates that between 10,000 and 15,000 Negro slaves from West Africa were landed in *Brazilian* ports in an *averagely* good year, the great majority of them coming from *Angola* during the last quarter of the sixteenth century" (italics mine). As early as 1530, he estimates (in the same work, p. 100), the annual export of slaves from the kingdom of Congo was some 4-5,000 prime slaves. On the number of slaves leaving Angola during 1575-1640, see also Birmingham, p. 26.

32. Mauro, p. 175. Of the remaining ships, 34 were bound for Brazil and 11 for São Tomé, with 7,454 and 1,184 slaves, respectively.

33. Curtin, pp. 106-15.

34. However, the Angola contract brought considerably more revenue to the Portuguese Crown than the Guinea contract did, for several reasons. Beyond the question of liability mentioned in note 27, above, Angola probably supplied the bulk of blacks intended for Brazil, thereby making the area the chief source of slave supply for America as a whole. In addition, Portuguese control of Angola in the face of foreign intrusion was much more secure than in Guinea in most of this period. See Mauro, pp. 159, 161; Galvão and Selvagem, 3: 55-63; and Boxer, *Salvador de Sá*, pp. 240ff.

35. Correia Lopes, pp. 2ff. On the 1454 bull of Pope Nicholas V authorizing the enslavement of Africans, see Greenfield, p. 47, n11.

36. Boxer, *Portuguese Seaborne Empire*, p. 31; Mauro, p. 164; Sandoval, pp. 101-4. Mauro observes that within various tribes quarrels over succession between the sons of a chief by different wives often resulted in the losers' being sold into slavery; thus many slaves, far from representing the dregs of African society, in fact came from the highest classes. Rodney, "African Slavery," argues persuasively for a careful reexamination of the connections between indigenous forms of slavery in Africa and the influence of the Atlantic slave trade.

37. As early as the 16th century the methods of slave procurement on the African coast scandalized perceptive observers on the Peninsula. However, the Jesuit casuist Tomás Sánchez, though he condemned those who bought Africans sucked into the trade by fraud or violence, claimed it was the responsibility of the first purchaser to determine if the enslavement of an individual

was legitimate. The effect of Sánchez's reasoning was to saddle the African middleman with the moral burden of the barter process while leaving European customers with clear consciences. See Davis, pp. 187-91.

38. Rodney, "Portuguese Attempts," p. 310.

39. Sandoval, p. 101; AHU, Cabo Verde, caixa 1, memorial on the Cape Verde contract, ca. 1615. On the importance of iron, see also Rodney, "Portuguese Attempts," pp. 310-12, 315, who includes in the list of barter goods tin and copper basins, kettles, knives, and horses and cattle from the Cape Verde Islands.

40. Senna Barcellos, 1: 211; document in the Biblioteca Nacional (Lisbon), Collecção Pombalina, códice 249.

41. Boxer, *Salvador de Sá*, p. 229, n15, states that the term *tangomao* signified an "exile or banished man, fugitive, or runaway." Rodney, "Portuguese Attempts," pp. 307 (n3), 320, observes that the word is of uncertain origin, "but it may possibly be connected to the fact that there were priests or medicine men known as Tangomaus by the people of Sierra Leone in the sixteenth century." As regards the term lançado, Rodney believes that it was derived from the Portuguese *lançar* ("to throw"), and he explains: "Many . . . were mulattoes, already linked to the Africans by blood, and there were those who had become so integrated into African life that they wore tribal tattoos. It was these who were the authentic *lançados*, literally 'those who had thrown themselves among the Africans.' "

42. Boxer, *Race Relations*, pp. 9-11. See also Rodney, "Portuguese Attempts," pp. 307, 314-15, 320-21; Mauro, pp. 164-65; and Sandoval, p. 101. Rodney observes that only those African tribes who wished to monopolize the goods obtained by barter made any headway against the tangomaos. For example, one tribe in control of the area around the important slaving port of Cacheu on the Guinea coast would let slave merchants cool their heels for a year or more if satisfactory barter arrangements could not be concluded. The Portuguese merchants, a close-knit group, solved this problem in part by sending one of their number for a more or less prolonged residence on the Guinea coast. The slave merchant Manuel Bautista Pérez, for example, remained at Cacheu from April 1617 to March 1618, during which time he handled the barter arrangements of several slave ships. This information comes from slavers' records cited in full in Chapter 3.

43. Boxer, *Salvador de Sá*, pp. 229-31. Sandoval, p. 89, implies that by the early 17th century the Angolans along the coast used East Indian cloth almost exclusively for their clothing. He also reports that contact with Europeans had introduced the keeping of dogs and cats as pets, "which they esteem so much that they do not hesitate to give a black for a cat or a dog if it pleases them." See also Birmingham, pp. 24-26.

44. See letter to Crown, ca. 1622, in Cordeiro, 1: 317-18. See also Birmingham, pp. 25-26; Curtin, p. 122; Sandoval, pp. 100-101; Boxer, *Salvador de Sá*, pp. 227-03; and Boxer, *Race Relations*, pp. 23-29.

45. Correia Lopes, p. 55, is convinced those ships along the Guinea coast

that reportedly carried from 800 to 1,000 slaves were in fact floating barracoons where the captives were kept prior to sale in smaller lots for shipment across the Atlantic.

46. Boxer, *Salvador de Sá*, pp. 230-31.

47. This account is based on a famous letter written in 1622 by the Jesuit Pedro de Espinosa in Córdoba (Tucumán) to Father Diego Ruiz in Seville, printed in Pastells, 1: 300-301. Espinosa, alarmed about the defective baptism of slaves brought into Tucumán from Buenos Aires, forwarded information passed on to him by various slave traders. His letter in turn precipitated a massive reexamination of defective baptisms among the slave population of the Archbishopric of Seville, and the furor caused by this move filtered back to Sandoval in Cartagena. Sandoval prints Espinosa's letter and other information sent him by Andalusian Jesuits in *De instauranda*, pp. 347-67, and evokes the sense of scandal that must have prevailed among enlightened contemporaries. For additional information on the baptism controversy, see Pastells, 1: 297-301; and Boxer, *Salvador de Sá*, pp. 230-31.

48. The quotation is from Boxer, *Race Relations*, pp. 7-8, who provides an excellent account of the failure of the Portuguese missionary movement on the African coast. See esp. pp. 7-9, 12, 19-23, 33-40. See also Sandoval, pp. 347-72. Some historians say that in 1639, perhaps moved in part by the baptism scandal and by the methods of slave procurement, Pope Urban VIII issued a bull prohibiting Catholics from taking part in the trade. Saco, p. 275, mentions the bull, but fails to cite his source; and Mellafe, *Esclavitud*, p. 97, accepts Saco's assertion. Ortiz Fernández, *Hampa afro-cubana*, p. 78, is skeptical of the bull's existence, however. If there was such a document, it had little effect, and its publication in Spain may have been blocked by the Crown.

49. Sandoval, p. 107.

50. *Ibid.*, pp. 107, 357. For a more detailed account of the miseries of the slave trade, see Mercado, pp. 63-68. Published in Salamanca in 1569, Mercado's work was one of the earliest denunciations of the slave trade.

51. See the appropriate clauses in Molinari, appendix. A royal decree of 1571, printed in Encinas, 4: 415, indicates that slave merchants had long been allowed to start out from Africa with more blacks than their licenses permitted to make up for the mortality rate on the crossing.

52. Sandoval, pp. 100, 422, from which the quotation is taken; Suardo, 2: 119. Huguette and Pierre Chaunu, 7: 118-23, provides interesting figures on shipwrecks in the Atlantic, but there is no way to single out slave ship disasters.

53. Available information on the cost of insurance for slaving vessels is scanty. A document in the Biblioteca Nacional (Lisbon), Collecção Pombalina, códice 249, states that in 1611 the insurance was 16 pesos on a slave carried from Guinea to Seville and another 18 pesos from Seville to Spanish America. I have found no figures on costs from the African coast to Spanish America. According to information obtained from the Amsterdam municipal archive by Professor Engel Sluiter, which he has been kind enough to share with me, some of this insurance was written in Holland despite continuing hostilities between that country and Spain.

54. Sandoval, pp. 107-8. He nevertheless sets the rate of slave mortality on the Atlantic crossing at 30 per cent.

55. Extract from a letter to the Crown from Matias de Albuquerque, gov. of the captaincy of Pernambuco, 20 Sept 1620, in AHU, Angola, códice 32; Mauro, pp. 167-68; Saco, p. 257.

56. Quoted and translated by Boxer, *Salvador de Sá*, p. 232.

57. Pérez to an associate, Cartagena, 30 July 1618, in Concurso/Pérez, leg. 34.

58. D'Elvas's asiento, for example, included this privilege (Scelle, 1: 432); and he and his clients seem to have exercised it in Mexico (Aguirre Beltrán, *Población*, pp. 36-37).

59. In addition to the sums owed the Crown, a merchant who sold his cargo of slaves in Cartagena also had to pay 2 local taxes, one to defray the costs of fortifications to protect the city, the other to finance the apprehension of runaway slaves. In 1629 the latter tax was set at 6 reales per slave. See the document cited in note 53, above; and Saco, p. 269.

60. Sandoval, p. 107.

CHAPTER THREE

1. Sandoval, p. 423.

2. *Ibid.*, pp. 105-10, 307-9. Miramón, pp. 180-81, provides a lurid description of the *feria de los negros*.

3. Chandler.

4. In addition to Sandoval and Chandler, I rely here on Hoeppli, pp. 15-16.

5. Sandoval, p. 109.

6. Sandoval's work, first published in 1627, is of paramount importance for the documentation of Jesuit efforts among the African arrivals. See esp. pp. xiv-xvi, 307-9, 329-40, 367-87, 402-8. See also Pacheco. For useful biographies of Claver, see Armas Medina; Picón-Salas; Porras Troconis; and Valtierra. A black man, presumably an interpreter for the Jesuits, may be wearing one of these medallions in the portrait of Claver in Posada (between p. 114 and p. 115).

7. Lewin, *Descripción*, pp. 121-22. Part of this observer's account is also printed in Vargas Ugarte, *Biblioteca Peruana*, 1: 39-67; and in *RANP*, 17 (1944): 3-44.

8. ANP, Consulado: Contencioso, 17th century, leg. 12.M, Alonso de Miranda v. Luis de Sanmillán. The two were partners in the operation of the ship.

9. RA/PC, 72 (1629-30), "Autos seguidos sobre los bienes del Capitán Gaspar Martín": 313-27, 427r-68r.

10. Mellafe, *Introducción*, pp. 163-69, observes that Chilean merchants rarely had the capital to purchase large lots of slaves directly in Cartagena or Panama, and therefore bought them at Callao in groups of 5 to 20 along with textiles and other European products.

11. Huguette and Pierre Chaunu, 4: 314.

12. *Ibid.*, 314-16, 346-48; 8.1: 212ff. Quote appears in vol. 4 at p. 314.

13. In the order of mention: AGIL 321, Fr. Miguel de Monsalve to Crown,

Lima 20 Feb 1600; Concurso/Pérez, leg. 34 (see note 19, below, for complete citation); AGIL 150, Rico to Council of the Indies. See also Huguette and Pierre Chaunu, 2: 566-68; 3: 14-15, 148, 171-75; 4: 213-15, 312-16, 345-48; 8.1: 212ff, 238-40; and Garcia, pp. 155-57, 160-62.

14. Encinas, 4: 413.

15. AGIL 36, Esquilache to Crown, Panama, 24 June 1615.

16. It should be emphasized, however, that the Holy Office was hardly an infallible instrument in the royal effort to ferret out commercial fraud. The inquisitors, charged with policing the religious orthodoxy and morals of Spanish America, could devote no more than a fraction of their time to the Portuguese merchants, and the tribunals of Cartagena and Lima were frequently short-handed. Nor were the inquisitors themselves above dishonesty. For example, Juan de Mañozca, inquisitor first in Cartagena and then transferred to the Lima tribunal, was alleged by some to be deeply involved himself in slaving frauds at Cartagena. See J. T. Medina, Historia . . . Cartagena, pp. 135-45; and the summary in Henry Lea, p. 475.

17. For this and additional information on Portuguese Jews active in the slave trade at Cartagena, see Tejado Fernández, pp. 148-54, 166-79, 184ff. See also J. T. Medina, Historia . . . Cartagena, pp. 221-28.

18. For a partial account of the proceedings against the accused Jews, see J. T. Medina, Historia . . . Lima, 2: 47-164; Henry Lea, pp. 425-33 (who relies on Medina); and Lewin, Santo Oficio, pp. 135ff.

19. These records include the account books and other business documents of Pérez, today preserved in ANP, Inquisición: Contencioso, leg. 3, 7, 10, 13, 17-19, 21-22, 26, 29-34, 36, 38-41, 43, 46, 49-50, 52-53, 59, 61-62, 64-71, 73-75, 77, 83, 87, 89, 93; Concurso/Pérez, leg. 34-39; Concurso/Silva, leg. 40; and Inquisición: Contencioso, 18 (1631), "Autos referentes a los bienes de Garçi Mendez de Dueñas, relajado." Since each legajo usually contains more than one volume, and since the folios of each are intermittently and confusingly numbered, I will not attempt a more precise citation of these records. The records of Sebastián Duarte's business dealings, which at one time must have formed part of the above archival material, are now housed in the Archivo Nacional de Chile, Archivo Vicuña Mackenna, books 77 (1 and 2), 78 (1 and 2), and 79. Duarte's accounts have been extensively summarized by Mellafe, Introducción, pp. 169-81, on which I here chiefly rely. See also Emeth.

20. Most of what is known about Pérez's personal life comes from J. T. Medina, Historia . . . Lima, 2: 150-51. However, from Pérez's own meticulous records, we also learn that at the age of 22 he sired an illegitimate mulatto daughter, born in the mission village (aldea) of Cacheu on July 2, 1612. Pérez never claimed the child formally, but in letters to his associates he scrupulously provided for her support. Concurso/Pérez, 34.

21. Concurso/Pérez, 34. If the listing in Huguette and Pierre Chaunu, 4: 508-9, is correct, Pérez made the trip from Guinea to Cartagena in the Nuestra Señora del Vencimiento, which vessel he later sold, in poor condition and along with some supplies, for 2,000 pesos in Cartagena.

22. Mellafe, *Introducción*, p. 170. As late as 1634 Barreto and Pérez were in partnership for the sale of 70 slaves in Lima. Concurso/Pérez, 35.

23. Both quotations come from Henry Lea, p. 431.

24. Concurso/Pérez, 34, 36. On commercial contacts between Peru and the Orient via Mexico, see Borah, *Early Colonial Trade*; Schurz; and Chaunu, *Philippines*.

25. Concurso/Pérez, 34, 36. Pérez and Duarte seem to have sold most of the dry goods they purchased in Lima, but in 1623 they sent nearly 7,500 pesos' worth of fabrics to be sold in Potosí.

26. For example, in a letter to a Portuguese associate sealed 26 July 1620, Pérez lamented the fact that a certain slaver had not yet arrived from Africa. *Ibid.*, 34.

27. *Ibid.*, 36.

28. *Ibid.*

29. *Ibid.*; Mellafe, *Introducción*, p. 180.

30. Concurso/Pérez, 34, 36. It is clear from these figures that 17th-century Portuguese complaints about increases in barter prices in Guinea must be viewed with skepticism. Moreover, even the above prices are slightly inflated, since it was customary in negotiating the purchase of large slave parcels to agree on a set price per black, to multiply that figure by the total number involved, and then to deduct a small percentage for *daños*, i.e., slaves who had been "damaged" in transit.

31. *Ibid.*, 36.

32. *Ibid.*

33. Mellafe, *Introducción*, pp. 175-78. Mellafe's interpretation that Duarte's *fes* (p. 173) concerned slave children born after arrival in Spanish America, orphaned after leaving Africa, or sold apart from their parents is surely mistaken. For example, he would have Duarte buying 87 infants in a slave cargo of 258 blacks in 1626, a proportion of young children to adults rarely found in the slave trade in this period.

34. My information on Puerto Belo in the following discussion is based largely on the sources cited in note 19, above.

35. On the disturbances that prompted the Crown to ban slave importation into Tierra Firme, see Saco, pp. 193, 205-7, 221-25. Precisely when the prohibition was proclaimed is unclear, but it was incorporated in all the asientos of the period and was suggested as early as 1573 by Viceroy Toledo, who urged the Crown to restrict sharply slave importations into Tierra Firme to prevent possible alliances between runaway blacks and English corsairs. Levillier, 5: 212-13, Toledo to Crown, La Plata, 30 Nov 1573.

36. For a brief period of time in the late 1630's, slave traders were also required to pay a head tax of 1.5 pesos in Panama for the construction of a bridge. This tax, called the *sisa de la puente de piedra*, was collected on 900 slaves who passed through the city during 1637-93. AGIC 1476-77, Caja de Panamá, treasury accounts for 7 Jan 1637 to 7 Jan 1639. These are the only legajos for Panama that contain a record of the collection of this revenue.

37. The details are in the *declaración* that divided the profits in SN 67 (1625), 24 Sept: 1151-60.

38. RA/PC, 43 (1618-19), Pedro Gómez v. Francisco Guissado et al. In this suit Gómez claimed that he had agreed with Guissado and others to care for the slaves on the journey from Cartagena to Lima in return for free passage for himself, a cousin, and a servant. When the cargo sickened, he was persuaded to remain at Paita to care for them, but his employers refused to pay him for his time, which he valued at 600 pesos. Ultimately, Gómez was awarded a third of this sum.

39. This account is based on Mellafe, *Introducción*, pp. 169-81. Similar standards of slave care are reflected in archival documents.

40. Sandoval, pp. 569-70. The incident seems to have occurred in 1617 or shortly thereafter.

41. AGIL 42, Chinchón to Crown with an accompanying report, Lima, 12 Mar 1632. These documents are printed in Muzquiz de Miguel, pp. 88-90, 231-32, 273-74. The accident is also reported, with minor variations in detail, in Suardo, 1: 213.

42. Concurso/Pérez, 36.

43. *Ibid.*, 34, 36.

44. LCL, 18: 792-93, session of 14 Feb 1620. Similar quarantine measures were taken elsewhere in Spanish America. See Hoeppli, p. 16; and Chandler, "Health and Slavery."

45. LCL, 19: 826-28, session of 18 Mar 1624.

46. AGIL 1618.

47. Suardo, 1: 62; Concurso/Pérez, 34, where a medical inspection of 1633 is recorded.

48. AGIL 44, Chinchón to Crown, 24 Apr 1633.

49. Escalona Agüero, pp. 261-63; Rubén Vargas Ugarte in the introduction to Suardo, 1: xvi.

50. The head tax was 4 pesos per slave from its inception in 1549 until 1591, when the rate was cut in half. Concerning this tax, see Appendix A.

51. On the "Union of Arms" concept and its application to Spain's European possessions, see Elliot, pp. 326-28, 332, 336-37. Haring, pp. 287-88, states that the proceeds from this tax in America were intended to support the military escort of the convoy system.

52. AGIC 1679, almojarifazgo receipts collected by the treasurer Alonso Riquelme (1542).

53. My account of the imposition of the almojarifazgo is based on AGIJ 447, fiscal proceedings for 1574, "Son los del fiscal con los mercaderes de la ciudad de los Reyes . . ."; AGIC 1684, decree of 14 Oct 1565 (unnumbered folios); AGIC 1687, treasury accounts for 1572-75, pl. 131; AGIL 570.14: 28v-29r, 35v-37r; Levillier, 7: 10-11, 179-80, 185; and Encinas, 3: 453-54. In the early 1580's the city of Lima urged the Crown to reconsider the question of customs duties, but the appeal was rebuffed. See AGIL 108, "Instrucción de esta ciudad de los Reyes . . . para la enviar a corte de Su Majestad . . . para que conforme

a ella se suplique... las mercedes siguientes." Undated, but annotated in Madrid on 14 July 1583.

54. My information is based on a document concerning the audit of Lima treasury records for 1573-75 in AGI L 112: 48v-79r *passim*; and on a detailed examination of the almojarifazgo accounts for the years 1570-1600, 1614-21, and 1625-35, in AGI C 1687-90, 1692-1702, 1705a, 1706-8, and 1710-20. The gaps in these accounts represent those years when separate treasury officials were stationed at Callao and the periods when the duty was farmed out to the Lima merchant guild. In both instances, no almojarifazgo records have survived.

55. See, for example, AGI C 1699, "Data de real hacienda extraordinaria," pl. 120, entry of 24 Feb 1592.

56. Concurso/Pérez, 34, letters dated in Lima, 24 Apr 1619, and 22 and 30 Apr 1623.

57. *Ibid.* re slave sales in the wine-growing areas; ANP, Real Hacienda, 2 (1619-35), "Registro del navío nombrado San Bernardo...": 108r-9r, which records that Pérez sent 7 slaves to Arica for delivery to a resident in the Moquegua Valley.

58. Concurso/Pérez, 36.

59. RA/PC, 4 (1601), Garci Barba Cabeza de Vaca to Hernando Alonso del Villar, 8 May 1595: 44v-45r.

60. See the letters of 22 and 30 Apr 1623 in Concurso/Pérez, 34. Pérez indignantly declared that his competitors even accepted wine as payment for blacks.

61. *Ibid.*, 36. Slave sales on credit inevitably meant occasional bad debts and a certain amount of litigation to collect overdue accounts. Pérez usually insisted on a co-signer or bondsman when dealing with someone whose credit was dubious or who was unknown to him, but even this did not entirely solve the problem. Other slavers and private individuals who sold blacks on credit encountered similar difficulties. See, for example, RA/PC, 86 (1635), Juan Rey de Fontuoso v. Juan Bautista Moreno; and ANP, Inquisición: Contencioso, 21 (1633-34), Gregorio López de Salazar v. Catalina de Herrera.

62. Pérez's bookkeeping for the two years, in Concurso/Pérez, is given on p. 372.

63. *Ibid.*

64. LCL, 18: 794-95, 808, sessions of 17 Feb and 9 Mar 1620.

65. The vast majority of the slave licenses granted by the Spanish Crown specify no destination more precise than Cartagena or New Spain, and many merely designate the Indies as the general destination of the African cargoes. The records of the almojarifazgo, which was collected at Callao after 1572, shed little light, since cargoes were taxed in toto, without distinguishing slaves from other merchandise except on rare occasion. Moreover, as we have seen, the duty on blacks varied with the estimated quality of the slave, so that the number of slaves in the occasional cargo that included no other merchandise cannot be calculated from the lump-sum customs payment. The records of

Tabulation for Note 62

1630

Cost of 189 slaves in Cartagena (1629)	73,680
Price of fes purchased to cover illegal entries	2,114
Expenses from Cartagena to Callao	11,287
Expenses in Lima (maintenance, freight charges, royal and municipal taxes, medical expenses, legal fees)	10,730
Sales tax and freight on slaves shipped for sale outside of Lima	408
Freight charges on the silver carried to Cartagena	1,500
Miscellaneous	308
	100,035
Realized from sales in Lima	100,500
Accounts receivable	7,770
Charged against Duarte for 3 slaves he sold where proceeds retained	1,000
Value of remaining 3 slaves to be sold	1,550
	110,820
Less expenses as listed above	100,035
Net profit	10,785

1631

Price of 140 slaves in Cartagena	49,889
Expenses from Cartagena to Callao	6,858
Expenses in Lima	3,196
Freight charges, Panama to Callao	2,007
Sales tax	315
	62,266
Realized to date from sales in Lima	65,861
Accounts receivable	15,320
	81,181
Less expenses as listed above	62,266
Net profit	18,915

the head tax collected by the city of Lima survive only in an abridged, distorted form to about the year 1588 (see Chapter 8 and Appendix A); and the records of Pérez and other slave traders, useful as they are for the study of the Peruvian slave trade, tell us very little about its total volume. Only for parts of the 1620's and 1630's, when the Lima head tax was taken over and administered by the Crown, do we have comprehensive records of the number of blacks imported through Lima.

66. Ángel Valtierra, in Sandoval, p. xiv. I employ the method used by Mellafe to arrive at the probable number of slaves (see Chap. 2, note 24).

67. In the order of mention, Konetzke, 2.1: 179-80, decree of 10 Sept 1615; Vázquez de Espinosa, p. 310; Sandoval, p. 107. With respect to the estimate of Vázquez de Espinosa, assuming that 10 slave ships a year came from Angola and 8 from Guinea, by the Mellafe method of multiplying an average of 118 nautical tons times three blacks a total of 6,372 slaves would have been imported annually. This may have been the case in an exceptional year, but the total is too high to serve as a long-term annual average.

68. In the order of mention, Rodney, "Portuguese Attempts," p. 313; AGI, Indiferente 2975, "Relación de las partidas que por cuenta del asiento de esclavos se han traído de las Indias este año de [1620]. . . ." The details of the 1619-20 figure also well illustrate the complexities of the slave trade. Three of the ships had been granted a total of 580 licenses for New Spain by the Crown, and instead imported 415 blacks into Cartagena. Another 80 Africans were contributed by a ship bound from São Tomé to Madeira, whose master used a dodge common at the time and arrived at Cartagena, claiming to have strayed off course and to be in need of supplies. Still another merchant, with licenses for 180 slaves, carried 332 more for a total of 512.

69. Based on the notarial records listed in the Bibliography, pp. 420-21.

70. LCL, 7: 103, session of 29 Mar 1571; almojarifazgo accounts of merchandise from Mexico for the years 1583-85 in AGIC 1694; and RA/PC, 36 (1596), will of Doña Ana de Veras Barrasa. In her will, Doña Ana lamented that the 6 slaves she sent from Panama for sale in Peru, part of the dowry brought to her second husband, did not bring their appraised value in the Peruvian market.

71. On the blacks sent from Mexico, see the "Cargo de real hacienda extraordinaria" account in AGIC 1703 for the years 1603, pl. 38, 40-41; 1604, pl. 37-38; 1605, pl. 26; and in AGIC 1704, for 1606, pl. 68. On the captured runaways, see AGIC 1690.4, "Relación de algunas adiciones que resultaron contra los oficiales reales de la ciudad de Lima . . ."; AGIC 1692, "Cargo de extraordinarios [1581]": 38; AGIC 1721, treasury accounts for 1636-37; "Cargo de los derechos de almojarifazgo del Consulado" and "Data de real hacienda extraordinaria," pl. 136-37, 520-21, 528-29; AGIC 1723, treasury accounts for 1638-39, "Cargo de real hacienda extraordinaria," pl. 101; and for 1639-40, 1724, pl. 95-96. For information on the relationship between the black runaways of the Isthmus and the English raiders, see Wright.

72. LCL, 7: 469-70, session of 12 June 1573.

73. "Cargo de real hacienda extraordinaria" for 1604, AGIC 1703, pl. 35; for 1610-11, 1705b, pl. 52; for 1611-12, 1705b, pl. 59; for 1621-22, 1708, pl. 35; and for 1633-34, 1718, pl. 96.

74. My account of the 1629 incident is based on an exchange of correspondence between the Crown, the viceroy, and several members of the Lima Audiencia, which lasted until 1637. AGIL 45, 48, 99, and 572.21: 1604.

75. Levillier, 3: 106, Gov. Garcia de Castro to Crown, Lima, 23 Sept 1565; LCL, 12: 422, session of 29 Jan 1596.

76. AGIL 301, prepared by order of the Archbishop of Lima in March 1611.

77. In the order of mention, AGIL 109, city to Crown, 20 May 1640; AGIL 53, petition backed by cover letter from the viceroy Marqués de Mancera, Callao, 7 July 1646; AGIL 54, Viceroy Salvatierra to Crown, 28 Mar 1650.

78. I rely for what follows on a list of expenses (excluding salaries) submitted by the city as testimony in the lawsuit, now to be found in AGI, Escribanía de Cámara 500a, "El Consejo, Justicia y Regimiento de la ciudad de los Reyes con los mercaderes . . .": 79v-93r; and on a detailed analysis of a mass of pinpoint evidence in the volumes of *LCL* for the period 1555-88.

79. AGIL 112; AGIC 1687, 1689, 1692, 1694, 1698. In the suit cited in the previous note, the city claimed (fol. 148) that an average of perhaps 100 slaves entered Lima in any given year, though as many as 400 or as few as 30 were imported annually in exceptional circumstances. The slave merchants involved put annual importation at some 1,500 to 2,000 blacks, which figure may have been true for an exceptional year in the 1580's but seems much too high for most of the period in question.

80. AGIL 41, Viceroy Guadalcázar to Crown, Lima, 15 Mar 1628.

81. One observer, writing in precisely 1623, stated that 2,000 blacks were imported into Lima annually. That figure is fairly close to the 1,501 entered in official records, but there is no way to determine if it is reliable as a long-term annual average for the years prior to that date. AGIL 154, Capt. Don Pedro Gutiérrez Calderón to Crown, 2 Apr 1623.

82. For example, between 1601 and 1612, when treasury officials were stationed in Trujillo to collect customs duties on merchandise and slaves passing through the coastal ports of Guanchaco, Santa, and Saña, only 47 Africans were imported during the whole period. AGIC 1820. Similar but less specific accounts are available for Arequipa for the years 1599-1605 and 1631-33 in AGIC 1822. Yet, as we have seen, Pérez and Duarte occasionally landed relatively large shipments of slaves at Paita and Trujillo. Some of the blacks were sold in these areas, but most were taken by land to Lima for sale. In these cases it appears that payment of the municipal head tax (and therefore official enumeration) was successfully evaded. With the advent of royal administration of the tax in 1636, this ruse would probably not have worked, but by then Pérez and Duarte were in jail.

83. Additional evidence to this effect comes from two contracts signed in 1648 and 1651 assigning the collection of customs duties on all merchandise to the Lima merchant guild. The guild agreed to pay a flat 56,000 *pesos ensayados* a year for the privilege, but added an interesting stipulation. Though the slave trade was in abeyance at this time, its revival was expected at any moment. The guild therefore stipulated that their payment was to be reduced by 3,000 pesos if fewer than 800 blacks arrived in any one year, with duties on all slaves below that figure going intact to the Crown. The guild made no estimate of the upper limits of the volume of the Peruvian slave trade, but we may infer that a return to normal conditions did not mean the importation of 2,000 blacks annually. Otherwise, why add a stipulation that used a minimum

number of 800 slaves, since the demand of Peruvian consumers, who had been unable to buy bozales for around a decade, would presumably have pushed the volume of the trade up to at least the best levels of the 1630's, i.e., 1,000 to 1,500 blacks per annum?

84. Their geographical origins were Peru (location unspecified but more than likely Lima), 385; Lima, 297; Trujillo, 22; Ica, Pisco, and Cuzco, 7 ea.; Guánuco, 6; Cañete, 5; Saña, 4; San Miguel de Piura, Santa, Arica, Chancay, and Callao, 3 ea.; Arequipa and Guamanga, 2 ea.; and Nazca, Cajatambo, Lunaguana, and Cajamarca, 1 ea.

85. Of the 167, 86 came from the Cape Verde Islands, 72 from São Tomé, 6 from the Canary Islands, and 3 from the Azores.

86. The percentage for African-born slaves is slightly high, since the origin of a tiny minority of the blacks who figure in the bills of sale, perhaps one-half of 1 per cent, cannot be determined; in all cases, African origin has been presumed. The reader will also notice that the number of bozales recorded in Table 2, p. 42, is less than the number mentioned here. This is because bozales were sometimes sold in large blocks identified merely as "bozales of various castes and ages."

87. Poma de Ayala (1936), p. 704.

88. RA/PC, 83 (1634), Doña Francisca de Balbastre v. Alonso Sánchez, bill of sale dated 30 Mar 1621: 44r. With regard to the religious orders, to cite only one of numerous examples, in 1620 the prior of the Augustinian convent of Lima purchased 14 bozales from Francisco Rodrigues Barreto, a prominent slave dealer. SN 63 (1620), bill of sale of 6 May: 915-19.

89. Herrera (1934), 2: 176.

90. For a list of the tachas recorded in the sample, see p. 376.

91. *LCL*, 7: 258, 268-69, 289, sessions of 11 and 28 Apr and 30 May 1572.

92. I depend for the definition on Ortiz Fernández, *Hampa afro-cubana*, p. 175.

93. I rely here on Concurso/Pérez, 34; and on a mass of examples culled from Lima notary records.

94. Occasionally, however, Pérez chose to do legal battle. See, for example, RA/PC, 63 (1625-26), documenting a case in which Doña Francisca de Guzmán y Quintana successfully claimed that Pérez had knowingly sold her a slave with a long-standing kidney ailment and was awarded a refund of the purchase price plus the medical expenses incurred.

95. Two cases taken from SN 2 (1600): 349, 640-41, will illustrate. In the first, the buyer negotiated a price reduction of 50 pesos after discovering that the black had ringworm. In the second, the buyer claimed that the slave was a drunkard and runaway; the seller won the initial decision in the lower courts but reduced the purchase price by 50 pesos when the case was appealed to the Audiencia.

96. In addition to the examples cited in note 95, my discussion is based on several cases. In AGI, Escribanía de Cámara 567a, Juan de Amaya Fonseca v.

Tabulation for Note 90

Physical infirmities (388)			
Missing teeth	61	Castrated	4
Sick (unspecified)	48	Unspecified eye trouble	4
Lame; maimed or missing		Various abscesses	3
hands/limbs/feet	38	Scabies	3
Finger(s) missing or		King's evil	3
disfunctional	34	Sexual difficulties *(enfer-*	
Ulcers/sores on various parts		*medades secretas)*	3
of body	31	Swollen legs	3
Wounds and/or scars on body	18	Bed-wetters *(mea en la cama)*	3
Buboes	16	Blind	3
White spots *(nubes)* on cornea	13	Measles	2
One-eyed	13	Deaf in one or both ears	2
Ruptures and hernias	13	Spits blood	2
Missing toes	13	Chest pains	2
Heart trouble *(gota coral)*	11	Asthma	2
Unspecified fevers	9	Quartan fever	1
Epilepsy	8	Headaches	1
Loose bowels	8	Mental instability *(loco)*	1
Clay-eaters *(come tierra)*	6	Stomach trouble	1
Phlebitis	5		

Moral defects (459)			
Drunkard, thief, and runaway	134	Thief	10
Runaway	103	Drunkard	7
Has fled several/many times	62	Habitual liar	5
Has fled once	53	Drunkard and thief	5
Has fled and not apprehended		Compulsive gambler	4
at point of sale	26	Murder suspect	3
Thief and runaway	18	Runaway and drunkard	2
Argumentative	15	Possessed of the devil	
In jail for running away	10	*(endemionado)*	2

Doctor Avendaño and his son, esp. fols. 3v-5r, 14v-15r, 16r, 17v-18v, 20r, 21r, and 38v. From RA/PC, 4 (1556-60), Francisco Baliu v. Don Juan Guillermo; 35 (1595-96), Francisco de Herbas v. Juan de Urrutia; 29 (1612), Juan Gallardo de Afuera v. Pedro Fernández Palomino; 38 (1617), Juan González v. Sancho de Ávila; 93 (1636), Doña María de Guevara v. Francisco de Vergara; RA, Esclavos, 1 (1633-1774), María Evangelista v. Doña Josefa de la Cueva; Inquisición: Contenciosos, 19 (1631-32), Don León de Alcayagua Lartaun v. Antonio de Mendoza. In addition, 9 cases in the *Causas de negros* section of AA were consulted. This section of the archive is in process of being reorganized, so I am unable to cite legajo numbers on these cases.

97. Both cases come from AA, Causas de negros.

98. RA/PC, 67 (1627-28).

99. E.g., *ibid.*, 22 (1580-82), María de Rabaneda v. Luis Godoy.

CHAPTER FOUR

1. Lockhart, pp. 147-48, 186-87. My statements about the employment of free persons of color in Peruvian agriculture are based on a study of a considerable number of employment contracts in Peruvian notarial records. Ordinarily, such contracts provided for perquisites in addition to a small salary. In 1575, for example, the free mulatto Domingo signed on as a vaquero for a year with a Spanish employer for 70 pesos plus board, fodder for his horse, medical care, and a certain amount of clothing. SN 33 (1575), 17 Jan. Often the contract also allowed the free black the use of a plot of land on which to grow corn and other crops.

2. In the order of mention (all from RA/PC), 97 (1637), "Autos seguidos por los acreedores á los bienes de Lorenzo Pérez Noguera"; 26 (1610-11), will of Alonso de Estrada; and 124 (1650), "Autos hechos a pedimiento de Juan de Otacer...."

3. In the order of mention, RA/PC, 25 (1585-86), Álvaro de Torres v. Juan Gil de Montenegro; SN 46 (1635), inventory of the estate of Miguel de Taraçona, 26 Feb: 683v-87v; RA/PC, 64 (1626-27), Alonso Gómez de la Montaña v. Juan Delgado Crespo.

4. For an example in the case of wheat cultivation, see RA/PC, 1 (1600), Pedro Pablo Marón v. Doña Ana Venegas.

5. RA/PC, 34 (1594), Hernando Velásquez de Talavera v. Don Francisco de Cárdenas and Juan Daza de Olivares: 61r-73r.

6. RA/PC, 120 (1647), "Miguel de Medina, curador de Don Lorenzo Dávila...": 7r-23r; *ibid.*, 104 (1639-40), "Autos seguidos sobre los bienes que quedan por fin y muerte de Bartolomé Verdugo": 859-66; AGIL 212, petition to Crown from Bartolomé de Heredia, 14 Feb.

7. E.g., RA/PC, 53 (1622), "Autos referentes a los bienes de Juan Rodríguez Acevedo, difunto": 4v-33v, 101r-2r; AGI, Escribanía de Cámara 510c, "Andrés de los Reyes...": 167r-89r.

8. RA/PC, 86 (1635), Juan Rey de Fontuoso v. Juan Bautista Moreno: 89r-92r; *ibid.*, 1 (1600), Miguel Hernández de Bonilla v. Francisco Carrasco: 3r-6r.

9. E.g., Torres v. Gil de Montenegro (see note 3); "Autos... Pérez Noguera" (see note 2); RA/PC, 48 (1620-21), Doña Florencia de Aliaga v. Melchior de Salazar.

10. Vargas Ugarte, *Biblioteca Peruana*, 5: 183.

11. The prohibition also extended to employment in textile mills. The royal endeavor was not inspired entirely by humanitarian considerations. With regard to wine and cloth, the Crown was anxious to limit American production so that Spanish output would find colonial markets, but this policy was never very successful. For a general discussion of the subject, see Haring, pp. 253-54,

260-61. My information for Peru comes from AGIL 1; Levillier, 10: 139-40; 12: 173; 13: 161; 14: 119; Mellafe, *Introducción*, p. 154; and Silva Santisteban.

12. The attempted reforms of 1601 applied not only to Peru, but to the entire American empire, with appropriate modifications to fit each area. See Haring, pp. 65-66. A copy of the decree for Peru will be found in Levillier, 14: 302-22.

13. AGIL 156, Juan Muñoz de Hoyo to Crown, 2 Feb 1626. Muñoz proposed that the mita be suspended for a period of 10 or 12 years to arrest the decline of the native population, and that Africans be used instead.

14. AGIL 154, Gutiérrez Calderón to Crown, 2 May 1623; AGIL 47, Chinchón to Crown, 11 Oct 1636.

15. AGIL 53, petition backed by cover letter from Marqués de Mancera, 7 July 1646. Mancera likewise stressed to his successor that the resumption of the slave trade was a matter of extreme urgency if the colony were to avoid even greater economic damage. Beltrán y Rózpide and Altolaguirre, 2: 149.

16. Lewin, *Descripción*, pp. 25-26; Vargas Ugarte, *Biblioteca Peruana*, 3: 86-87. In 1626, the priest Muñoz de Hoyo (as cited in note 13, above) claimed that there were 12,000 blacks "in this city of Trujillo and the surrounding district" in contrast to "more than sixty thousand" in Lima. According to the ecclesiastical census of Lima of 1619 (see Appendix A), this estimate is at least five times too high for Lima, but if we assume that Muñoz's general impression of the proportion of blacks in each city was correct, this would mean a black population in Trujillo of some 2,000 in 1626.

17. Lewin, *Descripción*, p. 28.

18. Vázquez de Espinosa, pp. 478-80.

19. AGIL 330, the Society of Jesus v. the dean and cabildo of the Lima cathedral (1627): 7r-9r, letter of donation of 6 Apr 1622. For an example of a Pisco estate of similar size, see the mortgage instrument in AGIL 329 between Juan Rodríguez Guerrero and wife and the heirs of Bartolomé Sánchez, 15 June 1622.

20. Lewin, *Descripción*, pp. 106-7; Vázquez de Espinosa, pp. 482-83.

21. AGIL 155, proof of services of Don Juan de Padilla y Pastrana, a greatgrandson of Gutiérrez de Contreras (1624); Vázquez de Espinosa, pp. 472-73. I am inclined to agree with Lockhart, p. 185, who regards the more than 300 slaves supposedly employed on this plantation as an exaggerated figure.

22. Vázquez de Espinosa, pp. 472-73.

23. RA/PC, 17 (1607-8), Don García de Vera v. Cristóbal Muñoz: 126-29. For additional examples of slaveholding in these valleys, see AGIL 324, a petition to the Crown in 1606 from the Dominican convent of Nuestra Señora de los Remedios in Lima, owner of a vineyard in the area; and Suardo, 2: 148-49.

24. Vázquez de Espinosa, pp. 515-16.

25. AGIL 307, "Los autos que el Ilustrísimo Señor Maestro Don Fray Am-

brosio Vallejo, Obispo de Trujillo ... hizo en razón de la necesidad que tienen de cura ... los vecinos de la villa de Cajamarca...." Vargas Ugarte, *Biblioteca Peruana*, 2: 124-27, printed totals from this census that differ slightly from mine.

26. Lewin, *Descripción*, pp. 31-32.

27. Vázquez de Espinosa, pp. 523-24.

28. Doña Leonor proposed to found with this estate a convent in Cuzco dedicated to Our Lady of Carmen. The letter of donation is part of a batch of documents in AGIL 333 that refer to the proposed convent.

29. Vázquez de Espinosa, pp. 597-98. For occasional mention of blacks in 17th-century Cuzco, see also the notarial documents printed in "De la vida colonial."

30. RA/PC, 102 (1639), will of Esteban González, Quillabamba, 3 Sept 1637, together with an inventory of his estate; *ibid.*, 103 (1639), Doña Mencia de León Garabito v. the Society of Jesus: 277r-78r.

31. In the main, the generalizations in this paragraph are based on a mass of scattered data in RA/PC and SN.

32. In addition to various data in RA/PC and SN, I rely here on a document in AA, Causas de visitas, leg. 1.10, which records the confirmations of the baptisms of 1,067 Africans in the agricultural valleys south of Lima in 1632.

33. Lockhart, pp. 109, 184; Lewin, *Descripción*, pp. 89-90.

34. For examples of mule trains and slave muleteers owned by agriculturalists, see SN 46 (1635), Miguel de Taraçona, inventory of 26 Feb: 683v-87v; and in RA/PC: 53 (1622), "Autos referentes a los bienes de Juan Rodríguez Acevedo"; 85 (1634), Doctor Julián de León v. creditors of Hernando de la Concha; 94 (1636-37), inventory of estate of Don Juan Gutiérrez Flores; and 102 (1639), Baltasar de Tinco v. heirs of Andrés de Arevalo. On the sale of mule trains and muleteers as a unit, see SN 105 (1605), bill of sale of 13 July recording the sale of 2 black muleteers and 14 mules together with tackle.

35. AGIC 1710, DGG (1624-25), pl. 313.

36. *Ibid.*, pl. 259-60.

37. See the treasury records in AGIC as follows: 1713, "Data de proveeduría" (1628-29), pl. 509-11; 1715, DGG (1630-31), pl. 295-96; 1716, DGG (1631-32), pl. 268-69, 353, 411-16; 1717, DGG (1632-33), pl. 434-36; 1718, DGG (1633-34), pl. 365; and 1723, DGG (1638-39), pl. 486-87.

38. Lewin, *Descripción*, p. 64.

39. See Lockhart, pp. 114ff, for greater detail.

40. ANP, Consulado: Contencioso, 17th century, leg. 12.M, Don Alonso de Miranda v. Don Luis de Sanmillán (1629): 94r. For other examples of black sailors on the Callao-Panama run, see RA/PC, 26 (1587-89), Licenciado Torres and Miguel Redondo v. Alvar Yañez; and AGIC 1698, "Data de hacienda real"; 145v-46r, entry of 11 Jan 1590.

41. Mellafe, *Introducción*, pp. 68-70; RA/PC, 38 (1596), Juan de Lumbreras

v. estate of Anton César; ANP, Consulado: Contencioso, 17th century, leg. 14.O-P, Don Antonio de Oseriu v. Captain Don Juan Pérez de Vargas: 27r-113r.

42. Suardo, 2: 75-76.

43. Vázquez de Espinosa, pp. 452-53.

44. AGIC 1683, extraordinary receipts collected by the treasurer Bernardo Ruíz, entry of 6 Feb 1564; *ibid.*, extraordinary receipts collected by the treasurer Hernandarias de Saavedra, entry of 7 Aug 1565. Both entries concern the sale of royal vessels and the disposition of the slave crew members.

45. The following discussion about the employment of blacks in the royal fleet is based on treasury records in AGIC 1694, 1696-98, 1703-4, 1707-8, 1711-17, and 1721-25, and particularly the DGG account.

46. The Crown was even reduced to the expedient of obliging Spaniards convicted of serious crimes to furnish slaves to man the galleys. See AGIC 1686, "Cargo de penas de cámara" (1571): 40; and AGIC 1726, "Cargo de lo venido de fuera" (1641-42), pl. 19-22.

47. AGIC 1694, treasury accounts for 1584, pl. 87-89; and list of expenditures for 1587 in AGIC 1696: 90; for 1588, AGIC 1697: 138, 144; for 1589, AGIC 1698: 74, 79, 89; and for 1590, AGIC 1698: 146-47, 195.

48. Correspondence on this proposal is in AGIL 112, 127, and 570.15: 45v; and Levillier, 10: 124-25; 11: 172, 217-18.

49. Levillier, 12: 100-101, 290; 13: 23-24.

50. Lewin, *Descripción*, p. 68.

51. AGIC 1694, 1696-98, 1703-4, 1707-8, 1711-17, and 1721-25.

52. AGIL 41, Guadalcázar to Crown, 15 Mar 1628.

53. AGIL 50, Mancera to Crown, 29 May 1640.

54. Lewin, *Descripción*, pp. 39-40; Suardo, 2: 166.

55. In 1611, for example, the royal treasurer in Arequipa was served by 2 African slaves, a mestizo girl, 2 Indian women, 4 Indian children, and a mitayo who brought wood and water to the house. AGIL 116, Don Pedro Chacón de Luna to Crown, 22 Feb.

56. SN 67 (1620), will of 1 Aug: 1616-28; SN 68 (1640), will of 21 Aug: 1188-1216. On Africans and household service, see also Lockhart, pp. 159-60, 180-82.

57. E.g., AGIL 160, Licenciado Varona de Incinillas (Crown attorney to the Audiencia) to Crown, Lima, 30 May 1629.

58. AGIL 47, Chinchón to Crown, 11 Oct 1636.

59. See Parry, *Sale*.

60. SN 81 (1635): 896-900; SN 93 (1615): 489r-94r.

61. Lewin, *Descripción*, p. 74.

62. SN 51 (1615): 42v-45r (Hidalgo bequeathed a bed and some clothing to one of the slaves); SN 67 (1625): 421r-26r, 617-19.

63. In addition to extensive evidence discovered in Peruvian notarial records, I rely here on the following works by Emilio Harth-terré: "Carta india"; "Esclavo negro"; and *Informe*.

64. AGIL 310, Lima cathedral chapter to Crown, 6 May 1622.

65. Blacks figured in *cartas de dote* with such regularity that I soon ceased to record such documents. However, notes taken on 24 of them involving 64 slaves show the total value of the properties and goods assessed at 129,171 pesos. The slaves accounted for about 29 per cent of this amount (38,320 pesos).

66. SN 93 (1615): 159-61.

67. See, for example, RA/PC, 90 (1636), "Autos ejecutivos seguidos contra los bienes de Doña Sebastiana de Arana . . .": 454r-57r. Doña Sebastiana here pledged, among other things, 4 slaves toward the repayment of loans totaling 1,800 pesos. See also ANP, Inquisición: Contencioso, 19 (1631-32), Juan de Navarrete v. Pedro de la Hoz, in which a small boat and the slave who manned it were pledged to satisfy a debt.

68. I base this assertion on a mass of pinpoint evidence in Peruvian notarial registers. See also Lockhart, pp. 159-60.

69. Poma de Ayala (1936), p. 707.

70. SN 63 (1610): 484v-93r, 837v-40r.

71. RA/PC, 117 (1645-46), Doña Ana Riquelme v. Francisco Mexía; 24 (1610), offspring of Hernando Garrido v. Hernando de Aguilar.

72. RA/PC, 22 (1580-82), María de Rabaneda v. Luis Godoy; RA/PC, 119 (1646-47), Martín de Aranda v. estate of Martín de Basavil. It is worth noting that slaves could be hired out in payment of debts. E.g., Doña Magdalena Fernández Pardo, who hired out a slave to a creditor for 8 pesos a month to satisfy an obligation of 400 pesos. SN 60 (1620): 191-94.

73. LCL, 23: 317, session of 11 Feb 1636.

74. There were exceptions. In 1645 Pedro Criollo (aged 40) was hired out by his mistress for 9 years at 6 pesos a month, with the employer assuming responsibility for medical care. But this was an unusual case, since the mistress purchased the slave only to hire him out to his former owner on the same day. The one-time owner may well have been in need of cash and found in this a way to obtain it without losing his slave's services. SN 38 (1645), 31 Oct: 12.

75. This paragraph relies on the notarial records listed in the Bibliography, pp. 420-21.

76. Lewin, *Descripción*, pp. 58-59.

77. AGIL 326, from a series of documents relating to the services of Bachiller Juan Manuel Carrasco, first chaplain and then majordomo of the hospital.

78. Levillier, 1: 287, 380; AGIL 134, letter of donation signed by Sánchez de Bilbao and wife, forming part of a larger petition to the Crown. See also AGIL 50 (1641), list of goods and ornaments given the convent of Nuestra Señora del Prado by Angela de la Encarnación, its founder.

79. SN 29 (1564): 1287-89; SN 11 (1572), Rojas letter of donation of 6 Nov, no foliation. The munificent donation of Dueñas was challenged by his creditors: see the lawsuit in RA/PC, 15 (1573).

80. This paragraph is based on *LCL*, 5: 277-78; 8: 179, 182; and 19: 935-36; on AGIL 95, Viceroy Montesclaros and Audiencia to Crown, 5 Feb 1609; and on a wide variety of government accounts in AGIC 1680, 1689, 1693-94, 1698-1707, 1709, 1713-16, and 1723-25. Of particular importance are the DGG accounts and those entitled "Data de real hacienda extraordinaria."

81. Lockhart, pp. 122, 184.

82. Vázquez de Espinosa, p. 454. Re Meneses, see AGIC 1705a, the "alcance de cuentas" account for 1614-15, pl. 23; and for 1615-16, AGIC, 1706, pl. 32.

83. *LCL*, 4: 239, 241, 548-51. On the royal navy, see the source cited in note 45, above. Lockhart, p. 108, asserts that "most practitioners of the trades connected with food production were not artisans in the usual sense of men with special training and equipment." This situation may have changed somewhat after 1560.

84. Lockhart, pp. 108-9, 160, 193; AGIC 1680, "Los gastos ordinarios para la provisión del campo de Su Majestad . . . ," entry of 15 Jan 1554; RA/PC, 46 (1620), "El defensor de los bienes de Cristóbal Ruiz . . .": 1-7. Africans also worked the salt mines on the Punta de Salinas near the present town of Huacho, some 60 miles from Lima. The salt was cut in large blocks ("as much as a black can carry") and shipped by sea to the capital. Lewin, *Descripción*, p. 30.

85. *LCL*, 6.1: 197, 8: 216-17; 9: 420-21.

86. For this example and others, see *LCL*, 4: 330, 336; 5: 616-17; 6.1: 197, 9: 421; and 17: 664-65.

87. Levillier, 7: 29-30.

88. *LCL*, 7: 234, 329; 8: 35-36.

89. *LCL*, 19: 381.

90. *LCL*, 17: 292-93.

91. Salinas y Córdova, pp. 252-54. Lockhart, p. 188, mentions that as early as 1547 black vendors were commonly engaged in these activities in Lima's main square.

92. Ricardo Palma, cited by Ortiz Fernández, "Cabildos," p. 9n.

93. *LCL*, 6.2: 541; Levillier, 8: 101-3, ordinances issued by Toledo in Checacupi, 18 Oct 1572.

94. *LCL*, 12: 247, 275; 18: 461-62.

95. SN 35 (1645): 145. See also SN 35 (1650): 1056v-57v. Space for the pulperías operated by persons of color was frequently rented only for short periods. See SN 89 (1620): 416; SN 94 (1640): 311v-12r; and SN 45 (1645): 9v, 41. The modest nature of the black-operated pulperías is clear from the rent charged for one—4.5 pesos monthly. Cited in SN 94 (1640): 311v-12r.

96. AGIL 47, Chinchón to Crown, 11 Oct 1636.

CHAPTER FIVE

1. In addition, all mines let to other individuals by the Crown were to fall under Espino's administration on expiration of the lease. However, the mercury mines of Huancavelica were excluded from the contract and were to

continue under the rental agreements concluded by Toledo. The Espino contract and various decrees implementing its clauses will be found in AGIL 579.5: 272v-81r; and 579.6: 72r-74r, 86r-100r, 109v-10r, 235r.

2. AGIL 579.6: 233r-35r, 271r-72r.

3. The remainder of my account comes largely from a petition in AGIL 1632, "Juan de Medina Avellaneda y otros . . . ," which incorporates documents from 1586-89 about the contract. See also Lohmann Villena, *Minas*, pp. 110-11.

4. AGIL 127, treasury official Manrique de Lara to Crown, 25 Apr 1585.

5. Haring, pp. 303-4, provides an account of the relationship between these two councils.

6. Konetzke, 1: 573-79, recommendation of 22 Feb 1587.

7. My account of the Estrella venture is based on documents spanning the years 1588-92 in AGIL 1; 1351; and 1632. Pedro de Estrella, as he was commonly called, was the son of Cristóbal Calvete de Estrella, official chronicler to both Charles V and Philip II.

8. RA/PC, 39 (1596-97), Gerónimo de Velasco et al. v. Pedro de la Estrella. This document sheds some light on Estrella's financial difficulties but makes no mention of the mining project.

9. AGIL 123, Francisco Muñoz to Crown, 2 Aug 1574.

10. AGIL 318, Durán y Ribera to Crown, 20 Apr 1591.

11. My account of the Apurímac project is based mainly on Harth-terré and Márquez Abanto, *RANP*, 25: 43-52.

12. As standardized by Viceroy Toledo, every sizable community in Peru was to have a Protector of the Indians, an official who settled minor disputes and guarded the native population against possible abuses inflicted by the Spanish or by their own caciques. Presumably, the person appointed for Lima, who spoke for the natives before the viceroy and the Audiencia, carried the title of Protector General. See Haring, p. 61.

13. According to Haring, pp. 174-75, such funds were "accumulated from the produce of certain common lands or labor of the village, or derived from quitrents of communal lands let out to Spanish or Indian farmers. The income was used to defray municipal expenses such as legal services, support of a hospital, aid to widows and orphans, repair of roads and bridges, or to pay the tribute of members who were ill or absent."

14. AGIL 570.15: 224-25r, Crown to Cañete, 23 Dec 1595.

15. AGIL 571.17: 56-57, decree of 13 Mar 1610, which states that the money to buy the blacks was put up entirely by the Crown; AGIL 141, treasury accounts audited by the Tribunal of Accounts (13 Feb 1607-20 Apr 1611): 12v.

16. AGIL 570.15: 143v-44r, Crown to Cañete, 22 Sept 1593.

17. Levillier, 13: 232, Cañete to Crown, 20 Jan 1595; AGIL 570.15: 228r, Crown to Cañete, 23 Dec 1595.

18. Konetzke, 2.1: 24-30, from the instructions issued to Velasco on 22 July 1595.

19. The term zambaigo (eventually shortened to zambo) is of uncertain

origin. Mörner, *Race Mixture*, p. 59, n22, cites Alexander von Humboldt, *Ensayo político sobre el reino de la Nueva España* (6th ed., Mexico, 1941), 2: 140-41, to the effect that in the 18th century a cross between an Indian and a black was called a *chino* in Peru and Mexico and a zambo in Venezuela. Ortiz Fernández states that in Cuba a chino was a cross between a mulatto and a black (*Hampa afro-cubana*, p. 173, n1). But these terms were used quite differently in the 16th and 17th centuries. My researches in both Peruvian and Mexican notarial records indicate that zambo was widely used for Afro-Indians in Peru as early as the 16th century, though in Mexico they were still referred to as "mulattoes" as late as 1650. Since Venezuela was hardly the *arbiter elegantiae* of racial terminology at this early date, it seems likely that zambo was a term coined either in Peru or on the Isthmus. However, its usage may very well have spread first to Venezuela and thence to Mexico, since commercial ties between the two colonies were relatively strong. With regard to chino, at least until 1650 this term was used in both Peru and Mexico only in reference to Orientals, usually qualified by *"de tierra Malabar," "de India Portuguesa,"* or *"indio natural de Goa"* to make the origin of the individual more precise. On racial terminology, see also Mellafe, *Esclavitud*, p. 56, and the sources there cited. The presence of Orientals in Peru is discussed in Appendix A.

20. Konetzke, 2.1: 47.

21. My discussion of the 1601 decree relies mainly on Haring, pp. 65-66; and the copy of the orders for Peru in Levillier, 14: 302-22.

22. Biblioteca Nacional (Madrid), mss. 19282 [Gayangos Collection]: 128r-30r.

23. AGIL 570.16: 92v-93r, instructions dated 19 May 1603; AGIL 582.14: 171r, decree of 21 Nov 1603.

24. Konetzke, 2.1: 134-35, decree of 16 Aug 1607.

25. Fox, pp. 66-67.

26. AGIL 570.16: 252-53, decree of 26 July 1608.

27. Konetzke, 2.1: 148, decree of 10 Apr 1609.

28. *Ibid.*, pp. 154-68. This copy, the one issued for New Spain, is identical except for minor details to the decree for Peru. For the Peruvian decree, see AGIL 571.17: 1ff.

29. Konetzke, 2.1: 153-54.

30. AGIL 571.17: 17r.

31. AGIL 36, Viceroy Montesclaros to Crown, 3 and 8 Apr 1611.

32. What follows is based on documents about the bridge in AGIL 38 and 149; and on Harth-terré and Márquez Abanto, "Histórico," pp. 27-38, 52-61.

33. AGIL 97, Tribunal of Accounts to Crown, 19 Apr 1622; Audiencia to Crown, 6 May 1622.

34. AGIL 43, Tribunal of Accounts and Audiencia to Crown, 11 July 1629; AGIL 572.20: 265r, Crown to Chinchón, 22 Apr 1632.

35. E.g., Juan de Estrada, who played an important part in the drainage projects at the Huancavelica mercury mines in the 1620's, mentioned that

black slaves had assisted him in certain technical operations. AGIL 320, proof of services, 5 July 1633.

36. AGIL 51, Mancera to Crown, 10 June 1642; Beltrán y Rózpide and Altolaguirre, 2: 151-52, where Mancera's stress is more on the improvement in mail service than on the lightening of Indian labor obligations.

37. AGIL 573.23: 110r-12r, decree of 8 June 1648 addressed to Salvatierra and a royal reply to Valenzuela of the same date informing him of the government's action.

38. AGIL 54, Salvatierra to Crown, 28 Mar 1650.

39. AGIL 573.23: 300.

CHAPTER SIX

1. See the interesting discussion of this point in Freyre, pp. 278-403.

2. Lockhart, p. 183.

3. RA/PC, 94 (1636-37), inventory, estate of Don Juan Gutiérrez Flores.

4. Lewin, *Descripción*, pp. 109-10.

5. SN 14 (1595), *carta de dote* of 30 Nov: 1290-95; RA/PC, 65 (1627), will of Doña Melchora de Luna, Arequipa; RA/PC, 106 (1640), heirs of Pedro de Segura v. estate of Juan Gallardo and his wife: 377. On some vineyards the division of labor was so specialized that even the grape-treaders (*pisadores*) were singled out for mention. See SN 46 (1635), inventory, estate of Miguel de Taraçona, 26 Feb: 683v-87v.

6. For examples of these skills: RA/PC, 97 (1637), "Autos seguidos por los acreedores a los bienes de Lorenzo Pérez Noguera"; and 124 (1650), "Autos hechos a pedimiento de Juan de Otacer...." See also SN 96 (1640): 619-21.

7. Unless otherwise noted, all my information on shipbuilding is based on the following legajos in AGIC: 1698, receipts collected by Luis de Alfaro (1587-88): 4-7; 1698, listing of expenditures by the factor Don Francisco Manrique de Lara (1589): 5-8, 16, 18, 26; 1703, DGG (1603): pl. 82-83, 86-87; 1704, "Data de la armada y guerra" (1608-9): pl. 94-96; "Data de los gastos para la fábrica de los galeones" for 1609-10, 1705b, pl. 149-51; for 1611-12, 1705b, pl. 120; and for 1613-14, 1705a, pl. 87, 91, 93-94, 98-101, and 1705b, pl. 111-12; 1705a, "Cargo de real hacienda extraordinaria" (1614-15), pl. 29; "Data de la fábrica de los galeones" for 1614-15, 1705a, pl. 160-61, for 1619-20, 1708, pl. 262, 265, 271, for 1620-21, 1708, pl. 201, and for 1621-22, 1708, pl. 142; 1710, DGG (1624-25), pl. 213, 276-77; 1711, DGG (1626-27), pl. 276-77, 311, 326; 1713, DGG (1628-29), pl. 356; 1713, "Data que pagaron y remitieron al dicho tesorero Don Sebastián Hurtado de Corcuera que asista en el puerto del Callao para la paga de la maestranza" (1628-29), pl. 241-42; 1715, DGG (1630-31), pl. 471-94; 1716, DGG (1631-32), pl. 323-26, 414-16; 1717, DGG (1632-33), pl. 437-40; 1722b, DGG (1637-38), pl. 505-10, 714-26; 1723, DGG (1638-39), pl. 641-52; 1724, DGG (1639-40), pl. 509-20; 1725, DGG (1640-41), pl. 530-42, 629-38.

8. AGIL 50, Mancera to Crown, 29 May 1640; AGIL 572.22: 163r, Crown to Mancera, 4 Apr 1642. There is some evidence that black shipwrights and

caulkers who serviced private ships were paid roughly the same wages as the amount paid by the Crown, at least before 1640. See RA/PC, 95 (1637), "Concurso de acreedores a los bienes del Capitán Don Juan Gutiérrez y Otone": 211-23.

9. Lockhart, p. 108.

10. AGIC 1685 (1569), monies received by the factor Nuflo de Romani to build the Lima mint. The Lima mint was established in 1568, but the principal mining centers were so far away that it did not receive enough silver to pay for its operation. Consequently, the mint was officially transferred to Potosí in 1572, though sporadic operations continued in Lima until at least 1590. See Haring, p. 309.

11. See the following accounts in AGIC: 1689, list of expenditures from the *penas de cámara* for 1579: 222; 1698, "Los gastos que estaron por las libranzas del Licenciado Alonso Maldonado de Torres": 32-33; 1698, "Data de la real hacienda" (1590): 187; 1699, "Data de los pesos de oro que de cuenta de real hacienda se gastan en el reparo de estas casas reales" (1591), pl. 95; 1708, DGG (1621-22), pl. 82; 1717, DGG (1632-33), pl. 440; 1723, DGG (1638-39), pl. 490; 1724, DGG (1639-40), pl. 520; and 1725, DGG (1640-41), pl. 542.

12. For a general view of the problem, see Lohmann Villena, *Defensas*.

13. AGIL 226, proof of services of Don Sancho de Prado, corregidor of Ica at the time of the Dutch threat, Lima, 22 Feb 1625.

14. AGIC 1710, DGG (1624-25), pl. 309-13.

15. In the order of mention, AGIL 225, proof of services of Gerónimo López de Saavedra, 12 Apr 1625; AGIL 230, proof of services of Don Antonio del Castillo Enríquez, Lima, 12 Oct 1634.

16. My information on this project comes from AGIL 157, proof of services of Capt. Rodrigo Montero de Uduarte, who directed construction and who was also in charge of fortifications at Pisco and Callao during the 1624 emergency. Montero implied here that he had had previous experience in this sort of work in Spain and the Netherlands.

17. AGIC 1715, DGG (1630-31), pl. 527.

18. AGIL 465, Mancera to Crown, 14 Feb 1641, letter and supporting documents.

19. *LCL*, 4: 156, 158; 7: 664-65; 8: 94-95; 13: 176; Harth-terré and Márquez Abanto, *RANP*, 25: 44-50. For additional information, see the 1611 will of Juan del Corral, who was overseer of all municipal construction in the early 17th century, printed as an appendix to Harth-terré and Márquez Abanto, "Puente."

20. *LCL*, 6.2: 334, 352, 358-59, 366, 513; 7: 33, 90, 606-7.

21. *LCL*, 5: 579-80. Between the action of the river and the wear of heavy traffic, the bridge required extensive repairs from time to time. In 1598, for example, the city had the black mason Francisco de Gamarra restore one of the span's pillars. Harth-terré and Márquez Abanto, *RANP*, 25: 49-50.

22. AGIC 1705b, "Data de la fábrica de Guayaquil" (1609-10), pl. 151,

which records the sale of the city's slaves to the Crown; Harth-terré and Márquez Abanto, "Puente."

23. E.g., Suardo, 2: 189.

24. AGIL 566.5: 21r-22r, 23r; 566.6: 168r; 579.5: 127v-28r.

25. SN 85 (1625): 1579v-89v.

26. AGIL 337, from a notarized copy of the minutes of a San Marcos fac-
ulty meeting; AGIL 148, from a document submitted to gain royal approval
for the construction of the Saña convent.

27. AGIL 324, from a petition of Francisco de Saldaña to Crown, 1606.

28. Harth-terré and Márquez Abanto, *RANP*, 22 (1958): 194-217.

29. For these and other examples, see *ibid.*, 25: 10-11, 45-47, 53-56.

30. SN 37 (1600): 512v-13v.

31. Harth-terré and Márquez Abanto, *RANP*, 25: 8, 46-48.

32. SN 105 (1605): 576-77; SN 49 (1605): 129-30; Harth-terré and Márquez Abanto, *RANP*, 26: 50-53. As Harth-terré and Márquez Abanto make
clear, Spanish artisans also often secured the services of black slaves as part
of their contracts.

33. Sandoval, pp. 64-65.

34. On slaves as smiths in the early colonial period, see Lockhart, pp. 105-
6, 182-83. As early as 1535-36 the Lima authorities forbade the African slaves
of blacksmiths to cut trees in the area for charcoal. *LCL*, 1: 23, 116.

35. Vázquez de Espinosa, p. 408; AGIC 1684, list of expenditures for 1567,
entry of 22 Nov. In 1565 a representative of the governor of Tucumán was
advanced 1,000 *pesos ensayados* from the royal treasury at Lima for the purchase of an African blacksmith and other equipment necessary to pacify the
Indians of that province. See AGIC 1683, record of expenditures for 1565,
entry of 18 Aug.

36. AGIC 1680, "Los gastos ordinarios para la provisión del campo de Su
Majestad por libranzas del proveedor Bernaldino de Romani . . . ," entry of
19 Feb 1554.

37. *LCL*, 4: 402-3, 581-82, 588.

38. SN 47 (1625), shop rental agreement of 7 Feb: 869v-70r.

39. Lockhart, p. 182.

40. *LCL*, 23: 244-45, 261-64. For another example, see *ibid.*, 247-48.

41. *Ibid.*, 151-52.

42. In 1625, for example, the goldsmith Cristóbal Sánchez described the
two slaves who assisted him as silversmiths. SN 67 (1625), Sánchez will of 4
Oct: 1038r-45r. In the sixteenth century some slaves were also used in the
sporadic operations of the Lima mint. See AGIC 1685, list of expenditures
for 1568: 184, 202v; 1686, "Cargo de real hacienda extraordinaria" (1570),
no foliation, n.d.; 1699, same account (1593), pl. 71.

43. Salinas y Córdova, p. 255. However, Suardo, 2: 23, writes of a mulatto
silversmith whose store was robbed of over 1,000 pesos in 1634.

44. Lewin, *Descripción*, p. 58; Harth-terré and Márquez Abanto, *RANP*,
22: 435.

45. RA/PC, 73 (1630), creditors v. estate of Pedro de la Barrera.

46. SN 26 (1574), Juan Manzano rental agreement of 1 Oct: 176r-77r; RA/PC, 16 (1573-74), Hernández de Medinilla, will of 13 Mar.

47. AGIC 1705b, "Data de los gastos de Huancavelica" for 1611-12, 1705b, pl. 82, 85; for 1612-13, 1705a, pl. 90-92; for 1613-14, 1705b, pl. 126-27; and for 1614-15, 1705a, pl. 99, 108.

48. *LCL*, 5, 592; Konetzke, 1: 611-12; 2.1: 108-9, 189-90.

49. *LCL*, 11: 454; Salinas y Córdova, pp. 255-56.

50. AGI, Escribanía de Cámara 567a, Juan de Amaya Fonseca v. Dr. Avendaño and son: 3v-5r. See also AGIL 95, "Testimonio de la causa contra Juan Pérez de Cumeta . . . ," 20 Apr 1611. Pérez was a barber-surgeon who owned a small hat factory operated by African slaves.

51. SN 67 (1625): 1001-32; RA/PC, 119 (1646-47), "Autos sobre el testamento . . . de Antonio de Rivera Zambrano": 4v-19v; Salinas y Córdova, p. 255.

52. One of the very few references to African participation in the manufacture of cloth elsewhere in the colony comes from the 1571 will of Francisco Velázquez Talavera, a prominent encomendero, who employed 5 black slaves in his textile mill in the valley of Santa Lucia de Chanchan. RA/PC, 34 (1594) Hernando Velázquez de Talavera v. Don Francisco de Cárdenas: 61r-73r.

53. Lockhart, p. 182.

54. *Ibid.*, pp. 98-99, 183.

55. RA/PC, 68 (1628), Doña Inés de Salazar v. estate of Pedro de Saavedra y Aguilera: 20-40; RA/PC, 47 (1620), "El defensor de los bienes de difuntos por los de Francisco Hernández Irola contra Francisco Ruiz de Usenda y otros sus albaceas": 10r-26r; RA/PC, 26 (1610-11), will of the cleric Alonso de Estrada.

56. SN 57 (1645): 2091-94.

57. Except where otherwise noted, the discussion of prices paid for skilled blacks and their earning power relies on Harth-terré and Márquez Abanto, *RANP*, 25: 18-27.

58. SN 73 (1610): 478r-79r; SN 47 (1620): 265v-66v; SN 68 (1640): 1089-90.

59. On Valenzuela, see SN 17 (1577): 469-70. For examples of older slaves, see AGIC 1689, "Cargo de real hacienda extraordinaria" (1578), entry of 19 July; and SN 41 (1615): 150.

60. In 1640, for example, Francisco Caravali, a journeyman blacksmith, was sold for 470 pesos, a surprisingly low price considering the craft. In part, Francisco's age (40) and the depressed state of slave prices lowered his value, but his owner also refused to give legal assurances against any defects except ill-health. As another example, in 1615, at the end of a long period of stability in slave prices, the leatherworker Juan Criollo (age 20) was sold for the relatively modest price of 500 pesos, probably because his shoemaker master described him as a runaway. SN 102 (1640): 1047r-48r; SN 47 (1615): 73r-74r.

61. SN 68 (1650): 74r-75r.

62. E.g., SN 45 (1620), bill of sale of 10 Dec, no foliation; SN 63 (1620): 1433r-34r; SN 93 (1615): 12-14; SN 105 (1605): 188r-89r; SN 37 (1605): 807v-10v. See also Harth-terré and Márquez Abanto, *RANP*, 25: 18-20.

63. For examples of fatal accidents involving blacks in the construction industry, see Suardo, 1: 279; 2: 125.

64. Harth-terré and Márquez Abanto, *RANP*, 25: 7-8, 14-15.

65. SN 42 (1605): 548r-49r; SN 19 (1581): 173.

66. For examples of voluntary apprenticeship by free colored adults, see Harth-terré and Márquez Abanto, *RANP*, 25: 12, 14-15, 57-59.

67. SN 54 (1615): 792v-93r.

68. Harth-terré and Márquez Abanto, *RANP*, 25: 15-18.

69. In 1613 the Lima guild of printers and engravers forbade blacks to practice the craft except in the shop of a Spanish master. Konetzke, 2.1: 185. At least one prominent Lima printer used both blacks and Indians in his operations. See Márquez Abanto, "Don Antonio Ricardo."

70. Levillier, 8: 101; *LCL*, 10: 361.

71. *LCL*, 7: 268, 270. The effectiveness of this prohibition is open to debate. For example, on the death of the pharmacist Francisco de Alva in 1576, an inventory of his possessions listed one Mateo Negro "who serves in the pharmacy." RA/PC, 18 (1575-76), creditors v. estate of Francisco de Alva: 7v.

72. Lockhart, pp. 183-84; SN 63 (1610): 681.

73. *LCL*, 5: 265-66; 8: 101-2; 15: 197; Harth-terré and Márquez Abanto, *RANP*, 25: 44-45. This is not to say, however, that momentary outbursts of prejudice did not occur, and these sometimes succeeded if the black had set up shop without first passing the examination or presenting his credentials. In 1634, for example, the carpenters guild persuaded the Lima city council to deny examination as a lathe operator to the slave of a Spanish surgeon, apparently because the black had been found guilty of setting up shop without first obtaining municipal approval. Nevertheless, in a rare departure from customary practice, the council based its refusal not on violation of the law but on the dual grounds of race and slavery. *LCL*, 23: 68.

74. Harth-terré and Márquez Abanto, *RANP*, 25: 12-13, 48-51.

75. Lockhart, pp. 182-83; Harth-terré and Márquez Abanto, *RANP*, 25: 9-11, 46-50.

76. Lockhart, p. 183.

CHAPTER SEVEN

1. Ayala, 4: 372.

2. Herrera (1934), 2: 97, 124; Larrazábal Blanco, pp. 143-45; Díaz Soler (1965), p. 203; Haring, pp. 221-22; Davidson.

3. Konetzke, 1: 80-81; Aguirre Beltrán, *Población negra*, pp. 113, 160; *CDIU*, 10: 141-42; Encinas, 4: 384; Ortiz Fernández, *Hampa afro-cubana*, p. 426. Sporadic efforts continued to be made to enforce these laws. In 1562, for example, Baltasar de Loaysa was permitted to carry 2 mulattoes from Seville to Peru only on certification that both were the offspring of a *negra*

atezada (i.e., a very dark black woman, presumably an African and not a *morisca*) and a "white Spanish Old Christian" man. AGIL 567.10: 249v, 253r.

4. Encinas, 4: 388; Konetzke, 1: 213-14.

5. The only known contemporary copy of this document is to be found in AGI, Patronato 171, no. 2.10. The copy is undated, but the ordinances are assumed by Konetzke, 1: 237-40, to have been drawn up around 1545. The ordinances are also printed in *CDII*, 11: 82.

6. In local matters city councils were allowed to formulate ordinances consistent with the general principles of Castilian law. Subsequent royal approval was required, but in the interval such ordinances enjoyed the full force of law. See Altamira y Crevea, p. 52. With regard to the control of blacks, it is clear that Spanish municipal law was often a model for Peruvian legislation. For example, compare the concerns of the Seville city fathers (as expressed in Pike, *Aristocrats and Traders*, p. 181) with those expressed by Peruvian town councils as discussed in this and the following chapter.

7. *LCL*, 1: 22-25, 47. In 1536 the cabildo again forbade blacks to enter the Indian markets, and 2 years later the prohibition was specifically extended to black women and moriscas. *LCL*, 1: 116-17.

8. AGIL 565.2: 241. Printed in Barriga, *Documentos*, 3: 4-7; and in Porras Barrenechea, 2: 283.

9. AGIL 566.4: 252; Konetzke, 1: 206-7, 213; Levillier, 1: 154; *LCL*, 4: 93-94.

10. AGIL 567.7: 40r-48r; Herrera (1934), 4: 160. In 1555 the city of Trujillo adopted local ordinances on Afro-Indian relations that echoed the royal will. See Harth-terré and Márquez Abanto, *RANP*, 25: 23-24.

11. Konetzke, 1: 297, 321; AGIL 121, Cristóbal de Montalvo to Crown, Lima, 1 Feb 1566; *LCL*, 6.2: 486-87, resolution of the cabildo of 10 Mar 1567.

12. Haring, pp. 142-44; Rowe, "The Incas," pp. 161-70; Lohmann Villena, *Corregidor*, pp. 81-96.

13. On these and other measures, see AGI, Patronato 189, ramo 11, ordinances issued by Dr. Gregorio González de Cuenca, *oidor* (judge) of the Lima Audiencia, during an inspection of northern Peru on 29 Aug 1566; Levillier, 3: 121, and 8: 351, 370; Konetzke, 1: 422; and *LCL*, 8: 19. In 1570 the Crown also took the extraordinary step of forbidding African slaves to hold Indians in encomienda, a move provoked by events in Quito. See AGIL 569.13: 128v.

14. Konetzke, 1: 513, 527-28, 586-87, 598-600; 2.1: 24-30, 47, 401-2; AGIL 570.16: 92v-93r; AGIL 572.22: 352v-53r; AGIL 573.23: 66v-68r; AGIL 584.20: 269r-70r.

15. Levillier, 9: 66. Enríquez' claim of strong efforts on the part of the authorities is not particularly convincing when one considers that 9 short years later, in 1590, there was thought of moving the natives who had settled in the San Lázaro district of Lima across the Rímac River to the Indian compound called the Cercado to spare them from abuse by passing blacks and

mulattoes. Proposal of Don Pedro de Santillán, *alcalde ordinario*, in *LCL*, 11: 457-60, session of 15 Oct. Santillán added that blacks who lived in the city but worked in the countryside were accustomed to spend time in the shacks of the San Lázaro Indians engaged in "drinking and other dealings." In the same year Viceroy Cañete echoed these charges and added that the colored population of Lima was accustomed to concealing the fruits of their robberies in San Lázaro. Levillier, 12: 176.

16. AGIL 140, Serrano to Crown, Chucuito, 16 Mar 1609.

17. AGIL 138, Dr. Alonso Pérez Merchán to Crown, Lima, 20 May 1607. In this connection, see also AGIL 318, Fr. Tomás Durán y Ribera to Crown, Lima, 20 Apr 1591; and Levillier, 13: 173-74.

18. Poma de Ayala (1936), p. 710.

19. Lewin, *Descripción*, p. 40. Other sources used in this discussion are *LCL*, 1: 203, 287; 4: 55-56; 5: 265; 7: 566-67; Konetzke, 1: 290-91, 299-300, 384-88, 420, 436-37, 479; Encinas, 4: 388; Levillier, 3: 267; 10: 143; *Recopilación*, 7.5, laws 7, 15; AGIL 567.7: 40r-48r, 86; AGIL 570.14: 34r-35r, 337r; AGIL 583.17: 285v-86r; AGIL 801, decree of 10 July 1637.

20. Beltrán y Rózpide and Altolaguirre, 2: 266-67.

21. Konetzke, 1: 384-88; *LCL*, 4: 11; 5: 217; 12: 66off, ordinance 69; 23: 317.

22. *LCL*, 4: 55-56; 7: 580; 13: 774-75; Levillier, 10: 160; Konetzke, 1: 612-14.

23. *LCL*, 4: 11, 470-71; 12: 66off, ordinance 122; Poma de Ayala (1936), p. 708.

24. Lockhart, p. 191. In 1548 the city council of Cuzco also saw fit to forbid slaves access to the homes of free coloreds. "Actas," pp. 280-81, session of 25 Oct.

25. This discussion is based on Konetzke, 1: 384-88; Levillier, 1: 531; *LCL*, 1: 297; 4: 12-13, 28, 72-73; 5: 157-58, 162; AGIL 118, Pedro Rodríguez Puertocarrero to Crown, Lima, 30 Sept 1557, denouncing the Carabaya project.

26. Levillier, 3: 429-30; 7: 61-64; 8: 103-6; *LCL*, 7: 211; 13: 774-75; AGIL 569.13: 343; AGIL 108, "Instrucción de lo que Gerónimo de Mercado, regidor de esta ciudad de los Reyes, ha de hacer y pedir en los reinos de España a Su Majestad ...," 22 Dec 1574, item 23; AGIL 579.5: 226, royal request for a viceregal opinion on the proposal to relocate the free coloreds.

27. Lockhart, p. 188.

28. Poma de Ayala (1936), p. 707.

29. Lockhart, p. 182.

30. SN 13 (1565): 524.

31. SN 17 (1573): 193v-94v; SN 17 (1578): 465.

32. SN 29 (1560): 778; SN 27 (1569), no foliation; SN 33 (1575): 61r-62r.

33. RA/PC, 38 (1617), Juan González v. Sancho de Ávila. For additional examples of redhibition cases involving unruly slaves, see AA, Causas de negros, unnumbered legajos: Don Jusepe de Castilla Altamirano v. Bachiller

Diego de Morales; Licenciado Juan Sigler de Bustillo v. Doña Luisa de Montalvo; and Don Pedro de Castilla Manrique v. Licenciado Bernabé López de Burgos.

34. For a full discussion of the *alcalde ordinario*, see Bayle, pp. 159-74; Haring, pp. 162-70; and Moore, pp. 99-105.

35. The Callao alcalde could impose the penalties provided in law on the colored population for petty theft or curfew violation, and was also empowered to place vagrant free blacks and mulattoes with Spanish employers. In more important cases suspects and the cases prepared against them were still referred to the Lima magistrates for determination. The second Marqués de Cañete (1590-96) decreed that the alcalde must be a resident of Callao, and thereafter the magistrate was appointed by a complicated system that involved selected inhabitants of the port, the viceroy, and the Lima city council. *LCL*, 6.2: 390-94, 470; 7: 227-28; 11: 228-29; 12: 244-47; 15: 121-25, 629-31.

36. In Spanish law the *alguacil mayor* was a member of the city council and served at its pleasure, but this was not true of Peru. Francisco Pizarro was given the privilege of appointing these officials in Peruvian municipalities, and on his death the Crown claimed the prerogative. The post was a lucrative one and was among those ordered sold by the financially hard-pressed government in 1591. For more information, see *LCL*, 1: 52, 146; Bayle, pp. 189-95; Haring, pp. 162-66; Parry, *Sale*, pp. 24-29; and Moore, pp. 110-11.

37. The Audiencia's decision was final in criminal cases, whether heard on appeal or in the first instance, a rule specifically applied to blacks and Indians in 1534. Konetzke, 1: 163, decree of 27 Oct. But there were rare exceptions. In 1602, for example, a Licenciado Delgado and his slave, both condemned to death by the tribunal for murder, escaped to Spain and obtained a royal pardon. AGIL 136.

38. For more detail on the judicial role of the Audiencia, see Haring, pp. 129-37. The rest of Peru enjoyed a different relationship with the Audiencia. As we have seen, in the 16th century the Indian areas of the colony came to be ruled by corregidores, and the same was true of the principal Spanish towns and their surrounding districts. In judicial matters these officials acted as an intermediate court of appeal between municipal magistrates and the Audiencia, though criminal cases involving blacks were rarely appealed to the high tribunal from other parts of the colony because of the distance and expense. For a brief period a corregidor was also appointed for Lima, but the office was abolished in 1568 because of the proximity of the Audiencia and viceroy. On the role of the corregidor, see Bayle, pp. 155-69; Moore, pp. 261-62; and Castañeda, pp. 446-61.

39. AGIL 127, Ramos to Crown, 26 Apr 1584; *LCL*, 18: 101-2, 434-36; Salvatierra to his successor, in Beltrán y Rózpide and Altolaguirre, 2: 266-67.

40. *LCL*, 6.2: 57-59, 87, 544; 8: 326-27, 659-64; 12: 372-74, 423-24; 13: 557-58; 14: 189-90; 18: 710; 19: 534-35.

41. AGIL 108; *LCL*, 18: 741.

42. Normally, the curfew hour varied with the season. In 1624, for exam-

ple, from November 1 to April 30 the bell rang for blacks between 8 and 9 P.M. and for Spaniards between 10 and 11; and from May 1 to October 31 the respective hours were 7-8 and 9-10. In the beginning curfew was tolled by a bell in the municipal jail, but later the chimes of the cathedral were used since they carried a greater distance. *LCL*, 19: 769.

43. AGIL 38, Esquilache to Crown, 18 Apr 1618.

44. AGIL 571.18: 98v-99r, 100v-101v.

45. AGIL 96, Audiencia to Crown, undated letter; AGIL 571.19: 47, Crown to Audiencia, 28 May 1621.

46. For this and similar complaints about the blacks of the Holy Office, see Levillier, 7: 24-25, 237-38, 403-4.

47. AGIL 165. The decree is included among the petitions and testimony presented to the Council of the Indies by Don Diego de Ayala, *alcalde provincial* of the Hermandad, in 1640.

48. AGIL 95, "Testimonio de la causa que se siguió contra un negro de Juan de Robles, familiar del Santo Oficio," Lima, 26 Apr 1611; Suardo, 1: 132, 243-44.

49. AGIL 1631, testimony of Juan Gutiérrez de Molina, clerk of the Audiencia; AGIL 570.14: 336v, decree of 19 Nov 1586, approving the sentence of exile; Levillier, 10: 143-44; 221-22, Villar to Crown, 25 May and 23 Dec 1586.

50. Suardo, 2: 85.

51. AGIL 97, *alcaldes del crimen* and Luis Enríquez to Crown, 26 and 28 Apr 1621.

52. AGIL 571.20: 139r-43r.

53. AGIL 156, Mexía to Crown, 18 Feb 1626.

54. AGIL 572.20: 94v-95v.

55. Suardo, 2: 17-19, 66, 89, 100; AGIL 99, Audiencia to Crown, 18 May 1636; AGIL 572.21: 274r.

56. In the main this paragraph is based on bills of sale and bail bonds in those Peruvian notarial records that mentioned crimes committed by blacks in credible detail. Two other sources were also used: a document in AGIL 1633 that lists the criminal suits pending before the Audiencia when Toledo became viceroy in 1570; and Suardo, who mentions both major and minor crimes committed in Lima between 1629 and 1639.

57. AGIC 1686, record of expenditures for 1570: 103-4; Sater; Mellafe, *Introducción*, pp. 95-102.

58. On the debate over the Acuña proposal and the realities of galley service at Callao, see Lewin, *Descripción*, p. 68; Suardo, 2: 121; AGIL 95, Acuña to Crown, 20 May 1607, and Audiencia to Crown, 30 Mar 1609; AGIL 571.17: 51v-52r, Crown to Audiencia, 24 Jan 1610; AGIL 97, Acuña to Crown, 2 May 1623; AGIL 154, Capt. Don Pedro Gutiérrez Calderón to Crown supporting Acuña, 2 May 1623; AGIL 571.19: 259r-60r, Crown to Guadalcázar, 13 Nov 1626; AGIL 41, Guadalcázar to Crown, 15 Mar 1628; Konetzke, 2.1: 328, decree of 18 Feb 1631 ordering implementation of proposal; AGIL 162,

memorial from mine operators of Huancavelica forwarded to Crown, 20 May 1636.

59. AGIL 154, Gutiérrez Calderón to Crown, 2 May 1623.

60. Biblioteca Nacional (Madrid), mss. 2010. The memorial is undated, but additional correspondence from Monsalve to the Crown in AGIL 321 suggests it was written around 1600. For biographical information on Monsalve, see Lohmann Villena, *Minas*, pp. 249-50, where the Dominican is described as "restless, wild-eyed, and possessed with a mania for writing."

61. Poma de Ayala (1936), pp. 704-10.

62. Levillier, 3: 106, 240-41; AGIL 313, Corral to Crown, 4 Mar 1567.

63. In 1586 Viceroy Villar reported rumors of a plot by some mulattoes in Potosí, but he minimized the potential dangers of such a plot supposing there was one. Levillier, 10: 158-59.

64. AGIL 228, proof of services presented in 1628 by Luis Fernández de Córdova, grandson of the slain official.

65. AGIL 276, Visitor-General Juan Gutiérrez Flores to Crown, 29 Oct 1626; Suardo, 2: 65. Beginning in 1634 the Crown granted to the highest bidder the exclusive privilege of supplying Lima's inhabitants with snow, which was brought down from the surrounding mountains and was packed hard like ice. See Escalona y Agüero, book 2, part 2, chap. 20.

66. AGIL 158, proof of services of Aguilar; AGIL 138, a similar document prepared by Diego García de Paredes, gov. of the area during the 1604 revolt.

67. Levillier, 3: 257-58; AGIL 108, Lima city council to Crown, 20 Apr 1619; AGIL 571.18: 246v-47r, Crown to Esquilache, 28 Mar 1620.

68. Lewin, *Descripción*, p. 40.

69. AGIC 1688, record of expenditures for 1577, *passim*; LCL, 8: 442-48; Konetzke, 1: 489-90; Wright, *passim*; Newton, pp. 86-93.

70. AGIL 125, Ramírez de Cartagena to Crown, 27 Apr 1579.

71. Levillier, 12: 290.

72. *LCL*, 12: 422.

73. The same point was made some years earlier by Lewin's anonymous observer: "What most assures those of the city that the blacks will not revolt is that the latter are of many nations and castes and almost all are enemies of one another." *Descripción*, p. 40. In 1615 Viceroy Montesclaros said as much to his successor Esquilache, and stated that even under threat of Dutch attack he had been most reluctant to organize blacks and mulattoes into militia units lest it increase their sense of community and accustom them to obeying the orders of a few men. Beltrán y Rózpide and Altolaguirre, 1: 169.

74. AGIL 135, Vázquez de Loaysa to Crown, 29 Apr 1601; AGIL 145, letter of 30 Apr 1615.

75. *LCL*, 17: 664.

76. AGIL 37, Viceroy Esquilache to Crown, 30 Apr 1616; AGIL 146, Cacho de Santillana to Crown, 19 May 1616.

77. AGIL 38, Álvarez de Paz to Esquilache, 25 July 1618.

78. AGIL 108, decree of 30 Aug 1618. Violations were to be punished by a fine equal to the value of the slave; free blacks were to receive 100 lashes.

79. AGIL 582.18: 277v-78r.

80. LCL, 19: 163, 381.

81. AGIL 154, memorial from Gutiérrez Calderón.

82. AGIL 40, Guadalcázar to Crown, 6 June 1624.

83. LCL, 19: 908-9.

84. Beltrán y Rózpide and Altolaguirre, 2: 43.

85. AGIL 160. However, the Crown continued to push for a curtailment of the number of armed black lackeys. Konetzke, 2.1: 317, decree of 4 Apr 1628.

86. Suardo, 1: 57-58.

87. AGIL 162, Esquivel Triana to Crown, 12 May 1634.

88. AGIL 47, Chinchón to Crown, 11 Oct 1636.

89. Real Academia de la Historia (Madrid), Colección Muñoz, 89: 293v, Chinchón to Villena, 3 June 1637.

90. Beltrán y Rózpide and Altolaguirre, 2: 86.

91. AGIL 572.22: 6v-7v, 113r. In 1645 the Crown again urged that the slave population be closely watched, a decree printed in Ortiz Fernández, *Hampa afro-cubana*, p. 448.

92. AGIL 50, Mancera to Crown, 21 May 1640.

93. AGIL 51, Mancera to Crown, 20 and 23 July 1642. Mancera admitted to his successor, Salvatierra, that so many Portuguese claimed exemption from the decree of expulsion from Lima that their cases had to be judged one by one, and many seem to have remained in the city. Beltrán y Rózpide and Altolaguirre, 2: 147-49.

94. Beltrán y Rózpide and Altolaguirre, 2: 179.

95. On arms and the colored population during Salvatierra's time, see also AGIL 100, Don Pedro Vázquez de Velasco to Crown, 15 Sept 1651; and Mugaburu and Mugaburu, 1:29.

CHAPTER EIGHT

1. AGIJ 451 (1546), "Residencia tomada de los Licenciados Diego Vázquez de Cepeda, Pedro Ortiz de Zárate, Alonso Álvarez y Lisón de Tejada...": 1074v, 1103v, 1131r, 1142r, 1154; Rafael Loredo in the prologue to Borregán, p. 15, n5.

2. Lockhart, p. 189; Guillot, pp. 254-55.

3. LCL, 4: 4-5, 111-12.

4. Borregán, pp. 91, 97, 101.

5. Lockhart, pp. 189-90.

6. Both cases in AA, Causas de negros: Dr. Francisco Calvo de Sandoval v. Licenciado Juan de Bonifacio; and Juan Ochoa de Aranda v. Doña María de Prado.

7. RA/PC, 53 (1622), estate of Juan Rodríguez Acevedo; 92 (1636), estate

of Francisco Rodríguez del Padrón; 94 (1636-37), estate of Don Juan Gutié-rrez Flores. Often, the names of runaway blacks were carried on plantation inventories for years after their flight.

8. SN 14 (1591): 970-71.

9. SN 45 (1620): 228-29; SN 17 (1585): 1152; SN 2 (1595): 90r-91r.

10. SN 38 (1645): 13r-14r; SN 68 (1650): 1083r-84r.

11. SN 46 (1610): 498r-500r; SN 85 (1615): 360v-61v.

12. Suardo, 2: 43, 45.

13. SN 17 (1566): 330; SN 3 (1591): 96r-97r; AA, Causas de negros, Cris-tóbal de Loayza v. Licenciado Cristóbal de Ortega. This was an age when jail space was very limited, and the accused was expected to pay for the costs of confinement—or, in the case of a black, his master. Viceroy Toledo, in his 1572 ordinances for the governance of Cuzco, for example, was at pains to ensure that blacks imprisoned for delinquencies be punished and set free with dispatch, and that their masters be made liable for all jail costs as well as judicial fines. Levillier, 8: 103-6. Given these circumstances, some masters signed what we would consider to be bail bonds, known as *cartas de depósito* or *fianzas de la haz*, promises that their slaves would appear at the date set for their trials and that the slaveholder would pay all judicial fines and costs in the event of a guilty verdict. In many instances, however, third parties performed this function for slaveholders of dubious financial resources and received the labor of the black in the interim as compensation. In 1645, for example, Francisco Gómez de la Estrella, the owner of a bakery (establish-ments that relied heavily on this device because the hard work and low wages involved attracted few takers even among slaveholders with idle blacks), was entrusted with the alleged runaway Marcos Jolofo, the slave of the Indian Pedro Felipe. SN 45, 15 Apr: 44. The danger here, obviously, was that the slave would run away again, exposing the bondsman to legal expenses and fines while denying him the use of the black's labor.

14. SN 13 (transaction of 1567 mixed with those for 1568): 1417; SN 14 (1591), no foliation; SN 29 (1564): 1174. On this point, see also Lockhart, p. 189.

15. SN 37 (1600), letter of agreement of 25 May: 640-41; ANP, Inquisición: Contencioso, 19 (1631-32), Gutiérrez Velázquez Ovando v. Bartolomé de Lanza.

16. SN 35 (1640): 51, 62-63; AA, Causas de negros, Luisa Velásquez v. Luis de Aguilar y Mora.

17. AA, Causas de negros, Nicolás de la Plana v. Doña María de Cervantes.

18. Poma de Ayala (1936), p. 711.

19. RA/PC, 42 (1618), Doña Michaela de la Torre v. estate of Francisco de Mendoza: 64r-68r. Interestingly, the apprehended blacks were allowed le-gal counsel during their trial.

20. SN 45 (1645): 45.

21. SN 17 (1573): 875-76; SN 37 (1625): 99r-100r; SN 85 (1625): 428-29.

22. SN 63 (1610): 105v-6v; SN 57 (1645): 2268-69.

23. SN 73 (1610): 652v-54r; SN 91 (1600): 1024; SN 43 (1630): 475-79.

24. LCL, 1: 24, 146; 4: 4-5, 12, 111-12; 5: 149; 6.1: 228-29; 6.2: 135-36, 159-60, 480-82.

25. LCL, 1: 298-99; 4: 4-5, 27, 47, 72-73, 75, 111-12.

26. LCL, 4: 118-25.

27. In general the government frowned on mutilation and death as suitable punishments for criminal blacks, and in 1536 forbade the death penalty for runaways as contrary to the laws of the realm. AGIL 565.2: 223v-24r. However, the Crown did not choose to overturn the contradictory provisions of the Lima ordinances, and (as we have seen in Chap. 7), mutilation for cases of Afro-Indian sexual relations received royal sanction in 1551. A further reversal of Crown policy occurred in 1571, when it was decreed that a black absent for more than 6 months and found consorting with other cimarrones might be hanged. Leaders of runaway bands who resisted capture might also be executed without trial. Klein, pp. 70-71.

28. In 1559 Viceroy Cañete lowered the tax to 2 pesos per head on cargoes of more than 30 slaves, but the original rate seems to have been reinstated shortly thereafter. AGI, Escribanía de Cámara 500a, "El Consejo, Justicia y Regimiento de la ciudad de los Reyes con los mercaderes... [1588-95]": 12v-14v.

29. This post was discontinued some twenty years later, in 1568.

30. Some 9 years earlier, a royal decree provided that runaways who voluntarily returned to their masters, presumably after any length of absence, were not to be punished, and this practice seems to have been adopted in Peru. Encinas, 4: 394, decree of 7 Sept 1540.

31. Mellafe, *Introducción*, pp. 82-83.

32. Though Bayle, pp. 170-71, says the *alcalde de la Hermandad* was nominally subordinate to the *alcaldes ordinarios*, i.e., he captured the criminal and prepared the case whereas the others passed sentence, this was not the practice in Peru, where the head of the Hermandad had the authority to try all cases under his jurisdiction and to carry out the sentences. In 1623 the Lima city council provided that the legal counsel (*asesor*) appointed to advise the municipal justices render the same service to the head of the Hermandad. The decisions of both judges were subject to review by the Audiencia. LCL, 5: 563; 6.1: 151, 478-81; 19: 484-85.

33. LCL, 5: 481, 611, 613, 615; 6.1: 160-61. For a brief period colored cuadrilleros were also titled *alguaciles de negros*. In an interesting case of 1566, 2 mulatto constables were invested with the title, one for the city and one for the countryside. The appointment carried the proviso that on fiesta days they assemble and guard the wooden barriers for the city's bullring. For this they received a bonus of 25 pesos plus the 4 bulls that were allotted for the year. LCL, 6.2: 345, 385.

34. This measure was re-proclaimed in 1571. LCL, 7: 191.

35. Konetzke, 1: 384-88.

36. AGI, Patronato 189, ramo 11, ordinances framed by González for the

villa of Jayanaca in the Saña area, 29 Aug 1566; AGIC 1685, list of expenditures for 1568: 150.

37. LCL, 7: 125-26, 258, 268-69, 289.

38. Levillier, 4: 447; 5: 339-40; 8: 103-6; Biblioteca Nacional (Madrid), ms. 19282, Gayangos Collection: 163r-64v.

39. These totals are based on an examination of the Lima city council records for the appropriate years and on a list of expenses taken from the headtax records by Blas Hernández, city clerk, on 7 Apr 1588, which was entered as testimony in the lawsuit cited in note 28, above.

40. Suit cited in note 28, fols. 61-62, testimony of 10 Apr 1588. Ampuero mentioned other expeditions of 1560 and 1570.

41. LCL, 5: 209; 6.2: 435, 449; 7: 421, 457, 463.

42. LCL, 4: 648-49, 652-53, 663; 7: 14, 41, 87, 496; 8: 192-95; 10: 216-17, 478-79. The Crown too borrowed from the caja, taking nearly 3,000 pesos in 1554 to help finance the suppression of the Hernández Girón rebellion, but this money was almost certainly repaid. AGIC 1680, "Cargo de los pesos de oro que recibió Sancho de Ugarte . . . ," entry of 15 Feb 1554.

43. For examples of this practice, see the suit cited in note 28, fols. 54r, 57v-58r, 73r; and LCL, 4: 300-301, 545-48.

44. LCL, 7: 469-70; 8: 577; 10: 145; suit cited in note 28, fols. 31, 38r, 72r.

45. LCL, 5: 687-88; 7: 336-37; 8: 175, 200, 222.

46. LCL, 6.1: 160-61, 298, 301, 318, 357; 6.2: 8, 74, 76, 99, 104-5, 113, 121, 133, 139-40, 155, 174, 272, 365, 385. One unsalaried free black was also appointed in 1565.

47. LCL, 6.2: 324-25; 7: 134, 189-90, 218; suit cited in note 28, fols. 77-92.

48. LCL, 7: 126, 344-45, 422; 8: 24, 31, 258-59, 333, 655-56, 678; 9: 115, 183, 223, 233-34, 339, 414-15; 13: 112.

49. LCL, 8: 127.

50. AGIC 1680, "Cargo de penas de cámara," entry of 22 Dec 1557.

51. Suit cited in note 28, fols. 30, 33-35, 36v-37r, 133, 141, 147v-48r, 155v-56r.

52. LCL, 7: 243; 9: 270, 272-73, 507.

53. The office was so unattractive that the *alcaldes de la Hermandad* for 1563 were compelled by the city council to exercise their duties under threat of a 200-peso fine. LCL, 6.2: 113.

54. LCL, 6.1: 151, 346-48, 478-81, 486-87; 6.2: 84, 96, 171-72, 289, 378, 449; 7: 25, 80, 86-87, 124-25, 206, 420, 551; 8: 92-93; 9: 424-25; 10: 307.

55. LCL, 10: 321-24, 394; Levillier, 10: 155; suit cited in note 28, fols. 6r, 93-95, 151, 158v-59v, 167v-68r.

56. AGIL 568.9: 411v, decree of 7 Feb 1560; AGIL 569.11: 69r-70r, decree of 14 Nov 1563; AGIL 580.9: 141v-42r, decree of 17 Mar 1589.

57. Suit cited in note 28, fols. 170r-71r; AGIL 1, opinion of Council of the Indies, 25 Jan 1597; AGIL 581.12: 89r-90r, decree of 18 Feb 1597.

58. Figueroa, p. 89. A similar picture is given in Lewin, *Descripción*, pp. 31, 45-46.

59. Levillier, 12: 168-69, 273.

60. AGIL 110, various correspondence between Cuzco and the Crown (1594-1601); Bayle, pp. 170-71.

61. LCL, 11: 59, 165, 229, 318-22, 359ff, 454, 491-95, 500, 530, 548, 625-27, 640-41, 738, 767; 12: 564, 583, 66off [nos. 212 and 213]; 13: 175; suit cited in note 28, fols. 93-95, 151.

62. AGIL 108, city of Lima's instructions of 1574 and 1583 to its representative in Spain; LCL, 11: 693, 695.

63. LCL, 12: 458; 13: 9-10, 317; 14: 595-96; 15: 517-19; 18: 811. However, contrary to practice in Spain, the Lima alcalde was denied a place on the city council.

64. LCL, 13: 90-91, 175, 340-41; AGIL 163, a bundle of petitions and testimony presented by Don Diego de Ayala, provincial of the Hermandad, to Council of the Indies in 1637. Among these documents are various titles of authority issued to the heads of the Lima constabulary in 1606, 1621, 1630, and 1635, confirming his expanded jurisdiction.

65. LCL, 13: 317, 327-28, 340-41, 377-78, 390, 404-6, 509; 14: 27-29; 16: 13, 312.

66. LCL, 13: 14, 69, 166-67, 200, 395-96, 642, 644-45, 731; 14: 281, 941-42; 15: 533-34, 747.

67. LCL, 18: 321, 327, 329-30, 751, 754, 762-63; 19: 458. On the rancheadores of Cuba, see Klein, p. 70.

68. LCL, 19: 322, 486; AGIL 97, Enríquez to Crown, 28 Apr 1623.

69. AGIL 571.20: 256v-57v, Crown to Guadalcázar (1626); AGIL 41, Guadalcázar to Crown (1628); AGIL 572.20: 147v, Crown to Chinchón (1630).

70. AGIL 41, "Certificación del recetor de la avería de los negros bozales que entran en Lima. . . ."

71. AGIL 45, Chinchón to Crown, 20 Apr 1634; AGIL 105, Valencia to Crown, 14 May 1633.

72. AGIL 572.21: 80r-81r, Crown to Chinchón, 30 Mar 1635; AGIL 45, Chinchón to Crown, 20 Nov 1635.

73. AGIL 163, Ayala material cited in note 64; AGIC 1723, "Cuentas de real hacienda desde el despacho de la armada de 1638 hasta la de 1639," pl. 793-96. The office of *escribano de la Hermandad*, i.e., the clerk who prepared the legal documentation associated with the institution, had been sold as early as 1606 for 3,000 pesos and was disposed of again in 1621 for 2,000. LCL, 15: 205-14; 19: 271-75.

74. AGIL 572.21: 263; AGIC 1721, "Cuentas de real hacienda desde el despacho de la armada de 1636 hasta la de 1637," pl. 581-92; LCL, 16: 543.

75. Information on the career of Valladolid Mogorón can be found in AGIL 166; and Konetzke, 2.1: 470-71, prints a Council of the Indies opinion on his petition for advancement. The Cañete incident is reported by Suardo, 1: 216.

76. Accounts of these and other incidents involving cimarrones in the Lima area will be found in Suardo, 1: 198, 254, 296-97, 299, 301; 2: 20, 22, 24, 49, 88. See also AGIC 1725, treasury accounts for 1640-41, pl. 737.

77. Suardo, 2: 192.
78. AGIL 165, from Ayala material presented to Council of the Indies in 1640.
79. Suardo, 1: 246, 250.
80. AGIL 163, Ayala material of 1637.
81. Though Ayala did not mention it in his appeal to the Council of the Indies, he found no allies among the members of the Lima city council. Rather, at a meeting of 30 Jan 1637 the council members voted to ask Chinchón to reconsider his ruling and lower the fees that the Hermandad might charge for the capture of runaways. *LCL*, 23: 423.
82. AGIL 163, Ayala material of 1637; AGIL 165, Ayala material of 1640.
83. AGIC 1720-33, "Data de la avería de los negros bozales."

CHAPTER NINE

1. Konetzke, 1: 237-40.
2. Sandoval, pp. 192-94; Martín, pp. 68-70.
3. Martín, p. 69.
4. Sandoval, pp. 194-97.
5. Poma de Ayala (1936), pp. 704-12, 925-26.
6. Muzquiz de Miguel, pp. 116-17.
7. Lewin, *Descripción*, pp. 48-50; Harth-terré and Márquez Abanto, *RANP*, 25: 3-73 *passim*, who indicate that even wine was usually provided to the craftsmen's assistants.
8. *LCL*, 6.2: 352; 7: 494-95; Harth-terré and Márquez Abanto, *RANP*, 25: 18-27, and *RANP*, 22: 202-5.
9. RA/PC, 48 (1620-21), Doña Florencia de Aliaga v. Melchior de Salazar: 4r-8r; 97 (1637), creditors v. estate of Lorenzo Pérez Noguera: 7v-8r, 29v, 318r, 392-95, 557-77.
10. *LCL*, 6.2: 370, 513; 7: 49, 214, 228-29, 294, 503, 606-7.
11. Martín, p. 70; Lewin, *Descripción*, pp. 23, 29, 58.
12. See the accounts cited in note 9. Similar expenses in the rural areas are reported in RA/PC, 4 (1601), Hernando Alonso del Villar v. Garci Barba Cabeza de Vaca: 66v-67r.
13. Lewin, *Descripción*, p. 38. Several references, primarily in plantation inventories in RA/PC, make mention of this type of rural housing for blacks.
14. Levillier, 11: 221-22, 284, 285; 12: 89 (various letters from Viceroys Villar and Cañete to Crown, 1589); AGIL 94, Audiencia to Crown, 19 Aug 1606.
15. Martín, pp. 70-71.
16. *LCL*, 4: 292; 7: 160, 218, 465, 583.
17. AGIL 584.20: 288v-89v, decree of 26 Mar 1640.
18. RA/PC, 4 (1601) Hernando Alonso del Villar v. Garci Barba Cabeza de Vaca: 30r, 44v-45r, 66v-67r, 75v.
19. AGIC 1692, "Data de tributos de Tiaguanaco del cargo del tesorero Pedro de Vera [1580]": 165.

20. Martín, pp. 69-70; Poma de Ayala (1936), pp. 706, 925; AGIL 42, Chinchón to Crown, 31 Oct 1629.

21. AGIC 1682, judicial fines owed the Crown and collected by the treasurer Bernardo Ruíz, 1555, entry of 7 Dec; Suardo, 2: 45.

22. AGIC 1680, "Cargo que se hace al tesorero Juan Muñoz Rico ... de condenaciones de penas de cámara [1557]," entry of 21 Jan; AGIC 1683, same account for 1564, entry of 20 Apr.

23. However, the case soon became entangled in a dispute between Church and state over jurisdiction. Levillier, 7: 335-36, Licenciado Álvaro de Carvajal, royal attorney for the Lima Audiencia, to Crown, 7 May 1576.

24. For example, in AGIL 1633 a list compiled in 1571, "Testimonio de los pleitos civiles y criminales que ha seguido y sigue el Señor Licenciado Ramírez de Cartagena después que es fiscal de S.M.," *passim*, contains numerous instances of Spaniards brought to justice for cruel treatment of blacks.

25. AGIJ 453, *residencia* of Licenciado Bautista Monzón, *fiscal* of the Lima Audiencia, testimony of Juan de Aos, 9 June 1568: 120v-21v.

26. LCL, 6.2: 144-45.

27. Quoted by Guillot, p. 268.

28. Archivo Histórico Nacional (Madrid), Sección de Inquisición, Relaciones de fe (Lima), book 1027, memorandum of cases tried and sentences (1571-73): 29v.

29. LCL, 7: 619, session of 12 July 1574.

30. Phelan, p. 57.

31. Konetzke, 1: 231, 237-40.

32. Guillot, pp. 271-72; Levillier, 8: 52.

33. Sandoval, p. 89. The rest of this section is based on pp. 197-212, 280-81, 335-47, 400-401, 421-58. Father Sandoval's missionary labors among the Africans were centered in the great slaving port of Cartagena, where conditions may have been harsher than elsewhere in Spanish America with regard to Christianization and slave existence in general. Nevertheless, Sandoval had lived in Lima and had studied at the Jesuit College of San Pablo there, and the remarks in his work were phrased in such a way as to give them general application to the American colonies. For biographical detail, see the remarks of Valtierra in the introduction to *De instauranda*, pp. x-xxii. On the reception given the book by the Jesuits of Lima, see Martín, pp. 51-52.

34. AA, Causas de negros, Antonio Rodríguez de la Cruz, attorney of the archepiscopal court of Lima, v. Bartolomé Sánchez.

35. Encinas, 4: 392; AGIL 300, Archbishop to Crown, 23 Apr 1572.

36. This and the following paragraph are based on the relevant documentation in AGIL 1.

37. Konetzke, 2.1: 99-100.

38. AGIL 94, Audiencia to Crown, 20 May 1606; AGIL 570.16: 165, royal reply, 13 Feb 1607.

39. AGIL 302, Archbishop to Crown, 27 May 1632; AGIL 572.21: 34, Crown to Chinchón, 12 Aug 1634.

40. AGIL 47, Chinchón to Crown, 29 Apr 1636, with accompanying copies of his exchange of correspondence with the Archbishop.
41. AGIL 572.21: 240v-41v, decree of 30 Mar 1637.
42. AGIL 308, 15 July 1652.
43. AGIL 312 and AGIL 1618, various letters of 1649-50 from the Mercedarians, the Jesuits, and the dean and members of the Lima cathedral chapter.
44. AGIL 329, Fr. Francisco Crespo to Crown, about 1625.
45. Vázquez de Espinosa, p. 478.
46. AA, Causas de visitas, leg. 1.10, Cañete (1632).
47. AGIL 571.19: 228v, Crown to Enríquez, 14 Oct 1626; Mörner, *Race Mixture*, p. 60n.
48. E.g., RA/PC, 1 (1600), "Pedro Pablo Morón ... contra Doña Ana Venegas, su segunda mujer, sobre el remate de los bienes de Antonio de la Cueva, difunto," will of the deceased, Lima, 1 July 1600, listing 2 Bioho slaves, both without Christian names, "who are not Christians."
49. E.g., RA/PC, 102 (1639), Baltasar de Tinco v. heirs of Licenciado Andrés de Arevalo: 406; 94 (1636-37), inventory of estate of Don Juan Gutiérrez Flores, unnumbered folios.
50. RA/PC, 1 (1600), Miguel Hernández de Bonilla v. Francisco Carrasco: 3r-6r; 48 (1620-21), Doña Florencia de Aliaga v. Melchior de Salazar: 69r, 72v-73r.
51. RA/PC, 97 (1637), creditors v. estate of Lorenzo Pérez Noguera: 573v.
52. Vázquez de Espinosa, p. 442.
53. For additional detail about San Martín (who was canonized in 1962), see Chap. 11; and Cassinelli; Bernardo Medina; and Preher.
54. Vázquez de Espinosa, p. 436.
55. Sandoval, p. 584; Vargas Ugarte, *Biblioteca Peruana*, 4: 112-13, letter from Fr. Antonio Pardo to Fr. Diego Álvarez de Paz, Trujillo, 19 Oct 1618.
56. Martín, p. 51.
57. *Ibid.*, pp. 51-52, 132, 137; Guillot, p. 272.
58. The information in this paragraph and the next is drawn from Vázquez de Espinosa, p. 438; Guillot, p. 272; Martín, pp. 142-43; and Vargas Ugarte, "Nuevos documentos," pp. 209-11.
59. Vázquez de Espinosa, p. 432.
60. *LCL*, 4: 55-56.
61. Konetzke, 1: 612-14; 2.1: 88.
62. *LCL*, 10: 180-81, session of 29 Apr 1585.
63. AGIL 34, Dominicans and Jesuits to Crown, 4 and 11 Apr 1603.
64. Harth-terré and Márquez Abanto, *RANP*, 25: 34-35.
65. Martín, pp. 133-34.
66. Archivo Histórico Nacional (Madrid), Sección de Inquisición, Relaciones de fe (Lima), book 1027: 11, 111v, 146, 198.
67. Lewin, *Descripción*, p. 73.
68. The investigation is entered as testimony in AGIJ 451, "Residencia tomada de los Licenciados Diego Vázquez de Cepeda, Pedro Ortiz de Zárate,

Alonso Álvarez y Lisón de Tejada por el Licenciado Pedro de la Gasca [1549]": 623, 877-89. On Don Francisco de Ampuero and Doña Inés Yupanqui, see Mendiburu, 2: 3-6.

69. AGIL 1633, "Testimonio de los pleitos civiles y criminales que ha seguido y sigue el Señor Licenciado Ramírez de Cartagena [1570]"; Tejado Fernández, pp. 53, 82-85, 130, 295-302.

70. AGIL 300, "Información contra el Padre Luna sobre haber querido dar hechizos a Su Excelencia."

71. See Davis, pp. 102-6, and the sources there cited. The Crown was particularly anxious that married slaves not be separated by transfer of one of the partners from Spain to America, as expressed by a 1570 decree published in Konetzke, 1: 451, and there was some attempt to enforce this measure. See various permits for slave couples to come to Spanish America for the years 1570-79 in AGIL 569.13: 184v; AGIL 578.14: 83v-84r; and AGIL 578.5: 95v.

72. Vargas Ugarte, *Concilios Limenses*, 1: 227, 338; AGIL 308, "Constituciones sinodales de este obispado ... ordenadas por el Reverendísimo Señor Don Francisco Verdugo [5-6 Aug 1629]": 16.

73. Poma de Ayala (1936), pp. 704-5; Sandoval, pp. 197-202. In law, children born of slave mothers (in or out of wedlock) assumed slave status, as reaffirmed for America by a decree of 1526 published in Konetzke, 1: 81-82.

74. RA/PC, 53 (1622), estate of Juan Rodríguez Acevedo: 32-33; 124 (1650), "Autos hechos a pedimento de Juan de Otacer ...": 61; 97 (1637), creditors v. estate of Lorenzo Pérez Noguera: 318r.

75. RA/PC, 25 (1585-86), Licenciado Álvaro de Torres v. Juan Gil de Montenegro: 5v; 94 (1636-37), inventory of estate of Don Juan Gutiérrez Flores, unnumbered; 85 (1634), Dr. Julián de León v. creditors of Hernando de la Concha: 177v-79r, 200r-201r.

76. AGIL 300, city of Lima to Crown, 26 Apr 1584. The city here urged confirmation of the resolutions of the ecclesiastical council despite the council's rebuff of the city's complaint on slave marriages.

77. The housing of married couples who belonged to different masters was more easily arranged in the countryside. One of the Ayala documents in AGIL 163, for example, cites the case of the ladino Damián Mozambique and his wife, both of whom were owned by landowners on the outskirts of Lima. Damián worked for his master by day, but lived in his wife's hut on her owner's estate.

78. Suardo, 1: 292-96.

79. SN 14 (1590): 1700.

80. AA, Causas de negros. A similar change of heart occurred in 1638 involving 2 mulatto slaves of different mistresses. The woman, Luisa de Villarroel, had consented to marry Felipe de Guerra but changed her mind at the last moment, and the license was not granted. *Ibid.*

81. For 1649 alone, for instance, I found records of 2 marriages between widowed slaves, one uniting Miguel and Monica Angola, and the other Felipe Mandinga and Catalina Jolofa. *Ibid.*

82. These licenses are housed in the Archivo Arzobispal in Lima. From their chronological distribution (see tabulation below) it is clear that many of those issued during the period have not survived. Indeed, on the basis of such obviously fragmentary data, one would not even want to hazard a guess as to the probable number of slave marriages in Lima in any given year during this period.

Year	No. of licenses	Year	No. of licenses	Year	No. of licenses
1600	4	1634	11	1643	4
1605	2	1635	5	1645	2
1614	1	1636	3	1646	2
1615	1	1637	32	1647	4
1617	1	1638	54	1648	4
1620	1	1639	36	1649	35
1621	1	1640	42	1650	5
1632	1	1641	10		
1633	1	1642	27		

83. E.g., SN 93 (1630), bill of sale of 24 July: 414-15, in which Lucrecia Angola, age 30 and "married to another slave of mine," was sold by her master to the parish priest of San Marcelo.

84. SN 17 (1578): 557v-58v; SN 14 (1590 and 1591): 176v-77v, 970-71, respectively; SN 46 (1610): 397.

85. E.g., ANP, Inquisición: Contencioso, 24 (1635), "Auto referente al ne-gro de Tomé de Quaresma, relajado," which concerns the case of the basket-maker Francisco Angola, owned by Quaresma and sent in 1635 to the mines of Bombón in the asiento of Santiago de Guadalcázar for delivery to Rodrigo de Navajada. Francisco was married to a slave owned by Navajada, who had agreed to buy Francisco for 425 pesos, payable by the armada of 1635. In the meantime the slave was to earn a peso a day in wages. However, Navajada was unable to raise the money, Quaresma was imprisoned by the Holy Office, and Francisco, who had been employed in the forge of one of the mines, was sold to someone else by the Inquisition for 500 pesos. The fate of the marriage is unknown. See also Harth-terré, "Esclavo negro," p. 320.

86. The cases that follow all come from AA, Causas de negros, unnumbered legajos.

87. In a similar case of 1635 the mulata slave Jacinta de Orosco claimed that she was married to a black held in bondage in Quito, but that she had been taken "with treachery and violence" to Lima by her master and sold to Diego Frens de la Fuente even though Frens knew the circumstances. Jacinta charged that her new master treated her badly when he learned she intended to appeal to the ecclesiastical authorities. As a result, she pleaded not only to be returned to Quito and sold there, but also to be given in bond to a third party so that Frens could harm her no further. A period of legal sparring followed, during which Frens refused to reply directly to Jacinta's charges until she and her 3-year-old mulatto son returned to his service. Jacinta re-

plied that her status as a slave made her too poor and powerless to assemble the witnesses necessary to prove her charges, and the sympathetic ecclesiastical *fiscal* felt that Frens should be compelled to send the woman to Riobamba, where her husband was. Instead, the vicar general, perhaps acting on the basis of information not included in the transcript of the case, ruled that Jacinta must return to serve Frens; but the case was to continue, and Frens was to allow the slave an hour each morning and each afternoon to assemble her witnesses. No further documents on this case survive.

88. SN 67 (1625): 695-96, 1139-40; SN 33 (1575): 53r-54r; SN 35 (1650): 1-3; SN 73 (1610): 652v-54r.

89. SN 14 (1590): 860; SN 35 (1650): 121r-23r; SN 34 (1570): 714, 721.

90. SN 28 (1595): 398v-99v; SN 43 (1630): 475-79; SN 68 (1650): 929-30.

91. SN 95 (1650): 15-18; SN 47 (1625): 888; SN 51 (1640): 407. In what may also have been a case of economic necessity, Gaspar de Mendoza sold María Criolla, only 14 months old, to Doña Ana Jiménez for 80 pesos with the proviso that the mother, his slave Francisca Folupa, could keep the child another 6 months, until she reached the age of 2. SN 93 (1640): 30v-31v.

92. SN 5/ (1640): 675v-76r.

93. SN 102 (1630): 662v-63v; SN 47 (1625): 880v-81v; SN 35 (1650): 690v-92r. For more detail on the colored militia, see Chapter 10.

CHAPTER TEN

1. See the Author's Note, pp. xiii-xiv, on the racial terminology used in this chapter. Some of this material has appeared in altered form in David Cohen and Jack P. Greene, eds., *Neither Slave Nor Free*, pp. 19-58.

2. AGIL 568.10: 102v. Lockhart, p. 191, provides a similar example; and Pike, *Aristocrats*, pp. 189-90, mentions other free coloreds who came to Peru as servants, often in the company of their former masters.

3. Lockhart, p. 191.

4. Mörner, *Race Mixture*, p. 35.

5. In the words of Davis, p. 103: "It is important to note . . . that as a body of ideal law, *las Siete Partidas* had little relation to the living law of Castile."

6. *Las Siete Partidas*, Part 3: title 2, law 8; title 5, law 4; title 14, law 5; title 33, rule 1; Part 4: title 5, prologue; title 21, law 1; title 22, laws 1 and 13.

7. Helps, 2d ed., 4: 250.

8. As Davis, pp. 102-6, observes, it was philosophically difficult to reconcile the slave's marital obligations with the master's claims to absolute authority, but in neither Spain nor Spanish America was marriage considered sufficient grounds for freedom. *Las Siete Partidas* proclaimed the right of the slave to marry even against his owner's will but did not go so far as to recommend that he be given free status. The same reconciliation of marital responsibility and slaveholder authority was stated for Spanish America in decrees of 1526, 1538, and 1541, printed in Konetzke, 1: 81-82, 185, 210.

9. Harth-terré and Márquez Abanto, *RANP*, 24: 55-74 (will of 1611); SN 89 (1620): 245-46; SN 61 (1605): 6.

10. SN 35 (1650): 687v-89r.

11. E.g., Jacoba Criolla (age 15), who was freed in recognition of her mother's 30 years of service. SN 81 (1635): 132-33.

12. RA/PC, 37 (1616-17), Bachiller Alonso de Torres v. Pascual de Aranda, codicil of 2 May 1616.

13. In many cases, the circumstances surrounding the manumission of the old and the sick and the intentions of the masters are not known. In 1592, for example, one slaveowner freed a black woman described in his will as old to the point of senility (*vieja sin juicio*), but what seems an exceedingly callous act has to be weighed against the meticulous provisions in the same document for the care and upbringing of a mulata of 14, who was also manumitted. RA/PC, 13 (1569-70), Francisco Caro de Macuecos v. executors for Jorge Griego: 30v-36v.

14. RA/PC, 102 (1639), will of Esteban González; SN 35 (1640): 637v-40r; SN 43 (1630): 422-25; RA/PC, 46 (1620), will of Doña Juana Ravanal.

15. RA/PC, 60 (1625), will of Rodrigo García Carnero.

16. RA/PC, 68 (1628), Doña Inés de Salazar v. estate of Pedro de Aguilera y Saavedra (*sic*), will of 1616 and codicil of 1620: 20-40. Saavedra also attempted to provide for the welfare of slaves who were not manumitted. One, Catalina Bioho, was charged with the care of his infant son, who on reaching manhood was implored to treat her "as a mother and not as a slave." The codicil provided for Catalina's manumission after 20 years of service to the son. Another slave youth was also charged with serving the son, who was to repay the black by apprenticing him as a blacksmith or cobbler and was "to treat him well for such is his care."

17. RA/PC, 13 (1569-70), Francisco Caro de Macuecos v. executors for Jorge Griego; SN 63 (1610): 837v-40r; SN 68 (1640): 847-52.

18. SN 38 (1650): 36v-38v. There is some evidence that the kindly intentions of ex-masters were not always honored by the responsible parties, as illustrated by two examples from AA, Causas de negros. The first, from 1639, concerns the complaint lodged by Doña Juana de Aguilar about the treatment accorded Ageda Criolla by Ana María de Collasos, a nun in Encarnación convent. According to Doña Juana, the black had been freed at the age of seven by her dead husband to serve Ana María, but the latter had been treating Ageda poorly, almost as though she were a slave. However, Doña Juana's efforts to help the child, then fourteen and who supposedly had fled from the convent, were frustrated, first by a constable who reclaimed her for Ana María and then by a sworn statement from the girl that she preferred service under that mistress. In the second case, a year later, the free black Diego de Castillo petitioned the ecclesiastical court that he had obtained the necessary licenses to marry Francisca Baçau, likewise black and free, but that she was within the convent of Concepción and was not permitted to leave by order of one Doña Aldonça de Garay. In the investigation that followed, we learn that Francisca, a girl of twelve or thirteen, had been freed recently by the will of her mistress, left a small sum of money and a few other possessions, and

entrusted to the care of executors who were to arrange for her either to follow a religious life or marry. One of the executors seconded Diego's complaint, and stated that the nuns were putting undue pressure on Francisca to remain in the convent. The girl, however, declared that she wished to stay where she was and denied that she had ever even met her suitor.

19. SN 35 (1635): 159v-62v; SN 68 (1650): 1797-1800.

20. SN 17 (1573): 972r-74r.

21. SN 57 (1645): 2156r-60r; SN 52 (1615): 1-7. Isabel Cataño also owned María Bran, Francisca's mother, who was not freed.

22. The will of Don Pedro Ysasaga, dated in 1623, is among the documents in RA/PC, 62 (1625), "Autos referentes al testamento del Licenciado Don Manuel de Castro y Padilla": 20-40.

23. SN 17 (1585): 566-67; SN 68 (1650): 1392-93.

24. See Harth-terré and Márquez Abanto, *RANP*, 25: 27-31, for the details of these examples.

25. SN 42 (1605): 561v-63v.

26. E.g., Juana de Espinosa, self-described as an old woman, who agreed to free at her death her slave María Negra, purchased 15 years previously, and María's daughter Isabel (age 10). SN 26 (1576): 467v-69v.

27. SN 30 (1583): 250v-52r.

28. *Siete Partidas*, Part 3: title 2, law 8; title 29, law 3; Part 4: title 21, law 7; Part 5, title 5, law 45.

29. Konetzke, 1: 88.

30. Lockhart, p. 190.

31. SN 68 (1645): 511r-12r.

32. SN 30 (1583): 222r-24r; RA/PC, 47 (1620), "El defensor de los bienes de difuntos por los de Francisco Hernández Irola contra Francisco Ruiz de Usenda y otros sus albaceas": 26r.

33. SN 3 (1593): 92v-93v; SN 37 (1615): 299r-301r, 816-17.

34. SN 30 (1585): 1361-63; SN 93 (1615): 610-15; SN 63 (1620): 88v-90v.

35. SN 46 (1610): 414; SN 35 (1620): 117-20. In the second case, the letter of manumission noted that the mulata had always paid her assigned wages to her master "with great punctuality."

36. RA/PC, 37 (1616-17), will of Asencio Pérez de Longarte; SN 67 (1625): 151-57; SN 37 (1625): 55.

37. SN 86 (1645): 143v-44r, 247-49, 743.

38. SN 102 (1640): 660r-62r; SN 35 (1650): 823v-24v.

39. SN 45 (1635): 929-33.

40. Harth-terré and Márquez Abanto, *RANP*, 25: 7-8, 10-11, 27-31, discuss the case of Polonia and other cases of blacks who were allowed to apply a portion of their time and wages toward freedom. The example of Domingo Congo comes from SN 40 (1635): 409r-14r.

41. SN 101 (1640): 392; SN 19 (1595): 203r-4r.

42. For one example of each situation among many, see the following. Free husband pays to liberate slave wife: SN 55 (1635): 2521v-22v, by which Fran-

cisco Bioho, a retainer (*criado*) of the master, gave 350 pesos to liberate his wife; the money was borrowed from a Spanish peddler. The reverse: SN 14 (1595): 49. Free parents liberate child: SN 85 (1620): 63v-64v.

43. SN 57 (1645): 2247-48; SN 35 (1645): 18.

44. SN 38 (1645): 38-40; SN 35 (1650): 918r-2or.

45. SN 67 (1625): 387v-88v; SN 94 (1640): 446v-47v. See also SN 37 (1600), promissory note of 15 May, fol. 566, by which Antonia Criolla pledged to repay the 300 pesos she was loaned by Beatriz Magdalena, an Indian woman who helped her purchase her freedom.

46. SN 41 (1620): 41r-42r. It should be observed that on occasion blacks were less than charitable toward one another about freedom. In 1647, for example, the *fiscal* of the Audiencia considered the case of the free black couple Antón Mina and Juana Martel. When Juana died, she had provided that her slave Magdalena Conga serve her husband for the rest of his life and then be free. But the husband, who had been having a long-term affair with Polonia Biafara, attempted in his will to sell Magdalena to his mistress for a nominal sum. The spurious sale was rejected by the *fiscal* when challenged, and it is to be presumed that Magdalena gained her freedom. RA/PC, 121 (1647-48), "Libro de pareceres del Señor Fiscal, 1647": 157r-6or.

47. Levillier, 7: 287-88, Licenciado Ramírez de Cartagena to Crown.

48. See the minute racial and physical descriminations and terminology recorded in Mörner, *Race Mixture*, pp. 58-59; and in Aguirre Beltrán, "Races."

49. On this question, see also Mörner, "Teoría."

50. Levillier, 10: 139-40, Villar to Crown (1586); AGIL 41, Guadalcázar to Crown (1628).

51. Levillier, 10: 198-99; 13: 173-74.

52. *Ibid.*, 4: 127-30, 384-85.

53. AGI, Patronato, 43, "Papeles pertenecientes a los servicios del Conde del Villar": 14r; Konetzke, 2.1: 308-14, summary of Deza's memorial (1626) and attached recommendation of the Council (1628).

54. López de Velasco, p. 43.

55. For examples of marriages between black slaves and Indian women, see Harth-terré and Márquez Abanto, *RANP*, 25: 15; SN 17 (1577): 561; and SN 51 (1615): 183r-84r, 214r-15r. Occasionally, one reads of zambos born of black slave women, who had only bondage as their future, barring the charity of others. There is, for example, the 1605 case of Lázaro Negro, the child of Simón Indio and Ursula Negra, the latter a slave of the Indian noblewoman Doña Constanza Corxachumbi. Lázaro was freed by his father and raised by Doña Constanza, who sold his mother for reasons that are not stated in her will. In this document Doña Constanza instructs her husband to apprentice the boy, then 5 years old, at the appropriate time, and wills him 150 pesos. SN 61 (1605): 266-76.

56. Mörner, *Race Mixture*, p. 60; Konetzke, 2.1: 480.

57. However, some colonial authorities took a more tolerant view. Viceroy Chinchón, for example, felt that mulattoes, many of whom were reared side

by side with the Spanish father's legitimate children, helped to cement relations between Spaniard and African. The mulattoes considered it a mark of honor to be the children of Spaniards, and most, Chinchón stated, were so ignorant as to accept slave status without question. AGIL 47, Chinchón to Crown, 11 Oct 1636. Unions between Spanish women and African men were rare. Suardo, 2: 35-36, reports one case. Another is to be found in SN 46 (1610): 461, recording the sale of a mulatto slave, Pedro Alonso, who was born in Spain and was married to María Martín, a white woman, likewise a native of the Peninsula. Pedro was sold for the handsome sum of 787.5 pesos.

58. Lewin, *Descripción*, p. 39.

59. Quoted in Rosenblat, 2: 97. On crimes of passion involving colored women, see Suardo, 1: 114, 154, 285, 302; 2: 60, 91, 155.

60. *Recopilación*, 7: title 5, law 6.

61. SN 27 (1581), no foliation; SN 33 (1575): 204-5; SN 17 (1578): 652v-53v.

62. SN 41 (1625): 18r-21r; SN 38 (1650): 4-7.

63. SN 17 (1585): 1071. In the same year and before the same notary (fols. 1267r-68r), Luis Hernández de Sepúlveda purchased the liberty of Salvador Mulato (age 7), the son of his dead brother and Francisca Criolla, who remained a slave.

64. SN 17 (1566): 169v-70v.

65. SN 61 (1600): 991; SN 93 (1615): 116-17. We read also in the will of Doña Francisca de Chávez of the mulata Andrea de Vargas (age 20), former slave of Don Diego de Vargas y Ballesteros (dean of the cathedral of Panama) and daughter of a slave of Doña Francisca's. Andrea had been freed by Vargas on condition that she serve first Doña Francisca and then himself during their lives. Doña Francisca provided that at her death Andrea was to be sent to a convent until Vargas reached a decision on her future. SN 57 (1645): 1483-86.

66. SN 102 (1630): 653-54. In other instances Spanish men purchased colored infants with no mention of liberation, but it is difficult to envision any other motive. E.g., Don Francisco de Garnica, who bought María de San Francisco, a 1-month-old zamba, from the mother's master. SN 37 (1630): 100v-101v.

67. For these and other examples, see SN 6 (1583): 16v-17r; SN 17 (1595): 721-22, 1110-12; SN 63 (1610): 1511-52r; SN 35 (1630): 240; SN 40 (1635): 390; SN 94 (1640): 518r-19r; and SN 86 (1645): 985v-86r.

68. RA/PC, 8 (1565-66 [*sic*]), Juana Mulata v. Alonso Beltrán; 70 (1629), "Autos seguidos sobre los bienes de Luis de Morales."

69. RA/PC, 10 (1605), Juana Navarro and her son Lorenzo Navarro v. estate of Canon Navarro.

70. AA, Causas de negros, Flores v. Flores.

71. RA/PC, 121 (1647-48), "Libro de pareceres del Señor Fiscal, 1647."

72. RA/PC, 59 (1624-25), Juan Vaez de Quesada v. Francisca Mulata.

73. RA/PC, 28 (1611-12), Capt. Pedro de Vera Montoya v. Juan Ramos.

74. AA, Causas de negros. Hernando's error probably stemmed from the fact that María had been sold to her current master for 200 pesos (she was by then a woman of 48). But this did not oblige her owner to accept the lower figure as the legal price for liberation.

75. SN 37 (1600), letter of apartamiento of 26 Apr: 468-69.

76. RA/PC, 31 (1593), Isabel Martín v. Francisco Martínez.

77. RA/PC, 33 (1614), Juan Ruiz de Avendaño v. heirs of Alonso Ruiz Bonifacio. In his appeal, the slave stressed that his wife had the resources to have paid 600 pesos for his liberty: houses and land in the province of Guamachuco in Cajamarca, "and . . . she is an industrious woman . . . who knows how to make money as a seamstress." Both husband and wife seem to have practiced their trades in Trujillo.

78. AA, Causas de negros.

79. RA/PC, 36 (1596), Juan Calvo v. Pedro Calvo.

80. AA, Causas de negros.

81. *Ibid.*

82. The question of whether the attitudes of masters toward manumission fluctuated through time in response to economic forces needs further investigation. The sample from notarial records in my study is too small to generalize from. For a summary of what little is known on this point, see my article in Cohen and Greene.

83. RA/PC, 37 (1616-17), will of Asencio Pérez de Longarte; 97 (1637), creditors v. estate of Lorenzo Pérez Noguera.

84. It is clear from the inventories of plantations I have examined for this period that the rural residences on Peruvian estates were often in an alarming state of disrepair, indicating that the owners certainly did not live on such properties. Moreover, a large number of the wills of landowners dictated in Lima (and some from Cuzco, Trujillo, Arica, Ica, and elsewhere) list both urban and rural property, and indicate that the owners resided in the towns.

85. E.g., RA/PC, 25 (1585-86), Licenciado Álvaro de Torres v. Juan Gil de Montenegro and Licenciado Sánchez de Paredes. An inventory of 1576 submitted in this suit lists 4 plantation slaves married to Indian women (fol. 5v).

86. For examples of free coloreds in agricultural service, see Chap. 4; and SN 17 (1573): 742v-43r; SN 9 (1579): 94, 330v-31r; SN 66 (1600): 50v-60r; and SN 40 (1625): 177. For a discussion of the free rural black based on evidence for colonial Spanish America in general, see my paper in Cohen and Greene.

87. Lockhart, p. 191. In a 1592 census of the highland mining town of Huancavelica only 10 free coloreds, the majority of them women, were counted in a total population of 253. AGIL 116, Alonso de Vargas Pecillín to Crown, 7 Aug 1592.

88. Biblioteca Nacional (Madrid), mss. 3178, "Descripción de todos los reinos del Perú, Chile, y Tierra Firme . . . 1586": 9v.

89. AGIL 95, "Testimonio de las diligencias hechas por el Señor Carrasco

del Saz ...," with a cover letter of 22 Apr 1611. On the 1614 census, see Appendix A, p. 340.

CHAPTER ELEVEN

1. Both quotations are from Lockhart, p. 196.

2. Konetzke, 1: 467; Levillier, 5: 339; 6: 274-75; AGIL 570.14: 118v-19r.

3. Konetzke, 1: 482-83, 502-3; Levillier, 7: 294.

4. E.g., AGIL 127, letter of royal accountant Tristán Sánchez to Crown, 2 Mar 1585, admitting that nothing had been done to collect the tax.

5. This figure is too low, since the accounts for many years have not survived, and sometimes colored tribute is lumped with other revenue. For revenues from Arequipa deposited in the Lima treasury, see the "Cargo de lo venido de fuera" account in AGIC as follows (by legajo, year, and pliego). 1705a (1609-10): 37; 1705b (1610-11): 29; 1708 (1619-20): 12-13; 1708 (1620-21): 20-21; 1709 (1623-24): 21-22; 1710 (1625-26): 19; 1714 (1629-30): 22; 1717 (1632-33): 58-59; 1718 (1633-34): 28; 1719 (1634-35): 27; 1721 (1636-37): 38-39; 1722a (1637-38): 35-37; 1723 (1638-39): 31-32; 1724 (1639-40): 20-22; 1725 (1640-41): 29-31; 1727 (1642-43): 42-43; 1729 (1644-45): 20; 1732 (1647-48): 4-5; 1735 (1649-50): 6; and 1737 (1650-51): 5-7. See also various accounts specifically for the Arequipa treasury in AGIC 1822.

6. The exact amount paid by the free coloreds of Ica in 1596 cannot be determined, since their tribute was lumped with that of the yanacona Indians. AGIC 1700, treasury accounts (1596): pl. 111; AGIL 122, treasury official San Juan de Velaóstigui to Crown, 23 Apr 1597.

7. AGIC 1820, treasury accounts (1601-8, 1608-11): pl. 58-60 and 39-40, respectively; AGIC 1820, Caja de Trujillo, "Relación de lo que ha entrado y salido [1624-29]"; AGIL 117, Trujillo treasury officials to Crown, 23 Feb 1627.

8. See the "Cargo de lo venido de fuera" account in the Lima treasury records in AGIC as follows (by legajo, year, and pliego). 1705a (1609-10): 41; 1705a (1612-13): 16: 1705b (1610-11): 32; 1705b (1611-12), pl. nos. illegible; 1710 (1624-25): 11-12; 1710 (1625-26): 17-18; 1711 (1626-27): 27; 1712 (1627-28): 48; 1713 (1628-29): 30-32; 1719 (1634-35): 26-27; 1720 (1635-36): 24; 1721 (1636-37): 36-37; 1723 (1638-39): 34-35; 1726 (1641-42): 26-27; 1727 (1642-43): 34; 1728a (1643-44): 29-30; 1729 (1644-45): 22; 1730 (1645-46): 44-45.

9. AGI, Patronato 190.43, from Villar's report to his successor; Levillier, 12: 164-65 and 13: 14, Cañete to Crown, 1590 and 1593; AGIC 1700, treasury accounts (1595): pl. 98, where a deposit of 994 pesos is recorded; AGIC 1703, treasury accounts (1603): pl. 71, which records a deposit of 227 pesos of 9 reales.

10. AGIC 1713, treasury accounts (1628-29), "Cargo de los tributos de los negros y mulatos horros": pl. 196, which provides a good summary of the government's efforts to collect the revenue.

11. AGIC 1704, treasury accounts (1608-9), "Cargo de alcances de cuen-

tas": pl. 3, records a payment by Rivera of 773 pesos, but an audit completed in 1611 showed that he still owed over 1,140 pesos. See AGIL 141, "Relación de las cuentas . . .": 7r.

12. AGIL 36, Montesclaros to Crown, letters of 1611-12; AGIL 571.18: 31, 147r, Crown to Montesclaros, letters of 1610 and 1612; AGIL 95, Licenciado Carrasco del Saz to Crown, 22 Apr 1611. Carrasco, Crown attorney for the Tribunal of the Santa Cruzada, had been commissioned by Montesclaros to put the tribute payment decree into effect.

13. AGIC 1705a, "Cargo de real hacienda extraordinaria" (1612-13, 1613-14): pl. 44, 66.

14. The "Cargo de la tasa de negros y mulatos" account for 1613-18 in AGIC 1705a, 1706, and 1707 records this information.

15. AGIL 571.18: 158-59, decrees of 1619 to viceroy and Audiencia; AGIL 39, Esquilache to Crown, 24 Apr 1620; AGIL 97, Tribunal of Accounts to Crown, ca. 1621; Biblioteca Nacional (Madrid), mss. 19282, "Papeles varios relativos al Perú, Potosí y Chile"; 61v-62v, part of an *acuerdo* of 31 Oct 1619.

16. AGIC 1709, "Cargo de real hacienda extraordinaria" (1623-24): pl. 53; and AGIC 1710, same account (1624-25): pl. 64, summarize the payments made under the contract.

17. Beltrán y Rózpide and Altolaguirre, 1: 287.

18. AGIL 97, Audiencia to Crown, 26 Apr 1621; AGIL 39, "Relación de lo que importa el servicio gracioso y emprestido que se ha hecha a Su Majestad . . . ," contributors' list compiled on 16 June 1623. The black group's contribution was listed as a gift.

19. AGIL 571.19: 271.

20. It is not clear if the guild was to include only mulattoes strictly defined or all free persons of African descent. My information comes from AGI, Escribanía de Cámara 1023b, Pedro Martín Leguisamo v. Guild of Mulattoes, 1632, *passim*. Leguisamo's mother was a mulatto, but his father was a Basque and a *hidalgo*. On the strength of his father's noble status, Leguisamo successfully avoided both the payment of tribute and service in the colored militia. He appealed to the Council of the Indies for certification of his status as a Spaniard and as a member of the guild of silversmiths, but the Council directed him to petition the viceroy instead. The testimony introduced by Leguisamo revealed that his brother was a secular priest in Panama.

21. Suardo, 1: 133-35, 137-42, describes the festivities.

22. See the account "Cargo de los tributos de los negros y mulatos horros" for the years 1623-24, 1628-29, and 1633-36 in AGIC 1709, 1713, and 1718-20.

23. AGIL 158, petition from those serving in the militia companies of 18 Mar 1627. According to the document, tribute collection had been farmed out to 3 constables for 400 pesos a year, but it is doubtful that the contract was fulfilled; AGIL 99, *fiscal* and Audiencia to Crown 17 Mar 1627 and 6 June 1630. The communication from the Audiencia was in response to the Crown's request in 1629 for more information. AGIL 572.20: 162v-63r.

24. Konetzke, 2.1: 333-35. But this was as far as the Crown was prepared

to go in rewarding free coloreds for military service. In 1648, for example, the Crown provided that they could not claim the *fuero*, i.e., the right to be tried in military courts, which were presumed to be more lenient to soldiers than civil courts. *Ibid.*, pp. 433-34.

25. SN 33 (1575): 16v; SN 26 (1574): 130v; SN 26 (1575): 310.

26. Lockhart, pp. 193-95, at p. 194.

27. *LCL*, 5: 356-57; 7: 338-39; 9: 174-75; 11: 113-14. See also Lockhart, p. 191.

28. AGIL 163, Ayala petitions and testimony as cited in Chap. 8, note 64.

29. SN 105 (1605): 1982; SN 52 (1615): 16v-18v; SN 94 (1640): 297v-98r.

30. For examples of artisans who lived where they worked, see SN 2 (1595): 489v-90v, the mulatto tailor Francisco de Sevilla; and SN 96 (1640): 7, the master shoemaker Antonio de Monroy, a mulatto. For an example of one who did not, see SN 46 (1610): 423, in which Antón Bran, a free black clothier, rented "a store where he has his office of tailoring in the *calle de los roperos*."

31. Vázquez de Espinosa, p. 457.

32. This information comes from AGIL 158, free coloreds of Lima to Crown, 18 Mar 1627; and AGIL 584.20: 365v-66v, decree of 3 Dec 1641, exempting the colored militia of Piura and Paita. To claim their exemption, the northern Peruvians were first obliged to pay a fee of 6 pesos, the equivalent of their tribute assessment for a year.

33. The career of Valladolid, which reflects the activities of the colored militia during this period, can be traced in Konetzke, 2.1: 470-71; and in AGIL 166, which contains a batch of petitions and titles to office presented by Valladolid. On the Spanish officers of these forces and their salaries, see *LCL*, 19: 513; and AGIC, DDG, as follows: 1713 (1628-29): 324-35; 1715 (1630-31): 545-46; 1724 (1639-40): 346, 449-53, 532-33; and 1725 (1640-41): 428-31.

34. Konetzke, 1: 435-36, 444-45, 449, 566; 2.1: 135, 365. An interesting decree of 1623 provided that free, married black women could not be forced to attend the public dances held on religious holidays. *Ibid.*, 2.1: 278.

35. AGIL 96, Cristóbal Cacho de Santillán to Crown, 16 Apr 1617; *LCL*, 17: 506-7, 526.

36. Encinas, 4: 387.

37. AGIC 1692, "Cargo de penas de cámara": 48.

38. *LCL*, 19: 401.

39. AGIL 160, Licenciado Varona de Incinillas to Crown, 30 May 1629; Suardo, 1: 17, 155.

40. Lewin, *Descripción*, pp. 68-70.

41. Mörner, *Race Mixture*, pp. 40, 68.

42. AGIL 305, Bishop of Cuzco to Crown, 11 Feb 1577; Lanning, p. 47.

43. AGIL 323, from a 1608 copy of the school's charter issued by Viceroy Cañete on 8 Aug 1592.

44. "Libro de Cabildo de los Huérfanos . . . ," partially printed in Vargas Ugarte, *Biblioteca Peruana*, 3: 143-52.

45. Martín, pp. 36-38.

46. Konetzke, 2.1: 134-35, decree of 16 Aug 1607; AGIL 35, Montesclaros to Crown 25 Mar 1609. Martín, p. 70, mentions that the Jesuits recognized an obligation to give some of their slaves a "religious and human education. Some of the slaves at San Pablo became accomplished musicians, bakers, vintners, and even pharmacists." However, it cannot be determined how many of these blacks eventually became free.

47. Konetzke, 1: 256, decree of 27 Feb 1549, addressed to the Audiencia of New Granada but obviously of general application, where reference is made to still earlier "laws and pragmatic sanctions of our kingdoms" to the same effect. The decree is also printed in Encinas, 2: 226. In some instances this general prohibition was extended to specific posts. In 1584, for example, when the Crown attempted to raise money through the sale of minor public offices, that of reporter (*receptor*) of the Audiencia was barred to mulattoes "insofar as possible." Konetzke, 1: 555-56. This decree is likewise addressed to the New Granada Audiencia, but again it is of obvious application elsewhere, as testified by its inclusion in *Recopilación*, 2: title 27, law 1.

48. AGIL 96, Audiencia to Crown, 24 Apr 1619; Konetzke, 2.1: 251, 259-60. During the early decades of the colony, as Lockhart, p. 193, indicates, free blacks in remote areas of Peru were sometimes able to gain access to greater opportunities in this connection. In Puertoviejo, for example, "a member of the city council and royal official was said to be a Negro and former slave." As Lockhart also observes, "many of the town criers and executioners in Peruvian cities were free Negroes, because few Spaniards would consent to hold the post."

49. AGIL 100, Audiencia to Crown, 28 May 1637, with accompanying documents from which the above information is drawn.

50. AGIL 49, Chinchón to Crown, 29 May 1639, with attached copies of correspondence between the viceroy and the professor.

51. Konetzke, 1: 607-8; 2.1: 356-67.

52. Posada, pp. 128-29. His actual phrase, whose tone is difficult to capture in translation is "de sangre muy azul, castellano puro, natural de Burgos, y persona muy principal."

53. In 1619, for example, it was reported that the archdeacon of the Lima cathedral had had several children by various colored women and was currently keeping a mulata mistress (AGIL 327, Fr. Alonso Díaz to the Patriarch of the Indies [?], 8 Apr). Examples of marriages between Spanish men and African women are rare. For two cases, see AGIC 1710, DGG (1625-26): pl. 165, where the free black woman Beatriz González de Hoyos is described as the widow of a Spanish soldier; and AGIC 1704, "Cargo de alcances de cuentas" (1608-9): pl. 20, which mentions the free mulata Ana López, widow of a vineyard owner in Pisco.

54. Urteaga, "Conquistador," will of 24 July 1542; RA/PC, 73 (1630), creditors v. estate of Pedro de la Barrera: 179v-80v. Barrera also left his clothing and bed to his son. From the will, it is clear that the female slave also had

a mulata daughter, Francisca Rodríguez (age 25), but she was apparently not of Barrera's seed. In any event Francisca was mortgaged for 500 pesos, and no provision was made for her freedom.

55. AGI, Escribanía de Cámara 510c, "Andrés de los Reyes . . . ."
56. Lockhart, pp. 193-95.
57. SN 8 (1595): 445v-48r. Isabel also provided that María Espinosa, a free mulata, might choose a site on the recently purchased lot, build a dwelling, and live there for the rest of her life, "since this is a debt that I owe her." As with many free coloreds, Isabel accepted the savings of slaves for loan to others with interest, in this case the pathetic sum of 28 reales given her by Luisa Berbesi, which had been loaned to various mulattoes.
58. SN 14 (1590): 589; SN 89 (1620): 247-48. The second register (fols. 404r-6r) also contains the will of Elena de Vega, a married free mulata, who listed a house with an annual mortgage payment of 47 pesos as the principal possession she owned in common with her husband.
59. SN 51 (1615): 27v-29v, 49v-51v.
60. Lockhart, p. 193.
61. LCL, 8: 325.
62. SN 94 (1640): 267-69; SN 17 (1566): 661-64.
63. RA/PC, 31 (1593), Isabel Martín v. Francisco Martínez and Hernán Pérez: 26r.
64. SN 101 (1640): 915v-17v; SN 68 (1630): 531-35; SN 17 (1573): 1141-42.
65. AA, Causas de negros.
66. SN 17 (1578): 521r-23r; SN 24 (1589): 34-35.
67. SN 17 (1566): 50r-51r, 926-28; SN 17 (1578): 378r-80r.
68. LCL, 22: 252, session of 4 Feb 1633.
69. Lockhart, p. 192.
70. AGIL 316, Tiruel to Crown, 1 Feb 1585.
71. SN 86 (1645): 279-81.
72. SN 17 (1566): 50r-51r, 661-64.
73. SN 37 (1600): 971v-72v.

CHAPTER TWELVE

1. AGI, Estado 75, from a copy provided me by Prof. James F. King. The precise figures of the 1792 census show a total population of 1,076,122 people, of whom 40,337 were slaves and 41,404 were *"gente de color libre."* Romero, pp. 377-78, cites different figures—1,232,122, 40,336, and 41,256, respectively —which are based on the preliminary census data for 1791 printed in Paz Soldán. The major difference in the two sets of figures lies in the number of Indians in the totals: 764,894 in 1791 and 608,912 in 1792. Only additional research can explain the discrepancy, but I presume that the 1792 census results were more accurate since these were sent to Spain. Clearly, however, the 1792 totals assign a higher percentage of Peru's population to people of color.
2. King, "The Colored Castes," p. 55.

Bibliography

Bibliography

I have relied on a wide range of manuscript material for the preparation of this book. A considerable portion of the documentation came from the Archivo General de Indias (Seville), where I worked for seventeen months in 1963-64. The sections of the Archive that hold the greatest interest for students of African slavery in Peru during the sixteenth and seventeenth centuries, in approximate order of importance, are Gobierno (Audiencia de Lima); Contaduría; Escribanía de Cámara; Justicia; and Patronato. In Madrid, I used the Biblioteca Nacional, the Real Academia de la Historia, and the Archivo Histórico Nacional, all of which contain scattered but valuable materials concerning the Afro-Peruvian. In Portugal, I devoted several weeks of research to the collection in the Archivo Histórico Ultramarino (Lisbon); most of my material from this and other Portuguese archives, however, was taken from microfilm transcriptions in the possession of Professor Engel Sluiter.

Nine months of intensive research were spent in Lima during the summers of 1964, 1968, and 1969, in the Archivo Arzobispal, the Biblioteca Nacional, and the Archivo Nacional. The records housed in the first repository are particularly useful for information on slave marriages and on suits concerning liberty or mistreatment brought before the ecclesiastical courts by Afro-Peruvians. The once-valuable collection of documents in the Biblioteca Nacional was severely damaged in a fire, and many records lucky enough to have escaped destruction are so singed or water-soaked as to be practically useless. The Archivo Nacional houses a considerable amount of documentation that is priceless for the history of the Afro-Peruvian, particularly in the sections labeled Real Audiencia, Tribunal de la Inquisición, and Sección Notarial.

Special mention must be made of the notarial records in the Sección Notarial, which I made heavy use of in researching this book. The registers of the following notaries were examined in some detail:

SIXTEENTH CENTURY

1. Adrada, Diego de, 1575
2. Aguilar Mendieta, Cristóbal de, 1595
3. Aguilar Mendieta, Cristóbal de, with Diego de la Torre Sabá and Agustín Atencia, 1589-93
4. Alejandro, Francisco, 1595
5. Álvarez, Diego de, 1560
6. Arias Cortés, Pedro, 1582-83, 1595
7. Bello, Diego, 1571
8. Bote, Ramiro Francisco, 1595
9. Cueva, Alonso de la, 1577, 1579-80
10. Fornizedo, Diego de, 1561-62
11. Franco de Esquivel, Marcos, 1569-73, 1575-77, 1581-83
12. Frías, Juan Cristóbal de, 1560-62
13. García, Juan Tomino, 1560, 1565, 1568-70
14. Gómez de Baeza, Rodrigo de, 1585, 1590-91, 1595
15. Gómez de Garnica, Martín, 1595-97
16. Grados, Nicolás de, 1560
17. Gutiérrez, Juan, 1565-66, 1573, 1576-78, 1585, 1595

18. Hernández, Alonso, 1585
19. Hernández, Blas, 1569-72, 1581-83, 1590-91, 1595, 1600
20. Herrero, Alonso, 1583
21. López, Esteban, 1591, 1595-98
22. López, Gaspar, 1576
23. López de Arrieta, Juan, 1562
24. Manuel, Francisco, 1588-90
25. Manuel, Juan, 1585-90
26. Morales, Juan de, 1574-77
27. Moscoso, Ambrosio de, 1560, 1565, 1570, 1575-77, 1579-82, 1584-87
28. Núñez de la Vega, Sebastián, 1593-95
29. Padilla, Juan, 1560, 1564
30. Pérez, Esteban, with Bartolomé Gascón, 1560-62, 1564, 1571-72, 1575, 1583-85, 1589
31. Ríos, Pedro de los, 1589-90
32. Ruiz, Diego, 1560, 1565
33. Salamanca, Juan de, 1571-72, 1575
34. Valencia, Alonso de, 1570

SEVENTEENTH CENTURY

35. Acuña, Francisco de, 1620, 1625, 1630, 1635, 1640, 1645, 1650
36. Aguila Bullón, Juan, 1630
37. Aguilar Mendieta, Cristóbal, 1600, 1605, 1615, 1625, 1630
38. Aguirre Urbina, José de, 1645, 1650
39. Alcocer, Pedro Luis de, 1620
40. Aldana, Cristóbal de, 1625, 1635, 1640, 1645
41. Alférez, Miguel de, 1610, 1615, 1620, 1625
42. Altamirano, Juan, 1605
43. Álvarez de Quiroz, Pedro, 1625, 1630, 1635
44. Aparicio de Urrutia, Juan, 1605, 1609-10
45. Arauz, Cristóbal de, 1605, 1610, 1620, 1630, 1635, 1640, 1645
46. Arroyo, Pedro de, 1601-2, 1605, 1610, 1635
47. Atencia, Agustín de, 1615, 1620, 1625
48. Balcázar, Martín de, 1640, 1645
49. Barrientos, Cristóbal, 1605, 1610, 1615
50. Bello, Juan, 1600-1602

51. Bustamante, Francisco de, 1615, 1640
52. Cámara, Bartolomé de la, 1615, 1620
53. Carbajal, Juan de, 1645, 1650
54. Carrión, Alonso de, 1615, 1620
55. Cívico, Bartolomé de, 1625, 1635
56. Fernández, Fabián, 1645
57. Figueroa, Marcelo Antonio de, 1645
58. Florez, Cristóbal, 1605, 1610
59. García de León, Diego, 1645
60. Gómez, José Felipe, 1620, 1625
61. Gómez de Baeza, Rodrigo, 1600, 1605
62. Gómez de Garnica, Martín, 1600-1601, 1605
63. González Balcázar, Francisco, 1605, 1610, 1620
64. González Pareja, Juan, 1615, 1620
65. González de Soto, Alonso, 1630
66. Grados de Lícera, Miguel, 1600
67. Hernández, Francisco, 1620, 1625
68. Herrera, Juan Bautista, 1630, 1640, 1645, 1650
69. Ita Hervás, Baltasar de, 1635
70. Jácome Carlos, Juan, 1645

71. Jaramillo, Diego de, 1645
72. López, Esteban, 1600, 1605
73. López de Almagro, Pedro, 1610
74. López Chico, Gregorio, 1630
75. López Lízar, Diego, 1620, 1630
76. López Mallea, Pedro, 1615
77. López de Mendoza, Juan, 1630
78. López Salazar, Diego, 1610
79. Luna, Miguel de, 1630
80. Martínez, Francisco, 1610, 1615
81. Martínez Llorenta, Juan, 1635
82. Medina, Melchior de, 1625, 1630
83. Mendieta, Juan de, 1600
84. Mota, Antonio de la, 1650
85. Nieto Maldonado, Diego de, 1610, 1615, 1620, 1625, 1630, 1635
86. Ochandiano, Martín de, 1645
87. Ordoñez, Francisco, 1640, 1645
88. Pérez Gallegos, Diego, 1625, 1630, 1640

89. Pineda, Cristóbal de, 1610, 1620
90. Postiga, Luis del, 1610
91. Quesada, Cristóbal de, 1600
92. Quintero, Martín de, 1640, 1645, 1650
93. Rivera, Juan de, 1615, 1630, 1640
94. Rodríguez, Cristóbal, 1610, 1640
95. Rosa, Luis de la, 1650
96. Samudio, Juan, 1610, 1640, 1645
97. Sánchez Vadillo, Diego, 1635
98. Santisteban, Marcos, 1645, 1650
99. Sobarzo, Juan de, 1650
100. Taboada, Francisco de, 1645, 1650
101. Tamayo, Antonio de, 1620, 1640
102. Toro, Bartolomé de, 1630, 1640
103. Valenzuela, Juan de la, 1630
104. Vargas, Cristóbal de, 1610
105. Vargas, Cristóbal de, with Clemente de Obregón, 1605

With regard to printed manuscript materials, the collection dealing with social developments edited by Konetzke is particularly useful for the study of the person of color, since the editor has gathered together in several volumes documents from the AGI that were previously unpublished or published in widely scattered sources. Roberto Levillier, ed., *Gobernantes del Perú*, was helpful because it contains virtually all surviving government correspondence from officials in Peru to the mother country during the sixteenth century. The *Libros de cabildos de Lima* are important for many aspects of African slavery in the capital, but particularly with respect to the control of the colored population. Mention must also be made of Rubén Vargas Ugarte's *Biblioteca Peruana*, which is not only useful as a bibliographical tool, but also valuable for the documents that are wholly or partially printed there.

I have also relied heavily on the published observations of several colonial writers, and perhaps most of all on the pungent comments of the *Nueva corónica* by Felipe Guamán Poma de Ayala. The *Compendium* of Antonio Vázquez de Espinosa and the work of the anonymous observer edited by Boleslao Lewin are also very valuable for their insights into the status of the black man in the economy and society of colonial Peru. Further, the two authors complement each other nicely, since the former takes a cheerful view of the African's lot, whereas the latter (perhaps a foreign Jew) is harshly critical of Spanish treatment of the black man. The work of Alonso de Sandoval is without peer for its information concerning the slave trade and the Jesuit missionary effort among the blacks arriving at Cartagena, and the passionate uneasiness with which this great Jesuit viewed the institution of African slavery is very moving. The *Diario* kept by Juan Antonio Suardo is indispensable for a picture of social conditions in seventeenth-century Lima. In general, extensive use of the work of other historians has been impossible for the simple reason that so little research has been done in the field of colonial Peruvian history, and still less on matters relating to the person of color. The outstanding exception is James Lockhart's invaluable *Spanish Peru*. I am also indebted to Emilio Harth-terré, Alberto Márquez Abanto, and Rolando Mellafe for their contributions to the history of the Afro-Peruvian.

Two abbreviations are used below: *HAHR* for *Hispanic American Historical Review* and *RANP* for *Revista del Archivo Nacional del Perú*.

WORKS CITED

"Actas de los Libros de Cabildos del Cuzco, años de 1545 a 1548," *Revista del Archivo Histórico del Cuzco*, 9 (1958): 37-305.

Aguirre Beltrán, Gonzalo. *La población negra de México, 1519-1810*. Mexico, 1946.

———. "Races in 17th Century Mexico," *Phylon*, 6 (1945): 212-18.

Altamira y Crevea, Rafael. "La aprobación y confirmación de las leyes dadas por las autoridades coloniales españolas," in *Contribuciones para el estudio de la historia de América*. Buenos Aires, 1941.

Andrade e Silva, José Justino, comp. and ed. *Collecção cronológica de legislação portuguesa, 1603-1700*. 10 vols. Lisbon, 1854-59.

Angulo, Domingo, ed. "El Capitán Gómez de León, vecino fundador de la ciudad de Arequipa," *RANP* 6 (1928): 95-148.

Armas Medina, Fernando de. "El santo de los esclavos," *Estudios Americanos*, 40-41 (1955): 55-61.

Ayala, Manuel Josef de, comp. *Diccionario de gobierno y legislación de Indias*, ed. Laudelino Moreno, in *Colección de documentos inéditos para la historia de Hispano-América*, vols. 4, 8. 14 vols. Madrid, 1927-32.

Barriga, Víctor M., ed. *Documentos para la historia de Arequipa*. 3 vols. Arequipa, Peru, 1939-55.

———. *Los Mercedarios en el Perú en el siglo XVI: Documentos inéditos del Archivo General de Indias*. 5 vols. Rome and Arequipa, Peru, 1933-54.

Basadre, Jorge. "El régimen de la mita," *Letras*, 3 (1937): 325-64.

Baudet, Henri. *Paradise on Earth: Some Thoughts on European Images of Non-European Man*, tr. Elizabeth Wentholt. New Haven, Conn., 1965.

Bayle, Constantino. *Los cabildos seculares en la América española*. Madrid, 1952.

Belaúnde Guinassi, Manuel. *La encomienda en el Perú*. Lima, 1945.

Beltrán y Rózpide, Ricardo, and Ángel de Altolaguirre, eds. *Colección de las memorias y relaciones que escribieron los virreyes del Perú*. 2 vols. Madrid, 1921-31.

Birmingham, David. *The Portuguese Conquest of Angola*. London, 1965.

Blake, J. W. *European Beginnings in West Africa, 1454-1578*. London, 1937.

Borah, Woodrow W. *Early Colonial Trade and Navigation Between Mexico and Peru*. Berkeley, Calif., 1954.

———. *New Spain's Century of Depression*. Berkeley, Calif., 1951.

Borah, Woodrow W., and Sherburne F. Cook. *The Aboriginal Population of Central Mexico on the Eve of the Spanish Conquest*. Berkeley, Calif., 1963.

Borregán, Alonso de. *Crónica de la conquista del Perú*. Seville, 1948.

Bowser, Frederick P., pp. 19-58 in David W. Cohen and Jack P. Greene, eds., *Neither Slave Nor Free: The Freedmen of African Descent in the Slave Societies of the New World*. Baltimore, Md., 1972.

Boxer, C. R. *The Golden Age of Brazil, 1695-1750: Growing Pains of a Colonial Society*. Berkeley, Calif., 1962.

———. *The Portuguese Seaborne Empire, 1415-1825*. New York, 1969.

———. *Race Relations in the Portuguese Colonial Empire, 1415-1825*. Oxford, Eng., 1963.

————. *Salvador de Sá and the Struggle for Brazil and Angola, 1602-1686*. London, 1952.

Cassinelli, Catalina. *El mulato Martín, pródigo de América: Vida del beato Fray Martín de Porres*. Lima, 1942.

Castañeda, C. E. "The Corregidor in Spanish Colonial Administration," *HAHR*, 9 (1929): 446-70.

Castillero C., Alfredo. *La sociedad panameña: Historia de su formación e integración*. Panama, 1970.

Céspedes del Castillo, Guillermo. *La avería en el comercio de Indias*. Seville, 1945.

Chandler, David L. "Health and Slavery: A Study of Health Conditions in the Slave Trade Through New Granada," in Robert Brent Toplin, ed., *The Afro-Latin American: Burdens of the Past*. Forthcoming in 1974.

Chaunu, Huguette and Pierre. *Séville et l'Atlantique, 1504-1650*. 8 vols. in 11. Paris, 1955-59.

Chaunu, Pierre. "Le Maroc et l'Atlantique, 1450-1550," *Annales: Économies, Sociétés, Civilisations*, 11 (1956): 361-65.

————. *Les Philippines et le Pacifique des Ibériques, xvie, xviie, xviiie siècles: Introduction méthodologique et indices d'activité*. Paris, 1960.

Clemence, Stella R., ed. *The Harkness Collection in the Library of Congress: Calendar of Spanish Manuscripts Concerning Peru, 1531-1651*. Washington, D.C., 1932.

————, ed. and trans. *The Harkness Collection in the Library of Congress: Documents from Early Peru, the Pizarros and the Almagros, 1531-1578*. Washington, D.C., 1936.

Colección de documentos inéditos relativos al descubrimiento, conquista y organización de las antiguas posesiones españolas de América y Oceanía, sacados de los archivos del reino, y muy especialmente del de Indias. 42 vols. Madrid, 1864-84.

Colección de documentos inéditos relativos al descubrimiento, conquista y organización de las antiguas posesiones españolas de Ultramar. 25 vols. Madrid, 1885-1932.

Cook, Noble David. "La población indígena en el Perú colonial," pp. 73-110 in *América colonial: Población y economía. Anuario del Instituto de Investigaciones Históricas*. Universidad Nacional del Litoral, Rosario, Argentina, 1965.

Cook, Sherburne F., and Woodrow W. Borah. *The Indian Population of Central Mexico, 1531-1610*. Berkeley, Calif., 1960.

Cook, Sherburne F., and Lesley Byrd Simpson. *The Population of Central Mexico in the Sixteenth Century*. Berkeley, Calif., 1948.

Cordeiro, Luciano. *Questões histórico-coloniais*. 3 vols. Lisbon, 1935-36.

Correia Lopes, Edmundo. *A escravatura: Subsídios para a sua história*. Lisbon, 1944.

Cortés, Vicenta. *La esclavitud en Valencia durante el reinado de los Reyes Católicos*. Valencia, 1964.

Crosby, Alfred W. "*Conquistador y Pestilencia*: The First New World Pandemic and the Fall of the Great Indian Empires," *HAHR*, 47 (1967): 321-37.

Curtin, Philip D. *The Atlantic Slave Trade: A Census*. Madison, Wis., 1969.

Davidson, D. M. "Negro Slave Control and Resistance in Colonial Mexico, 1519-1650," *HAHR*, 46 (1966): 235-53.

Davis, David Brion. *The Problem of Slavery in Western Culture*. Ithaca, N.Y., 1966.

"De la vida colonial en el siglo XVII: 271 fichas y documentos de primera noticia," *Revista del Archivo Histórico del Cuzco*, 5 (1954): 159-252.

Diaz Soler, Luis M. *Historia de la esclavitud negra en Puerto Rico, 1493-1890*. Madrid, 1953. 2d ed., rev., Rio Piedras, Puerto Rico, 1965.

Dobyns, H. F. "Estimating Aboriginal American Population: An Appraisal of Techniques with a New Hemispheric Estimate," *Current Anthropology*, 7 (1966): 395-449.

————. "An Outline of Andean Epidemic History to 1720," *Bulletin of the History of Medicine*, 37 (1963): 493-515.

Dodge, Peter. "Comparative Racial Systems in the Greater Caribbean," *Social and Economic Studies*, 16 (1967): 249-61.

Elliott, J. H. *Imperial Spain, 1469-1716*. London, 1963.

Emeth, Omer [Emilio Vaisse]. "El libro de cuentas de un negrero en 1621," *Revista Chilena de Historia y Geografía*, 6 (1913): 274-86.

Encinas, Diego de. *Cedulario indiano: Reproducción facsimil de la edición única de 1596*. 4 vols. Madrid, 1945-46.

Escalona Agüero, Gaspar de. *Gazofilacio real del Perú [Gazophilacium regium Perubicum]: Tratado financiero del coloniaje*. 4th ed. La Paz, 1941.

Escobar Gamboa, Mauro, and Noble David Cook, eds. *Padrón de los indios de Lima en 1613*. Lima, 1968.

Figueroa, Cristóbal. *Hechos de Don García Hurtado de Mendoza, cuarto Marqués de Cañete*, pp. 1-206, in vol. 5 of *Colección de historiadores de Chile y documentos relativos a la historia nacional*. 50 vols. Santiago de Chile, 1861-1948.

Fox, K. V. "Pedro Muñiz, Dean of Lima, and the Indian Labor Question," *HAHR*, 42 (1962): 63-88.

Freyre, Gilberto. *The Masters and the Slaves (Casa grande and senzala): A Study in the Development of Brazilian Civilization*, tr. Samuel Putnam. 2d ed. New York, 1956.

Galvão, Henrique, and Carlos Selvagem. *Império ultramarino português*. 4 vols. Lisbon, 1950-53.

Garcia Sampaio, Rozendo. "Contribução ao estudo do aprovisionamento de escravos negros na América Espanhola, 1580-1640," *Anais do Museu Paulista*, 16 (1962): 5-195.

Garcilaso de la Vega, El Inca. *Historia general del Perú: Segunda parte de los Comentarios reales de los Incas*, ed. Ángel Rosenblat and with an essay by José de la Riva Agüero. 3 vols. Buenos Aires, 1944.

Góngora, Mario. *Los grupos de conquistadores en Tierra Firme, 1509-1530. Fisonomía histórico-social de un tipo de conquista*. Santiago de Chile, 1962.

Greenfield, Sidney M. "Slavery and the Plantation in the New World: The Development and Diffusion of a Social Form," *Journal of Inter-American Studies*, 11 (1969): 44-57.

Guillot, Carlos Federico. *Negros rebeldes y negros cimarrones: Perfil afroamericano en la historia del Nuevo Mundo durante el siglo XVI*. Buenos Aires, 1961.

Gutiérrez de Santa Clara, Pedro. *Historia de las guerras civiles del Perú (1544-1588) y de otros sucesos de las Indias*, ed. Manuel Serrano y Sanz. 6 vols. Madrid, 1904-29.

Haring, C. H. *The Spanish Empire in America*. New York, 1947.

Harth-terré, Emilio. "Carta India." 14 mimeo. pages dated Lima, April 1962.

————. "El esclavo negro en la sociedad indoperuana," *Journal of Inter-American Studies*, 3 (1961): 133-42.

————. *Informe sobre el descubrimiento de documentos que revelan la trata y comercio de esclavos negros por los indios del común durante el gobierno virreinal en el Perú*, with English translation by Jean Fitch Costa. Lima, 1961.

Harth-terré, Emilio, and Alberto Márquez Abanto. "El artesano negro en la arquitectura virreinal limeña," *RANP*, 25 (1961): 3-73.

————. "Las bellas artes en el virreinato del Perú en el siglo XVII: Azulejos limeños," *RANP*, 22 (1958): 411-45.

————. "Las bellas artes en el virreinato del Perú en el siglo XVI: Las casas del Real Tribunal de la Inquisición," *RANP*, 22 (1958): 194-217.

————. "Historia de la casa urbana virreinal en Lima," *RANP*, 26 (1962); and offprint, Lima, 1962.

————. "El histórico puente sobre el Río Apurímac," *RANP*, 25 (1961); and offprint, Lima, 1961.

————. "El puente de piedra de Lima," *RANP*, 24 (1960), and offprint, Lima, 1960.

Helps, Arthur. *The Spanish Conquest in America and Its Relation to the History of Slavery and to the Government of Colonies.* 4 vols. London, 1855-61. 2d ed. edited by M. Oppenheim. 4 vols., London, 1900.

Herrera y Tordesillas, Antonio de. *Historia general de los hechos de los castellanos en las islas y tierra firme del mar océano.* 9 vols. in 5. Madrid, 1726-27. 17 vols. Madrid, 1934-57.

Hoeppli, R. *Parasitic Diseases in Africa and the Western Hemisphere: Early Documentation and Transmission by the Slave Trade.* Basel, 1969.

Hoetink, Harry. *The Two Variants in Caribbean Race Relations: A Contribution to the Sociology of Segmented Societies,* tr. Eva M. Hooykaas. New York, 1967.

James, Preston. *Latin America.* 3d ed. New York, 1959.

King, James F. "The Colored Castes and American Representation in the Cortes of Cádiz," *HAHR*, 33 (1953): 33-64.

————. "Evolution of the Free Slave Trade Principle in Spanish Colonial Administration," *HAHR*, 22 (1942): 34-56.

Klein, Herbert S. *Slavery in the Americas: A Comparative Study of Virginia and Cuba.* Chicago, 1967.

Konetzke, Richard, ed. *Colección de documentos para la historia de la formación social de Hispanoamérica, 1493-1810.* 3 vols. in 5. Madrid, 1953-62.

Kubler, George. "The Quechua in the Colonial World," pp. 331-410 in vol. 2 of Julian H. Steward, ed., *Handbook of South American Indians.* Washington, D.C., 1946.

Lamb, Ursula. *Frey Nicolás de Ovando: Gobernador de las Indias, 1501-1509.* Madrid, 1956.

Lanning, John Tate. "Legitimacy and *Limpieza de Sangre* in the Practice of Medicine in the Spanish Empire," *Jahrbuch für Geschichte van Staat, Wirtschaft und Gesellschaft Lateinamerikas,* 4 (1967): 37-60.

Larrazábal Blanco, Carlos. *Los negros y la esclavitud en Santo Domingo.* Santo Domingo, 1967.

Lea, Henry Charles. *The Inquisition in the Spanish Dependencies.* London, 1908.

Lee, Bertram T., ed. "El General Francisco Velásquez Vela Núñez," *RANP*, 8.2 (1935): 225-32.

Levillier, Roberto, ed. *Gobernantes del Perú: Cartas y papeles, siglo XVI. Documentos del Archivo de Indias.* 14 vols. Madrid, 1921-26.

Lewin, Boleslao. *El Santo Oficio y el más grande proceso inquisitorial en el Perú.* Buenos Aires, 1950.

————. *Descripción del virreinato del Perú: Crónica inédita de comienzos del siglo XVII.* Universidad Nacional del Litoral, Instituto de Investigaciones Históricas, Colección de Textos y Documentos, series B, no. 1. Rosario, Argentina, 1958.

Libros de cabildos de Lima, ed. Bertram T. Lee and Juan Bromley. Vols. 1- , Lima, 1935- .

Lockhart, James. *Spanish Peru, 1532-1560: A Colonial Society.* Madison, Wis., 1968.

Lohmann Villena, Guillermo. "Apuntaciones sobre el curso de los precios de los artículos de primera necesidad en Lima durante el siglo XVI," *Revista Histórica* (Lima), 29 (1966): 79-104.

————. *El corregidor de indios en el Perú bajo los Austrias.* Madrid, 1957.

————. *Las defensas militares de Lima y Callao.* Seville, 1964.

————. *Las minas de Huancavelica en los siglos XVI y XVII.* Seville, 1949.

————, comp. "Índice del 'Libro becerro de escrituras,'" *RANP*, 14 (1941): 211-40; 15 (1942): 87-96, 215-20; 16 (1943): 59-100, 173-219; 17 (1944): 51-69.

López de Velasco, Juan. *Geografía y descripción universal de las Indias, recopilada . . . desde el año de 1571 al de 1574.* Madrid, 1894.

Márquez Abanto, Alberto, ed. "Don Antonio Ricardo, introductor de la imprenta en Lima: Su testamento y codicilio," *RANP*, 19 (1955): 290-305.

Martín, Luis. *The Intellectual Conquest of Peru: The Jesuit College of San Pablo, 1568-1767.* New York, 1968.

Mauro, Frédéric. *Le Portugal et l'Atlantique au xviie siècle (1570-1670): Étude économique.* Paris, 1960.

Means, Philip Ainsworth. *Fall of the Inca Empire and the Spanish Rule in Peru, 1530-1780.* New York, 1932.

Medina, Bernardo. *San Martín de Porres, biografía del siglo XVII.* Mexico, 1964. From the 1675 Madrid ed.

Medina, José Toribio. *El descubrimiento del Océano Pacífico: Vasco Núñez de Balboa, Hernando de Magallanes y sus compañeros.* 4 vols. in 3. Santiago de Chile, 1914-20.

————. *Historia del Tribunal del Santo Oficio de la Inquisición de Lima, 1569-1820.* 2 vols. Santiago de Chile, 1887.

————. *Historia del Tribunal del Santo Oficio de la Inquisición en Cartagena de Indias.* Santiago de Chile, 1899.

Meléndez Chaverri, Carlos. "Los orígenes de los esclavos africanos en Costa Rica," pp. 387-91 in vol. 4 of *XXXVI Congreso Internacional de Americanistas: Actas y memorias.* Seville, 1966.

Mellafe, Rolando. *Diego de Almagro y el descubrimiento del Perú.* Santiago de Chile, 1954.

————. *La esclavitud en Hispanomérica.* Buenos Aires, 1964.

————. *La introducción de la esclavitud negra en Chile: Tráfico y rutas.* Santiago de Chile, 1959.

Mendiburu, Manuel de. *Diccionario histórico-biográfico del Perú.* 8 vols. Lima, 1874-90.

Mercado, Tomás de. *Suma de tratos y contratos de mercaderes y tratantes decididos y determinados.* Seville, 1587.

Meza Villalobos, Nestor. *La formación de la fortuna mobiliaria y el ritmo de la conquista.* Santiago de Chile, 1941.

Miramón, Alberto. "Los negreros del Caribe," *Boletín de Historia y Antigüedades* (Bogotá), 31 (1944): 168-87.

Molinari, Diego Luis. *La trata de negros: Datos para su estudio en el Río de la Plata.* 2d ed. Buenos Aires, 1944.

Moore, John Preston. *The Cabildo in Peru Under the Hapsburgs: A Study in the Origins and Powers of the Town Council in the Viceroyalty of Peru, 1530-1700.* Durham, N.C., 1954.

Mörner, Magnus. *Race Mixture in the History of Latin America.* Boston, 1967.

————. "Teoría y práctica de la segregación racial en la América colonial española," Academia Nacional de la Historia (Caracas), *Boletín*, 44 (1961): 278-85.

Mugaburu, Josephe de, and Francisco de Mugaburu (hijo). *Diario de Lima (1640-1694): Crónica de la época colonial,* ed. Horacio H. Urteaga and Carlos A. Romero. 2 vols. Lima, 1917-18.

Murphy, Robert Cushman. "The Earliest Spanish Advances Southward from Panama Along the West Coast of South America," *HAHR*, 21 (1941): 3-28.

Muzquiz de Miguel, José Luis. *El Conde de Chinchón, virrey del Perú.* Madrid, 1945.

Newton, Arthur Percival. *The European Nations in the West Indies, 1493-1688.* London, 1933.

Ortiz Fernández, Fernando. "Los cabildos afro-cubanos," *Revista Bimestre Cubana,* 16 (1921): 5-39.

——. *Hampa afro-cubana: Los negros esclavos. Estudio sociológico y de derecho público.* Havana, 1916.
Otte, Enrique, and Conchita Ruiz-Burruecos. "Los portugueses en la trata de esclavos negros de las postrimerías del siglo XVI," *Moneda y Crédito: Revista de Economía,* no. 85 (1963); and offprint, Madrid, 1963.
Pacheco, Juan Manuel, S.J. "El maestro de Claver: P. Alonso de Sandoval," *Revista Javeriana,* 42 (1954): 80-89, 146-55.
Parry, J. H. *The Sale of Public Office in the Spanish Indies Under the Hapsburgs.* Berkeley, Calif., 1953.
——. *The Spanish Seaborne Empire.* New York, 1966.
Pastells, Pablo, S.J., ed. *Historia de la Compañía de Jesús en la provincia del Paraguay (Argentina, Paraguay, Uruguay, Perú, Bolivia y Brasil) según los documentos originales del Archivo General de Indias.* 9 vols. Madrid, 1912-49.
Paz Soldán, Mariano Felipe. *Diccionario geográfico-estadístico del Perú.* Lima, 1877.
Phelan, John Leddy. *The Kingdom of Quito in the Seventeenth Century: Bureaucratic Politics in the Spanish Empire.* Madison, Wis., 1967.
Picón-Salas, Mariano. *Pedro Claver, el santo de los esclavos.* Mexico, 1950.
Pike, Ruth. *Aristocrats and Traders: Sevillian Society in the Sixteenth Century.* Ithaca, N.Y., 1966.
——. *Enterprise and Adventure: The Genoese in Seville and the Opening of the New World.* Ithaca, N.Y., 1966.
Poma de Ayala, Felipe Guamán. *Nueva corónica y buen gobierno: Codex péruvien illustré.* Paris, 1936. (Modern Spanish ed., tr. Luis Bustíos Gálvez. 3 vols. Lima, 1956-66.)
Porras Barrenechea, Raúl, ed. *Cedulario del Perú.* 2 vols. Lima, 1944-48.
Porras Troconis, Gabriel. *Vida de San Pedro Claver, esclavo de los esclavos.* Bogotá, 1954.
Posada, Eduardo. *La esclavitud en Colombia,* bound with Carlos Restrepo Canal, ed., *Leyes de manumisión.* Bogotá, 1935.
Preher, Leo Marie. *The Social Implications in the Work of Blessed Martin de Porres.* Washington, D.C., 1941.
Prescott, William H. *History of the Conquest of Peru.* Various editions.
Ramón, César, et al. *La comunidad de Chuschi.* Instituto Indigenista Peruano (mimeo.). Ayacucho, Peru, 1967.
Recopilación de leyes de los reynos de las Indias: Edición facsimilar de la cuarta impresión hecha en Madrid el año 1791. 3 vols. Madrid, 1943.
Rodney, Walter. "African Slavery and Other Forms of Social Oppression on the Upper Guinea Coast in the Context of the Atlantic Slave Trade," *Journal of African History,* 7 (1966): 431-43.
——. "Portuguese Attempts at Monopoly on the Upper Guinea Coast, 1580-1650," *Journal of African History,* 6 (1965): 307-22.
Romero, Fernando. "The Slave Trade and the Negro in South America," *HAHR,* 24 (1944): 368-86.
Rosenblat, Ángel. *La población indígena y el mestizaje en América.* 2 vols. Buenos Aires, 1954.
Rowe, John Howland. "Inca Culture at the Time of the Spanish Conquest," pp. 183-330 in vol. 2 of Julian H. Steward, ed., *Handbook of South American Indians.* Washington, D.C., 1946.
——. "The Incas Under Spanish Colonial Institutions," *HAHR,* 37 (1957): 155-99.
Rumeu de Armas, Antonio. *España en el Africa Atlántica,* 2 vols. Madrid, 1956-57.
Saco, José Antonio. *Historia de la esclavitud de la raza africana en el Nuevo Mundo y en especial en los países américo-hispanos.* Barcelona, 1879.
Salinas y Córdova, Fray Buenaventura de. *Memorial de las historias del Nvevo Mvndo Pirv.* Lima, 1957.

Sandoval, Alonso de. *De instauranda Aethiopum salute: El mundo de la esclavitud negra en América*, ed. Ángel Valtierra. Bogotá, 1956.

Saraiva, A.-J. "Le Père Antonio Vieira S.J. et l'esclavage des Noirs au xviiᵉ siècle," *Annales: Économies, Sociétés, Civilisations*, 22 (1967): 1289-1309.

Sater, William F. "The Forgotten Race," in Robert Brent Toplin, ed., *The Afro-Latin American: Burdens of the Past*. Forthcoming in 1974.

Sauer, Carl Ortwin. *The Early Spanish Main*. Berkeley, Calif., 1966.

Scelle, Georges. *La traité négrière aux Indes de Castille: Contrats et traités d'assiento*. 2 vols. Paris, 1906.

Schurz, William Lytle. *The Manila Galleon*. New York, 1939.

Senna Barcellos, Christiano José de. *Subsídios para a historia de Cabo Verde e Guiné*. 2 vols. Lisbon, 1899.

Las Siete Partidas del Rey Don Alfonso el Sabio cotejadas con varios códices antiguos por la Real Academia de la Historia. 3 vols. Madrid, 1807.

Silva Santisteban, Fernando. *Los obrajes en el virreinato del Perú*. Lima, 1964.

Smith, Clifford Thorpe. "Depopulation of the Central Andes in the Sixteenth Century," *Current Anthropology*, 11 (1970): 453-64.

Spalding, Karen. "The Colonial Indian: Past and Future Research Perspectives," *Latin American Research Review*, 7 (1972): 47-76.

Suardo, Juan Antonio. *Diario de Lima*, ed. Rubén Vargas Ugarte. 2 vols. Lima, 1936.

Tejado Fernández, Manuel. *Aspectos de la vida social en Cartagena de Indias durante el seiscientos*. Seville, 1954.

Torquemada, Juan de. *Monarquía indiana*. 3 vols. Mexico, 1943.

Urteaga, Horacio H., ed. "El conquistador y poblador del Perú Diego [sic] de Destre," *RANP*, 8 (1930): 29-39.

———. "Cristóbal de Burgos: Conquistador del Perú y Regidor del Cabildo de Lima," *RANP*, 11 (1938): 97-110.

———. "Don Diego de Agüero y Sandoval, conquistador y poblador del Perú," *RANP*, 6 (1928): 149-70.

Valtierra, Ángel. *El santo que libertó una raza: San Pedro Claver, S.J., esclavo de los esclavos negros. Su vida y su época, 1580-1654*. Bogotá, 1954.

Vargas Ugarte, Rubén, comp. *Biblioteca Peruana*. 12 vols. Lima and Buenos Aires, 1935-57.

———, ed. *Concilios Limenses, 1551-1772*. 3 vols. Lima, 1951-54.

———. "Nuevos documentos sobre el Ven. P. Francisco del Castillo, S.J.," *RANP*, 6 (1928): 203-20.

Vázquez, Mário C. "Immigration and *Mestizaje* in Nineteenth-Century Peru," pp. 73-95 in Magnus Mörner, ed., *Race and Class in Latin America*. New York, 1970.

Vázquez de Espinosa, Antonio. *Compendium and Description of the West Indies*, tr. Charles Upson Clark. Washington, D.C., 1942.

Veitia Linage, Joseph de. *Norte de la contratación de las Indias Occidentales*. Buenos Aires, 1945. From the 1672 Seville ed.

Verlinden, Charles. *L'esclavage dans l'Europe médiévale, 1: Péninsule Ibérique-France*. Bruges, 1955.

von Hagen, Victor Wolfgang, ed. *The Incas of Pedro de Cieza de León*, tr. Harriet de Onis. Norman, Okla., 1959.

West, Robert C. *Colonial Placer Mining in Colombia*. Baton Rouge, La., 1952.

Wiedner, Donald L. "Forced Labor in Colonial Peru," *The Americas*, 16 (1969): 357-83.

Wright, Irene A., ed. *Documents Concerning English Voyages to the Spanish Main, 1569-1580*. London, 1932.

Index

Abancay Valley, 94
Abanto, Márquez, Alberto, viii, 138, 250
Acapulco, 64, 97
Accounts, Tribunal of, 122, 214
Acuña, de, Alberto, 173
aduanilla, 361
Africa: as source of slaves, 1-3, 26-51, 58, 79, 111, 144-48 *passim*, 326f, 355; baptism of slaves in, 54, 238-39; slavery within, 364
Afro-Indian relations, *see under* Indians
Afro-Spanish sexual unions, 286-89
age, of slaves, 95, 137, 298, 305, 344-45, 388
agriculture: Indian labor in, 12, 117f, 120, 123, 324-28 *passim*; black labor in, 88-96, 100, 109, 126, 146, 182, 223, 317, 377; menaced by runaways, 147, 187, 193, 216f; blacks turning to, 317. *See also chácaras*; plantations
Aguilar, de, Diego, 176-77
alcabala, 68, 347
alcaldes, 161-70 *passim*, 174f, 196-99 *passim*, 209-19 *passim*, 304, 347, 397
Aldana, de, Lorenzo, 187-88
Alexander VI, Pope, 2
Alfonso the Wise, 273
alguaciles, see constables
Almagro, de, Diego, 4f, 7, 10-11, 356; the Younger, 8-9
almojarifazgo, 68, 73-74, 76, 347, 370f
Alonga, 40-41 (Table 1), 346
Alvarado, de, Pedro, 4
Álvarez de Paz, Diego, 180
Ampuero, de, Francisco, 202, 252
Añaquito, 9
Anchico, 40-43 (Tables 1 and 2), 346
Angola, 30-33 *passim*, 38-49 *passim*, 72, 80, 145, 250, 364f, 373; language of, 234-35, 245
Antilles, 195, 355
apprenticeship, 125, 126-27, 136-46 *passim*, 329
Apurímac, 114-15, 121-22
Arabs, 1f, 325
Arara (Arda), 40-43 (Tables 1-2), 346
Araucarian Indians, 172, 309n, 358
archbishops of Lima, *see under* Church
Arequipa, 10, 21, 78, 106, 159, 177, 253, 267, 303-4, 374f
Arica, 93f, 179, 265, 280, 299, 304, 371
Aristotle, 223
Armenians, 1
arms and weapons: prohibitions against, 149, 155f, 174, 179; bearing of arms by persons of color, 149f, 154-56, 175-81 *passim*, 309-10; use of, by persons of color, 155-56, 163-64, 168, 171f, 182-88 *passim*, 217
army, blacks in, 8-9. *See also* militia
Arnedo, 211
artisans, colored, 9, 125-46, 159, 250, 307; living conditions of, 158, 225, 309, 317, 329, 413; and freedom, 260, 281, 288, 300
asentistas and *asientos*, 31-37, 44-46, 48-49, 55, 61f, 326-27, 347, 361f, 369
asesor, 347, 397
asientos, see asentistas
assimilation, viii, 220, 272, 305n, 321f, 331, 333f, 340
asylum, 157f, 169, 171, 187, 199ff
Atahualpa, 252
Audiencia, 162-67 *passim*, 347; and treatment of slaves, 84, 105, 115, 122, 132, 173, 229; and lawsuits, 101, 231,

239, 242, 253, 259, 263, 392, 397; and
mine labor, 111f, 119; control of slaves,
149-57 *passim*, 182, 197, 200, 206f, 211,
218f; in law enforcement, 168-71; and
taxes, 208, 212, 303-7 *passim*; and
sale of offices, 215, 314; and freedom
cases, 274, 291-96 *passim*; and discrimination, 283, 310, 313, 414
Augustinians, 98, 127, 130, 170, 175,
243, 249, 320
avenças, 30, 347
avería de los negros bozales, 219, 347,
361f
Ayacucho, *see* Guamanga
Ayala, Poma de, Felipe Guamán, *see*
Poma de Ayala
Ayala y Contreras, Diego, 214-19, 400
Azores, 2

Balanta, 40-43 (Tables 1 and 2)
Baltasar Carlos, 306
Bañol, 40-43 (Tables 1 and 2), 346
Bantu tribes, 38
baptisms, slave, *see under* Church
Barbarán, de, Juan, 188
barracoons, 47, 366
Barreto, Luis Gomes, 57-58, 59, 369
bastardy, *see* illegitimacy
beating of slaves, *see* punishment
Benguela, 40-41 (Table 1)
Benin, Bight of, 38, 346
Berbers, 360
Berbesi, 40-43 (Tables 1 and 2), 346
Biafra, 38, 40-43 (Tables 1 and 2), 346
Bioho, 40-43 (Tables 1 and 2), 44, 346
birth rate, 75, 337-38
Black Sea, 1
Bleblo, 40-41 (Table 1), 346
Bocanegra, 217-18
Bolivia, ix, 73
Borregán, Alonso, 188
bounty on runaway slaves, 197-205
passim
Boxer, C. R., 38n, 39, 44ff, 364
bozales, 39, 42-43 (Table 2), 73f, 130,
196, 203, 235-39 *passim*, 250, 347;
on the market, 77-84 *passim*, 342-45,
355, 374f
Bran, 40-43 (Tables 1 and 2), 346
branding of slaves, 83-84, 201, 224, 357
Brazil, vii, 3, 29-33 *passim*, 38, 57, 73,
89, 111, 185, 364
brotherhoods, colored, *see* sodalities
Buenos Aires, 39
Bulgarians, 1

bulls, Papal, 2, 366
burials, 223, 230, 241, 248, 310, 320

Caballos, 93
cabildos, 149ff, 156, 165, 212, 260, 347,
390
Cáceres, de, Juan, 14-15
Cacho de Santillana, Cristóbal, 180
caja de los negros, 203-6 *passim*, 210-13
passim, 398
Cajamarca, 94, 262, 264, 293
Cajatambo, 211
Callao, 151, 162, 248, 301, 392; and
slave trade, 54f, 62-77 *passim*, 96-100
passim, 203f, 213, 367, 371f; blacks
working in, 104ff, 126-27; fortifications
of, 128-29, 180-85 *passim*, 309f;
criminality in, 173, 177, 190-96 *passim*,
215, 232f
Camaná Valley, 93-94
Cañari Indians, 176
Canary Islands, 2, 35
Canelas Albarrán, Juan, 339, 341
Cañete, 89, 92, 193, 208, 211, 215, 241
Cañete, de, Marqués: First, 17, 22, 105,
156f, 178, 199-208 *passim*, 232, 317,
397; Second, 90, 98-100, 114ff, 208ff,
239, 285, 391f
Cape Verde—Guinea, 30
Cape Verde Islands, 2, 78, 363, 365
Capitulations of Toledo, 4
Carabaya, 13, 17, 113, 157f, 317, 359
Carabayllo Valley, 101, 202
Caravali, 40-43 (Tables 1 and 2), 346
Caribbean, vii, 3, 5, 26-87 *passim*, 148
Cartagena, 91, 173, 253; as slave trade
center, 31f, 36, 39, 48-87 *passim*, 367,
371f; missionary work in, 238f, 401
cartas de alquiler, 104, 347
Casa de la Contratación, 34, 55-56, 361
Casamance, 346
Casanga, 40-43 (Tables 1 and 2), 346
Casas, de las, Bartolomé, 12, 26, 325
Casma Valley, 126, 211
Castilla, Criado de, Alonso, 339
castration and other forms of mutilation,
150-55 *passim*, 174, 179, 196-201
passim, 397. *See also* branding of
slaves; punishment
Castro, García de, Lope, 20, 153, 175
Castrovirreina, 93
Cathedral parish of Lima, 75, 249f, 339f
Catholicism, *see* Christianity; Church;
*and individual religious orders and
rites by name*

censuses, 23, 239, 300-305 *passim*, 334n, 338-41, 378, 410, 415. *See also* population
Central America, 5, 97. *See also individual countries by name*
Cercado district, 305, 340, 390
chácaras, 88ff, 101, 348
Chachapoyas, 17
Chagres River, 63
Chancay, 196, 202, 208, 256
Charcas, 111, 157
Charles V, Emperor, 28, 110, 149
chasquis, 116, 123, 348
chicha, 108-9, 224
Chichima, Francisco, 176-77
Chiclayo, 304
Chilca, 192
children: and family ties, 81, 254-55, 268-70, 317; of mixed parentage, 139, 151, 257f, 285-93 *passim*, 315-16, 321, 332, 403, 409; apprenticed, 139-40; and manumission, 274-77 *passim*, 281f, 298, 300; in slave trade, 369
Chile, 5, 55, 73, 77, 172, 200, 309n, 310, 367
Chincha Valley, 19
Chinchón, de, Conde, 168, 171, 220; on treatment of blacks, 65-66, 67, 224, 240, 408-9; on *mita* labor, 91; on African labor, 99-100, 101, 109, 122; on control of blacks, 182-85, 218, 231, 311, 400; on sale of offices, 214-15, 216, 314; and census, 341
Chinese in Lima, 341
chinos, see zambos
Chircay, 125, 256
Christianity, 1, 27-28, 222-23, 233-71 *passim*, 274-77 *passim*, 310, 326. *See also* Church; missionaries; *and individual religious orders by name*
Chucuito, 153
Chunchanga Valley, 242
Chupas, 8-9, 357
Church, Catholic, 34, 181, 312, 315, 320; and slave baptisms, 3, 28, 47-48, 54, 65, 148, 234-42 *passim*, 256, 366, 379; role in New World, 53f, 232-71; and law enforcement, 163, 165, 169-71; archbishops of Lima, 169f, 212, 237-41 *passim*, 248, 295, 310, 339ff, 360; and assimilation, 283, 285, 310, 321, 331. *See also* Christianity; missionaries; *and individual religious orders by name*
Cieza de Léon, de, Pedro, 19

cimarrones, see runaways
Circassians, 1
civil wars, 5, 8-10, 12, 18, 25, 132, 151
Claver, Saint Peter, 53
climate, 13-17, 20, 22, 113f, 119f, 122, 173
clothing, 226-27, 271, 311, 331f, 358
coartación system, 279n
coast: labor problems, 20-21, 23-25, 123, 201; decline of Indian population, 18-19, 324f, 328; black population, 110, 119, 124, 186f, 273, 300, 327-28, 338
Cocoli, 40-43 (Tables 1 and 2), 346
cofradía, see sodalities
Colegio Real de San Felipe y San Marcos, 312
College of San Pablo, 90, 231, 245ff, 269, 312-13, 401, 414
Columbus, Christopher, 1f
communion, 236, 239, 246ff, 251
Concepción convent, 275, 281
Conchucos, 195
Condor Valley, 92
confraternities, *see* sodalities
Confraternity of the Prisons and Charity, 228, 243
Confraternity of the Saints Peter and Paul, 243
Congo, 38, 40-43 (Tables 1 and 2), 80, 145, 346, 364
conquest of Peru, role of blacks in, 25, 132, 135, 272-73
conquistadores, 3-13 *passim*, 19-20, 25f 150f, 273, 321, 356
constables, 162, 164ff, 174-79 *passim*, 196-214 *passim*, 219, 221, 304, 347. *See also cuadrilleros;* Hermandad; law enforcement
Constantinople, 1
construction, blacks in, 114-15, 121-22, 127-31 *passim*, 135, 146, 225f, 229, 267, 386
contraband, 35ff, 51, 56, 61f, 72ff, 77, 326-27, 362
contracts: labor, 111-13; apprenticeship, 139-41, 145-46, 268; employment, 307-8, 377; rental, 308-9
Contratación, Casa de la, 34, 55-56, 361
convents: and slavery, 7, 104-5, 130-31, 260, 267, 269; served by children, 270, 312; examples of manumitted slaves in, 275-81 *passim*, 288, 290, 406
convoy taxes, 75, 348, 361-62, 370
Córdoba, 126
Corral, del, Francisco, 175

corregidores de indios, 12-13, 153-54, 177, 198, 215, 285, 305, 348, 361, 392
Corsica, 10
Cortés, Hernando, 3
costs: care of slaves, xiv, 223-30 *passim*, 240, 358; mining, 13-17; in slave trade, 61-71 *passim*, 366; litigation, 85-87; apprehending runaways, 187, 191, 195-203 *passim*, 213-14, 219; manumission, 275, 278-82 *passim*, 288-300 *passim*, 315; jail, 396. *See also* prices, slave
couriers, India, 116, 123, 348
courts, 162-68 *passim*, 192, 236-37, 259-69, 279, 287-97. *See also* lawsuits
Coutinho, Gonzalo Vaez, 362
Coutinho, João Rodrigués, 32-33, 362
craftsmen, *see* artisans
credit, 61, 69-70, 71, 81f, 112f, 119, 122, 371
creoles, *see* criollos
criminals, *see* law enforcement; punishment
criollos, 78-80, 91, 145, 159, 193, 250f, 342-45, 348, 355
Crown, Portuguese, 30, 45
Crown, Spanish: role in slave trade, 3-9 *passim*, 26-51, 55-57, 61, 63, 67f, 71-77 *passim*, 362, 369; use of Africans, 10, 13-17, 96-101 *passim*, 110-34 *passim*, 145, 412-13; attitude toward Indians, 12-13, 90-91, 110-24 *passim*, 135, 325-28 *passim*; sources of revenue, 23, 212f, 220f, 303-7, 310, 328, 398; attitude on care of slaves, 82, 224-31 *passim*; and Church, 169-71, 222, 233-57 *passim*; tax dispute with Lima, 210-15. *See also* decrees; Spain
cuadrilleros, 105-6, 199-211 *passim*, 218f, 348, 397. *See also* law enforcement
Cuba, 73, 212, 279n, 362
Cumaná, 362
curfew, 149f, 156, 164, 166-67, 172, 309, 392f
Curtin, Philip, 39, 362f
Cuzco: labor in, 23-24, 64, 114f, 121, 134, 141f; control of blacks, 158, 161, 169, 201, 209, 391, 396; under siege, 356

Dahomey, 346
dances, 156, 163, 183, 232, 239, 248, 413
daños, 369
death penalty, 160-74 *passim*, 193-202 *passim*, 231, 252, 397
decrees: on control of blacks, 21, 149, 155, 165-66, 183, 222; on residence

requirements, 23, 157; on importation, 35, 81, 148, 254, 355f, 360-66 *passim*; on *mita* system, 111, 116-17, 120; on control of runaways, 199, 214f, 218-19, 397; on welfare of blacks, 233, 242, 248, 303, 310, 313, 403, 413; on discrimination, 313, 414. *See also* legislation
defects in slaves, 81-87, 137, 174, 190f, 376, 388
demography, *see* censuses; population
diet, 224-26, 227
diseases, *see* sickness and disease
divide-and-rule policies, 162, 169, 249, 285
doctors, *see* medical care
domestics, *see* household servants
Dominicans, 130, 169f, 174, 243, 248-50 *passim*, 258, 315, 318
donativo, 306
Drake, Francis, 178
drinking and drunkenness, 81, 85, 108-9, 150, 156-59 *passim*, 163, 172, 239, 247, 321, 376, 391
Duarte, Sebastián, 58-71, 73, 78, 369, 372, 374
Dudum siquidem (Papal bull), 2
Durán y Ribera, Tomás, 114
duty, *see* taxes
dynastic union, 29-36 *passim*, 50-51, 239, 326

economy: contribution of Africans to, viii, 3, 9, 23, 88-109, 119, 124, 146; and institution of slavery, ix, 24-25, 33, 76, 172, 183, 201, 324-28; and the Indian, 13-18, 110, 118, 120, 123, 326-28
Ecuador, 55, 73, 77, 122, 296, 315
education, 270, 312-13, 315, 333, 414
d'Elvas, Antonio Fernandes, 31n, 33
employment regulations, 303, 307-8, 332
Encarnación, La, convent, 105, 166f, 270, 276, 280, 406
encomienda and *encomenderos*, 7f, 10, 12, 18-21, 117, 150-54 *passim*, 203, 318, 348, 358, 390
England, 37, 73, 97, 178, 201, 330, 369
Enríquez, Luis, 170, 212-13, 242
Enríquez, Martín, 112, 153, 390
epidemics, 308, 339
esclavos blancos, 355
esclavos chinos, 340
escribano de la Hermandad, 399
Espino, Ventura, 111-13, 382-83

Espinosa, de, Pedro, 366
Espinosa, Vázquez de, Antonio, 241f, 339
Esquilache, de, Príncipe, 56-57, 165-70
  passim, 179f, 182, 212, 305f
Esquivel Triana, Juan, 183
Estrella, Cornejo de, Pedro, 112-14, 383
Ethiopia, 26f
ethnic origins of Afro-Peruvians, 40-43
  (Tables 1 and 2), 78-80, 346
exclusion laws, 3, 148-49
excommunication, 259, 262, 265
executions, *see* death penalty;
  punishment
exile of slaves, 150, 153f, 172, 199f,
  232, 253

family life, 254-71, 331
farms, *see* agriculture; *chácaras*;
  plantations
fathers of mixed-blood children, 287-89,
  295, 315-17, 332, 409
fe de entrada, 61-62, 348, 369, 372
feast days and festivals, 232-41 *passim*,
  245f, 248, 276
female slaves: life of, 67, 108f, 151-56
  passim, 229, 246, 255-68 *passim*, 287,
  298, 300; ratio to male slaves, 81, 95,
  254, 340-41; prices, 343-45. *See also*
  mothers; women
Ferdinand VI, King, 2
fines: of slaves, 147, 153, 160, 168, 179,
  263; to support constables, 162, 200,
  206f, 210, 214, 218f; of masters, 198,
  200, 231, 234
Florines, Bernabé, 121-22
Folupo, 40-43 (Tables 1 and 2)
food: blacks in production and sale of,
  106-9; for slaves, 224-26, 227, 271,
  321, 331, 358
forasteros, 24, 90, 348
forced labor, *see mita* system
France, 37, 148, 178
Franciscans, 98, 160, 248f, 320
free persons of color, viii, 272-323; as
  laborers, 17, 22-23, 88, 97f, 116-24
  passim, 377; and runaways, 105, 196,
  199f, 204; as skilled labor, 106, 108-9,
  125-46 *passim*; numbers of, 147, 174,
  186, 339; control of, 151-59 *passim*,
  220, 230f; life of, 175, 260f, 268, 279,
  330-33 *passim*, 405, 414
freedom: promised, 9, 147f, 177f, 181f,
  197; by purchase, 125, 127, 139,
  278-82, 315ff, 407f; voluntary
  manumission, 223, 272-78; role of

racial mixture, 282-301, 405;
  difficulties after achieving, 317, 329,
  331-32
Fregenal, de, Juan, 308, 317
Fuente, de la, Francisco, 121f
Fula, 40-43 (Tables 1 and 2), 346
funerals, *see* burials

galleys, 97-100, 123, 172f, 184, 191, 215,
  295, 380
Gama, da, Vasco, 3
Gambia Valley, 346
gambling, 150, 153, 159f, 165, 172, 233
Gasca, de la, Pedro, 14-15, 151, 197
Gelofes, 28, 148, 319, 346, 348, 360
Georgians, 1
German slavers, 29
gift money, 278ff, 332
Girón, *see* Hernández Girón, Francisco
Godoy, de, Francisco, 241f
godparents, 280, 282, 289
gold: as monetary unit, xiii; mining of,
  3, 5, 13, 17, 24, 112-13, 122f, 176, 317
González de Cuenca, Gregorio, 201
grumetes, 97, 99, 104, 348
Guadalcázar, de, Marqués, 66f, 99,
  128-29, 181, 213, 283
Guamanga, 10, 93f, 241, 254, 294f
Guanchaco, 64
Guánuco, 276
Guara Valley, 89, 255
Guarina, 9
Guatemala, 4, 73, 290, 296, 319
Guauray, 267
Guayaquil, 126, 193, 195, 296
Guaylas, 89, 227
Guevara de Armenta, Pedro, 122
guilds: Sevillian merchant guild, 30,
  34-37, 45, 50-51, 55-56, 208, 362;
  for blacks, 108, 306; artisan, 134, 141-
  43, 146, 329, 374, 389, 412
Guinea: slave trade from, 28, 33, 37-50
  passim, 54, 58, 72, 364f, 373; prices
  of slaves from, 61, 361, 369; quality of
  slaves from, 79f, 132, 145, 363
Guinea-Bissau, 40-43 (Tables 1 and 2),
  80, 145, 346
Guinea-Conakry, 346
Gutiérrez de Contreras, Pedro, 93

Ham, curse of, 27, 360
hanging, *see* death penalty; punishment
Hapsburgs, 29, 162, 363
Harth-terré, Emilio, viii, 137f, 250
Havana, 148

head tax, *see* taxes
health: and climate, 20, 113f, 120, 122; of slaves, 39, 47-50, 53-54, 66-67, 71, 223, 376; as quality on slave market, 80, 81-87, 137. *See also* sickness and disease
Herbay, 255
Hermandad, 187, 190, 199, 200-221, 330f, 400
Hernández Girón, Francisco, 9-10, 93, 337, 398
Herrera y Tordesillas, de, Antonio, 338-39
hiding of runaways, 157, 169, 171, 187, 199ff
highlands: labor problems in, 13-24 *passim*, 113f, 120-24 *passim*, 324f, 327f; and criminals, 176, 189, 201
hiring-out of slaves, 103-5, 126-27, 136, 139, 307-8, 381
Hispaniola, 55, 73, 148, 197, 362
Holland: and slave trade, 36f, 49, 51, 366; as threat in Pacific, 96f, 101; and Peruvian blacks, 122, 128, 179-84, 186, 306-10 *passim*, 330, 394
holy days, *see* feast days and festivals
Holy Office, 191, 218, 225, 253, 259, 269, 312, 368; and law enforcement, 57-59, 72, 168, 232, 302; and Sandoval, 236
Honduras, 73, 362
hospitals, 105-6, 130, 191, 228-30, 247f
household servants: Indians as, 5, 7; blacks as, 91f, 100-105, 182, 360; life of 125, 146, 223, 227, 260, 270, 300, 317; loyalty of, 159, 184
housing, 227, 271, 303, 308-9, 317ff, 331ff, 403
Huacho, 382
Huananguilla Valley, 94
Huancavelica, 23, 93, 99, 123, 133, 173, 382-83, 384, 410
Huánuco, 94, 136
Huara, 188
Huarochirí, 215f
Huaylas, 211
Huayna Capac, 252
huidors, see runaways

Iberia, *see* Portugal; Spain
Ica, 56, 211, 242, 304, 411
illegitimacy, 139, 151, 257f, 268, 302, 312, 315, 321, 331; cited cases, 288-89, 296, 408-9. *See also* fathers of mixed-blood children

illness, *see* sickness and disease
importation, slave: limitations on, 22-23, 148, 178-79, 183, 360, 367; volume of, 72-78, 220, 337-38, 354f, 361f, 374
Incas, 7-8, 11, 19-20, 114, 282, 287, 326, 356. *See also* Indians
Incinillas, de, Varona, 182
India, 2-3
Indians: relations with blacks, vii, viii, 7, 103, 147-54 *passim*, 176, 276f, 282-86, 313, 317f, 390f; as slaves, 5-7, 12, 358; Spanish control of, 8f, 176, 178, 180, 184, 356, 358f, 392; as labor force, 11-24 *passim*, 88-100 *passim*, 110-25 *passim*, 134-44 *passim*, 158, 173, 183, 232f, 303, 324-28 *passim*, 359, 385; decline of, 18-19, 75f, 87, 114-21 *passim*, 227, 229, 243, 340f, 415; Christianization, 26-27, 34, 234-43 *passim*, 248, 251f, 321; sexual mingling of, 254, 256, 261, 313, 332, 408; segregation of, 282-87, 293, 299f
Indies, Council of the, 15-16, 112-17 *passim*, 166, 182, 188, 218, 238, 247, 286, 316
inheritance, 291-92, 316-19 *passim*
Inquisition, 57-58, 131, 168, 225, 251, 253
insurance on slaving vessels, 366
insurrections, *see* rebellions
Inter caetera (Papal bull), 2
invasion, fear of, 97, 128, 178-86 *passim*, 220
investment, slaves as, 14, 103, 136-39, 147, 187, 225, 232, 329, 356
Isabella, Queen, 2
Islam, 27f, 148, 222, 251, 283, 360. *See also* Moors
Isthmus, *see* Panama
Italian slavers, 1, 29

Jails, 172, 203, 214, 232, 234, 243, 247f, 359, 396. *See also* law enforcement; punishment
Jamaica, 49, 73
Jauja, 20n, 150, 211
Jesuits: and care of slaves, 47, 52ff, 227ff; and baptism of slaves, 65, 238, 366f; as slaveowners, 90, 98, 127, 223; and law enforcement, 169f, 217f; instruction of blacks, 239-51 *passim*, 312-13, 414
Jews, 34, 57-59, 222
Jolofo, 40-43 (Tables 1 and 2), 346
juros, 32, 348

King, James F., 39n

labor, forced Indian, viii, 5, 7, 12-13, 18-22, 76, 87, 110-24 *passim*, 183, 358f, 385. *See also mita* system
ladinos, 78-79, 148, 184, 235f, 238, 250f, 268, 348, 355; prices of, 342-45
La Magdalena, port, 92
lançados, 45, 365
language, 73, 78, 196, 259, 321; instruction, 149, 222, 234; and Christianization, 235, 237, 245, 249
La Paz, 160
La Quinua Valley, 94
Lati, 90
law enforcement, 147-79 *passim*, 187-221 *passim*; agencies, 161-68 *passim*, 175, 187, 190, 199-221 *passim*, 330f, 400
laws of exclusion, 3, 148-49
lawsuits: between buyers and sellers, 82-87 *passim*, 191-93, 371; to abolish head tax, 204-15 *passim*; involving manumission, 287-97 *passim*
Lea, Henry Charles, 59
legislation: in labor reform, 117-19, 124; to meet black threat, 148-58 *passim*, 185, 197-99, 200-201, 207, 390, 397; sumptuary laws, 232f, 311. *See also* decrees
Lewis, Boleslao, 339
licenses: for importation of slaves, 3f, 9, 25-37 *passim*, 44-49 *passim*, 55f, 61f, 68, 148-49, 172, 326-27, 360-73 *passim*; for working slaves, 107-13 *passim*, 143, 182; for blacks to bear arms, 155, 179, 182-83; for slave marriages, 260-61, 404; for emigration, 273
Lima: as slave market, 10, 50, 54-87 *passim*, 254, 268, 342-45, 370; colored population of, 11, 77, 182, 337-41, 378
Lisbon, 2, 30, 35f, 50, 55, 238, 361
litigation, *see* lawsuits
Lockhart, James, viii, 5-8 *passim*, 10, 378; on slave occupations, 13, 88, 106, 126f, 132, 135-36, 142, 144-45; on control of blacks, 157f, 160, 189; on status of blacks, 279, 308, 320, 414
Loja district, 122
López, Luis, 243, 245
López de Lara, Pedro, 212
Los Reyes, 209
loyalty of colored population, 7-8, 158-59, 178-81 *passim*, 186, 224, 236, 310, 334

Luanda, 38f, 46f, 49
Lucena, de, Alonso, 180
Lucumi, 40-43 (Tables 1 and 2)
Lunaguán Valley, 92
Lurigancho Valley, 89
Luso-Spanish union, 29-36 *passim*, 50-51, 239, 326

Madrid, 30, 306
Magellan, Strait of, 99, 309n
mail delivery, 116, 123, 385
Mala Valley, 225f, 242
Malamba/Malemba, 40-43 (Tables 1 and 2), 250
Malambo, 67, 243
Maldonado de Torres, Alonso, 115
male slaves: ratio to female slaves, 81, 95, 254, 340-41; prices, 343-45
Mancera, de, Marqués, 91, 99-100, 123, 127, 129, 184-85, 310, 378, 385, 395
Manco Inca, 7, 356
Mandinga, 40-43 (Tables 1 and 2), 287, 346
Mañozca, de, Juan, 368
manumission, *see* freedom
Maranga, 202
Maranhão, 49
marriages, 254-67, 271, 331, 340, 403-9 *passim*, 414
Martín, Gaspar, 54-55
Martín, Luis, 228, 312-13
matriarchy, *see* mothers
medical care, 63-71 *passim*, 85f, 91, 138, 205f, 223f, 228-30, 236, 243, 372
Mediterranean, 2, 27
Mellafe, Rolando, 363, 373
Mercedarians, 7, 141, 170, 249, 296, 322
merchants: blacks as, 106-9, 250, 318; and head tax, 204-14 *passim*
mercury mines, 23, 99, 123, 133, 173, 382ff
mestizos, 94, 105, 177f, 228, 313, 331, 334n, 348, 359; as work force, 23, 108, 116-19 *passim*, 123, 134; numbers of, 75, 94, 147, 153, 175; and Indians, 209, 285
Mexía, Alonso, 169-70
Mexico, vii, viii, 3, 16, 64, 73, 148f, 153, 330, 360, 362, 384
militia, colored, 181f, 219, 247, 271, 302, 306-10 *passim*, 332f, 412-13
mills: textile, 89, 135, 247, 377, 388; sugar, 90, 92, 94, 116; grain, 92-93; woolen, 229
Mina, 40-43 (Tables 1 and 2)

mines, 12-24 *passim*, 110-23 *passim*, 325, 328, 356, 359, 382. *See also specific metals by name*
Mint, Lima, xiii, 127, 386f
Miranda, de, Alonso, 54
missionaries, 7, 47f, 147, 234ff, 245, 249, 360, 401. *See also* Church; Christianity; *and individual religious orders by name*
mita system, 18-24 *passim*, 90-91, 110-24, 173, 283, 303, 324-28 *passim*, 378
mitayos, see mita system
mixed blood, *see* racial mixture
mochileros, 45, 348
monasteries, 104-5, 118, 127, 130, 141, 166f, 175, 212, 248; as refuges, 160, 169, 258
Monsalve, de, Miguel, 174
Monterrey, de, Conde, 118-19, 212, 239
Montesclaros, de, Marqués, 119-21, 180, 212, 305, 309, 313, 340, 394, 412
Moors, 1, 27, 148, 222f, 251, 355, 360. *See also* Islam
Moquegua Valley, 89, 371
Morales, de, Tomás, 169
morality of slavery and slave trade, 12, 18, 24-27 *passim*, 110, 223f, 244, 270, 273-74, 325
Mörner, Magnus, 273, 384
Morro Quemado, 93
mortality rate: in mines, 13-14, 117, 121; of black cargos, 47-58 *passim*, 64-70 *passim*; of slaves, 75, 77, 95-96, 100, 103, 227-28, 230, 338; of *mitayos*, 91, 114
Mosanga, 40-41 (Table 1)
mothers: slaves as, 256, 258, 268-70, 287, 403; and cases of manumission, 274-82 *passim*, 288, 291-97 *passim*, 307
Mozambique, 40-43 (Tables 1 and 2), 346
Muhammadanism, *see* Islam
mulattoes, xiv, 384; as labor force, 17, 22-24, 45f, 97ff, 108f, 116-21 *passim*, 158, 205; numbers of, 75, 94, 147, 174f, 301, 321, 339ff; as artisans, 131-36 *passim*, 140-45 *passim*, 314-20 *passim*, 412; legislation against, 148, 156f, 164, 182, 310-12, 392, 414; relationship with Indians, 153f, 209, 285ff, 390; as lawbreakers, 165, 177ff, 189, 199; social standing of, 183-84, 224, 312, 333, 408-9; life of, 234, 243, 246-55 *passim*, 303-13 *passim*; and freedom, 277-81 *passim*, 288-98 *passim*
municipal control of blacks, 149-50, 161-

68, 201-16. *See also* law enforcement; Hermandad
Muñiz, Pedro, 119
music, 232, 246, 414
mutilation, *see* branding of slaves; castration of slaves; punishment

Nalu, 40-43 (Tables 1 and 2), 346
navy, 97-100, 104, 382
Nazca, 10, 93, 196, 241
negros congos, 248f
New Granada, vii, viii, 26, 54, 73, 242
New Laws, 8, 12, 116, 358
Nicaragua, 73, 77n, 296
Nieva, de, Conde, 21f, 157
Niger, 37
Noguera, Pérez, 227, 230, 243, 255
Núñez Vela, Blasco, 8ff, 13

offices, sale of, 213-15, 313-15, 392, 399, 414
oidores, 155, 166-67, 170, 176-80 *passim*, 239, 348, 360f. *See also* Audiencia
Orient, 60, 64, 340
orphanages, 105, 312
orphans, 307, 313

Paita, 54, 64f, 78, 179, 283, 307, 310, 374
Palma, Ricardo, 287
Panama: slavery in, 3-5, 149, 169, 369; and slave trade, 10, 54-74 *passim*, 96-100 *passim*, 178; runaways in, 187, 195, 199, 201, 330
Pancorvo, de, Juan, 8
Paraguay, 73
parents, role of under slavery, 268-70. *See also* mothers
Partidas, see Siete Partidas, Las
"passing," 305n, 321, 340
peculium, 278
Pérez, Manuel Bautista, 49-50, 58-71, 73-87 *passim*, 365-76 *passim*
Perico, 64, 66
permits, *see* licenses
Pernambuco, 49
peso, value of, xiii-xiv
Phelan, John, 233
Philip II, King, xiii, 29, 230
Philip IV, King, 110
physicians, *see* medical care
"piece," 39n
Pike, Ruth, xiii
Piquirí River, 63
Pisco, 96, 128, 181, 191, 195, 241f, 265f, 318

Pisco Valley, 92f
Piura, 106, 307, 310
Pizarro, Francisco, 3-8 *passim*, 19, 150, 196, 392
Pizarro, Gonzalo, 8-9, 10, 14, 151, 188, 252, 356f
Pizarro, Hernando, 16
plantations, 20, 38, 89-96 *passim*, 120, 123, 126, 176-77, 189, 225-33 *passim*, 238-43 *passim*; 298-30
Poma de Ayala, Felipe Guamán, 79, 103, 154-59 *passim*, 174-75, 193, 224, 226, 230f, 254f
pombeiros, 46, 348
Popayán, 253
population: slave, 11, 76-78, 147, 149, 182f, 186, 215, 221, 237; Indian, 18-20, 283, 324, 360, 378; colored, 300-305 *passim*, 333, 337-41, 359. *See also* censuses
Porco, 14-15
Portugal: and slave trade, 2f, 10, 26-51 *passim*, 55-59, 110, 326f, 362ff, 369; relations with Spain, 71-72, 77, 123, 185, 219, 326f
Portugal, Council of, 33, 238
Potosí, xiii, 14-15, 23-24, 121, 240, 386
prejudice, racial, 27, 109, 141, 143, 176 283, 302, 332, 389
prices, slave, 11, 16, 30-31, 37, 45f, 54-87 *passim*, 92, 121, 342-45, 369, 372; ceilings on, 71, 361; of skilled labor, 97, 115, 126, 132, 134, 136-38; influences on, 161, 191, 195, 235, 258, 268, 388
priests: as slaveowners, 7, 90, 98, 127, 223; work among slaves, 47-48, 65, 248, 251; work among Indians, 91; and control of slaves, 153-54, 165, 169-71; availability of, 234-43 *passim*, 339, 341; blacks excluded as, 315. *See also* missionaries; religious orders
prisons, *see* jails
prostitution, 104, 107, 156, 255, 307, 311
Protector, for slaves, 184, 224
Protector General of the Indians, 114, 123, 383
Puerto Belo, 50, 56, 62f, 65
Puerto Rico, 73, 197, 362
pulperías, 108-9, 156, 217, 258, 319, 348
punishment: of masters, by authorities, 83-84, 231, 234, 254, 262, 401; of slaves, for crimes and less serious infractions, 98f, 123, 149-56 *passim*, 165-79 *passim*, 196-201 *passim*, 209,

251, 308, 397; of free persons of color, 157f, 217, 309n; of slaves, by masters, 159, 161, 184, 193, 222ff, 230-32, 255. *See also* fines
purchase: of slaves, 78-87, 261; of manumission, 275, 278-82, 288-300 *passim*, 315, 331-32. *See also* offices, sale of

quadroons, 145, 171, 288, 298, 305f, 314, 333
Quito, 111, 135, 227, 261, 267, 390

racial mixture, 272, 274, 282-323 *passim*, 332f. *See also individual racial types by name*
racial terminology, xiv, 39n, 383-84
Ramírez de Cartagena (*oidor*), 178
rancheadores, 212
rape, 151, 153, 172
rebellions: Indian, 7, 11f, 333; role of blacks in, 8-11; Girón, 9, 93, 398; Pizarro, 10, 14, 252; potential among blacks, 147-48, 175-86 *passim*, 222, 247, 321, 330
recapture of runaways, *see* law enforcement
receptor, 414
Recogimiento de Divorcio, 260
redhibition suits, 82-87 *passim*, 193, 256
reforms: of Indian labor system, 117-24 *passim*; of law enforcement, 163-64; in head tax collections, 212; of baptism methods, 238-40
religion, *see* Christianity; Church; missionaries; religious orders; sodalities
religious instruction, 223, 233-48 *passim*, 255, 277, 323
religious orders: use of slaves by, 81, 98, 105, 361, 375; and law enforcement, 169-71; care of slaves by, 228, 239, 242f, 247-50 *passim*. *See also individual orders by name*
repartimiento, *see mita* system
residence requirements, 307-9, 332
revolts, *see* rebellions
Rico, Gregorio, 56
Rímac River, 67, 129, 209, 308
Río de la Hacha, 362
Ríos de Guinea, 37
Ríos y Berriz, de los, Juan, 164-66
Rivera, de, Salvador, 169
robbery, *see* thievery
Rodney, Walter, 39, 364f
Rodríguez, Gerónimo, 64
Rosenblat, Ángel, 339

runaways: troublesomeness of, 63, 147,
   176, 365, 369; control of, 68, 106, 149,
   185-221 *passim*, 330-31, 367, 396f, 400;
   moral defects of, 81-87, 376, 388; rate
   of, 172; and marriage, 259-67 *passim*;
   insurance against, 358

sadism, 223, 231-32
salaries, *see* wages
Saldaña, de, Francisco, 130
sale of offices, 213-15, 313-15, 392, 399,
   414
Salinas y Córdova, de, Buenaventura,
   108, 133, 135, 340
Salvatierra, de, Conde, 75, 123f, 156, 164,
   185
San Andrés hospital, 105, 229, 281
San Lázaro district, 67, 135, 209, 247,
   309, 390f
San Marcelo parish of Lima, 75, 171,
   248f, 340
San Martín de Porres, 243, 315
San Sebastián parish of Lima, 75, 249,
   318, 339f
Sana, 64, 130, 304
Sánchez, Tomás, 364-65
Sandoval, de, Alonso, 40n, 49, 52f, 65,
   72, 223; on types of slaves, 79, 132,
   346, 363; on mistreatment of slaves,
   224-30 *passim*, 255, 257, 275; mission-
   ary work of, 234-39 *passim*, 243, 245,
   366, 401
Santa, 54, 64, 190f, 230, 304
Santa Ana hospital, 105, 130, 191
Santa Ana parish of Lima, 75, 248ff, 339f
Santa Clara convent, 130, 189, 267, 269,
   318
Santa Cruz y Padilla, Gerónimo, 241
Santa Hermandad, *see* Hermandad
Santa Marta, 58, 362
Santiago, 173, 251
Santillán, de, Pedro, 391
Santo Domingo, 5
São Jorge de Mina, 30
São Paulo de Luanda, 38f, 46f, 49
São Tomé, 30, 38, 57, 78
Sarmiento y Gamboa, de, Pedro, 309n
sedition, 175-88 *passim*. *See also*
   rebellions
segregation, 169, 222, 249, 260-61, 283-86
self-government of blacks, 174-75
Senegal, 346
Senegal River, 37
Senegambia, 40-43 (Tables 1 and 2), 80,
   145, 346

separation of slave families, 193-95, 254f,
   259-70 *passim*, 403
Serrano, Pedro, 153
Serrato, Cristóbal, 64
servants, *see* household servants
Seville merchant guild, *see under* guilds
sexual contact between races, vii, 150-51,
   154, 254, 283-87 *passim*, 297, 397
shipwrecks, 48-49, 65, 113, 366
sickness and disease, 3, 18-20 *passim*,
   47-54 *passim*, 66-67, 71, 81-86 *passim*,
   227-30 *passim*, 358, 376, 406
sierra, *see* highlands
Sierra Leone, 346, 365
Siete Partidas, Las, 273-74, 278, 405
silver: mining, ix, 13-18, 23-24, 118, 122f,
   359; demand for, xii, 29, 326-28 *passim*;
   and slave trade, 32, 50f, 55, 61, 76,
   326-28, 372; competition for, with
   Portugal, 33f, 36, 110, 326-28 *passim*
skilled labor: slaves, 111, 125-46; free
   persons of color, 125-46 *passim*, 268,
   276-77, 281, 299-300, 317, 329, 332
slave prices, *see* prices, slave
slavecatchers, 212, 220
smuggling, *see* contraband
Society of Jesus, *see* Jesuits
sodalities, colored, 156, 183, 247-51, 261,
   282, 306, 318f, 322
sorcery, 252-53
Soria, de, Jerónimo, 16
Soso, 40-43 (Tables 1 and 2), 322, 346
Southern Africa, 145
Spain: and Portugal, 2-3, 55-59, 71-72,
   77, 123, 185, 219, 328; and Dutch,
   96f, 101, 128, 179-84 *passim*, 186,
   306-10 *passim*, 394. *See also* Crown,
   Spanish
status, legal, 272-74, 286f, 403
sumptuary legislation, 232f, 311
superstition, 241, 251-53, 321, 331
Surco, 309

tachas, *see* defects in slaves
Tacna, 94
tangomaos, 45, 349, 365
Tarija, 24
Tartars, 1
taverns, 108-9
taxes, 68, 73-78 *passim*, 121, 179, 198-221
   passim, 337, 361ff, 369-74 *passim*, 397.
   See also tribute
terminology, xiv, 39n, 383-84
Terranova, 40-43 (Tables 1 and 2), 346
thievery: and slaves, 82-87 *passim*, 104-8

passim, 147, 151-74 *passim*, 233, 376; and *cimarrones*, 187ff, 195, 201ff, 209, 217f, 331
tiangues, 150, 349
tiendas, 109, 349
Tierra Firme, *see* Panama
Tiruel, José, 321
Toledo, Capitulations of, 4
Toledo, de, Francisco, 178, 230, 253, 285, 369; and labor problems, 22-25, 76, 110-11, 120, 324f, 383; and revenue, 68, 207, 303, 359; and control of blacks, 108, 142, 153, 157-58, 162, 201, 238, 396; on Christianity, 234, 245
Tordesillas, Treaty of, 2-3, 29f, 36, 50-51
Torquemada, de, Juan, 360
Torres Fresnada, de, Antonio, 114f
trade, slave: in Middle Ages, 1-4; volume, 72-85 *passim*, 338, 354f, 363f, 372, 374; cessation and resumption of, 91, 95-96, 124, 148, 219, 230, 378; complexities of, 110, 123, 178, 301, 373f
Treasury, Council of the, 112-13
trials, 161-68 *passim*, 193, 196ff, 206. *See also* lawsuits
Triana district, 243
tribute, 410, 412; Indians, 7, 10-21 *passim*, 117, 286, 313, 358; persons of color, 23, 120f, 139, 175, 301-10 *passim*, 332, 341, 359; exemptions from, 182, 193, 413
Trujillo: 64, 78, 94, 228, 241, 243, 304, 374; labor in, 20, 92, 94; census, 378
Tucumán, 73, 366, 387
tumbeiros, 48
Túmbez, 4
Túpac Amarú, 333
Turkey, 1-2

Union of Arms tax, 75, 348
universities, 130, 312ff
University of San Marcos, 130, 312, 314
Upper Guinea, 45
Upper Peru, 77, 133
uprisings, *see* rebellions
Urban VIII, Pope, 366
Ursua-Aguirre expedition, 132

vagrancy, 156f, 187, 307
Valdivia, 310
Valdivia, de, Pedro, 5
Valencia, de, Hernando, 214
Valenzuela, de, Francisco, 123
Valiente, Juan, 5

Valladolid Mogorón, de, Juan, 215, 310
value of slaves, *see* prices, slave
Vargas y Mendoza, de, Juan, 165
Vázquez de Loaysa, Juan, 179
Velasco, de, Luis, 115-23 *passim*, 180, 210-22, 303-4, 305, 313
Venezuela, 55, 73, 362, 384
Veracruz, 32, 36, 39
viceroys, 166, 173, 180f, 212-15 *passim*, 242, 283, 311, 360f; and control of blacks, 155-57 *passim*, 163, 182, 206, 221. *See also individual viceroys by name*
Vilcabamba, 94, 123, 176
Villar, del, Conde, 90, 98, 112, 169, 208ff, 283f, 304, 394
Villena, de, Marqués, 184
Viñaca Valley, 94
Vitor Valley, 93
volume of slave trade, *see under* trade, slave

wages, 98, 103-4, 141-42, 146, 303; of Indians, 118; of artisans, 125-31 *passim*, 138-40, 329; and cases of freedom, 281, 291, 295; of orphans, 312
weapons, *see* arms and weapons
weddings, *see* marriages
West Africa, 30, 37-44 *passim*, 80, 145, 354
West Indies, 54, 89, 149, 187, 220, 326
Westphalia, Treaty of, ix
whipping of slaves, *see* punishment
witchcraft, 252-53, 331
Wolofs, *see* Gelofes
women: as slaveowners, 98, 103-5, 127, 136; Indian, 154, 189, 286, 303; and freedom, 268, 298, 317; allure of blacks for Spaniards, 286-89, 311, 315, 332f, 408-9, 414. *See also* female slaves; mothers

yanaconas, 18, 21, 90, 94, 349, 411
Yucay Valley, 94
Yupiay, 188

zambaigos, see zambos
Zambianpungo, 235
zambos, 116-20 *passim*, 151, 178, 209, 349, 383-84, 408; status of, 145, 285f, 298f, 303, 306, 312, 332; numbers of, 174, 301
Zape, 40-43 (Tables 1 and 2), 346
zimbo, 46, 349